CADOGAN GUIDES

"Intelligently organized and obviously well researched, these books strike a balance between background and sightseeing information and the practicalities that travelers need to make a trip enjoyable. As a travel bookseller, I am happy to see guides focusing on destinations that people would like to visit but have been unable to gather enough information until now."

—Harriett Greenberg, *The Complete Traveller Bookstore, New York City*

"Rochelle Jaffe, owner and manager of Travel Books Unlimited in Bethesda, Maryland, attributes (Cadogan Guides) popularity to both their good, clean-looking format and the fact that they include 'information about everything for everyone'. . . ."

—*American Bookseller* magazine

Other titles in the Cadogan Guide series:

THE CARIBBEAN
GREEK ISLANDS
INDIA
IRELAND
ITALIAN ISLANDS
ITALY
SCOTLAND
THE SOUTH OF FRANCE
SPAIN
TURKEY

Forthcoming:
BALI
MOROCCO
PORTUGAL
THAILAND &
BURMA
TUSCANY &
UMBRIA

ABOUT THE AUTHOR

NICHOLAS LUSH was born in Sydney, Australia, in 1953 and educated by the Society of Jesus on the shores of Sydney Harbour within gawking distance of the Sydney Opera House and the Harbour Bridge. He later attended Sydney University where, after 12 years of intermittent study, he was awarded a Bachelor of Arts degree. In the meantime he whiled away a decade by singing, acting, dancing and playing his way through musical shows and theatre restaurants around Sydney, Melbourne and other parts of Australia. He then went to work for a publisher and wrote for the *Sydney Morning Herald*, the *Daily Telegraph*, the *Sunday Telegraph* and other Sydney newspapers as well as editing the travel guides *Inside Sydney* and *Dollarsmart Overseas Travel* plus a string of similar consumer publications. He spent a large part of 1987 on the road and in front of the computer for the *Cadogan Guide to Australia*. He is married and has one small daughter.

CADOGAN GUIDES

AUSTRALIA

NICK LUSH

Illustrations by Pauline Pears

A Voyager Book

The
Globe
Pequot
Press

Chester, Connecticut 06412

ACKNOWLEDGEMENTS

My thanks go first to Jane who helped tremendously and organised the holiday after everything was done, to Leora who gave practical assistance when it was most needed and to Stephen for his fast printers (Thank God!). Tourism Queensland, The Northern Territory Tourist Bureau, Tasbureau and The South Australian Department of Tourism were also instrumental as were East–West Airlines and Air NSW. Thanks all.

The publishers would also like to thank Jenny Fielding for her many helpful contributions at the 10th hour.

Copyright © 1988 by Nick Lush
Illustrations copyright © 1988 by Pauline Pears
Cover design by Keith Pointing
Cover illustration by Povl Webb
Maps by Thames Cartographic Services Ltd
Series Editors: Rachel Fielding and Paula Levey

First Edition/Second Printing

Library of Congress Cataloging-in-Publication Data

Lush, Nicholas.
    Cadogan guides, Australia/by Nicholas Lush.
        p.   cm.—(A Voyager book)
    Includes index.
    ISBN 0–87106–796–X (pbk.)
        1. Australia—Description and travel—1981—Guide books.
I. Title.
DU95.L87   1988   919.4′0463—dc19   87–32998

Manufactured in the United Kingdom

CONTENTS

Introduction

LIST OF MAPS

PLEASE NOTE

Every effort has been made to ensure the accuracy of the information in this book at the time of going to press. However, practical details such as opening hours, travel information, standards in hotels and restaurants and, in particular, prices are liable to change.

We intend to keep this book as up-to-date as possible in the coming years. Please write to us if there is anything you feel should be included in future editions.

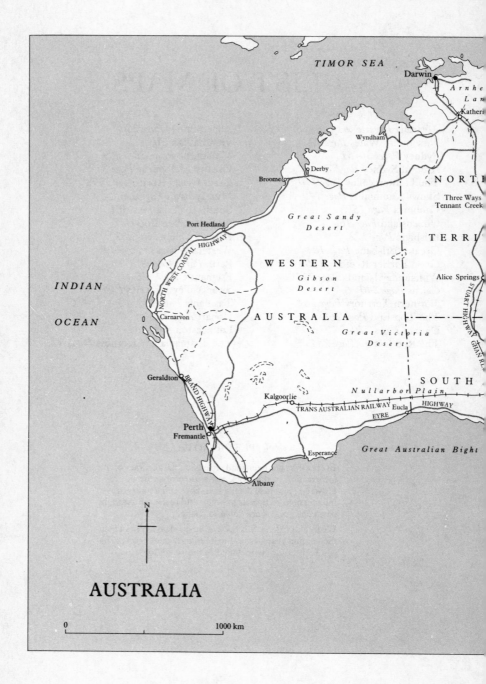

AUSTRALIA

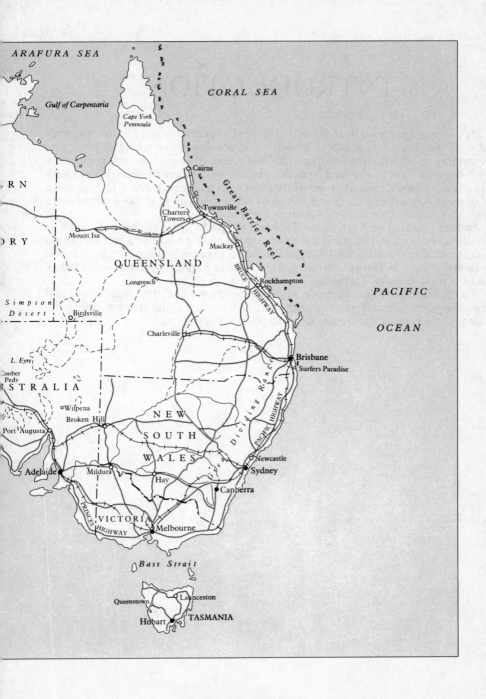

ARAFURA SEA

Gulf of Carpentaria

CORAL SEA

Cape York
Peninsula

RN

Cairns

ORY

Charters
Towers

Townsville

Mount Isa

Great Barrier Reef

Mackay

QUEENSLAND

Longreach

Rockhampton

PACIFIC

Simpson
Desert

Birdsville

Charleville

OCEAN

L. Eyre

Coober
Pedy

STRALIA

Brisbane
Surfers Paradise

Wilpena

Broken Hill

NEW

SOUTH

Port Augusta

Dividing Range

WALES

Adelaide

Mildura

Hay

Newcastle

Sydney

PACIFIC HIGHWAY

Canberra

VICTORIA

PRINCES
HIGHWAY

Melbourne

Bass Strait

Queenstown

Launceston

Hobart

TASMANIA

INTRODUCTION

This guide is a personal introduction to Australia backed up by a lifetime's knowledge of the Australian scene. You won't find absolutely everything in here, just everything good: wineries detailed to the last grape, Aboriginal artists, restaurants with the best food in the land, outback ghost towns, mountain guesthouses with breathtaking views, cabins in rainforests, coral reefs and seaside cities. If these and a glimpse of Australian history and culture—richer than you probably imagine—are your idea of travelling well, this guide is for you.

Sydney, the Barrier Reef, Ayers Rock and the Red Centre are here of course as are the kangaroos and koalas but they are spread among a host of lesser known no less extraordinary fascinations like the Flinders Ranges in South Australia, Kakadu National Park near Darwin, the long, wide beaches of northern New South Wales and the mountains of Tasmania.

You'll find bushwalks, ski trails, sailing tours, four-wheel drive adventures and crocodile cruises inside too but at the end of each is a comfortable bed and the balance of a night at the theatre or an afternoon in a gallery.

Part I
GENERAL INFORMATION

Platypus

It may be stating the obvious but sometimes it doesn't hurt to do so—Australia is very big and very far away. That is part of its attraction, but it means that travelling to and around the country takes time, more time than Europe for example. Australia is also quite thinly settled. It has about 16,000,000 inhabitants living in an area roughly the size of all Europe (excluding the USSR) or the whole of the United States. By far the greater proportion of the citizens lives in large, prosperous cities on the east coast. Much smaller concentrations gather in the south west and one small city stands on the north coast. Outside the major cities are wide tracts of farming land which, as one moves towards the centre of the continent, turn into deserts, vast empty distances stretching between urbanised coastal enclaves on whose uncrowded maps a few roads string from small town to small town sustaining very infrequent traffic. This is the outback and parts of it contain some of the country's most fascinating, unusual and typical terrain.

Since there is no changing the geography to suit the traveller, anyone who wants too see a goodly slice of Australia will find that time is his most precious commodity and those contemplating only a short stay would be well served to choose carefully and not be too ambitious. These caveats in mind, the traveller will find that transport, especially in the air, is adequately organised if rather over-regulated and, when compared to similar distances elsewhere in the world, not as costly as it is reputed to be.

1

Getting to Australia

Getting to Australia is easy but the only way to do it is by air and it takes longer than almost any other flight in the world. None the less, Australians do it in the reverse direction at the drop of a hat so it can't be all that harrowing. Travellers arriving from London will find their journey takes about 24 hours, from Los Angeles 18 hours and from Tokyo 9 hours.

From the UK and Europe

Departure points
Flights on the Kangaroo route from the UK and Europe depart from London, Manchester, Amsterdam, Frankfurt, Rome, Athens and Belgrade.

Which airline?
Qantas is the main carrier on the route in association with Alitalia, British Airways, Lufthansa, Thai International, Olympic Airways and JAT. Others flying to Australia from Europe are UTA, KLM, Iberia and Singapore Airlines.

Which fare?
All economy fares are seasonal. First and business class fares remain the same throughout the year except in the case of special promotions. Planes from European and UK ports are least full from January to March and are most patronised in October and around Christmas (especially from London, Athens and Rome). Other times of the year tend to be regarded as shoulder seasons. The high season fares are around £1100 and low £850 London–Sydney return full economy with shoulder fares falling between these figures. Apex fares cut this by many per cent.

Seats are available for less at bucket shops (discount travel agents who buy airline tickets in bulk). Such discount sellers are common in the Earls Court area of London and in Buckingham Palace Road. If you buy one of their tickets, it may be wise to ring the airline 24 hours or so later to check that your booking has gone through. For the latest information on the discount fares available look at the travel ads in the *Sunday Times*, *Time Out* or the give-away papers such as *Lam*.

Entry Points
Flights from UK & Europe enter Australia through Sydney, Melbourne, Perth and Darwin, in some cases continuing from those cities to other state capitals. Garuda flies into Port Headland in north-west Western Australia once a fortnight on Saturday from Bali. That flight continues to Darwin.

Information sources
The Australian Tourist Commission, now called **Tourism Australia**, is the main source of information for travellers coming to Australia. Its UK office is on the 4th Floor, 20 Saville Row, London W1X 1AE (01) 434 4371/2. The European office is at Neue Mainzer Strasse 22, D-6000 Frankfurt am Main, Federal Republic of Germany, (069) 23 5071. This office can put you in touch with representatives in

2

other European countries. The ATC has a list of travel agents specialising in Australia.

The major UK office of Qantas is at Qantas House, 395–403 King Street, London W6 9NJ, phone (0345) 747 767. Other British Isles offices are in Manchester, Dublin, Glasgow, Leeds, Birmingham, Bristol and two more in London at Regent Street and The Strand. Qantas has European offices in Frankfurt, Amsterdam, Rome, Paris, Athens, Vienna, Zurich, Stockholm and Belgrade.

Jetabout, the holiday wholesaling wing of Qantas, is at Brook House, 229/243 Shepherds Bush Road, London W6 7AN, phone (0345) 010900. Other travel companies specialising in Australia include: **Kuoni Travel**, 33 Maddox Street, London W1R 9LD, and 84 Bishopsgate, London EC2N 4AU (0306) 885044; **Trailfinders Ltd**, 42–48 Earls Court Road, London W8 6EJ, (01) 937 9631; **Jetset Tours**, 64–67 New Oxford Street, London WC1A 1EU; **AAT Kings Australian Holidays**, 4th Floor, 7–9 Swallow Street, London W1R 8DU, (01) 434 3868; **Australian Destination Centre**, 27-28 High Street, Windsor, Berkshire SL4 1LH, (0753) 855457; **Austravel**, 62 Trafalgar Square, London WC2N 5EW, (01) 930 4751; **Insight International Tours**, 26 Cockspur Street, Trafalgar Square, London SW1Y 5BY, (01) 839 7060; **Newmans Tours**, 42 Harrow View Road, Ealing, London W5 1LZ, (01) 998 4612; **Travel Machine**, 7 Maddox Street, London W1R 9LE, (01) 499 8366; **Horizon Travel Centre**, 1st Floor, 49 Old Bond Street, London W1X 3AF, (01) 493 7446. The last company also has offices in Birmingham, Coventry, Derby, Leicester, Nottingham, Cardiff, Bristol, Manchester, Leeds, Newcastle upon Tyne and Glasgow.

A collection of Australian tourism and airline offices inhabits the 4th floor of Heathcote House, 20 Saville Row, London W1X 1AE. As well as Tourism Australia, there is the **Northern Territory Tourist Commission**, (01) 439 2727, **Western Australian Tourism Commission**, (01) 437 8951, and **Ansett Airlines**, (01) 748 4444. Other information offices are in the Strand: **Queensland Tourist and Travel Corporation**, Queensland House, 392 The Strand, London WC2R 0LZ, (01) 836 1333; **South Australian Department of Tourism**, South Australia House, 50 The Strand, London WC2N 5LW, (01) 930 7471; **Tourism Commission of New South Wales**, New South Wales House, 66 The Strand, London WC2N 5LZ, (01) 839 6651; **Victorian Tourism Commission**, Victoria House, Melbourne Place, The Strand, London WC2B 4LA, (01) 836 2656.

From the USA & Canada

Departure points
Qantas flights to Australia from North America leave from Vancouver, Los Angeles, San Francisco, Houston and Honolulu.

Which airline?
Airlines serving Australia from the US are Qantas, United and Continental. Qantas and CP Air operate from Vancouver through Honolulu. Some services from west-coast USA travel through Tahiti and Auckland to Sydney.

Which fare?
High season is from December through March, shoulder is October through November and low is April through September. Fares are generally around US$1350 high season, US$1000 low season Hawaii to Sydney return full economy. Apex fares reduce the cost somewhat and are very popular. Sunday travel sections of the *Los Angeles Times*, *San Francisco Examiner* and *New York Times* advertise discounted fares.

Entry points
Flights from North America enter Australia through Sydney, Melbourne, Brisbane and Cairns, in some cases continuing from those cities to other state capitals.

Information sources
The **Australian Tourist Commission** has offices in North America at Suite 1200, 2121 Avenue of the Stars, Los Angeles, California 90067, phone (213) 552 1988; and at 489 Fifth Avenue, New York, New York 10017, phone (212) 687 6300.

Qantas has offices in North America at Suite 1304, 3550 Wilshire Boulevard, Los Angeles, CA 90010, (231) 217 2007; 512 Fifth Avenue, New York, NY 10036, (212) 764 0214. There are also offices in San Francisco, Seattle, Houston, Honolulu and Boston. The Vancouver office is at Four Bentnall Centre, Suite 1714, 1055 Dunsmuir Street, Vancouver BC V7X 1L3, phone (604) 684 1441.

Jetabout, the holiday wholesaling wing of Qantas, has offices at 9800 Sepulveda Boulevard, Los Angeles, CA 90045, (213) 641 8770; and in Canada at 80 Bloor Street West, Suite 505, Toronto, Ontario, Canada M5S 2V1, phone (416) 967 5306. Other tour companies specialising in Australia include **Associated Tours (Australia) Pty. Ltd,** c/o Pacific Delight, 132 Madison Avenue, New York, NY 10016, (212) 684 7707 NY City & State, (800) 221 7179 USA; **Atlantic & Pacific Travel**, 230 N Maryland Avenue, Glendale CA 91706, (818) 240 0538, (800) 421 9020 USA, (800) 228 7238 Canada; **Jetset Tours**, 8383 Wilshire Boulevard, Beverly Hills, CA 90211, (213) 651 4050, (800) 252 2035 Canada; **Landmark (South Pacific)**, 850 Colorado Boulevard, Los Angeles, CA 90041, (213) 256 1991, (800) 621 1633 CA, (800) 621 7242 USA; **Austravel**, 51 East 42nd Street, Suite 4 413–415, New York, NY 10017, (212) 972 6880 NY State, (800) 544 0212 USA & Canada.

Tax
A departure tax of $20 per head is placed on all persons leaving Australia. An entry tax is also soon likely to be levied.

Essentials

Legal

To enter Australia you must have a valid passport which remains current throughout your stay. Visas are necessary from all countries except New Zealand. There are four kinds: Visitors' Visa valid for six months or less, a Working Holidaymakers' Visa valid usually for a maximum of twelve months, a temporary residents visa and a student's visa. Multiple entry visitor's visas are available. Visas are free.

Visas are obtained from Australian Government offices. The main ones are The Australian High Commission, Visa Section, Australia House, The Strand, London, WC2B 4LA, phone (01) 836 7161; Australian Consulate General, 611 North Larchmont Boulevard, Los Angeles, CA 90004, (213) 469 4300; Australian Consulate General, International Building, 636 Fifth Avenue, New York, NY 10111, (212) 245 4000; Australian Consulate General, 800 Oceanic Plaza, 1066 West Hastings Street, Vancouver, BC V6E 3X1, (604) 684 1177. There are further offices in San Francisco, Houston, Chicago, Washington, Ottawa and Toronto.

Working Holidaymakers' Visas are only available to 18–25-year-old single people or married couples without children from the UK, Canada, Japan and the Netherlands. They entitle their holders to do casual or temporary work whilst holidaying in Australia.

Australian **customs** regulations relating to dutiable goods are complicated. Information about them can be obtained from Australian Government offices. Some matters, however, are straightforward. Drugs of dependence, certain weapons and firearms, cordless telephones, plants, wildlife and endangered species, the food that you get on the aeroplane, birds and certain other animals are not allowed into the country. You may bring in personal effects, 200 cigarettes, 1 litre of alcohol and dutiable goods up to the value of $400 without incurring duty.

Money

Australian money is decimal, ie, it consists of dollars and cents. Coins are $2, $1, and 50, 20, 10, 5, 2 and 1 cents. Notes are $100, $50, $20, $10 and $5. There is no limit on personal funds you bring in. You must take out no more than you brought in. In no case may you take out more than $5,000 in notes and coins of Australian currency.

Credit cards are common, the most widely accepted being Amex, Mastercard, Visa and associated cards and Diners Club. Americans will find, however, that credit card use is less widespread than in their home country. They do not generally extend to supermarkets and are less used altogether the farther you go from large cities. Travellers' cheques can be cashed in banks and hotels but there are not many independent *bureaux de change*. Few retail outlets will change foreign currency travellers' cheques.

Clothes

Light clothing is sufficient for almost all places in Australia during the summer except in the southern parts of the country during evenings when a light jacket or cotton sweater is sometimes necessary. Winter can be cold and the wind cutting, especially in Melbourne and even more in Hobart but Sydney can also be cold, wet and windy. Umbrellas are always a good idea.

Electricity

Australian current is 240 to 250 volts AC 50hz and the three pin socket in our power points is of a different design to that in most other countries. Most large hotels have international sockets but carrying your own adapter is a good idea.

Medicines

Patent medicines such as aspirin and other non-prescription pain killers are easily available in Australia. They can be bought at pharmacies (chemists) along with other preparations related to health. Two analgesics, amidopyrine and dipyrone, are illegal and may not be brought into Australia. If you are in Australia during summer, especially in the tropics, insect repellent is essential as is suntan lotion and a hat.

Insurance

Theft is by no means unheard of in Australia, especially in Queensland and accidents will happen, sometimes to your luggage and, worse still, to you. Travel insurance including cancellation rebates, luggage rebates and health cover should be bought before you come to Australia. It is worth remembering that once a person has been in Australia six months, he or she automatically comes under the provisions of the national low cost health care scheme called Medicare.

Climate

Australian climes range from cool temperate to wet tropical to alpine to desert. The seasons are the reverse of northern hemisphere countries, ie, spring is September to November, summer December to February, autumn March to May and winter June to August. In most parts of the country seasons are less marked than in Europe and North America, although this is less so in Tasmania. The in-between seasons are often the best times to come as they have neither the extremes of heat nor cold experienced at other periods. High summer, even in Melbourne, can swelter, and winter can rain and blow. In the tropical north there are really only two seasons, 'Wet' from November to May and 'Dry' from April to October. The wet is hot and sticky, the dry warm and clear. Day to day weather is forecast nightly on television and radio news bulletins throughout the nation.

Here are some seasonal statistics for major centres of population; temperatures are in °C (°F) and rainfall is in millimetres (inches).

		Summer		Autumn		Winter		Spring	
Sydney	Max Temp	25	(77)	22	(72)	17	(63)	22	(72)
	Min Temp	18	(64)	14	(57)	9	(48)	13	(55)
	Rainfall	97	(4)	126	(5)	105	(4)	74	(3)
	Water Temp	21	(70)	19	(66)	16	(61)	17	(63)
Melbourne	Max Temp	26	(79)	20	(68)	14	(57)	20	(68)

	Min Temp	14	(57)	11	(52)	6	(42)	9	(48)
	Rainfall	52	(2)	57	(2)	48	(2)	61	(2)
	Water Temp	17	(63)	16	(61)	13	(55)	14	(57)
Perth	Max Temp	29	(84)	24	(75)	18	(65)	22	(72)
	Min Temp	17	(63)	14	(57)	9	(48)	12	(53)
	Rainfall	11	—	61	(2)	166	(7)	52	(2)
	Water Temp	20	(68)	21	(70)	19	(66)	18	(64)
Brisbane	Max Temp	29	(84)	26	(78)	21	(70)	26	(78)
	Min Temp	21	(70)	16	(61)	10	(50)	16	(61)
	Rainfall	152	(6)	100	(4)	58	(2)	73	(3)
	Water Temp	25	(77)	24	(75)	20	(68)	21	(70)
Darwin	Max Temp	32	(90)	32	(90)	31	(88)	34	(93)
	Min Temp	25	(77)	24	(75)	20	(68)	24	(75)
	Rainfall	321	(13)	126	(5)	2	—	63	(3)
	Water Temp	29	(84)	28	(82)	25	(77)	28	(82)
Adelaide	Max Temp	29	(84)	23	(73)	16	(61)	22	(72)
	Min Temp	16	(61)	13	(55)	8	(46)	11	(52)
	Rainfall	22	(1)	47	(2)	67	(3)	42	(2)
	Water Temp	19	(66)	18	(64)	14	(57)	15	(59)
Cairns	Max Temp	31	(88)	29	(84)	26	(78)	29	(84)
	Min Temp	24	(75)	21	(70)	18	(65)	21	(70)
	Rainfall	336	(13)	244	(10)	37	(1)	57	(2)
	Water Temp	28	(82)	26	(78)	23	(73)	25	(77)
Hobart	Max Temp	21	(70)	17	(63)	12	(53)	17	(63)
	Min Temp	12	(53)	9	(48)	5	(41)	8	(46)
	Rainfall	47	(2)	49	(2)	53	(2)	58	(2)
	Water Temp	14	(57)	14	(57)	12	(53)	12	(53)
Canberra	Max Temp	27	(80)	20	(68)	12	(53)	19	(66)
	Min Temp	12	(53)	6	(42)	1	(34)	7	(44)
	Rainfall	59	(2)	50	(2)	40	(2)	60	(2)
Alice Springs	Max Temp	36	(97)	28	(82)	20	(68)	30	(87)
	Min Temp	21	(70)	14	(57)	7	(44)	14	(57)
	Rainfall	35	(1)	17	(1)	14	(1)	16	(1)

To convert Centigrade to Fahrenheit: multiply by 9, divide by 5, then add 32.
To convert Fahrenheit to Centigrade: subtract 32, multiply by 5, then divide by 9.

Time

Australia has three time zones, **Eastern Standard Time** (Queensland, New South Wales, Victoria and Tasmania) is 10 hours behind GMT, **Central Standard Time** (South Australia and the Northern Territory) is one half hour behind EST and **Western Standard Time** is two hours behind EST. Some Australian states adopt daylight saving in the summer months. This throws the system into chaos because not everyone likes the idea. Queensland, for example, sticks to Eastern Standard

Time and falls an hour behind NSW, Victoria and Tasmania which adopt Eastern Summer Time. They in turn move three hours ahead of Western Australia which chooses not to daylight save either. South Australia and the Northern Territory save and so remain a half hour behind NSW, Victoria and Tasmania, a half hour ahead of Queensland and two and a half hours ahead of Western Australia.

Getting Around Australia

By Air

Flying is the main form of transport between Australian states. It is dominated by two airlines, **Ansett** and **Australian**. The first is a private company, the second a government instrumentality but their operations are so bound by governmental regulation that they fly almost identical schedules and set identical fares. Both offer generous reductions on their rather expensive economy fares to travellers who book their internal flights ahead of time, with some return fares cut by as much as 45 per cent on major routes. Various conditions apply to such reduced fares, including the possibility of having your flight delayed by one or two days if full-paying passengers fill the service you originally booked and the inconvenience of not knowing precisely which flight you're on until the day before you travel. Smaller but still large reductions apply to other advance purchase options and stand-by flights.

Some special air passes are available to overseas visitors only. These are the **See Australia** fare and the **Go Australia** air pass. The first knocks 30 per cent off the cost of your fare provided you travel over 1000 km, very easy to do in Australia, and the second takes off 40 per cent on average for journeys between 6000 and 10,000 km. They are available on Ansett, Australian and Air NSW. The major restriction is that you must enter Australia on a promotional airfare, for example Apex, Excursion or a special promotion. These passes must be bought overseas or within 30 days of arrival.

Two smaller operators, East West Airlines and Air NSW run between Sydney, Melbourne, Brisbane and Ayers Rock. They fly smaller aircraft and offer less on board service than the majors but their fares are often considerably cheaper and they too have similar special offers. Both are owned by Ansett. Flying from place to place within New South Wales is also the preserve of these two. Other small airlines of which the biggest are Air Queensland, Ansett NT, Ansett WA and Skywest (WA) operate in other states.

East West Airlines offers the **Trans-Continental,** a one-way pass from east to west or west to east starting in Cairns or Perth; the **YSS** airfare which gives 30 per cent discount on normal fares over all sectors but must be purchased overseas or within 14 days of arrival; **Coastal** airpass which carries you from Cairns to Hobart via Brisbane, Sydney and Melbourne, but within 60 days only. Air Queensland offers ten per cent discount to all overseas passengers flying on Qantas.

Qantas passengers can also take advantage of their stop-over entitlements for travel within Australia provided that they have not exhausted those entitlements on the way here.

By Rail

Trains in Australia are quite good, though not a match for those in Europe or Japan where small distances make inter-city train travel extremely attractive. In general, they are leisurely by comparison and not particularly well funded although major services are well patronised.

Railways of Australia is the organisation responsible for train travel throughout the country. Most of its rail network is in the south. There are trains from Sydney to Canberra, Melbourne, Brisbane, Perth, Adelaide and Alice Springs; from Melbourne to Sydney and Adelaide; from Adelaide to Sydney, Alice Springs and Perth; from Perth to Adelaide and from Brisbane to Sydney, Rockhampton and Cairns. Each state except Tasmania and the Northern Territory has a passenger rail network, the most wide-ranging being NSW, followed by Victoria and Queensland. Services are not very extensive in South and Western Australia. Most trains offer first- and economy-class seating and, where applicable, sleeping and dining cars.

Purchasing in advance can also reduce your rail fare on some services. Savings of up to 30 per cent are possible on 'CAPER' (Customer Advance Purchase Excursion Rail) fares booked and paid for at least seven days in advance but you must ask for a CAPER fare.

Austrail passes are available overseas or on arrival if you can produce your passport and a return ticket. They entitle holders to travel on any government rail service in Australia or on road coaches operated by the railways. There are two kinds, First Class and Budget and they range in price from $520 for 14 days first class and $320 for 14 days budget to $1290 first class 90 days and $820 budget 90 days. Seven day extensions cost $260 first class and $160 budget and there is a $35 per sector sleeping berth charge on interstate trains.

By Road

Express coach services are frequent, reliable and comfortable throughout Australia. They are also relatively inexpensive but, because of the sheer distance between cities, can be a slow and tiring way to travel. Operators with national networks are **Ansett Pioneer, Greyhound, Deluxe** and **Bus Australia** (known as **McCafferty's** in parts of NSW and Queensland). They travel right round the Australian coast and into the Red Centre, serving all major centres of population and many minor ones. Greyhound has the most comprehensive network but the difference between it and its rivals is really minimal.

Cheap passes are available for those contemplating extended coach travel on Greyhound, Deluxe, Ansett Pioneer and bus Australia. They run from 7 to 90 days, cost from around $165 to $1100 and are excellent value. Some include accommodation and only Greyhound and Ansett Pioneer extend to Tasmania. There are also routing restrictions on some passes.

Hiring a car
Car hire is dominated by Avis, Hertz and Budget who have offices throughout the country and desks in all airports. Thrifty is only a little below the big three as is National both of which also have wide networks.

Small cut-price car rental companies exist in most cities and tourism centres. They can be worthwhile if you are not intending to travel very far and will be able to return the car you hire to the place from which you hired it but some of their deals are too good to be true. Be sure to check that mileage charges, collision damage waivers, personal insurance, delivery charges and any other costs are included in the price you are offered before you compare it with the majors. Small vehicles such as Mini Mokes and motor cycles can usually be hired in tourist places and four-wheel drive vehicles are available where they are needed.

Driving Regulations

Australians drive on the left hand side of the road, opposite to the USA and European countries, the same as the UK. To drive whilst here you will need a valid overseas driving licence or an International Driver's Permit and it must be carried whenever you are driving. Drink driving laws are extremely strict and the best advice is not to drink and drive. International road signs are used on most roads. The speed limit in built-up areas is commonly 60 km per hour and on major highways 110 km per hour. Between these, the most common are 80 and 100. Petrol (gasoline) is not expensive by European standards, being about 50 cents per litre in the big cities. The price is higher in the outback—up to 75 cents—and in Tasmania where the rule is around 60 to 65 cents.

By Sea

In days gone by, Australians and visitors to Australia could take advantage of a considerable coastal shipping network, especially along the eastern seaboard but all these services are long gone and the only regular sea service remaining crosses Bass Strait from Melbourne to Devonport in Tasmania. It is a passenger and car ferry called the *Abel Tasman*. Details are given in Part X, Tasmania.

Federalism

This may seem an esoteric subject for a travel guide book but it impinges on the lives of everyone moving around Australia. The nation has six states and a Federal Government which results in far too many and not very uniform laws. State governments, for example, have control of liquor laws and shopping hours which means that these are slightly different from state to state. So are driving regulations, particularly the amount of alcohol you can have in your blood before its illegal to drive and whether you can be pulled up at random to be tested for it. States also have separate transport systems but their borders are unregulated, except for a prohibition on the carrying across of fruit and vegetables.

Where to Stay

Accommodation choices in Australia are wide but there is a jungle of terminology concerning them and they are not rated by any governmental body or central tourist authority. Americans should note that people who want twin and not double beds should ask for them in advance of their arrival at most hotels and motels.

Hotels

The word 'hotel' has two widely divergent meanings in Australia. Regents, Hyatts, Sheratons and their like, to be found in all major cities and tourist destinations, are called hotels, but so is the corner pub. The word refers to the liquor licence held by these institutions which allows them to have a public bar no matter what their status in other matters. The Regent will also have restaurants, cabaret room, coffee shops and high class accommodation. The corner pub too may have a restaurant or bistro but its accommodation usually leaves a lot to be desired, probably consisting of a few dark narrow rooms without bathrooms.

Chain hotels are increasingly common in Australia but their standards vary. The Regents and Hyatts are top of the heap, often because they have the newest establishments. Sheraton and Hilton, also with some new hotels, are next as well as a few Oberois. The lesser chains are Southern Pacific and Four Seasons. In all chain hotel accommodation you will find, besides the requisite bedding and bathroom, electric jug with tea bags and instant coffee, a fridge full of alcohol, a colour television, bedside radio, telephone and often a lounge or easy chair, table and chairs. Hotels offer room service. In some it is 24 hours, in others often less, especially for meals. They generally have 24-hour reception. The decor in chain hotels is rarely hideous, rather it ranges from bearable to luxurious.

In the wilder reaches of Australia, the country pub is an institution and a legend. Unlike its city counterpart it usually offers liveable if sometimes rough rooms but it is rapidly being replaced by the motel, in many cases attached to existing pubs, a useful compromise. In towns where country pubs offer decent accommodation, I have tried to list them in this guide.

There is another altogether different kind of hotel called a **Private Hotel**. Establishments of this designation may not serve liquor and, these days, are often called guesthouses. British travellers will know them as bed and breakfast accommodation. **Country House Hotels** are another minor permutation. Exceedingly up-market, some of them are among the loveliest places to stay in Australia. They are usually established in grand old country homes and offer high standard accommodation backed up with gourmet food.

Motels

Motels exist in almost every Australian town and in the suburbs of many cities. They tend to be owner operated, usually by a married couple or individual and their quality can vary widely. Age is the other determinant of standard with those over ten years old showing signs of obsolescence in the face of ferocious new competitors but, generally speaking, motels are cheaper than chain and international style hotels and in many country towns, the best available accommodation. The best are absolutely excellent for their market but even the worst probably won't cheat you.

Certain matters are guaranteed. No liquor is served except if the premises has a licensed restaurant and then only in the restaurant. Rooms have a small, separate bathroom either at the front or the back which will have a shower but often no bath,

11

there will be an electric jug, tea bags and instant coffee, a fridge frequently containing fresh milk, a colour television (considered essential even in the remotest parts of Australia), a place to put your suitcase and a bedside radio. Many motels have a swimming pool and restaurant although their food is rarely anything but ordinary to amateurish. There is either no room service or room service only for breakfast and dinner. Decor in motels can be outrageously tasteless and almost universally features a bare brick wall somewhere in the room. More recently built places are less offensive in this department. Some motels offer family suites of more than one room sometimes containing kitchenettes (called 'cooking facilities') or full kitchen.

One road to reliability in motel selection is to stick with a 'chain'. These are groups of motels, independently owned but linked for advertising, booking and rating purposes. The biggest are Flag Inns and Homestead Motor Inns (linked to the US group Best Western). Each publishes a directory of its establishments, rated and described and giving tariffs. They also offer cut price deals, free nights and other inducements for frequent use of their motels as well as reservations from just about anywhere in the country. Contact Flag in Australia by ringing 008 335 005 and Homestead on 008 222 116. Flag Inn directories can be obtained from ATC offices.

Guesthouses
Sometimes called private hotels as mentioned above, these are roughly equivalent to the British bed and breakfast hotel, being small establishments with not more than about 20 rooms and shared facilities—the average is one bathroom to two rooms. The better ones offer private bathrooms. All serve breakfast and very many also offer dinner and/or lunch. Some house top-flight restaurants and they are particularly prevalent on the outskirts of big cities where people spend weekends out of town.

Serviced Apartments
These are the coming thing in city accommodation. They pitch themselves either to the family market or the up-market hotel patron looking for a change. In keeping with this situation they can be like an average home or absolutely Vogue. They come with one, two, three or sometimes four bedrooms, a kitchen and at least one bathroom and are ideal for extended stays in one location. Service is usually daily or weekly and means a change of sheets and towels and a general clean-up in the hotel chamber maid manner. Room service and 24-hour reception is lacking in almost all, only in Melbourne which has begun to feature the up-market end of this style, does service extend to delivered restaurant-prepared meals and such like.

Outdoors
Camping grounds and caravan (trailer) parks are the forms of outdoor accommodation in Australia. Caravan parks are numerous, especially in beachside locations where the local population goes for school and summer holidays. They sometimes offer very cheap accommodation in on-site vans from as little as $7 to $10 per night. Camping grounds, some with powered sites, exist in the same areas, often as adjuncts to caravan parks. Camping is also possible in National Parks and similar

public recreation areas but it is restricted to designated grounds. Anyone intending to sleep under the stars in the wilderness should ask park rangers where it is legal to do so. Also keep in mind that parts of Australia have distinct bushfire seasons and the lighting of fires is likely to be banned if the danger is high.

Farm Stays
Farm holidays have a tremendous air of romance but either the farm or the holiday has to be a sideline for the people running them. The quality of accommodation varies from what to do with the shearers quarters when it isn't shearing time to motel-style rooms and full board but guests are often expected to supply their own linen and food. My suggestion if you intend taking a farm holiday is to investigate the deal thoroughly, not because there's likely to be any dishonesty but because the outback is a hard place and people live simple, tough lives with a minimum of citified comforts. The amount of 'farm' in your holiday can vary too. Some places simply offer accommodation on the property while others encourage guests to involve themselves in—or at least observe, seasonal activities. Farm holiday stations (ranches) are listed in the sections on places where they occur. See Outback New South Wales, The Snowy Mountains and Inland Queensland.

Others
Very cheap accommodation is available in **Youth Hostels** and privately run back-packers hostels, YMCAs and YWCAs and in the residential colleges of some universities during academic holidays, especially November through February. Students receive preference for university accommodation.

Eating and Drinking

Licensed vs. BYO

Australian licensing laws will baffle those who come from countries where the population is allowed to drink whatever it likes, wherever it likes, 24 hours a day. The Australian situation is almost bizarre in the permutations of permission to drink but its essentials can be explained sufficiently to place the traveller in a 'forewarned is forearmed' condition.

Premises described as 'licensed' may sell and serve liquor. They range from pubs to bars to restaurants. There is a second division in the restaurant trade known as BYO (Bring Your Own). In places wearing this label you may drink whatever you bring but liquor is not for sale. Usually, a waiter will take your bottle, open it and serve it just the same as if it had come from a wine list. This division between restaurants has been raised from merely a different way of serving booze to a class war. BYO restaurants are distinctly different from licensed premises in most cases. They are smaller, less expensive, less decorated and less fussy but they often serve very good food. BYOs mean that diners can eat and drink less expensively than otherwise would be the case and they are well worth trying, especially in Melbourne and Sydney. The Eating Out sections of this guide include lots of them.

Plenty of other rules apply to the business of drinking in Australia and because liquor licenses are doled out by state governments, they change somewhat from state to state. Pubs mostly serve for ten hours a day, 10 am to 10 pm or 11 am to 11 pm and in some cases noon to midnight but they can, indeed must, serve 'bona fide travellers'—anyone who has travelled 25 miles, at any time. Other licenses, for example bars, nightclubs and some restaurants can extend drinking hours up to 3 am but there is almost no 24-hour trading anywhere. There are also rules about drinking in licensed premises which serve food, often you may not be served liquor unless you have something to eat. Anti-discrimination laws have disallowed the old exclusion of women from public bars and in cities their presence no longer excites comment but in the nether reaches of the country a woman who breezes into a public bar is still a focus for stares and jokes among the old time drinkers.

Dress Codes
Australia prides itself on being a free and easy place but some rules do apply to what you wear when socialising. In public bars almost anything is acceptable, down to bikinis and swimming costumes outdoors at beachside spots but once into the lounge or other kind of bar at least t-shirts, shorts and some footwear is expected. Some nightclubs will not allow you through the door in jeans or t-shirt, thongs are out anywhere but the pub but ties are rarely required and even if they are the doorman usually has a few spare.

The Ethnic Explosion
Melbourne and Sydney particularly but also other cities have benefited enormously in their cuisines from the presence of European and Asian migrants. The arrival of thousands of people from Italy and Greece during the 1950s and '60s and of many from Thailand, Vietnam and other parts of South-East Asia during the last decade has changed the eating habits of the average Australian city dweller from meat pies and peas to *yum cha*, green curry or taramosalata. The restaurant scene is constantly on the move, one fad taking the place of another every few months but a basis of high quality cooking and an increasingly discerning public ensures that eating in cities is one of the great pleasures of an Australian holiday.

The same cannot be said of the countryside where the further out you go, the less appetising your fare is likely to become. It is not wise to expect to eat well in remote towns, Australia has no tradition of regional cooking and isolated places in such a large and far-scattered country struggle to gain access to good quality ingredients.

Oz Nouveau
Under the influence of those new Australians who came from Europe and Asia, the country has lately begun to develop a cuisine of its own. It is only an infant and has no completely definite characteristics except a wide eclecticism and a tendency to apply the precision and design of modern European cooking with flavours from Asia and ingredients native to the regions in which individual restaurants are found. It does not consist of kangaroo tail soup and buff (buffalo) burgers, although these can be found in some places.

The new style goes by snappy titles such as *Oz Nouveau* and *Australienne* and is found in and around the big cities of Melbourne and Sydney. Generally speaking, it does not come cheap.

Grazing

Eating on the run and at odd hours is done more and more in Australia these days. The formality of eating hours has broken down most extensively in cities where travellers will find all kinds of fast-food outlets including MacDonalds, Pizza Huts and similar places as well as small hamburger shops (often called milk bars) and sandwich-making bars.

Restaurant Prices

Restaurant prices are not especially high in Australia but neither are they especially low. The cheapest way to eat is at small BYO restaurants but this has already been stressed. In this guide meal costs are designated low price range, mid price range and upper price range. Low is up to $25 per person but can be a good deal less in the big cities, mid is up to $40 per person and upper is over that amount. The cost presumes a three-course meal but does not include wine. One way to eat less expensively at some of the higher cost places is to leave out one course.

Tipping

This is not common or necessary in Australia as many workers are paid high penalty and overtime wages for working out of hours.

Australian Wine

Australia produces large quantities of excellent domestic wine and even larger quantities of lesser quality vintage which is sold in cardboard casks. Bottled wine is nearly always better than the drink sold in bulk. Here are some tips for understanding how it is labelled. Labels show the name of the wine-maker and either the variety of grape from which the wine is made (varietals) or the style of wine (generic) which the bottle contains. Common varietals include riesling, chardonnay and semillon in .whites and cabernet, hermitage and shiraz in red but there are many, many others. Any wine which wears a varietal label must have at least 85 per cent of that grape variety in its make-up. Labels on generic wine styles do not need to say what grape varieties they contain or how much, consequently they are more variable. Chablis, moselle and claret are common generics.

There are three major centres of wine production, the Barossa Valley in South Australia, the Hunter Valley in New South Wales and the Swan and Margaret River Valleys in Western Australia. Wines are also produced in Victoria and Tasmania. Barossa Valley wines are the most famous and, certainly in reds, the best. Whites from this region are good too but are run close by those from the Hunter Valley. The Western Australian vineyards also produce very drinkable white wines, including a much drier style of riesling than those from other regions. The best way to taste wines is to tour the vineyards recommended in relevant sections of this guide. All vineyards are open up to seven days a week for tasting and generally supply free from their whole range, although sometimes premium wines are charged for. There is no pressure to buy and many wine-makers are happy to place you on a mailing list.

15

Recommending wines is a hazardous pursuit in Australia. Individual vintages drop in and out of the market year by year and hit wine-makers are targets for take-over merchants who keep the label but not the inspired individual. In general terms, chardonnay is the best white drinking and cabernet and shiraz the best red. Dessert wines from botrytis-affected semillons to rich tokays and muscats are also excellent. Australian champagne, though often talked of and more often drunk, is no match for its French counterparts but very cheap. You will pay around $10 at a bottle shop for good red or white, about one and a half to twice that in a licensed restaurant.

Australian Beer
A national reputation for consuming a Sydney Harbour full of beer annually is something Australians have to put up with. In reality, it's a bit of a rumour. Australian do drink a lot of beer but a good deal less than some others. The beer is always served freezing cold which relieves your thirst and heat but means you can't really taste it. It used to be the case that each state had its own brewery and there was some regionalisation of beer styles but this has lately gone by the board since all breweries are now shared by two giant Australian based transnational companies, Swan and Carlton United which makes Fosters.

An independent-minded response to this new uniformity has emerged in the form of 'boutique' breweries—individual hotels which brew their own beer. You'll find them in Sydney and Perth. The beer they serve comes in a wide range of eccentric varieties and is generally only available across the bars of the hotel which brews it.

Spirits
Australians do not drink spirits in the same way as Americans, mostly because they are so expensive. A bottle of scotch from the liquor shop shelf will set you back well over $20 and in a bar you will pay several dollars for a nip not much more than half the size of the American standard. People who want to have spirits will thus find it by far the most expensive way to drink.

Shopping

Retail hours throughout Australia are limited compared to the United States. Shops open around 9 am in the morning and generally trade until 5 or 5.30 pm during the working week. There are extended trading hours on one or two nights each week, usually Thursday and/or Friday. Weekend trading is 9 am to noon on Saturday and not at all on Sunday but in Sydney and Melbourne some shops and shopping centres stay open throughout the weekend. Sydney shops trade until 4 pm on Saturday.

There is a domestic fashion industry which generally follows European trends although colour plays a stronger role, especially in summer. Look for clothes by Trent Nathan, Jenny Kee, and Stuart Membery in the exclusive shopping districts of Sydney and Melbourne. The style will be there but Australian fabrics are not equal to those from Italy, for example. The tourist to Sydney will become sick of the sight of t-shirts, tea towels, posters and other paraphernalia bearing designs by Ken

Done whose clever use of bright colours, simple forms and slogans makes his work unique but whose marketing skills have led to extreme overkill. Aboriginal artefacts including paintings are common in Central Australia and are also sold in the major cities. More about them is to be found in the section on Alice Springs.

Banking

Banking hours are 9.30 am to 4 pm Monday to Thursday and to 5 pm on Friday throughout Australia. Banks are closed on weekends. Although banks are highly computerised, this seems to have had little effect on their speed of service. Do not expect them to do anything quickly and you will not be disappointed.

Mail and Phones

Post Offices open 9 am to 5 pm Monday to Friday and not at all on weekends. Overseas and interstate phone calls can be made direct from your hotel room in most large cities and from public phone boxes, provided you have enough coins. A local call costs 30 cents (one 20 cent coin and one 10 cent coin only) from a public phone.

Newspapers, TV and Radio

Daily newspapers are published in all major cities and towns and there are two national dailies, *The Australian* and *The Australian Financial Review*, and one national weekly, *The Times on Sunday*. Television and radio stations are either commercial—supported by advertising, or run by the Australian Broadcasting Corporation, a government funded, independently-run network modelled on the BBC. The latter is the only truly national network in either radio or television; others, although owned by a few big companies, are regionally based. There is also a station called SBS TV which broadcasts in languages other than English although its news and current affairs programmes are in that language.

Public and School Holidays

Australia has a reputation for having lots of public holidays. It certainly has more than some countries but less than others. They can have a devastating effect on holidaymakers as museums, restaurants, shops and just about everything closes on the days when they occur. Here is the list:

New Year's Day
Australia Day (January 26)
Hobart Cup (February 4, Hobart only)
Regatta Day (February 10, Hobart only)
8 Hour Day (March 2, Tasmania)
Labour Day (March 2, Western Australia)
Labour Day (March 9, Victoria)
Canberra Day (March 16, ACT)

Good Friday
Easter Monday
Easter Tuesday (Victoria only)
Bank Holiday (Easter Tuesday, Tasmania)
Anzac Day (April 25)
Labour Day (May 4, Queensland)
May Day (May 4, Northern Territory)
Adelaide Cup Day (May 18, Adelaide only)
Foundation Day (June 1, Western Australia)
Queen's Birthday (June 8 all states except Western Australia)
Alice Springs Show Day (July 3, Alice Springs only)
Darwin Royal Show Day (July 24, Darwin only)
Bank Holiday (August 3, ACT and NSW)
Picnic Day (August 3, Northern Territory)
Brisbane Exhibition Day (August 19, Brisbane only)
Melbourne Show Day (September 24, Melbourne only)
Queen's Birthday (October 5, Western Australia)
Labour Day (October 5, ACT and NSW)
Labour Day (October 12, South Australia)
Melbourne Cup Day (First Tuesday in November, Melbourne only)
Christmas Day
Boxing Day
Proclamation Day (December 28, South Australia)
Additional Holiday (December 29, Northern Territory)

School Holidays occur four times a year in Australia. The longest break begins in the second week of December and finishes in early February. There are shorter breaks from mid-April to mid-May, late June to late July and mid-September to mid-October.

Tourist Information

Tourist information agencies abound in Australia. There is one to be found in almost every town where tourists even so much as show their faces. They are staffed by local people and full of informative if sometimes ill-produced brochures that are unavailable anywhere else, as well as information about accommodation and tours. You will find them indicated by the international 'i' sign. They are generally open 9 am to 5 pm Monday to Friday and 9 am to noon on Saturday. In some cases these hours extend to all day Saturday and Sunday.

Emergencies

Police, fire and ambulance services can be contacted by dialling 000 from anywhere in Australia.

Embassies

All foreign embassies are in Canberra. Some useful addresses are:
UK: Commonwealth Avenue, Yarralumla; (73 0422)

Ireland: 20 Arkana St, Yarralumla; (73 3022)
USA: State Circle, Yarralumla; (73 3711)
Canada: Commonwealth Avenue, Yarralumla; (73 3844)
New Zealand: Commonwealth Avenue, Yarralumla; (73 3611)
   Government representation in major state capitals is at consular level with
addresses and phone numbers listed in local telephone directories.

Itineraries

Fast travel

The following 10 itineraries mostly presume that travellers will have two to four
weeks' holiday and will therefore fly from one large destination to another, using
each as a base for touring a given district. Although they represent convenient
'modules' they don't exhaust the possibilities; they can also be combined to build
longer holidays.

Sydney and the Barrier Reef

This is the most common itinerary. You arrive either at Sydney or Cairns International airport. Cairns is a base for travel to nearby islands, the Barrier Reef, the
Atherton Tableland and Cape Tribulation. Activities include boat trips, diving,
fishing, scenic flights, bush walks and rainforest tours. In Sydney you will see the city
sights, the Blue Mountains, the beaches and enjoy a couple of nights on the town. A
day trip to Canberra is also a possibility. Activities include city and bush walking,
harbour trips under steam or sail, swimming, dining out and theatre-going. Two
weeks or slightly less is sufficient for this itinerary.

Sydney–Reef–Red Centre

This option adds Ayers Rock alone or Ayers Rock and Alice Springs to the itinerary
above. Arrival is again at Sydney or Cairns from where you fly to the Rock or to Alice
Springs and take coach transport to the Rock. This is a very good itinerary for the
fast traveller because it gives the maximum spectacle and fun in the shortest time,
combining Australia's best city, the fabulous reef and the startling inland in one trip.
Only include Alice Springs if you want to visit the gorges of the Macdonnell Ranges.
This itinerary can be done in two weeks at a cracking pace but close to three is kinder
to your blood pressure.

Sydney–The Barrier Reef–Northern Territory

This is very much like the Sydney–Barrier Reef–Red Centre itinerary but adds the
Top End of the Northern Territory, extending the trip by around a week. It
combines Sydney, Cairns, Alice Springs and Darwin. In the Top End you will see
Darwin, Kakadu National Park and possibly Katherine Gorge. Activities include
looking at park wildlife (crocodiles, buffaloes and thousands of birds) and boating
through the deep gorge at Katherine.

Big Cities

This is a two week trip for drivers or train travellers. The Sydney–Canberra–

Melbourne axis in the south east is Australia's most settled, civilised and historical area but it also offers plenty of beautiful and varied countryside including the Snowy Mountains, the South Coast of New South Wales, the Murray River and the Victorian Gold Fields. Arrival is either at Sydney or Melbourne and the first and last days should be spent there. Go south down the coast from Sydney, inland to Canberra for an overnight or two night stop, down through the mountains, across the Murray, through central Victoria to Melbourne. From Melbourne simply reverse the process. This holiday covers the best art galleries, theatres and restaurants in Australia as well as some good wine-growing areas and historical sites.

Including Tasmania
If you have an extra week or so, the island state of Tasmania can be added to the Sydney–Canberra–Melbourne trip. Visitors to the small state will be able to see Hobart and the nearby Tasman Peninsula, the wild national parks of the west and the state's second city of Launceston. A pleasing balance of activities is available from city sight-seeing to picnics in an historical village, great bushwalking and spectacular river trips. Australia's only regular passenger ship, the *Abel Tasman*, which plies Bass Strait from Melbourne to Tasmania is an added inducement.

Perth–Ayers Rock–Sydney
This itinerary is a good way to make the best of a landing in Perth which is a long way from everything else in Australia, especially Sydney. Allow yourself around three weeks or close to four if you wish to include Alice Springs. Two to three days is sufficient for Perth itself and its port of Fremantle where the 1987 America's Cup was sailed. Using Perth as a base you can also explore the wine-growing districts of the Swan Valley to the north east and the Margaret River to the south west. Wild flowers abound in the south west during September and October and there are attractive beaches as well. Anyone choosing to visit only Ayers Rock in the Red Centre will need a minimum of two days. If the Macdonnell Ranges and other gorge country around Alice Springs is included, this will stretch to about a week. Sight-seeing is the major activity in the centre but you can also go camel riding and meet Aboriginals. This itinerary finishes with a week in Sydney. It can, of course, be reversed if you would rather to finish in Perth.

Melbourne–Ayers Rock–Adelaide
This is definitely a 'second time around' option. A week in Melbourne, eating out, shopping, going to the theatre, taking day trips into the countryside is followed by either two days at Ayers Rock alone or extra days in Alice Springs and a few days in Adelaide including a visit to Australia's best wine-growing district, the Barossa Valley. Those with more time can tack Perth onto the end of this itinerary. Those un-excited by Melbourne or Adelaide can remove one of those cities and go to Perth at the beginning or the end of their trip instead. The time taken will be much the same.

Queensland Alone (maybe with Sydney)
Queensland has so much to offer that you can easily limit your Australian holiday to

that state. Two weeks can be pleasantly spent by arriving in Brisbane and spending a couple of days there before departing for a southern island like Heron for diving or the Whitsunday Islands, halfway up the reef, for sailing. Flying on to Cairns gives an opportunity to see the jungles and rainforest of the hinterland as well as take Queensland's best reef viewing boat, the *Quicksilver*, from Port Douglas. Hankerings for the outback can be satisfied at Winton or Mount Isa in the west. Anyone who wants to extend the tour to Sydney can fly to that city from Cairns and finish their stay there.

Northern Territory Alone
A week in the Top End and a week in the Red Centre will show you the Australia of cinematic legend, the outback of celluloid dreams. The scenery varies from tropical wetlands filled with birds and fish to flat dry red deserts to ironstone gorges and Ayers Rock. You can meet buffalo hunters in Darwin or tribal aborigines at Alice Springs.

Perth–Broome–Darwin
This offers something unusual for anyone who has already 'done' Ayers Rock. Huge desert gorges and the eccentric Bungle Bungle Range lie inland from Broome and the town itself is worth visiting for its outlandish natural colours and racial melting-pot character. You will need about three weeks, maybe more depending on the season, to land in Perth, have a look around, fly to Broome and go by road to Darwin via the desert sights.

Slow Travel

The itineraries here are deliberately expansive, allowing the opportunity to add some lesser known places mentioned in this guide to the tourist spots everybody knows. One way to cut the expense of these longer holidays is to tow a caravan (trailer) or stay in camping grounds.

Around Australia
It takes six months to drive around Australia but one sees just about everything. You may start at any point on the route I am about to give but I have chosen to begin and end in Sydney as that's where most international travellers land. The question of whether to head north or south depends on which time of year you arrive. If arriving in winter (June to August), turn north, if in summer (December to February), turn south. I shall presume a winter arrival.

Basically, the route is Sydney–North Coast New South Wales–Gold Coast–Brisbane–Sunshine Coast–Rockhampton–Whitsunday Islands–Townsville–Cairns–Charters Towers–Mt Isa–Three Ways–Alice Springs–Ayers Rock–Alice Springs–Tennant Creek–Katherine–Kakadu–Darwin–Katherine–Kununurra–Broome–The Pilbara–Perth–Kalgoorlie–The Nullarbor Plain–Adelaide–Melbourne–(divert to Tasmania if you want)–Canberra–Sydney. Travelling this route means almost no dirt roads and six months allows some time to stop in and circulate around most places. Provided that you land in or near most of the towns listed, a good road map and reading this guide will allow you to plan your own variations on the route.

The Eastern Circle
The same rules for departure times and directions apply to this route which is identical as far as Ayers Rock. From here you turn south to Coober Pedy and Adelaide before heading for Melbourne, Canberra and Sydney. Allow yourself ten weeks to three months at minimum.

The Western Circle
This one begins and ends in Perth, Darwin or Adelaide. Once again, try to go north for the winter and south for the summer. It also involves long sections of desert road including the Stuart Highway from Adelaide to Darwin, the Eyre Highway across the Nullarbor Plain and sections of the Great Northern Highway in Western Australia. It is best for those who want a long experience of Outback Australia. Beginning in Darwin, the route is Darwin–Kakadu–Katherine–Kununurra–Broome–The Pilbara–Perth–Kalgoorlie–The Nullarbor Plain–Adelaide–Coober Pedy–Ayers Rock–Alice Springs–Tennant Creek–Darwin. Allow three to four months.

The East Coast
You can drive the length of Australia's east coast from Melbourne to Cairns in about two months. Although the highways may seem very close to the coast on maps, except for short sections, they run well out of sight of the sea so true aficionados of coasts must frequently divert from the road to the sea. Once in Queensland, make sure to set aside some time for trips to the Barrier Reef and its islands.

The Stuart Highway
The Stuart Highway runs over 3,000 km (1860 miles) from Darwin to Adelaide. Four weeks should be sufficient to cover it and see, as well as the two cities, Kakadu National Park, Katherine Gorge, Alice Springs and its surroundings, Ayers Rock, Coober Pedy and the Flinders Ranges. After that you should have had enough outback for a lifetime. For a change of scene, extend this trip through western Victoria to Melbourne and depart from Australia there. The extra distance will add about a week to ten days.

As Much of Oz as You Can See from a Train
You can't travel right around Australia by train. You miss Darwin and the Top End of the Northern Territory, all but the far south of Western Australia and all of Tasmania. The *Indian Pacific*, the longest single route in the country, travels mostly through outback country from Sydney to Perth but to see the maximum in the south travel from Sydney to Melbourne, Melbourne to Adelaide, Adelaide to Kalgoorlie, Kalgoorlie to Perth. The Red Centre is accessible from Adelaide via *The Ghan*.

Train travel extends north of Sydney as far as Cairns. It runs close to but not along the coast and branch lines extend west into the outback from Sydney to Broken Hill (and Adelaide), Rockhampton to Longreach and Townsville to Mt Isa.

Festivals and Events

January
The Sydney Festival occupies all of January each year. It is a wide ranging celebration of the city's delights which includes lots of theatre, film, music and art, but also a great deal of eating, drinking and raucous fun. The festival opens on New Year's Eve with fireworks over the harbour and concerts in various spots around town. Hyde Park is filled with amusements and rides for the duration of the celebrations.
Australia Day, January 26, is Australia's official national day and remembers Captain Phillip's 1788 landing at Sydney Cove. There is usually a re-enactment of the landing in Sydney Harbour.

February/March
Moomba Festival is Melbourne's annual, long established letting down of hair. A float parade through the city, lorded over by a celebrity who has been appointed 'King of Moomba', is the festival's highlight.
Festival of Perth is Western Australia's annual arts extravaganza. Local and overseas performers, writers and artists assemble and exercise their talents for a month.

March
Canberra Festival is the Australian Capital Territory's equivalent of festivals in other major capitals. Theatre, music, film and art are the main foci.
Adelaide Festival is Australia's premier arts festival by a long chalk. It takes place only in even numbered years and specialises in attracting an array of the best overseas talent as well as fostering local performers.

April
Barossa Valley Vintage Festival is Australia's major wine-making celebration. The usually peaceful valley gives way to an orgy of drinking, eating, grape treading and general falling about.

May
Bangtail Muster is the first of the big events in the Northern Territory each year. It takes place in Alice Springs and includes float parades and sporting events.

June
Beer Can Regatta, along with the Henley-on-Todd Regatta, is among Australia's most eccentric events. Rafts and boats made entirely of empty beer cans race in the waters off Darwin. Most sink.

August
Henley-on-Todd Regatta, on the other hand, has never lost a boat because the river it uses is dry. The Todd River in Alice Springs is the venue and the boats are

23

only mock-ups, made of cloth and paper. Racers stick their legs through the bottom, hold the 'boats' waist high and run along the river bed.

September
Spoleto Melbourne is Melbourne's arts festival, an offshoot of Giancarlo Menotti's Italian and American Spoleto festivals. It runs music and theatre, some with a distinctly Italian flavour.
VFL Grand Final is the annual Australian Rules football final in Melbourne. Attended by over 100,000 fans.

October
Australian Formula One Grand Prix takes place through the streets of Adelaide at this time each year. The event generates tremendous noise and excitement and fills the city with people who would have no reason to visit it at other times.

November
Melbourne Cup, on the first Tuesday in November, is the only horse race in the world for which an entire nation stops. Hundreds of millions of dollars are gambled, Victoria takes a public holiday and the whole population watches the race on TV or listens on radio.

December
Sydney to Hobart Yacht Race departs Sydney Harbour on Boxing Day each year. The greatest ocean race in a nation which loves ocean races, it is contested by huge yachts from around the world. They sail down the east coast, across Bass Strait and into Sullivan's Cove at Hobart.

The Bicentennial

Australia officially turned 200 years old on January 26, 1988 when the anniversary of Captain Arthur Phillip's landing is celebrated. A year long party has been planned and wherever anyone goes, there's almost bound to be something on. This is particularly so in New South Wales where the anniversary has more reality than in other states. Most prominent among Bicentennial projects are the redevelopment of Sydney's Darling Harbour and Brisbane's Expo '88 but there are literally thousands of events in small communities. The Australian Bicentennial Authority, 88 George Street, Sydney, (02) 236 1988, has information and programmes.

Australia's Top Ten

This very random and thoroughly subjective list is my pick of the absolute best that Australia has to offer.
Beaches: The beaches of northern New South Wales are unsurpassed anywhere in the world for physical beauty and sheer number. They offer year round swimming but you do have to be able to cope with the surf.

Cities: Sydney is the best Australian city by miles. No other has its beauty of setting or lively approach to life. Adelaide has the prettiest plan and Perth the best weather.
Convict Sites: Port Arthur in Tasmania far outstrips any other for location, historical significance and state of preservation.
Country Towns: Richmond near Hobart in Tasmania is the prettiest and has loads of fascinating colonial history. The once wealthy gold towns of Ballarat and Bendigo in Victoria are also fascinating.
Food: Melbourne has the best restaurants in Australia. Sydney runs a close second.
Islands: Lizard Island is the best small, elegant getaway, Hayman is the most luxurious and Heron has the best diving.
Natural Sights: The rainforested slopes of Mt Warning in northern New South Wales (especially in the rain), Ayers Rock despite the tourists, the Twelve Apostles off the southern coast of Victoria and the corals and fish of the Barrier Reef.
Sports: A cricket test at Adelaide Oval, 18-foot sailing boat races on Sydney Harbour, surf boat races on any beach.
Waterways: Hinchinbrook Passage in north Queensland is hardly ever heard of but astonishingly beautiful and the nearby Whitsunday Passage is good competition for the Bahamas. The waterways of Broken Bay, Pittwater and the Hawkesbury River near Sydney are the best close to any city.
Wine: The Barossa Valley has the best wine and the best scenery of any Australian wine-making area.

Animals

Australia's animals are an oddly schizoid lot, being either outrageously cute, cuddly and appealing—at least in appearance—or hideously poisonous and dangerous. Many a wildlife park on city outskirts is happy to show you scads of koalas, wombats, kangaroos and emus but taipans and crocodiles are more rare, especially in the south. Here are some tips on what you'll be looking at and what they are really like.

Marsupials

Many of Australia's unique animals are marsupial, **koalas and kangaroos,** among them but also their relatives the **wallabies** and **wombats, Tasmanian devils** and **possums** of all types. They give birth to their young in embryo and the tiny creatures then crawl into a pouch on the mother's stomach where they suckle and grow for many months before leaving completely. Baby kangaroos (joeys) will continue to hop in and out of mother's pouch at what seem outrageous sizes. The young are not born in litters but occur one at a time.

Hence, koalas are not bears, their nearest relation being the ground dwelling, bumbling, burrowing wombat. They are also rather grumpy, don't really like to be touched and have long, sharp claws. Kangaroos come in lots of sizes and colours from red to brown and grey and have many relatives, among them the various species of wallabies. There is even a tree-dwelling family member. Seeing kangaroos in the wild is not uncommon as in the countryside they exist in huge numbers. Koalas have to be searched for but are around if you know where to look. Possums only come out at night but can be found in any leafy suburb.

Visitors to wildlife parks will often find marsupials disappointingly sluggish. This is because they are nocturnal or saving their energy. After all, only mad dogs and Englishmen go out in the mid-day sun.

Platypus

The Platypus is a monotreme, something halfway between a reptile and a marsupial, the only such beast in the world and a true missing link except that it's not missing anymore. It is about a foot long, has a duck-like beak, fur and webbed feet (males carry poison injecting spines on their back ones). Females lay eggs and when the young hatch, they suckle them. Platypuses live in small streams and come out in the cool parts of the day, especially early morning.

Birds

Australia's variety of native birdlife is startling. The raucous laugh of the kookaburra (a member of the kingfisher family) is the closest we have to an aural flag and the emu, tall, stately and flightless, is almost as well known as the kangaroo.

Parrots are universal, varying from the large white sulphur crested cockatoo to fantastically bright rosellas and lorikeets and tiny, desert dwelling budgerigars. The noisy grey and pink galah is a byword for idiotic behaviour.

Each environment has unique species: bower birds and other ground nesters live on rainforest floors while tiny, brightly coloured insect eaters flit through the canopy; rare frigate birds and boobies live along the coastal mangroves; in the wetlands waders such as jabirus spoonbills dominate; drylands and mountains are the preserve of birds of prey, the wedge-tailed eagle, the bustard and the kite.

Crocodiles

Crocodiles come in two kinds, salt-water and freshwater, sometimes called Johnson's River crocodiles, but it makes no real difference as the really dangerous ones, salt-water crocs, are perfectly at home in fresh water. They are incredibly dangerous and consider all humans fair game. Warnings about them are to be taken very seriously. Johnson's River crocodiles will generally not attack unless threatened but what they take to be a threat is up to them.

Marine Life

What it lacks in land-based predators like lions and bears, Australia makes up in sea-borne nasties. Box Jelly Fish, also known simply as stingers, float into the coast of Queensland and northern Australia between October and May each year. They have very long tentacles whose sting is enough to kill a child and severely injure an adult. Even walking on the water's edge during stinger season is inadvisable as their tentacles can extend into the shallowest water. Swimming is out of the question although panty hose are said by some people to be an effective defence.

Other deadly marine creatures include stone fish which dwell on the Barrier Reef and are so well disguised as to be almost invisible. Reef walkers who don't wear shoes step on them and are injected with poison by the spines along their backs. This also happens to people who pick up odd-looking rocks. The blue ringed octopus, a small octopus found in rock pools right along the east coast can also sting you to death. Sharks are common in Australian waters but rarely behave like 'Jaws' despite their hideous reputation. One or two unlucky swimmers are injured by them each summer season.

Snakes

Snakes generally stay well away from people and are unlikely to attack you unless feeling threatened but some can be deadly if they do strike. Keep away from taipans, tiger snakes, death adders, copperheads, brown snakes and red bellied black snakes.

Spiders

Two deadly spiders are found in Australia, the funnel-web and the red back. The funnel-web is found in and around Sydney only, especially in the leafier parts. It used to be the case that if one bit you, you made your farewells and went but now there is a successful anti-venene—provided you get to a hospital fast enough. The more widespread red back is not quite so deadly and its bite too can be chemically overcome.

National Parks

Australia has no Parthenon and no Empire State Building but it possesses extraordinary landscapes which Australian governments have begun to treat the way other governments treat their cathedrals. National Parks take in vast tracts of land which are ostensibly protected from unwise development but opened to community and visitors for recreational enjoyment as well as being used for scientific study. Among them are the great parks of Uluru (Ayers Rock) and Kakadu in the Northern Territory and the whole of the Barrier Reef which attract hundreds of thousand of visitors each year but there are also parks in places as remote and unvisited as the Simpson Desert and the Kimberleys. Almost every one has one extraordinary feature worth seeing, some have many. Their facilities for visitors vary from huts and camping grounds to nothing at all. Despite being called National Parks, they are state run, a National Parks and Wildlife Service or similarly named body has charge of them in each state. The state tourism authorities can provide contacts for these bodies in each state and should be able to give you general information about seeing National Parks.

Language

Australians speak English although other speakers of that language might baulk at such an assertion. The native Australian accent is sometimes a little difficult to follow but it is by no means the only accent common to Australia. Careful listeners will hear Italian, Greek and Eastern European accents in many places and Asian English is becoming more common by the day. It is also certainly true that Australians use some colourful expressions not heard elsewhere. Here are some you might come across:

Avago: Have a go, give it a try, also rendered 'avagoyermug', ie, have a go you mug.

Amber fluid: beer

Barrack: Cheer on, root for

Battler: one who struggles to make ends meet.

Billabong: Ox-bow lake (or water-hole).

Billy: Tin can with wire handle in which water is boiled on a campfire for making tea.

Bloke: Man, guy.

Boomerang: Aboriginal curved throwing stick.

Buckley's Chance: No chance (sometimes just Buckley's).

Bulls Roar: long distance, as in 'No-one in a bulls roar of him.'

Carn: Come on as used for sports barracking, eg, 'Carn the Pies' (Come on the Magpies, a Melbourne football team).

Chook: Chicken.

Cobber: Has been replaced by Mate. No one under seventy calls his mate his cobber anymore.

Cockie: Farmer.

Damper: bush bread made from flour and water and cooked in a pit.

Didgeridoo: Aboriginal wind instrument made from a hollow log.

Dilly Bag: All-purpose carrying bag woven of grass by Aboriginal women.

Dingo: a yellow dog.

Dinkum: Honest, also Fair Dinkum.

Donkey's Years: Ages.

Drongo: a stupid person.

Fair go: equal or just opportunity, also Fair crack.

Galah: Fool, especially 'stop acting like a galah'.

G'arn: Go on! You're kidding!

G'day: Good day, the universal Australian greeting.

Good oil: Right idea, useful information, as in give someone the good oil.

Grazier: big sheep or cattle farmer.

Kangaroos Loose in the Top Paddock: Unhinged.

Knockers: people who criticise tall poppies (see below).

Mate: Friend but sometimes abusive, as in 'Listen, mate!' introducing a violent argument.

Middy: middle sized beer glass.

Milk Bar: cross between an old fashioned drug store and a diner.

Never Never: distant outback.

Not the Full Quid: intellectually handicapped.

Ocker: Loud, rude Australian.

Ol' Bastard: A friendly greeting, as in 'Ow ya going, ya ol' bastard' or possibly an expression of admiration, as in, 'You ol' bastard!'

On the Piss: Out drinking.

'Ow ya goin': How are you going, an inquiry after one's well-being.

Pastoralist: even bigger than a grazier.

Piss: booze.

Pissed: Drunk.

Plonk: Wine, especially cheap wine.

Pom: English person, also Pommy, also Pommy Bastard.

Pony: Small beer glass.

Randy: Horny.

Right: OK.

Ripper: Terrific, great.

Rolling: Drunk.

Rotten: Drunk.

Schooner: Large beer glass.

Sheila: Girl but not often used these days.

She'll be Right: No problem.

Sherman Tank: rhyming slang for Yank.

Shout: Buy a round of drinks.

Stone the Crows: An expression of surprise.

Stone Motherless: Broke.

Starve the Lizards: Equivalent to Stone the Crows. In extreme surprise say, 'Stone the crows and starve the lizards.'

Tall Poppies: successful people. The Australian tendency to denigrate such successes is known as the 'tall poppy syndrome' and is oft-discussed with disapproving sighs.

True Blue: honest, straight.

Tucker: food.

Ute: Utility, pick-up truck.

Whinge: complain endlessly about every little thing.

Wowser: active prude.

Part II
PEOPLE AND HISTORY

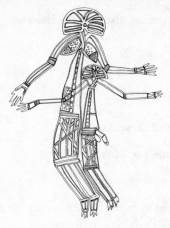

Aboriginal painting

Australian history was once thought dull because it lacked the invasions, military squabbles, giant personalities and revolutionary uprisings of European development. It seemed there was no mass destruction and megalomaniacs were few. This view failed completely to take into account the position of the Aboriginals for whom mass destruction was a reality and to whom every white man must have seemed a megalomaniac but the experience of Australia's native people is only just beginning to be brought into the national consciousness as history.

The Aboriginal People

The Australian Aboriginals are a very ancient people. Estimates given for the age of their occupation have been lately extended, on the basis of archaeological finds in Victoria, to 80,000 years although there may have been a break in continuity. The present race probably entered Australia during the last great Ice Age about 30,000 years ago via land bridges and short stretches of water from South-East Asia. Some theories relate them to the people of the Indian sub-continent. They became completely isolated 5000 years ago when the sea rose sufficiently to form Torres Strait. The first arrivals would have found a rather more favourable environment than is the case today, as well as existing native animals there were giant marsupials such as 'Procoptodon', a 10-foot kangaroo, and the whole continent was better watered. As the people spread through the land over thousands of years they developed physical characteristics which, while all groups remained similar, reflected the differing environments in which they came to live. This is also the case

30

with Aboriginal culture which, while it has certain uniformities, differs from region to region throughout Australia. For example there were probably 300 separate languages as well as many dialects and although they had similarities of sound system and vocabulary, their grammatical structures were quite distinct. In colder parts of the country, the people wore skins but in the deserts they went largely naked. Body-scarring was universal but patterns differed from tribe to tribe. Ways of burial, religious ceremonies and art differed from one place to another but Aboriginal religion was basically totemistic and mythological.

Tribal Society

Aboriginal tribal society before the coming of Europeans was highly organised, extremely disciplined and spiritually rich. Its people lead a hunting and gathering life and day to day activity, especially in less fertile areas, was devoted almost entirely to securing sustenance. Men hunted, women and children gathered, moving in small groups of close relatives called bands usually numbering about 20 to 50 people. Bands were led by senior men who enforced strict and complicated rules on marriage and childbirth—effective defences against in-breeding and over-breeding, and passed on tribal mythology. Each band was a sub-group of a larger tribe which shared ceremonial occasions and land. Although bands moved from place to place, tribes trespassed on one another's territory rarely as such actions could lead to war. Many features of tribal life remain among the Aborigines of the Northern Territory and Western Australia although they have been somewhat broken down by European influence.

The Land

Relationship to land was and is basic to the structure of Aboriginal society although there is no concept of individual ownership. Aboriginals will rather say that land owns them than that they own land. They speak of 'Our Mother, the Land' and finding separation from their birth place difficult to bear. General dispossession has placed their society under extreme strain. Their husbanding of land is deliberate and more interventionist than was once thought. Fire, for example, is used as a husbanding tool in Central Australian desert communities but whatever the method, the aim is to maintain rather than exploit a supportive environment.

Ceremonies

Aboriginal literature is verbal and ceremonies play a vital role in passing on cultural information, especially in the lives of men who carry the burden of mythological and practical education—though the separation is hardly distinct; Aboriginals can attach a story to almost anything. The sexual separation of their society extends to religion where men and women both have secret rituals, often to do with initiation into adulthood but there are also frequent joint ceremonies. Art is vital to all religious occasions extending from complex body and sand paintings to carved poles, figurative images and engraved stones. Apart from their informative role, ceremonies were believed to ensure the fertility of the land as effectively as any practical measures for its preservation.

31

The Dreaming

Individuals held their place in the spiritual whole by means of what has come to be known as their 'dreaming'—a misnomer to say the least since it has nothing to do with being asleep. It is more a state of knowledge relating all objects in the exterior world to each other, the individual and his relatives, by a complex of myths which began with the formation of the world by powerful spiritual beings. The spirits of those beings continue to control universal destiny. The idea of stewardship under such powerful forces is central and disasters are often seen as resulting from failure to carry out individual or collective duties to the land. It is not hard to imagine the personal and collective damage that dispossession does to people ruled by such beliefs.

The European Settlers

When the first European settlers arrived in Australia in 1788 it is estimated that there were about 250,000 to 300,000 Aboriginals, although this amounts to no more than a rather ill-educated guess. Policy towards them was officially benevolent but they were considered 'savages' and the cultural distance between the two races made understanding impossible. It soon emerged that the common attitude was rarely as 'Christian' as the official one. Aboriginals who resisted what they could only see as invasion were shot or imprisoned. Finally a legal fiction known as *Terra Nullius*, the empty land, which presumes Australia to have been unoccupied at the time of white settlement, was imposed to legitimise the occupation. It remains a foundation of Australian law today.

Far worse than deprivation and outright killing was the effect of white man's diseases which did the greatest initial damage. By 1798 smallpox had reached plague proportions among tribes around Sydney and rapidly spread south and west along the inland rivers as far as South Australia. In a terrible warning of what was to come it decimated tribes in places where white men had never been seen. When the whites arrived they drove the weakened and ill-armed tribes away or gathered them into urban centres to be 'civilised'. In Tasmania where Aboriginal resistance was organised almost to guerrilla level, they were hunted down and virtually wiped out. Only in the deserts where white men and their diseases could not survive did tribal life continue relatively undisturbed until the twentieth century but it too was eventually damaged and distorted.

The Present

Today there are around 50,000 Aboriginals of unmixed descent but well over 100,000 people identify themselves as Aboriginals. Many live poorly in towns and cities where misunderstanding still prevails between both cultures but many also alternate with varying success between white and tribal societies. Some remain or have chosen to become almost fully tribal. In the 1970s and '80s Australian Aboriginals have developed a national consciousness similar to that of first peoples in other parts of the world and have begun a new fight for recognition and especially for land rights. Some small but encouraging gains have been made in this area, especially in the Northern Territory but a long and difficult struggle remains.

White Australia

White Australia's history is one of discovery and development, a very successful one given the odds against the first arrivals of 1788. It bespeaks, in part, the energy and ingenuity of the British Enlightenment and the dutiful dedication of its empire builders. It is also full of the bitter struggles of small individuals who acted for their own advancement at great personal risk in coming freely to a new land and making it their home.

Discovery

The great south land was speculated about and almost discovered on and off from as long ago as the twelfth century. The spread of Islam into South East Asia came within 480 km of Australia's northern shores and Chinese and Arab documents of the 1400s show that a south land was either known or presumed to exist. The Portuguese raised the issue of *terra australia incognita* during their time as the world's great voyagers and the Spanish actually came as close as the New Hebrides (now Vanuatu) in the early 1600s but it was the Dutch who first set European feet on Australian soil in 1616.

Dirk Hartog, a Dutch sea trading captain carried too far east on his journey from the Cape of Good Hope to Java, landed at Shark Bay in Western Australia on 25 October 1616. He marked his brief stay by engraving a plate and tacking it to a tree on the island. The plate resides today in the Western Australian Maritime Museum in Fremantle. Hartog was followed by deliberate Dutch explorers who drew charts of the whole west coast and large sections of the north and south. In 1626–27 Pieter Nuyts explored almost 1000 miles of the south coast and in November 1644 Abel Tasman came as far as modern day Tasmania which he named Van Diemen's Land in honour of the Governor General of the Indies. In the same year, the north coast was also charted and the land mass so jigsawed together named New Holland. It stretched from Cape York to southern Tasmania but the east coast remained a mystery. The Dutch, however, disappointed at finding no gold or spices gave up their explorations and turned their attention elsewhere.

The first Englishman to make his mark in New Holland was a pirate named William Dampier who took refuge on the north coast in 1688 and, like many a criminal in modern times, wrote an account of his exploits when he returned home. Published under the title *Voyages*, the work excited such interest that Dampier was able to persuade the Admiralty to back him on a second voyage in 1699. On that occasion he explored 1000 miles of the west coast but returned with a damning report of the infertile country and its savage, ill-fed populous whom he described as 'the miserablest people in the world'. Interest flagged and did not revive again until the mid-eighteenth century when Rousseau-esque ideas of the noble savage were at their height and the South Seas voyages of Captain James Cook added reality to their philosophical speculations.

James Cook

Cook, perhaps the greatest navigator of his time, was dispatched in 1768 to observe the Transit of Venus at Tahiti and to establish the existence or otherwise of the great south land. He achieved the first but always believed himself to have failed in the second of his purposes. Having made observations in Tahiti, he sailed south and came first to New Zealand, the whole of whose coastline he charted before heading off to see what else he might discover. On 20 April 1770, he sighted the coast of Victoria, naming the point first seen, Hicks, after an officer of his ship the *Endeavour*. He proceeded north along the coast of present day New South Wales, attempting a landing near Wollongong but being driven back by heavy surf. On 29 April he landed at Botany Bay, shot at a couple of inquisitive Aboriginals and walked some distance inland with a party of officers. The visit lasted only five hours but led eventually to the founding of a colony at New South Wales. Cook, meantime, sailed on up the coast past Port Jackson, Broken Bay and Port Stephens, arriving on 16 May at Point Danger where modern NSW is divided from Queensland. Passing Morton (now Moreton) Bay he entered the Whitsunday Passage on 6 June and, puzzled by the calm water surrounding the islands, sailed east discovering the Barrier Reef. Continuing up the coast inside the reef, he came almost as far north as present day Cooktown before running aground and doing severe damage to the *Endeavour* on 11 June. The ship, patched with its own sails, limped to the mouth of the Endeavour River where Cooktown now stands where, beached, it remained for a month undergoing repairs. On 6 August, the journey was resumed, Cook found a way out of the reef and sailed into Torres Strait, certifying that it did indeed separate Australia from New Guinea. His final act on the epic voyage was to land on Possession Island off the tip of Cape York on 20 August 1770 and claim the whole of the east coast for England, calling it initially New Wales which he later amended to New South Wales.

The Colonial Period

Gulags

The year 1776 had a profound influence on the history of Australia. England's American colonies successfully revolted and the chronically poor habitual criminals of urban Great Britain could no longer be dispensed with by shipping to the west. By 1783 His Majesty's Government had to admit the new and uncomfortable situation as the hulks on the Thames filled to bursting point with the products of a newly 'enlightened' legal system. After considering Africa and one or two other possibilities, it looked to New South Wales as a site for penal settlement. The penal settlement idea was the publicly admitted position on the settling of Botany Bay but it was privately hoped that from this South Seas base English trade might build a sphere of influence in the Pacific region. Cook had pointed out that the presence of plentiful timber and probably flax would make the area useful to shipping.

The convict scheme was officially endorsed in 1786 under the aegis of Thomas Townshend, Lord Sydney, Secretary of State for Home Affairs who appointed a retired naval captain named Arthur Phillip as Captain-General of the expedition. On 13 May 1787 a fleet of 11 ships, 6 of them chartered transports, set out from Portsmouth under his command carrying 759 convicts, 13 of their children, 252 marines, 20 officials, 210 Royal Navy seamen and 233 merchant seamen. It is known in Australian history as the First Fleet and by the time it reached Botany Bay in January 1788, its members numbered 1030. They landed, hoisted the British flag and drank toasts to the Queen on January 26 which date is now annually celebrated as Australia Day.

Trouble came instantly. Botany Bay proved sandy and without fresh water. Phillip left the fleet and took a small boat north, discovering Port Jackson which he straightaway saw was much more suitable both as a harbour and a place of settlement. The first settlement was thus established not at the site chosen by Lord Sydney but at a cove which Phillip named after the lord in Port Jackson where there was a deep anchorage and a small, freshwater stream. Sydney Cove was, however, long known in England as Botany Bay.

The first years were difficult. Phillip had to contend with convicts who would not work unless strictly supervised, military personnel who were more interested in the women convicts than their duties, argumentative subordinates and, due to a lack of farming skills combined with an unknown and so far infertile land, eventually starvation. The colony, believing itself neglected or perhaps even forgotten by England, was saved by the arrival of the Second Fleet in dribs and drabs during June 1790. After that time, new land was opened up at Parramatta and successfully farmed so that the colony could provide for some of its immediate needs. Phillip departed in 1792, having done his duty as fully as could be expected.

The Second Fleet also brought the first detachment of the New South Wales Corps, a regiment especially established for duty in New South Wales. Its members came to be a lasting influence on the colony for, where governors were regularly changed, the regiment remained, at times constituting the only authority. Its members had little to engage them militarily. They indulged instead in trade, farming and politics, enriching themselves and squabbling with successive governors. They rebelled against Bligh (of Bounty fame), frustrated the visionary Macquarie and opposed the growing emancipist party, made up of pardoned convicts who had become traders in their own right.

Convict labour was the backbone of the community. By 1830, 53,000 had arrived, 50,000 of them men. They fell into various classes, most were professional urban petty thieves, a few—mainly Irish—were socio-political offenders and still fewer were true political radicals. They constituted a virtual slave labour force which worked either in government gangs or for free individuals to whom they were assigned. Well-behaved convicts were given tickets of leave which conferred certain rights on them including some freedom of movement and the right to earn money. Repeating offenders were consigned to a growing line of prison camps which stretched by the 1820s from Moreton Bay to Tasmania. In many the treatment was so harsh and the conditions so unhealthy that death sentences were thought a release. Of those convicts who served out their sentences or were pardoned (emancipists), many chose to remain and make a life in the new land with varying degrees of success. Some grew rich and powerful, others returned to crime.

Settlement or Invasion?

The Australian continent was not invaded by an organised array of military forces but to its Aboriginal inhabitants the effect was the same. Despite an officially benevolent policy there was no understanding of Aboriginal society and its attachment, individual and collective, to land. Poorly armed and soon riddled with European diseases, especially smallpox, the natives fell rapidly to the advancing whites despite noble and often desperate resistance. On the other hand, the new arrivals perceived the land, apparently undeveloped, as unoccupied and its people as savage wanderers. They saw themselves as exploring and settling an empty wilderness.

The first substantial explorations were undertaken by sea. Naval Surgeon George Bass and his fellow officer Matthew Flinders sailed into harbours near Botany Bay in 1795 and '96. Bass went south alone to Western Port in Victoria in 1797–98 and together in late 1798 they circumnavigated Tasmania, proving it to be the island Cook had denied it was. Port Phillip, later the site of Melbourne, was discovered in 1802. Flinders followed up by charting the whole of the Australian coast in 1802–4 and urged that the land be given the name Australia, a proposition officially endorsed in 1817.

In the meantime, settlement was spreading to places away from Sydney Cove. In 1803 David Collins, former Judge Advocate of New South Wales who had sailed on the First Fleet but returned to England in 1796, arrived in Port Phillip Bay aboard HMS *Calcutta* with 300 convicts. He soon abandoned that site and removed to Tasmania where he established Hobart Town in 1804.

Around Sydney itself farmers and graziers spread out over an arc of about 150 to 200 miles following the exploratory feats of journalist William Charles Wentworth, the son of an emancipist, who led an expedition over the rugged Blue Mountains in 1813. John Oxley, New South Wales Surveyor General, moved further inland to map the courses of the Lachlan and Macquarie Rivers and explored the coast south of Moreton Bay in 1823 while Allan Cunningham explored the hinterland in 1827, penetrating as far as the Darling Downs. Hamilton Hume and William Hovell went overland south to the western side of Port Phillip, discovering the Murray River on the way, in 1824–5. Most famous of all was Charles Sturt who sailed that river from its source in the southern alps to where it flowed into Lake Alexandrina, now in South Australia. He solved the riddle of Australia's inland rivers, ascertaining that the Murrumbidgee and the Darling, the greatest of them, flowed into the Murray and not into an inland sea as had been speculated, but into the Southern Ocean via the lake.

By 1830 settlements had been established at Albany (Western Australia), Moreton Bay (Queensland), Hobart Town (Tasmania) and Port Phillip (Victoria). The first colonists arrived in South Australia in 1837 and Port Essington near present day Darwin was established in 1838, though abandoned in 1849. Neither did it take long for the separate settlements to divide into separate colonies. Victoria, South Australia and Tasmania were individual by 1851, Queensland followed in 1859. The steps to self-government occurred in stages between this period and 1860. Bicameral legislatures on the British model were set up and, except in Tasmania, adult male franchise introduced by that date. The only real laggard was Western Australia which did not become self-governing until 1890.

The transport of convicts continued but, especially in the more prosperous states, had become a source of some embarrassment whose stigma had begun to outweigh its value as de facto slave labour. This latter aspect of the system was also under criticism from enlightened circles in British politics and combined pressure from both colony and home ended transportation to the eastern states in 1852. It continued, however, to Western Australia until 1868. That colony had begun without convict support but a severe labour shortage led to transportation commencing in 1848 on the demands of the colonists themselves. Convicts were never brought to South Australia and very few helped to found Victoria. In all 161,000 were transported, 151,000 to the east and 10,000 to the west.

Wool

Once discovered, the pastures of New South Wales and Victoria gave birth to a wool growing industry which was to become the world's major source of fine merino fleece. The story begins with John Macarthur who arrived on the Second Fleet in 1790 as an officer of the New South Wales Corps and became one of the wealthiest and most influential members of colonial society. He settled at Camden south-west of Sydney in late 1790 and soon came to believe that wool might be a major source of income for the still shaky colonial economy. He received a substantial land grant in 1805 to pursue his interest and began to develop a substantial merino flock. Indeed, he claimed to be the first to import merinos to Australia though he probably knew the assertion to be untrue. By this and other exaggerations—he was guilty of many—Macarthur persuaded the British Government that fine wool could easily be grown in New South Wales and so far as that government was concerned, the option was preferable to Europe or North America, provided that the wool was cheap enough. The truth, however, was less sanguine and the pastoral industry grew slowly while Macarthur fought political battles with successive governors, heading the 'exclusive' party against William Charles Wentworth and the 'emancipists'. His continual politicking and a developing case of megalomania which caused one government official to seriously question his sanity, affected Macarthur's health and eventually isolated him even from his own party. He died at Camden in 1834 without seeing his dreams for the wool industry realised but he had been right in predicting how it would grow.

The settlement of Port Phillip in the 1830s was crucial to this process. It completed an arc of pastoral development 200 miles wide and extending from Brisbane and the Darling Downs to Adelaide but centring on Melbourne which prospered enormously as the wool trade grew. Only the Aborigines suffered, falling to the guns and diseases of the whites. In Tasmania they were effectively wiped out, on the mainland they were driven off their land, murdered or collapsed into miscegenation. The burgeoning pastoral industry gave a fillip to exploration which continued apace. Sir Thomas Mitchell opened the way from New South Wales into Victoria in 1836. George Grey and Edward John Eyre mapped the Western Australian coast and in 1862 John McDowell Stuart crossed from Adelaide to the north coast over the Red Centre, forever quashing speculations of an inland sea.

Gold

No event had quite the same impact on Australian history as the gold discoveries of the 1850s. California had made the mid-nineteenth century the age of the gold rush and when gold discoveries were revealed almost simultaneously in New South Wales and Victoria in 1850–51 people poured out of the cities into the diggings. Australia was changed at a stroke from a place of exile to a place of golden attraction.

The precious metal had been found in its alluvial form as early as 1823 but the first substantial find was made in the Lithgow area of New South Wales in 1841 by a geologist and clergyman the Reverend W. B. Clarke who showed specimens of it to Governor Gipps and a few members of the Legislative Council in 1844. Gipps was set hard against any publication of the discovery and is reported to have said: 'Put it away Mr Clarke or we shall all have our throats cut.' He feared the convicts. That argument lost force by 1850, the end of transportation was imminent, a large slice of the population had rushed off to California anyway and a rural depression had been savaging the economy for more than a year. A new governor, Fitz Roy, urged that the mineral resources of New South Wales be exploited. Geologists and experienced prospectors were brought in and Edward Hargraves, who had seen service on the Californian fields, found gold at Ophir near Bathurst in February 1851. In April on the same site two of his associates produced the first payable gold in Australia.

The ensuing rush so deprived Melbourne of its adult male population that a Gold Discovery Committee was immediately established and £200 reward offered for a find nearer to the city. The prize was rapidly won when James Esmond discovered gold at Ballarat in June 1851 and led the way to the opening of one of the richest gold fields ever mined. After these successes the search for gold became a feature of Australian public life and was made in all states with general success but nowhere did the rushes reach the heights of the first two. The precious mineral was discovered at Gympie in Queensland in 1867 and at fields which still produce at Kalgoorlie in 1892–3. Other smaller fields developed in the Northern Territory (then part of South Australia) and Tasmania.

The Best Place on Earth

The discovery and production of gold rocketed the Australian colonies into a period of sustained growth. Population poured in from Britain, Europe, the United States and China, bringing skills that the colonies had sadly lacked. While pastoralism continued to stride ahead, secondary industry grew at a phenomenal rate, multiplying itself ten times between 1860 and 1900 and accounting for 25 per cent of national product in the 1880s. Building in the major cities of Sydney and Melbourne became ornate and stylish, ostentation prevailed among the rich and the average man thought himself to be living well under the kind antipodean sun. Cultural life of a specifically Australian character came into its own as a nascent nationalism began to express itself in art and literature. Novelists such as Marcus Clarke, poets Adam

Lindsay Gordon and Henry Kendall and painters Tom Roberts and Frederick McCubbin delineated the new Australian landscape, its people and history in their work.

By the 1890s, this trend had developed into an identifiable nationalist movement of which the most prominent manifestation was Sydney's *Bulletin* magazine. It published the verse and prose of Henry Lawson and Joseph Furphy and political cartoons by the young Norman Lindsay, all of whom, especially Lawson, became colossi in the construction of Australian self-image. The magazine was nationalist and even republican in tone and expressed the view that Australians lived in the promised land, free men at heart chafing under the colonial yoke—but the promise did not come true. The 1880s had also been a time of speculation and Australians had borrowed heavily from English banks in the expectation that high commodity prices would continue, instead, in the early 1890s they crashed. The Australian economy was savaged, unemployment exploded and a new political consciousness emerged among the working classes, resulting in the formation of labour parties throughout the land. To sensible nationalists these events only strengthened the case for the six colonies becoming one nation and the movement pushed on undaunted through the hard times.

Federation

It must be admitted that not all motives for federation were altruistic. Fear of invasion from the north played a strong part as did the desires of smaller colonies, hit hardest by the depression of the '90s, to gain as much as possible from association with their larger counterparts. New South Wales, the most prosperous, was most reluctant; Victoria, particularly badly damaged by the collapse of rural prices, pressed hardest. Commissions met and argued between 1891 and 1898 and in the end submitted constitutional drafts to referendum. The majority was in the affirmative and Australia federated, by an act of the British Parliament, on 1 January 1901.

The Twentieth Century

The early years of the new century saw the new nation drawn into conflicts far beyond its shores and struggling with a reality of nationhood far from the nationalist ideal. Expected and expecting themselves to be exemplary members of the British Empire, its citizens either saw loyalty to Australia as indistinguishable from loyalty to Great Britain or actively set the mother country's interests above their own. When war came to Europe in 1914, the mass of Australians rallied to the British flag without a second thought.

Other People's Wars

Australia developed the means for war in the first decade of the century and learned the feel of it in South Africa where Australians fought beside the British against the Boers. Those who died there were the first to pay for a dependence on great powers which remains crucial to Australia's idea of itself as a nation in a world of nations. The 60,000 lost in World War I, in the name of empire, cemented and ennobled a tradition of fighting other people's wars, of which those who died as lately as Vietnam were also part. In each case, but especially the first, the call to arms was seen as a test of national spirit, the kind of test not met by literature and art but only by feats of arms. In modern times the dancing partner has changed but the song remains the same. United States military personnel based on Australian soil in joint communications facilities perhaps make Australia a nuclear target.

Of all the wars, and they are not many, in which Australia has played a role, only World War II came really close to her soil. It changed the old great power dependence on Britain to the new one on the USA. The crucial event in this was the Battle of the Coral Sea, May 1942, in which US and Australian aircraft turned back the Japanese invasion fleet. Though never fighting on their own soil, Australians battled closer to it than they ever had before, driving back the Japanese along the Kokoda Trail in New Guinea's jungle-covered mountains. Darwin was bombed and, for a time, there was a real fear of invasion. That war took half the number of lives lost in World War I.

Other People's People

After 1945 Australia entered a period of prosperity such as it had not known since the 1850s. The Anglo-Australian bourgeoisie, almost without being aware of it, enjoyed one of the highest living standards among wealthy developed nations. The prosperity was underpinned by huge migration from a shattered and exhausted Europe. From 1946 until 1974 when migration restrictions were introduced approximately 100,000 migrants entered Australia every year and, though the majority came from Britain they were still less than a third. A sixth, for example, came from Italy, a tenth from Germany and the Netherlands. These people had no ties with mother Britannia and served more effectively than any other means to de-Anglicise the Australian consciousness. Sydney and Melbourne especially turned into polyglot communities with little Italies and Greeces, more like the United States of the 1920s than anything to be found in Great Britain at the time.

Following the Vietnam War, a fall-off in European migration and the abandonment of the infamous 'White Australia' policy, the country has opened more to its true neighbours than ever before, discovering that not all of them are New Zealanders. Although by no means the majority, Asian migrants—whose way was paved, like the Europeans, by war refugees—are finding a secure place in the Australian community of the 1980s. More than welcome, such people are essential to our future which seems increasingly to lie on the Pacific Rim and not in a European idyll at all.

The Last Twenty Years

Australians feel they have altered tremendously in the last twenty years. The period is perhaps not considerably different to the 1880s and '90s in the emergence of a refreshed and broadened idea of 'Australianness'. That it also bears worrying

40

economic similarities with that dangerous time may not be altogether coincidental. Until the late sixties, Australian artists and writers, hating the smallness and mediocrity of their home environment abandoned the native soil and chose, yet again, to strive for places in a European, often English, context. It has to be said that, for Australian artists in the fifties, their own nation provided hardly any social context at all. When they returned, as many did, they helped to broaden the local view. In their absence a new generation of intellectuals grew up and made their mark at home, some contributing work of international significance. The seventies saw new writers emerge; specifically, sometimes aggressively, Australian characters trod the boards and a national film industry mythologised colonial history. The marketers of Australia, beer sellers and tourism touts, are late-comers to this new confidence. Perhaps they show us to the northern hemisphere in digestible form but intending visitors would do themselves a favour by ignoring it. Those who want a truer glimpse of the Australian heart will turn to Albert Facey's *Fortunate Life*, Elizabeth Jolley's wry novels and Peter Carey's satires of our urban desperation. After all, Australia is the most urbanised nation on earth.

A Little Politics

There are three main political parties in Australia: the Australian Labor Party, the Liberal Party and the National Party (often known as the Country Party as it draws its main support from rural areas). Until recently, the conservative Liberal-Country coalition has been the predominant force in post-war politics, with a brief interlude in the early 1970s when Gough Whitlam's short-lived Labor government (1972–1975) ended in the dissolution of parliament amidst much controversy. However, the Australian Labor Party is enjoying an unprecedented run in the 1980s under the leadership of Prime Minister Bob Hawke as it heads for its one hundredth year of battling with what it calls 'conservative forces'.

Part III
NEW SOUTH WALES

Sydney Opera House

New South Wales has the nation's most colourful and vibrant city, huge curves of deserted beach, tiny historic towns, superb vineyards, snow mountains, temperate rainforests and a wide outback. The state is the engine room of Australia's economy and accommodates around one third of the country's population (5.4 million) but there's plenty of space for them all and for the hundreds of thousands of tourists who arrive each year.

The coastline is over 1000 miles long, separated from vast inland plains by the Great Dividing Range, a spine of ancient, rugged and low mountains extending along the entire eastern edge of Australia. In the south the mountains rise high enough to attract snow. Beyond them lie rich slopes of grazing land, wheat-growing plains and finally the dry, flat, hot outback where mining is the main source of livelihood. On the coast north and south of Sydney are surf beaches unequalled anywhere in Australia, backed by dramatic forested escarpments or undulating dairy farms.

Climate

The climatic mix includes temperate to sub-tropical coasts, snowy alpine environments, green riverlands and thoroughly inhospitable deserts. In most of New South Wales the weather is warmer for longer than northern hemisphere dwellers are used to but in winter, May to August, there are sub-zero temperatures in the mountains and the south-west. It can get pretty cold when the wind blows in Sydney as well. Generally speaking, temperatures are hotter in the north than the south and also increase and become more extreme generally as you move inland.

History

New South Wales was the first settled of the Australian states and was the first name given to eastern Australia. The coast was explored by Captain James Cook in 1770 who sailed in from the South Pacific, up the side of present day New South Wales and into Queensland waters, discovering Botany Bay as he went. It was Cook's glowing but inaccurate report of Botany Bay that led to it being chosen for the penal colony actually established at Sydney Cove, a short distance north, in January 1788 by the 1500 members of the First Fleet, mostly convicts.

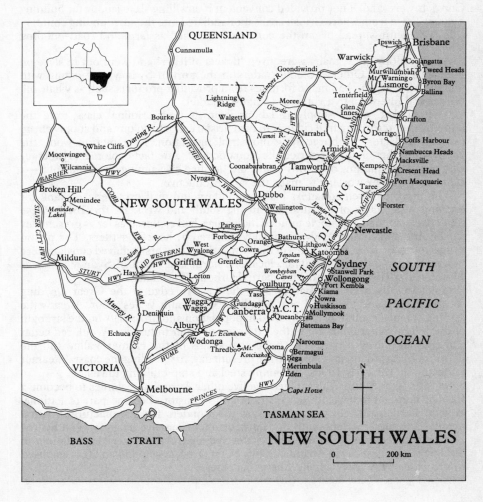

Neither the criminals nor their officers had any appreciable skill in farming, a necessity under the circumstances, and neither did they learn anything from the Aboriginals who had been surviving very comfortably around Sydney for tens of thousands of years. The prisoners and their rulers came close to starvation and were supported only by the arrival of the Second Fleet with supplies from the motherland in 1790.

Initial obstacles were overcome by low rations, dedicated governors, and the opening up of fertile land in the vicinity of Parramatta west of Sydney (now part of the metropolitan area) where successful farms were established in the 1790s. Convicts were vital. They provided convenient if unwilling slave labour for building Sydney Town from where British civilisation radiated into the surrounding country-side. When the spread began the convicts were used as farm and road-building labour.

As the colony grew, many were given 'tickets of leave' and went out to slave on their own behalf. Others became traders in the port of Sydney, competing with military officers who had made fortunes from providing products such as whale oil, timber and fine wool to a voracious English market.

That market, whilst supplying labour from its poor criminal class, gave the impetus to enterprising free citizens to turn prison camp to colony and supply cheap raw materials for the burgeoning industrial revolution. Fine merino wool, the greatest product of all, supported the 'squatocracy', a de facto colonial aristocracy who began by squatting on Crown Land and finished by claiming ownership of it—a claim they won by working to make the land productive.

The market-driven squatters had the military and civil explorers to thank for opening wide tracts of grazing land in the south and west. By the 1820s these rugged, disciplined and single minded individuals had explored as far as present day Melbourne and Brisbane, always quickly followed by hopeful settlers. The prison camps too spawned prison camps of their own when the worst behaved convicts were moved to less and less hospitable locations north and south of Sydney as far as Moreton Bay (Brisbane) and Macquarie Harbour (Tasmania).

Gold was discovered at Bathurst on the western edge of the Great Dividing Range in 1850 and the world beat a path to New South Wales' door. Already the leading colonial economy, it ballooned in population and prosperity on the strength of the yellow mineral but not to the exclusion of other industries. Wool, red cedar and coal all played a part. The huge coal seams of the Hunter Valley and the Illawarra Escarpment have lasted to the present day, first feeding the coastal steamer trade and, in the early 1900s, becoming steel and ship building towns.

In 1901 New South Wales joined the five other Australian colonies to become a state of the Commonwealth of Australia and its history became part of national growth. Participation in two world wars did wonders for manufacturing. Rural wealth continued to climb with the construction of massive irrigation and hydro-electricity schemes in the south of the state. Sydney grew beyond all expectations to become the biggest city in Australia, a place of relaxed, cosmopolitan life recognised world-wide as the jewel among Australian cities.

GETTING TO AND AROUND

By Air
New South Wales' only port for international air traffic is Sydney. Flights from interstate on Ansett and Australian Airlines also use Sydney as their gateway. Air NSW and East West Airlines fly between Sydney and major country centres in New South Wales as well as important towns in Queensland, Victoria and Tasmania. **East West Airlines,** has its office at 323 Castlereagh Street, phone (02) 20 940, and **Air NSW** is in the Ansett building on the corner of Oxford and Riley Streets, Darlinghurst, phone (02) 268 1214. **Australian Airlines** is at 70 Hunter Street, Sydney, phone (02) 693 3333.

By Rail
New South Wales has a wide rail network linking Sydney with major country towns. A 'fast' train called the XPT (it can do up to 160 km (100 miles) per hour) operates to major country centres including Murwillumbah, Newcastle, Tamworth, Bathurst, Dubbo, Goulburn and Albury. Trains also operate between many country centres but tend to be infrequent as patronage is universally low outside the main routes.

By Road
Express coach services in New South Wales are poor when compared with other states. Sydney is connected to all other state capitals and Canberra by daily services but there are very strict limits on where these services can set down on the way to their interstate destinations. Generally, they may not drop passengers at all along New South Wales section of their routes so you can't, for example, take a coach from Sydney to Brisbane and get off in Newcastle. This is a way of protecting the railways from competition; only the holders of around Australia bus passes and travellers from interstate are not subject to it and can get on and off wherever the bus stops. Local bus services operate between towns in the country.

Roads in New South Wales are the best and the worst in Australia. Superb freeways run between Sydney and Newcastle and Sydney and the Southern Highlands and then peter out into pot-holed winding nightmares. Sometimes they suddenly change character from four lanes to two and back again. Generally speaking, however, the roads are sealed and driveable which makes them better than many Australian tracks, but keep your foot off the accelerator.

TOURIST INFORMATION
The **Tourism Commission of New South Wales** is responsible for informing tourists about the state. It distributes regionalised booklets which together cover the whole of New South Wales. Among them are Sydney, Leisure Coast, Holiday Coast, South Coast, Snowy/Canberra, Outback and North-West country. The booklets are general and contain a fair bit of blather but they are accompanied by useful inserts listing attractions and accommodation with very brief details of each. The Commission's main outlet is on the corner of Spring and Pitt Streets in Sydney, (02) 231 4444. Bookings for travel and accommodation can be made there and at the Commission's interstate offices:

Corner Queen and Edward Streets, **Brisbane**, (07) 31 1838
353 Little Collins Street, **Melbourne**, (03) 67 7461
7th Floor, Australian Airlines Building, 144 North Terrace, **Adelaide**, (08) 51 3167.

Rail and bus transport information is available from the State Rail Authority Travel and Tours Centre on the corner of York and Margaret Streets in Sydney.

MAJOR SIGHTS

If the three rules of real estate are position, position and position, then the three sights of New South Wales are **Sydney**, Sydney and Sydney. No city has a better location although some locations may have a better city. One should not neglect the areas close to its sprawling width, especially the **Blue Mountains** for spectacle and the **Southern Highlands** for history. The **North Coast** and its hinterland in the Great Dividing Range are of tremendous natural beauty, especially the beaches of Byron Bay and the forests at Dorrigo and Mount Warning. The **Shoalhaven River** region on the South Coast has a majestic landscape of white river beaches, high bushy bluffs and green dairy fields. **Mount Kosciusko**, Australia's highest peak, and its fellows in the Snowy Mountains are ideal for summer bushwalking and provide skiing when the snow is good.

ACCOMMODATION

Accommodation in New South Wales is generally good. It follows the Australian trend from international hotels in the state capital to caravan (trailer) parks at coastal resorts but there is a motel in every town, hundreds in and around popular holiday spots. Recent developments include luxury accommodation in some centres north of Sydney and in the Blue Mountains. There are also good small guesthouses offering bed and breakfast or full board in the mountains and the Southern Highlands. The areas shortest of accommodation are the west, the north-west and Sydney. **Farm Holidays** are available in all country regions of New South Wales but tend to be concentrated in the Snowy/Canberra, north-west and north coast areas.

FOOD AND DRINK

New South Wales is not distinguished for any particular culinary delight as is, say, Queensland for tropical fruits and mud crabs or Tasmania for crayfish, but some areas of it are among the best places to eat in the country because the competition is fierce, almost as fierce as pride in culinary art, and the rewards of success are great. Sydney has more restaurants than you could cover in five years of continuous dining, some are excellent, many are good and very many are inexpensive. Equally outstanding are the best eating houses in the Blue Mountains and the Hunter Valley, and Canberra has one or two. The quality dips outside these areas except for the occasional gem and even in some big country towns, a really good meal can be hard to come by. Steak tends to be the great stand-by in such circumstances.

The Hunter Valley is the main **wine**-producing region in New South Wales and the second most prominent wine-growing district in Australia after the Barossa Valley. It produces a good range of varietal wines with distinctive regional character, especially among the whites. Hunter Valley wines are available throughout Australia.

ACTIVITIES AND SPORTS

Spectator sports in New South Wales are Rugby League and Rugby Union football in winter and Cricket in summer. International matches in these codes take place in Sydney at the Sydney Cricket Ground, the Sydney Sports Ground and Concord Oval and there are vigorous local competitions in all towns. You will frequently see cricket matches in parks on summer weekends. Tennis is also played everywhere and each town has courts, usually available to the public. The more expensive and newer accommodation houses also have them. Golf courses are frequent, as are lawn bowling clubs.

Outdoor activities include bushwalking in the many national parks throughout the state, the best surfing in Australia, sailing, water skiing, snow skiing, grass skiing, ballooning, fishing in coastal and inland waters, white-water and smooth-water canoeing, horse riding and hunting.

SYDNEY

Sydney is Australia's biggest and most exciting city but this happy situation is more an accident of history than a triumph of planning. In fact planning is a word rarely associated with Sydney at all; the city has the chaotic structure and vibrant spontaneity one would expect from a place which, to use an old Australianism, 'Grew like Topsy'–fast and furious.

The story of Sydney's first 20 years is the story of Australia's first 20 years. A tough struggle in which officers, officials and convicts strove mutually for survival and only just succeeded. After that risky time, settlers moved further afield, especially to Tasmania, but Sydney remained the centre of colonial administration until the mid-1800s when the colonies of Victoria and Queensland were bitten off the bottom and the top of New South Wales. It was a severe reduction as the latter colony had previously extended from the south to the north of the continent.

The first settlers were lucky in their choice of a city site, although they would hardly have thought so at the time. After an initial failure to provide for themselves, they learned how to exploit the fertility of the surrounding land and the colony was able to provide for some of its needs. It was, however, the decision of Major Grose, the interim head of the colony between governors Phillip and Hunter, to allow the military officers under his command to trade and own land that provided a real kick-start. The rum they traded effectively oiled the works of the new colonial economy.

The burgeoning trade attracted free settlers and the city soon divided into high, low and in-between classes. Top of the heap was the military governing class which included a few religious ministers and high civil officials, the bottom was occupied by convicts; in between were free settlers who established themselves in business, ex-convicts who did the same and labouring people free or ex-convict. The lowest lived on the harbour's edge around the Rocks, the highest among the spreading fields of Parramatta, fifteen miles from the dirty port. While the harbour's edge was left to convicts, the greatest builder among New South Wales' early Governors, Lachlan Macquarie, set to work on the street that bears his name in the city heart, bequeathing to Sydney a swag of fine colonial buildings, many designed by forger, convict and architect Francis Greenway.

The port, now Sydney's city centre, grew up wild and narrow with its streets putting function before appearance. Allowing it to do so meant that a slum as bad as any in London occupied the Rocks and its surrounds, a sink of disease and drinking where black plague soon broke out. Exciting at the time, it did little long term damage. A convict population of about 750 at the first landing had grown to 58,000 by 1852 when convict transportation was stopped.

The natural excellence of its port and the wealth of its hinterland determined that Sydney should always prosper and it has continued to 'Grow like Topsy' from its first days to the present. Its nearly 4 million residents live in a vast sprawl of suburbs stretching north, south and especially west, of a city centre almost unoccupied by true residents. High-rise temples of commerce tower over colonial quaintnesses and the city sky-line echoes those of modern US and Asian trading ports. It has the traffic snarls and air pollution that are the main diseases of such hearts of enterprise but they don't seem to make a dent in its sunny beauty.

The weather is best in March, April, September and October when temperatures are mild; summer from December to February is hot and gets progressively stickier; Sydney winter days can sometimes be cold and wet but are often relieved by clear, cool and sunny conditions.

GETTING TO AND AROUND

By Air
Around 60 per cent of travellers to Australia choose Sydney as their first port of call. Major international airlines landing there include British Airways, Alitalia, Lufthansa, Singapore Airlines, Continental, United and Qantas. Ansett and Australian Airlines fly direct to Sydney from all mainland capitals as well as Alice Springs, Queensland coastal cities, Hamilton Island (Ansett only) and the Sunshine Coast. The fares from mainland capitals are Melbourne $171, Brisbane $176, Adelaide $234, Perth $444, Darwin $453. East West Airlines flies direct to Sydney from Brisbane, Melbourne, Hobart, Perth (via Ayers Rock) and the Queensland Sunshine Coast; Air NSW from Melbourne and the Sunshine Coast as well as Ayers Rock via Broken Hill. The last two also serve Sydney from country towns in New South Wales.

All these aircraft land at Sydney Airport, sometimes called Kingsford Smith Airport, in the suburb of Mascot about ten km (six miles) from the city centre. The airport has a single terminal for international traffic. Ansett and Australian Airlines have separate terminals. East West shares with Australian and Air NSW with Ansett. Sydney Airport's arrival hall is badly in need of updating. Progress through immigration and customs is extremely slow and baggage takes ages to arrive. The staff are officious and sometimes rude and there are not nearly enough baggage trolleys. Being at the head of the queue when you disembark improves matters somewhat but it's a bad introduction to Australia.

The Urban Transit Authority of New South Wales operates an **Airport Express** bus to and from the city which costs $2.20 and runs every 20 minutes from 7 am to 6 pm and every 30 minutes from 6 pm to 9 pm and 6 am to 7 am seven days a week. It picks up from the three main terminals. The drivers provide a commentary on places of interest during the journey but seem to be chosen for their good humour rather than their qualities as historians. The bus drops passengers at Central Railway Station and at points along George Street which runs through the city centre, and finishes near Sydney's harbour foreshores in Phillip Street, Circular Quay.

Sydney **taxi** drivers frequent the airport in large numbers. They are generally honest and chatty but some render their English in exotic accents with varying degrees of clarity. Their licences require them to know where major hotels are and the shortest practicable routes by which to reach them. Fares are rung up on a meter, starting with a hiring charge and increasing by so many cents per kilometre. The meter must be set running as soon as the taxi departs for its destination. There is an extra charge for luggage and crossing the Harbour Bridge costs $1 (you do not have to cross when going to town from the airport). If the total fare to the city exceeds $15, begin asking questions. There is no train from Sydney Airport.

By Rail

Trains terminate at **Central Station** at the southern end of town recognisable by its distinctive sandstone clock tower. Interstate services to Sydney are the *Brisbane Limited* from the city of the same name, the *Sydney Express* (overnight) and the *Inter-Capital Daylight Express* from Melbourne ($67 both), the *Indian Pacific* from Perth ($516) and Adelaide ($186) and the *Alice* from Alice Springs ($506). Intrastate and suburban services also arrive at and depart from Central.

By Road

Ansett Pioneer, Greyhound, Deluxe and Bus Australia **express road coaches** serve Sydney direct from Melbourne ($40 to $45 some services via Canberra), Brisbane ($40 to $45 and Bus Australia uses McCafferty's coaches) and Adelaide ($70 to $75). Ansett Pioneer and Greyhound offers Canberra to Sydney services ($15 and $18). Coaches terminate at Oxford Square near Hyde Park if they are Ansett Pioneer or Greyhound operated. Deluxe Coachlines set their passengers down at a terminal on the corner of Hay and Castlereagh Streets at the southern end of the city close to Central Station. These big companies are not the only ones driving the busy routes from Melbourne and Brisbane to Sydney, there are a number of low-budget operators whose buses leave their passengers on the street at Central Railway, wherever they can find a spot.

Getting around the city

Buses to the southern suburbs leave from **Eddy Avenue** on the northern side of Central Station and to the eastern suburbs from **Railway Square** to the west. **Circular Quay** at the northern end of town is where buses to the western suburbs depart. The other main bus terminus is beside **Wynyard Park** in Carrington Street

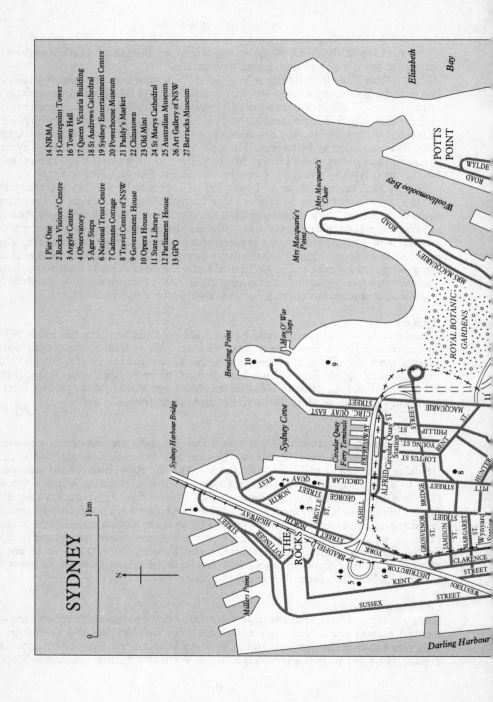

SYDNEY

0 |——————| 1 km

N

1 Pier One
2 Rocks Visitors' Centre
3 Argyle Centre
4 Observatory
5 Agar Steps
6 National Trust Centre
7 Cadmans Cottage
8 Travel Centre of NSW
9 Government House
10 Opera House
11 State Library
12 Parliament House
13 GPO
14 NRMA
15 Centrepoint Tower
16 Town Hall
17 Queen Victoria Building
18 St Andrews Cathedral
19 Sydney Entertainment Centre
20 Powerhouse Museum
21 Paddy's Market
22 Chinatown
23 Old Mint
24 St Marys Cathedral
25 Australian Museum
26 Art Gallery of NSW
27 Barracks Museum

where buses heading north across the Harbour Bridge leave town. Bus fares begin at $1.20 which is enough to carry you to most places in the city area.

An **underground railway** called the City Circle links city stations from Central to Circular Quay. Its stations are convenient to all parts of the city, including the Town Hall and Wynyard where trains to the suburbs depart, and it is not difficult to decipher although changing trains from platform to platform can be confusing. Platforms are not labelled except at entry and exit points. Riding on suburban and city trains in Sydney is generally safe up to quite late at night. The fare is $1.20 throughout the City Circle.

Circular Quay is Sydney's **ferry** terminus. Harbour ferries travelling to Taronga Zoo, Neutral Bay, Mosman, Balmain and Hunters Hill depart from its middle wharves, Manly ferries and the hydrofoil to Manly leave from the wharves at the Opera House end and tourist cruises from the wharf at the other end. Single ferry fares are $1.20 for the inner harbour and $1.50 to Manly. Ferries depart continually at intervals of fifteen minutes to an hour and from around 6 am to midnight each day.

Cars for use in the metropolitan area can be hired cheaply from **Rent-A-Bomb**, 67 New South Head Road, Rushcutters Bay, (02) 327 7699, east of Kings Cross. The offices of the major car hire companies are in William Street below Kings Cross.

Main roads into and out of Sydney are the Pacific Highway to the north coast and Queensland, the Princes Highway to the south coast and Victoria, the Hume Highway which is the main route to and from Melbourne and the Great Western Highway carrying traffic to and from the Blue Mountains and beyond.

Although **cycling** has become something of a trend lately, Sydney is not kind to cyclists. The city is hilly, the main roads are often choked with traffic and the drivers are universally unsympathetic. Consequently, cycle hire is not a large field of endeavour. Centennial Park is one of the few places where it is safe to cycle because cars are restricted. **Centennial Park Cycle Hire**, 50 Clovelly Road, Randwick, (02) 398 5027 has bicycles for hire.

TOURIST INFORMATION

Your first stop should be the **Travel Centre of New South Wales** on the corner of Pitt and Spring Streets in the city. The helpful people there can supply hundreds of brochures on all parts of New South Wales and make bookings for accommodation and travel. Ask for the **Sydney Visitors Map** which is excellent for finding your way around the city as well as out of it. The centre is open from 9 am to 5 pm, Monday to Friday. Phone (02) 231 4444. **Tourist Newsfront** in Playfair Street, The Rocks, provides information and a vast range of booking services including entertainment and tours. It is open the more helpful hours of 9 am to 5 pm every day. Phone (02) 27 7197. Information on all government-run transport in the Sydney metropolitan area is available every day from 7 am to 10 pm by phoning (02) 29 2622. The **Rail and Travel Centre** on the corner of York and Margaret Streets is the central booking and information office for New South Wales public transport.

Orientation

The city of Sydney extends from its oldest sections around Circular Quay and the

Rocks on the southern harbour foreshores to Central Railway station about a kilometre south. It occupies a relatively narrow strip with its western boundary marked by Darling Harbour and eastern by Farm Cove, the Botanic Gardens and the Domain. It is entered from the north, across the harbour, by the Harbour Bridge which runs onto York Street, and from the south by George Street which runs through the centre of the city. Its main north–south streets are George, Pitt, Elizabeth and Macquarie; Martin Place and Market, Park and Oxford Streets are the major east–west streets.

The Harbour

The city's two most famous landmarks, the Opera House and the Harbour Bridge, dominate its unrivalled harbour. The first is an architectural masterpiece, the second a triumph of engineering to the exclusion of all elegance, justly known to the city's people as 'the old coathanger'. Together, they neatly depict the town's divided soul. The scramble of sky-scrapers and the blank suburbs beyond them can make one despair, but in the face of the harbour, all is forgiven.

Sydney Harbour, actually named Port Jackson by Captain James Cook when he sailed past its heads in 1770, is a long, deep and very safe anchorage with the advantage of considerable width despite its narrow entrance way. It is Australia's leading port and has many bays breaking off north and south of its main channel as well as several small islands, some of which are public recreation areas. **Fort Denison**, the castellated island in mid-channel, was originally used as an 'exile-away-from-exile' for intractable convicts. It won the pseudonym *Pinchgut* for the poor rations doled out to those consigned there. It was later fortified to protect the city against invasion by enemies of Britain such as France and Russia. The **Maritime Services Board** organises tours of it for which bookings are necessary months in advance. Phone (02) 240 2036.

The **Sydney Harbour Bridge** spans one of Port Jackson's narrowest channels, between The Rocks and North Sydney. Before the 1930s, punts and ferries were the only way to cross to the north from the city which clustered around Circular Quay on the harbour's southern shore. The bridge, opened on March 20, 1932 in the sight of 750,000 people, was considered a great feat of engineering at the time. Its dedication was enlivened by Captain Henry de Groot, a member of a right wing movement called 'The New Guard', who pre-empted the official ribbon-cutting by riding up on a charger and slashing the ribbon with his ceremonial sword. De Groot was arrested, the ribbon was hastily repaired and state Premier Jack Lang recut it with due ceremony.

As a traffic artery, the bridge is overdue for a by-pass operation so a controversial harbour tunnel is planned to supplement it. The present $1 bridge toll, paid when travelling north to south, is supposed to meet the cost of the tunnel.

A second major business district has sprouted at the northern end of the bridge living on the city over-flow of the last ten years. It's thick with advertising agencies and insurance companies. The foreshore suburbs east of the city are Sydney's best where water-front mansions bring up to, and sometimes more than, $10 million. The northern foreshores are not so expensive because most of the houses face south, the least preferred direction, but prices can still be well in the millions. Where there is no residential development, the foreshore land is often part of **Sydney Harbour Foreshores National Park** and dedicated to public use.

The best and cheapest way to see Sydney Harbour is by ferry from Circular Quay. Small, modern, twin and single hulled vessels cover inner harbour destinations such as Neutral Bay, Cremorne and Taronga Park Zoo to the north-east, and Balmain, Greenwich and Hunters Hill to the west and north-west. Return trips on these routes take less than an hour and cost $1.20 each way. Large, leisurely old ferries and speedy hydrofoils ply the waters to Manly. Take the slow boat out, about 45 minutes for $1.50, and the fast one, about 15 for $2.40, back. Returning by bus is also possible.

City Sights

A great proportion of the major architectural, historical and cultural sights of Sydney can be covered on a single walk beginning at Agar Steps in Kent Street and finishing at the Australian Museum in College Street.

Observatory Hill
Agar Steps lead to Observatory Hill, named for the observatory which dominates its summit. The **National Trust Centre**, built as a military hospital by Governor Macquarie in 1815 and used as Fort Street School from 1850, occupies the southern end of the hill. It houses the **S. H. Ervin Museum and Art Gallery** which specialises in retrospective shows of Australian painting, and has a shop and offices. When exhibitions are running, the gallery is open from Tuesday to Friday, 11 am to 5 pm and on Saturday and Sunday from 2 pm to 5 pm. Admission price varies with exhibitions but is usually around $2.

The **Observatory** on the hilltop was designed by colonial architect Alexander Dawson, constructed in 1858 and remained in service until 1983 when it became part of the **Museum of Applied Arts and Sciences**, a widely scattered institution which includes the **Mint and Barracks Museums** and the **Power House Museum** among its other venues. Until 1942, the time ball atop the Observatory tower dropped at 1 pm each day and a cannon was fired from Dawes Point under the Harbour Bridge.

Observatory Hill affords a close view of the Harbour Bridge on its eastern side. The view on a western arc takes in the Walsh Bay wharves, Millers Point, Darling Harbour and Pyrmont, the heart of Sydney's port. Upper Fort Street runs along the eastern edge of the hill and joins Watson Road at Bridge Stairs. Watson Road leads down to Argyle Street and the Rocks proper.

The Rocks
The Rocks is where Australia began. Today it's a neat collection of tastefully restored warehouses, nineteenth-century terraces, restaurants and tourist attractions but it began life as a prison camp where the 'criminal classes' of England were dumped to be kept in line and provided for by a regiment of soldiers and a naval governor. It had a rough adolescence during which it accommodated press gangs,

prostitutes, drunks and sailors of every creed and colour from square-rigged ships berthed at Circular Quay on one side and Darling Harbour on the other. 'Pushes' or razor gangs arose there early in this century and terrorised the quieter residents with their energetic gang warfare and disregard for the law.

Argyle Place at the bottom of Watson Road is a fine circle of Georgian and Victorian terraced houses with **The Garrison Church**, built in 1840, at its eastern end. The church was in part designed by Edmund Blackett who built many of Sydney's nineteenth-century sandstone churches. **Argyle Cut** which leads under Cumberland Street was hewn out of solid rock between 1843 and 1859 to provide a passage through the steep hill separating the Circular Quay and Walsh Bay wharves. The work was begun by convicts not long before transportation to NSW breathed its last, and completed by hired labour. Argyle Steps lead up from its centre to the Harbour Bridge.

The cut brings walkers down to the **Argyle Arts Centre**, a conglomeration of art and craft shops carrying merchandise for tourist consumption and housed in the 1880s Argyle Bond Stores. Short, well signposted detours to many points of interest in the Rocks are possible from here. The **Rocks Visitors' Centre** at 102 George Street has information and maps on the area. To reach George Street, turn left along Playfair Street, a pedestrians-only thoroughfare where Argyle Terraces, built in the 1870s and now carefully restored, house shops and fast food bars. **Tourist Newsfront**, a good place for information, maps and tour and entertainment bookings, is at the southern end of Playfair Street. The northern end runs into George Street; the Rocks Visitors' Centre is to the right. To continue the walk, cross George Street and proceed down Hickson Road to its junction with Circular Quay West and turn right.

Circular Quay

The western flank of Circular Quay is the old quayside of Sydney, now largely occupied by the Overseas Passenger Terminal where cruise ships berth. Water police headquarters stand by the waterside. The restaurants in the old bond stores opposite have wonderful views but variable food quality. Customs Officer's Stairs bring walkers from the bond stores up to George Street which runs past **Cadman's Cottage**, Sydney's oldest dwelling built in 1815, that excellent watering hole the **Oriental Hotel** and the Maritime Services Building where many of the day tour buses depart. A left turn past the Maritime Services Building and down through a small park leads to Circular Quay itself where the ferry wharves accommodate public ferries and harbour cruising boats.

The Quay is a day-time bustle of workers, tourists, buskers and shopkeepers; at night it thrums to concert, opera and theatre-goers on their way from ferries and buses to the Opera House which is approached by a covered walk-way from its eastern end. Behind the Quay along Alfred Street, where buses arrive from and depart to the eastern and western suburbs are pubs, shops and **Customs House**– the oldest building left standing where Australia first made camp, completed in 1885 and still in use. It is not open to the public.

The Opera House

Bennelong Point, named after the Aboriginal who first established communication with the colonisers, is the site of the **Sydney Opera House**. The building was commissioned by a world-wide competition held in the 1950s when the point was a tram depot. Danish Architect, Joern Utzon won with the sail design which has become Sydney's most clichéd symbol. Despite its success, everything associated with the building's construction was controversial—its appearance, its cost which rose from $7 million to $102 million, the sixteen years from original planning to completion and especially the building itself which was such a focus of political storms and ended so changed from Utzon's first conception that the architect withdrew and has not since returned to see his vision complete. The building houses a Concert Hall, Opera Theatre (also used for ballet), Drama Theatre, Recording Hall, Playhouse Cinema, Exhibition Hall, two restaurants, a coffee shop, a souvenir shop, a library of performing arts and rehearsal and administration facilities. **Guided tours** cost $3.50 and depart on demand with the last tour leaving at 4 pm every day. Saturday afternoon is not a good time for tours as matinee performances fill the theatres. Backstage tours ($6) occur on Sunday also on demand, ring and check to see if rehearsals have closed any theatres on the day; (02) 250 7111 ask for the Guides' Desk. Join all tours at the Guides' Desk in the Exhibition Hall. There is also a full evening outing including tour, supper and show available.

The Opera House is flanked on three sides by harbourside broadwalks. They afford superb day and night views of the harbour and the bridge, and on Sundays jazz bands, dance troupes and others add entertainment to the scene. Altogether, it's a superb place to soak up the feeling of Sydney on a sunny day or a balmy evening when the sky is flooded with stars.

The Royal Botanic Gardens

Farm Cove lies on the eastern side of the Opera House edged by the Royal Botanic Gardens, a swathe of labelled greenery which stretches east to Woolloomooloo Bay and south to the Cahill Expressway where the Domain begins. **Government House** where the governor of New South Wales lives today is located at the northern end of the gardens behind and above the Opera House; the **New South Wales Conservatorium of Music**, once Government House stables, is further south at the beginning of Macquarie Street.

The Royal Botanic Gardens occupy the site where the first colonists tried and failed to grow themselves a food supply. Its luxuriance does little credit to their ability. It has ponds with ducks and swans, walkways and the harbour shore at its low end; a restaurant in the middle and a Visitor Centre and glass pyramid for tropical species at its high end. Eastern entrances and exits are along Mrs Macquarie's Road, where one also finds the Visitor Centre. The main gate with its exceedingly out-of-place Italianate fountain is at the lower end of Macquarie Street. An exit and right turn into Mrs Macquarie's Road will take you across the expressway bridge to the Art Gallery of NSW and the Domain. A left turn leads down to **Mrs Macquarie's Chair** also known as Mrs Macquarie's Seat, a rock cutting made in 1816 to commemorate the completion of Mrs Macquarie's Scenic Road and the part played by Elizabeth Macquarie, Governor Lachlan Macquarie's wife, in beautifying colonial Sydney.

The Art Gallery of NSW

The Art Gallery of NSW houses the state's art collection. It is also home to touring blockbuster exhibitions and has a good little café and an interesting book shop. The facade, entrance hall and old wing are what is left of the original building constructed in 1885 to accommodate an international exhibition. Additions were made up to 1919 and then again in 1972. A further wing is being built.

Two smallish galleries in the old wing house Australian art from the nineteenth and early twentieth centuries. Here one can find the Sydney Impressionists' sublime paintings of their harbour as it was in the late nineteenth and early twentieth centuries. The remaining old section is given over to European pre-twentieth-century paintings and sculpture and the rest of the gallery is devoted to its modern collection which includes Picasso and other famous Europeans as well as a large number of works by the best Australian painters. Gallery hours are 10 am to 5 pm Monday to Saturday and noon to 5 pm on Sunday. Admission to permanent exhibitions is free.

Domain

The Domain lies between the Art Gallery and Macquarie Street. It was originally 'The Governor's Domain' and stretched down to the Botanic Gardens and up to Hyde Park. These days political speakers gather on weekends, lunchtime joggers run during the week and the Australian Opera entertains outdoors during the annual Festival of Sydney on its reduced expanse of grass and trees.

Macquarie Street

Macquarie Street, on the western side of the Domain, is the seat of New South Wales government and the site of many elegant colonial buildings including the Mint and Barracks Museums, Parliament House, Sydney Hospital and the **State Library**. The latter houses the earliest colonial records including lists of First Fleet passengers and the journals of governors, explorers and officers. Small exhibitions of historical documents are regularly held there.

Mint Museum, at one time part of Australia's first permanent hospital (known as the Rum Hospital from the sales of rum which helped to pay for it) houses Australian decorative arts. Domestic oddities such as highly decorated, silver encased emu eggs are exhibited with more commonplace furniture and fabrics tracing the growing influence of Australian landscape and materials on public and domestic design. It is open 10am to 5 pm Monday to Sunday except for Wednesday when hours are noon to 5 pm. Admission is free.

Barracks Museum, also free and open the same hours, traces the history of Sydney with special reference to domestic architecture and the development of civic life through celebratory occasions such as the centenary of NSW in 1888, the opening of the Harbour Bridge, Royal visits and the annual Easter Show.

Parliament House is the oldest public building in Australia and was originally also part of the Rum Hospital. It houses a parliament known throughout Australia as 'The Bear Pit' for the unrestrained verbal savagery of its debates. Though often denigrated as a circus, it is the mother of Australia's rumbustious parliaments and its boots-and-all traditions affect the tone of every political house. Visitors are admitted to the Public Gallery after 7.30 pm on sitting days.

Sydney Hospital, next door, is built in the Late Victorian style and was a replacement for the central wing of the Rum Hospital. Once of central importance to the Sydney medical establishment, its role has lately been reduced to that of a small inner city hospital.

Queens Square occupies the southern end of Macquarie Street. The square holds **St James Church**, a Georgian structure designed by Francis Greenway and dating from 1819, around which are clustered the old and new buildings of Sydney's main legal precinct. Across the paved square is the modern **Supreme Court Building** and behind the church is that court's Georgian companion in law, recently restored with considerable attention to detail.

Hyde Park

Hyde Park, an oasis of tree-lined promenades, lawns, formal gardens and statuary, lies across the road. The **Archibald Fountain** dominates its northern section and could be mistaken for a high Victorian extravaganza despite having been donated to the city by a prosperous notable in 1932. The sandstone cathedral to the east of Hyde Park is **St Mary's**, an incomplete nineteenth-century gothic revival version of the great English cathedrals. Although it has no spire, it is internally impressive. A guided tour takes place on the first Sunday of every month at 2 pm but the building is open every day. Each January when the **Festival of Sydney** takes place, Hyde Park is filled with rides, outdoor theatres, amusement tents and fast food vans. Some say this is a misuse of the usually quiet park but the city's people and especially its children keep coming back. At other times the park accommodates lunching workers and shoppers escaping the city bustle. It is cut in half by Park Street which joins the sweep of William Street up to Kings Cross. A war memorial and unkempt pool of remembrance dominate the southern end between Park and Liverpool Streets. East of this section of park, across College Street, is the Australian Museum.

The Australian Museum

The museum is Australia's largest repository of natural history and features biological, evolutionary and anthropological displays. Walkers who find themselves completely exhausted (such a condition would not be unexpected) can take tea on the lower ground floor of the museum and consider the great feat they have just accomplished.

Anyone fascinated by the variety of unique, charming and sometimes dangerous fauna which the isolation of the Australian continent has spawned will delight in an hour or two spent in this museum. The ground floor displays show marsupials in habitats varying from the western desert to metropolitan Sydney. The same floor houses an Aboriginal gallery which is the museum's most fascinating offering, describing the life of Aboriginal people from the undisturbed traditions of the bush to urban living. It shows cultural objects, medicine, life-styles and some of the 700 languages spoken in Australia before white dominance. Other floors present fish, mammals and birds as well as displays of cultural material from other Pacific and South-East Asian countries, especially New Guinea.

Taylor Square and Paddington

Rapacious sightseers will continue to Liverpool Street and catch a bus (380, 381) to Taylor Square to see the **1888 court buildings**, still serving their original function, and, behind them, the **Old Darlinghurst Jail** which now houses East Sydney Technical College. The same bus continues to **Victoria Barracks** completed in 1819 as convict quarters and now occupied by the military. It has a fine colonial parade ground and a military museum. The barracks are open on Tuesdays from 10 am to noon when there is a ceremonial changing of the guard and a guided tour.

A walk up Oxford Street from the barracks brings you to **Paddington** shopping centre where antique, book, curio, clothing and furniture shops, restaurants and pubs compete for the custom of Sydney's trendiest people. A lively **market** takes place each Saturday in the grounds of The Paddington Village Church.

Centennial Park, a vast open space dedicated to celebrate the first one hundred years of Australian history, is found at the top of Oxford Street, Paddington.

Other Sights

Sydney Tower

Anyone who wants to take in the big picture before going anywhere should catch the lift up Sydney Tower which rises like a one-legged spaceship over the Centrepoint shopping complex in Pitt Street. At 270 metres (about 900 feet), the tower summit is the city's highest point and has a revolving observation deck and two restaurants in which the view is the best feature. On a clear day you can see as far as the Blue Mountains, the Central Coast and Wollongong. Admission cost $4.

Colonial Houses

Sydney has preserved two of its best colonial houses, Elizabeth Bay House and Vaucluse House. **Elizabeth Bay House** is at 7 Onslow Avenue, Elizabeth Bay, just below Kings Cross on the eastern side amongst some of the city's most valuable real estate. It was built between 1835 and 1838 to a design by John Verge, the leading architect of the time and is furnished in mid-nineteenth-century style. It also houses exhibitions depicting colonial life and is open from Tuesday to Sunday 10 am to 4.30 pm. Admission cost $2.

Vaucluse House is in Wentworth Road, in the eastern suburb of Vaucluse about eight km (five miles) from the city. The house was built in stages, beginning in 1803, as a home for explorer and politician, William Charles Wentworth whose descendants are still prominent in Sydney society. It has beautiful gardens and elegant tea rooms attached where picnic hampers are available. Nielsen Park, a pretty and popular harbour beach is a short walk away.

Darling Harbour

The re-development of Darling Harbour is the state of New South Wales' principal contribution to the Australian Bicentenary. The harbour was originally a thriving cargo port on the opposite side of the city from Circular Quay but had become a broken down and unsightly wreck until the current project was undertaken. It consists of parks, a Chinese garden, exhibition and convention buildings and waterside walkways flanked with places to shop and eat. The new precinct formed by Darling Harbour is linked to the city by a mono-rail train which runs down George and Pitt Streets.

Museums

The **Power House Museum**, is a very large museum exhibiting triumphs of engineering and applied sciences and housed appropriately in the old Pyrmont power station on the western side of Darling Harbour. It contains objects such as aeroplanes, trams and boats which would be hard to see in any other kind of building. Less overwhelming exhibits include musical instruments, steam engines and a famous pie cart called Harry's Café de Wheels that used to serve sailors at Woolloomooloo. The old power house is a new site for a collection which has been partly exhibited in smaller venues during past years. Its opening, due in March 1988, is part of the celebrations for Australia's Bicentenary. Phone (02) 217 0111 to find out if the opening made it on time. The museum stands on the western edge of the Darling Harbour re-development.

Other museums in Sydney include the **Geological and Mining Museum** at 36 George Street, the Rocks, which pays tribute to the almost incalculable influence that mining has had on the history of Australia. Open 9.30 am to 4 pm Monday to Friday, 1 pm to 4 pm Saturday and 11 am to 4 pm Sundays and public holidays. Free. The **Sydney Maritime Museum**, at Birkenhead Point, Drummoyne, has a number of old steamships moored at its quay as well as displays on land. Open 10 am to 5 pm Tuesday to Saturday and 1.30 pm to 5 pm Sunday. Admission $4. The **Nicholson Museum** on the south side of the Main Quadrangle at Sydney University, is Sydney's only museum specialising in classical antiquities and archaeology. Open 10 am to 4.30 pm Monday to Thursday, closes at 4.15 pm on Friday. Free.

Taronga Zoological Park

This beautifully sited zoo is gathered on the harbour foreshores at Mosman, one of Sydney's most prestigious northern suburbs, a short ferry ride from Circular Quay. It has its own wharf. Parts of the zoo are in the traditional mould with monkeys in cages, lions and tigers in pits, a nocturnal house, an aquarium and a walk-through aviary. Its most unusual feature aside from a glorious setting is a new seal pool constructed in the waters of the harbour. The zoo is also the closest place to town where you can see koalas and kangaroos. Open 9 am to 5 pm seven days. Admission $7.50.

Beaches Close to Town

It is sheer luck that Sydney's founding fathers pitched their tents a few miles from beaches which make other citizens of the world turn emerald with envy. Their concentration was on fresh water and a sheltered anchorage and they cared nothing for the feature which modern Sydneysiders regard as one of their city's best. After all it's impossible to grow maize on a surf beach.

Swimming at any ocean beach should be approached with care as dangerous currents called rips can carry swimmers out to sea. Only swim between the red and yellow flags displayed on any beach when it is patrolled by surf lifesavers. Swim elsewhere or when the beach is not patrolled and you may be taking your life in your hands.

Bondi and Manly are the best known of the beaches and suffer from that familiarity to a certain extent. They are no longer and have not been since the beginning of this century pristine stretches of naked nature. Nonetheless, they have charm.

Bondi

Bondi (take the 380 or 381 bus from the city or a train to Bondi Junction and change to a beach bus) is the racier of Sydney's two most famous beaches but there is still no being blasé about its beauty. Even if it is egregiously urbanised, slightly tatty and sometimes not as clean as it might be, it expresses the energy and variety of Sydney life to the full. The city's beautiful bodies come out to promenade and lie about on the esplanade and the beach, wearing as little clothing as possible—bikini tops are passé when sun-baking. The collected generations of migrant families congregate for picnics on the grassy hill behind the beach and the fish restaurants and ice-cream parlours of Campbell Parade are always thick with customers. Jazz concerts, plays, exhibitions and children's entertainments take place in the beachfront pavilion.

Manly

The scene at Manly is different. A more dedicated attempt has been made to catch and hold the day tripper in a 'fun for all the family' atmosphere. Getting there by ferry from Circular Quay is best. Fish and chips shops scramble for weekend custom along the Corso, a pedestrians-only mall with a small amphitheatre in the middle. The beachfront with its still impressive and famous, though now depleted, stand of Norfolk Island pines is not so open as Bondi but offers a lengthier prospect. The sand is golden rather than white. Young sidewalk and surf board-riders gather along the esplanade which is a lovely place to stroll in the early evening. **Manly Underwater World** in West Esplanade has an enormous tank full of sharks, stingrays, gropers and less threatening sea life as well. It has recently been reconstructed so that visitors can 'walk underwater' among the fishes through perspex hallways.

Marine Parade, a seaside pathway running from the southern end of Manly Esplanade, around the foreshores to Shelley Beach, a protected, west facing, still water beach, is a lovely walk. It gradually brings you round to face back towards the full length of Manly Beach and, along the way, gives views of the Pacific Ocean beaches as they step north to Palm Beach. Shelley Beach has a small grassy headland behind it, ideal for kite flying or just appreciating the ocean vista. Walking around the harbour side of the district from Manly Wharf affords a new angle on the harbour and the heads.

Other Beaches

Other than the two famous names, Sydney's surf beaches stretch north to **Palm Beach** and south to the **Royal National Park**. Each is one of nature's masterpieces but those close to the city suffer from over-population and, sometimes, sadly, pollution. Keeping this in mind, there are good, patrolled **surf beaches** south of Bondi at **Bronte**, **Clovelly** and **Coogee** and north of Manly at **Harbord** and **Curl Curl**. They are all crowded on sunny summer weekends but much less so on working days.

Sydney has **still water** swimming in the eastern and northern suburbs. In the east, **Neilsen Park** at Vaucluse and **Camp Cove** at Watsons Bay are small strips of sand where the water falls gently and the crowds press hard. **Lady Bay** on South Head near Camp Cove is for naked swimmers. **Balmoral Beach** at Mosman is the best of the northern harbour beaches having wide sand and a pleasant esplanade but it tends to be crowded too. The very small and almost inaccessible **Obelisk Beach** on Middle Head is the northside's concession to nudity.

True escape from the weekend crowds (remember, there are four million people in Sydney) can be gained only at beaches far from town which are covered in the section called 'Around Sydney'.

SHOPPING

Shopping for stuffed koalas and opals is no great challenge but tasteful and unique Australian products are more likely to come your way at the **Aboriginal Artists' Gallery** on the corner of Market and Clarence Streets in the city where urban and tribal painters and crafts people sell their works on consignment. The **National Trust shops** on Observatory Hill and in Paddington sell books, calendars and merchandise related to their preservationist work. You can buy reproductions of Australian art, and books on the subject, at the **Art Gallery of NSW** book shop and the **Australian Museum** shop offers reproductions of antiquities from Asia and Africa, jewellery based on Australian flora and toys.

People with money to spend and an eye for art should head for the commercial galleries of Paddington and Woollahra which have changing exhibitions and stocks of work by well-known local painters. **Holdsworth Galleries**, 86 Holdsworth Street, Woollahra, (02) 32 1364, is one of the largest commercial galleries in Sydney and specialises in the works of Australian artists, changing its show about once a month. **Roslyn Oxley 9 Gallery**, 13–21 MacDonald Street, Paddington, (02) 331 1919, exhibits contemporary Australian art. **Ray Hughes Gallery** 124 Jersey Road, Woollahra, (02) 32 2533, is a gallery for good quality Australian work from the 1950s to the 1980s.

The city's most prestigious shopping arcades are the **Strand** which runs from Pitt to George Streets and the **Queen Victoria Building** opposite the Hilton Hotel. They house fashion and jewellery stores and give entrance to the city's leading department stores via underground walkways and overpasses. **Double Bay** in the east has the most exclusive high fashion shops of all. Catch the 324 bus in Elizabeth Street, City or a train to Edgecliff Station. **Oxford Street**, Paddington, is also a fascinating place to shop. Catch the 380 or 381 bus also from Elizabeth Street.

Duty free shops in Sydney offer relatively good value although they do not compare with Hong Kong or Singapore for variety and quantity of merchandise. You will get good prices on what is sold provided you buy in the city and not at the airport.

NIGHTLIFE

'Kulture Vultures', as Australians label those interested in brain and soul-teasing pastimes, can take their pick of theatre, music or ballet. Those dedicated to a mere good time are catered for in nightclubs and in the 'gin joints' of Kings Cross. The best way to find out what's on in these and many other places is to buy the *Sydney Morning Herald* on Friday and consult the entertainment listings in *Metro*, the insert printed on blue paper. It lists theatre, music, film and just about anything else that's happening.

Theatre

Sydney's theatre scene is busy and eclectic. Mainstream productions from **The Sydney Theatre Company**, the major state funded acting company, show at the Opera House Drama Theatre and The Wharf. The latter venue, constructed in an old wharf west of the Harbour Bridge at Walsh Bay, is newer and more intimate than its formal Opera House counterpart and has one of Sydney's best night-time views as well as a good restaurant. Productions at both theatres maintain an even, professional standard. Australian movie stars such as Judy Davis and Mel Gibson pop up in Sydney Theatre Company shows much less often than they once did. Hollywood has them now. Other theatres well worth a visit include the **Belvoir Street** in Surry Hills, **The Stables** in Kings Cross which specialises in new Australian writing, the **Marian Street** at Killara in the northern suburbs and, for experiment, **The Performance Space** in Cleveland Street, Redfern. Sydney's commercial houses, **The Theatre Royal**, **The Regent**, **Her Majesty's** and **The Footbridge Theatre** usually carry big musicals, farces or comedies with old American and English actors in leading roles. The other substantial theatrical venue is the **Seymour Centre**, a two theatre complex to the west of Railway Square. It houses touring productions from other states or overseas and **Nimrod**, a theatre company which engendered the theatrical revival of the 1970s but which has lately fallen upon artistic and financial hard times.

Cinema

George Street between Bathurst and Goulburn Streets is Sydney's cinema strip. The **Village, Hoyts** and **Greater Union** centres, each containing several cinemas, screen popular movies, both local and overseas productions. The **Roma Cinema** opposite the Hoyts complex is the only art house on George Street, the other city high-brow picture theatre is the **Dendy** in Martin Place at the entrance to Mid-City Centre shopping arcade. The **State Theatre** in Market Street between George and Pitt is Sydney's major representative of the great age of movies. A picture palace in the 1920s style, it even has a pit organ which is still played at some showings.

The most noteworthy suburban cinemas are the **Academy Twin** in Oxford Street, Paddington, a couple of minutes walk from Taylor Square, and the Australian Film Institute's **Chauvel Cinema** in the Paddington Town Hall. Both are art houses but the former offers by far the most accessible of this kind of movie. The **Walker Street Cinema**, 121 Walker Street, North Sydney is the city's leading cinema for re-screenings and revivals and also has some fringe first releases as does the **Valhalla Cinema**, 166 Glebe Point Road, Glebe.

Opera and Classical Music

Serious music centres on the **Opera House** where the Australian Broadcasting Corporation holds symphony concerts and recitals, the Sydney Philharmonia Choir performs choral works and the Australian Opera sings. When the Australian Opera goes to Melbourne, the Australian Ballet takes its place and in between times the justifiably much-vaunted Sydney Dance Company fits in a shortish season or two. A series of chamber music concerts called **Music and Heritage** takes place through-out the year in some of Sydney's grand old houses and public buildings. Phone (02) 32 4891 for information about these. Lunchtime and evening concerts also take place regularly in the **Conservatorium of Music**. Phone (02) 230 1263.

Jazz

Sydney has two well-established jazz clubs. **The Basement**, 29 Reiby Place, Circular Quay, lives up to the smoke-filled room image and hosts a combination of the best local bands and overseas artists; The **Don Burrows Supper Club**, is where Don Burrows, the grand and very smooth old reeds man of Sydney holds court with invited guests from the upper echelons of mainstream. He occasionally gives way to very exclusive visitors such as Steve Ross from New York's Algonquin Hotel. The club is in the Regent Hotel, 199 George Street—dress up and bring your money with you. For less formal jazz sessions **Soup Plus Restaurant**, 383 George Street on any night except Sunday, and the **Tilbury Hotel**, 22 Forbes Street, Woolloomooloo, and the **White Horse Hotel**, 381 Crown Street, Surry Hills, on Saturday afternoons are good bets.

Rock and Folk

Big rock concerts take place either at the **Hordern Pavilion** on Anzac Parade east of the city or at the **Sydney Entertainment Centre**, a venue for all kinds of spectaculars, sited in Chinatown. Day to day rock hangs out in pubs and sweaty discos. The **Hip Hop Club**, 11 Oxford Street, Paddington, has dance club (once called disco) some nights and rock bands late at night as well as comedy shows Wednesday to Saturday from 7 pm. **The Piccadilly Hotel**, 171 Victoria Street, Kings Cross, selects its bands from the more eccentric but sometimes fascinating edges of the Sydney rock scene. **Hotel Manly**, opposite Manly Wharf, features main-stream rockers and **The Hopetoun Hotel**, 416 Bourke Street, Surry Hills, is where you'll see the spikiest haircuts in town.

Nightclubs

Kings Cross is strip joints, peep shows, female impersonators, brothels, illegal gambling clubs and sleazy street life but compared to similar places in other cities, it's relatively easy-going, good humoured and not too dangerous. It has late opening nightclubs and bars such as **Jo Jo Ivory's**, in the Hotel Sheraton, 40 Macleay Street, which is also Sydney's best Cajun food restaurant, and **The New Orleans Restaurant and Cabaret**, 24 Darlinghurst Road, and some good after-midnight coffee houses, especially in Kellett Street. **The Cauldron**, 207 Darlinghurst Road, is a famous late-opening place with a bar, restaurant and dance floor but is very crowded on weekends—try a week night if you want to get in.

Nightclubs not in the Cross include **Kinsela's**, Bourke Street, Taylor Square, which has a restaurant and cabaret room, **Jamison Street**, a smart dance club at 11 Jamison Street in the city and **Steps** in the Metropole Hotel, at 287 Military Road, Cremorne on the north side of the harbour.

SPORT

Australians make a great deal of fuss about sport though Sydneysiders do it less than Melbournites. The **Sydney Cricket Ground** and the brand new **Sports Ground** next door to it host international cricket and football matches as well as the best of local contests. The Cricket Ground was once quite distinguished-looking but new concrete stands, an electronic scoreboard and lighting towers have made it the same as any other giant arena. The best of the old stands have been moved to North Sydney Oval which takes the cake for looks from any other in the city although the local Rugby League team leaves something to be desired in its on-field performances. The new Sports Ground has not turned out to be as horrid as one might expect.

The most eye-catching and unusual of Sydney sports is **surf lifesaving**. Summer lifesaving carnivals are a delight. The sight of 16 man rowing boats crashing out through the waves, striking to round their buoys and surfing to the shore where the crew swarms out and runs to the finish line is positively Homeric. To find out when the carnivals occur, ring the Surf Life Saving Association of NSW on (02) 663 4298. Sundays on Sydney Harbour, when 18-foot skiffs—the fastest small sailing boats in the world—compete, are a similar thrill but without any classical connotation. Take the specially organised ferry from No. 2 Wharf, Circular Quay, at 1.45 pm for a close-up view. Bookings on (02) 32 2995.

A flutter on the nags, or horse race gambling, is exceedingly popular in Sydney. **Randwick Racecourse** is the leading track, three others, **Rose Hill**, **Canterbury** and **Warwick Farm**, provide enough venues for racing to be held every weekend and on other days of the week as well. The details of race days can be found on the sports pages at the back of any newspaper.

Sydney's international **tennis** venue is **White City** at Rushcutters Bay but members of the general public can't play there. The nearest tennis courts to the city are at **Moore Park** near Paddington, (02) 662 7005 and **Rushcutters Bay** near King Cross, (02) 357 1675.

If you want to go boating on the harbour under your own steam, **Walton's Boatshed**, 2 The Esplanade, Balmoral Beach, (02) 969 6006, has vessels from cruisers to rowboats and sailboards for hire. They also run a sailboarding school.

WHERE TO STAY

Sydney can be a tough place to find a bed at any time. It is the most expensive Australian city and doesn't have much accommodation in the mid to low price range.

Prices are also rising because of high demand for rooms especially from October to April. Wise travellers will book their accommodation before arriving, it's cheaper and hassle free.

Anyone who hasn't booked before arriving should contact the **Travel Centre of New South Wales**. Its friendly counter staff give advice and make bookings from 9 am to 5 pm Monday to Friday at the corner of Pitt and Spring Streets in the city centre, phone (02) 231 4444. They can, of course, also handle advance bookings for Sydney and for other parts of New South Wales.

Over $200
Regent of Sydney, 199 George Street, Sydney, (02) 238 0000; is Sydney's best hotel and a very formal establishment it is indeed, with a somewhat intimidating marble foyer overlooked by a balcony where one can take luxurious teas. The rooms are all one would expect and many have fabulous views of Circular Quay and the Harbour Bridge. So far as the city itself is concerned, the Regent is close to history and Opera House but a little far from the rest of the action. Standard rooms $245, city view $270, harbour view $320.

Hilton International Sydney, 259 Pitt Street, Sydney (02) 266 0610; is bang in the middle of town and especially loved by shoppers for its proximity to the Queen Victoria Building, the city's most exclusive shopping arcade. The hotel was built long enough before the Regent and Intercontinental to possess an almost establishment air. Single $245, double $265.

Intercontinental Hotel Sydney, 117 Macquarie Street, Sydney, (02) 230 0200; facade-ism reigns supreme here where the old Treasury Buildings have been converted to foyer, shops and restaurants at the base of this high riser sitting above Circular Quay on the opposite side to the Regent. The Intercontinental has been reported to have some difficulty maintaining the standard of service expected in a hotel of such a pedigree. Single $240, double $245.

Sheraton Wentworth, 61–101 Phillip Street, Sydney, (02) 230 0700; was the grand dame of Sydney hotels until the above-mentioned trio came along and retains an atmosphere of quiet elegance appropriate to that position. Its rooms are stacked horseshoe shape over Phillip Street, a couple of blocks from Martin Place, some have showers only in their bathrooms. The hotel is well known among city late nighters for its piano bar. Single $190, double $240.

Sebel Town House, 23 Elizabeth Bay Road, Elizabeth Bay, (02) 358 3244; is very popular with visiting celebrities, especially rock and film stars. Located near the middle of Kings Cross. Single $220 to $250, double $235 to $265.

Hyatt Kingsgate Hotel, Top of William Street, Kings Cross, (02) 356 1234; is the one with the flashing advertising attached to its front. Despite this eyesore, it has lots in its favour, including great views and Kings Cross, and has recently been refurbished. Single $150 to $220, double $170 to $250.

Holiday Inn Menzies, 14 Carrington Street, Sydney, (02) 2 0232; is built above Wynyard railway station but this won't disturb your sleep, especially as the Menzies is one of the best value places to stay in central Sydney both for location and the size of your room. $225.

Boulevard, 90 William Street, Sydney, (02) 357 2277; is between the city and

Kings Cross and its top rooms overlook the Woolloomooloo wharves. No longer among the first rank of Sydney hotels. $220.

Old Sydney Park Royal, 55 George Street, Sydney, (02) 2 0524; is a surprising smallish hotel in the middle of the Rocks. Rather undistinguished looking outside, inside it has the atrium which seems to be required of all new hotels but manages greater intimacy than its bigger competition. The hotel is justly popular. $205.

Under $200

Wynyard Travelodge, 7–9 York Street, Sydney, (02) 2 0254, is very central, being opposite Wynyard Park and about ten minutes walk from the Rocks. Rooms refurbished in 1987. Double beds only. $195.

Park Apartments, 16–23 Oxford Street, Sydney, (02) 331 7728; good value, pleasantly furnished one- and two-bedroom serviced apartments with nice kitchens. $145 to $195.

Manly Pacific International Hotel, 55 North Steyne, Manly, (02) 977 7666, is the only 'international' hotel outside the city area. It overlooks Manly Beach in a superb position right opposite the beach. $195 oceanside, $165 elsewhere.

Stanford, 1 Hollywood Avenue, Bondi Junction, (02) 389 8700; located one suburb further east than Paddington. Two- and three-bedroom apartments plus a penthouse if you're feeling rich. Towels daily, serviced twice weekly, extra $10 for daily service. Security parking and heated pool. Two bedroom $160, three bedroom $180.

Olims Sydney Hotel, 26-34 Macleay Street, Potts Point, (02) 358 2777, is just down from the heart of Kings Cross and has nicely decorated if small rooms. Quite good value for a Kings Cross hotel. $135 to $170.

Gazebo Ramada Hotel, 2 Elizabeth Road, Elizabeth Bay, (02) 358 1999, is perhaps not the best in Kings Cross but one to turn to as a definite second or third choice. Court rooms (recently refurbished) $168. Tower rooms (older and smaller) $156.

Cambridge Inn, 212 Riley Street, Surry Hills, (02) 212 1111; a hotel with excellent spacious and tastefully decorated rooms situated close to Oxford Street in the city. $146.

Central Plaza Hotel, corner George and Quay Streets, Sydney, (02) 212 2544, is at Railway Square right at the southern end of Sydney's city area. Rooms have exposed brick walls and are furnished in brown. The decor elsewhere in the hotel has rather too much green. There is a bar, restaurant and pool. Single $135, double $145.

Meriton Plaza, 2 Springfield Avenue, Kings Cross, (02) 356 3255; smart one- and two-bedroom apartments right in the heart of Kings Cross. One bedroom $125, two bedroom $145.

Hyde Park Plaza, 38 College Street, Sydney, (02) 331 6933, overlooks the southern end of Hyde Park and has a range of self catering accommodation from bed-sits to two-bedroom units, all of good size. There is a restaurant for those who don't fancy cooking for themselves. Single $125, double $140.

The York, 5 York Street, Sydney, (02) 264 7747, is one of Sydney's few inner city apartment blocks and has some apartments turned over to high quality tourist accommodation. Can be difficult to get into. Studio apartments single $130, double $140. One and two bedrooms substantially more.

Hotel Sheraton, 40 Macleay Street, Potts Point, (02) 358 1955, is not a member of the international Sheraton hotel chain but a small hotel close to Kings Cross with rooms of about motel standard. Single $118, double $128.

Pensione Sydney, 27 Georgina Street, Newtown, (02) 550 1700, is located in a close suburb south of the city but within easy bus access. It is more like a quality European pensione than a hotel and occupies a Victorian house built in 1888. Some rooms have private facilities, others do not. $105 to $125 per room.

Russell Hotel, 143a George Street, Sydney, (02) 241 3543, is a small private hotel in the heart of the Rocks, furnished in simple but tasteful style with high Victorian beds. Fourteen rooms, six only double. Single $75 to $101 (share facilities) $113 (ensuite), double $82 to $111 (share) $123 (ensuite).

Greetings Oxford Koala, corner Oxford and Pelican Streets, Darlinghurst, (02) 269 0645, close to the city and Taylor Square above the Ansett Pioneer coach terminal. Standard rooms are furnished in cotton and cane. Some family rooms with kitchens. Single $94, double $105 standard. The **Greetings Oxford Towers** next door has self-catering apartments.

City Gardens, 1 Myrtle Street, Chippendale, (02) 690 9100; weekly serviced studio and one-bedroom apartments facing busy City Road and Victoria Park near Broadway about ten minutes' bus ride from the city. Studio $95, suite $105.

Under $100

The Manhattan, 8 Greenknowe Avenue, Potts Point, (02) 358 1288; a lower end of the market option but good value for the price since it has benefited from a pleasing renovation. Some rooms have private facilities, others do not. Single $73, double $88.

The Jackson, 94 Victoria Street, Potts Point, (02) 358 5801; a small private hotel taking up two Victorian terrace houses in the leafier part of Kings Cross. Its twenty rooms are furnished in appropriate style. Single $65 share facilities, $75 private facilities, double $75 share, $85 private.

Greetings Bondi Beach Apartments, 136–138 Curlewis Street, Bondi Beach, (02) 365 0155; close to the beach about half an hour's bus ride from town, these apartments are ideal for families or long term visitors as they have full kitchens and plenty of suburban shopping nearby. Single $76, double $83.

Greetings Paddington Gardens, 21–25 Oxford Street, Paddington, (02) 360 2333, is in Sydney's trendiest suburb about fifteen minutes bus ride from the city. Rooms are furnished in cool blues, perhaps to make them look a little larger than they are. Single $68, double $74.

Astoria, 9 Darlinghurst Road, Kings Cross, (02) 356 3666; an older establishment with small rooms but low prices for Sydney. Single $55, double $62.

EATING OUT

It's a feast. Any other description could not do justice to eating in Sydney. Fierce competition between hundreds of small restaurants serving a huge variety of cuisines keeps quality high and prices generally low.

Asian migrants, who began arriving in significant quantities after Australia helped

America lose the Vietnam War, have had a most profound and immediate influence on Sydney's eating habits. There are Vietnamese, Thai, Laotian, Kampuchean, Korean, Japanese, Indonesian, Malaysian, Mongolian, Burmese, Singaporean, Indian and Chinese eating houses. The previous migration wave brought southern Europeans, especially Italians and Greeks. The Italians have been contributing to our food culture ever since. Greeks and Spaniards have added to the pot, the latter seizing on our seafood with delight and skill—you'll find many of them in Goulburn Street, City. The truly insufferable foodie can also chase down Mauritian, African, Russian, Balkan, Mexican and Cajun establishments.

The irony of this culinary invasion is that Australia is said to have no cuisine of its own beyond the meat pie. This is nonsense. Sydney's food fascination has sewed its own crop of young chefs who approach our wealth of quality fresh ingredients and eclectic influences with dedication and style. Their cooking has coalesced into a fashion variously called *Oz Nouveau, Aussie Nouvelle* and *Australienne.*

Finding Sydney's eating places is not hard, as our restaurateurs often stick together along well established eating strips. The best are Oxford Street from the south east corner of Hyde Park to the end of Paddington; Glebe Point Road just west of railway square by the 431 bus from George Street, City; Bondi Road from Waverley Oval to the beach (catch the 380 bus from Elizabeth Street, City); and, on the north side of the harbour, Military Road through Neutral Bay and Cremorne which lies on the routes of buses departing from Wynyard Park. Dixon Street, Haymarket, is Sydney's Chinatown where there are many Chinese restaurants and a couple of Singapore style food stall arcades.

Australian
The Wharf, Pier 4, Hickson Road, Walsh Bay, (02) 250 1761; perfectly sited in an old wharf which has been converted to house the Sydney Theatre Company's new venue and rehearsal rooms, this restaurant has one of the city's best views, looking straight at Blues Point on the northern harbour foreshores, with the Harbour Bridge on the right. It is rather meanly furnished with chairs and tables that ought to belong outdoors but the light and tasty, quickly served meals make such a mild discomfort easy to forget. The menu changes regularly and uses ingredients of the season to original effect in dishes like cold zucchini omelet with tomato mayonnaise and warm salad of brains, capers and cucumbers. Pre-theatre dining is a speciality. Licensed. Low to mid price range.
Bayswater Brasserie, 32 Bayswater Road, Kings Cross, (02) 357 2794; full of hustle, bustle, noise and action with waiters darting to and fro at a frantic pace in keeping with the Italian café decor, giving excellent and friendly service from a menu of notable originality whose influences extend from Europe to Asia. Licensed. Mid price range.
The Left Bank 1 Burton Street, Darlinghurst, (02) 33 5129; the food is sometimes at war with the service in this restaurant. Do not expect to eat quickly but do expect to eat well on fresh ingredients prepared under the combined influence of Italy, France and Asia. The establishment is housed in an old sandstone bank building which adds to its charm. Especially good for lunch and for suppers after 9.30 pm. Licensed. Low to mid price range.

Chez Oz, 23 Craigend Street, Darlinghurst, (02) 332 4866; this most celebrated of city restaurants has a reputation for all sorts of things from celebrity spotting to leisurely service to some of the best food in town. It was established by the proprietors of the Melbourne restaurant Glo Glo's which has almost as great a reputation. The decor is exceedingly cool, lots of blues and low tone pinks, and the frequently changing menu has a heavy Californian influence with its concentration on fresh, seasonal ingredients cooked rapidly. Licensed. Upper price range.

The Bennelong, Sydney Opera House, Bennelong Point, (02) 241 1371; you can almost eat the view here but the food is good enough to deserve equal concentration. It doesn't leap to the heights of originality topped by some of the preceding restaurants but maintains consistent quality aimed at its enforcedly general clientele. You are likely to find such dishes as crayfish bisque and peppered fillet and cress salad among the entrées, cassoulet of seafood and char-grilled loin of lamb among the main courses. Set price menus are available for lunch and pre-theatre dinner. Licensed. Mid price range.

Fare Go Gourmet, 69 Union Street, North Sydney, (02) 922 2965; the exclusive preserve of Hungarian chef Kim Kertez who turns his hand to the cuisine of many nations with equal aptitude. His salads tend to the Japanese, main courses make use of local delicacies used simply such as tuna, grilled in steaks and served with pickles but he really lets go on desserts. BYO. Mid price range.

French

Berowra Waters Inn, Berowra Waters, (02) 456 1027; generally accredited with being Sydney's best restaurant, it makes a feature of lunch from Friday to Sunday. To do justice to it, you must set aside a whole day as it is far from the city and the food, especially desserts, should be savoured all afternoon. Dinner is on the same days from 7.30 pm. The menu changes every day. The restaurant overlooks Berowra Waters, a leafy bay near the Hawkesbury River. You cannot get in without a booking. Accessible by road, river or flying boat. Licensed. Upper price range.

Claude's, 10 Oxford Street, Woollahra, (02) 331 2325; another of Sydney's best, resident in a closely furnished room behind a white wall in Woollahra where the emphasis is on an excellent monthly menu. The menu is displayed on the wall outside and is enough temptation to draw anybody in. Game paté with pickled plums, saddle of venison roasted with juniper berries, hot nectarine soufflé have appeared. Licensed. Upper price range.

Puligny's, 240 Military Road, Neutral Bay, (02) 908 2552; another establishment burdened with accolades. Its chef, Greg Doyle, became quite a star when the place opened; he has maintained a high standard though the spotlight is now trained elsewhere. The style is classic French and the decor contemporary in grey. Licensed. Upper price range.

Au Chabrol, 248 Glenmore Road, Paddington, (02) 331 2551; a long serving stalwart of the Sydney restaurant scene which specialises in French provincial cooking with offerings such as duck liver paté, veal mignonettes with French mushrooms and, of course, profiteroles for dessert. BYO. Mid price range.

Italian

Taylor's, 203–205 Albion Street, Surry Hills, (02) 33 5100; the restored cottage where this restaurant lives and its garden dining area are not all the reasons for its being so good but they add considerable charm to the carefully studied northern Italian food served here which some say is Sydney's best such offering. The owners find it necessary to make regular trips to Italy just to make sure they have everything authentic and up-to-date. Licensed. Mid price range.

Senso Unico, 437 Elizabeth Street, Surry Hills, (02) 212 6199; a restaurant that winds its way from one room to another in a narrow, old Surry Hills shop-front terrace, belying its age with decor drawn from Mondrian. The menu makes much of Sydney's good seafood and steers clear of heavy sauces. Service has flair even if it is a little hammy. Licensed. Mid price range.

Mephisto, 30 Burton Street, Darlinghurst, (02) 33 5931; another which doesn't drown itself in oil and tomato, despite its orange walls. You won't find them too terrifying, especially when introduced to house specialities such as *petto de pollo* and *tiramisu*. Licensed. Mid price range.

The Restaurant, 88 Hackett Street, Ultimo, (02) 211 5895; a great deal of interesting pasta is made here, follow it with fish or offal dishes and home-made ice cream. The place can be hard to find, it's down a rather dingy lane and then down some stairs but the struggle is worth it. Open dining area with partly exposed kitchen which is chic these days. Licensed. Mid price range.

The Mixing Pot, 178 St Johns Road, Glebe, (02) 660 7449; has been on the Italian dining scene in Sydney for ages. Ask to eat in the courtyard if the weather is fine and keep your ears well tuned for the list of specials, recited at breakneck speed by thoroughly Italian staff. Grab whatever you like the sound of. Licensed. Mid price range.

Forbes Ristorante, 155 Forbes Street, Woolloomooloo, (02) 357 3652; to eat best here, go to town on the vast selection of good quality antipasti to which you help yourself—sardines, mussels, calamari, prosciutto etc. It's not hard to see how its done, just watch one of the scores of people squeezed into the place, breast the buffet and then stagger back to the table with a groaning plate. You sometimes need to be an artful dodger. Main courses are a rather unspectacular selection of pasta and veal dishes. BYO. Low price range.

Other European

Balkan Seafood and Continental, 215 Oxford Street, Darlinghurst, (02) 331 7670; a distinct division in the menu here between traditional Balkan sausages and some of Sydney's best fish prepared with lashings of garlic. Grilled baby calamari, mussels, char-grilled fish of the day and similar simple preparations are tops. The service can be slow when the restaurant is busy. BYO. Low price range.

Diethnes, 336 Pitt Street, Sydney, (02) 267 8956; Greek food on an encylopaedic menu in Greek and English where one will find such things as octopus, vine leaves and lots of lamb specials. Large servings, good value if you're hungry. Licensed. Low price range.

Sir John Young Hotel, 557 George Street, Sydney, (02) 267 3608; a Spanish restaurant hides in the back of this hotel. Select your fish from the display counter or your dish from the blackboard menu. Pay at the bar and don't forget your sangria.

Fish you won't usually get in Sydney restaurants such as garfish and sardines are on the menu here. Licensed. Low price range.

Chinese

Imperial Peking Harbourside, 15 Circular Quay West, The Rocks, (02) 27 7073; Chinese chic with a view and the food to match. Famous people such as Luciano Pavarotti have eaten here and raved. Sydney restaurant reviewers regularly do the same. A tank holds live lobsters awaiting execution and resurrection as lobster-head soup, *sashimi* or barbecue. There are around 200 dishes on the menu. Don't be indecisive! Licensed. Mid to upper price range.

East Ocean, 421 Sussex Street, Sydney, (02) 212 4198; and **Marigold**, 299–305 Sussex Street, Sydney, (02) 264 6744; these are here because they serve great *Yum Cha*, the Chinese version of brunch in which trolleys of delicacies travel from table to table and diners make their choice. They are very big restaurants seating many hundreds of people but you still need to book. Licensed. Low price range but depends on how much you eat.

Wei Song, 96 Bronte Road, Bondi Junction, (02) 389 3108, and 125 Military Road, Neutral Bay, (02) 90 6471. These two restaurants specialise in Chinese vegetarian food with no MSG in a smoke free environment. Beancurd is used a lot and rice is brown. BYO. Low price range.

Indian

Mayur, MLC Centre, 19 Martin Place, Sydney, (02) 235 2361; the long time doyen of Sydney's Indian eating houses. There is nothing unusual about the food, tandoori dishes and curries, except its consistent high quality. The decor, cool, thoughtful blue, and the punctilious service as well as the sight of tandoori cooks at work make dining here a fully rounded experience. Licensed. Mid to upper price range.

Amar's, 39 Goulburn Street, Sydney, (02) 211 4165; Indian restaurants charge separately for each side dish which makes dining expensive if you don't watch every cucumber and roti. This is certainly the case here where the menu seems to have taken on a life of its own but disciplined selection can keep the price down and doesn't affect the quality. Tandoori dishes are especially good as are the prawn and lamb curries. Licensed. Mid price range.

Indian Experience, 2 Sydney Road, Manly, (02) 977 7086 and The Quay Apartment Building, 2 Albert Street, Circular Quay, (02) 27 9323; the Manly venue has a disturbingly Spanish decor and that at the Quay, once a French restaurant, suffers from a similar problem but the ethnic confusion does not affect the food. Lovers of truly hot curries, those who like to cry and sweat for their love, come to these restaurants because when they say hot, they mean it. Manly also serves excellent tandoori. Licensed. Mid to upper price range.

Indian Excelsior, 314–316 Victoria Street, Darlinghurst, (02) 33 0693; run by some Indians who seem to come from London, this restaurant has not suffered from the round about route taken by its proprietors but is busy showing Sydney that good Indian food can be prepared inexpensively. Once again the menu mixes tandoori oven specialities with a selection of lamb, beef and prawn curries, usually quite mild. BYO. Low price range.

Japanese

Suntory, 529 Kent Street, Sydney, (02) 267 2900; one of the world-wide chain which specialises in up-market Japanese dining. The chefs are part of the show here, trained to fixate visually as well as orally, they do wonders with eggs and prawn heads on a giant hotplate surrounded by salivating customers. The restaurant is full of sliding screens and low tables like a Japanese rural house. Licensed. Upper price range.

Hanaya, 42 Kellett Street, King Cross, (02) 356 4222; you will find more than the usual run of a Japanese menu here, specialities include *saimaki*, vegetables rolled in beef and grilled, served with a fruit, vinegar and chilli sauce and *sankai nabe*, a soup of seafood, chicken and vegetables. Licensed. Upper price range.

Origami, 150 Liverpool Street, Darlinghurst, (02) 331 3373; possibly the best value among Sydney's Japanese eateries but small so book early. The menu does not range widely but has a hint of the unusual with breadcrumbed calamari and an interesting mixed *sashimi* as well as squid legs with ginger. BYO. Low price range.

Edosei, 74 Clarence Street, Sydney, (02) 29 8746; downstairs from a doorway in the street, this restaurant is used to catering for the business trade, both Australian and Japanese, and is essentially a *sushi* bar. Licensed. Mid to upper price range.

Kabuki, 185 Bourke Street, East Sydney, (02) 357 5050; lunch trays are the speciality in this hole-in-the-wall place just off William Street. They are a convenient way to eat a selection of Japanese delicacies such as *sashimi*, *tempura* and drumsticks. BYO. Low to mid price range.

Sushi House, 258 Pacific Highway, Crows Nest, (02) 439 1494; whatever is good at the fish markets on a given day is likely to turn up as *sushi* here. When it's not *sushi*, it's *tempura* or *teriyaki*. A selection of all is available in lunch box style. Licensed. Low to mid price range.

South-East Asian

Thai Orchid, 628 Crown Street, Surry Hills, (02) 698 2097; when Thai restaurants began to appear in Sydney, this was ahead of the pack. The pack has caught up lately but the Orchid has not lost its bloom. Open with a soup of seafood or chicken and coconut milk or an entrée of winter crab or golden triangles, main courses include tiny quails cooked in chilli or green and red curries of chicken and beef. Decor has always been a poor cousin here. Licensed. Low to mid price range.

Sala Thai, 778 Military Road, Mosman, (02) 969 9379; a splendid amalgam of spicy cooking and sidewalk café, this restaurant manages to do best what is best about Thai food, spice with complexity and subtlety the basic ingredients of chicken, beef and fish. Licensed. Mid price range.

Spice's Thai Kitchen, 148 Norton Street, Leichhardt, (02) 569 5828; stranded in the midst of little Italy in Sydney's inner west, this popular place does wonders with chicken wings and seafood, especially squid. BYO. Low price range.

Kim Van, 147 Glebe Point Road, Glebe, (02) 660 5252; Vietnamese cuisine came in the wave before Thai and is best represented by this shop-front eatery in the restaurant-thick Glebe Point Road. The food is delicate, including quails in five spices, seafood combination and minced pork barbecued on skewers and served on transparent noodles. BYO. Mid price range.

Malaya, 761 George Street, Sydney, (02) 211 4659; this formerly dark and chaotic haunt of journalists and academics has moved to better lit and more salubrious headquarters just down the road from its old site. It has a vast Chinese menu that you take no notice of, heading straight for the rough but honest Malayan noodle dishes such as *kwai du* and *laksa*, there's a no nonsense beef *rendang* (hot curry) and a milder *opor ayam* (chicken in coconut milk). Licensed. Low price range.

Korea House, 171 Victoria Road, Kings Cross, (02) 358 6601; one of Sydney's few Korean restaurants, this one displays plastic models of the food it serves at the restaurant door in Japanese fashion. Pan-fried items are especially worth trying. Licensed. Mid price range.

Borobudur, 263 Oxford Street, Darlinghurst, (02) 331 3464; named after the greatest of Java's temples, Borobudur presents a goodly selection of food from the Indonesian archipelago that couples can eat in tasty and filling plates for two. BYO. Low price range.

Safari Seafare, 26 King Street, Newtown, (02) 51 4458, specialises in charcoal grilled seafoods spiced with chilli but also serves the usual *gado-gado*, *satay* etc. Service ranges from leisurely to immobile but the excellence of the seafood is sufficient compensation. BYO. Low price range.

Breakfast

All the foregoing will set you right for dinner, almost all serve lunch as well but few manage breakfast. Here are some suggestions for escaping hotel cereal and eggs. Enterprising summer breakfasters will grab a 380 bus to Bondi Beach and settle in around 7.30 am at one of the **Lamrock Café's** outdoor tables. Lamrock breakfasts are hearty and original and the coffee is fine but you're really there for the prospect of Bondi in the morning, its best time. The **Roma Café** in Hay Street, Haymarket, near Railway Square bustles from 7 am with media, young execs and a layabout writer or two. Your breakfast will be Italian cakes, coffee and conversation. **Ashanti French Café**, 19 The Esplanade, Balmoral Beach, offers a northside version of the Lamrock's views and breakfast with a French flavour.

Grazing

At other times, lunch or in between, graze. Sydney is well set up for this kind of eating-on-the-move and it suits the traveller who will have a great deal to see, generally in far too short a time. City and suburban sandwich bars abound. Good places in town for a sit down lunch are the **Barracks Café** in the grounds of Hyde Park Barracks just off Queens Square and the noisy **Rossini's Rosticceria** under the Qantas International Centre, corner George and Jamison Streets, which is usually full of stock exchange types fresh from the hurly-burly of the trading floor.

Pub Food

The days of the counter lunch, served at every pub in town and usually consisting of a meat pie and whatever else was going—all at negligible cost, have succumbed to the power of takeaway food but many hotels are battling the food-warmer invasion with barbecues and bistros. The pub lunch these days is halfway between a food bar and a restaurant and a pretty good compromise at that. Patrons buy their steak, chicken or sausages uncooked and throw them on the open grill themselves or, at some places, the cook will do them to your liking. The price of the meal includes as much as you can eat from a groaning salad bar. A couple of good places to try this kind of lunching are the **Dolphin Hotel** 412 Crown Street, Surry Hills, and **The Oaks Hotel**, 118 Military Road, Neutral Bay.

Cafés

Coffee, usually backed up with a huge creamy or chocolatey cake, is an anytime option in Sydney. Here are some places to try.

Pudding Shop, 144a Glebe Point Road, Glebe, and 26 Spit Road, Mosman; famous for its pies and, after all, meat pies are to some the apogee of Australian cuisine. They also make sweet pies, cakes and other light meal fare and serve good coffee. The Glebe venue is decidedly undergrad, Mosman appeals more to the yuppie brigade.

Bagel Coffee House, 5 Flinders Street, Darlinghurst; known Sydney-wide for bagels cooked on the premises and filled to overflowing with chopped liver, tuna and mayonnaise and, of course, lox as well as other exotica. The chocolate mud cake is a challenge.

New Edition Tea Rooms, 328a Oxford Street, Paddington; an addition to the New Edition Bookshop and packed out on Saturday mornings when the Paddington Village Market is open and Oxford Street is alive. Arrive early with your newspapers and there may be a table free by the window where the parade passes.

Sloane Rangers, 312 Oxford Street, Paddington; a small distance down the road from the previous listing, this is a less bookish spot, offspring of a hairdressing shop. It has a sunny courtyard out the back and offers light vegetarian meals and cakes.

Vienna Gold, 121a King Street, Newtown; a long narrow, high ceilinged shop in Sydney's Greek quarter, specialising in rich Austrian cakes as well as that nation's hearty approach to more substantial meals.

Bar Via Venetto, corner Parramatta Road and Norton Street, Leichhardt; Norton Street is Sydney's little Italy, get your short black and Sienna cake here and practise your Italian.

Drinking

Drinking outside meal times is done in pubs and bars. Pubs in Sydney used to be distinguishable by tiles on the walls inside and out, a U-shaped bar in a big street-level room and men in blue singlets drinking beer. Such places still exist, especially near the wharves and in old working class suburbs but in the city they've either been knocked down or dressed up for the invasion of the suit and tie set. They open about 11 in the morning and close about 11 at night in summer and do both an hour earlier in winter. Pubs serve beer, mixed drinks and wine. You can buy potato crisps and packaged nuts from the bar. There are also American style bars in Sydney, mostly in Kings Cross. Some stay open until 3 am. They serve what pubs serve and charge more for it because of their low lights and late hours, otherwise the main difference is they'll make you a cocktail and they have stricter dress codes—no jeans and no thongs!

TOURS

The Urban Transit Authority runs a comprehensive and inexpensive tour of inner city sights. It is called the **Sydney Explorer**, costs $7.50, visits 20 famous spots around the city and your ticket allows you to alight from and rejoin the bus at will. A special ticket called 'Day Rover' which entitles the holder to almost unlimited travel on buses, ferries and trains throughout Sydney for a day is available from the **Rail and Travel Centre**, corner of York and Margaret Streets for $6.

Bus tours of Sydney and the surrounding countryside depart every day from outside the Maritime Services Building in George Street, the Rocks. The buses will also pick you up from your hotel if you book the tour beforehand. The main operators are AAT Kings, phone 669 5444; Ansett Pioneer, phone 268 1331; Australian Pacific, phone 693 2222; Clipper Tours, phone 888 3144; and Murray's Australia, phone 319 1266. Don't be alarmed if an AAT Kings coach picks you up for an Australian Pacific Tour as both companies are part of the same group.

The most popular half day tours take in the city sights and southern beaches including Bondi. Full day tours go further afield to the Blue Mountains, usually dropping in at a wildlife park on the way.

Maureen Fry, phone (02) 660 7157 and Sydney Footnotes, phone (02) 679 1513 operate **guided walking tours** of the city's historic sights. Ms Fry's tours are best for anyone with an interest in the detailed history of the Rocks and other old parts of Sydney.

Undoubtedly the most unusual and thrilling way to see Sydney is from a Tiger Moth aircraft. Red Baron **Scenic Flights** flies over the city sights and the beaches from the south western suburb of Bankstown, phone (02) 771 1333. Helicopter scenic flights can be booked at **Tourist Newsfront**, 22 Playfair Street, The Rocks.

Captain Cook Cruises operate morning, lunchtime and dinner cruises as well as a full day tour from No. 6 Jetty, Circular Quay. Southern Cross Cruises runs a similar service from Jetty No. 2. The Urban Transit Authority which operates the ferries also runs special tourist cruises on Wednesday, Saturday and Sunday at 1.30 and 2.30 pm from No. 4 Jetty, Circular Quay, and a river cruise up the Lane Cove and Parramatta Rivers from No. 5 Jetty on Sundays and public holidays at 2 pm.

FESTIVALS

Sydney dedicates itself to a summer celebration each January. The occasion, called **The Festival of Sydney**, is a programme of art and fun deliberately timed to coincide with the summer holiday period. Acting companies, musicians and other performing artists come from overseas to keep everyone amused for a month and local talents lend their expertise to the proceedings. The festival officially opens on New Year's Eve with fireworks displays; its big events are opera, classical and jazz concerts in the Sydney Domain and it peters out in the last week of January by which time most of the visiting celebrities have moved on to other cities and more festivals.

The oldest annual ritual is **The Royal Easter Show**, an agricultural extravaganza held at the Sydney Showground in Paddington every Easter. Hundreds of thousands and sometimes over a million people attend it rather more for the rides, sideshows and fairy floss than the wheat, meat and wool displays. It brings *squatters* (landed gentry) and *cow cockies* (cattle farmers) into the big smoke in droves (you'll recognise them by their low crowned, broad brimmed hats; some say 'The bigger the brim, the smaller the property') and, while mum and the kids go shopping, dad hopes his prize animal wins a ribbon and consoles himself in the squatters' bar if it doesn't. The show is intolerable if you like quiet, space and good manners but in many ways, despite the space rides and electronic games of recent years, it's a mark of continuity with older and simpler times.

Around Sydney

The best way to explore the Sydney hinterland is to hire a car and make a series of day trips, some of which may extend to two or even three days if you feel inclined. Trains are a good alternative. They stop at many of the places mentioned in this chapter. Those who choose to explore will find a rugged balance for inner Sydney sophistications in the grey-green, sometimes suddenly flowering bush, the beetling sea cliffs and sheer sandstone escarpments which characterise outer Sydney.

This section covers these areas. **North and North-West of Sydney**: the Peninsula, the Hawkesbury Region and the Central Coast; **South of Sydney**: The Royal National Park, Wollongong and The Southern Highlands. **West of Sydney** Parramatta.

GETTING OUT OF THE CITY
Trains travel to all areas mentioned in this chapter except the beaches of the Peninsula which are served by buses. They generally leave from Central Station but some can also be picked up at Town Hall and Wynyard in the city. Train travel can be planned and booked at the **Rail and Travel Centre** on the corner of York and Margaret Streets in the city, phone (02) 290 4743.

The way north for motorists lies across the Harbour Bridge, along the Pacific Highway, through the northern suburbs and down Mona Vale Road to the coast or down Bobbin Head Road which turns off a little further up the highway and leads into Ku-ring-gai Chase. Drivers heading south should proceed through Railway Square, along Broadway to City Road and through Newtown to the Princes Highway. Those going west take Parramatta Road (the Great Western Highway) from Broadway.

TOURIST INFORMATION
Judicious visiting of some offices in town is an excellent preparation for a country jaunt. The **National Parks and Wildlife Service**, 189 Kent Street, provides brochures, walking maps and advice on transport; open Monday to Friday from 9 am to 5 pm. Good maps for drivers are available from the **National Roads and Motorists Association (NRMA)**, 151 Clarence Street, Sydney; open the same hours.

North and north-west

The Peninsula, Broken Bay and the National Parks of Ku-ring-gai Chase, Brisbane Water and Bouddi lie to the north of Sydney; Wiseman's Ferry, the Hawkesbury

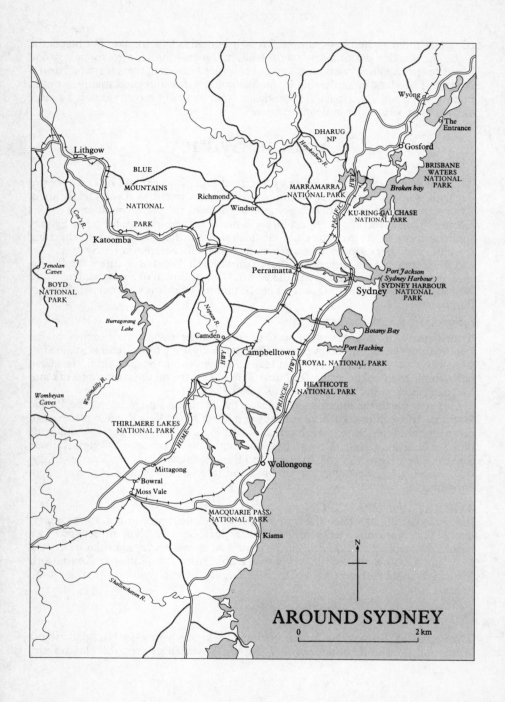

Wyong

The
Entrance

DHARUG
NP

Lithgow

Gosford

BRISBANE
WATERS
NATIONAL
PARK

BLUE

MOUNTAINS

MARRAMARRA
NATIONAL PARK

Broken bay

NATIONAL

Richmond

Windsor

KU-RING-GAI CHASE
NATIONAL PARK

PARK

PACIFIC HWY

Cox's R.

Hawkesbury R.

Katoomba

Jenolan
Caves

Perramatta

Port Jackson
(Sydney Harbour)
SYDNEY HARBOUR
NATIONAL
PARK

BOYD
NATIONAL
PARK

Sydney

Burragorang
Lake

Nepean R.

Botany Bay

Camden

Port Hacking

Campbelltown

ROYAL NATIONAL PARK

Wollondilly R.

Wombeyan
Caves

PRINCES HWY

HEATHCOTE
NATIONAL PARK

THIRLMERE LAKES
NATIONAL PARK

HUME HWY

Mittagong

Wollongong

Bowral
Moss Vale

MACQUARIE PASS
NATIONAL PARK

Kiama

Shallowhaven R.

N

AROUND SYDNEY

0   2 km

River and Dharug National Park to the north-west. When northern Sydney residents 'go bush', which usually means a bushwalk, a picnic and a swim, these are the places they choose. Thus they are relatively crowded on weekends but almost deserted during the week.

The Peninsula

A narrow spur of land, bounded by the surf on one side and a bay called Pittwater on the other, lies about an hour's drive along the coast north of Sydney. It is known as the Peninsula and, although strictly part of the outer suburbs, is famous for a recreational feel and a slower pace of life than the town. Locals concentrate on surf and sand and the city seems very far away.

GETTING TO AND AROUND
The beaches of the Peninsula are probably the perfect destination for day-trippers from the city. They are easy to reach, various and beautiful, well serviced and civilised. Although no trains serve them, buses depart regularly from the York Street side of Wynyard Park in the city. The Palm Beach bus, number 190, which runs right along the coast to the last and, some think best, of the beaches is a good choice. On a fine summer's day, it is one of the most scenic public bus rides in the world. It takes about 45 minutes to reach Mona Vale where the Peninsula truly begins, passing through the beachside suburbs of Manly Vale and Dee Why and covering the extra distance, beach by beach, to Palm Beach in about the same time.

Drivers cross the Harbour and Spit Bridges and follow the coast or take the Pacific Highway and Mona Vale Road.

WHAT TO SEE
The Peninsula is where Sydney's well-to-do writers, artists and film people live, including the likes of Bryan Brown and Thomas Keneally. Seeing the sweep of fine beaches scalloping its coast from Mona Vale to Barrenjoey Head it's not hard to understand why. The surf beaches of Bungan, Newport, Bilgola, Avalon, Whale Beach and Palm Beach form the Peninsula's eastern side and the long narrow bay of Pittwater, the western. The beaches vary from long, flat, open stretches of sand in sight of the passing traffic to tight crescents walled in by steep cliffs and hills. The more open beaches, among them Newport and Avalon are often crowded; the harder to reach like Bungan and Bilgola attract fewer people but on hot weekends nearly all are flocked with lovers of sun and surf. Here are some of the best.

Mona Vale

A generous stretch of fairly flat, golden sand and well-behaved surf thankfully far enough from the traffic to make crossing the road to it almost safe. It has a large, surf-fed swimming pool at the northern end which gets afternoon sun, a rarity along these beaches. The beach is lovely for late afternoon walks, returning along the golf course which runs behind it. Parking is ample if not profligate.

Warriewood

A small beach south of Mona Vale. Approachable by road or by walking around the rocks from the north. Very lovely and often less crowded than other, more fashionable Peninsula swimming places.

Bungan

The last beach not accessible by car. You must park on the high hills above and walk down a steep but well paved and stepped track to the beach. Many Peninsula locals say its isolation and spectacular surroundings make Bungan the most beautiful of the northern beaches, though by the same token it's the least provided with creature comforts.

Bilgola

Has lately begun to get very crowded on weekends with refugees from Avalon and looks quite 'in' since Tom Keneally took to swimming in its well-kept but rather ugly pool. A great beach for the early morning but can become fiercely hot during the day. The surf is sometimes rough, the sand wide and flat. You are right to be jealous of those whose houses front directly onto it without the interruption of a roadway.

Avalon

Once one of the Peninsula's jewels, Avalon has suffered the weather's ravages in the last decade and its surf should be avoided by the inexperienced. The coarse sand runs into it on a treacherously steep incline. The beach has, nonetheless, great scenic qualities, from its majestic northern head to the sand-hills, unlike many another beach, in part preserved and cared for.

Whale

A useful compromise for those scared-off by the inaccessibility of Bungan Beach. Whale is also bounded by steep hills but has a road down, parking, a local shop and regular patrols. Sand is whiter and less coarse than its southerly companions. The surf has a gentler flow which means a solid weekend crowd.

Palm

The most famous and popular of all Peninsula beaches. Flat, long and arching all the way to Barrenjoey Head, green and lumpy and topped by its little white ligi♦ house overlooking the mouth of Broken Bay. It supports some staggeringly expensive real estate, one or two ageing bastions of Sydney establishment families, a golf course, a caravan park, a stand of Norfolk Island pines and still manages to retain the charm which has made it a drawcard since the 1920s. But look out for the crowds, this is no place for anyone who hates children, dogs and surfboard riding teenagers.

Pittwater

The protected bay of Pittwater lies under the lee of the Peninsula. Especially around Newport, it resembles a parking area for yachts where the value of stacked up boat flesh seems almost incalculable. The bay has two distinct sides. The eastern shore is highly populated and directs its serious attention to maritime fun. Ku-ring-gai Chase National Park takes up the western shore, except for a few settled enclaves approachable only by water, and so is bushy and beautiful. On holidays and weekends, east invades west for picnics, sunbaking and lounging around on boats which diminishes its natural beauty but makes it lively.

The eastern shore of Pittwater offers an escape for non-surfers and families with small children. The narrow, still-water beaches have fine white sand, and are mostly surrounded by yacht and power boat moorings. Their water can be weedy. Here is a selection.

Clareville
Frequently crowded with picnicking families on the weekend on account of the fireplaces, permanent tables and shady trees bordering its sand. The beach is beloved of small children who don't mind the oily water caused by many, many boats moored just off shore. Parking can be a problem. The beach is due west of Avalon.

Paradise
Also west of Avalon, is distinguished by the presence of an enclosed swimming area with a boardwalk. The beach is attractive at high tide but the low reveals its muddy bottom and surfeit of weeds.

Little Palm
A cleaner alternative to Clareville but less spacious. The small park attached to a section of the beach has adequate parking for which, I am sure, the very good fish and chip shop across the road is forever grateful. The view over Pittwater's boats and forested hills is nice but the Barrenjoey Road traffic occasionally mars the aural environment.

Church Point
Not a beach but a lovely place from which to take a ferry ride around the lower reaches of Pittwater and Scotland Island which sits at the end of the bay. Small boats in which to go fishing or cruising around the inlets can be hired from the Church Point Wharf. To reach Church Point, continue along Pittwater Road at Mona Vale instead of taking Barrenjoey Road.

WHERE TO STAY
Because the Peninsula is very much an area for day-trips, there is little overnight accommodation.

Villa Jonah, 69 Bynya Road, Palm Beach, (02) 919 5599; spectacularly sited on a cliff overlooking Whale Beach where the view is among Sydney's most memorable. Rooms come with full or partial views. The house restaurant is well known for its Italian-style cooking. $120 and $140.

Pasadena Lodge Motel, Pittwater Road, Church Point (02) 99 3007; has quite comfortable double rooms with private facilities although some are a little elbow-to-elbow. Ask for a room overlooking the water. The motel has a restaurant. $60 waterfront rooms, $50 roadside, includes continental breakfast.

Barrenjoey House, 1108 Barrenjoey Road, Palm Beach (02) 919 4001; is better known for its food than its accommodation but it does have small simple rooms which are clean and neat. Shared facilities. $65.

EATING OUT
Reflections, 1075 Barrenjoey Road, Palm Beach, (02) 919 5893; is ranked among Sydney's best five eating houses. It puts forth a selection of classic French dishes from entrées such as game consommé with morels, or quail breasts in quail jelly to main courses as elaborate as boned saddle of hare with sauce poivrade, garnished with poached and spiced pear. Desserts are a delight, often featuring fruit. Licensed. Upper price range.
Barrenjoey House, 1108 Barrenjoey Road, Palm Beach (02) 919 4001; literally across the road from Reflections, its decorative tone is higher with white tablecloths and napkins, spaciously arranged seating and a romantically vine-covered terrace for summer dining. The food, though never disguising its French antecedents, turns to local ingredients for extra inspiration. Entrées may include warm salad of smoked scallops and vermicelli with sesame oil dressing or lamb-brain beignets with peppercorn sabayon; main courses, salad of guinea fowl stuffed with ricotta and sun-dried tomatoes or whole poached crayfish with hazelnut oil dressing; desserts, passion-fruit parfait with lemon curd or rockmelon mousseline with rhubarb ice cream. Trades Friday to Sunday only. Upper price range.
Clareville Kiosk, 27 Delecta Avenue, Clareville, (02) 918 2727; is about half as expensive as and less than half the size of the two places mentioned above. The restaurant is housed in a tiny former local post office and rumour has it that, being stretched for space and furniture, the proprietors have extended a 'bring your own table' invitation to some regulars, thus making certain they don't have to wait. Clareville Kiosk food is renowned in the district for its quality and low price. The restaurant does wonders with local Blue Swimmer crabs and its desserts are famous. Low to mid price range.

Bookings are essential for all these restaurants but there is absolutely no need to book for fish and chips from the **Palm Beach Fish Shop**, a couple of doors down from Barrenjoey House. It serves the best fish and chips in Sydney.
Newport Arms Hotel, Kalinya Street, Newport, (02) 997 4900; is the most famous local pub and very popular with weekend sailors who come to cook their own barbecue and eat in the beer garden overlooking Pittwater. The pub also has a bistro which specialises in seafood. It's a good place for lunch. Low price range.

BOAT HIRE
Gibson Marina, 1710 Pittwater Road, Bayview, (02) 997 1566; hires out aluminium fishing dinghies.
Gonsalves Boatshed, 1151 Barrenjoey Road, Palm Beach, (02) 919 5755; does likewise.
Pittwater Yacht Charter, Lovett Bay via Church Point, (02) 99 3047; hires out eight-berth cruising yachts.
Anderson's Newport Yacht Charters, Queens Parade, Newport, (02) 99 1170; has yachts to 35 feet with three double-berth cabins.

The Hawkesbury Region

Broken Bay, of which Pittwater is the southern arm, is the entrance to the Hawkesbury River which winds its way around the north-western outskirts of the Sydney metropolitan area. The points of interest along its length are about one to two hours journey from the city. The river's lower reaches are bounded by large and small national parks of which Ku-ring-gai Chase to the south and Dharug to the north are the largest. The towns of Windsor, Richmond, Wilberforce and Pitt Town, known as the Macquarie Towns in honour of the colonial governor who established them, stand beside or near the river in the west. Windsor is rich in colonial history and architecture.

The river and its plains played a prominent role in early colonial history. Governor Arthur Phillip explored it in 1789 while searching for decent farming land to provide for his starving charges. Twenty-two settlers moved there in 1794 and by 1796 there were 1000 acres under cultivation. When Governor Lachlan Macquarie established his five towns in 1810, he confirmed the area as being of lasting importance to the prosperity of Sydney. The agricultural land on the river banks is used today for turf farming and fruit growing and there are many oyster leases on the river itself.

National Parks

Although it has been a farming area since the earliest times of white settlement, the river is still surrounded by large areas of untouched bush useless for farming, rugged and inhospitable in some places but where it is approachable, used by the people of Sydney and the Central Coast for those physical, open-air pursuits typical of Australians.

Ku-ring-gai Chase

This 14,712-hectare (36,353-acre) park was set aside in 1894 by some far sighted urban planning which left a portion of Sydney's landscape very much as the first settlers would have found it. The suburbs along the northern railway line penetrate into the park. It extends west to Berowra Creek and the Hawkesbury River is its northern boundary. Entry to the park costs $4 which entitles you to the use of all its facilities from dawn to dusk.

GETTING THERE
The northern suburban railway line from the city runs along the edge of Ku-ring-gai Chase National Park. The stations of Mt Ku-ring-gai ($1.80), Berowra ($2.30) and Cowan ($2.30) give immediate access to it. Drivers take the Pacific Highway and Bobbin Head Road to Ku-ring-gai Chase and the lower reaches of the Hawkesbury. Anyone in a boat can land on the edges of the park and take walks into it.

TOURIST INFORMATION
Information and maps of walking trails can be obtained at the **Kalkari Visitors' Centre**, Ku-ring-gai Chase Road, between Bobbin Head Picnic Area and Mount Colah, where the staff will explain the best trail to take depending on the time you have available, your fitness and what you want to see. The Kalkari Centre's staff will also also give advice about fire regulations and safety and other rules of park use.

There is a second information centre on West Head Road near West Head look-out.

Aboriginal engravings

The Aboriginals who occupied the virgin bush were called *Guringai* and a corruption of their name labels the park. A few of their **rock engravings** and **hand stencil paintings** remain within its bounds. The mostly figurative engravings are etched onto flat rocks and are thought to have been drawn in charcoal and then cut into the rock surface with a sharp stone. It is likely that the engravings were renewed on ceremonial occasions. Their precise significance escapes us now as the artists who drew them, with their fellow *Guringai*, have long since disappeared, taking their unwritten culture with them. Some engravings can be seen near the beginning of the Elvina Track which runs off West Head Road.

West Head

Those without time for walking will drive along **West Head Road** which runs through park's centre, to West Head where there are spectacular views of Pittwater, Lion Island and the Pacific Coast but such behaviour hardly does the park justice. It is far better to walk. Some hard but very rewarding trails lead down from West Head Road to the small, white beaches on the edges of Pittwater, Cowan Creek and the Hawkesbury River. They pass through low, dry forest at the roadside, down rocky slopes to the beaches and rock platforms at the waterside. At low tide, exposed tidal pools pit the faces of the platforms and are full of marine life from small fish to hermit crabs and sea anemones.

Bobbin Head

Bobbin Head Road and **Ku-ring-gai Chase Road**, which descend into the park from the Pacific Highway, meet at Bobbin Head Picnic Area on Cowan Creek where more walking trails lead off into the bush. The picnic area is made to handle crowds. There are lots of barbecue fireplaces and a children's play area. One of the best trails, though also one of the most used, lies near the Kalkari Visitors' Centre on Ku-ring-gai Chase Road just before Bobbin Head. It is an easy, flat walk which gives a useful introduction to the bush and passes the park's animal compound, home to emus and other native creatures.

Waratah Park

Waratah Park is a native animal zoo on Namba Road, Terry Hills, on the edge of Ku-ring-gai Chase. It is the home of marsupial TV star, Skippy the Bush Kangaroo, impossible to distinguish from other kangaroos and wallabies but who, like the Phantom, seems to be immortal. As well as Skippy, there are koalas to touch and learn about, a wombat, wedge-tail eagles and lots of cockatoos, emus and other natives. Waratah Park is probably the best of such places in Sydney because the kangaroos, wallabies and emus roam free in a wide enclosure where the public is also welcome but this doesn't mean that the animals are in anything like their natural state. Open 10 am to 5 pm. Entry $7.

CAMPING OUT

The main camping area in Ku-ring-gai Chase is at The Basin on the foreshores of Pittwater. Access is by ferry from Palm Beach or by walking from West Head Road. The area has toilets and showers and a netted swimming area. Phone (02) 457 9853 for more information.

Brisbane Water and Dharug

The national parks on the northern Hawkesbury shore do not come down to the water quite so often as their southern counterparts. They are also somewhat more rugged and less well serviced.

GETTING THERE

Brisbane Water National Park can be reached from Wondabyne ($3.20) train station where a track leads off to the Aboriginal rock engravings at Bulgandry. Drivers can enter the park from the Pacific Highway at Girrakool.

Dharug can only be reached by car. Proceed west along the Great Western Highway and take the turn-off through Dural to the river town of Wiseman's Ferry at the south-western corner of the park.

TOURIST INFORMATION

Neither park has its own information centre. The National Parks and Wildlife Service office in Gosford at 168 Main Street (043) 24 4911 can help you or contact the service's Sydney office on (02) 237 6500.

Brisbane Water

The **Bulgandry Aboriginal Engraving Site** is the item of greatest interest in Brisbane Water National Park. The engravings were first recorded in 1951 and the site declared a reserve in 1961. It was finally opened to the public in 1978 after being carefully prepared for visitors. The site is surrounded by a walkway and contains engravings of fishes, kangaroos and human figures. It can be reached either by walking from Wondabyne Station or from a track off Bambarra Road in the park. Brisbane Water Park is also known for its displays of the waxy red native flower, waratah, in August and September.

Dharug

Dharug is the largest national park on Sydney's north-western outskirts. A disused section of the Great North Road, called the **Old Great North Road**, runs along its north-western boundary and two km (one and a quarter miles) of it is included in the park. The convict-built road linked Sydney with Newcastle and was among the first large engineering projects undertaken by the colonial government. Building work on the road began in 1826 and was completed in 1829. A gang of up to 520 convicts carved the road out of solid bedrock and built massive 12-metre (40-foot) high retaining walls from 600-kilogram (1323-pound) sandstone blocks, supported by huge buttresses every 20 metres (65 feet). Despite their efforts, the lower section of the road fell into disuse by the end of the century as coastal steamers and a better road starved it of traffic. Its fate meant it was never upgraded and it remains untouched for moderns to marvel at. The section contained in the park can be reached from Ten Mile Hollow.

The rest of Dharug consists of jumbled sandstone country of which **Mill Creek** is the most accessible part. To reach it take the road to Wiseman's Ferry, take the ferry, which carries cars as well as people, and turn right along Spencer Road. There is a ranger's office at Hazel Dell about five km (three miles) from where the ferry lands. Mill Creek with its good picnic grounds and quiet walks is a little further east. **Wiseman's Ferry** also marks the start of the pretty **Colo River**. Those who don't mind rough driving will find superb riverside picnic spots off the Putty Road.

CAMPING OUT
Camping is allowed at **Mill Creek** in Dharug where there are pit toilets, water and barbecues. Bookings must be made beforehand on (043) 24 4911.

The Macquarie Towns

Macquarie's idea in creating his towns was that each should be something like an English village, centred on a church and school house. Their surroundings have little in common with England and they have grown to something probably unimagined by their founder but the churches and other buildings of those early times remain.

GETTING THERE
The main suburban train line to the west branches off at Blacktown ($1.80) for Windsor ($2.80) and Richmond ($3.20). Drivers can turn off the Great Western Highway to the Macquarie Towns.

TOURIST INFORMATION
The **Hawkesbury Regional Tourist Centre**, Windsor Road, McGraths Hill, (045) 77 5915, has maps of the towns and guide books as well as a tea room and toilets. There is also a tourist information centre in Thompson Square, Windsor.

Windsor

Thompson Square, named by Macquarie in 1811, and once central to Windsor is one of the oldest public squares in Australia. The main buildings in the square are the Doctors' House, a two-storey sandstone and brick terrace house built in 1844 and occupied by doctors almost ever since—it also houses an art gallery; the Hawkesbury Museum built in 1843 as Coffey's Inn and the Macquarie Arms Hotel, parts of which date from 1815 although the facade is later. **St Matthews Anglican Church** in Moses Street was designed by emancipist colonial architect Francis Greenway and is considered one of his masterpieces. It was built by convicts between 1817 and 1820. Its rectory is the oldest such building in Australia. Other old buildings include the **Courthouse** in Court Street, completed in 1822 by William Cox who built much in the district using convict labour. The building is fully restored and still used for court hearings. **George Street** contains Loder House (now Lachlan's Restaurant) built by explorer George Loder in 1843 and **North Street** has cottages and a pub dating from the 1840s.

Richmond

There is not as much very early architecture in Richmond as in Windsor. The buildings in Windsor Road date from the mid to late nineteenth century. **Chapel Street** has Josieville, a farmhouse built in the 1830s by former convict Joseph Onus, and Clear Oaks formerly a farm cottage and one of the town's oldest buildings, dating from 1820. **Toxana** at 157 Windsor Street was built in about 1840 and has both Regency and Georgian features. It was home to William Bowman a member of the first NSW Parliament and has been restored.

Pitt Town and Wilberforce

The main area of historical interest in **Pitt Town** is around Bathurst, Grenville and Buckingham Streets where there are colonial churches (Scots Church 1862 and St James Anglican 1857) and two old inns, The Macquarie Arms at number 104 Bathurst Street and the Bird in Hand on the corner of Bathurst and Eildon Streets. Neither trades any longer. **Ebenezer Church**, built between 1807 and 1809 and thus the oldest building in the area is the main drawcard at **Wilberforce**. The **Australiana Pioneer Village**, centred on Rose Cottage, a timber house built in 1811 and now surrounded by replicas of colonial buildings from a bank to a shearing shed, is also in the town. Open 10 am to 5 pm except Monday and Saturday. Entry $5.

WHERE TO STAY
There is a three motel chain called **Colonial Motels** in this area. They are Windsor Colonial Motel, 54 George Street, Windsor, (045) 77 3626, a colonial style building; Windsor Terrace Motel also in George Street, Windsor, (045) 77 5999, a more modern but not unattractive three-storey slope-faced building; Richmond Colonial Motel, March Street, Richmond, (045) 78 1166, an everyday motel.

EATING OUT
The Richmond, 315 Windsor Street, Richmond, (045) 78 3914; French influenced food with the occasional Asian dish wandering onto the menu in a restored old house. Licensed. Low to mid price range.

Boating on the River

The Hawkesbury River is among Sydney's favourite recreational waterways and is a wonderful place to spend some quiet time on a hired cruiser or a luxury river boat. The river runs into Broken Bay from the west and is decidedly fancied by owners of pleasure craft, fishermen and weekend boat hirers who wander from Pittwater to the Hawkesbury and back. It is a wide waterway with many bays and subsidiary streams branching from its main course and, around its lower reaches, small sandy beaches backed by bush. Forested hills and leafy suburbs surround it.

Boating on the Hawkesbury is a gentle experience on weekdays when the crowds are not out but can be hectic on weekends. The river is wide in its lower reaches between Brooklyn and Pittwater and grows somewhat narrower as you head upstream to Wiseman's Ferry. The car ferry that still operates there marks the line beyond which most hire boats may not go. Water skiers use the still water at Wiseman's Ferry on weekends.

GETTING THERE
The rather scruffy town of **Brooklyn** near the Hawkesbury River Bridge on the Freeway north of Sydney is the main centre on the lower Hawkesbury. It has a railway station and many places to hire boats. Trains to Brooklyn (the station is called Hawkesbury River) run from Central Station, Sydney ($3.20). Drivers take the Pacific Highway and the Sydney to Newcastle Freeway.

BOAT HIRE
Cruisers (motor launches) and houseboats are available in quantity on the Hawkesbury. Brooklyn has most but they are also available at Akuna Bay, Berowra Waters and Bobbin Head. When hiring, you pay a basic charge for the boat which is always much more on weekends than during the week, petrol is additional and you either bring your own food and drink or contract for provisioning. Houseboats are large and comfortable but slow, cruisers are faster but more cramped. All boats have stoves and fridges, toilets and showers. No licence is required to drive them.

Holidays-a-Float, 65 Brooklyn Road, Brooklyn, (02) 455 1368; cruisers and six berth houseboats.

Baymac Marina, 87 Brooklyn Road, Brooklyn, (02) 455 1359; cruisers, houseboats sleeping up to eight and runabouts.

Hawkesbury River Boat Hire, Lot 2, McKell Park, Dangar Road, Brooklyn, (02) 455 1252; houseboats sleeping up to eight and half cabin runabouts.

Fenwick's Hawkesbury River Houseboats, 31 Brooklyn Road, Brooklyn, (02) 455 1333; houseboats only.

Skipper a Clipper, Clippers Anchorage, Akuna Bay, (02) 450 1888; four, six and eight berth fly bridge cruisers. All inclusive packages.

Halvorsen Boats, Bobbin Head Road, Turrmurra, (02) 457 9011; the original boat hire company on the Hawkesbury which builds its own cruisers. Some are a little old. Four to eight berths.

Hawkesbury River Holidays, River Road, Wisemans Ferry, (045) 66 4308; six and eight berth houseboats.

Luxury Homecruisers, Cruise Craft Marina, Berowra Waters Road, Berowra Waters, (02) 456 2866; eight to ten berth houseboats.

CRUISES
Joining the **Hawkesbury Riverboat Mail Run** is a delightful way to see the river and its people. The boat which delivers mail, milk and groceries to riverside residents departs from Brooklyn at 9.30 am and takes a three hour run on the river.

The fare is $14 which includes morning tea, and bookings can be made at the Travel Centre of NSW, phone (02) 231 4444.

Lady Hawkesbury, a luxury river cruiser with 60 cabins takes four day and weekend trips up-river. It is operated by Captain Cook Cruises. A twin-share cabin (bunks) costs $522 per person for four days and $291 per person for the weekend, staterooms (twin beds) $610 and $335 and deluxe staterooms (double bed) $709 and $385, transfers from Sydney are extra. Phone (02) 27 4548 for bookings.

Windsor River Cruises, (02) 621 4154; operates a number of cruises from Windsor Public Wharf including a morning cruise every Wednesday and a day cruise from Windsor to Brooklyn at various times.

EATING OUT ON THE RIVER

Akuna Bay Restaurant, Clipper's Anchorage Marina, Coal and Candle Creek, (02) 450 2660; has uninterrupted views of the water and specialises in seafood. Accessible by boat. Mid price range.

Peat's Bite, Peats Bight, Brooklyn, (02) 455 2040; a riverside restaurant accessible only by boat or amphibious aircraft. Simple but good quality fare, delightful views. Mid price range.

Berowra Waters Inn, Berowra Waters, (02) 456 1027; covered in the Sydney chapter and generally regarded as the city's best restaurant, overlooks and arm of the river and is accessible to Hawkesbury River sailors. Upper price range.

The Central Coast

Crossing Broken Bay or the Hawkesbury means one is officially on the Central Coast and no longer in the Sydney Metropolitan Area. The difference is becoming harder to recognise as Sydney's urban tentacles reach further and further north and the Central Coast becomes a prosperous city of its own, typified by greenery, low comfortable-looking, modern brick houses, new schools, garish shopping centres and lots of teenage children.

GETTING THERE

The Central Coast Line from Sydney crosses the river at Brooklyn and passes through Brisbane Water National Park to the towns of the Central Coast. Trains stop at Woy Woy ($3.70), Gosford ($4.10), Wyong ($5.50) and towns in between.

The Pacific Highway runs through Gosford and Wyong, the major Central Coast towns, along an old, scenic and winding route. The new, speedy, Sydney to Newcastle Tollway (toll is 60 cents for a car) has exits running off to both towns.

TOURIST INFORMATION

Information centres fall over each other to help you in this part of the country. They can be found at 200 Main Street, Gosford; on the Esplanade near the surf club at

Terrigal; in Marine Parade, The Entrance on the Tuggerah Lakes and on the corner of Main Road and Victoria Street, Toukley near Norahville.

Gosford

This is the Central Coast's biggest town but it is not actually on the coast. It stands at the head of Brisbane Water which breaks off Broken Bay to the north. The last fifteen years have seen it grow from a small town to a small city as the Central Coast has attracted more and more residents. The new city has begun to overwhelm all the small places you see named around it on any road map. Poet Henry Kendall, who wrote 'Bellbirds' a rhyme taught to every Australian school child, made his home at Gosford. The house he lived in is at Henry Kendall Street, West Gosford. The building has a romantic past, having been constructed in a definitely *ad hoc* fashion by Peter Fagan who settled a grant of 100 acres at the junction of the Broadwater and Narara Creek in 1835. Fagan used it as a homestead and later as a pub called the Red Cow Inn. The house has walls two feet thick, made of rubble and a roughish mortar.

Tourist Attractions

Gosford's popularity has attracted not merely tourists but amusements designed to keep them busy. **Old Sydney Town**, on the Pacific Highway at Somersby near Gosford is a re-creation of Sydney in its earliest days including buildings of timber and sandstone, a ship, bullock carts, actors performing the roles of grovelling convicts and cruel soldiers, mock whippings and other pseudo-colonial nonsense. It is open 10 am to 5 pm Wednesday to Sunday and admission costs $9. The **Australian Reptile Park**, also on the highway, features the undesirable but very exciting poisonous creatures native to Australia's countryside. Visitors can see funnel web spiders and poisonous snakes milked of their venom at 2 pm on Wednesdays and 2 pm Sundays respectively. Crocodiles are hand fed at 3 pm on Saturdays during the summer. The park is open 8 am to 5 pm each day, sometimes later in summer, and admission is $5. **Askania Park** is not nearly so disturbing an environment. It is a stand of rainforest plants developed along the banks of a small stream in a neat little valley on Ourimbah Creek Road, Ourimbah, north of the Reptile Park. All the plants are very educationally labelled and many birds have been encouraged to reside in the forest. Open 10 am to dusk Wednesday to Sunday, admission $3.50.

Terrigal and Avoca

Terrigal and **Avoca Beach** are two almost legendary resort towns on this coast. Terrigal owes its fame as much to the Sydney crowds which congregate there on summer weekends as to its wide, attractive beach. The beachfront Florida Hotel was the venue for Labour Party conferencing before the days of campaign launches in the Sydney Opera House. It saw a brawl or two. In their determination to obliterate these memories, the new owners have demolished the old Florida and are replacing it with a glossy new resort hotel. Avoca is not so raunchy and has latterly become so full of young families and sweet faced school children as to be unreproachably suburban but its two-km beach, backed by Bulbararing Lagoon, where sailboards are for hire, tends to relieve the suburban malaise.

Bouddi National Park is a small but beautiful coastal park with fine beaches and coastal valleys where stands of rainforest survive. It is accessible from The Scenic Road running from Kincumber a short distance south-west of Avoca through McMasters Beach to Pretty Beach. A track beginning at the Rangers' Station, on the Scenic Road inside the park, leads down to Maitland Bay where a steamer was wrecked on 6 May 1898 with the loss of 26 lives, mostly in the forward section of the vessel which disintegrated in the raging seas. Two boilers remain on the beach as mute witnesses to the tragedy. The mayor of Gosford at the time, Manasseh Ward, led 15 horsemen through country previously thought impassable to reach the wreck, he was later joined by some Sisters of St Joseph from Kincumber who brought supplies to care for the victims. The dead were buried at Booker Bay near the mouth of Brisbane Water.

Tuggerah Lakes

The lakes are actually one lake with two names, depending which end you're at. The north is sometimes called Lake Budgewoi and the south Tuggerah Lake. Whatever the case, the waters lie close to the coast north of Terrigal and are much loved by pelicans which flock there in thousands although they rarely move about in large groups, often appearing alone or in pairs on the water, in the air or just sitting around on wharf piles.

The old Pacific Highway (ie, not the new Sydney to Newcastle Tollway) runs close to the lakes' western shore and in the east, long sweeping beaches form a barrier between them and the sea. **Norahville** on the north-east corner of the lakes is the town where Edward Hammond Hargraves, the first man to discover gold at Bathurst in 1823, built a house using the £15,500 reward he was given for his discovery. The house is a replica of his Grandfather's English home and took three years to build. It stands in Elizabeth Drive, on the cliff overlooking Jenny Dixon Beach. Hargraves used to bring parties of friends up from Sydney in a chartered steamer, landing them at Cabbage Tree Wharf, close to the house a little north of Norah Head. While he and his party remained in residence, the Union Jack would always fly over the house. The house is not open for public inspection. Norah Head itself suffers from trail bike riders but has a charming small beach. The lighthouse is opened to the public on Tuesdays and Thursdays. Consult the Visitors' Centre at Toukley for details of times.

Tuggerah Beach swings south from Norah Head to Lakes Entrance where the Pacific and the lake join forces. The beach is long, narrow and mostly unpatrolled with a continuously pounding surf, loud enough to drown out passing traffic on the road only a few steps away. Lakes Entrance brings one into the highly populated areas of the central coast.

WHERE TO STAY
There is plenty of motel, hotel and caravan (trailer) park accommodation along the Central Coast because the area is a summer holiday magnet for Sydneysiders. The

Tienda Motel, single $32 to $50, double $36 to $53, and the **Aquarius Motel**, single $34, double $42, both in The Entrance Road, The Entrance, on Tuggerah Lakes, are reliable.

Kim's Camp, Charlton Avenue, Toowoon Bay, (043) 32 1566; is a collection of beachside cottages close to The Entrance with a central dining room where plain but good quality meals are served, is more interesting than many other places. $99 to $160 per person per day full board.

EATING OUT

The Galley, Terrigal Sailing Club, The Haven, Terrigal (043) 84 6333; hardly what you'd expect from a sailing club galley but this little beauty dishes up delicacies as inspiring as the views from its balcony on the club's top floor. Seafood is the house speciality but it's not just thrown on the barbie, examples are gateau of John Dory and prawns and scallops with nantua cream. BYO. Mid price range.

Tilbury's, 80 Ocean View Drive, Terrigal, (043) 84 2044; selections are from the blackboard here and usually include plenty of seafood. BYO. Mid price range.

CRUISES

The rather fancifully named **Starship Cruises**, (043) 23 1655, operates small cruising ferries on Brisbane Water and Tuggerah Lakes. The slow-paced cruises take around two hours.

South

A southerly trip from Sydney takes you initially to the Royal National Park, about an hour's drive from the city and thence through a string of coastal coal-mining towns to Wollongong, New South Wales' third largest city. The coastal scenery is some of the best that the state has to offer and there are plenty of opportunities for safe swimming in the surf.

The Royal National Park

This is the great coastal park on Sydney's southern fringe. The Royal National is Australia's longest established effort at conservation of the natural environment and includes beaches, rainforest stands, heathland and Aboriginal rock engravings within its confines. Gazetted in 1879, it was among the progenitors of the world-wide national parks movement, being the second such park established after Yellowstone in the United States.

GETTING THERE

Royal National Park is easy to reach by train. There is a station in the park ($1.80) or a short walk from the stations at Engadine ($1.80), Heathcote ($1.80) or Waterfall ($2.30) will bring you into it.

Drivers simply take the Princes Highway and follow the signs to the turn-off just past Loftus.

TOURIST INFORMATION

The Visitors' Centre is located at the park railway station in Farnell Avenue, a short distance from the northern park entrance, off the Princes Highway.

Beaches

Roads lead from the entrance to the main beaches at Garie, Wattamolla and Bundeena, a small settlement with shops, a pub and some beachside accommodation. **Wattamolla Beach** has kept its rugged appearance because it is surrounded by high ground. It is very pretty. A waterfall drops from beside the picnic area above the beach down to a stream which runs across the cream coloured sand and out to sea. The beach is reached by tracks running from the picnic and parking area which one is grateful cannot be seen from the sand. **Garie Beach** is an established surfing beach with parking right beside it and is often crowded.

Walks

The **Coast Walk** is the best bushwalk in Royal National Park but it is very long. It begins at Bundeena in the North and runs south to Otford, a distance of around 26 km (16 miles). Though it can be traversed in a day, two makes it easier and more enjoyable. The track traverses Big Marley and Little Marley beaches and Wattamolla Inlet then passes through Curracurrang and Curracurrong, two confusingly named but quite separate inlets, and rises to a flat cliff-top section before dropping again to Garie Beach. A short trek brings walkers to the beaches of North and South Era beyond which lies the final section of the track past Burning Palms beach and the Figure Eight Pool, through the Palm Jungle and on to Otford. A great deal of the walk is along the tops of sheer cliffs with beaches and dry rainforest gullies in between. It can be shortened by taking one of the many access tracks leading down from Bundeena Road or Sir Bertram Stephens Drive.

Perhaps the best **short walk** runs about three km (two miles) from the Marley Car Park on Bundeena Road to Big or Little Marley Beach. It falls from a wildflower studded heath through banksia and eucalypt forest to the beach.

CAMPING OUT

Bush camping, that is pitching your tent anywhere in the park provided you are one km from any road or picnic area, is allowed if you have a permit. These can be obtained free from the Visitors' Centre. Wood fires are banned and, on occasion, sections of the park may be closed to campers.

Stanwell Park to Wollongong

A string of coastal towns, now almost a ribbon of low level urbanisation, runs down the coast between Royal National Park and Wollongong. The towns, from Stanwell Park to Thirroul are coal mining centres that have been digging away at the cliffs behind them for nearly one hundred and fifty years. Since the railway between Sydney and Wollongong was electrified, many have begun to attract commuters and for a much longer time they have been summer resorts for the Sydney school holiday crowds.

According to his journals, had it not been for the heavy surf along this coast, Captain James Cook, would have landed here and who knows what would have happened to Botany Bay? The first white folks to make ground were George Bass and Matthew Flinders on their way south to Bass Strait. A party of shipwrecked sailors struggling back towards Sydney in 1796 found loose coal along the coast and Bass returned with some of them in 1797 to discover the seam at Coalcliff. Sixty years passed before it was seriously worked. A drought in 1815 drove explorers south again, this time in search of grasslands which they duly found. Fine stands of red cedar were a bonus which brought timber getters, the hardest of men, south as well. The military followed in 1826, establishing themselves first at Port Kembla and later at the present site of Wollongong.

GETTING THERE
The Illawarra Line which runs along the western edge of Royal National Park turns eastward here and follows the road through the coastal settlements. It is one of the most scenic stretches of track in New South Wales, enjoying the best of the coast on one side and the escarpment on the other. It also gives easy access to the beaches. The fares are $3.20 to Stanwell Park and $4.10 to Wollongong.

Leaving the Royal National Park at Otford, Lawrence Hargraves Drive winds down the coast to Thirroul where it once again joins the Princes Highway.

Views
The Lawrence Hargraves Memorial and Look-out at Stanwell Park commemorates the inventor of the box kite who was a considerable personage in the region during the 1890s. The spot where he loved to go fly his kite is a precipitous cliff overhanging the Pacific and offering the best coastal view south of Sydney. The contrast it gives to the bush of the park, only a minute or two away, is startling. These days the area is favoured by sky sailors who drop from the surrounding cliffs to the beach below with alarming sang-froid.

Beach Towns
The towns of Coalcliff, Clifton, Scarborough, Wombarra, Coledale and Austinmer, despite their almost holiday air, are in the gritty business of feeding blast furnaces with coal mined from the face of the Illawarra escarpment. Coal heaps and cranes on the hillsides above rocky beaches with gold sand make a jarring contrast. The beaches are smallish and flat, washed by Pacific surf and surrounded by houses, some old weatherboard weekenders' and miners' cottages, others modern brick boxes. They retain an air of Australia 20 years ago when life was less complicated and a weekend out of town with the family was more important than the state of the economy. Austinmer is the most attuned to visitors since it has long been a popular holiday destination.

Wollongong

The city is a steel making centre with a population of over 200,000. It has Australia's largest **steel works**, owned by BHP the nation's largest company, and some fine

94

surf beaches close by. Tours of the works can been arranged at the Australian Iron and Steel Works Visitors' Centre in Gladstone Street. Some fishing is done out of Wollongong although not nearly so much as from towns further south. The fishing fleet shelters in a small harbour under the lee of an old lighthouse built in 1872. There is a **City Gallery** on Burelli Street which is open Tuesday to Sunday from noon to 5 pm and an **Historical Museum** in Market Square open 10 am to 1 pm on Wednesday and 1.30 pm to 4.30 pm on weekends.

WHERE TO STAY
Northbeach International, Cliff Road, Wollongong, (042) 27 1188, overlooks the beach and Wollongong Harbour. Single $72 to $89, double $82 to $99.

Southern Highlands

A cool and less crowded alternative to the Blue Mountains, the Southern Highlands lie south-west of Sydney on the way to Canberra. History, horses and horticulture characterise the highlands. Compared to the wind-blown coast they are elegant mountain hideaways where people grow English-style gardens, run guesthouses and fat farms, and hold flower festivals. The local ritual is gymkhana of which there seems to be at least one if not half a dozen every weekend. Dressage is a religion; Toyota Landcruisers with horse floats attached are *de rigeur*; there are some quite good restaurants and acres of money. In truth, aside from the Blue Mountains, the Southern Highlands is the loveliest non-beach place near Sydney to drop out of sight for a weekend or a couple of mid-week days and, as the mountains become more and more crowded, may soon surpass them.

GETTING THERE
Trains travel from Sydney to all the places mentioned in this section except Berrima and Kangaroo Valley which is only accessible by car. The fares are Mittagong $7.60, Bowral $9.20, Bundanoon $16.50.
  The Hume Highway, the main route from Sydney to Melbourne passes through Mittagong and Berrima and close to Bowral and Bundanoon. The Kangaroo Valley is reached from the Illawarra Highway which joins the Southern Highlands with Wollongong.

TOURIST INFORMATION
There is a bustling information centre on the Hume Highway at Mittagong which is open 9 am to 5 pm every day.

Mittagong and Bowral

Mittagong and Bowral together form a moderately urbanised area used early this century as a retreat by very rich Sydney families such as the newspaper-owning Fairfaxes and the retailing Horderns, and by orders of Roman Catholic nuns and priests who set up retreat houses and schools. The area retains the restrained tone imposed upon it by such inhabitants although much of their property is now in the hands of more commercial concerns such as guesthouses, health farms and retirement homes.

The area is famous for its gardens and in October each year, during the Australian Spring, a Tulip Time festival is held. The oddly European tulip appears all over town but especially in Corbett Gardens in the centre of Bowral which is planted out with tulips of all colours. It's a tasteless exhibition of horticultural overkill but draws thousands. The gardens of some local houses, especially the exquisite **Milton Park**, now a ritzy guesthouse, are also open during Tulip Time. Open at no other time, they provide a tantalising alternative to the garish tulips. The tourist information centre has details of which houses are open and at which times.

WHERE TO STAY AND EAT

Milton Park, Horderns Road, Bowral, (048) 61 1862; is a truly fabulous country house hotel and restaurant occupying the former Ḥordern residence a discreet distance from Bowral. The house is a remarkably fine example of the Federation style of domestic architecture and is surrounded by a world famous garden. Modern, luxury accommodation has been added in as sensitive a manner as possible. Standard rooms $155. The restaurant serves *nouvelle cuisine*. Licensed. Upper price range.

There is a string of motels on the Hume Highway at Mittagong. The **Poplars Motel**, (048) 89 4239, is well appointed and has the advantage of a fairly good restaurant in a pretty building constructed in 1845. Single $40 to $49, double $44 to $49.

EATING OUT

Hume House Garden Restaurant, 84 Hume Highway, Mittagong, (048) 71 1871; interesting menu to which the label international is not an insult, friendly service and colonial surroundings. Licensed. Mid price range.

Wombeyan Caves

The caves are about 72 km (45 miles) west of Mittagong along some unsealed and tortuous road. If you can stand the rough drive—the scenery alone is probably worth it—there are five cave tours to choose from, all through vast caverns cluttered with weird and colourful limestone formations bearing quaint names like *Lots Wife* (the reason is obvious), the *Cockatoo*, *Pine Forests* and *Fortifications*; 'frozen' waterfalls and giant stalagmites abound. The caves have good pathways, stairs and handrails and all tours except one are guided. Bookings are not necessary. For more information contact the Superintendent's Office on (048) 53 5976.

Joadja

Joadja, a former kerosene shale mining village, now a ghost town, is reached by a turn-off on the way to the caves. A cemetery, School of Arts, schoolhouse and miners cottages still stand in the town and there is a picnic ground. The ghost town is only open on weekends and public holidays; is closed during the bushfire season from December to the beginning of March and may be closed at any time because of wet weather. The best idea is to check with the Mittagong Tourist Information Centre.

Berrima

Berrima, 122 km (76 miles) from Sydney, is something of a tourist trap but its jaws are gentle and its perfectly preserved sandstone colonial buildings make the town of genuine interest.

The jail, courthouse, pub and a couple of original houses are the main attractions backed up by a plethora of tea houses, craft and antique shops and other cashers-in on the tourist trade. The town owes its time-warp quality to being left behind by the march of progress when the railway passed it by in 1867, a favour which the planners of the time certainly did not intend for future generations but one which we appreciate none the less. Less appreciated is the Hume Highway whose traffic, including scores of pantechnicons an hour, roar right through the middle of town.

The **courthouse**, Berrima's most impressive structure, occupies a grassy hill next to the jail, one street back from the frenetic highway. The building was constructed between 1833 and 1838 to a design by Colonial Architect Mortimer Lewis. It had a short legal life, being used for only seven years as a Court of Assizes and entirely given up for legal purposes in 1889, becoming a venue for council meetings and concerts after that time. Now classified by the National Trust, the building has been restored to its original appearance save for the lanterns which provided daylight to the court and jury room; they have been replaced by skylights. The neo-classical sandstone portico, complete with columns and pediment gives entrance to a rotunda and tries hard to look like a Roman temple. The court room houses a rather tacky group of dummies at bar table, bench and in the dock, supposed to give an impression of authenticity. Other rooms contain glass cases of stuffed animals and insects which is also rather a shame but the building itself is fine. Outside is the only sandstone toilet block I have ever seen.

Berrima Jail is next door to the courthouse. It was constructed between 1834 and 1839 at a cost of £10,847 7s 5d. Its gate and beautiful front garden are all that the tourist sees; the jail still operates under the title Berrima Training Centre, a 'progressive establishment dedicated to the rehabilitation of its inmates'. The inmates have varied over the years from convicts to prisoners of war and foreign internees. From 1919 to 1939 the jail was empty and open to tourists but much was knocked down and rebuilt in the 1940s and it now houses low security prisoners. The facade was constructed in 1866 and tries to be appropriately intimidating.

Surveyor General Inn is still Berrima's pub after well over a century of service. It was established in 1834 and is Australia's longest continuously licensed inn. It serves a hearty lunch and a good cold beer in a pleasant garden where patrons can admire the proportions of its colonial construction. **Harper's Mansion** on the corner of Wilkinson Street is a fully restored property owned by the National Trust. The building, constructed for local policeman James Harper in 1834, is an excellent example of a middle-class Australian home of the 1830s. It has five rooms upstairs and five downstairs and can only be called a mansion in relation to other accommodation available at that time. The trust has undertaken a detailed restoration of the house and uses it as its Berrima headquarters. It is open Saturday, Sunday and Monday from 11 am to 4 pm.

Jellore Street, just past the Surveyor General, is flanked by art galleries and antique dealers and has the local Historical Society Museum at the Hume Highway end. Among the museum displays are Tyrolean canoes made by German prisoners during World War I. The prisoners were allowed considerable latitude and spent their days by the river where they built Tyrolean cottages and made boats. They were on such good terms with the townsfolk that they invited them to a regatta on the river.

Bundanoon

This small town at the south-western extremity of the highlands is an access point for Morton National Park. It has a convenient railway station and **cycling** is immensely popular there, though you have to be fit to manage it. Cycles hired from **Ye Olde Bicycle Shoppe** in Church Street can be ridden into the park and surrounding mountain countryside.

Morton National Park

The road through the park leads to **Grand Canyon Look-out** and other places to observe the steep wooded gorges of the Morton Ranges. Well marked walking trails take you down into the forest. Try to see Morton National Park on a week day, chances are you will have the views to yourself and the bush will be so quiet you can hear every bird and blowfly for miles. The Grand Canyon Look-out is breathtaking; huge, steep valleys topped by sandstone cliffs without a sign of humanity stretch away to the horizon. Birds cry to each other from the spaces. A short walk from the look-out to Fern Glen passes primeval banksia trees, eucalypts and plants with leathery and serrated leaves, green and grey against trunks blackened by the last bushfire. Startling red flowers stand out and points of fine white acacia blossom dust the gully like snow. The temperature drops noticeably as you descend to a rock wall of the glen which is covered with ferns. The surroundings give the feeling of living in a distant geological age.

Glow Worm Glen, a small sandstone grotto at the end of William Street is inhabited by thousands of tiny larvae of the fungus-gnat which glow blue in the dark. The walk to the glen takes about 25 minutes and should be done at sunset with a torch and strong shoes.

Kangaroo Valley

This valley runs down from the Southern Highlands through Morton National Park to Berry and Nowra on the Shoalhaven River near the coast. **Fitzroy Falls** at the upper end of the valley plunge over 75 metres (250 feet) to the valley floor of the park. The falls are close to the Nowra Road leading into the valley. There is an information centre, covered picnic facilities, a camping ground and parking area by the road, all rather untidy. Tracks lead to the escarpment on either side of the falls and to their base. Anyone suffering from vertigo should stay away from the edge of the look-out. Lyre birds, parrots and other native birds are often seen in the falls area. The Hampden Bridge, a sandstone suspension bridge, crosses the Kangaroo River at the middle of the valley and has become a focus for other tourist attractions including a pioneer 'village' museum and a pottery. The town of Kangaroo Valley lies a little way beyond the bridge. It is surrounded by high green hills, has a couple of tea rooms, a restaurant and a marvellous workshop making wooden toys.

Just beyond the town a left turn onto the Berry Mountain Road, marked as a tourist drive, takes you high over the valley on a winding journey continually revealing astonishing views of the valley floor and the mountains.

Horse Riding
There are 14 riding schools in Southern Highlands area any of which will show you the beauties of the region from horseback. A list is obtainable from the Travel Centre of NSW in Sydney.

West

When the first colonists discovered they couldn't grow enough to eat on the shores of Port Jackson, they headed west and began to farm the land around **Parramatta**, 20 miles from the port. There, they had a great deal more success and by the early 1800s had established a productive farming community. The area has much to offer in historical terms. Today, it is the heart of Sydney's western suburbs, a vast suburban wasteland of quarter-acre blocks and red brick housing developments which reaches almost to the Blue Mountains and is still growing. The preserved history of the district is represented by a number of colonial buildings all within easy walking distance of Parramatta Railway Station. These include Governor Phillip's **Old Government House**, built in 1799, in Parramatta Park (open 10 am to 4 pm); and the oldest farm building in Australia, **Elizabeth Farm Cottage** in Alice Street, built in 1793 (open 10 am to 4.30 pm, Tuesday to Sunday, $2 entry).

Wildlife Parks

Koalas, those cute but somewhat overdone representatives of Australian fauna, are exhibited in the company of kangaroos, emus, Tasmanian devils and the like at two commercial animal sanctuaries in Sydney's west. They are **Koala Park**, Castle Hill Road, West Pennant Hills and **Featherdale Wildlife Park**, 217 Kildare Road, Doonside, both within striking distance of Parramatta. These places are designed to attract crowds and usually do, but as it takes time, effort and luck to spot a koala, a kangaroo or a wombat—let alone an echidna—in the bush around Sydney these days they serve a useful purpose. A few of the animals are tame and touchable, which thrills the kids, but they are often caged and lethargic too because many are nocturnal. Any day tour by bus from Sydney will take you to one of these 'attractions'. Featherdale, in keeping with its name, has lots of birds.

TOURS AROUND SYDNEY

If your time is short, day tours by tourist bus to all points described in this chapter and beyond are available from Sydney city on the same bus companies which run city tours. As befits an organised occasion, very little of the touring time is truly your own and somebody else has decided what's supposed to interest you but you get there efficiently.

The State Rail Authority sells organised tours which include accommodation and bus trips as well as train tickets.

The Blue Mountains

These are where Sydneysiders escape their city's exhaust fumes and slow down for a weekend or a few days. It is also perfectly acceptable and not very taxing to see them on a day trip. They are at their best in spring and autumn when their height makes a true division between seasons which hardly exist for people on the coast. In summer they are warm but not humid and in winter, wet and cold.

Despite being known as the City of the Blue Mountains the region consists of a string of small resort towns surrounded by 200,000 hectares (494,194 acres) of national park. The mountains' blueness is real. It comes from tiny droplets of eucalypt oil rising into the air on their forested slopes and reflecting the blue in sunlight's spectrum. They are part of the Great Dividing Range which strings its low and very ancient crests almost the entire eastern length of Australia from the Atherton Tableland west of Cairns to the Victorian Alps. What they lack in height, they make up in ruggedness.

The mountains defied attempts to penetrate them in early colonial years and were first crossed by William Charles Wentworth, George Blaxland and William Lawson in 1813. They only managed to reach Mt Blaxland. The trail was carried to Bathurst by George Evans. Reports of good grazing land on the other side caused Governor Lachlan Macquarie to immediately order the building of a road. It followed Evans' route and took a mere six months to cover the 160 km (100 miles) to the western slopes.

The rich folk of Sydney built grand Blue Mountains retreats in Victorian times and made grand gardens to go with them, a horticultural tradition which is vigorously maintained today. The rest of the population came up on the train for weekends in guesthouses. The 1920s and 30s were the mountains' last great heyday but during and after World War II, a generation chose to neglect their charms and stick to the coast. Lately they have grown fashionable again. Many of the fine old Victorian and early 1900s buildings have been repaired and restored to accommodate weekend or mid-week visitors; local authorities are paying attention to natural and historical attractions and tourism has come to support a good deal of the local population.

GETTING TO AND AROUND

There are daily trains to the Blue Mountains from the Central Station. Fares are Springwood ($4.10), Faulconbridge ($4.10), Lawson ($4.80), Wentworth Falls

($5.50), Leura ($5.50), Katoomba ($6.50), Blackheath and Mt Victoria ($7.60) and Lithgow ($10.60). Each town has a railway station close to its centre. The towns themselves are quite small and can be covered on foot without difficulty.

Drivers take the Great Western Highway, proceeding from Railway Square in the city and along Parramatta Road. An alternative route runs through the very pretty hills around Kurrajong. Turn off the Great Western Highway at the Richmond–Blacktown Road, drive to Kurrajong and take the Bells Line of Road to the mountains.

TOURIST INFORMATION
The best source of information is the Tourist Information Centre at Echo Point, Katoomba, (047) 82 1833. There is another such centre on the Great Western Highway at Glenbrook on the eastern side of the range.

Katoomba

Katoomba is the Blue Mountains' major town. It specialises in luring day-trippers with the promise of views, mountain air, picturesque walks and a thrill or two. The thrills consist of the **Scenic Skyway** and the **Scenic Railway**. Both depart from a station perched on a precipice in Cliff Drive. Neither is very much more scenic than anything else in the area but most passengers don't notice because they're busy hanging on to their stomachs. The railway is not really a railway at all but a devilish species of cable car that drops, at an angle of not much less than 90°, into the Jamison Valley. People always scream when they ride it. The skyway is an 'orphan rocker', that is, a car hanging from a couple of wires, not secured underneath. It wobbles out and back over the valley at a dizzy height. A wire mesh floor makes sure passengers fully appreciate the drop.

The Three Sisters
Echo Point is where visitors to Katoomba come to marvel at the splendour of the

The Three Sisters

Three Sisters, a stand of startlingly similar weathered sandstone columnar peaks marching one before the other into the valley. An Aboriginal legend explains their appearance. The *Katoomba* and *Nepean* tribes were at war and fighting a great battle. The Katoomba leader saw his fighters would be defeated and feared the enemy would carry off his three beautiful daughters so in the heat of the battle he invoked the mountain spirits and turned the three girls to stone, saving them from capture, but the foolish man was himself killed and his daughters have remained guarding the valley of his death ever since.

Although many brochures show admiring groups looking up at the sisters and give an impression of imposing size, the reality is that Echo Point looks down on them and somewhat diminishes their effect. The **Giant Stairway** which descends into the valley next to the sisters affords a better opportunity to appreciate their grandeur. It can be reached via a path leading from behind the Information Centre at Echo Point and is called the Giant Stairway because that's just what it is.

Walks

The **Prince Henry Walk** leads off in the opposite direction from the Giant Stairway around the cliff faces as far as Leura. It is a mostly level walk but has challenging stairs in some places. It leads past Katoomba Cascades where walkers can rest in a cool, ferny glade by a waterfall. Many fine look-outs occur along its length.

Walks on the valley floor haven't the views of their cliff-top companions but they are cooler, running past caves, cascades and mountain streams and giving some indication of the primeval forest floor typical of the surrounding bush. The **Federal Pass** which begins at the foot of the Giant Stairway is one such walk. Maps of all walks can be obtained at the Echo Point information centre.

Leura

Leura is close to Katoomba and is sometimes a little difficult to separate from it. The town is particularly famous for its gardens, although you have to be there at the right time of year to gain access to most of them. **Everglades** in Denison Street is the most reliable and is open most days from 10 am to 4 pm. The garden is constructed on a sloping site and includes much stonework, pools, an open-air theatre and, in keeping with the climate, some thriving European as well as native trees and shrubbery. **Leuralla** in Olympian Parade, houses a collection of nineteenth-century Australian art in the stately house which occupies its landscaped grounds. The collection is that of Dr H. V. Evatt, the first Australian to be President of the United Nations and one of a great political and legal dynasty. It is open Friday to Sunday as well as public and school holidays from 10 am to 5 pm. Private gardens in the same town are open during the **Leura Gardens Festival** in mid-October (spring) as are gardens in other mountain towns, especially Mount Wilson. Exact dates can be obtained from the Tourist Information Centres.

Arts, Crafts and Antiques

The **Norman Lindsay Gallery** at Faulconbridge commemorates Sydney's artistic *enfant terrible* of the Edwardian age who painted nudes of mythical voluptuousness in salacious poses calculated to outrage the 'wowsers' of his time. It also has a fine garden where Lindsay's masterful and humorous sculptures are set. Lindsay designed the garden and its wildness offers a relief from the English pattern which so preoccupied other mountain gardeners. The artist lived long and famously beyond Edwardian times, continuing to paint and outrage. He was a novelist and remarkable builder of model ships in addition to his painting talents. He also wrote and illustrated *The Magic Pudding*, an irreverent classic of Australian children's literature. The gallery, run by the National Trust, includes paintings, etchings (a technique of which Lindsay was more than a master), ships and works by other members of the Lindsay family, especially the superbly under-stated Lionel. Copies of *The Magic Pudding* can be purchased at the gallery shop.

More modern and less artistic kinds of galleries, established by 1970s refugees from Sydney who make everything from lace-work to macramé pot-plant holders and multi-coloured wax candles, are to be found in every town. So are antique dealers who began by buying up the old furniture and crockery of defunct rural families to sell to Sydney antique fanciers and who now import and reproduce as well as selling local pieces. Their trade has established itself in Glenbrook, Warrimoo, Valley Heights, Faulconbridge, Hazelbrook, Lawson, Wentworth Falls, Leura, Katoomba, Blackheath, Mount Victoria and Kurrajong.

Mt Victoria

This little mountain town west of Katoomba is one of the area's most charming. Station Street, its steep main street, is flanked by tea rooms, antique and curio shops, guesthouses and hotels. A museum operated by the local historical society takes up some rooms in the back of the Railway Station. It holds documents and photographs, clothing and implements from local history and is open 2 pm to 5 pm on weekends.

Hartley

Some of the best sightseeing in the Blue Mountains region is found west of Katoomba where the Jenolan Caves road breaks off from the Great Western Highway. **Hartley Historic Site** stands at the junction of the two roads. The site includes a number of colonial buildings, private and public, many of which have been restored to their original condition. The village they make up once stood at the fringe of a new territory and was the focus for settlers taking up land on the Western Plains.

The courthouse, a building in Greek Revival style with a triangular pediment supported by Doric columns, was designed by Colonial architect Mortimer Lewis and completed in 1837. Its sandstone exterior is a veneer. The construction was actually carried out in local granite. The courthouse saw the trial of many a bushranger during the gold rush but mostly served to keep the convicts, delivered as labourers to local farmers, in order. It ceased functioning in 1887. **St Mary's Church** across the road from the courthouse was completed in 1848 after six years of building and difficult fund-raising. It served a population then almost 90 per cent

Irish Catholic. The church is still consecrated but rarely used. Its Anglican counterpart on the outskirts of town has long surpassed it. An elegant presbytery, almost as grand as the church, is attached to St. Mary's.

Hartley's humbler buildings were constructed by those whose jobs kept them in the town. John Finn became courthouse constable in 1839 and, with his wife and children, built his first home of slabs, across from the courthouse. Next door, he constructed a more substantial brick building which became the district post office in 1846. The Finn family is also credited with constructing the Farmers Inn, the Magistrate's House (Ivy Cottage) and other town buildings.

Jenolan Caves

Jenolan Caves Road leads down into a valley and to **Jenolan Caves**, New South Wales best known system of limestone caves. Gawking tourists have tramped through them since the late nineteenth century and they are thus a little worse for wear but this does little to reduce their impact. They are open from 9.30 am to 5 pm every day with parties going in at regular intervals controlled by an attendant at the main entrance. Visitors are conducted along underground trails, beside waterways through a number of well-lit and thoroughly spectacular caverns, some the size of cathedrals. There is a guesthouse, established near the caves entrance in the 1920s, where it is possible to stay overnight or for a weekend and go walking in the surrounding bush.

Kanangra Walls beyond Jenolan, give a cliff-top outlook back over the valley to Katoomba. Picnics are possible there and you have a good chance of seeing wallabies, wallaroos, kangaroos, possums, wombats and, with a little luck, a koala.

WHERE TO STAY

The Blue Mountains have no international hotels but lots of good country guesthouses where the table is the heart of the home. The best are run by couples dedicated to the comfort of their guests and the preservation of a quiet, domesticated atmosphere and they need to be booked well ahead, especially at weekends.

Cleopatra Guest House, 4 Cleopatra Street, Blackheath, (047) 87 8456; a single storey Victorian house with a wide veranda and substantial garden but only 6 guest rooms. Such is the devotion to food here that the proprietors take one entire day per week to do the shopping. In warm weather, lunch is served in the garden, in cold weather, guests eat by the fire. $140 to $170 per person per night Friday to Sunday (full board), $100 to $130 weeknights (dinner, bed and breakfast).

Pegum's, 25 Honour Avenue, Lawson, (047) 59 1844; a building of 1892 which has nine rooms furnished in country style with antiques individually purchased by the owners. There are four bathrooms. The dining room and lounge area are just like the home you wish you had. $75 per person dinner, bed and breakfast, $300 weekend, BYO.

Little Company Guesthouse, Eastview Avenue, Leura, (047) 82 4023; is somewhat larger in accommodation and grounds, having been established in a former Little Company of Mary convent. It has a croquet lawn and proprietors willing to instruct you in the sport. Some rooms with private facilities, otherwise one bathroom to two bedrooms. $75 per person Monday to Thursday, $85 Friday to Sunday, dinner bed and breakfast.

Glenella, 56 Govetts Leap Road, Blackheath, (047) 87 8352; certainly best known for its legendary restaurant run by Michael Manners which serves an ever-changing menu of French delights but also has accommodation in the country guesthouse style. Share facilities. Thursday, Friday, Sunday $75 per person full board. Saturday $30 per person bed and breakfast.

Caves House, Jenolan Caves, (063) 59 3304; is a rambling, 1920s mock Tudor hotel complete with port cochere and uncountable little roof peaks. The hotel has been refurbished in recent years and the standard of food improved out of sight. It is a very relaxing place to spend a weekend in isolation. For rooms with private facilities the prices are single $65, double $90 bed and breakfast. There are less expensive rooms without facilities. A motel has been built behind Caves House and bush cabins can also be booked through the house management.

Fairmont Resort, Sublime Point Road, Leura, (047) 82 5222; is a brand new mountain hotel with over 200 rooms, each of which has a view. It has tennis courts, squash courts, heated swimming pools in and outdoors and a golf course. The four storey gabled complex is fronted by an ornamental lake and has eating and entertainment rooms towards one end. Single $120, double $130 room only.

The Blue Mountains also have motels of acceptable comfort and colourless modernity in the towns of Faulconbridge, Wentworth Falls, Leura, Katoomba, Blackheath and Mount Victoria. Holiday cabins, cottages and flats are available for anyone contemplating a longer stay. There is a **youth hostel** in Katoomba. Bushwalkers can camp in the Blue Mountains National Park.

EATING OUT

Tea, taken as high as one can manage it, is a great Blue Mountains tradition. Tea Rooms abound and all serve Devonshire Teas, consisting of scones and jam and a pot of tea. Nowadays it is fashionable to offer a choice of English Breakfast, Darjeeling, Earl Grey or other varieties of the leaf; some iconoclasts even take their scones with coffee to which the tolerant tea house proprietors make no objection. Your choice of tea house is frequently a matter of the view as the scones are much of a muchness.

Yester Grange, Yester Road, Wentworth Falls; is a pretty old house where you can take tea while looking out on an attractive garden. Open Friday to Sunday 10 am to 5 pm. Low price range.

The Paragon Café, Katoomba Street, Katoomba, is a perfectly preserved Art Deco café known for chocolates which are hand-made upstairs and for a great deal of atmosphere downstairs. Ask to see the ballroom which resembles a Busby Berkley film set and has a sprung floor. Choose to take tea and scones or maybe a waffle as the rest of the food is of the meat pie and toasted sandwich variety. Low price range.

Most guesthouse dining rooms are open to the public and offer the best meals in the mountains. Glenella and Cleopatra are the pick but all are good. Book well in advance.

TOURS

Because the area is close to Sydney, many day sightseeing tours leave from the city. Companies running such tours include AAT Kings (02) 669 5444, Ansett Pioneer

105

(02) 268 1331, Australian Pacific Tours (02) 693 2222 and Clipper Tours (02) 888 3144. The State Rail Authority operates **Day-away Tours** to the Blue Mountains on which passengers train up and bus around the sights. All these tours include the main Blue Mountains sights and either a visit to Jenolan Caves or to a koala sanctuary.

The **Blue Mountains Explorer Bus** is based in Katoomba and runs around 22 scenic and interesting spots on Saturdays, Sundays and Public Holidays once every hour. Golden West Tours operates buses from Katoomba as well as **four-wheel drive** 'adventures' in the park, (047) 82 1866.

ACTIVITIES
Three horse-riding establishments take trail rides through the Megalong Valley section of the Blue Mountains National Park. **Packsaddlers**, Green Gully, Megalong, (047) 87 9150, has accommodation at its base and takes riders out camping in the park or for day trips. Other riding tours are available from **Werri Berri Trail Rides**, Megalong Valley, (047) 87 9171, and **Mountain River Riders**, Megalong Valley, (047) 82 1926.

A number of organisations take abseiling and rock-climbing expeditions into the park. **Australian Himalayan Expeditions**, 3rd Floor, 377 Sussex Street, Sydney, (02) 264 3366; **Natural Perception**, 4 Norwood Street, Leura, (047) 82 4091; **Rockcraft Climbing School**, 195 Katoomba Street, Katoomba, (047) 82 2014; **Wilderness Expeditions**, 100 Clarence Street, Sydney (02) 29 1582.

Cycling tours are conducted by **Bush Experiences**, 49 Jersey Avenue, Leura, phone (047) 84 2361.

Newcastle and The Hunter Valley

The coastal steel-making city of Newcastle, north of Sydney, is the gateway to the Hunter Valley, a rich, undulating but sometimes quite dry-looking region between the coast and the great dividing range where most of New South Wales' wine is grown and a great deal of its coal mined. The area enjoys a temperate climate with warm summers and mild winters on the coast and only slightly more extreme conditions inland.

The Newcastle and Hunter region has three divisions: Newcastle itself, a lumbering, and lately teetering, giant of industry; the wine-growing areas of the Hunter Valley to the west and the coastline north and south of the city.

Newcastle

The coal mines of the Hunter Valley feed the steel-making plants of Newcastle, a city of 300,000 people which began life as a jail for convicts who wouldn't toe the line at Sydney. Its location was discovered by Lieutenant John Shortland RN while searching for escaped convicts in September 1797. Two attempts were required before a viable penal colony was established in 1804. It was soon known as a hellhole, stocked with second and third offenders, the worst of whom were set to making lime at Limeburner's Bay while the rest cut timber in the estuary and, eventually, in camps as much as 70 km (43 miles) up the Hunter river.

Throughout its short life the convict settlement was thought to be too close to Sydney, thus encouraging prisoners to abscond. When it was moved north to Port Macquarie in 1823, Newcastle became a free settlement. By 1825, 360,000 acres had been taken up in the Hunter Valley but the town remained small since coastal traders preferred the harbour at Morpeth. Even by 1851 Newcastle could not count 2000 in its population.

The city really grew up as a company town. In 1915 the first sheets rolled off the Broken Hill Proprietary (BHP) steel production line and the tone was set for the best part of a century. Since then, Newcastle has followed the ups and downs of steel and coal and BHP has become Australia's largest company. A terrible place in the Depression, it rose again after World War II and is now struggling purposefully with the problems of reconstruction in the face of South-East Asian competition.

GETTING TO AND AROUND
Aeropelican and Eastern Airlines fly from Sydney to Newcastle several times a day. The fares are $47.50 and $55 respectively. Aeropelican can be booked through Ansett, Eastern through Australian Airlines.

Trains run from Sydney to Newcastle taking about about two and a half hours. They leave Central Station Monday to Friday at 11 am and the fare to Newcastle is $11.90.

Drivers take the Pacific Highway (Route 1) north from Sydney to Hornsby, then the Sydney to Newcastle Tollway.

TOURIST INFORMATION
The tourist information centre for Newcastle is in a railway carriage standing on Wharf Road, Newcastle.

The Civic Centre
The centre is bounded by King Street and Laman Street with the **City Hall** across King and the **Newcastle Regional Art Gallery** across Laman. The park between the two contains the **Captain James Cook Memorial Fountain**, a wide abstract metal sculpture of wave-like shapes fanned by jets of water. The fountain was erected in 1970 to celebrate the bicentenary of Cook's sailing up the east coast of Australia. It faces City Hall which has benefited markedly from a renovation done in 1981 to show off its neo-classical sandstone façade and clock tower. The gallery, although housed in an undistinguished building with, God forgive, astro-turf in front, is a small gem with an excellent collection of representative Australian painters, especially of the early to mid-twentieth century. Best represented are the glowing impressionistic works of Grace Cossington Smith and Rupert Bunny; other paintings include Elioth Gruner's views of Mosman and Cremorne on Sydney's northern foreshores, a famous portrait called *The Strapper* by Sir William Dobell and some of Margaret Preston's distinctive still-lifes featuring native flora. More recent but no less fêted names represented in the collection include Drysdale, Tucker,

Olsen and Whiteley. You'll find these paintings hanging in the large ground floor gallery whose space is also occupied by displays of Japanese ceramics—the gallery carries Australia's largest collection, and some sculpture. Upstairs is reserved for travelling exhibitions. The gallery is open on weekdays from 10 am to 5 pm, Saturdays from 1.30 pm to 5 pm and Sundays and public holidays from 2 pm to 5 pm. Admission is free.

Fort Scratchley
The fort dates from the 1840s and stands high on a hill at the eastern end of Hunter Street, off Nobby's Road, overlooking the sea. The view west is a panorama of Port Hunter and the city from its grimy wharves and railway lines to its imposingly sited cathedral, dominating the hill above the city centre. Nobby's Beach and the lighthouse on Nobby's Head lie immediately below. The north breakwater across the mouth of Port Hunter, where many coastal vessels have come to grief, juts into Newcastle Bight with Stockton Beach stretching further north.

The fort itself contains military installations from various periods. The two guns facing seawards and the observation tower behind them date from World War II, the fort buildings date from last century and have been uniformly cement rendered. The **Newcastle Maritime Museum** occupies a small building to the left of the main gate. It gives the history of shipbuilding in Newcastle, a former centre of that industry, and contains a model of the *Sophia Jane*, first of the coastal steam packets which dominated trade between Sydney and the Hunter region from the 1830s to the 1920s. Other models show the fleet of J & A Brown, for many years the district's leading coal mining company which built and ran colliers and packets into the 1940s.

Memorial Drive
Begins at Prince Edward Park which lies south of Fort Scratchley and is a delightful place to take your lunch. The park is green, has wide Pacific views in front and Newcastle's most interesting domestic architecture behind, including Victorian terraces and freestanding mansions in the late Victorian Italianate style. A wedding-cake bandstand nestles in its centre. The drive runs south along the city's beach-fronts passing the surf at Bar Beach, Dixon Park and Merewether. There are three look-outs along the way. The beaches have surf clubs and are patrolled on weekends.

WHERE TO STAY
Newcastle has motels, motor inns and lots of old style Australian hotels. **Newcastle Parkroyal**, corner King and Steel Streets, Newcastle, (049) 26 37770; is the city's best modern accommodation, a recently built international hotel. Single $73, double $79.
Grand Hotel, corner Bolton and Church Streets, Newcastle, (049) 23 489; an old but refurbished hotel for a taste of local flavour. Has a motel attached. Single $20, double $30 (share facilities, basic rooms); single $30, double $40 (motel rooms).
The Novocastrian Motor Inn, 21 Parnell Place, Newcastle, (049) 26 3688; occupies an enviable site overlooking the sea near Nobby's Point. Single $60 to $75, double $65 to $75, Suites $80.

EATING OUT
Carrington House, 130 Young Street, Carrington, (049) 61 3564; is located in one of Newcastle's old working class suburbs in a restored guesthouse. The decor is modern but not aggressive and the food is good modern French. Licensed. Set price lunch is inexpensive. Dinner mid price range.

The Hunter Valley

The Hunter Valley, west of Newcastle, offers more sophisticated and sensual pleasures than the steel making city and the beach-strewn coast to its east. They are the products of human skill as much as natural endowments.

GETTING THERE
Eastern Airlines flies from Sydney to Maitland up to six times a day ($55) and Singleton Air Service to Cessnock up to three times a day ($52). Those who can afford it may like to consider Hunter Hire Cars, chauffered vehicles which will take you around the valley vineyards without your having to find the way. The company is located beside Newcastle Heli-pad, phone (049) 61 3313.

Trains to Maitland from Sydney ($14.60) leave daily and the trip takes about three hours.

Drivers who want to skip Newcastle should turn off the Pacific Highway at Peats Ridge and proceed through Central Mangrove to Wollombi and on to Cessnock.

Bicycles are for hire at the Trading Post, Broke Road, Pokolbin, in the middle of the wine-growing area. The restaurant at the Trading Post will prepare picnic hampers to take on your ride. Phone (049) 98 7670.

TOURIST INFORMATION
Tourist information is available from the **Hunter Valley Wine Society**, 4 Wollombi Road, Cessnock; **Hunter Tourist Association**, New England Highway, Hexham; **Manning Valley Tourist Association**, 250 Victoria Street, Taree.

Vineyards

Grape cultivation in the valley is thought to have begun in 1824 when James Busby planted vines at Kirkton, just north of Branxton on the banks of the Hunter River. The oldest winery in the valley is Wyndham Estate, established in 1828, and still making wines. There are over fifty others, most of which are recent 'boutique' establishments often run by former accountants, advertising executives, doctors and lawyers in love with making wine. They are a tightly knit, hard-working group, conscious of good standards and in some cases producing award-winning vintages. They welcome passing customers in tasting rooms where wines can be sampled at the bar. The rooms vary from simple open areas to elaborate displays of wine and souvenirs.

Visitors to the valley usually take two or three days to enjoy its qualities. They base themselves at a central motel or guesthouse and tour the wineries, tasting char-

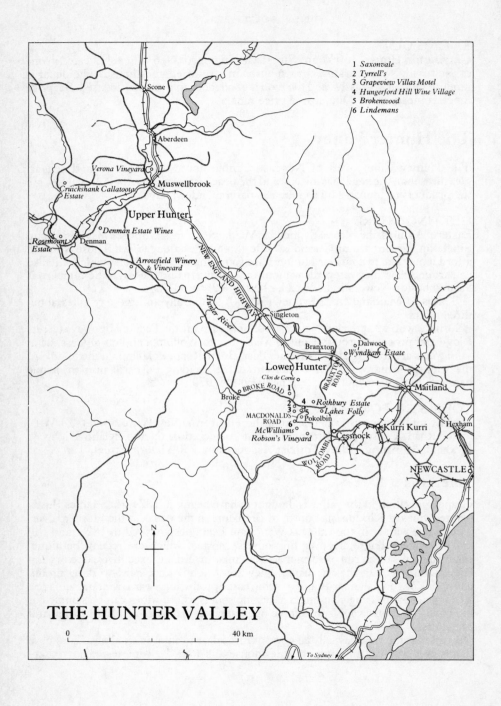

1 Saxonvale
2 Tyrrell's
3 Grapeview Villas Motel
4 Hungerford Hill Wine Village
5 Brokenwood
6 Lindemans

Scone

Aberdeen

Verona Vineyard

Cruckshank Callatoota
Estate

Muswellbrook

Upper Hunter

Denman Estate Wines

Rosemount
Estate

Denman

Arrowfield Winery
& Vineyard

NEW ENGLAND HIGHWAY

Hunter River

Singleton

Branxton

Dalwood

Wyndham Estate

Lower Hunter

Clos de Corie

BROKE ROAD

BRANXTON ROAD

Broke

1

2

3

4 Rothbury Estate

5 Lakes Folly

MACDONALDS
ROAD

Pokolbin

6

McWilliams

Robson's Vineyard

Cessnock

Kurri Kurri

Hexham

Maitland

WOLLOMBI ROAD

NEWCASTLE

N

THE HUNTER VALLEY

0   40 km

To Sydney

donnays, semillons, cabernet sauvignons, cabernet merlots and other varietals as well as a range of generic wine styles such as Chablis and White Burgundy. The region is especially well known for its white wines, chardonnays in particular, although reds are produced in quantity as well, with some vineyards making a speciality of them. The valley is conventionally divided into a lower and an upper section of which the former has the most vineyards.

The Lower Hunter

Many of the Lower Hunter wineries are in the Pokolbin area, a short drive from the town of Cessnock. The most developed for tourists is the **The Hungerford Hill Wine Village** on Broke Road near the corner of MacDonalds Road. Its public facilities are built in a rough colonial style meant to belie their recent origin and include cellars, tasting rooms, accommodation, a good restaurant, souvenir and food shops and a children's playground. Although it can get rather crowded and reeks of commercialism, it is a good place to begin a Lower Hunter tour because it is centrally placed and because its own wines are well worth tasting. From Hungerford Hill, you can strike out for some representative giants and tiddlers of the valley.

Lakes Folly, a small winery set a short distance off Broke Road near its junction with Branxton Road, is so called because it was considered in the 1960s to be the folly of its owner Max Lake. These days Mr Lake, a former surgeon, is considered to be among Australia's better wine-makers and the name-callers look a little foolish. Lake is one of Australian wine-making's great characters. Among his latest escapades was an appearance at the seventh annual *Symposium on Gastronomy* held at Oxford University in June 1987 where he spoke on the apparent propensity of some wines to cause mild sexual arousal. His winery is especially fêted for its cabernet.

Brokenwood, on MacDonalds Road, is the up and comer among small wineries of the Hunter. Chardonnay is the front runner there. Further down the valley off Mount View Road is **The Robson Vineyard**, another good small winery with varietals ranging from hermitage to semillon.

The Lower Hunter's giants are **Lindemans**, owned by multinational tobacco conglomerate Phillip Morris, **McWilliams**, one of the longest serving names in Australian wines and **Rothbury Estate** whose somewhat overbearing white temple is a modern landmark where wine ferments in gigantic stainless steel vats and oenophiles gather to exercise their palates in a 'baronial' hall. They are all worth visiting if you are still standing.

Tyrrell's Vineyard, Broke Road, although a famous name and a big producer, prefers to keep its facilities rustic and has a slab hut with a rammed dirt floor where visitors taste among old oak barrels. **The Wyndham Estate**, at Dalwood, via Branxton, is rather a drive from the rest of the vineyards but is very picturesque. Its old sheds, built during the first years of production there around 1830, are classified by the National Trust and their whitewashed walls contrast pleasingly with vines that come almost to the door.

These are by no means all the vineyards in the Lower Hunter. There is a signpost on Broke Road near Hungerford Hill that will direct you to many more.

Upper Hunter

Arrowfield Winery and Vineyard and **Rosemount Estate** are the major wineries in the Upper Hunter. Both just north of the Hunter River near the town of Denman, they are known for their high quality white wines, especially chardonnays and semillons.

The wineries give way to horse breeding, mining and dairying country around the towns of Singleton and Muswellbrook. This area contains some of the world's largest open-cut coal mines and the gigantic power stations of Liddell and Bayswater which keep Sydney lit and warm. The area has seen its share of drama in the past. An Aboriginal murderer, Joey Governor—the true subject of Thomas Keneally's novel, *The Chant of Jimmy Blacksmith*, made into a film by Bruce Beresford—is buried near Singleton. The notorious bushranger Captain Thunderbolt used to terrorise travellers on the road from Scone to Gloucester. **Bell Trees** homestead at Scone is one of New South Wales great country houses and was the location for much of the film *My Brilliant Career*.

WHERE TO STAY
Finding a room in the Hunter region should only prove difficult at the absolute height of summer holidays in late December and early January or, especially around the wineries, when there is a public holiday on Monday thus making the weekend three days long. There are motels in Cessnock and scattered elsewhere in the valley. Here are some interesting establishments.

Peppers Guest House, Ekerts Road, Pokolbin, (049) 98 7596; a colonial style building set in 11 hectares (25 acres) in the heart of the Lower Hunter wine district. The rooms are a blend of mod-cons and colonial furnishings and the restaurant is first class. Single $107, double $114.

Grapeview Villas Motel, Thompson Road, Pokolbin, (049) 98 7630; split level one- and two-bedroom units with kitchens and delightful views over the valley. Single $40, double $45.

Hunter Valley Quality Inn, Broke Road, Pokolbin, (049) 98 7600; right among the tourists but central to all the valley has to offer. Double $105.

Monte Pio Court, Dwyer Street, Campbells Hill, Maitland, (049) 32 5288; was formerly a Roman Catholic school. Though still owned by the church, it has recently been converted to a comfortable hotel with a few rather oddly shaped rooms, some with excellent valley views. Single $60, double $80.

EATING OUT
Restaurants in the Hunter Valley are very good and have excellent wine lists. They use local produce, including seafood from the nearby coast, to cook originally, often under the spell of French cuisine. Because trade is big during the day, many restaurants make a feature of lunch as well as dinner.

Clos de Corne, Hermitage Road, Pokolbin, (049) 98 7635; though somewhat out of the way is worth the drive to sample a menu which changes almost daily, taking account of what's at the market and the creative whims of chef Claude Corne who always strives for Haute Cuisine. Licensed. Mid to upper price range.

Cellars Restaurant, Hungerford Hill Wine Village, Broke Road, Pokolbin, (049)

98 7584; the setting is pleasantly conservatory-like with lots of hanging plants and tables placed well apart, and the cooking enhances rather than interferes with the fresh ingredients. Licensed. Mid price range.

The Cottage, 109 Wollombi Road, Cessnock, (049) 90 3026; the best restaurant in the town as opposed to among the vineyards, it consists of two unpretentious dining rooms in a renovated house where, once again, French style food of respectable quality is served. Licensed. Mid price range.

Old George and Dragon, 48 Melbourne Street, East Maitland, (049) 33 7272, occupies an 1837 inn, serves hearty French provincial food and has the best wine list in the district. Licensed. Mid price range.

Casuarina, Hermitage Road, Pokolbin, (049) 98 7590, goes perhaps a little further in other directions but the French still rule here. Has a delightful garden setting. Licensed. Mid price range.

The Satay Hut, Wollombi Road, Bellbird, (049) 90 1094; this South East Asian eatery in the Bellbird Hotel offers an escape from the French hegemony. Licensed. Low price range.

Peppers Guest House restaurant, one of the finest in the valley, is open for lunch seven days a week, see 'Where to Stay' for details. Licensed. Mid price range.

Wollombi Road

This old but driveable dirt road is an alternative route from the Hunter Valley to Sydney. It is mentioned here for its scenic value which very much surpasses that of the valley itself. The road winds like a snake around green hills and tiny valleys where unkempt and lonely farmhouses linger in the dusk. Handmade log fences along its sides show neglect in a place where nature is beginning to re-assert her authority. Driving it is like driving into another age.

EATING OUT

Le Café Wollombi, Wollombi Rd, Wollombi, (049) 98 3204; is not hard to find as Wollombi has only one big street and that's short enough. The restaurant is housed in a brightly decorated old weatherboard house and you can lunch on the balcony overlooking the valley and the few buildings which make up Wollombi. BYO. Low price range.

TOURS

The State Rail Authority runs a Hunter Discovery Tour in conjunction with the its fast XPT service to Newcastle. It picks up passengers from Newcastle and whisks them around the vineyards, stops for lunch and returns to Newcastle in time for an afternoon train to Sydney.

The coach companies AAT Kings, Australian Pacific and Ansett Pioneer run day tours to the valley from Sydney. The **Hunter Valley Vineyard Explorer** is a small bus service which tours the vineyards from the town of Rothbury, picking up passengers from surrounding motels, hotels, cabins and guesthouses; phone (049) 38 1573.

The Royal Newcastle Aero Club operates a range of aerial tours from its field at

Maitland, phone (049) 32 8888. Balloon flights over the Hunter are organised on weekends by Balloon Aloft, RMB 56, Hume Highway, Cross Roads, NSW 2170, phone (02) 607 2255.

Conducted weekend cycling tours of the Hunter Valley are available from Australian Himalayan Expeditions, 3rd Floor, 377 Sussex Street, Sydney, NSW 2000, phone (02) 264 3366.

Racing

Country race meetings are a long-standing Australian tradition and a great way to watch the nation's people indulging one of their universal passions. In the Hunter Valley they have the added attraction of showing off the region's fine bloodstock. There are country racecourses at Cessnock, Taree, Scone and Muswellbrook where meetings take place throughout the year. For information about specific race days, contact the Newcastle Jockey Club, phone (049) 61 1573.

Manning Valley

Between Scone and Taree lies the **Manning River Valley**. One hundred and fifty km (93 miles) of the river are navigable and in the nineteenth century it was the centre of a thriving timber industry. The piles of Sydney sandstone along its banks were dumped by timber boats which used them for ballast on their inward journeys before loading cargoes for return to the ports at Newcastle and Sydney. Nowadays its a recreational waterway. The **Barrington Tops** between Scone and Gloucester overlook the valley. Their height gives them an almost alpine climate good for horse riding and trout fishing. Wild horses (brumbies) are found in the more rugged parts. A walking track off the New England Highway between Scone and Murrurundi leads to Mt Wingen, a burning mountain which has been on fire for thousands of years. Aboriginal legend says that a man who lit a fire there was dragged off into the earth by an evil spirit and set the mountain burning as a warning to others.

Taree

The town of Taree at the north eastern tip of the Hunter was established in 1842 as a timber company town. When the railway arrived in 1913, it assumed its present role as a regional centre for dairying, meat, fruit, fishing, timber and tourism. The nearby stand of coastal rainforest called **Wingham Brush** is inhabited by thousands of flying foxes, a type of Australian native bat, which rise en masse into the evening air to go foraging for food from September to May. The Ellenborough Falls near Elands, north-west of Taree are one of the highest falls in the country.

TOURS AND CRUISES

Manning River Cruises runs two hour trips up the Manning River, (065) 52 4767.

Manning River Holidays Afloat, 36 Crescent Avenue, Taree, NSW 2430, phone (065) 52 6271, has houseboats for hire on the river.

White-water canoeing on the Barrington River as well as other adventurous pursuits such as abseiling and bushwalking are organised by **Adventure Outdoors**, P.O. Box 21, Tuncurry, NSW 2428, phone (065) 54 6429.

Short camping trips by four-wheel drive vehicles are available from **Manning Safaris**, Marchfield Road via Wingham, NSW 2429, phone (065) 53 4584. **Saddle Treks**, P.O. Box 14, Dungog, NSW 2420, phone (049) 92 1713, takes riders through the Barrington Tops on weekend as well as five-, six- and 12-day excursions.

The Coast

The Hunter coast and its attendant waterways, especially Lake Macquarie to the south of Newcastle and the Myall Lakes to the north, attract thousands of holidaymakers in the summer. Those of the locals who are not retired occupy themselves in commercial fishing and catering to visitors. The area is famous for prawns (shrimp) and oysters, the abundance and quality of which are celebrated in the **Myall Prawn Festival** on the second weekend in March each year. The festival includes an oyster punt race and the World Prawn Eating Competition among its cultural curiosities. A similar event, the **Forster–Tuncurry Oyster Festival** takes place on the October long weekend. Neither occasion is taken altogether seriously.

Historically speaking, cutting timber was the lifeblood of the coast in the early and mid-nineteenth century and opened the way for dairy farming to take over when the timber ran out. In the heyday of timber getting, steamers ran from port to port carrying loads of red cedar and regular boats brought passengers from Sydney to Newcastle and plied the Hunter and Manning.

GETTING THERE

Some trains to Newcastle stop close to the western shore of Lake Macquarie at Morrisset and Dora Creek ($9) but heading north from Newcastle, they swing away from the coast, by-passing the Port Stephens area and returning to the oceanside at Taree ($27.90). State Rail Authority Coaches run up the coast to Forster–Tuncurry from Newcastle, stopping at towns along the way.

Drivers will find that the Pacific Highway runs down the coastal side of Lake Macquarie south from Newcastle and north from the same city past Port Stephens and the Myall Lakes.

TOURIST INFORMATION

Tourist information centres are at Little Street, Forster, and Victoria Parade, Port Stephens.

Beaches

The beaches march up the coast from Lake Macquarie, past Newcastle and on to Port Stephens, Forster–Tuncurry and Taree, and the surf pounds away at them hard enough to have wrecked plenty of sailors in its time. They are wide strands of yellow sand, sometimes with hills covered in tough grass and low salt resistant shrubs and always with high green headlands between them. The largest is 40 km (25 miles) long, running from Hawks Nest to Seal Rocks. The Pacific Palms area

Egret

north of Seal Rocks has Elizabeth, Boomerang and Blueys Beaches, smaller but no less wild and beautiful, and Shelly Beach, a very secluded spot reached only by walking track from Elizabeth Beach. Swimming for the inexperienced is best done on weekends at beaches near the towns when there are lifesavers (lifeguards) around but surfers will want to work their way through the list given above.

Lake Macquarie

Lake Macquarie is the largest salt-water lake in Australia but, because close to Newcastle, is already surrounded by suburban sprawl—160,000 people live beside or near it. None the less, there are still many trees and some of the foreshore has been set aside for parks; a great quantity of 'boating facilities' such as launching ramps, wharves, pontoons and mooring are scattered around the lake shores. Recreational fishermen and sailors love it.

State route 133 to Morriset gives a relatively scenic run down the western shore of the lake. The small town of **Wangi Wangi**, reached by a short diversion about halfway along the route is famous as the location for a series of paintings by Sir William Dobell. It sits on a low promontory sticking out into the middle of the lake. In keeping with the area's uninhibited attitude to holiday accommodation, Wangi Point, the town's most picturesque and famous spot has been turned over to a crowded caravan (trailer) park. The prospect from the point retains the drama caught by Dobell who painted *Storm Over Wangi* there in the 1940s.

The Myall Lakes

These lakes north of **Port Stephens** are a wild contrast to Lake Macquarie and have been declared a national park. The park covers 31,000 hectares (76,600 acres) of which the lakes take up over 10,000 (25,000). They are mangrove edged and have ocean beaches on their eastern side. The best access to them is from the old timber

116

town of Bulahdelah on the Pacific Highway west of the lake system where house-boats can be hired and sailed down the Myall River into the lakes themselves. It is also possible to drive from Bulahdelah into the park but the unpaved roads can be dangerous in wet weather. The Myall Lakes attract large numbers of waterbirds including black swans, ducks and egrets; the land surrounding them is home to kangaroos, swamp and red-necked wallabies, possums, bandicoots, gliders and spiny anteaters.

Stroud

The nearest dose of colonial history is at Stroud where the local historical society has produced a Heritage Walk brochure with 30 significant locations marked on it. The surrounding countryside, part of the Great Dividing Range foothills is the kind of place where towns nestle rather than sprawl, memorable picnics are easily come by.

WHERE TO STAY

Since the area is so popular with local holidaymakers, the accommodation is largely aimed at families—motels and especially caravan (trailer) parks abound, many with on-site vans available for rent. The towns with the most accommodation are Lake Macquarie in the south and Forster–Tuncurry in the north, Nelson Bay near Port Stephens and Taree at the northern end of the coast also have plenty. Each of the other, smaller and often quieter towns has its one or two motels, a caravan park and the town pub.

Tudor House, 1 West Street, Forster, (065) 54 8766; is a guesthouse known for the quality of its food. It sits across the road from the beach and has eight rooms furnished in motel style with private facilities and balconies. There is a swimming pool but not very much garden. Oceanfront rooms $100.

EATING OUT

The wise eater is best advised to stick to seafood when dining along the coast. The area is famed for its prawns and oysters which should be eaten as fresh and plain as possible. In fact, they are best purchased at the fishermen's co-ops on the harbour fronts of most port towns. To·feel really Australian, eat your prawns on buttered fresh white bread and wash them down with a beer.

Cid's, Wharf Street, Forster, (065) 54 8055; has wide windows overlooking the river estuary and specialises in seafood. Licensed. Mid price range.

CRUISES

Day cruise boats on Lake Macquarie include the *Wangi Queen Showboat*, (049) 58 3211, and the MV *Marissa Anne*, (049) 59 1058. The *Nelson Bay Water Bus* tours Port Stephens and Tea Gardens, (049) 81 1887, as does the *Tamboi Queen* which also includes the Mayall Lakes, (049) 81 1959. A semi-submersible called the *Yellow Submarine* allows its passengers a view of the marine life in Nelson Bay, (049) 63 1701.

BOAT HIRE

Houseboats which you drive yourself can be hired from **Sunberg Holiday House-boats**, 60 Highfields Parade, Highfields, NSW 2289, phone (049) 43 1578 on Lake

Macquarie, and from **Mayall Lakes Houseboats**, 90 Crawford Street, Bulahdelah, NSW 2423, phone (049) 97 4221, on the Mayall Lakes. Cruisers (pleasure launches) are for hire on Port Stephens from **Lemon Tree Clipper Cruises**, P.O. Box 34, Lemon Tree Passage, NSW 2301, phone (049) 82 4027. The owners of houseboats and cruisers usually charge a basic hiring fee with extra costs for petrol and provisions added. Bare boat yacht charter on Lake Macquarie is available from **Marmong Cove Sail Cruise**, 11 Saint James Road, New Lambton, NSW 2305, phone (049) 57 1157.

Mayall Lakes Canoe Tours, Legges Camp, Bombah Point, NSW, 2423, phone (049) 97 4495, conducts two to six day camping and canoeing holidays on the Mayall Lakes.

The North Coast

Rainforest, waterfalls, river rapids, an old gaol or two, a lovers' breakwater and, of course, the shining sea are among the sights of this coast and its hinterland. Small beachside towns with a 'sans souci' air are interspersed among vast stretches of beach, each one named after its nearby headland: Crescent Head, Nambucca Heads, Evans Head, Brunswick Heads. The big towns of the North Coast are fishing ports, Port Macquarie in the south and Coffs Harbour halfway up, or prosperous rural centres with wide, generous streets such as Kempsey, Grafton, Lismore and Murwillumbah, placed 20 to 30 miles down river from the surf. Big, gentle rivers, the Clarence, Richmond, Nambucca, Hastings, Macleay and Tweed among them, run down from the high ground to the sea, creating shallow estuaries where fishing fleets shelter and pelicans sit like St Simeon on decaying wharf piles.

Where the rivers meet the sea, treacherous sandbars shift and change, waiting to wreck unwary sailors in their powerful surf. No sight on this coast matches a fishing fleet at first light riding the bar to the open sea or making that same risky traverse home with seagulls wheeling and cawing in its wake. To see it ask at the local wharf what time the boats go out, take your vantage on a head above the river mouth and, as the sun rises, you'll make close touch with the realities of life on a coast so often trivialised as yet another beer and skittles holiday playground.

In summer, at dawn or dusk, the beaches and the headlands have great power and mystery which tends to fade as the human world lifts its face into the heat of a full blown day. Unless you have a surfboard or a fishing rod tucked under your arm and a great deal of skill in the manipulation of either, summer on the endless beach can pall—well, after a week or two, and it does get hot! Still, there's always the pub, a cold beer and conversation with the locals.

The North Coast of New South Wales is a sub-tropical region stretching from the Hunter to Queensland. Its beaches, rivers and plateaux are best enjoyed during the in-between seasons of autumn and spring when humidity is lower, the sun kinder and the air clear but they have a superb climate throughout the year. The coast is long, over 800 km (500 miles), and can be conveniently divided into three parts, lower, mid and upper. Each part is dominated by a large coastal port providing a good base for exploring the surrounding beaches, historical sights and inland forests and towns.

The Lower North Coast

Port Macquarie is where the North Coast begins. It is a thriving coastal fishing port, thronged with holiday-makers whenever the weather is warm, especially during school holidays and in the early months of summer. The port began life as a penal colony in 1821, established to segregate the worst felons from Sydney and relieve Newcastle of having to intern them. The gaol was abandoned in 1830 and free settlers moved in establishing a small port. Trade grew sharply in 1840 when a road was cut from the New England tableland to the west causing the small town to become an important shipping centre for wool and timber.

GETTING THERE
East West Airlines flies to Port Macquarie from Sydney up to four times a day. The fare is ($104).

Port Macquarie is not accessible by rail but buses meet trains at Wauchope ($34.60), the nearest town with a railway station. The fare into Port Macquarie is around $4.

Port Macquarie is 13 km (eight miles) off the Pacific Highway to the east and Wauchope eight km (five miles) off the Pacific Highway to the west.

TOURIST INFORMATION
There is a tourist information centre in Horton Street, Port Macquarie.

WHAT TO SEE
Port Macquarie has a **museum** recalling its felonious past which is open from Monday to Saturday 9.30 am to 12.30 pm and 2 pm to 5 pm. **King Neptune's Park** at the mouth of the Hastings River, a ten minute walk from the town centre displays crocodiles, alligators and sharks. Its dolphins and sea lions give performances. Open daily 9 am to 5 pm, shows 10.30 am, 2 pm and 3 pm. Demonstrations of wood turning using rainforest timbers are given at **Old World Timber Art**, 120 Hastings River Drive, from 8.30 am to 5 pm Monday to Saturday and 10 am to 4 pm on Sunday. **Sea Acres Sanctuary**, three km (two miles) south of the town has 30 hectares of rainforest with marked trails and some wildlife about. Open daily 9 am to 5 pm. **Timbertown** at Wauchope, west of Port Macquarie, is a re-creation of a village from the days when cutting rainforest cedars was the economic lifeblood of the region. It has houses, shops, a sawmill, a steam railway and a newspaper office. Bullock teams drive through the town and costumed 'locals' demonstrate the crafts and working methods of the time including shingle splitting, pit sawing, wood turning and bullock driving.

WHERE TO STAY
Port Macquarie has over 40 motels which compete fiercely in off-season and drop their prices low but in summer they go up again as the rooms fill up. The following two places have something special about them.

Pelican Shores, Park Street, Port Macquarie, (065) 83 3999; on the waterfront two km (one and a quarter miles) from Port Macquarie town centre, high standard accommodation including double rooms and family suites. Every room has a balcony. Tennis courts. Swimming pool. Double $85 to $95.

Mount Seaview Resort, Oxley Highway, Yarra via Wauchope, (065) 87 7144; set on the banks of the Hastings River near Wauchope. It has motel style accommodation as well rooms without individual facilities. Single $18, double $22 share facilities, single $42, double $54 with facilities. Rooms with facilities also include kitchenettes.

TOURS AND CRUISES
Skennar's Coaches in Port Macquarie, phone (065) 83 1488, runs bus tours of areas surrounding the town. **Port Macquarie River Cruises**, (065) 83 3058, and the **Water Bus**, (065) 83 1293, take river cruises.

The Mid North Coast

This region is centred on the port of Coffs Harbour about halfway between Sydney and Brisbane, and is extremely popular with school holiday crowds. Hence it is thick with accommodation houses and 'attractions', ie, ways of amusing the children, and well-geared for travellers of all types. The wise will avoid it in high summer but in out-times such as spring and autumn when the kids are at school, it is quiet and there is room to appreciate its considerable beauties.

Coffs Harbour

The people of this town, one of the fastest growing in Australia, have seen fit to nominate it and its surroundings 'The Banana Republic'. Bananas are produced in vast quantities around Coffs Harbour.

Captain James Cook, who made sure he left none of Australia's eastern coast undiscovered, sighted the harbour while sailing north in 1770. Another seaman, Captain John Korff, first took a close look in 1847 when he sheltered there to escape the savage southerly storms which sometimes blow along this coast. His name was misspelled when government surveyors named the port in 1861 in preparation for the area's first permanent white settlers. The first and the hardiest were timber getters who came for red cedar, initially cut and floated down the region's rivers to the coast in the 1840s. They cleared the land and were followed by pastoralists, especially dairy farmers. A minor gold rush began in 1851 when the precious metal was discovered in the Clarence Valley. It petered out a little over 20 years later. Tourists appeared from as early as the 1880s, carried by coastal steamers from Sydney. Their arrival completed the main strands of the local economy which continue to support a very relaxed and prosperous population to the present day.

GETTING TO AND AROUND
Air NSW jets and Fokker Friendships fly from Sydney to Coffs Harbour every day. The fare is $107.

Trains run from Sydney's Central Station to Coffs Harbour at least four times a day between 8 am and 8.20 pm. The fare is $41.20 and the trip takes about 9 to 10 hours.

Drivers from Sydney or Brisbane take the Pacific Highway (National Route 1). The journey from either city takes about seven hours.

The town bus service runs to and from the Jetty, Park Beach and the town centre all days except Sundays and public holidays. Timetables are available from the Tourist Information Centre and the buses depart from Woolworths in Park Avenue. Taxis can be picked up from the High Street Mall.

Motor-cycles can be hired from Sports Motor-cycles, 70 Grafton Street (066) 52 7111 and bicycles from Fun Bikes, Northside Shopping Centre, Park Beach Road (066) 52 4593.

TOURIST INFORMATION
The tourist information centre is housed in a two-storey circular pavilion-like building in the middle of High Street Mall.

WHAT TO SEE
Coffs Harbour is a lively, modern town with a population of about 22,000. It has three sections, the town centre, the jetty area and the beaches. A pedestrian plaza with the Pacific Highway, also known as Grafton Street, at its western end, occupies the centre of town. It has lots of shops on either side and a tourist information centre in the middle. The post office is across Grafton Street. High Street heads east from the plaza, across the railway lines, to the jetty area and the main harbour where fishing and pleasure craft shelter behind a complex of massive, recently constructed breakwaters connecting the waterfront to **Mutton Bird Island**. The old wooden jetty, a relic from the late 1800s sticks forlornly out from Jetty Beach, abandoned in favour of the new shelter.

The green, wind-blown hump of Mutton Bird Island has been declared a wildlife sanctuary. A steep walking trail climbs from the breakwater to its summit. Though most often used by rod fishermen heading for the rocks on the seaward side, it is one of the finest places from which to look west over the town and east to the sea and the **Solitary Islands**, a group of small, uninhabited islands scattered up the coast. An easier look-out, approachable by car or foot, stands at the other side of the harbour on Victoria Street but is marred by the presence of a huge concrete tank.

High Street ends at the turn-off to the jetty. Orlando Street continues parallel with the railway line, across Coffs Harbour Creek where Ocean Parade leads off to the right and runs along **Park Beach**. The beach is fringed by a thicket of low trees which protects it from the road. It is Coffs' main surfing spot and runs north from the creek mouth to Macauley's Head, a wide, rocky headland covered with low scrub which gives access on its northern side to **Macauley's Beach**. Short tracks run from the roadside down to the sand. Walking tracks lead from one side of the headland to the other; there is no road over the headland. At low tide, it is possible to wade Coffs Harbour Creek and so walk from the harbour to Macauley's Headland.

The **North Coast Regional Botanic Garden** is located off High Street at the end of Hardacre Street, surrounded on both sides by arms of Coffs Harbour Creek.

121

It is open between 10 am and 5 pm. The Information Centre, next to the car park and open 10 am to 2 pm, provides brochures on how to identify plants used by the Aboriginal tribes who once inhabited the area and those the first settlers brought with them. There are displays of rare and endangered species and wild flowers. A picnic area has been constructed on the banks of the creek.

Amusements

Serious and idiotic amusements dot the Pacific Highway north of town. The **Big Banana** is the best known. It is a staggering bright yellow crescent stuck on a steep hillside three km (two miles) out of town in the midst of a banana plantation. Inside the banana is a photographic display showing how bananas are reared. A startlingly kitsch souvenir shop, a cheap clothes 'boutique' and a 'family' restaurant have been erected on either side of the piece of concrete fruit. The banana plantation is the real thing. Tractor borne tours of it depart regularly from the Big Banana. They climb through a jungle of banana trees while the ins and outs of banana cultivation are explained, and finish at a look-out which gives wide views over the town, the beaches and the islands. The **Orara East Forest Look-out** in Bruxner Park, off the highway a little further north, offers equal views in a natural setting where rainforest walks are possible and one may sometimes see lyre birds instead of bananas.

Further north are the **Kumbaigeri Wildlife Sanctuary** where you can cuddle koalas and see other native animals and the **Lake Russell Gallery**, the area's best art gallery which exhibits work by leading artists and craftspeople from throughout the north coast such as painters David Lane and Ken Delzoppo, potter Sandra Taylor and screen printer Lyn English. The gallery is housed in an award winning timber building beside Lake Russell and is open from 10 am to 5 pm every day.

WHERE TO STAY

Coffs Harbour could be called the town of a hundred motels and is well worth considering as a base for covering the whole mid-north coast. They cluster on the highway in and out of town and along Ocean Parade at Park Beach. There are a couple near the centre of town as well. Many display their rates on illuminated roadside signs which also tell you whether they have vacancies. Prices vary from about $30 to $40 a double per night, depending on the height of the season. Some bottom-of-the-market places drop as low as $25. The beachside motels have the best position but competition is fierce so their tariffs are not much more than the others. They are also close to restaurants and a popular pub called the Hoey-Moey.

Pelican Beach Resort, Pacific Highway, Coffs Harbour, (066) 53 7000; the place for a real splurge, about ten minutes drive north of Coffs. The resort has everything imaginable and is mostly in the best of modern good taste—a far cry from the decorative nightmares inside many a motel room. It is right on the beach. Family rooms are also available. Doubles $95 to $115.

Nautilus on the Beach, Pacific Highway, Coffs Harbour, (066) 53 6699; stands next door to Pelican Beach, fronting onto the same beach and is only a small step down in class. Its rooms come in four different sizes from doubles to three-bedroom suites. It has several tennis courts. Doubles $65 to $95.

Surf Beach Motor Inn, Ocean Parade, Coffs Harbour, (066) 52 1872; first motel on Ocean Parade, has clean but very basic rooms with private bath and a very helpful proprietor who knows the area well and can make useful touring and eating recommendations. Double $34.

Coffs Harbour Holiday Village, Park Beach Road, Coffs Harbour, (066) 52 2055; a new motel with a restaurant and limited room service. Better furnished than the Surf Beach. Double $47.

EATING OUT

Many restaurants cluster on **High Street** opposite the Treasure Island shopping complex. Most are licensed which tends to put the prices up and, perhaps because Coffs is a tourist town, there is an alarming uniformity to the cost of your dinner. Expect to pay about $20 to $30 each if you indulge in three courses. Lighter eating can let you out for around $12 to $16. At least there is variation in the available cuisines.

The Tandoori Oven, 398 High Street, Coffs Harbour (066) 2279; at the end of the strip, unfortunately beside the railway line, offers curries and tandoori. Air-conditioned. Licensed. Mid price range.

The Fisherman's Katch, 386 High Street, Coffs Harbour, (066) 52 4372; the strip's seafood specialist. BYO. Mid price range.

Chez Andree, 372 High Street, Coffs Harbour, (066) 52 5855; serves the best French food in town. BYO. Mid price range.

Oscars in the High Street Mall, a rather glossy nightclub-ish restaurant, offers a good value $15 set menu of French style dishes on some nights. Licensed. Low to mid price range.

There are many take away food shops, pizza bars and hamburger joints in and around town and motels with restaurants open to the public as well as guests.

A cheaper way to eat is to visit the **Fish Co-op** on the waterfront where freshly caught fish for barbecuing, or cooked prawns and crabs for a cold feast are sold from a small retail outlet next to the car park. The local yacht club in the same area has a good seafood restaurant.

TOURS

Tours around Coffs Harbour and its hinterland can be booked at the tourist information centre in the middle of High Street Mall. **North Coast Tours**, (066) 52 7193 operates a half-day excursion in and around the town for $16 and full day tours north to Grafton, south to Nambucca Heads and west to Dorrigo Plateau for $25. **Trents Tour and Hire Service**, (066) 55 2246 operates a seven-seater mini-bus on day tours to the same destinations and to Port Macquarie but the tours have a more personal quality. They cost $25. The **Coffs Harbour Aero Club**, (066) 52 2992 operates scenic flights throughout the Coffs area.

ACTIVITIES

Horse riding is available at **Kumbaingeri Wildlife Park** (066) 53 6246, 14 km (eight and a half miles) north of Coffs Harbour. Both trail rides and beach rides are conducted. They cater to various levels of skill. Bruxner Park Trails, Mt Coramba

Road, Coffs Harbour, (066) 53 6603, is another trail ride organiser and White Horse Riding School, RMB 42, Pacific Highway, Coffs Harbour, (066) 53 6343, will take you riding on a beach. Rides cost between $15 and $20 for around two hours in a conducted group.

Fishing trips from Coffs Harbour aboard the *Pamela Star*, a small ocean fishing vessel, can be arranged by ringing (066) 52 3045. **Wildwater Adventures**, (066) 53 4469, based in Bonville 14 km (eight and a half miles) south of the town, organises one day white-water rafting trips on the Nymboida River which drops from the Dorrigo Plateau rainforest over rocky rapids and through placid streams.

Wildwater Adventures, Lot 4, Butlers Road, Bonville, near Coffs Harbour, runs day rafting trips on the Nymboida River, riding the rapids in 14-foot rubber dinghies through gorges and rainforest from the Dorrigo Plateau to the sea. The trips take place on Wednesday and Friday, lunch is provided and bookings on (066) 53 4469, are essential.

Urunga

The small town of Urunga lies on the Bellinger River about 15 minutes drive south of Coffs Harbour. The road into town from the Pacific Highway runs along the riverside, past the estuary and out to **Hungry Head Reserve** which gives access to a beautiful beach chosen by boardriders for the quality of its surf. The reserve has parking space, picnic tables and fire places. There is also beachside parking. In the tiny township, the wide verandas of the fine old Ocean View Hotel look out over the turquoise water of the estuary to Urunga Island, a flat sand island in the river mouth.

WHERE TO STAY
Spartan **cabins** sleeping up to six people with a cooking areas and bathrooms are set in the reserve on Hungry Head close to the beach. They cost $40 per day or $100 a week in the low season. The same daily rate but a weekly cost of $185 is charged in school holidays and at Easter. Phone (066) 55 6208.

BOAT HIRE
There are two boat hirers in Urunga, **Urunga Marine Centre** under the Pacific Highway bridge a short distance along the Urunga turn-off, and **Urunga Boat Hire** on the estuary opposite the town tennis courts. They rent out row boats and motor boats for periods from an hour to a day or two for trips up river. Costs range from around $8 an hour to $20 per four hours for motorised craft. Row boats are about half the cost. Urunga Boat Hire also has windsurfers.

Bellingen and Dorrigo

In Bellingen and Dorrigo one comes especially close to the beginnings of white history on the north coast. The towns are hardly much more than 80 years old and it is still possible to meet the sons of pioneers who continue to occupy sections taken up and cleared by their fathers in the early 1900s. They live side by side with new settlers, refugees from big cities, many of them artists and craftspeople who came in the 1970s. The land itself is beautiful both in the rolling fields where calm cattle graze by the Bellinger River and especially in the remaining stands of giant rain-forest preserved in Dorrigo National Park.

GETTING TO AND AROUND
There are no trains to this area. The only bus service from Coffs Harbour is the daily school bus. Drivers should take the Pacific Highway south from Coffs Harbour to the Bellingen turn-off.

TOURIST INFORMATION
The Bellingen tourist information centre is in Doepel Street but Coffs Harbour tourist information office is more reliable.

Bellingen

The drive into Bellingen from the Pacific Highway runs along the left bank of the Bellinger River through rolling dairy farms with the Dorrigo Plateau rising in the western distance. The village itself stands on a hill overlooking the Bellinger River and its old, single lane, wooden bridge. There are green picnic grounds on the river bank and a lovely small island in mid-stream below the town. Bellingen's appearance is little changed from its early twentieth-century beginnings. Hyde Street which runs through the centre of town is flanked by shops and public buildings dating from the 1910s whose wrought iron decorated awnings shade the footpaths.

The old **Butter Factory** on the southern outskirts, built at the turn of the century when dairying was prosperous enough to justify it, has been taken over by wooden toy and furniture makers. It has a restaurant in the front of the main building, a herb garden and a Japanese garden in the grounds. Other artists sell their work from the Yellow Shed, nearer the main town. Pottery, paintings and woodwork make up the bulk of the display. Potters and other craftspeople work in the building while you shop and are happy to talk about their crafts.

WHERE TO STAY
Bellinger Valley Inn, (066) 55 1599; ordinary but comfortable motel units in a very beautiful setting one km (half a mile) west of Bellingen, looking out on the mountains. Single $37, double $46.

EATING OUT
Boiling Billy, Church Street, Bellingen, (066) 55 1947; uses local ingredients to good, simple and light effect. BYO. Low price range.
Oasis Cafe, (066) 55 2150; in the Old Butter Factory is simply furnished and generally unpretentious but has a fireplace for cold nights and an original and inexpensive menu. Its hours are a little unreliable. BYO. Low price range.
Mario and Martha's, Brierfield Street; hole-in-the-wall pizza and pasta eatery. BYO. Low price range.

In keeping with the proclivities of Bellingen's new settlers, there is a 'whole' food bar next to Mario and Martha's which has some tables on the footpath. It is very popular with local youth.

TOURS
Horse Drawn Discovery Tours take you around the town in a big tram-like carriage drawn by two draft horses. They include billy tea and damper at the Old Bellingen Saddlery where the tours depart between 10 am and 4 pm each day, weather and horses permitting. Phone (066) 55 1110. Tours cost $10.

ACTIVITIES
Bushwhacker Expeditions and Tours, based in Thora, a small town halfway between Bellingen and Dorrigo, operates canoe trips on the Bellinger River. Lunch is provided on the trip which begins in Thora at 9.30 am and finishes there at about 5 pm. They also hire out canoes and conduct rainforest walks. Phone (066) 55 8607 for bookings which are essential.

Dorrigo

While Bellingen hides in the valley made by its river, Dorrigo is folded around low hills on the top of a plateau where that river has its source.

GETTING THERE
Dorrigo is only accessible by car. The road through Bellingen continues to Thora where it begins to wind its way up the Dorrigo escarpment on a fairly tortuous drive, punctuated by glorious views of the valley and the sea.

Dorrigo National Park
About halfway up the mountain you enter the Dorrigo National Park, noted on a roadside sign. Public access to the park is from a roadside visitors' centre and ranger headquarters at the top of Dorrigo Mountain about four km (two and a half miles) east of Dorrigo township.

Dorrigo National Park is what remains of the rainforest that once covered this entire region and was logged out of existence by cedar getters and pastoralists. The life of these men was extremely hard and their work deadly dangerous. The trees of a rainforest are locked together by vines, some as thick as an ordinary tree trunk. Felling a 30- or 40-metre forest giant in such conditions can mean bringing a good measure of the surrounding growth down around your head. To avoid injury and death, axemen had to be extremely skilled and knowledgeable. They needed endurance and toughness as well, if only to bear their atrocious living conditions. Housed in rough camps pitched on the site of their work for six or seven months without a break, they depended on each other for company and, sometimes, life itself. Few ever became rich. The logs they cut, hauled by bullock teams to local mills, fetched a few shillings per super foot and the money often went on grog and women.

Richard Craig, an escaped convict, was reputed to be the first white man to explore the Dorrigo forests. When recaptured he offered to lead a party back into them to show the giant red cedars he had discovered there. Until he came the local Aboriginals had lived and hunted undisturbed for tens of thousands of years but his expedition soon led to a rush for the 'red gold' growing on the plateau. The natives were driven out without concern for the niceties of race relations. The forest which makes up Dorrigo National Park is among the few areas never to have been logged. It was saved by virtue of its steep hillsides which made the timber virtually impossible to bring out. Today it is given over to bushwalkers and picnickers.

The National Parks and Wildlife Service roadside visitors' centre at the top of Dorrigo Mountain contains a display showing implements used by nineteenth-century loggers, telling the story of Richard Craig and giving information about the forest animals and birds. Walking maps are also available in the centre.

Walks

Walking in Dorrigo National Park is an exhilarating experience. Tracks are well-marked and easy and the open forest floor means there is lots to see. **Wonga Walk** leads from The Glade, a picnic area near the visitors' centre, to Crystal Shower and Tristania Falls, a circuit which takes about two hours to complete. It runs through thick rainforest for the whole of its length past gigantic red cedars, yellow carabeen, rosewood, tallowwood, blackbutt and crab apple trees. Many of the trees are marked with their common and botanical names as are the vines which cling to their trunks. The track descends gently to Crystal Shower Falls about a kilometre and a half (a mile) from The Glade. The falls drop straight over a protruding rock ledge into a small round pool edged by spherical boulders. Thick-leaved vines grow in the midst of the falling water and hang below the ledge. The track crosses behind and underneath the falls so walkers can look through the vines and the sunlit falls down the steeply sloping creek bed which dips away into the forest, bounded by towering trees. Tristania Falls, further downstream, drop down a stairway-like wall and run under a wooden bridge. They mark the low point of the track which then begins a climb back up to The Glade through gullies scattered with mossy boulders and shot with green light.

A further 13 km (eight miles) of walking tracks taking in more waterfalls branch from the **Never Never Picnic Area**, 11 km (seven miles) into the park. It can be reached via a road leading from the visitors' centre. This area is more isolated and much further from the road and so presents more opportunity for a quiet, observant walker to see the pademelons (small wallabies), swamp wallabies, possums, lyrebirds, brush turkeys and bower-birds that live in the park.

Dorrigo Town

The town of Dorrigo is relatively undistinguished but it does have a small **museum** run by the local historical society which displays bric-à-brac, photographs and documents from the area's early days. They include photos of opening day at the Bellingen Butter Factory and of early settlers' families. A display of polished rainforest woods has been erected in a small room and Aboriginal tools are displayed in the entranceway. The museum is open from 11 am to 3 pm each day and is staffed by members of the society whose connections with Dorrigo date back to early this century. They can often be more interesting than their collection. Admission is 50 cents. There is also a grand but tatty old pub in the town.

WHERE TO STAY

The Lookout Motor Inn, (066) 57 2511, sits on the top of Dorrigo Mountain a very short distance east of the park entrance. It is large, new, comfortable and has spectacular views of the surrounding hills, the valley and the coast. A restaurant, bar, recreation room and 20 acres of grounds complete the facilities. Doubles $48 to $65. Surcharge during holiday periods.

EATING OUT

Dorrigo is not known for its restaurants. Wise diners prefer Bellingen.

The Nambucca Valley

This valley, about 40 minutes drive south from Coffs Harbour on the Pacific Highway is fed by the Nambucca River which joins the sea at Nambucca Heads. The towns of Macksville, Taylors Arm and Bowraville are worth a short visit when touring the valley.

Nambucca Heads

The town of this name is set on a hill overlooking the Nambucca River estuary, a short distance east of the Pacific Highway. It's barren contemporary style belies a fascinating history of coastal steamers and river boats which carried logs, dairy produce and passengers to and from Sydney and Newcastle as well as up river to Macksville and Taylors Arm.

GETTING THERE

Some but not all trains to the north coast stop at Nambucca Heads and Macksville ($38.40) although Nambucca Station is a fair distance from the township. Pell's Bus Service runs from Nambucca Heads to Macksville Monday to Friday and on Saturday mornings. They also run a bus to Coffs Harbour at 9.30 am each Thursday. There are no services on Sundays or public holidays.

TOURIST INFORMATION

There is a tourist information centre in the foyer of the School of Arts Hall, Ridge Street.

WHAT TO SEE

A small weatherboard **museum** next door to the RSL Youth Club on Nambucca Headland displays many photographs from that era including the wreck of the steamer *Nambucca* on South Beach in 1944 which presaged the end of Nambucca Heads as a coastal port. There are earlier pictures of the now demolished government wharf in its heyday. The museum is open from 2 pm to 4 pm on Wednesday, Saturday and Sunday.

Nowadays Nambucca's **beaches** attract surfers rather than sailors. Main Beach on the southern side of the headland is long, wild and open. It can be threatening to inexperienced swimmers but it has great grandeur. Shelley Beach, nestled under the lee of the headland on the northern side is smaller and quieter. It has safe swimming in clear, shallow water between rocky outcrops. Nambucca Heads beach itself is patrolled by lifesavers from the local Surf Lifesaving Club on weekends and, during school holidays, by local council life-guards. The best places to go surfboard riding are Nambucca Heads near the river entrance and along Main Beach.

The **Vee Wall** at the river mouth across White Albatross Lagoon is a burst of comic relief. Visitors are allowed to paint messages and slogans on the piled rocks and concrete blocks that compose it. The wall was begun in 1895 and continued on and off, mostly off, until finished by work gangs of unemployed people during the Depression. The messages cover all states of love and communication from 'menage à trois' to 'hello grandma'. The wall is at the end of Wellington Drive near the White Albatross Caravan Park.

WHERE TO STAY

Not a great deal of choice as Nambucca Heads is close enough to Coffs Harbour and Port Macquarie for most travellers to be just passing through. The worryingly named **Nirvana Village Motel**, Riverside Drive (065) 68 6620, has about the most convenient location for beach access but, as is often the case in beachside towns, all other good locations are taken up by caravan (trailer) parks. There are other motels are on the Pacific Highway a little outside town. Singles generally around $40, doubles $50.

Backpackers can stay at the **Nambucca Backpackers Hostel** in Newman Street, (065) 68 6360.

EATING OUT

A surprising number of restaurants survive, one presumes, on customers provided by the seven or so large caravan parks in and around Nambucca Heads which have no restaurants of their own. There are two good BYOs:

Matilda's, Wellington Drive, is a pretty lattice-covered building with tables on side veranda. Serves steaks and seafood without doing them too much damage. BYO. Low price range.

Grapevine Restaurant, Ridge Street, does much the same in not such pleasant surroundings. BYO. Mid price range.

TOURS

One of the best reasons for dropping in on Nambucca Heads is the *Nambucca Princess* which cruises the river on Tuesday, Wednesday, Thursday, Friday and Sunday. There are two-hour afternoon cruises and lunch cruises. The twin-hulled boat departs from a small wharf behind the RSL Club and takes you up river to Macksville through the dairying country. Passengers can sit on the open upper deck in sunny weather or inside if they prefer. Phone (065) 68 6922 for bookings.

ACTIVITIES

Boats for estuary fishing or just mucking about in can be hired from Nambucca Marine in Wellington Drive and The Beachcomber in Riverside Drive. The former also has paddle-boats and canoes and the latter aquabikes and sailboards. For **tennis court** hire phone (065) 68 6138.

Conducted **horse riding** along bush trails is available at Waldene Farm on Newee Creek, eight km (five miles) from Nambucca Heads. Phone (065) 68 1282.

Macksville, Bowraville and Taylors Arm

These are the three other towns of interest in the Nambucca Valley. Each has one or two reasons for a quick visit but they are not places in which to spend more than a couple of hours. They can probably be covered in a single day out from Nambucca Heads when you're not heading for the beach.

Macksville is sited on the Nambucca River where the Taylors Arm River branches off to the south-west. It can be reached by driving straight down the Pacific Highway from Nambucca Heads. The journey takes about 15 minutes. The town's main attraction is Mary Boulton's Pioneer Cottage, a replica of a wooden house typical of those inhabited by the valley's pioneers at the middle of last century. The building is set in a pretty garden next door to the home of its curator, Mary Boulton, a descendant of a pioneering family.

Its construction of rough-sawn timber, in part without nails which were scarce and expensive at the time, is a very accurate reflection of how the pioneers built. The cottage has two rooms, a bedroom and a combined kitchen and living area. Its wooden floor and indoor fireplace make it relatively luxurious. The interior is furnished with original objects from the time and contains all that the valley's first permanent white residents needed to create a home. Horse-drawn vehicles and old farm implements are displayed in a shed at the the rear of the cottage.

A half-hour drive north-west of Macksville brings you to **Bowraville**. The town's High Street is unchanged from last century with palm trees down the middle and rows of quaint veranda posts supporting the shop awnings on either side. Sullivan's Hotel, built in 1912 and still carrying all its glorious wrought iron, is the street's grandest sight.

The **Eliza and Joseph Newman Folk Museum**, housed in and around a cavernous old warehouse at the northern end of High Street, is unashamedly junky but also fascinatingly eclectic. Its collection includes an Irish settlers' tiny slab hut re-assembled, complete with furniture, inside the building, a 100-year-old white weatherboard church, a blacksmith's shop, horse drawn and steam driven vehicles and farm implements, a 1928 Dodge car in less than mint condition, a German World War II contact mine found off Nambucca Heads, the superstructure and façade of a wooden boarding house run by one P. Gibson during the late 1800s, a wool wagon, buttons, coins, medals, bottles, musical instruments and a 'Food for Britain' poster dated 12 July 1946 showing two thin and desperate children of the mother country. Open every day. Admission $1.

River Bend Farms, in South Bank Road on the way to Taylors Arm, is a complex of three dairy studs owned by the Brown family. The family opens its property to visitors on Sundays between 2 pm and 4 pm or by special arrangement, for demonstrations of what happens on a dairy farm. During holiday periods the farm is opened at the same times on Wednesday and Friday as well. Cost for the tour is $3 which includes afternoon tea. Phone (065) 69 6103.

Taylors Arm, about 40 minutes' drive south-west of Macksville is the site of an Australian legend,The Pub With No Beer, celebrated in song by Slim Dusty. These days the old country pub, actually called the Cosmopolitan, has plenty of beer. Its bar is decorated with memorabilia from the history of Australian country music, especially anything relating to the famous song; the neat lawns and occasional brick barbecue and picnic tables around it attest to its popularity with tourists. After all, who would pass up the chance to have a drink in the bar of the Pub With No Beer?

South-West Rocks

This town sits next to a very pretty small beach called Horseshoe Bay much favoured by families in search of safe swimming for their children. The much larger Trial Bay stretches away from the town to the east. Its unusual aspect makes it very popular with sailboarders, especially at its sheltered end under the lee of Laggers Point. The small settlement of Arakoon occupies the eastern end of Trial Bay.

GETTING TO AND AROUND
South-West Rocks is approached by turning off the Pacific Highway at Clybucca about 35 km (22 miles) south of Macksville. Trains do not reach the town.

Once in South-West Rocks, you'll find that most of the places mentioned here are within walking distance of the town.

Trial Bay Gaol
Laggers Point is the site of Trial Bay Gaol, a monument to the well-intentioned folly of the New South Wales government and its agencies at the turn of the century. The gaol is unused except as an occasional film set and has been so since the end of World War I. It is preserved by the National Parks and Wildlife Service as part of the Arakoon State Recreation Area and is well worth visiting. Despite its oppressive atmosphere, it was the result of a prison reform movement which began in the 1860s and sought to rehabilitate the best behaved inmates of the prison system by teaching them skills useful in the outside world. It was thought that prisoners sent to Trial Bay could be employed in the construction of a breakwater to provide a storm refuge for coastal shipping. Gaol construction, from locally quarried pink granite, was begun in 1877 after many years of debate and planning but the building was not ready to receive prisoners until 1886 after continual delays and cost overruns not to mention the death of the original contractor. Work on the breakwater, the original reason for building a prison, did not begin until 1889. During the intervening years, the prisoners added to their own prison while the planners re-assessed and changed the direction of the breakwater.

The giant blocks of stone, one weighing over 36 tons, of which the breakwater was made were quarried from a nearby hillside and carried to the shore on horse drawn rail trucks. It took a year to project the breakwater 63 metres (206 feet) into the bay. By 1902 its length was 299 metres (981 feet) but during the same period, washbacks had demolished a nearly equal length so that continual reconstruction was required.

The last straw was a huge storm in 1903 that reduced the main body of the wall to a shapeless mass. To make matters worse, by that year the entrance of the Macleay River had moved south and was considerably safer and the average coastal steamer was a much less dangerous vessel altogether. The entire project was abandoned and the gaol closed down in July 1903. It did, however, have a last hurrah when German nationals were interned there during World War I. They were a select band of highly-educated single men who whiled away their years of rather lax imprisonment with musical and theatrical pursuits and the enjoyment of extraordinarily beautiful natural surroundings. They were none the less decidedly chagrined at their cruel fate as relics of the internment displayed in the prison museum show.

The strongest impressions left on the contemporary visitor are the sheer folly of it all, the sound of the sea without the sight of it and the steady wind that penetrates all parts of the ruin despite its high stone walls.

Smoky Cape Lighthouse

Lighthouse Road leads from Arakoon to the area's other architectural monument, the Smoky Cape Lighthouse. It has enjoyed a longer and more useful life than the prison, shining since 1891. Both the lighthouse, the tallest on the New South Wales coast, and its surrounding buildings are protected by the National Trust. The Cape on which it stands was named by Captain James Cook for a fire he saw burning there on his journey up the coast in 1770. The road up to it through **Hat Head National Park** is unsealed and, after wet weather can be a mite challenging but the journey is rewarding. Beneath Smoky Cape is a truly unspoiled beach to which the road branches just before climbing up to the lighthouse. A walking trail through the surrounding scrub leads to a waterfall which drops into a sandy pool only a few metres from the surf. The lighthouse is open Thursdays only from 10 am to 11.45 am and from 1 pm to 2.45 pm.

WHERE TO STAY

Costa Rica Motel Resort and Lodges, Gregory Street, South-West Rocks, (065) 66 6400; has standard motel units and a lodge with a kitchen for self-caterers but you must supply your own linen and blankets. The motel has squash courts and a salt-water swimming pool. Single $27 and $37, double $35 and $45, includes light breakfast.

Motel South-West Rocks, Gregory Street, South-West Rocks, (065) 66 6330; similar standard to the above. Single $25, double $30.

Arakoon House, 2 Russell Street, Arakoon, (065) 66 6116 or (02) 437 6926; is a Victorian two-storey residence with wide verandas and lies a short walk from Trial Bay and the Arakoon State Recreation Area. It contains four two-bedroom units, each of which will accommodate up to five people. The daily rate is $25 plus a cleaning fee of $14 on departure.

EATING OUT

There are few restaurants not attached to motels in South-West Rocks. Two are **Benito's** in Livingston Street and **Gerry's Steakhouse** in Arakoon but otherwise you're limited to the motels. Try the **Bayroom** at Motel South-West Rocks if you want to eat in licensed premises. The dining room at the **South-West Rocks Country Club** in Phillip Drive is also open to the public.

ACTIVITIES
Boats are for hire at Leisure Craft Marine, New Entrance Road, South-West Rocks (065) 66 6192. The same place sells fishing tackle and bait.

Upper North Coast

Swathes of agricultural richness formed by the Clarence, Richmond and Tweed River Valleys typify the far North Coast from Grafton to the Queensland border. Along the coast, the beaches continue. Those around Byron Bay are the most famous and accessible. In the far north near the Queensland border is the glorious Scenic Rim, a range of mountains, high hills and valleys full of towering rainforests and misty hollows, where the hard light of the coast is softened and tinged with enchantment.

Clarence River Valley

The Clarence is the first of the great north coast rivers which rise in the Great Dividing Range and take meandering courses to the coast. It starts life in Queensland and winds 400 km (248 miles) through grazing country down to a rich coastal plain where it spreads widely enough to accommodate more than one hundred islands.

GETTING TO AND AROUND
East West Airlines flies daily from Sydney to Grafton. Fare $138. Grafton is also a major stop on the Sydney to Brisbane train line and the terminus for XPT services to the Far North Coast ($41.20).
. Coaches from the Gold Coast and Brisbane run to Grafton and Maclean and Kirklands Coaches run daily from Lismore to Grafton and Maclean.
The Pacific Highway from Sydney and Brisbane runs through Grafton as well as Maclean at the head of the Clarence River, a short distance from the coast.

TOURIST INFORMATION
Tourist information is obtainable in Grafton from a centre on the corner of Duke and Victoria Streets, close to the river. National Parks information is available from the NPWS headquarters at 50 Victoria Street, Grafton.

Grafton

This town of around 17,000 people was settled on the Clarence River in the 1850s and 60s and was originally a timber getting centre. It is renowned for its streets lined with Jacaranda trees that bloom lilac in spring and a festival is held in their honour on the last week of October each year. The town has many historic buildings including its **gaol** built in 1893 and, until recently a maximum security prison. It still houses less dangerous prisoners. **Christ Church Cathedral**, built in 1884, is the city's main religious building. It stands on Duke Street. **Schaeffer House Museum** in Fitzroy Street holds a comprehensive collection of artefacts recalling the exploration and development of the North Coast. It occupies an elegant homestead built in 1900. A large colony of fruit bats inhabits the nature reserve on **Susan Island** in the Clarence River.

Merino Mac's Agradome on the Pacific Highway 25 km (15 and a half miles) south of town is a sheep theatre which presents an hour long demonstration of shearing, wool classing and sheep dog cleverness at 2 pm on Tuesdays and Thursdays and at 11 am on Sundays.

WHERE TO STAY AND EAT
There are seven motels in Grafton and another six in Yamba as well as a couple in Maclean.
Motel Camden Lodge, 17–25 Villiers Street, Grafton, (066) 42 1822; comfortable motel rooms, restaurant, swimming pool, air-conditioned. Single $40, double $50 with loadings during school holidays.
Fitzroy Motel, 27–29 Fitzroy Street, Grafton, (066) 42 4477; a slightly lower standard than the previous establishment, no swimming pool but has air-conditioning and video machines. Single $34, double $40 with loadings during school holidays.

CRUISE
Clarence River Cruises, (066) 42 4835; leave from the Wharf One at the end of Prince Street in Grafton and cruises around some of the river islands including Susan Island and Woodford Island. Cruises take place on Tuesday, Thursday and Sunday and cost $8, lunch is extra. They leave at 11.30 am and take two hours.

Maclean and Yamba

Maclean, much closer to the river mouth than Grafton, is home to the local fishing fleet which trawls as much as 50 km (31 miles) upstream during the prawning season. Trawler owners can sometimes be persuaded to carry interested spectators on their morning runs. Their 6 am start may sound daunting but a prawner's breakfast of freshly cooked prawns and cold beer is the reward for such early rising. The fleet shelters on the western side of the levee wall in River Street. Maclean is also a **sugar-growing** town and, during the harvest season from May to December, whole fields of cane are set on fire to clear the pests before cutting. You won't forget the sight.

Yamba is a small coastal settlement west of Maclean which shelters the local ocean fishing fleet. It is also a popular holiday place for amateur fishermen who cast into the river from walls and dinghies. Oysters are grown here in quantity and although they mostly go to the overseas and metropolitan markets, some can be bought in the town. The town surf beach is patrolled in the summer months. **Micalo Island** off Yamba is the site of a prawn farm where salt-water ponds hold millions of fat crustaceans awaiting export to Japan.

National Parks

The Clarence Valley has two good coastal parks, Yuragir and Bunjalung and a highland park called Gibraltar Range, west of Grafton. **Yuragir** covers the coast east of Grafton and south of Yamba. It is in three sections and has succeeded in protecting most of the coast from development. Small villages on the park outskirts at Brooms Head and Wooli have camp sites, caravan (trailer) parks and motels. The section closest to Yamba has Angourie Point on the eastern side where surfers regularly risk their necks. Fresh-water swimming is possible at the Blue Pool, a few metres from the ocean. The pool was once a quarry but filled with water when an underground spring was exposed during mining. Wooloweyah Lake is a salt-water lagoon on the western boundary of the park where more sedate swimming is possible. Four-wheel drive vehicles can be hired at Yamba for journeys into Yuragir.

Bunjalung lies to the north of the Clarence, covering 38 km (23 and a half miles) of coastline between Iluka and Evans Head. Ten Mile Beach, in its centre, is approached by Gap Road, an unsealed 21 km (13 miles) track which breaks off from the Pacific Highway south of Woodburn. You will find there, as the name implies, ten miles of wide white surf beach which hopefully won't have been used as a racing track by reckless Range Rover drivers. The southern tip of the park encloses a section of the Iluka Peninsula where there is still water swimming as well as some fine surf beaches. **Gibraltar Range**, 72 km (45 miles) west of Grafton on the Gwydir Highway, takes up part of the large forest on the eastern margin of the New England Tablelands. It has an extraordinary skyline studded with huge outcrops of granite, bearing names like Old Man's Hat, Anvil Rock and the Needles. They are accessible by walking tracks and information about them is available from the park headquarters on the Gwydir Highway where there is also a picnic area.

Richmond River

That part of the North Coast around the next major town, Lismore, on the north arm of the Richmond River, includes the coastal towns of Ballina and Byron Bay and the inland 'hippie havens' of Nimbin and The Channon. Before, and since, hippies were called alternative lifestylers, this area has drawn such people from urban disillusionment to an imagined Rousseau-esque primitivism which, in present times, has gained a commercial, gently image-conscious edge. Bustling outdoor **markets** take place at Bangalow on Byron Creek on the fourth Sunday of each month and at The Channon on Terania Creek every second Sunday. The town of Nimbin has become so closely associated with 'alternatives' that the mere mention of its name expresses an entire life-style. The area is also home to many older rural Australian traditions which have managed, with intermittent tension, to tolerate and even learn from the dreaded hippies while by no means giving up their white Anglo-Saxon ways. While mantra's and murals on shopfronts and community centres, health food cafés, buskers and men with long hair are typical, there's still a solid right-wing vote in this area.

GETTING TO AND AROUND

Air NSW flies daily from Sydney to Casino from where the airline runs a shuttle bus service into Lismore. The airfare is $140.

Trains from Sydney stop at the towns of Lismore and Byron Bay ($46.80).

Kirklands coaches (02) 281 2233 run services to and from Sydney ($38) and Brisbane ($17.50) to Lismore as well as coach services from Lismore to other Far North Coast towns including Byron Bay ($4.80).

The Summerland Way from Grafton to Casino gives access to Lismore via the Bruxner Highway which then rejoins the Pacific Highway to Byron Bay. Access to this area of the New South Wales North Coast from Brisbane is via the Pacific Highway.

TOURIST INFORMATION

There are tourist information centres in Ballina Street, Lismore and in the Ballina Maritime Museum, La Balsa Plaza, Ballina on the Richmond River bank.

Lismore

Lismore is the rural centre of this district and is a prosperous but not a pretty town. It was the last point on the Richmond River to which the timber and trading schooners could come during the mid 1800s and thus became an important river port for shipping logs out of the 'Big Scrub'—the rainforests full of red cedar to the north and west. The town has an **historical museum** which holds a photographic collection covering its early days and Aboriginal artefacts from the *Bundjalung* tribe which inhabited the area before the whites took over. The museum is in Molesworth Street and open Tuesday to Friday, 10 am to 4 pm, admission costs 50 cents. The **Lismore Regional Art Gallery** where local painters exhibit is housed in the same building and is open Tuesday to Friday 10 am to 4 pm and Saturday 10 am to 1 pm. Admission is free. **Minyon Falls**, in the Minyon Falls Flora Reserve, Whian Whian forest, drop 400 feet into a palm filled gorge where there are lovely picnic spots. An **Aboriginal Bora ring**, once the site of sacred ceremonies, is located at Tucki cemetery, 16 km (10 miles) south on the Lismore to Woodburn Road. Nineteen km (12 miles) north at the town of Dunoon is Australia's largest **macadamia nut plantation and processing plant**. Inspections take place from Monday to Thursday 9 am to 3 pm and on Friday from 9 am to noon. The factory operates from May to December.

Nimbin Area

Nimbin lies about 30 km (18½ miles) north of Lismore and is the access point for **Night-cap National Park**. The park has good walking tracks, many of which once served pioneers driving pack horses between Lismore and Murwillumbah to the north. **Terania Creek Track** travels through a forest of Bangalow palms to **Protesters Falls** named for the conservationists who defended its surrounding rainforests from timber interests. There is also an enjoyable walk to **Mt Nardi** which gives a panorama of the surrounding coast. The mountain can also be reached by sealed road from Nimbin.

Ballina and Byron Bay

These are the two main coastal towns in this area. **Ballina**, 32 km (20 miles) east of Lismore on the Pacific Highway, has a **maritime museum** which shows how tough life was for nineteenth-century seafarers along this often unkind coast. The *Atzlan*, a balsa wood raft which drifted from Ecuador to Australia in 1973 as part of the Las Balsas expedition is also on display there. The town has many commercial art and craft galleries.

Byron Bay, about 30 km (18¹/₂ miles) north of Ballina, is more beloved of surfers than any other spot in NSW, even the taxis have surfboard racks. Byron's beaches face in different directions so whether the wind is blowing from the north or south, the waves still run. **Cape Byron** stands between the two beaches. Its tip is the easternmost point in Australia and accommodates the **Cape Byron Light**, constructed in 1901 and still going strong.

A well-established and signposted walking trail runs between **Captain Cook Look-out,** a short drive from town and the lighthouse, crossing the cape. The track leads down from the look-out to the beach and up again across the narrow, hilly and scrubby cape to the lighthouse. It can be traversed in the opposite direction as the light is also accessible by car. Cape Byron Light itself is not open to the public but anyone is welcome to wander the grounds where it and its surrounding buildings stand. Although architecturally undistinguished, the white painted buildings are kept in perfect order even to their blue chimney pots, the light, standing at the highest point on the cape, towers over them all.

A paved walk with three **look-outs** brings visitors from the light to the tip of the cape and Watego's Beach. The first look-out allows you to watch the Cape Byron goats clambering around the cliffs inches from a precipitous drop into the boiling sea. They are descendants of a herd which provided meat and milk for the original lighthouse keeper. The second look-out is for whale watchers. In winter, humpbacked whales migrate from the Antarctic and they can be seen passing Cape Byron in May and June. The last look-out stands at the easternmost point in Australia and overlooks Watego's Beach and Julian Rocks where large schools of dolphins can be seen playing in the surf.

Watego's Beach is a gem dropped neatly on the end of the cape and bounded by rocky outcrops at either end. It is not big but perfectly placed and to my mind is the most beautiful of Byron Bay's beaches. The paved track continues from the final look-out down to Watego's. **Julian Rocks** break the surface of the water some metres beyond the cape's end. They mark the point where cold southerly and warm northerly ocean currents meet and are occupied by a unique variety and combination of marine life from huge warm water tropical species, such as the Queensland gropers which occupy a sea cave among the rocks, to migrants from the chilly south.

Byron Bay township has a touch more sophistication than some of its North Coast counterparts but, because it is heavily influenced by the counter-culture, this self-awareness extends more to health food shops and vegie burgers than fashionable clothes or flash cars. Shops and supermarket windows are plastered with posters offering every conceivable form of psychic and spiritual reconstruction and the people pay more attention to conservation than they do to work.

WHERE TO STAY

Lismore is not a tourist town and offers little accommodation. Byron Bay and Ballina are better geared to receive visitors.

AZA Motel, 114 Keen Street, Lismore, (066) 21 9499; basic brick, three storey, no frills motel close to the centre of town. Air-conditioned. Double $39.

The motels in Lawson Street, Byron Bay have the advantage of being not too far, but far enough, away from the town and fairly close to Main Beach.

El Greco Motel, 32 Lawson Street, Byron Bay, (066) 85 6090; a smaller establishment but with comfort which places it close to the top of the motel range. Swimming pool and restaurant. Single $32 to $48, double $42 to $58. Holiday surcharge.

Byron Motor Lodge, corner Lawson and Butler Streets, Byron Bay, (066) 85 6522; is a pleasing homestead style low rise structure facing wide lawns near the beach. Single $40 to $90 (high summer), double $45 to $90.

Byron Bay Arts Factory Lodge, Skinner Shoot Road, Byron Bay, (066) 85 6197; is a 'young' place to stay in the grounds of Byron Bay Arts Factory. The factory is the town's centre of entertainment (usually rock and roll) and popular with surfers. Shared accommodation from $7.50 per night. Some family rooms available.

EATING OUT

There is fairly wide choice in Byron Bay and Ballina since they attract the tourists. Most of Byron Bay's restaurants are in Jonson Street which runs from the beach through the centre of town. About five minutes walking is enough to cover its length.

Il Duomo, (066) 85 7320; a *tavola calda* restaurant offering traditional Italian cooking, set in a pretty garden and possibly the only place on the far North Coast serving true *gelato*. Licensed. Mid price range.

Café Oz, light and airy place occupying a wide shopfront, specialising in breakfasts, snacks and light meals, locally popular. BYO. Low price range.

Annabella's Spaghetti Bar, down an arcade of Jonson Street, offers various spaghetti and basic Italian fare at high counters where you sit on stools. Also takeaway. BYO. Low price range.

South Indian Curry House, a very small restaurant close to the beach offering curries not authentic enough to do you any damage. BYO. Low price range.

Byron Bay Arts Factory, Skinner Shoot Road, Byron Bay, (066) 85 7276; lots of entertainment here including a dinner theatre and dancing. Food is from the sea. Licensed until 3 am. Low to mid price range.

In Ballina's restaurants the menus feature seafood, especially lobster (never cheap) and an occasional steak.

Ballina Beach Hut, Compton Drive, East Ballina, (066) 86 4221, offers a reasonable value seafood platter. BYO. Low price range.

Scampi's Restaurant, 181–183 River Street, Ballina, (066) 86 2267; here you can choose your lobster live from the tank—if you can stand the thought of it cooking. Licensed. Mid price range.

Don Valentin's Restaurant, 196 River Street, Ballina, (066) 86 2775, serves surf and turf (lobster on a steak) as well as plain seafood and has its own way of treating lobster. Licensed. Mid to upper price range.

There are also two good restaurants serving French influenced food outside the main towns.

Janot La Frite, 33 Byron Street, Bangalow, (066) 87 1181; light French cuisine including some uncommon ingredients such as pheasant, also seafood. BYO. Mid price range.

The Black Cockatoo, 26 Pacific Parade, Lennox Head, (066) 87 7392; lovely place close to the sea. Nearest thing to *Australienne* in the area. BYO. Mid price range.

CRUISES AND DIVING

The *Richmond Riverboat* runs lunch and dinner cruises up the Richmond River from Lismore Quay, phone (066) 21 3710.

The *Richmond Princess* sails from Ballina on Tuesday, Thursday and Sunday, (066) 86 3669, and MVB Charters operates cruises from Lismore Quay which include meals, (066) 21 3710.

Byron Bay Sportscene in Lawson Street, Byron Bay runs daytime dives on Julian Rocks at 9 am, 11 am and 1.30 pm.

The Tweed Valley

This river valley, not so grand as those lower down the North Coast but giving way in the mountains to some magical scenery, marks the end of New South Wales and the beginning of Queensland.

GETTING TO AND AROUND

The airport closest to the Tweed Valley is at Coolangatta on the southern Gold Coast in Queensland. It is only a short distance from Tweed Heads and all the major carriers land there every day from Sydney. The fare is $166.

The Pacific Coast Motorail Express train from Sydney terminates in Murwillumbah ($49.60).

Coaches run every day from Brisbane to Tweed Heads and Murwillumbah. Kirklands serves Murwillumbah and Tweed Heads/Coolangatta from Sydney ($38).

Drivers travelling in both directions should remain, as usual, on the Pacific Highway.

TOURIST INFORMATION

Tourist Information Centres are on the Pacific Highway in Tweed Heads and in Alma Street, Murwillumbah.

Tweed Heads

Tweed Heads, the northern tip of the New South Wales North Coast, is on the Queensland border and the advantages, penalties and eccentricities of such proximity are expressed in its life. The town has two enormous poker machine clubs, the Twin Towns Services Club placed 100 yards from the border, and Seagulls Rugby League club on the shores of Lake Terranora, both supported to the tune of close to $100 million a year by Queenslanders whose law bans one arm bandits but not border crossing. Tweed Heads is so close to the Queensland town of Coolangatta that it is more truly part of the brash and brassy Gold Coast than the quiet fishing and farming villages of northern New South Wales. Summer daylight saving which prevails in New South Wales but not in Queensland means a walk across the road makes you an hour younger or older. Since, culturally, they are more part of the Gold Coast than of the New South Wales North Coast, the gambling and nightlife of Tweed Heads are covered in the chapter on Queensland.

The **Minjungbal Aboriginal Cultural Visitors Centre** is the most interesting feature of the town. It stands in Kirkwood Road, South Tweed Heads, and is the site of a *Bora Ring* where males were intiated into the local tribe. A display in the centre gives details of how Aboriginals lived in this sub-tropical region showing what plants they gathered and how they hunted and fished as well as what tools they made. Cultural matters, including Aboriginal associations with Pacific Islanders brought to Queensland as indentured cane workers in the late 1800s, are also covered. The centre is open between 10 am and 4 pm Wednesday to Sunday and admission is $1.

WHERE TO STAY AND EAT
Accommodation and food in Tweed Heads/Coolangatta are covered in the Queensland chapter on page ??.

Murwillumbah

Murwillumbah, the town set below Mt Warning on the Tweed River and once a major timber centre still serves the rural interests of the Tweed valley. **Mount Warning**, 1756 metres (3500 feet) high was named by Captain James Cook as a navigational marker for a dangerous place on the coast. It is possible to climb to its peak, now part of the Mt Warning National Park, from Breakfast Creek a few miles north of Murwillumbah. The return walk takes four hours and is hard; chains attached to the final ascent are a help and the view from the top is fitting reward. The lower section of the walk travels through an imposing forest of giant red cedars. **Uki Village**, 11 km (seven miles) south-west on the road to Kyogle, is a rural valley settlement which retains much of the character of former times. A bazaar takes place there on the third Sunday of every month.

WHERE TO STAY
Murwillumbah Motor Inn, 17 Byangum Road, Murwillumbah, (066) 72 2022; quite a bit of astro-turf and concrete paving here also lots of plastic outdoor furniture but clean and comfortable. Rooms of ordinary and deluxe standard. Single $27, $40, double $32, $45.
Tweed River Motel, Pacific Highway, Murwillumbah, (066) 72 3933; close to tourist information and railway station. Swimming pool. Standard motel units looking out on the motel car park. Single $30, double $35. Holiday surcharge.

Mount Warning Lodge Country Resort, Mount Warning Road, Mount Warning, (066) 79 5161, is placed in 97 hectares (242 acres) of forest where activities include river swimming, riding, canoeing, bushwalking and gem fossicking. The resort has a 'colonial' restaurant which serves unpretentious but good quality fare. The accommodation is in basic prefabricated units. Single $32, double $48 bed and breakfast.

FARM STAYS
Midginbil Hill, Uki, via Murwillumbah, (066) 79 7158; a 400-acre property selected in 1904, specialising in horse-riding holidays. Accommodation in a lodge where each room has private facilities or at a campsite. Lodge $49 per person per day full board.
Tyalgum Tops, Top End of Tyalgum Creek Road, Tyalgum, via Murwillumbah, (066) 79 3370; almost on the border of New South Wales and Queensland at the base of the McPherson Ranges, this holiday farm offers horse riding, general farm activities, bushwalking, fossicking and similar outdoor pursuits. Accommodation is in five self-contained units with kichens. Each holds six people. Double $35. Linen extra, no meals provided. Store on the property.

EATING OUT
There are few restaurants in Murwillumbah but it is possible to eat in the dining rooms of the **local clubs**. Remember their hours are short and early, usually 6.30 pm to 8.30 pm or less and the food will be plain—roasts, grills and such like but the prices are low. The major clubs are Murwillumbah Services Memorial Club, Wollumbin Street, (066) 72 1388 and Mirwillumbah Golf Club, Byangum Road, (066) 72 4041. For a change, try:
Riverside Seafood Restaurant, 51 Pacific Highway, Murwillumbah, (066) 72 2921; serves fresh seafood plus daring stuff like pork fillet in strawberry sauce. Licensed. Mid price range.
Avocado Land, at Duranbah about 15 km (nine miles) north of Murwillumbah is an interesting place to visit if you have food in mind. It's the avocado equivalent of Coffs Harbour's Big Banana, a farm where tourists are invited to see how avocados are grown, and it has a dining room and sandwich bar that strive to extend the use of avocados further than you believed possible. Open 9 am to 5 pm daily.

TOURS
Pinnacle Four-Wheel Drive Tours, (066) 72 2698; takes one day guided tours of the Tweed Valley rainforests picking up from Tweed Heads at 8.15 am and Murwillumbah at 8.45 am. Bookings from Peter Weekes Real Estate, 131 Main Street, Murwillumbah. **Off The Beaten Track** in Dalley Street, Mullumbimby, (066) 84 2277, also operates four-wheel drive tours in the district's forest.

The Scenic Rim
This name is given to the high country which runs along the border of Queensland and New South Wales where the McPherson Range juts out from the Great Dividing Range. The **Border Ranges, Lamington, Gwongorella** and **Warrie**

National Parks are strung out along this startlingly beautiful border country which has many high green hills, cloud-topped when the weather is wet, and deep valleys where mist gathers in the early morning. The railway line from Lismore to Brisbane runs through this enchanted country as does the back road to Nerang and the Gold Coast. If you are continuing to Queensland from New South Wales, this route is well worth your consideration.

The South Coast

The South Coast begins at Nowra about 160 km (100 miles) south of Sydney and stretches to Eden 560 km (350 miles) further south. Its countryside is characterised by white sand beaches, bright blue seas and grassy hillsides populated by dairy cows. Fishing of all kinds from dropping a line off a wharf or a river bank to chasing Black Marlin in the open sea, is the chief recreation and occupation along its entire length. Those locals not engaged in commercial fish harvesting are mostly dairy farmers and timber getters.

The South Coast is a temperate region which people from Melbourne think warm enough for holidays but which Sydney folk often scorn in favour of the hotter north. Why they do so is a mystery since the south lacks nothing in beauty when compared to the north. The South Coast is at its best in summer when it is cooler than the tropics and less humid. In colder seasons the days are often fine but late afternoon can call for a sweater. In general there is less domestication on the south coast, the beaches are wilder and the highlands mistier than other parts of New South Wales.

Captain James Cook was first to sight the coast in May 1770 on his way north to Botany Bay. Its next exploration took place in the 1790s when naval surgeon and explorer, George Bass sailed down from Sydney. The south coast's first settlements were whaling stations at Eden which supported a bay whaling industry similar to that begun in Tasmania during the first decade of the 1800s.

Nowra to Bateman's Bay

Nowra is 159 km (99 miles) from Sydney and can be seen by stretching a day trip to the Wollongong area, although it marks the point where a day can easily turn into overnight or more. The area's greatest feature is the beautiful Shoalhaven River which has some dramatic cliffsides and crunchy river beaches. Painters and water-skiers love it.

GETTING THERE
Trains run from Sydney to Bomaderry (the station for Nowra) several times a day. The fare is $10.60. Drivers take the Princes highway from Sydney.

TOURIST INFORMATION
Shoalhaven City Tourist Centre, Princes Highway, Bomaderry, (044) 21 0778, is the place to go for information in the Nowra area. Bomaderry is the southern part of

Nowra town. The tourist centre in Bateman's Bay is also on the Princes Highway, (044) 72 4225.

Nowra

This substantial town, built on the banks of the Shoalhaven River is the commercial centre of the South Coast. The river winds its way down from the mountains through forests and grazing land. It is wide and inviting and there are beaches along its lower reaches. The best land views are from **Ben's Walk** which leads to Hanging Rock, an outcrop jutting over the Shoalhaven, and from **Cambewarra Look-out**. The town also has a naval aviation museum at the **HMAS Albatross Air Station**. Open every day. There is an animal park in Rockhill Road, open from 9 am to 5 pm every day. The town also has a botanic garden.

WHERE TO STAY
Pleasant Way Motor Inn, Pleasant Way, Nowra, (044) 21 5544; is a new motel on the banks of the Shoalhaven River just past the Princes Highway bridge. Has family units, an indoor heated pool and riverside restaurant. Single $36 to $40, double $40 to $44.

EATING OUT
The Baker and Bunyip, 23 Prince Alfred Street, Berry, (044) 64 1454; is close to the coast just north of Nowra. It carries a good selection of Australian and French vintage wines. The menu changes every week but is based on local seafood backed up with unusual meats such as venison and spatchcock. Licensed. Mid price range.

Resort Towns

Coastal resort towns near Nowra are Shoalhaven Heads, Sussex Inlet, Huskisson and Jervis Bay of which the last is home to the Australian Navy's Officer Training School. The **beaches** of Jervis Bay, especially Hyam's beach have, according to the *Guinness Book of Records*, the whitest sand in the world. One of them, Vincentia Beach, is nudist. Nowra gives access to the Southern Highlands via beautiful **Kangaroo Valley**. There are superb picnic spots along the Kangaroo River and a picturesque castellated suspension bridge at Hampden.

Milton/Ulladulla and Bateman's Bay

The towns of Milton and Ulladulla, 48 km (30 miles) further south have combined into one. Camping, swimming and fishing are available at Conjola Lake to the north and Burrill Lake to the south, where boats can be hired. Lake Tabourie **Museum** 16 km (10 miles) south of Ulladulla displays Aboriginal artefacts. **Bateman's Bay**, 53 km (33 miles) down the Princes Highway at the foot of Clyde Mountain has fishing trawlers for hire, cruises operate on the **Clyde River** and there is a bird sanctuary at Batehaven, five km (three miles) south, through which you can take a train ride. Much of the land which surrounds the Clyde is wildlife sanctuary. At Pebbly Beach tame kangaroos and wallabies will eat from your hands.

WHERE TO STAY

Mariners Resort Motel, Orient Street and Beach Road, Bateman's Bay, (044) 72 6222; is on the waterfront and has easy access to the centre of town. Single $33 to $39, double $39 to $47.

Reef Motor Inn, 27 Clyde Street, Bateman's Bay, (044) 72 6000; has some rooms which look across Clyde Street to a river bank park. Family units with cooking facilities available. Single $38 to $60, double $46 to $75.

CRUISES

Merinda Cruises and Charters, (044) 72 610, in Batehaven near Bateman's Bay, runs cruises up the Clyde River.

Clyde Valley

The gold rush of the 1850s which saw tens of thousands of prospectors descend on the South Coast was concentrated on the Clyde River, especially around the towns of Araluen and Nelligen. During the 60 years of its gold-mining prosperity, the **Araluen Valley** was famous for bushrangers such as the notorious Clarke Gang; nineteenth-century novelist Ralph Bolderwood set his *Robbery Under Arms* in the valley, writing for a time at the village of Kiora. Gold panning still takes place at Nelligen.

Moruya and Bega

The dairying industry comes into its own as one moves further south towards Bega, one of New South Wales' important cheese producing areas. Gold rush days are recalled at Central Tilba in the mountain foothills where many mid-nineteenth-century buildings remain.

GETTING THERE

Air NSW flies to Bega from Sydney ($107). The railway from Sydney finishes at Nowra from where the Pioneer Bus Service operates to towns as far south as Eden. State Rail Authority coaches run from Bungendore ($21.60) on the Goulbourn Line south-west of Sydney to Moruya and Bega.

Ansett Pioneer coaches run to Bega from Canberra. The fare is $25 and the trip takes close to three and a half hours. Drivers simply continue on the Princes Highway.

TOURIST INFORMATION

Tourist information is available from the Council Chambers in Moruya, the Bega Tourist Centre, Gipps Street, Bega, and the Bermagui Tourist Information Centre in the town post office.

Moruya Area

The granite which makes up the Sydney Harbour Bridge pylons was quarried at **Moruya** 27 km (17 miles) south of Bateman's Bay. The town has many historic buildings and a good surf beach. **Narooma**—the name meant 'clear water' in the local Aboriginal language—is the next coastal town and fishing port. It is built on a hilly peninsula overlooking the ocean, the river and the inlet which constitutes its port. **Montague Island,** just off the coast, was also granite quarry and contributed to the facade of many a Sydney building. The island is now occupied by a lighthouse surrounded by a wildlife sanctuary with penguins and seals inhabiting its northern end, circumnavigation but no landing allowed.

Central Tilba

Central Tilba, 16 km (10 miles) south, is an old gold-mining and grazing town. Its picturesque setting and good state of preservation have encouraged the National Trust to declare it an historical village and several mid-nineteenth-century buildings have been restored. The town also has a cheese-tasting bar in the main street. Tilba Valley Wines on the shores of Coruma Lake has tastings and a barbecue area. Mt Dromadery, the highest mountain on the New South Wales coast (792 metres: 2600 feet) stands behind Central Tilba. It can be climbed by four-wheel drive or partly by car and on foot.

Bermagui

Bermagui, off the highway past Central Tilba, is the South Coast's game fishing centre and has been so since the 1930s. Game fishing boats set out from the harbour with fishing parties aboard in search of marlin. Book one day ahead to join a boat, all gear is supplied. Durras Lake north of the town is popular for boating and fishing. The coastal road from Bermagui to Bega is not all sealed. If you don't like dirt roads return to the Princes Highway along the same route which leads into the town.

Bega

The inland dairying centre of Bega is the main town on the far South Coast. A cheese making plant on the northern side of the Bega River is open for inspection from Monday to Friday. There is a town museum on the corner of Auckland and Bega Streets. Kameruka Estate, off the Princes Highway between Bega and Merimbula, is a 2225-hectare (5500-acre) property which began life in 1834 and is now the largest rural enterprise in the Bega Valley, famous for its cheddar style cheeses. It is open daily. The hamlet of Candelo, 22 km (14 miles) south-west of Bega has an historic convent and a museum, both are open every day. The nearest beach is at Tathra, 18 km (11 miles) east of Bega.

WHERE TO STAY
There are four motels on the Princes Highway at Bega as well as more around other towns such as Narooma and Bermagui.
Princes Motel, Princes Highway, Bega, (0649) 21 944; on the highway south of the town centre. Single $33, double $39.
Bega Village Motor Inn, Princes Highway, Bega, (0649) 22 466; single $33, double $39.

EATING OUT
The **Northside Motel**, Old Princes Highway, North Bega, (0649) 21 640, has a licensed restaurant.

Merimbula and Eden

These two towns are 26 km (16 miles) apart right at the bottom of the south coast close to the Victorian border and are popular with holiday-makers from that southern state. Eden is also a major fishing centre whose history dates from the early nineteenth century when whalers worked the oceans between the southern corner of Australia and New Zealand.

GETTING THERE
Air NSW flies from Sydney ($107) and Kendell Airlines from Melbourne ($116) to Merimbula. Air NSW also flies from Sydney to Eden ($107).

Trains from Sydney run only as far as Nowra from where the Pioneer Bus Service schedules coaches as far as Eden. State Rail Authority Coaches run from Bungendore on the Goulburn Line as far south as Eden.

Melbourne to Sydney Greyhound coaches on the coastal route are allowed to set down passengers from interstate in Merimbula. The fare from Melbourne is $29.50. The Sapphire Coast Bus Service also runs from Melbourne to Merimbula. The Princes Highway continues through both towns.

TOURIST INFORMATION
There is a tourist information centre in the Merimbula town centre and on the Princes Highway South, Eden.

Merimbula

Merimbula, the most popular of the South Coast resorts is 26 km (16 miles) south of Bega. It is a prominent tuna-fishing port where the sophistications of the industry include spotter planes for sharks and fish. Boats can be hired along the waterfront and cruises joined for journeys in Merimbula and Pambula Lakes, where there are rich oyster leases, and up the Pambula River. Merimbula has a museum accommodated in an old school house and at nearby Pambula there is a crafts centre housed in 130-year-old building called, of all things, Toad Hall. Sixteen km (10 miles) south of Merimbula in the Ben Boyd National Park stands a rock formation known as The Pinnacles. There is a commercial wildlife park about eight km (five miles) north of the town which is open daily from 9 am to 5 pm.

WHERE TO STAY
Black Dolphin Motel, Princes Highway, Merimbula, (0649) 51 500, looks across the Merimbula Lake and has the ocean behind. Single $32 to $40, double $38 to $50.
Hillcrest Motor Inn, 97 Princes Highway, Merimbula, (0649) 51 578, is north of the main town but has one of the best views along the whole south coast, looking

down from a hilltop to a crescent of white beach. Single $42 to $44, double $46 to $49.

Kingfisher Motel, 105 Princes Highway, Merimbula, (0649) 51 595, occupies a similarly lovely position but is slightly less expensive. Single $35, double $44.

EATING OUT
The Black Dolphin Motel, listed above, has a licensed restaurant.

Eden

Eden, the last of the South Coast's towns and its best known fishing port, is also the centre of the region's wood chipping industry which is fast consuming local timber resources. A century of whaling which ended in in the early 1900s has left its marks on the town. Ben Boyd, the best known of the whalers, who was also a pastoralist and banker, built Boydtown on Twofold Bay, Eden's harbour, in the 1840s as a whaling centre. All that remains intact of his great project is **The Seahorse Inn**, a distinctive old white hotel which is open 9 am to 5 pm each day.

The whalers of the mid-nineteenth-century made strange bedfellows. Each year, one week ahead of the great migration of whales to the Antarctic, killer whales would gather in the bay. As their prey moved south past its mouth, some killers mustered in the unfortunate beasts to where others tried to drown them by hurling their bodies over the whales' air vents. The whalers joined the slaughter without ever having to pursue their quarry in the open ocean. The **Whale Museum** in Boydtown shows to what extent the symbiosis could go. It contains the giant skeletons of the killers, the teeth of one worn away by its habit of dragging whaling boats to the kill. The relationship was sealed in a gruesome pay-off, the whalers took the blubber and meat; the epicurean killers ate only the lips and tongues.

Wallaby

147

WHERE TO STAY
Halfway Motel, corner Princes Highway and Imlay Street, Eden, (0649) 61 178; is a two-storey average motel with the advantage of an ocean view from some rooms. Single $32, double $40.

EATING OUT
Light meals are available at the **Seahorse Inn**.

TOURS
Edwards Coaches, (0649) 61 780, of Eden runs a number of day and half-day coach tours in the area around Merimbula travelling as far as Bega Valley and including Ben Boyd National Park. They also run cruises on the Pambula River. The **Snug Cove Ferry Service**, (0649) 62 027, travels around Twofold Bay.

National Parks
The South Coast has seven national parks: Morton located south of Fitzroy Falls and so mostly in the Southern Highlands which has camping grounds with facilities blocks at Fitzroy Falls and Bundanoon; Murramarang a narrow coastal strip between Ulladulla and Bateman's Bay where kangaroos and wallabies are common, camping at Pretty and Merry Beaches, Pebbly Beach and North and South Durras; Deua west of Moruya which has wild rivers and offers remote camp sites, bushwalking and canoeing; Wadbilliga along the Tuross River which has a gorge and waterfall; Ben Boyd, north and south of Eden, fishing, swimming, bushwalking, camping; Mt Imlay south-west of Eden which has views from the mountain and delightful bushwalks; Mimosa Rocks, a small park north of Bega, swimming, fishing, bushwalking.

The Snowy Mountains

The Snowies, among them Mount Kosciusko, the country's tallest peak, are the only real alps in Australia. They are a wild, relatively unpopulated and unproductive expanse of open country which supports ski resorts in the winter, wild flowers in summer and is home to a huge hydro-electric system throughout the year. Australia's most famous bush ballad, *The Man from Snowy River* by Banjo Patterson, is set in the mountains. It tells a story of brumbies (wild horses) chasing over the steep and treacherous mountainsides and how the outstanding horsemanship of an unknown mountain man brought back a valuable colt where more reputed horsemen failed. Although the waters of progress have blotted out some hillsides where these mountain riders chased their brumbies, the wild horses still run on those that remain.

Winter snows are often unreliable and thin but in good seasons offer good skiing. At such times people flock to the mountains from Sydney in their thousands and don't baulk at paying exorbitant lift fees. Skiing gear can be hired at any ski shop in

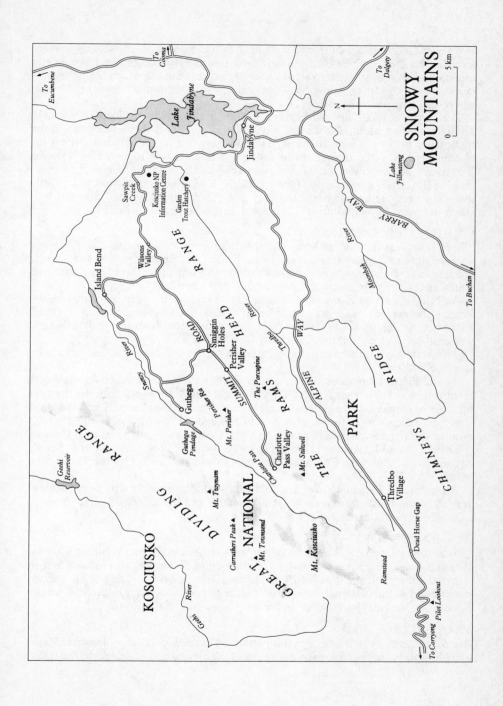

SNOWY
MOUNTAINS

5 km

N

To Dalgety

To Cooma

To Eucumbene

Lake
Jindabyne

Jindabyne

Sawpit
Creek

Kosciusko NP
Information Centre

Garden
Trout Hatchery

Island Bend

Wilsons
Valley

RANGE

ROAD

Smiggin
Holes

Perisher
Valley

SUMMIT

Snowy River

Guthega

Perisher Rd

Mt. Perisher ▲

The Porcupine
▲

HEAD

RAM'S

Perisher River

Charlotte Pass

Charlotte
Pass Valley

▲Mt. Stilwell

Thredbo River

ALPINE

WAY

Lake
Jillmatong

Moonbah River

BARRY WAY

To Buchan

THE

PARK

RIDGE

CHIMNEYS

Geehi
Reservoir

KOSCIUSKO

RANGE

Guthega
Pondage

Mt. Twynam ▲

Carruthers Peak ▲

NATIONAL

GREAT

Mt. Townsend ▲

▲Mt. Kosciusko

DIVIDING

Geehi River

Thredbo
Village

Dead Horse Gap

Ramstead

Pilot Lookout

To Corryong

Sydney or Cooma, the main large town near the ski resorts. Skiers who are used to Europe, the USA or New Zealand fields will find the Australian alps have shorter downhill trails, not such steep slopes and more trees than the much higher mountains of those countries. Some New Zealand fields, for example, begin at the height where those in Australia end.

P. E. Strzelecki, a Polish adventurer, was the Snowies' first explorer. Arriving in 1840, he named Mount Kosciusko after a Polish hero and wandered through the mountains nursing a broken heart. He had been prevented from marrying his chosen love by class differences in Poland. Strzelecki was followed by Thomas Townsend who surveyed the mountains in 1846 and by gold-discoverer the Reverend W. B. Clarke who examined their geology in 1851–2. But they proved of little interest to anyone except horse trappers and cattlemen until the 1950s and '60s when the huge Snowy Mountains Hydro-Electric Scheme was built.

GETTING TO AND AROUND
There is a great deal of traffic to and from the Snowy Mountains during the ski season (June to September), especially on Friday and Sunday nights, as it's quite feasible to take a skiing weekend from Sydney and very attractive to take one from Canberra. Transport drops off considerably in the summer.

Air NSW flies from Sydney to Cooma daily throughout the year. The fare is $104. During the ski season services increase on Friday, Saturday and Sunday. Kendell Airlines operates from Melbourne to Cooma daily throughout the year with extra weekend services during the ski season. The fare is $108.

The State Rail Authority runs a train/coach service to Cooma via Canberra. The fare is $31.50.

Ansett Pioneer operates coaches from Sydney to the snowfields via Canberra from June to October each year. They go every day of the week with the greatest number of services down on Friday nights and Sunday mornings. The last stop is Perisher Valley with a free shuttle bus to Smiggin Holes thrown in. The fare is around $45 from Sydney, $30 from Canberra. Coaches also meet planes at Cooma.

Drivers should take the Hume Highway from Sydney and join the Snowy Mountains Highway at Cooma. Tyre chains must be carried by law during the winter.

Thredbo and Perisher Valley are linked by an underground train called Skitube. It runs continuously from 6 am to 6 pm each day and less frequently from 6 pm to midnight. The return fare is $9.

TOURIST INFORMATION
Information centres for the Snowy Mountains are located in Sharp Street, Cooma; Petamin Plaza, Jindabyne; Thredbo Resort Centre, Thredbo; and Fitzroy Street, Tumut. Information about bushwalking and cross-country skiing trails can be obtained from the National Parks and Wildlife Service in Sydney or direct from the Kosciusko National Park Office in Sawpit Creek, phone (0645) 62 102.

WHAT TO SEE
Almost the entire mountain region is contained in the **Kosciusko National Park**, at 6900 square km (4278 square miles) one of the biggest national parks in Australia.

In the short skiing season from July to early September, the slopes around Thredbo, Charlotte Pass, Perisher, Smiggin Holes, Guthega and Mt Selwyn fill with weekend trippers; in the long summer, temperatures can soar to equal those in other parts of Australia and bushwalking is the main attraction. There are over 15 walking trails in the park for which the recommended season is November to April.

Ski Resorts

There are four well established resorts of which Thredbo Alpine Village is by far the biggest.

Thredbo

This is the only resort to bring in tourists winter and summer although winter ones predominate by far. It sits at the foot of Mt Crackenback, a little below the snowline and is the oldest, most established and best ski resort in Australia. Really a small town, it has lots of ski lodges, eating and drinking places and a couple of year-round accommodation houses. There is a main chairlift and a number of tows up the mountain. The chairlift which carries skiers in winter continues to operate in summer for the convenience of sightseers and walkers. Thredbo promotes itself as a conference and bushwalking centre when it is not overrun with skiers.

Perisher Valley

There are 40 km (25 miles) of trails here and a lift which rises higher than any other in Australia (2030 metres, 6660 feet). Perisher is a notch below Thredbo in entertainment facilities but argument rolls back and forth over which has the best runs, the award for variety going to Perisher.

Smiggin Holes

A companion resort to Perisher and not very far away. Shuttle buses run between the two and tickets combining use of the facilities at both are available.

Charlotte Pass

Charlotte Pass is in a lonely spot at the base of Mt Kosciusko where the roads can be deep under snow, requiring slow snow cat transport in. A good spot if you want to spend a week or so on the snow but rather inaccessible to weekend skiers. Cross-country skiing is done from here as well as downhill.

Cross-country

Cross-country skiing is often better than downhill in the Snowies because they are not tremendously high but offer long overland trails with enough downhill to keep you busy. This kind of winter bushwalking, provided it's done in a party, is safe and fascinating since it gives a view of Australia that few visitors ever expect to see. It is mainly done in the Cabramurra and Mt Selwyn areas. Organised cross-country skiing expeditions occur throughout the winter months.

Wilderness Expeditions, 100 Clarence Street, Sydney, (02) 27 8744, and 26 Sharp Street, Cooma, (0645) 21 587, organises all sorts of adventurous pursuits in the Snowy Mountains. They include cross-country skiing, white-water rafting and hiking tours. Trout-fishing trips can be arranged through Trout Trips, P.O. Box 374, Tumut, NSW 2720, (069) 47 1128.

The Mountains in Other Seasons
In seasons other than winter, especially in spring, the mountains open their rugged heart to walkers, riders and motorists. Walkers can tramp from the top station of the Thredbo chairlift to the peak of Mt Kosciusko. Merrit's Nature Track is a two hour downhill walk from the summit through fields of snow daisies, sunrays, buttercups and other alpine wild flowers. A 10-km (six-mile) track leads from Dead Horse Gap, five km (three miles) past Thredbo, to the Thredbo River on the valley floor. A sweater or windjacket is a good idea on any of these walks as the higher you climb, the lower the temperature drops.

WHERE TO STAY
Mountain ski lodges with shared facilities including big open living areas and fireplaces are the favoured winter accommodation in the Snowies. Those close to the best slopes fill up quickly so early booking is a good idea if skiing is your aim. Out of season, many lodges, especially those above the snow line, close down altogether, although some re-open during school holidays. The Travel Centre of New South Wales in Sydney (02) 231 4444 or Melbourne (03) 67 7461 can tell prospective visitors which lodges are open and when. Another useful accommodation contact for the skifields is **Thredbo Resort Centre**, PO Box 7 Thredbo Village, (0645) 76 360, which lets accommodation throughout Thredbo year round. There are also motels and hotels in some mountain towns and Cooma has a considerable amount of accommodation.
Thredbo Alpine Hotel, Thredbo, (0645) 76 333; is a comfortable base for exploring the Kosciusko region and is open year round, it has apartments attached which, together with the hotel make up quite a large complex. $64.
Perisher Valley Hotel, Perisher Valley, (0645) 75 030; has ten units and 11 suites as well as a three-bedroom 'Summit' suite and many other appointments including air-conditioning and videos. Single $220 to $320, double $370 to $520 dinner bed and breakfast.

EATING OUT
There are licensed restaurants in all the premises mentioned in 'Where to Stay.' Others to try are:
Alpenhorn Lodge, Buckwong Place, Thredbo, (0645) 76 223, and **Bernti's Mountain Inn**, Mowamba Place, Thredbo, (0645) 76 332.

Cooma
Although not actually in the mountains, Cooma is the commercial and administrative centre of the region and where the Snowy Mountains Scheme is headquartered. The scheme is Australia's biggest hydro-electricity project and was an

engineering achievement of vast proportions which gathered many skilled migrants from Europe to Australia following World War II. They drilled tunnels through mountains, dammed rivers, drowned valley and town and built power stations in underground caverns. Its engineering brilliance is explained at the **Snowy Mountains Authority** in Cooma North where visits to the scheme's most spectacular feats can be arranged. Cooma owes its modern existence to the hydro-electric scheme and reflects that in its stolid appearance. It is more a feeder for the Snowies than one of their best attractions and the roads which lead out of it to the picturesque countryside may be its best feature.

WHERE TO STAY

Salmon Motel, 237 Sharp Street, Cooma, (0645) 21 884; low roofed, single storey building with a swimming pool and mini golf as added inducements to the passing trade. Ski hire and the arrangement of tours are offered as well. Single $39, double $45.

Jindabyne

The road to Mt Kosciusko runs south-west from Cooma through Berridale and the new Jindabyne which replaced the town drowned by the hydro scheme engineers. Lake Jindabyne which overwhelmed the old town is, like all the man-made lakes in the Snowies, stocked with trout and haunted by parties of fly fishermen. There is a trout hatchery west of Jindabyne on the Kosciusko Road and fishing equipment can be hired in the town.

Tumut Valley

Kiandra and the Tumut Valley lie west of Cooma on the Snowy Mountains Highway. The remarkable **Yarongobilly Caves**, a couple of miles off the highway between the two towns, have four chambers open to the public. The largest, called the Glory Hole, contains a thermal pool with a constant temperature of 27°C. The caves are open every day from 10 am to 4 pm, guided tours take place at 1 pm with extra tours on weekends and holidays.

Tumut, 112 km (70 miles) north of Cooma, is the northern gateway to the Snowies. Adelong Falls, west of the town, the Talbingo and Blowering Dams to the east and the giant Tumut 3 Power Station at Talbingo are some of the area's features. Batlow, famous for Granny Smith apples lies south of Tumut. At Tumbarumba, further south, the **Hume and Hovell Walking Track** follows a portion of the route taken by the explorers after whom it is named. The town also has a vineyard, Rosemount Estates in Taradale Road, which specialises in champagne and has cellar door sales and tastings. It is open from 9 am to 4 pm daily.

FARM HOLIDAYS

Farm holidays provide an opportunity to enjoy the countryside of the Snowies and get to know some local people as well. Those which offer full board are best for the traveller from outside Australia. **Upsan Downs Guest Lodge**, Barry Way, Jindabyne, NSW 2627, (0645) 62 421, is a small farm which has rooms with private facilities and bunk rooms. **San Michelle**, Snowy Mountains Highway, Adaminaby, NSW 2360, (0645) 42 229, is a 610-hectare (1507-acre) sheep property with motel-style units. **Rose Valley Homestead**, Rose Valley Road, Cooma, NSW 2630, (0645) 22 885, has two- and three-bedroom cottages and offers full board on application; the 800 hectare property dates from 1860. **Reynella Holidays**, Bolaro Road, Adaminaby, NSW 2360, (0645) 42 368, has bunkhouse accommodation. **Litchfield Farm Holidays**, P.O. Box 48, Cooma, NSW 2630, (0645) 33 231, has family rooms and a bunkhouse on 485 hectares (1198 acres), 21 km (13 miles) from Cooma. All the farms mentioned offer horse riding, bushwalking and trout fishing, many have a swimming pool and tennis courts, Upsan Downs is half an hour from the snow fields. On most farm holidays guests can participate in the daily chores of farming if they find such things romantic and unusual.

Horse Riding
Many of the holiday farms mentioned above organise horse riding excursions through the mountains. Day horseback tours are available from Thredbo Riding School, Thredbo Alpine Village, (0645) 76 275.

TOURS
Coach operators, Ansett Pioneer (062) 42 6624 and Murray's (062) 95 3677 offer a wide variety of Snowy Mountains bus tours. Tumut Valley Tours (069) 47 1043 covers the Snowy River Hydro Electric Scheme. Nimmitybelle Launch Cruises (0645) 97 3133 tour Lake Jindabyne.

Outback New South Wales

On the western edges of New South Wales the state's outback shimmers in a haze of heat—dry, desert-like and challenging. It is the province of opal, silver, lead and zinc miners, from hardy individualists to feisty unionists employed by giant mining companies. The town of Broken Hill in the far west, an isolated community with a strong sense of identity encapsulates the spirit of today's outback. Bred on the fabulous wealth of its mines, it is now almost a city in the middle of the desert but many highly individual characters remain among its population.

Broken Hill

Broken Hill is the westernmost town in New South Wales, a legendary wild mining town and the only settlement of any size in the far west. It stands on a chain of hills which guard massive deposits of silver, zinc and lead. It's a union-run town where to cross the corporation, called the Barrier Industrial Council, can mean being driven out forever. The growth of BHP, Australia's biggest company, was fed by the wealth of its mines although that company ceased operating there in 1940. Four miners, North Broken Hill Limited, Minerals Mining and Metallurgy Limited, the Zinc Corporation Limited and New Broken Hill Consolidated Limited now operate the mines.

GETTING THERE

Air NSW flies to Broken Hill from Sydney ($194) and Ayers Rock ($252), Kendell Airlines from Adelaide ($113). Booking through Ansett.

Train travel to Broken Hill gives its passengers a long and fascinating look at the state on the way. The trip takes about 18 hours and the fare is $56.20.

Ansett Pioneer and Bus Australia coaches serve Broken Hill from Adelaide ($29) and Greyhound has a Melbourne to Broken Hill service ($52).

TOURIST INFORMATION

The major tourist information centre for far western New South Wales is at the corner of Blende and Bromide Streets, Broken Hill.

WHAT TO SEE

In contrast to its hard image, Broken Hill has become a breeding ground for bush painters who depict the surrounding countryside and sell their work from over a dozen galleries scattered throughout the town. Around 30 buildings including the Technical College, Court House, Police Station, Post Office, Trades Hall and the Palace Hotel have been classified by the National Trust. Underground Tours of **Delprat's Mine** take tourists down nearly 122 metres (400 feet) to see how mining was and is carried out. The tours begin at 10.30 am from Monday to Friday and at 2 pm on Saturday. They can be booked on (080) 88 1604. Surface tours of **North Mine** occur at 2 pm from Monday to Friday and can be booked on (080) 97 325. The town numbers a **mosque**, established for Afghan camel drivers in the 1890s, among its more unusual buildings. The **Royal Flying Doctor Service** is head-quartered north-east of the town and the School of the Air, a radio and correspond-ence school for isolated children, has its base in Broken Hill. The mosque is open on Sundays from 2 pm to 3 pm. Inspections of the Flying Doctor base can be booked at Silver City Travel, 35 Sulphide Street, (080) 2 564, and the School of the Air at the Tourist Information Centre (080) 6 077. The ghost town of **Silverton**, 20 km (15 miles) from Broken Hill, has served as a location for numerous films including *A Town Like Alice* and *Mad Max II*.

WHERE TO STAY

Broken Hill has at least a dozen motels plus a number of country pubs. Here are some recommendations near the centre of town:

Miners Lamp Motor Inn, Cobalt Street, Broken Hill, (080) 88 4122; is a high quality motel with a swimming pool, a licensed restaurant and an older hotel attached. Single $40, double $46.

Mine Host Motel, 102 Argent Street, Broken Hill, (080) 6 627; is another good standard place. Single $40, double $49.

The Lodge Motel, 252 Mica Street, Broken Hill, (080) 88 2722; is a little north of the town centre but includes an old stone country house as part of its accommo-dation. Single $38, double $44 includes breakfast.

Royal Exchange Hotel, corner Argent and Chloride Streets, Broken Hill, (080) 2 308; is the big hotel close to the centre of town and has rooms with private and shared facilities as well as a licensed restaurant. Single $15 and $25, double $24 and $36.

Around the West

The **Darling River** is the only watercourse of any volume near Broken Hill and though it is intermittently dry, it is a beautiful stream when flowing. **Wilcannia**, 196 km (121 miles) to the east and **Menindee**, 114 km (71 miles) south-east of Broken Hill are both on the river. The first town was once the third largest river port in Australia and has fine stone colonial buildings and the second is close to **Kinchega National Park** and a number of large lakes. North of Wilcannia another 98 km (61 miles), is **White Cliffs**, an opal-mining settlement where surface temperatures are so high that people live underground.

TOURS
Wanderer Tour of Silver City, (080) 7 750, takes in the main sights of Broken Hill including the mines and the Flying Doctor base, heading out as far as White Cliffs on a full day tour. The **Barrier Air Taxi Service** (080) 88 4307 takes paying passengers on its mail run to White Cliffs and includes a visit to the mines and lunch at the White Cliffs Hotel. The same air taxi carries passengers on its general mail run which visits 25 stations in the far west.

Part IV

AUSTRALIAN CAPITAL TERRITORY

Kookaburra

CANBERRA

Canberra is Australia's capital and the nation's most arrestingly neat city. The result of an award winning plan built by a persevering commission, it has hardly any smog or ugly factories, no really tall buildings and lots of bushland between its well-organised suburbs. Tremendous architectural effort has been spent on show palaces of law and culture which rank among Australia's best modern architecture, but the city exudes a distinct air of isolation from the 'real' Australia. Pristine, spacious, clean and flat, it can also seem artificial. Perhaps the man-made lake in its city centre says more about Canberra than any other single feature. It is principally ornamental.

Canberra occupies the Australian Capital Territory, a small area roughly halfway between Sydney and Melbourne, surrounded by New South Wales but not part of it. It is Australia's largest inland city, helped by government centralisation to reach nearly a quarter of a million people in the last twenty years. Its weather is famous for discomfort—very cold and windy in winter, very hot in summer but in autumn it puts on unusual grace as its thousands of trees change colour while temperatures are blessedly cool. The city lies close to the Snowy Mountains and its nearest coastal retreat is the area around Nowra, south of Wollongong.

History

Australia's separate national capital was created by the Commonwealth Constitution Act of 1901 which formed a nation from six colonies. Its location on the Canberra Plains, grazing land occupied by white settlers since the 1830s, is usually

157

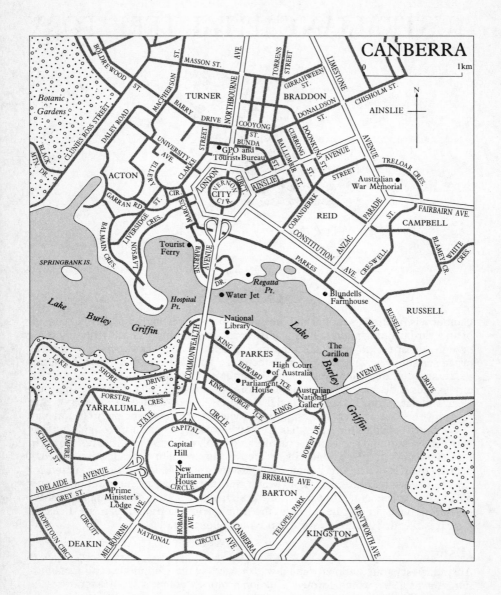

thought to be a compromise between Sydney and Melbourne but there were 20 other claimants and a final decision took nine years of bickering.

Canberra was designed by American architect and town-planner, Walter Burley Griffin. His plan for a city of small centres divided from each other by swathes of bush and linked by wide roads won an international competition in 1912 for which the prize was the equivalent of $3500. Following the competition the work was handed over to the National Capital Development Commission and the city slowly began to take shape.

The Australian Parliament, resident in Melbourne from 1901, arrived in 1927 after a 'temporary' building was erected to house it. The temporary structure was home until 1988. The city itself grew slowly up to World War II when a large defence and administrative establishment became entrenched. Now the population is over three times Griffin's original estimate of 75,000. Some might argue the designer had the right idea.

GETTING TO AND AROUND
Despite being Australia's capital city, Canberra has no international airport. Ansett and Australian Airlines fly there non-stop several times daily from Sydney ($95), Melbourne ($134), Brisbane ($206) and Adelaide ($208). East West Airlines ($85) and Air NSW also fly from Sydney a number of times each day. Canberra Airport is seven km (four and a half miles) from the city. There is an infrequent bus into town but plenty of taxis.

There are rail services to Canberra daily from Sydney. The XPT leaves at 6.35 pm and arrives in Canberra 10.40 pm, ordinary services leave early in the morning and take about five hours ($23). A rail-coach service which swaps from train to bus at Wodonga on the New South Wales border runs from Melbourne ($39).

Ansett Pioneer and Greyhound coaches travel to Canberra from Sydney ($15 and $18 respectively). Drivers should take the Hume Highway from Sydney and from Melbourne.

Buses are Canberra's only public transport other than taxis but they are frequent and well kept. For information about timetables ring (062) 51 6566.

TOURIST INFORMATION
The Canberra Tourist Bureau has its main office in the Jolimont Centre, Northbourne Avenue (062) 49 7555. The Sydney office is at 9 Elizabeth Street (02) 233 3180, and Melbourne, 247 Collins Street (03) 63 7737.

Orientation
Canberra can be confusing. It consists of separate points joined by long boulevards with Lake Burley Griffin rather than a true city centre at its heart. Capital Hill, the rise from which the new parliament house overlooks the lake, is a hub of radiating streets, the major ones being Commonwealth Avenue and Kings Avenue which bridge the lake at its narrowest points. Commonwealth Avenue runs between Capital Hill and Vernon Circle encompassing what, in Canberra, is designated City but really means shopping centre. Most of Canberra's major buildings lie within a triangle formed by Commonwealth Avenue, Kings Avenue and Constitution Avenue with Capital Hill as its apex and City on the northern corner.

Capital Hill

Capital Hill was always meant to be the site of Australia's **Parliament House**. The squat white building beneath it, never more than a temporary home, will be superseded in 1988 by a much grander affair carved out of the hill itself. The fate of the old building is yet to be decided but it continues in its former function until the new one is opened.

The temporary parliament has accommodated the House of Representatives and the Senate for over 60 years. Its entrance lobby, known as Kings Hall, is a colonnaded area decorated with portraits of former Prime Ministers and other politicians. It contains one of only three surviving copies of the *Magna Carta*, donated by the British Government as a token of the parliament's Westminster traditions. The Senate chamber is on the right and the House of Representatives on the left; both have visitors galleries. No admission ticket is required to witness Senate proceedings; for the House of Representatives gallery a couple of days' notice is required at the Inquiry Desk in Kings Hall. Inspection tours of whichever chamber is not sitting occur from 9 am to 5 pm Monday to Saturday and from 9.30 am on Sunday.

Lake Burley Griffin

The lake is the true centre-piece of Canberra. Important buildings from the Governor-General's residence to the National Gallery and Library surround it and monuments are set in or by its waters. The lake was created in 1963 by damming the Molongolo River into an 11 km long pool with 35 km (22 miles) of shoreline, much of it parkland. **Captain Cook Memorial Water Jet** which blasts six tons of water 150 metres (450 feet) into the air shoots up near Commonwealth Avenue Bridge. When it is switched on, it can be seen for miles and makes a useful focal point. The tall, squarish, white stack on Aspen Island at the northern end of Kings Avenue Bridge is the Canberra Carillon which was presented to the Australian people by the British Government in recognition of Canberra's 50th anniversary. Its 53 bells, ranging in weight from 15 to 53 lbs are played on Sundays and Wednesdays. The instrument is open for inspection from 1 pm to 4 pm on Saturday and 9 am to 2 pm on Sunday. Aspen Island is connected to the shore by a foot-bridge.

Australian National Gallery

Canberra's cultural jewel, the Australian National Gallery, stands on the shores of the lake in Parkes Place. It was opened in 1982 and is 23 metres (75 feet) high and with over 7000 square metres (75,000 square feet) of exhibition space throughout 11 exhibition galleries on three levels. It houses an outstanding collection of modern and post-modern art including works by Pollock, De Kooning and Leger. Sculptors represented include Rodin, Modigliani and Brancusi. There are is also a wide collection of Australian painters from McCubbin to Whiteley and the gallery is a major host of high quality exhibitions from overseas. It also has a restaurant overlooking the lake. Open every day 10 am to 5 pm.

The National Library

Despite being a modern building opened in 1968, the National Library shows a marked neo-classical influence. Forty-four square columns faced with white Carrara marble surround the exterior, giving an impression of classical Greek proportion and stasis with added severity. The foyer decoration includes three five-metre (16-feet) high Aubusson Tapestries and sixteen coloured glass windows by Leonard French who also designed the glass roof in Victoria's National Gallery. The building, on the lake shore at the other end of Parkes Place from the gallery, contains over two million books and thousands of recordings, photographs and films. Guided tours are available.

The Australian War Memorial

The Australian War Memorial is Australia's most visited museum, attracting over 1,000,000 people a year. It stands opposite Parliament House at the end of Anzac Parade and is an imposing but heavy and depressing grey Byzantine-inspired basilica, copper domed and faced with granite. It records and displays the history of Australians at war, in many cases on behalf of its powerful friends Great Britain and the United States, and focuses especially on the deeds and sufferings of the 200,000 Australians who died in World Wars I and II. Old aircraft, weapons and equipment such as biplanes, Spitfires, an Amiens gun, a Japanese midget submarine which attacked Sydney harbour in 1942, and tanks and landing barges are displayed, and dioramas depict where and how Australian soldiers fought their battles from Gallipoli to the Western Desert and the New Guinea jungle. The memorial is open every day from 9 am to 4.45 pm. Admission free.

Other Landmarks

The **Black Mountain Telecommunications Tower**, though hardly part of Walter Burley Griffin's original conception, offers spectacular views of the city and surrounding countryside. It has a glassed-in observation deck, a snack bar and a revolving restaurant. Good views of the city, in keeping with Griffin's vision, can be gained from **Mount Ainslie** behind the War Memorial. The remarkable modern building near Parliament House on the lake front is the **High Court of Australia**, opened in 1980. Its main feature is a 24-metre (78-feet) high public gallery from which ramps lead off to the courts. The building is connected to the National Gallery by a foot-bridge.

Historical buildings

Canberra is a quintessentially modern city, having come to its own only in about the last 20 years but some old buildings from its pastoral past remain. **Lanyon Homestead** on the outskirts, preserved by the National Trust as an example of early nineteenth-century rural living, has the bonus of a small modern museum housing a collection of paintings given to the trust by Sir Sidney Nolan, many among them from his outstanding Ned Kelly series. Other places to visit include **Blundell's Farmhouse** on the shores of Lake Burley Griffin and **Cuppacumbalong**.

Vernon Circle

Canberra's centre for shopping and business life is Vernon Circle, north of the lake, at the end of Commonwealth Avenue. Canberra's major retail centre, called **Civic**, is there as well as its main theatre, cinemas and some restaurants. Two pedestrian malls, Petrie Plaza and City Mall, make up the bulk of the shopping area.

WHERE TO STAY

Hyatt Hotel Canberra, Commonwealth Avenue, Canberra, (062) 81 5955, is Canberra's classy new hotel, just down the road from Parliament House and convenient to all the attractions on the south side of Lake Burley Griffin. $175.

Noah's Lakeside International, London Circuit, Canberra, (062) 47 6244, was for many years, perhaps too many, the leading hotel in Canberra, known as the place where many a politician or public servant leaked documents over lunch to a trusted journalist. The hotel, a tall building, stands close to Lake Burley Griffin and overlooking it in the heart of Canberra. $128.

Canberra International, 242 Northbourne Avenue, Canberra, (062) 47 6966, is a very classy motel rather than a true hotel but one of the best value places in town with comfortable rooms well above the ruling standard for motels plus an attempt at style. $125.

Canberra Parkroyal, 102 Northbourne Avenue, Canberra, (062) 49 1411, is a large hotel, recently refurbished and located on Canberra's main thoroughfare. Expect no inspiration but an acceptable standard of comfort and service. $120.

Canberra Rex, Northbourne Avenue, Canberra, (062) 48 5311; in the same street as the previous hotel in all senses of the expression. $116.

Olims Ainslie Hotel, corner Ainslie and Limestone Avenues, Braddon, (062) 48 5511; three long blocks from what Canberrans call their city centre, this old Canberra stand-by has benefited markedly from a thoughtful redevelopment which includes a charming courtyard garden and some rooms with kitchens as well as two-level suites. $105 standard rooms.

Canberra Capital Motor Inn, 108 Northbourne Avenue, Braddon, (062) 48 6566, is much better than your average motel on Canberra's street of motels and hotels. Three storeys overlooking shady lawns from spacious rooms with balconies. All but the most determined walkers will take a bus to the city. $96.

City Gate Motel, Corner Northbourne Avenue and Mouatt Street, Lyneham, (062) 47 2777, is at the far end of Northbourne Avenue on the northern fringe of Canberra's city area, a comfortable motel with 100 roomy units. Single $76, double $86.

The Diplomat International, corner Canberra Avenue and Hely Street, Griffith, (062) 95 2277, is east of Capital Hill and south of the lake so you'll need transport. The hotel has comfortable, spacious rooms set around an atrium which could do without its dreadful gold chandeliers. $85.

Eagle Hawk Hill Motel, Federal Highway, Watson, (062) 30 3404, is a brand new motel set in the bush 11 km (6 miles) from Canberra city. Units are laid out village style around a central complex containing restaurants and barbecues. There are tennis courts and a swimming pool. Single $48, double $56.

Motel 7, Jerrabomberra Avenue, Narrabundah, (062) 95 0755; an older motel south of Capital Hill with a swimming pool and children's play area. Rooms are smallish. Single $36, double $40.

EATING OUT

Canberra has a number of quality restaurants and one or two which serve ethnic exotica.

EJ's, 21 Kennedy Street, Kingston, (062) 95 1949, is the best of the city's restaurants serving modern Australian cuisine and is good for lunch and seeing the Canberra clutch of journos, pollies and spooks. Licensed. Mid price range.

The Charcoal Restaurant, 61 London Circuit, Canberra, (062) 48 8015, is a long established and popular grill room specialising in steaks and good red wines. Licensed. Mid price range.

Jean Pierre Le Carrousel Restaurant, Red Hill Lookout, Red Hill, (062) 73 1808; goes to the full length of Frenchness with such entrées as *Feuilleté de Ris et Crevettes 'Jean Pierre'* and *Rillette de Truite Saumonée et Saumon Fumé* and main courses like *Filet de Porc aux Epinards et Calvados* and *Suprême de Volaille au Camembert* but there are also barramundi and macadamia nuts in some dishes. Licensed. Upper price range.

The Tower Restaurant, Black Mountain Tower, (062) 48 6162, has the best night views in Canberra and an 'international' menu with a scatter gun approach to its customers' tastes. Licensed. Upper price range.

Con's Seafood Restaurant, Southlands Shopping Centre, Mawson Drive, Mawson, (062) 86 3753; has truly fresh seafood flown in from outside Canberra and kept alive in tanks. Try the seafood souvlaki. Premises are somewhat elbow-to-elbow. Licensed. Mid price range.

Imperial Court, 40 Northbourne Avenue, Canberra, (062) 48 5547, serves quality Chinese. Licensed. Mid price range.

Alanya, Style Arcade, Manuka, (062) 95 9678, is a popular Turkish establishment. If you're in the mood for a little adventure, cheese and filo cigars are a good starter. Licensed. Low price range.

TOURS AND CRUISES

The **Canberra Explorer** operated by Murray's Coaches, (062) 95 3677, is a pick-up and drop tour covering 24 stops from Capital Hill to well along Northbourne Avenue. Passengers can alight along the route and re-join the service after having a look around. Fare is $7. **Murray's Coaches** also operates full day ($34) and half day ($14) city tours as does **Ansett Pioneer**, (062) 42 6624, whose prices are a little lower but may not have as many inclusions. Murray's also operates to country places around Canberra including Gundaroo Pub and Burbong Sheep Station. **Canberra Charter Coaches**, (062) 41 1055, does evening tours in Canberra.

Lady Clare cruises right around the Lake Burley Griffin ($9) once a day and in the Parliament Triangle area ($6) once a day. The *City of Canberra* floating restaurant runs lunch ($9) and dinner ($15) cruises, meals extra. Book through Murray's Coaches.

163

Part V

QUEENSLAND

Fish of the Barrier Reef

Queensland is bold, profit driven and sometimes crazy but at the same time relaxed and expansive enough to cheerfully carry its contradictions. Central to its attractions is the Great Barrier Reef, sprinkled with islands and nurturing a forest of multi-coloured corals that shelters thousands of fishes as bright as bunting. Extremes and contrasts typify the state from the pseudo-Miami of the Gold Coast, all flashing neon and gold bikinis, to the luxurious seclusion of Hayman Island; from the blistering heat, red dust and toughness of an outback mining town to the deserted white beaches backed by dense tropical rainforest of the north.

It's hard to persuade Queenslanders that anywhere on earth is as good as their state. Its place in the consciousness of other Australians is more equivocal. Its people are known to be individually friendly and easy-going, but collectively the state is Australia's example of carpetbag politics, famous for its gerrymandered electorate, repressive laws on freedom of expression and paternalistic attitude to race relations. In the south of the country, it is frequently referred to as the 'deep north'. Though its neanderthal politics may be a laughing stock to the rest of the country, its sun, perpetually warmer than the south, draws thousands every year. Develop or die has become the state's tourism strategy. Hotel builders chase profit where they sniff it. During the 1960s and 70s they sniffed it strongly on the Gold Coast and erected a Disneyland of white, blue and grey holiday-unit towers. In the 1980s, Cairns has taken the front running in development though the town is still characterised by weatherboard houses rather than skyscrapers and new buildings are limited to 14 storeys.

In the face of this develop or bust strategy, Queensland has a great advantage—it

164

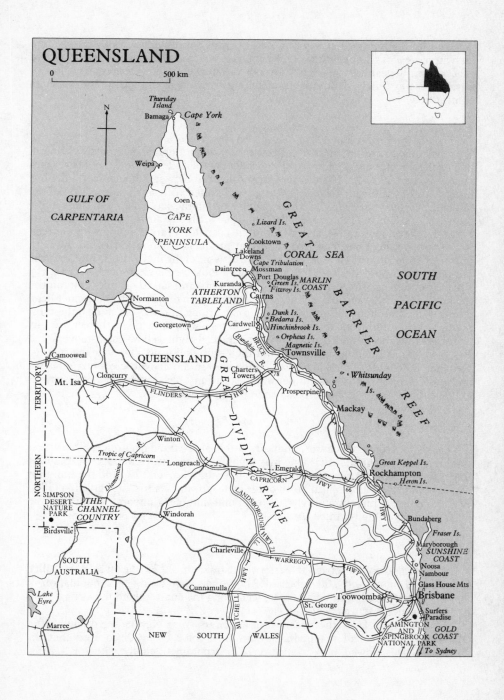

QUEENSLAND

0   500 km

N

Thursday Island
Bamaga   *Cape York*

Weipa

GULF OF

CARPENTARIA

Coen

CAPE
YORK
PENINSULA

Lizard Is.

GREAT

Cooktown
Lakeland
Downs
Cape Tribulation
Daintree   Mossman
Port Douglas
Kuranda   *Green Is.*
ATHERTON   *Fitzroy Is.*
TABLELAND   Cairns

CORAL SEA

MARLIN
COAST

SOUTH

PACIFIC

OCEAN

Normanton

Georgetown

Cardwell

Dunk Is.
Bedarra Is.
Hinchinbrook Is.
Orpheus Is.
Magnetic Is.
Townsville

Burdekin
BRUCE R.

BARRIER

Camooweal

QUEENSLAND

GREAT

Mt. Isa   Cloncurry

FLINDERS

Charters
Towers
78

Prosperpine

Whitsunday
Is.

REEF

Mackay

HWY

DIVIDING

Winton

Tropic of Capricorn
Longreach

Emerald

CAPRICORN   HWY
66

Great Keppel Is.
Rockhampton
Heron Is.

NORTHERN

TERRITORY

SIMPSON
DESERT
NATURE
PARK

THE
CHANNEL
COUNTRY

Windorah

LANDSBOROUGH HWY 71

RANGE

HWY 1

Birdsville

SOUTH
AUSTRALIA

Charleville

WARREGO

HWY

Bundaberg

Fraser Is.
Maryborough   *SUNSHINE*
COAST
Noosa
Nambour

Lake
Eyre

Cunnamulla

MITCHELL HWY

St. George

Toowoomba
54

Glass House Mts
Brisbane

Surfers
Paradise

Marree

NEW   SOUTH   WALES

LAMINGTON
AND
SPINGBROOK
NATIONAL PARK

GOLD
COAST

To Sydney

is very big. There are still some places, such as the Hinchinbrook Passage and anywhere west of Charters Towers, which have not caught the developers' eyes and others, mostly islands, where they are not yet allowed to go. Development has its advantages too. Queensland is very welcoming to travellers and accommodates them comfortably.

Geography

Queensland occupies the north-eastern corner of continental Australia. It is cut in half by the **Tropic of Capricorn**. The greater part of its 2.5 million people lives on a narrow, green 2000-km (1250-mile) strip squeezed between the coast and the low mountains of the **Great Dividing Range** and dotted with small cities. West of the range the country varies from fertile grazing lands in the south-east to deserts in the far west. The centre of the state is flat and dry. North of Cairns, tropical rainforests cover the mountains and stretch down to the coast for a rare meeting with the reef.

Sugar cane, beef and coal are important products. As one moves northwards, grass-green and fawn cane looms by the roads in eight foot stands, blocking the immediate view and stretching straight to where dark emerald mountains rise. Big square wooden houses, decorated with lattice work and raised on stilts to minimise the heat rise weirdly above the cane, seeming to float in the simmering summer heat. Around the mountain valleys near the Tropic are giant open-cut mines, the most efficient coal producers in the world—holes so wide and deep that entire city suburbs could be buried in them without trace. Bright yellow earth movers and trucks as big as buildings crawl around their spiralled walls like drunken insects, throwing up clouds of choking dust. To the west in the dry cattle country all is flat and endless, open to a vast sky under which occasional beasts graze in dusty pastures and shelter beneath scrawny trees in the burning midday sun.

Climate

To the visitor from cool climes, humidity and heat are the most noticeable features of Queensland's climate. Brisbane may be officially sub-tropical but try explaining that to a Londoner in January when the temperature is over 30°C and the humidity 80 per cent. The truly tropical north of the state, around Cairns, is enervating (30°C to 35°C and very high humidity) and wet in mid-summer (January), warm (20°C to 30°C) and dry in mid-winter (August).

History

When James Cook discovered eastern Australia in 1770 the area now called Queensland supported 200 tribes of Aboriginals amounting to a population of 94,000. They fished, hunted and lived well along the coast; inland the struggle was harder but their life was peaceful.

The first white faces to appear were explorers from New South Wales. After Matthew Flinders had mapped Moreton Bay, John Oxley discovered that the Brisbane River flowed into it and in 1823 recommended the site for a penal

166

settlement. Convicts, the worst in the colony, soon followed but free settlers—although a few had drifted to the rich Darling Downs in the west in the late 1820s—were strictly forbidden at Brisbane itself until 1839. The first of their kind arrived from New South Wales in 1842 but the small remote settlement, a collection of timber huts and a few stone buildings on the mangrove-edged banks of a sluggish greeny-brown river, was a minor consideration in the minds of British colonial administrators.

This changed when immigrants began to arrive directly from Britain in the 1850s. Years of rapid growth, especially in the grazing industry followed. Brisbane and inland towns gained an air of permanence and the new colonists began to dislike being represented from Sydney. They said so loudly and after much wrangling, Queensland was made a separate colony in 1859. Gold discoveries similar to those in Victoria and New South Wales were made first at Gympie and later, stepping northwards, at Ravenswood, Charters Towers and the Palmer River. Each new town boomed into a muddy and drunken riot of gold fever, tent and bark cities sprang up in weeks then fell away again, leaving the difficult but profitable mining to those who knew how to do it. Much of the gold population stayed, turning old skills to the general good so that by 1880 the colony supported over 200,000 residents.

Though some early attempts at cattle and sheep grazing had failed, westward advance into well watered country was rapid and by the same year three million cattle and seven million sheep populated the pastures. Sugar was first planted in the 1860s and quickly became a strong industry in the tropical north, developing its own plantation culture complete with quasi-slaves press-ganged from the South Sea islands. The boom came to a shuddering halt in the 1890s when a nationwide depression hit, reducing the economy to a shambles and threatening the livelihoods of all working people. In the new, harsher climate, Australian labour politics was born among the shearers of central Queensland who went on strike to protect their wages. The time could not have been more ripe for labour to emerge as a political force and Queensland quickly became the first colony to have a labour dominated government.

Despite this early history of radicalism, Queensland today is Australia's bastion of conservative politics, some say it is the nearest we have to a loony right. Development and anti-unionism are its cries and the scene is totally at odds with older traditions.

GETTING TO AND AROUND

By Air
Queensland has three international air gateways, Brisbane, Townsville and Cairns. Brisbane is easily the largest but some flights from west coast USA and Japan operate direct into Cairns.

Australian and **Ansett Airlines** fly into all major towns of the state from the rest of Australia.

East West Airlines flies from Sydney to Brisbane, the Gold Coast, Sunshine Coast and Cairns, **Air NSW** does the same except for Cairns.

Ansett and Australian serve the coastal cities and fly west to Mt Isa. Australian

Airlines is the major carrier to smaller centres in the west of the state. **Air Queensland** and **Lloyd Aviation** also operate intra-state services.

Flights to Barrier Reef islands with airports operate on Ansett, Australian, **Air Whitsunday** and Lloyd Aviation.

By Train

Travelling to Queensland by train can only be done via Sydney.

The *Sunlander* and *Queenslander* trains run up the coast from Brisbane to Cairns, calling at coastal towns along the way. The full journey takes two days.

The *Capricornian* follows the same route but terminates at Rockhampton from where services leave for Longreach and Winton in the central west. Townsville is the departure point for trains to Charters Towers and Mt Isa; Brisbane for points in the south-west of the state as far as Quilpie about 200 km (124 miles) west of Charleville.

By Road

All major coach companies enter Queensland from the south via Brisbane and from the west via Mt Isa and Townsville, connecting the state with the rest of the nation. They also run city to city between Brisbane and Cairns (full journey 24 hours) with **Greyhound** doing most of the work between the coastal towns and western Queensland.

Drivers can travel almost the whole of Queensland's coast (just over 1800 km: 1125 miles) along the Bruce Highway, all sealed and usually two lanes, much of it running between cane fields, not much within sight of the coast. The major highways into the west are sealed as are plenty of minor roads in the south-east but in the south-west, far west and especially Cape York, bring your four-wheel drive.

TOURIST INFORMATION

Tourism Queensland is the official new name for the Queensland Government's instrument responsible for providing information about the state although it is sometimes better known by its old name, the Queensland Travel and Tourist Corporation. It operates offices in all Australian state capitals which are called **Queensland Travel Centres**. Yes, I'm confused too but that's bureaucracy. Here is where to find them:

196 Adelaide Street, **Brisbane**, (07) 31 2211
75 Castlereagh Street, **Sydney**, (02) 232 1788
25 Garema Place, **Canberra**, (062) 48 8411
257 Collins Street, **Melbourne**, (03) 654 3866
10 Grenfell Street, **Adelaide**, (08) 212 2399
55 St George's Terrace, **Perth**, (09) 325 1600

Time

Some cruel commentators have said that Queensland is 100 years behind the rest of Australia. Whatever your opinion, the fact remains that the state does not indulge in daylight saving and so, during the summer, is one hour behind New South Wales and Victoria, half an hour behind South Australia and the Northern Territory.

MAJOR SIGHTS

Queensland's major sight is the **Barrier Reef** but it's not exactly self-contained. Seeing all of it could take a lifetime. Some guidance on how to select an island or coastal destination, the major differences between islands and what the big coastal resorts have to offer is included in the guide to the Barrier Reef beginning on page ??. **Cairns** is the Barrier Reef town that everybody has heard of but it has little to offer in itself besides places to sleep and eat. It is, however, close to a generous dose of islands and reef, backed by steep green mountains and within striking distance of coastal rainforests—what people used to call jungle. Too much reef also tends to blot out places such as **Fraser Island**, an island made entirely of sand but supporting fresh water-lakes, unique and extensive vegetation and huge beaches, and the **Hinchinbrook Passage**, a hidden stream of silvery sea framed by coastal and island mountains. The southern part of the state has **Brisbane**, an unsophisticated but likeable capital city, and the **Gold Coast**, Australia's attempt at Hawaiian style development.

ACCOMMODATION

Nearly everything in Queensland is a 'resort'. Indeed, 'resort' is possibly the most corrupted word in the Queensland tourism vocabulary and can mean anything from a luxury beachfront hideaway to a down at heel motel facing the highway five km (three miles) from the nearest beach. Take no notice of the word whenever it appears and your margin of safety in selecting accommodation will be greatly increased. This warning in mind, the true range is as wide as you care to name from big hotels to camping grounds, farm stays to wilderness lodges and even true resort hotels. Places to stay do, however, cluster on the coast and in the tourist areas and thin out considerably in quantity and comfort the further off the beaten track you go. I have yet to discover a true deluxe hotel in Queensland, not for the want of new exotic buildings but because the standard of service has not yet reached the required excellence. This is not to say that it is bad but rather that it sometimes fails to put the customer first and when that happens Queenslanders' famous relaxed approach can degenerate into neglect and off-handedness. The only places where this observation might not hold true is on the very posh islands such as Lizard, Hayman and Bedarra.

FOOD AND DRINK

Queensland produces vast quantities of delicious tropical fruit. Millions of mangoes, pawpaws (papayas), pineapples, avocados and macadamia nuts appear on its tables as well as acquired tastes such as plantains, rambutans, guanobanas, carambolas, caimitos, pommelos and manney sapotes. A grand parade of seafood is led by the Queensland mud crab, a huge black mangrove-dwelling crab, the size of your plate and red when cooked. The Barrier Reef yields parrot fish and the delicate coral trout (not a true trout) as well as other fine, sweet species. I have often been disappointed by the quality of steak in the sunshine state, perhaps the best of it also ends up in other places.

Booze is the proper word for Queensland's alcoholic output which consists of Bundaberg Rum, made in the coastal city of Bundaberg, known universally as 'Bundy' and the traditional beverage of old time Queenslanders, and XXXX (pronounced Four Ex) beer.

The best food is served in the restaurants of Brisbane, the Gold Coast, the Sunshine Coast and Airlie Beach as well as in the dining rooms of the more exclusive islands.

ACTIVITIES
Water Sports dominate the coast from surfing along the southern beaches to scuba diving, snorkelling, sailing, windsurfing, parasailing, waterskiing and just fooling around off the Barrier Reef Islands. Boom netting in which one rides a rope net hung at right angles into the water from a speeding boat is a favourite with bruise-loving tourists to the reef. Bruises are also freely available by rafting the fast falling streams around Tully in the state's north. Cairns is the biggest game-fishing centre but fishing anywhere on the reef is easy, cheap and nearly always successful.

Bushwalkers will be surprised by how much they can tramp about the islands and by the beauty of the south-east hinterland west of Brisbane and the Gold Coast.

The most exciting spectator sports are surf lifesaving carnivals on the Gold Coast and rodeos that move from town to town in the west.

BRISBANE

The saying used to go 'Brisbane's a big country town'. Not any more. Now it is planning the tallest building in the world and Expo '88 glitters away on its southern river front but the old wisdom holds true in the slow pace and friendliness of the city's people for, despite a 1.1 million population, Brisbane is scattered and doesn't bustle like Sydney or Melbourne.

The city is built on the Brisbane River which winds around a business centre set 25 km (15½ miles) upstream from its port at Moreton Bay on the site of a penal colony established in 1824. Capital of Queensland, it has its share of skyscrapers but retains an air of the exotic colonial outpost where palm trees wave in front of neo-classical façades and wide squares accommodate few sightseers. It is also hotter than the southern capitals, slowing the pace of life and making a good place to visit when the south is cool.

History

Ungovernable convicts, flogged, starved and worked to death were the first citizens of Brisbane. English military men ruled them with varying degrees of ferocity from 1824 to 1839, the most infamous being Captain Patrick Logan, whose brief reign began in 1829. He erected the city's first substantial buildings but was killed by Aboriginals in 1830 while exploring the surrounding countryside.

After 1839 no further prisoners were sent north and the Brisbane area was opened to free settlers, the first arriving in 1842. At the same time the first regular steamer service between Sydney and Brisbane began to operate. In 1843 Alexander McLeay was elected to represent Brisbane in the New South Wales Legislative Council. The colony of Queensland became independent of New South Wales on

December 10, 1859 and Brisbane, which then had a population of 5000, was declared the capital.

GETTING TO AND AROUND

By Air

Brisbane has an international airport where, among others, Qantas, Air New Zealand, British Airways and Singapore Airlines land. Domestic carriers Ansett Airlines, Australian Airlines, East-West Airlines and Air NSW fly in from Sydney. Ansett and Australian also fly direct from Melbourne, Adelaide and Darwin as well as linking Brisbane to Queensland's coastal cities and islands. Flying from Sydney takes about one and a quarter hours, Melbourne two, Adelaide three, Darwin four and Perth four and a half. One way economy fares from mainland capitals are Sydney $176 ($166 on East-West), Melbourne $261, Adelaide $289 and Darwin $410. Brisbane airport is also a centre for departures to south-east and western Queensland on the intra-state services of Australian Airlines, Air Queensland, Eastern Airlines and Sunstate Airlines.

The journey from the airport to town takes about half an hour. Skennars Coaches runs a service to the city, departing half hourly between 6 am and around 7 pm. The fare is $2.70 one way and the bus stops at major hotels and transport terminals. The same service operates in the opposite direction. Taxis abound at the airport. Average fare $10.

By Road

Coach services into Brisbane from Melbourne and Sydney are operated by Ansett Pioneer, Greyhound, Deluxe and McCafferty's coaches. Ansett Pioneer and Bus Australia operate from Adelaide. The journey from Melbourne takes about 28½ hours and from Sydney, about 17 hours. Fares are $80 from Melbourne, $40 from Sydney and $105 from Adelaide.

By Rail

A train called the *Brisbane Limited* runs daily from Sydney to Brisbane, departing from Sydney at 6 pm and arriving in Brisbane at around 10 am the next day. First class berths cost $132 and seats $97, economy $69 sit-up only. Passengers from other states must make their way to Sydney in order to catch the Brisbane train. Intra-state trains the *Queenslander* ($258.80 first, $89.90 economy) and the *Sunlander* ($134.80 and $89.90) from Cairns and *The Capricornian* ($73.50 and $46.20) from Rockhampton serve Brisbane via other major coastal cities.

GETTING AROUND THE CITY

Once in Brisbane, your legs should be sufficient to carry you around the city area. The City Bus service picks up in town for suburban destinations at large, well signposted stops which include bus identification numbers, destinations and route maps. A single sector adult bus fare is 60 cents. Ferries ply the Brisbane River from side to side and up and downstream. The main wharves are at the southern end of Edward Street and the northern end of Charlotte Street and Queen's Street in the city area. Fares are the same as buses. There are plenty of taxis in town.

171

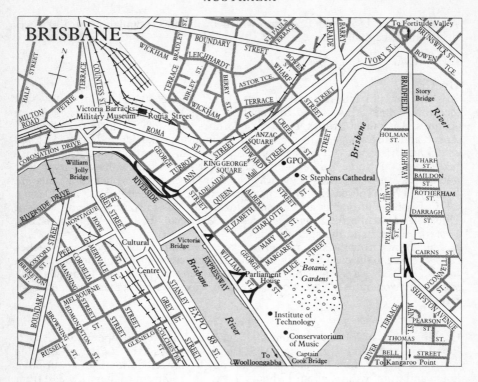

No railway serves the inner city but trains to suburban destinations can be joined at Central Station in Ann Street. Services by train and coach to places farther afield leave from the Roma Street Transit Centre under the Brisbane City Travelodge hotel. The tri-level centre includes a large railway station and a coach terminal where tickets can be bought and coach tours booked.

The major car hire companies have airport desks and city offices. Cheap car hire, generally from as little as $30 per day, is available from Express Auto Rent (07) 52 9461, Crown Car Rentals (07) 854 1848 and AA Bargain Inedell Car Rentals (07) 350 2353. Make sure you ask about extras such as insurance, mileage charges and damage waiver fees. Where drivers are aged under 25, there may be extra conditions on the rental and some companies do not rent to anyone under 21 years old. Cheap car hire companies usually insist that you return the car to the point from which you picked it up. Some will bring your car to the airport or your hotel. Bicycles can be hired at Brisbane Bicycle Hire, 214 Margaret Street.

TOURIST INFORMATION
Maps of, and information about, Brisbane are available from the **Sunmap Centre** in Anzac Square and from the **Brisbane City Council** booth in Queen Street Mall.

The Queensland Government Travel Centre, 196 Adelaide Street, (07) 226 5255 has information on all parts of Queensland and can make bookings throughout the state.

Orientation

Brisbane's city centre noses out into a bend of the Brisbane River with its Botanic Gardens at the southern end and Albert Park to the north. Its streets are arranged in a simple grid between Turbot and Alice Streets. Queen Street runs through the centre of the city to Victoria Bridge which gives access to the south bank of the river. The Riverside Expressway runs past the edge of the city along the north bank.

The city's historical buildings, which are concentrated in the city area, are generally not as old as those of other Australian cities and the Queenslanders, who have more respect for free enterprise than history, tend to demolish them if they stand in the way of progress. Nonetheless, Brisbane has some fine city squares, a number of elegant colonial buildings and, despite its Philistine reputation in the southern states, a high quality cultural centre combining the state's art gallery, museum and major theatres.

The City Sights

Anzac Square is an ideal place in which to start exploring the city. It is the heart of Brisbane and expresses that heart well. Where Sydney shows off around its harbour and Melbourne wears a respectable pin-stripe, Brisbane devotes its city centre to war dead from a succession of conflicts, beginning in colonial servitude and continuing with great power allegiances. The chain of deadly encounters, defined as tests of nationhood, focuses on the World War I battle fought by Australian and New Zealand troops at Gallipoli on the Turkish coast in 1914. Lost but commemorated each year on Anzac Day, 25 April, it is regarded as Australia's finest martial hour.

The square's high end, bounded by Ann Street and directly across from the entrance to Central Railway Station and the Brisbane Sheraton Hotel, is dominated by a memorial to the Anzac fallen of World War I. The memorial takes the form of a small circular Greek temple but has neither roof nor walls. A catalogue of great European battles in which Australians participated is lettered in bronze around the inside and an eternal flame burns in the middle of the floor.

Stairs set on either side of the shrine arc down and meet in the narrow square below. It is planted out with Queensland bottle trees, palms and plots of annuals. A subterranean Shrine of Memories beneath the little temple contains regimental plaques and a grotesquely coloured mosaic of idealised death whose meaning is elusive but whose sentimentality is clear. High governmental buildings fronted with walkways leading into Central Station loom somewhat on either side of the square. Tourist information is available on the ground floor of the building on the right if you are facing Adelaide Street. A statue of an unknown horseman stands at the lower end of the square, recalling the Australian dead of the Boer War. A tunnel drops from in front of it, under Adelaide Street, emerging on the other side in Post Office Square.

Post Office Square is named for the colonial building facing across Queen Street. It is still Brisbane's General Post Office and is a masterpiece of restorative work which shows off the subtle cream, pink, mauve and honey colours of its porphyry freestone facade to the best advantage. This delicate and optimistic building was constructed in stages from 1872 to 1879 to plans by colonial architect F. G. D. Stanley. It contrasts startlingly with Anzac Square. The northern wing was erected first, followed by the southern wing and tower. The building's two storey façade consists entirely of freestone with arches fronting the ground floor and elegant narrow columns supporting the second storey veranda roof. The arch of the Italianate central tower, decorated with bronze plaques showing the names of glorious dead who worked for the postal service, leads into a lane between the north and south wings. The lane comes out at the Elizabeth Street footpath, across from **St Stephen's Catholic Cathedral**, a building constructed of identical stone but rough hewn and left undressed on the outer surface so lending much stronger tonality to the natural colours. The gothic style church is smallish for a cathedral, some if its construction dates from as late as 1921.

Brisbane's modern salute to square making is the **Queen Street Mall**, a section of Queen Street between Edward and Albert Streets, set aside for pedestrians. It is a relaxed, trafficless place where one can sip coffee in an outdoor café while watching the city's people go about their daily business. The mall is flanked by exclusive shops, shopping arcades and department stores. The city's cinemas are to be found in and around it.

Brisbane's **Botanic Gardens** occupy a point jutting out into a bend of the Brisbane River at the south eastern end of the city. Entrance to them is gained from the end of Edward Street beside the river, or from Alice Street near Parliament House. The gardens have wide lawns, many palm trees, lots of *bohinia* (the Queensland state tree which flowers purple and white at the middle of the year) and other tropical plants but the display is not exceptional. The public uses the lawns and river banks for picnics, walks and cycling. Concerts take place on weekends in the centre of the park where a stage has been constructed. A short boardwalk leads from the riverside path among the mangroves which grow at the river's tidal edge.

Old Government House overlooks the Botanic Gardens from the east. It is now surrounded by the buildings of The Queensland Institute of Technology and stands next to the modern Conservatorium of Music. The building has been restored by the National Trust of Queensland. It is of a simpler, lighter, less imposing but more serene design than its civic counterparts, having a semi-circular entrance flanked by two wings. Its narrow, straight columns and feeling of openness seem to combine the institutional and the domestic in equal and harmonious proportions. This could hardly be said of **Parliament House**, a lumpy French Renaissance style structure just outside the college grounds on the corner of Alice and George Streets where institutionalism is utterly triumphant. Built in 1868, it lacks even the softening effect of those swaying palms so frequently planted against the fronts of Brisbane buildings. It has been done up in recent days and is open when parliament is not sitting. This is more often than you might think as the Queensland Parliament has the least sittings of any Australian Parliament. Tours of the building take place at 10.30 am and 2.30 pm on weekdays. George Street, heading back to the city centre, is the main governmental precinct. **Queen's Square** two blocks beyond the parliament is home to the State Library but only until it moves to the new Cultural Centre across the river. The library building, dated 1903, is stylistically in keeping with its monumental companions flanking the street. The row of six pretty terrace houses across from Parliament House, called the Mansions, was built in about 1890 and has been restored to house shops, restaurants and offices.

One square remains, **King George Square**, the centre of civic administration, bounded by Ann and Adelaide Streets with Edward Street at its north-eastern end. The ornate sandstone building facing the square is Brisbane City Hall, built in 1930 to a then modish English neo-classical revival design. Its columned portico and majestic wings are topped by a Florentine clock tower at that time the city's tallest structure which still provides a good city view. The foyer has ornate vaulted ceilings, intricate plaster work, floor mosaics and woodwork turned from Queensland timbers. The **City Hall Art Gallery and Museum** is located on the left of the foyer. It houses historical documents, photographs, ceramics and furniture as well as a collection of paintings by Richard John Randall who depicted nineteenth-century life in the outback. The gallery is open from 10 am to 4 pm Monday to Friday. The building also contains a circular concert hall with a grand pipe organ.

Ann Street Presbyterian and **Albert Street Church** border the square. The former is a simple, low, white, unpretentious colonial church established in 1849 and makes a welcome contrast to the elaborate City Hall. Albert Street Church is a red brick building with white stucco ornament in what can best be described as a gothic mockery.

Cultural Centre

The **Queensland Cultural Centre**, the most important new building in Brisbane, is set on the south bank of the river at the end of Victoria Bridge. The centre looks like a huge layer cake, stacked, stepped and staggered on either side of the bridge's southern end. Its right half contains the Queensland Art Gallery and the Queensland Museum and its left the Performing Arts Complex.

The interior of the **Queensland Art Gallery** shows some of the best qualities of modern building. Space and light abound and a shallow, wide rectangular pool reflects the surroundings, giving an atmosphere of peace to the whole. The collection is in keeping with the contemporary architecture, holding some challenging works by living Australian and especially Queensland artists such as painters William Robinson and Stephen Killick and sculptor Tom Risley. More senior painters such as Leonard French are also represented. Sections of the gallery are set aside for touring exhibitions from around Australia and overseas. The capacity to properly exhibit large modern works, including sculpture, is a particular delight of this gallery but it does not do quite so well in showing smaller, more domesticated, nineteenth- and early twentieth-century material. Its collection of such material from Australian sources is representative but small, holding a few paintings each from the best Australians of that time including Arthur Streeton, Frederick McCubbin and Rupert Bunny as well as the women painters Grace Cossington Smith, Grace Cowley and Margaret Preston. Mid to late twentieth-century masters such as William Dobell, Russell Drysdale, Lloyd Rees and Sidney Nolan are represented in the same fashion. The gallery is open from Monday to Sunday 10 am to 5 pm, entrance is free except for special exhibitions. Guided tours take place at 11 am, 1 pm and 2 pm from Monday to Friday and at 2 pm and 3 pm on Saturday and Sunday.

The Queensland Museum, located in the rear of the same building and entered separately, has a wide range of exhibits but it could not be accused of great depth. It covers palaeontology, anthropology, biology, zoology and applied science on three floors. A section devoted to the great aviators Bert Hinkler and Sir Charles Kingsford Smith and showing the important part they played in diminishing Australia's tyranny of distance as well as swashbuckling around the world on hitherto unheard-of aerial journeys, is the museum's best feature. Individual exhibits include a *Muttaburrasaurus* skeleton, named after Muttaburra near Winton in Western Queensland where its fossilised bones were found; three-metre (10-foot) high termite citadels; the life of rainforest dwelling *Jirrbul* Aborigines; fish and birds and other objects of natural fascination. Museum hours are 9 am to 5 pm seven days a week.

A walkway over Melbourne Street leads from the gallery and museum to the **Performing Arts Complex**. The complex contains three auditoria, a **Concert Hall** holding almost 2000 people, used for live music concerts, it is home to the Queensland Symphony Orchestra; **The Lyric Theatre**, a 2000-seater used by opera and ballet companies and **The Cremorne Theatre**, a smaller more flexible space where new works and theatrical experiments tend to take place. It is often used by the Queensland Theatre Company. Guided tours of the Performing Arts Complex leave from the Tour Desk in the Ticket Sales Foyer on the hour from 10 am to 4 pm, Monday to Saturday. Cost is $2.50.

Convict Buildings

Few convict-built structures remain in Brisbane. The **Old Windmill** on Wickham Terrace, north of King George Square, is one and the **Old Commissariat Store** between William Street and Queens Wharf Road is another. The Windmill, also known as the Observatory was built in 1828 and has served both functions in its time. During 1930 it was the first television transmitting tower in the city. The Old Commissariat stands over the site of Brisbane's original wharf and was the colony's first stone building. It is the headquarters of the Royal Historical Society of Queensland and is open Tuesday to Friday 11 am to 2 pm and on Sundays from 11 am to 4 pm.

Earlystreet Village

Earlystreet Village tries to make up for the lack of Brisbane colonial architecture remaining in situ. It is a group of old buildings gathered in the grounds of the mid-nineteenth-century gentleman's residence, Eulalia, in the suburb of Norman Park which shows the strata of domestic life in colonial times. Besides Eulalia, it includes parts of Auchenflower House, an elegant mansion dating from the 1890s which saw service as a residence for two Queensland premiers, a boys' school and a monastery during its former life. At the other end of the social scale is a pioneer's slab hut complete with household and farm implements and a general store which at one time sold everything and even issued its own token money. The village is open on weekdays from 9.30 am to 4.30 pm and on weekends from 10.30 am to 4.30 pm. It is at 75 McIllwraith Avenue, Norman Park, a few kilometres south of Brisbane City. Admission costs $6.

Other Sights

Other Brisbane city sights include the **Wilderness Walk**, an indoor display of bush habitats located in Koala House on the corner of Creek and Adelaide Streets where live koalas are kept in the trees (open Monday to Friday from 9.30 am to 5 pm and until noon on Saturday) and the **Queensland Maritime Museum** on the south side of the river in Stanley Street which houses the World War II frigate *Diamantina* in its old dry dock (open Wednesday 10 am to 3.30 pm and weekends 10 am to 4.30 pm).

New Farm Park in Brunswick Street, New Farm, is renowned for its roses (12,000 in all), avenues of jacaranda and poinciana trees, in bloom from October to December.

Brisbane also has an elaborate **Chinatown** centred on Chinatown Mall along Duncan Street with its main entrance facing Wickham Street in the suburb of Fortitude Valley, north of the city heart. The mall is a collection of buildings, archways and gardens said to be constructed after the style of the Tang Dynasty (618 to 907 AD) on the theme of peace and tranquillity. It houses restaurants, supermarkets, stalls and shops. The foods available include Chinese, Korean, Malaysian, Singaporean and Thai. See the 'Eating Out' section for further details of these.

History near the City
Some historical buildings can be found a short distance from the city area. The **Victoria Barracks Military Museum** in Petrie Terrace dates from the 1860s. Its collection recalls the role of military personnel in colonial times and includes uniforms, photographs and written material. Open 11.30 am to 4.30 pm on the second Sunday of each month, admission free. **Miegunyah** in Jordan Street, Bowen Hills, a house built in 1884 is a museum showing the lives of colonial women. Open Tuesday, Wednesday and weekends from 10.30 am to 3 pm. **Newstead House** in Breakfast Creek Road, Newstead, is Brisbane's oldest residence. It is surrounded by a park overlooking the river and is now a place of public recreation. It is open Monday to Thursday from 11 am to 3 pm and on Sundays from 2 pm to 5 pm when afternoon tea is served. Admission $1.

Mount Coot-tha
This is the nearest bush area close to Brisbane city. The mount, really a high hill, is in the suburb of Toowong about six km (four miles) from town. Mt Coot-tha Rd winds up its forested slopes where there are picnic spots and parkland. There is a charmingly sited restaurant and tea rooms on the top. The Mt Coot-tha Botanical Gardens on Mt Coot-tha Road feature sub-tropical plantings in a new garden which also has areas set aside for arid environment plants and an impressive 'tropical

dome' which provides an especially humid atmosphere throughout the year. A planetarium and tea rooms are included in the gardens. Open daily 7 am to 5 pm, admission free. Take bus 39 from the city.

Wildlife Sanctuaries
Lone Pine Koala Sanctuary in Jesmond Road, Fig Tree Pocket, 11 km (seven miles) from the city was established in 1927 and claims to be the oldest koala sanctuary in the world. It occupies over 20 hectares (50 acres) of land and as well as the koalas has kangaroos, wallabies, a platypus and other native animals on public show. The sanctuary is open from 9.30 am to 5 pm every day. The platypus is best seen when fed at 11.30 am and 3 pm. Admission $7. **Bunya Park Wildlife Sanctuary**, Bunya Park Drive, Eatons Hill, about 20 minutes drive north of the city is the competition. It also makes a feature of koalas, even extending to a koala kindergarten. Open daily 9.30 am to 5 pm, admission $8.50. Both these places compete head to head in the 'cuddle a koala' stakes, actively encouraging visitors to hold and be photographed with koalas.

Theatres
Brisbane has some reputable theatres outside those housed in the Performing Arts Complex. **La Boite**, 57 Hale Street, Milton, (07) 369 1622, is a small house where the prices are not so great as elsewhere. Its productions deviate somewhat from the mainstream and do not necessarily play every night of the week. **Twelfth Night Theatre**, 4 Cintra Road, Bowen Hill, (07) 52 5287, tends to have nightly perform-ances of touring shows, sometimes musicals. **Suncorp Theatre**, Turbot Street, City (07) 221 5177, is the closest to the city, also often housing musicals and touring plays.

World Expo '88
World Expo '88 is the great once-only attraction of Brisbane in 1988. Although it's not a permanent feature of the city, it's hard to ignore. The Expo has been established on the South Bank of the Brisbane River on a 40-hectare (99-acre) site next door to the Queensland Performing Arts Complex, populated by over 50 display pavilions representing nations and corporations. Among those represented are the USA, the USSR and many European nations. The theme is 'Leisure in the Age of Technology' and as well as exhibitors' pavilions, the site includes a 'High-Tech' amusement park and 2.3 km (one and a half miles) of monorail. World Expo '88 runs from April 30 to October 30, 1988, and the site is open 12 hours a day, seven days a week during that time. You will recognise it by the five giant tent-like structures providing shade for various activities and the flat-roofed, box-like exhi-bition buildings. All day tickets cost $25 and evening tickets, allowing admission after 5 pm, $14.

WHERE TO STAY
Sheraton Brisbane Hotel and Towers, 249 Turbot Street, (07) 835 3535; has two sections of which the Tower, a black glass monolith looking down on Anzac

Square has the best rooms and views. The Hotel, adjoining Central Station is partly located in a highly renovated old building. Every mod-con down to free in-house videos and a heated outdoor swimming pool. Tower rooms $230, Hotel $165.

Hilton International Brisbane, corner Queen Street Mall and Elizabeth Street, (07) 231 3131; just as central as the Sheraton and with practically the same facilities on 27 floors. Single $135 to $175, double and twin $155 to $195.

Brisbane City Travelodge, Roma Street, (07) 238 2222; set on top of the Roma Street Transit Centre about five minutes walk from King George Square. Good value with very comfortable rooms and polite service. The rooms at the back of the hotel are little too near the railway station. $85.

Mayfair Crest International, King George Square, (07) 229 9111; another big central city hotel, 440 rooms of various classes including penthouses and luxury suites. It has two swimming pools and is very popular as a mid-market hotel. Single $123, twin and double $138, all standard rooms $86 on weekends.

Gazebo Ramada Hotel, 345 Wickham Terrace, (07) 831 6177; on the western edge of the city area overlooking a park. Each room has a balcony. 24-hour room service. Parking. $70 Monday to Thursday, $63 Friday to Sunday.

Brisbane Parkroyal, Corner Alice and Albert Streets, Brisbane, (07) 221 3411; across the road from the Brisbane Botanic Gardens. $125.

Olims Kangaroo Point Motor Inn, 355 Main Street, Kangaroo Point (07) 391 5566; a smaller hotel which stands on the opposite side of the river to the city and so has pleasant views from those rooms which overlook the water. Its location necessitates taking a ferry into town, a journey of about 5 minutes. $85 to $95.

Lennons Hotel Brisbane, 66–76 Queen Street, (07) 222 3222; central city location, unpretentious accommodation. $65.

Bellevue Hotel, 103 George Street, (07) 221 6044; the furniture and style of the rooms is not Vogue Magazine but the location is good and the facilities adequate. Single, twin, double and executive suites with lounge rooms. Single $49, double $65.

Gateway Hotel, 85–87 North Quay, (07) 221 0211; a square block of a building overlooking the expressway and the river. Its front rooms have small balconies. Single $85, double $95 Monday to Thursday, all rooms $64 Friday to Sunday.

Ridge All-Suites Inn, 189 Leichhardt Street, (07) 831 5000; west of the city area about 10 minutes walk to town, has motel suites and family rooms with kitchens. Single $73, double $78 Monday to Thursday, all rooms $55 Friday to Sunday.

Wickham Terrace Motel, 491 Wickham Terrace, (07) 839 9611; newish motel, some rooms with balconies, 10 to 15 minutes walk from the city. Clean and simple. Single $46, double $48.

Annies Shandon Inn, 405 Upper Edward Street, (07) 831 8684; this is the most central of Brisbane's budget places, a guesthouse located a couple of streets back from the Sheraton in a recently renovated late nineteenth-century building. Single $22, double $30, bed and breakfast.

Pacific Coast Budget Accommodation, 513 Queens Street, (07) 832 2591 (also known as the Atcherly Hotel). $32 a double.

Youth Hostel, 309 Upper Roma Street, (07) 221 0961. $7 per person per night.

EATING OUT

Brisbane is not nearly so well endowed with restaurants as Melbourne and Sydney and those it has are widely scattered. There are concentrations in Chinatown, around the city and in the suburb of Paddington to the west but nowhere are restaurants gathered along single streets except in Chinatown.

City

La Grange, 303 Adelaide Street, Brisbane, (07) 221 5590; it has had a long life on the Brisbane restaurant scene and remains one of the best smaller restaurants in the city cooking French food on a menu which changes every two or three days. BYO. Mid price range.

Jo-Jo's, Pavilion Building, Queen and Albert Streets, Brisbane, (07) 221 1221; two dining areas upstairs and down. The former is self-service but not to be scoffed at: food is better than one might expect and the prices reasonable. Downstairs the à la carte operation is smooth and professional with a varied menu including a seafood platter, huge steaks and Pritikin dishes. Licensed. Low to mid price range.

Little Tokyo, 85 Bowen Street, Brisbane, (07) 831 7751; one of the few Asian restaurants in Brisbane city. The house speciality is Teppan lobster and the place is popular with Japanese business types so it must be authentic. Licensed. Mid price range.

Kookaburra Queen, Customs House Wharf, Petrie Bight Marina, Edward Street, Brisbane, (07) 52 3797; the last thing you might expect to find on a river cruising paddlewheeler is a really high quality menu with more than a whiff of Asian spice about it but its all here along with decor and atmosphere appropriate to the occasion and the setting. Licensed. Mid to upper price range.

Milano, 78 Queen Street, Brisbane, (07) 229 3917; Brisbane's classic Italian with excellent pastas and interesting diversions such as baked smoked rack of lamb and Moreton Bay bugs grilled with ginger sauce. Licensed. Mid price range.

The Fountain Room, Queensland Cultural Centre, South Brisbane, (07) 240 7111; this is the restaurant in the Art Gallery section of the cultural centre and overlooks the river to the city and is delightful for evening dining. The food draws its influences from a breadth of European sources. There are separate pre- and post-theatre menus. Licensed. Mid to Upper price range.

Chinatown

Brisbane's new Chinatown has drawn many Asian restaurants into its orbit and is the best place to go in the city if you have a craving for this kind of food.

Vungtau, 143 Wickham Street, Fortitude Valley, (07) 52 9810; run by Chinese Vietnamese who escaped during the fall of Saigon, this restaurant is very popular with the Chinese themselves. The mussels in black bean and chilli sauce are hot and tasty. BYO. Low to mid price range.

Singapore, 196 Wickham Street, Fortitude Valley, (07) 52 2006; Singapore steamboat, in which diners cook their own meats and vegetables in a boiling broth is the speciality here but the menu ranges across South-East Asia from Malaysia to Canton. Licensed. Low price range.

Home Made Chinese Meal Kitchen, 257 Wickham Street, Fortitude Valley, (07) 52 2831; very small but serves delicious fresh Chinese vegetables as well as seafood in Chinese sauces. Essential to book. BYO. Low price range.

Sala Thai, Shop 56, Valley Plaza Centre, Wickham Street, Fortitude Valley, (07) 854 1198; the staff here will explain the mysteries of Thai food to diners and then serve it in authentic style. A big menu of fascinating delights. Licensed. Mid to upper price range.

Paddington

This suburb and its surrounding areas of Milton, Red Hill and Rosalie are where one finds some of Brisbane's best dining.

Le Baron, 261 Given Terrace, Paddington, (07) 368 1620; has the taste of Europe down to a 't' and the service and wines to go with it. The large menu travels widely from Hungary and Yugoslavia to France and Germany as does the eclectic wine list. Licensed. Mid price range.

Kookaburra Café, 280 Given Terrace, Paddington, (07) 369 6760; Italy and France both have a hand in stirring the pot here to various but consistent effect, for example, pan fried calamari with avocado or creamy crab sauce over veal are among the choices. BYO. Mid price range.

Le Chalet, 26 Great George Street, Paddington, (07) 369 7397; great northern French food in a tiny converted shop. From stuffed mushrooms to pepper steak in brandied sauce, all is straight forward but delicious. BYO. Mid price range.

Chevalier's, 55 Railway Terrace, Milton, (07) 369 6271; is perhaps Brisbane's best BYO whose menu is rich with imagination leading to intriguing items such as ravioli filled with duckmeat and spinach purée in watercress and broccoli sauce and filleted lamb flavoured with rosemary and served on spinach pasta tossed with pinenuts and a hint of garlic. Desserts include home-made ice-cream in a biscuit tulip served on fresh berry sauce. BYO. Mid price range.

Harrowers', 249 Coronation Drive, Milton, (07) 368 1200; a restored century-old terrace house is home to this stylish, special occasion restaurant where the food is inspired by French models and includes such items as tipsy oysters and turkey paupiette. Licensed. Mid to upper price range.

Night of the Iguana, 111 Haig Road, Rosalie, (07) 371 9031; whoosh go your sinuses as you tuck into chilli-hot foods from Mexico and the Caribbean. Try spiced Jamaican pork or chicken calypso. BYO. Low price range.

Gambaro's, 33 Caxton Street, Petrie Terrace, (07) 369 9500; a Brisbane seafood institution on the border of the city and Red Hill. It used to be almost a fish and chip shop but became so famous that it moved over the road and grew into a gigantic, brick-fronted cavern where you have to ignore the decor for the sheer quality of the oceanic fare. Licensed. Mid price range.

TOURS AND CRUISES

Koala Cruises (07) 229 7055 depart from Riverside, near the Edward Street entrance to the Botanic Gardens, and North Quay, next to Victoria Bridge, each day at 12.50 pm and 1.15 pm respectively. The cruise goes up the river to Lone Pine Koala Sanctuary and costs $9 not including admission to the sanctuary.

Those who would like to see more can join a coach at Lone Pine which travels to the Mt Coot-tha Botanic Gardens and other sites, returning to Riverside at 5.30 pm. This costs an extra $5.

Brisbane City Ferries cruise up and down the river on Saturday and Sunday from Riverside at 1.15 pm, cost $5. This tour must be booked beforehand on (07) 399 4768.

The *Brisbane Paddlewheeler* does river trips each Sunday which include lunch and a jazz band. Cost is $18, phone (07) 846 1713 for bookings.

Brisbane City Council operates a half day tour called **Lookabout** which leaves from 69 Ann Street each day at 9.30 am and 1.30 pm. The fare is $10. Bookings on (07) 225 5555.

Day tours which go further abroad to such places as Moreton Bay, the Gold Coast and even the Sunshine Coast are operated by **Sunliner Boomerang Day Tours**, **Scenic Tours**, **Aladdins Tours**, **Ansett Pioneer** and **Sunstate Tours**. The booking offices for these tours are all at the Roma Street Transit Centre from where they also depart.

Lovely! Champagne Balloon Flights takes passengers from Gatton, west of the city, for flights over Brisbane. Champagne and Breakfast or Brunch are served following each flight. Phone (07) 844 6671 for bookings.

Moreton Bay

The Brisbane River flows east into Moreton Bay which, if you count every rock pushing up out of the water, has 300 islands. The bayside residential areas of Redlands to the south-east of Brisbane and Redcliffe to the north-east give access to the water and islands. They are easy places for daytrips.

GETTING THERE
The settlements around Moreton Bay are about 45 minutes road journey from Brisbane city. Redcliffe Bus Lines buses leave Roma Street Transit Centre for Redcliffe and Redlands.

TOURIST INFORMATION
The Greater Brisbane Region has an information centre on the Shopping Mall Level of the Roma Street Transit Centre. It also has an office at 30 Herschel Street, Brisbane, (07) 221 1562.

WHAT TO SEE
Since Brisbane has no beaches, these islands are the places where Brisbanites come to swim and lie in the sun. The bay and the western sides of the islands have still water. The eastern shores of the islands feel the Pacific surf.

Redcliffe and Redlands

Redcliffe is 35 km (22 miles) north of Brisbane on the edge of Moreton Bay and gives access to about 20 km (12 miles) of coastline. Although it was the site of

Queensland's first settlement, no evidence of this remains and the area has become a suburban outpost of quarter-acre blocks and undistinguished modern homes favoured by retirees, daytrippers and fishermen. The beaches are calm, bayside strands characterised by waterside parks, parking lots and boat launching ramps. Their tree-lined esplanades and narrow lengths of yellow sand where few waves fall tend to give them a somewhat European feel. When the weekend weather is warm, they fill with people, trailer sailors, hobie cats (both small beach launched sailing boats) and windsurfers.

The **Redlands** area, south-east of Brisbane is an enclave of suburbs and market gardens stretching south from Wellington Point to Redlands Bay. It has attracted a coterie of craftspeople, especially **potters** who exhibit in Cleveland at the Hitching Post Gallery, 119 Russell Street, and the Mellerish Gallery, 120 Queen Street, as well as at Victoria Point Potters Gallery, Masters Avenue, Victoria Point, Wellington Point Pottery, 536 Main Road, Wellington Point and other galleries in the district.

Ormiston House in Wellington Street, Ormiston was built in 1862 for Captain Louis Hope, the district's first cane farmer who also had the dubious distinction of being the first man in Queensland to import Pacific islanders as cheap labour for his fields. His labour importing habits extended to his house, constructed of handmade bricks manufactured by Scottish labourers brought to Australia for the purpose. Ormiston House has been restored and furnished in its original style and is open 1.30 pm to 4.30 pm on Sunday afternoons from March to November. You can take afternoon tea there.

An old wooden lighthouse known as the **Cleveland Light** stands in Cleveland Point Reserve. It was built in 1864 and used to guide small boats and timber-carrying rafts into the bay. The concrete lighthouse on Cleveland Point replaced it in 1976.

North Stradbroke Island lies within sight of Redlands, about 10 km (six miles) out to sea. There are many smaller islands in Redlands Bay.

WHERE TO STAY

Waltzing Matilda Motel, 109 Margate Parade, Margate Beach, Redcliffe, (07) 284 5171; air-conditioned units, some looking straight out at the beach which is across the road. Has a swimming pool and restaurant. Single $30 to $35, double $35 to $40.

CRUISES

Redland Bay Cruise and Charter Company, (07) 206 4881; operates a ferry out of Redland Bay on a day cruise around Moreton Bay and the islands. $25 includes lunch. **Bay Cruises**, (07) 207 7287; runs a cruise from Victoria Point at 11 am on Wednesdays, returning at 4 pm. $15 includes lunch.

Moreton Bay Islands

The big islands are **North Stradbroke**, **Moreton** and **Bribie**. They are used by Brisbane's people for rest and recreation but are strictly last gasp for the tourist. North Stradbroke is long, narrow and close to the coast but not quite so close as

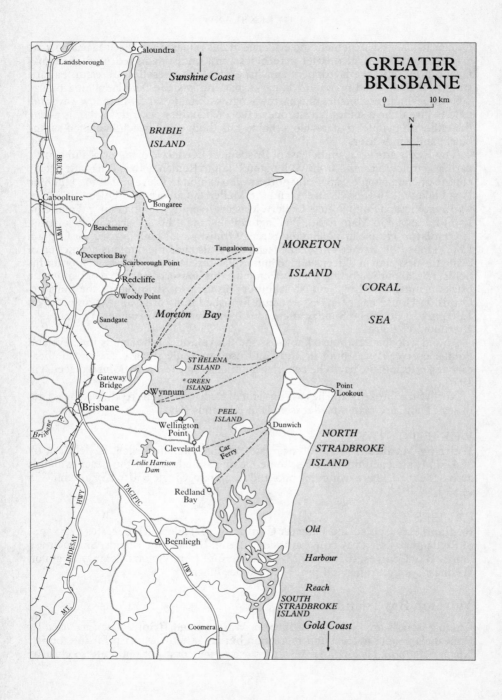

GREATER
BRISBANE

0   10 km

N

Caloundra

Landsborough

Sunshine Coast

*BRIBIE
ISLAND*

BRUCE

HWY

Caboolture

Bongaree

Beachmere

Deception Bay

Scarborough Point

Redcliffe

Woody Point

Sandgate

Moreton   Bay

Tangalooma

MORETON

ISLAND

CORAL

SEA

*ST HELENA
ISLAND*

*GREEN
ISLAND*

Gateway
Bridge

Wynnum

Brisbane

Brisbane R.

Wellington
Point

*PEEL
ISLAND*

Point
Lookout

Dunwich

*NORTH
STRADBROKE
ISLAND*

Cleveland

Car
Ferry

*Leslie Harrison
Dam*

Redland
Bay

Old

Harbour

PACIFIC

Beenleigh

Reach

*SOUTH
STRADBROKE
ISLAND*

Gold Coast

LINDSAY

HWY

MT.

Coomera

South Stradbroke, just beneath it. Together they stretch from the Gold Coast halfway across the broad mouth of Moreton Bay. Moreton Island, 24 km (15 miles) east of Redcliffe, is the furthest from the coast and holds the middle position. Its northern end is opposite Bribie Island.

GETTING THERE

Barges taking cars and people operate between Middle Street, Cleveland and Dunwich on North Stradbroke Island seven days a week at least nine times a day and usually more. Day trips to the resort at Tangalooma on Moreton Island leave Brisbane every day from Hamilton Game Fishing Wharf, Kingsford Smith Drive, Hamilton, usually at 9.30 am. The cost is $25. Phone (075) 48 2666. Bribie Island is reached by a bridge from the mainland. The smaller islands of Coochiemudlo and St Helena are reached by ferry services from Victoria Point and Manly Boat Harbour respectively. Regular passenger ferries also run to McLeay, Lamb, Russell and Karragarra islands in the southern part of the bay.

WHAT TO SEE

South Stradbroke has a resort on its western side, away from the ocean but as the island is narrow, the surf is only a short walk away. The very much larger **North Stradbroke** has three settlements, Dunwich, Amity Point and Point Lookout. Dunwich, the oldest, dates from 1828. There are two freshwater lakes, Brown Lake and Blue Lake, and a 35-km (22-mile beach which runs south from Point Lookout. The main resort on North Stradbroke is Anchorage Village on the beachfront at Point Lookout. **Moreton Island**, is a large sand island whose main attractions are Mt Tempest National Park and Tangalooma Resort. The park is dominated by a gigantic sandhill called Mt Moreton, though it is hardly a mountain. **Bribie Island** has good surf beaches on its eastern side and a large flora and fauna sanctuary, the rest of it is residential.

RESORTS

Tangalooma Moreton Island Resort, Moreton Island, (075) 48 2666; very much for the young, energetic and committed funster, this resort consists of two beach-front blocks, one three storeys, the other two. Rooms have balconies overlooking the swimming pool, the beach or the road behind. $85 to $98 full board.
Anchorage Village Beach Resort, Point Lookout, North Stradbroke Island, (075) 49 8266; a complex of three-storey buildings overlooking its own swimming pool, gardens, outdoor eating area and the beach beyond, or the road. The units have kitchens and come as bedsitters or with one or two bedrooms. Twin-share bedsitters $50, one bedroom $63, two bedroom $87. Less expensive for more people per room.

The Gold Coast

This coast, about an hour's drive south of Brisbane, was first called gold for its miles of beautiful beaches but is now better known for sky-scraping property developments, luxury cars raffled in the streets, pin-ball parlours, gambling, bikini boutiques and Japanese honeymooners. Hideous but fascinating, it attracts over two million holidaying Australians each year and is making an effort to catch the overseas market as well. The population is divided between the retirees housed in high-rise unit blocks or on artificial waterfronts, servants of the tourist industry and the frenetic tourists themselves, giving the place an odd atmosphere of ferocious self-indulgence mixed with bored languor.

The main attractions are the average summer temperature—28°C without the humidity of Brisbane and the beaches—beautiful when compared to other countries' seaside spots but not what they might have been with a little more care. They stretch from Coolangatta on the New South Wales border to Southport, a stone's throw from South Stradbroke Island at the bottom of Moreton Bay, a distance of about 25 km (15 miles). Practically all the beaches face due east to the Pacific and are generally safe for swimming. Any prospect north along them is dominated by the pile of high-rise apartments and hotels on the beachfront at Surfers Paradise which gleams bright orange, gold and green as the sun sets behind it but is otherwise an ugly *eminence grise*—unless you're in the middle of its action. A host of man-made diversions from fun parks to massage parlours has sprung up along the beachside Gold Coast Highway to alleviate sun and surf ennui.

GETTING TO AND AROUND

By Air
Two airports serve this region, Brisbane International and Coolangatta, a domestic airport close to the New South Wales border at the southern end of the coast. They are about equi-distant from Surfers Paradise, the beachfront area considered to be the centre of activity on the Gold Coast. Coolangatta is perhaps the closest but you can expect to spend 40 minutes to an hour travelling by road from either airport to Surfers Paradise. Ansett and Australian fly direct to Coolangatta from Sydney and Melbourne. The fares are $166 and $255. Air NSW and East-West also fly from Sydney. The fare is $152. Flights take one hour and 10 minutes.

The Skennars coach serving Brisbane airport drops off at the Roma Street Transit Centre in Brisbane City from where Greyhound, McCafferty's and its own coaches to the Gold Coast depart. The trip from Brisbane costs around $10. Skennars also runs a service to the Gold Coast from its company terminal. More information about Brisbane International Airport is given in the section on Brisbane. Ansett Pioneer buses run regularly from Coolangatta airport to Surfers Paradise ($5) and Kenny's buses serve Coolangatta itself ($3).

By Road
Ansett Pioneer, Deluxe, Greyhound and McCafferty's coaches from Sydney (14 hours) and Melbourne (26 hours) set down at Coolangatta and Surfers Paradise. The fare is generally the same as travelling to Brisbane.

A local bus service operates up and down the Gold Coast Highway taking passengers from beach to beach between Southport and Tweed Heads, just over the

NSW border. The buses are called Surfside and make regular stops along the highway at all beaches. All day tickets are available for around $5.

The major car hire companies have offices in the centre of Surfers Paradise around Cavill, Orchid and Elkhorn Avenues. Cheaper cars are available from Half Price Rent-a-Car, 3142 Gold Coast Highway on the corner of Beach Road, (075) 92 0456, where you can rent from as low as around $30 a day. Those with a tendency to show off can rent drop-tops from Cruiser Convertibles, (075) 54 9191 for $44 to $49 a day. There are restrictions on the distance you can travel without generating extra charges on these cars.

Wherever you stay along the Gold Coast, you'll be within walking distance of the beach.

TOURIST INFORMATION

Information is readily available from the Queensland Government Tourist Bureau, TAA Building, Cavill Avenue, Surfers Paradise, (075) 92 1033; Monday to Friday 9 am to 5 pm, and from the Gold Coast Visitors and Convention Bureau Information Centre, Cavill Mall, Surfers Paradise, (075) 38 4419; Monday to Friday 8 am to 4 pm and Saturday 10 am to 4 pm.

Surfers Paradise

Surfers Paradise is a built environment in every sense of the words. The only natural feature remaining is its lovely long beach. Hotels, unit blocks, shopping centres, eateries and tourist diversions are jammed along the narrow stretch of ivory sand where the Pacific rolls impassively. The **Broadwater**, a long inlet into the Nerang River, lies across the Gold Coast Highway to the west. Its southern section has been divided into residential islands called 'Canal Estates' with names like Paradise Waters, Isle of Capri and Rio Vista where wealthy retirees park their boats and their bodies and await their ends. Some of its developments are so security conscious that a careless resident who lost his card key might never gain re-entry. Geographically speaking, **Southport** stands to the north of Surfers on either side of the breakwater and the **Spit**, a tongue of sand accommodating some tourist attractions and more beach, finishes off the seaside area to the north, but in reality, there is no visible separation between these areas, Surfers just has more tower blocks than the others.

Beaches

The beaches in and near Surfers, from north to south, are Main Beach (at Southport) Surfers Paradise Beach, Northcliffe Beach, Broadbeach and Kurrawa Beach. The division between them is arbitrary; they are all merely names scattered along one straight sandy fringe but each can be identified by a surf lifesaving club bearing the name of the beach it guards. All are patrolled. Swimming is generally safe if you stick to these beaches and swim between the red and yellow flags. The Gold Coast is not known for strong surf. Surfers Paradise Beach is usually the most populated and swinging and the further south you go, the more sand you get to yourself but the less access you have to other amusements.

Amusements

A staggering array of diversions from amusement parks to animal and fish shows has gathered around Surfers Paradise. They vary from absurd and embarrassing to educational and fun. Here are some you might like to visit.

Seaworld, in Seaworld Drive on the north end of the Spit, is a fun park specialising in performing marine animals and humans. It encompasses a small lake, a 'Theatre of the Sea', a pool for performing sea lions, dolphins and whales, rides, waterslides and a big swimming pool. The 'Theatre of the Sea' is the highlight. Constructed like a cinema with a large window instead of a screen looking into an aquarium where sharks, stingrays, groper and other sizeable sea creatures swim in splendid freedom, it is the venue for an underwater show telling the story of diving from its eighteenth-century beginnings to modern scuba equipment. Divers appear from the gloom wearing primitive apparatus and an ancient diving bell descends into the aquarium while the role of persons ranging from Alexander the Great to Edmund Halley is explained. In other shows, the sea mammals do just as one would expect—jump through hoops, leap out of the water for food and applause and carry people around on their backs. A water-skiing troupe performs in the artificial lake complete with clowns, acrobatic ski-jumpers and pretty girls who perform their tricks even in raging thunderstorms.

Other diversions, including a roller coaster, a watery ride through a drowning mine complete with stiffly animated, life-size puppets and a swimming pool dominated by precipitous slides long enough to propel the foolhardy into the water at speeds up to 90 km (56 miles) per hour, are included in the hefty $18 admission. Seaworld also has fast food outlets, doughnut stalls, soft and hard drink bars spread throughout its grounds. The parts of its considerable area are linked by an overhead monorail train. It is open every day from 10 am to 5 pm.

Fisherman's Wharf, a complex of shops and restaurants built on the margin of the Broadwater next door to Seaworld and taking its example from the development of the same name in San Francisco, and **The Great White Shark Expo**, also in Seaworld Drive are other places worth a look. The Expo displays the biggest great white shark ever caught in Australia as well as other gruesome shark memorabilia and folklore. It is open every day from 9 am to 5.30 pm.

Dreamworld on the Pacific Highway at Coomera, north of Surfers Paradise, is for children. It incorporates eight 'themed' areas with titles such as Koala Land and Gold Rush Country, each with associated rides. Lovers of the bizarre will get a kick out of the Koala Theatre where huge computer-animated kangaroos and koalas sing traditional Australian songs. It proves that computer animation has a long way to go! The one-price-covers-all entry fee is around $20 and hours are 10 am to 5 pm every day. **Magic Mountain**, further south on the Gold Coast Highway at Nobby Beach, is the other big fun park on the Gold Coast. It includes a 'Castle of Magic and Illusion' and lots of rides and is open from Sunday to Thursday 10 am to 5 pm. A man-made riverside park called **Cascade Gardens** located just north of Broadbeach shows off artificial waterfalls and still water pools. It is designed to attract picnickers.

NIGHTLIFE

Surfers Paradise has a plenty of nightlife; until recently the range of entertainment has been limited to cabarets, nightclubs and discos but culture has lately reared its venerable head in the construction of **The Centre**, a new entertainment and arts complex in Bundall Road, about five minutes drive from Surfers Centre. The Centre has two theatres, two art galleries and other exhibition areas as well as a restaurant and bar. It houses musicals, plays, comedy shows and ballet. Phone (075) 91 3600 for information about what's on there.

Surfers' major disco/night-clubs are **Melba's** at 46 Cavill Avenue; **Private Music** in the Ocean Pacifique Resort, 19 Orchid Avenue; and **Twains**, **Bensons** and **Penthouse**, also in Orchid Avenue. The last has live entertainment as well as disco music.

Jupiters Casino in the Conrad International Hotel, Gold Coast Highway, Broadbeach is the only legal gambling den on the Gold Coast and its most visible building. A giant glass and steel wedge set in front of the high-rise hotel, inside it has all the welcome of a shopping centre. Gambling is continuous and all-intrusive, 24 hours of table and video games but no poker machines. The uniquely Australian coin-flipping game of 'Two Up' is played there as well. Besides its casino, the Conrad has a showroom in which Las Vegas-style song and dance shows are presented. Phone (075) 92 8303 for bookings.

SHOPPING

Cavill Avenue, Orchid Avenue and Elkhorn Avenue are the main shopping streets. They are joined by a network of arcades and flanked with clothing boutiques which are well known to have better fashions and accessories than Brisbane.

WHERE TO STAY

At first sight, sorting out accommodation on the Gold Coast, especially in Surfers Paradise where almost everyone stays, can be a nightmare—just about everything standing is available for short-term rental. In fact, there are few true hotels, more than half the accommodation consists of units aimed at families who like to spend school holidays in the sun. These are equipped with full kitchens, laundries and other family necessities but are only worthwhile if your stay is long, around two weeks or so. They are generally not serviced and it is a good idea to check if the one you rent comes with air conditioning. **Accommodation Unlimited** on the corner of the Gold Coast Highway and Elkhorn Avenue in Surfers Paradise, (075) 38 3311, is a central booking agency for many self-contained apartments.

There is almost no choice in the style of building you stay in; everything is high-rise, mostly over 20 storeys, except the small motels along the Gold Coast Highway. The Gold Coast has lately become very popular with Japanese tourists which means that some rates listed below can be expected to increase with the demand for rooms, especially in the summer (December to February). Easter and Christmas/New Year are the high seasons for Australian holidayers and prices go up then as well.

Conrad International Hotel, Gold Coast Highway, Broadbeach, (075) 92 1133; actually run by the Hilton chain, this huge horseshoe shaped luxury hotel, sited a couple of kilometres south of the Surfers bustle, has become the most recognisable building on the Gold Coast, known especially for the glass wedge in front of it which houses Jupiter's Casino. A bus service operates from the hotel to the town centre during the day but not at night. Gambling does rather intrude if you don't like that sort of thing but the rooms have every comfort and wonderful views. All the usual bars and eating places are there as well as several tennis courts and a very large pool which the hotel management insists is in ancient Roman style. I can't see it myself. $115 to $140 for standard rooms, depending which floor you are on. Prices range from there up to $850 for the penthouse.

Gold Coast International Hotel, corner Gold Coast Highway and Staghorn Avenue, Surfers Paradise, (075) 92 1200; a couple of streets north of Surfers centre very close to the beach, 24 levels with 300 rooms. Squash and tennis courts. $125 to $145.

Holiday Inn Surfers Paradise, 22 View Avenue, Surfers Paradise, (075) 59 1000; just as close to the beach, even closer to the action, 22 levels, 408 rooms, two tennis courts and a children's playground. $110 to $135.

Ramada Hotel, Paradise Centre, Surfers Paradise, (075) 59 3499; brand new tower block, international style hotel bang in the middle of town. Single $90 to $105, double $100 to $115.

Chevron Paradise Hotel, Ferny Avenue, Surfers Paradise, (075) 39 0444; this hotel has two sections, an older, less expensive low rise and a 22-storey tower. It also has a couple of swimming pools but no tennis courts, and is a little further from the beach. Low rise single $42 to $62, double $50 to $73, tower $90 to $101.

Beachcomber Quality Inn, 18 Hanlan Street, Surfers Paradise, (075) 50 1000; serviced apartments close to beach and shopping. One bedroom $80, two bedroom $115.

Iluka Quality Inn, corner Esplanade and Hanlan Street, Surfers Paradise, (075) 39 9155; this building has motel units and self-contained one-bedroom apartments. It is as close to the surf as possible. Units, single $65 to $100, double $70 to $105; apartments $85 to $120.

EATING OUT

Squeezed into the square mile or so around Surfers are as many restaurants as could safely fit in that space while leaving a little room for other kinds of business. They have some common features nearly always found in places heavily frequented by tourists. On the downside, most are licensed which raises the food and drink prices and its hard to find the kind of reasonable BYO which Australian city dwellers are used to. On the upside, there is an interesting variety of food and most restaurants display their menus on the street or in the front window so you can make an informed choice. Here are some suggestions:

Chevaliers, Aegean Building, 30 Laycock Street, Surfers Paradise, (075) 38 3100; Americans should feel at home here eating American Salad with four different types of lettuce or being adventurous with a seafood salad including Moreton Bay bugs (small crustaceans). There are souffles for dessert and an excellent, interesting wine list. Licensed. Upper price range.

Forrests Restaurant, Condor Building, 2 Riverview Parade, Surfers Paradise,

(075) 38 5683; like the previous restaurant in that it's housed on the ground floor of a tower block. The menu changes every night but is always a terrific read, as is the wine list. The food is in modern Australian style. Licensed. Mid to upper price range.

Royal Thai Restaurant, Shop 8 Centrepoint Arcade, 3290 Gold Coast Highway, Surfers Paradise, (075) 38 0205; a small, good quality restaurant at the end of the arcade, opposite a more expensive Indian establishment. Comfortable seating and a pseudo-plush atmosphere in deep blues. Food quality is even without any standouts but general good value. BYO. Low price range.

The Typical Japanese Restaurant, Elkhorn Avenue, no phone; aimed at Japanese visitors and so serving authentic Japanese home cooking especially soup and noodle dishes. Decor is minimal but the service is jolly. BYO. Low price range.

Cavills Italienne Ristorante, Cavill Avenue, Surfers Paradise, (075) 50 2887; an up-market Italian, good for a splurge. Licensed, dinner only. Upper price range.

Gino's Osteria, 2563 Gold Coast Highway, Broadbeach, (075) 55 3966; cleanly decorated in fawns and dark green lattice screens, this spacious restaurant serves traditional and flavoursome Italian dishes. Licensed. Mid price range.

Bavarian Steakhouse, corner Cavill Avenue and Gold Coast Highway, Surfers Paradise, (075) 31 7150; good for plain eaters who veer away from spicy food. The atmosphere is jolly German beer hall with a big bar and simple dark wooden tables and chairs. Licensed. Low to mid price range.

Fisherman's Wharf, Seaworld Drive, The Spit, (075) 32 7944; not a restaurant but a waterfront complex of eating places, bars and shops where, for diners, the accent is on seafood from fish and chips to lobster and chardonnay. Can be cheap or expensive, depending on your mood. The leading restaurant in the complex is Fisherman's Wharf Yacht Harbour Restaurant. Licensed.

Tandoori Taj, 3100 Gold Coast Highway, Surfers Paradise, (075) 39 9433; rather overdone on the cheap Indian decor but the food is as authentically Indian as it's likely to be in this part of the world. Licensed. Mid to upper price range.

The River Inn, 32 Ferny Avenue, Surfers Paradise, (075) 31 6177; diners in by 6.30 pm and out by 7.50 pm receive 20% discount here. The restaurant strives for a nautical atmosphere and specialises in seafood. Licensed. Mid to upper price range.

TOURS

The entire Gold Coast is so easily accessible from Brisbane that nearly all coach tours from that city include it on their routes. The names and numbers of these companies are given in the section on Brisbane. Their tour buses depart from the Roma Street Transit Centre where their booking offices are also located.

The major Gold Coast based coach tour operators are **Trans Otway Good Times Tours** (075) 50 1455 and **Intertour EET** (075) 38 0000. They send their buses out from Surfers Paradise to points north (including Brisbane) south and west. There are tours to the fun parks Seaworld and Dreamworld, tours to the mountains and the Lamington National Park and night tours taking in the discos, casino and bars of the coast. Some cross the border into northern New South Wales.

Water tours also depart from Surfers Paradise to South Stradbroke Island and around the canals of Surfers' residential islands.

Chevron Princess (075) 39 9833, **Shangri-La** (075) 38 1444 and **Sir Bruce** (075) 32 5031, cruise the canals, the Nerang River and the Broadwater. Their basic cruise price is $12. Stradbroke Island is served by four boats, **Jet-a-Way** (075) 38 3400, **Maranoa,** an old 60-foot, two-masted, island lugger, (075) 50 3228, **Shangri-La** again but with a bigger boat and **Stradbroke Star** which also cruises the Tweed River near Coolangatta. The price for Stradbroke Island is a uniform $30 which includes lunch.

Helicopter joyflights operate continually from Seaworld, costing around $40. Phone (075) 32 1055.

BOAT HIRE
Golden Boat Hire, 1 Hooker Boulevard, Broadbeach, (075) 52 3322; outboard motor boats for fishing and exploring $60 per day, $40 half day.

Complete Watersports Activities, river end of Cavill Avenue, Surfers Paradise, (075) 38 0022; self-drive half-cabin cruisers, fishing tackle and waterway maps. These people arrange waterskiing as well, phone (075) 38 0055.

Burleigh Heads and Currumbin

Both these places are a short distance south of Surfers Paradise on the Gold Coast Highway. They can be reached by Sunliner bus or by car.

Burleigh Heads is the only National Park on the Gold Coast. It is a small, rocky, bush-covered headland which neatly divides the north half of the coast from the south and marks the point where the bustle of Surfers Paradise and its surrounds give way to something quieter. The headland is home to a very few koalas and is criss-crossed by three km (two miles) of walking trails. The best views of the coast are to be had from its summit. Burleigh Heads Beach often has very good surf and is the site of an annual international surfboard-riding competition each March.

Currumbin lies halfway between Burleigh Heads and Coolangatta. It is the home of one of Australia's best known tourist attractions, the **Wildlife Sanctuary** just off the Gold Coast Highway in Tomewin Street, where sick and injured native animals have been cared for since the 1940s. Currumbin Wildlife Sanctuary was originally an apiary owned by Alex Griffiths who, when he wasn't relieving bees of their honey, created a beautiful flowering garden. The garden attracted lorikeets, brightly plumed green and red parrots, which, in their enthusiasm to drink nectar from the blooms, threatened to destroy it. Griffiths solved the problem by feeding them on a mixture of honey, bread and water to which they took in such numbers that bird feeding times at Currumbin became famous.

Griffiths made a gift of the sanctuary to the National Trust of Queensland in 1976.

Its spacious green grounds, filled with healthy, friendly animals, are a delight to visit. The birds fly down in hundreds at early morning and late afternoon and are tame enough to land on visitors' arms, shoulders and heads. About the only thing that will keep them away is the sight of a bird of prey circling over their feeding ground. Other animals, including kangaroos and koalas, roam freely about wide enclosures open to visitors. At feeding times, animal keepers give talks on their charges. Water birds are fed each day at a small lake in the grounds where eels, some as much as 2.5 metres (eight feet) long, also live. At feeding times, the eels swarm riotously on the water surface, battling for the leftovers. Opening hours are 8 am to 5 pm every day. Admission $8.

Currumbin also has a very attractive beach, not so long and sweeping as those around Surfers Paradise but white, gently curving and not too crowded.

WHERE TO STAY

Rocks Resort, Pacific Parade, Currumbin Beach, (075) 34 4466; ocean front block of two-bedroom, self-contained apartments close to the junction of Currumbin Creek and the Pacific. Not quite so many storeys as other blocks but longer. Doubles $84 to $135. Weekly rates are considerably cheaper.

Fifth Avenue Motel, 1949–1953 Gold Coast Highway, Burleigh Heads, (075) 35 3588; close to the beach, a medium-sized motel with pleasant pool area and adequate rooms. Single $35 to $47, double $38 to $75.

Aussie Resort, corner 3rd Avenue and Gold Coast Highway, Burleigh Heads, (075) 56 2877; serviced apartments built around a heated swimming pool. Linen is supplied and the rooms are serviced weekly but otherwise you take care of yourself. Close to beach. $60 per night, weekly rates cheaper.

EATING OUT

Paragon, (075) 35 2300; one of the Gold Coast's better seafood restaurants. Licensed. Upper price range.

Coolangatta and Tweed Heads

These two southern Gold Coast centres are known as the Twin Towns. Coolangatta stands in Queensland, Tweed Heads in New South Wales but it has become impossible to separate them. Their Siamese twinning is due to the eccentricities of state politics in the matter of poker machines. Poker machine gambling is a feature of New South Wales working men's clubs where the machines provide revenue and entertainment and, every so often, make a payout to their players but Queensland, despite its casinos, won't have them. At the border this dichotomy has become a farce. Queenslanders roll over the line by the bus load for the delights of pulling the 'pokies' in Tweed Heads. On the back of its gambling trade that town has grown into its Queensland neighbour, creating one centre with two names.

GETTING THERE

The Sunliner bus from Southport takes an hour to reach Coolangatta and can be picked up at any of its many stops along the Gold Coast Highway. Air services to Coolangatta are described in Getting to and Around the Gold Coast.

TOURIST INFORMATION

Information from Beach House, Marine Parade, Coolangatta, (075) 36 7765; Monday to Friday 8 am to 4 pm, Saturday 10 am to 4 pm and Travel Centre of New South Wales, Pacific Highway, Tweed Heads, (075) 36 2634; 9 am to 5 pm daily.

WHAT TO SEE
Tweed Heads has two gargantuan gambling clubs which come complete with cabaret rooms for 'international' entertainers and local stars, restaurants and sporting facilities.

Seagulls Rugby League Football Club in Gollan Drive, Tweed Heads, (075) 36 3433, makes the most of its luck by being open 24 hours a day. It has 430 poker machines, four restaurants, a disco, cheap breakfasts and its own Rugby League football team.

Twin Towns Services Club, Tweed Heads, (075) 36 1977, though not open 24 hours has extended to two venues. The original club has two restaurants and a coffee shop, lounge and cocktail bars, a sports room and hundreds of poker machines. Its extension, the Twin Towns Sports Complex, Banora Point, is six km (four miles) south of the parent club and has a golf course, more poker machines, two restaurants and a drinking lounge. You do not need to be a member to enter these clubs as they accept what are loosely known as 'bona fide visitors', ie, anyone they see fit to allow in. Because gambling finances all their operations the shows and food they offer are cheap compared with other Gold Coast places.

Seagulls and Twin Towns clubs are not the only ones in Tweed Heads, there is also the **Terranora Lakes Country Club**, Marana Street, Bilambil Heights, (075) 54 9223, set in the hills behind Tweed Heads, and the newly refurbished **Coolangatta Tweed Heads Golf Club**, (075) 54 4544 which has a 36-hole golf course.

Coolangatta provides an airport, accommodation and particularly beaches which Tweed Heads, set on a river mouth, lacks.

WHERE TO STAY
Almost all accommodation here is in apartments which are available for weekly rental only and are not serviced.

Seascape, 53 Bay Street, Tweed Heads, (075) 36 0300; a tower rising above Tweed River Boat Harbour, has self-contained, two-bedroom apartments, two tennis courts and a beach out the front. $425 to $735 per week or $80 to $110 per night for at least three nights plus $30 cleaning fee.

Bahamas Motel, 7 Hill Street, Coolangatta, (075) 36 1824; across the NSW border close to the Tweed Heads clubs. Doubles $40.

EATING OUT
Oskar's on the Beach, Marine Parade, Greenmount Beach, Coolangatta, (075) 36 4621; a beautifully sited, beachfront, seafood restaurant of extremely high reputation. Licensed. Upper price range.

TOURS
Joy flights in a two-passenger biplane are run by a gentleman called Ken Keane from Coolangatta Airport, phone (075) 36 3877.

The Hinterland
Escape from the unceasing gaiety of Gold Coast life is possible by venturing inland to the comparatively untouched forest gorges and waterfalls of Springbrook and Binna Burra close to the border of New South Wales.

GETTING THERE

Car is the only option other than taking a package tour. Take the signposted routes inland from the Gold Coast Highway to the destinations mentioned below.

TOURIST INFORMATION

Local information from Tambourine Mountain Visitor Information Centre, Doughty Park, North Tambourine; 10.30 am to 3.30 pm every day except in very wet weather, and from Canungra Visitor Information Centre Lamington National Park Road, Canungra, (075) 43 5156; Sunday to Friday 10 am to 4 pm, Saturday 10 am to 12.30 pm.

Springbrook

This small town around 40 km (25 miles) west of Coolangatta is higher and cooler than the coast. The distance and height replace sea colours with the greens and rusty browns of the land and flamboyant and aggressive buildings are absent. No sky-scrapers, rather modest, weatherboard stores and houses. Coastal and Tweed Valley views can be gained from vantage points around the town, especially off **Lyrebird Ridge Road**. A number of bushwalks lead to **Purlingbrook Falls** in the **Springbrook National Park**; one trail takes intrepid walkers under the cataract. An historic village erected in the town from pioneer buildings includes the 1889 Nerang Railway Station among its sights. An English garden set in Springbrook Road amidst the rainforest is possibly the town's most eccentric delight. It is open all days except Mondays from 10.30 am to 4 pm.

On the Lamington Plateau, the town of **Binna Burra** is approached from Southport via Nerang and the Beechmont Road, a journey of about 45 km (28 miles) which ends at the eastern entrance to **Lamington National Park**. The park has 500 waterfalls, a great deal of sub-topical jungle where huge trees and thick vines carpet the hillsides and over 140 km (87 miles) of walking tracks graded from easy to difficult. Greatest of its attractions is the **Natural Arch**, a bridge of stone carved out by a roaring cataract that, after heavy rain, rises to a deafening pitch of ferocity.

Tambourine Mountain is further north in the Darlington Ranges 20 km (12 miles) west of Coomera. The town of Tambourine has restaurants, art galleries, roadside stalls selling arts and crafts and antique shops. It is one of the get-away settlements where hippies went to hide and then discovered they had to make a living.

WHERE TO STAY

O'Reilly's Guest House, Green Mountain via Canungra, Lamington National Park (075) 45 1611; despite its name, a complex of low, country buildings set in a big rainforest clearing. The dining room is licensed and there is a tennis court. $60 to $82 per person including full board and activities.

Binna Burra Mountain Resort, Beechmont via Nerang, (075) 33 3622; 41 cabins, licensed dining room, guided walks from the resort into Lamington National Park. $86 per person with own facilities, $74 per person with vanity unit but no bathroom, $60 per person budget accommodation. All rates include full board and activities.

Mountain Lodge Guesthouse, Southport Avenue, Eagle Heights, (075) 45 1484; simple, traditional guesthouse in Tambourine Mountain, nine rooms only. $20 per person bed and breakfast, $35 per person includes dinner.

EATING OUT
There are plenty of tea rooms and small restaurants in the small highland towns including: **English Country Gardens Restaurant**, Springbrook Road, Springbrook, (075) 33 5244; **Old Colonial Restaurant**, Springbrook Road, Springbrook, (075) 33 5200; **Falls Licensed Restaurant**, Eagle Heights Road, Tambourine, (075) 45 1267; **Old Post Office Restaurant**, Mt Tambourine Road, Upper Coomera, (075) 53 1286.

TOURS
The tour companies mentioned under Surfers Paradise also conduct tours to the hinterland.

From Brisbane to The Sunshine Coast

The Bruce Highway and the coastal railway run north from Brisbane through the **Glass House Mountains** to the southern border of the Sunshine Coast. Dairy farms keep many of the locals occupied providing milk for Brisbane. The countryside is a combination of grassy green slopes and forested water courses.

The way the Glass House Mountains jut out of this settled landscape was an oddity noted even by Captain James Cook who is reputed to have named them after glass kilns in his home of Yorkshire. They are long extinct volcanoes of which only the hardened cores remain, poking straight into the sky from low forested slopes like giant fingers of grey stone. The modern highway runs straight by the mountains, cutting off its former more scenic route but it is still possible to take the old road, now called the **Glasshouse Mountains Tourist Drive** from Glasshouse Mountains township on the highway. The drive rejoins the Bruce Highway nine km (six miles) north of Landsborough. Its route passes through Glasshouse Mountains National Park and the towns of **Beerwah** and **Landsborough**. The **Queensland Fauna and Reptile Park** in Beerwah displays a range of Australia's deadliest snakes including death adders and taipans, along with crocodiles and some native marsupials. Open daily. There is an historical museum in Maleny Road, Landsborough which is open Sundays only from 1 pm to 4 pm.

The Sunshine Coast

The Sunshine coast has two faces, wide white beaches open to the sun, the breeze and the Pacific Ocean that rolls in sometimes green, sometimes blue but always with ranks of white breakers at the shore, and, west of the beaches, a green range of low hills and mountains where small farmhouses nestle in the laps of gentle undulations, enjoying misty mornings and cool evenings.

People dispense with their shoes on the Sunshine Coast and often with most of their clothes as well. They may put them on again to walk in a national park or along a back country road but that is only a temporary measure. Garments remain off, especially in the psychological sense, until the wearer returns to the normal course of life.

The coast extends from Caloundra, just over 100 km (62 miles) north of Brisbane, to Fraser Island. It is about 140 km (87 miles) long and the climate is sub-tropical, over 30°C in summer (December to February) but not as humid as north Queensland. Winter temperatures average around 20°C. There is a great deal of rural as well as tourist industry—sugar cane growing begins here and runs all the way up the Queensland coast. A huge variety of tropical fruit and nuts are also grown.

A kind of miniature Gold Coast is trying to spring up along the strip between Caloundra and Noosa, especially at Noosa, but it is comparatively low-rise and unlikely ever to match the monstrosities of Surfers Paradise. Because the Sunshine Coast is part of Queensland, it also inevitably bears some naive eccentricities of tourist promotion, of which the Big Pineapple is the most prominent example.

GETTING TO AND AROUND

By Air
Air NSW and East West airlines fly to Maroochydore from Sydney ($177) and Melbourne ($270) daily. The flight takes slightly longer than that to Brisbane. Air NSW flies from Sydney to Caloundra ($183) and Henerbery Aviation from Brisbane ($33). Sunstate Airlines flies from Brisbane to Noosa daily ($46).

By Train
The *Queenslander* and *Capricornian* trains from the same centre stop in Nambour, the main inland town on the coast but there are no rail lines to the coastal towns.

By Road
Skennars Coaches run three services daily from the Roma Street Transit Centre in Brisbane to Caloundra, Mooloolaba, Maroochydore, Noosa and Tewantin on the Sunshine Coast. This service can also be used to hop from town to town along the coast. The fare is $13 to Noosa, less to places closer to Brisbane. The trip takes about an hour and a half.

Motorists can reach all the Sunshine Coast's main towns from the Bruce Highway.

TOURIST INFORMATION
There are tourist information centres at Alexandra Parade, Alexandra Headland near Mooloolaba, open 9 am to 5 pm Monday to Friday and on the Noosa Tewantin road outside Noosa, open the same hours seven days. The National Parks and Wildlife Service's Kinaba Information Centre, located at the northern end of Lake Cootharaba is only accessible by water from Elanda Point on the western shores of the lake.

The Big Pineapple

Caloundra

The coastal town of **Caloundra**, 12 km (seven miles) east of the highway, marks the true beginning of the Sunshine Coast. It has four **surf beaches** within easy distance: Kings Beach, Bulcock Beach, Dickey Beach and Kawana Beach. Captain James Cook's ship the *Endeavour* is reproduced at two-thirds its true size in a display on Landsborough Parade, Golden Beach, open 9 am to 4.45 pm each day. One of the town's odder attractions is **World of Matchcraft** at 108 Nicklin Way, where matchstick models of the Sydney Harbour Bridge, the Eiffel Tower and the Spanish Armada are exhibited among other curiosities. A beachside road runs from Caloundra to Mooloolaba and Maroochydore about 16 km (10 miles) north.

Mooloolaba and Surrounds

Mooloolaba, at the mouth of the Mooloola River shelters the coast's prawning and fishing fleets as well as Brisbane's pilot vessels and is a base for sports fishermen who trip out to the near offshore reefs. **Alexandra Headland** is the best local surfing beach. **Maroochydore**, five km (three miles) north, at the mouth of the Maroochy River, has been a beach resort town for many years and has its share of ugly high-rise unit blocks. The road through Buderim, eight km (five miles) inland from Maroochydore, leads back to the Bruce Highway.

In **Buderim** the soil is good enough to grow lovely tropical gardens where frangipani, pointsettias, hibiscus, bougainvillaea and poincianas appear in quantity. The town has an historical museum called Pioneer House, contained in a slab hut dating from 1876 and located in Ballinger Road. Primitive agricultural and domestic implements and furniture are displayed there. Open daily from 10 am to 4 pm. A short drive brings you back to the highway near Tanawha. The next place of interest on its northward run is **Woombye**, site of the Sunshine Plantation and the CSR Macadamia Nut Factory.

The pineapple-growing **Sunshine Plantation** is a monument to Queensland's unmistakable style of tourist development. British royalty are frequently subjected to it when visiting Australia so they may understand how local industry and tourism can combine in perfect commercial harmony. The plantation is dominated by the Big Pineapple—an exhibition hall in the shape of a pineapple with a viewing platform under the leaves from which the whole plantation can be seen. Visitors ride through the neatly laid out fields in a sugar cane train, may eat up to 50 varieties of tropical fruits in the restaurant and buy souvenirs from the plantation shop. An animal nursery and rainforest walks are also part of the fun. The Sunshine Plantation is open every day from 9 am to 5 pm. Its near neighbour the **CSR Macadamia Nut Factory** can be reached on foot or via the 'nutmobile', which carries passengers from the plantation. You can see macadamias being processed from cracking to packaging at the factory. Open 9 am to 4.30 pm each day.

Montville, about 13 km (eight miles) west of the Bruce Highway is the highest mountain town in the region. **Rainforest Tourist Park**, a short distance from the Montville turnoff, is an arrangement of formal gardens and enclosed rainforest with a restaurant and superb views of the coast and farmland. Artists and restaurateurs congregate at Montville to profit from the tourist traffic in an understated way. There are galleries, places to eat and a museum. It is possible to continue north along the top of the range through Flaxton to Mapleton or to head east back to the Bruce Highway via Palmwoods.

EATING OUT

There are two good restaurants in Montville: **Misty's**, Main Road, Montville, (071) 42 9264, was once the town general store and upstairs enjoys fabulous views of the coast. The menu changes each month but generally includes flavours of the Sunshine Coast's delicious fruits. BYO. Mid price range; **Pottingers**, Main Road, Montville, (071) 42 9407, offers more original fare and can be relied upon always to surprise and please with dishes such as mud crabs in ginger and lemon sauce with mango, and Thai pepper chicken. BYO. Upper price range.

Nambour

The Bruce Highway continues north to **Nambour**, the main rural centre on the Sunshine Coast, famous for the cane trains which wind through its wide, awning edged main street. The trains, drawn by a small yellow diesel engines, consist of open topped, wire sided bins filled with straw coloured stalks of ripe sugar cane. About 25 cars long, they run on tracks hardly two steps wide, rocking up the street to the **Moreton Central Sugar Mill**. Their journey begins in the fields, themselves networked with rail lines, where cane is dumped into bins as it falls to the harvesters. July to December is harvest period. Tours of the crushing mill are conducted during harvest time on Tuesday, Wednesday and Thursday. Phone (071) 41 1411. A turning two km (one mile) north from Nambour takes you back to the coast via Bli Bli and across the Maroochy River. The strip of coast between the river mouth and Noosa is skirted by the **David Low Way** which runs through beach towns including Coolum and Peregian Beach but all roads at this end of the Sunshine Coast lead to Noosa.

Noosa Heads

Noosa Heads, usually just called Noosa, is the best town in which to base yourself on the Sunshine Coast. The town rests right on the beach facing blue Laguna Bay and spreads up the surrounding green hillsides. **Hastings Street**, separated from the beachfront by low-rise apartments and the only street of any consequence, is a strip of sidewalk cafés, restaurants and boutiques, shaded by enough trees to make it bearable in the summer heat. Noosa's north-facing beaches are among the best anywhere in Queensland; their aspect means protected waters and all-day sun but the main beach has become a victim of over-development, damaging its profile and resulting in severe sand loss. This has been remedied by a crude bulwark of stones laid almost the whole length of the beach which is a bad disappointment if one comes upon it unexpectedly.

Noosa National Park to the east of the town rises and falls around coves and rocky headlands. Its coastal walking trail leads to Tea Tree Bay and Granite Bay, to tidal pools and, south from Noosa Head, Alexandria Bay, a kilometre of wild beach where the pounding surf is better appreciated from the land than the sea.

The Noosa River runs west of the town through its sister settlement of **Noosaville** and past Tewantin to Lake Cooroibah and Lake Cootharaba. A ferry from Tewantin takes four-wheel drive vehicles (available for hire in Noosa) across the river to **Teewah Beach** and Cooloola National Park. The beach, where the Aboriginals are said to believe the world-creating Rainbow Serpent came to die, stretches away to the north; its gold, orange, snow-white, pink and purple sand hills are the Sunshine Coast's greatest sight, changing colour by the day as rain washes them and the sea eats at their edges. Organised daytrips to see them depart regularly from Noosaville (see Tours below). Launches leave in the early morning and motor up the river through the everglades and mangroves to Lake Cootharaba. After lunch, passengers plunge into Cooloola National Park in jeeps travelling through towering rainforest to the ancient extinct volcano at Double Island Point to look back past the multicoloured sands to Noosa.

WHERE TO STAY

The best accommodation is at Noosa which, surviving almost entirely on tourism, provides a considerable quantity of it. You can choose to stay in either a resort hotel or a holiday unit but they are a little hard to tell apart as most are two-bedroom, two-bathroom units, often with a dining area, kitchen and sometimes laundry built in. Units tend not to have staff except for a caretaker but some do extend to receptions and such. Most places have swimming pools surrounded by small or large tropical gardens. There is often a barbecue. The hotels have maids, valets etc. Most accommodation is on Hastings Street, either fronting onto the beach or across the road from it. One or two places are set back on the hill overlooking Laguna Bay.

Accom Noosa, Hastings Street (071) 47 3444; is an agency which handles about ten unit blocks in Noosa. It can provide you with a place to stay on the beachfront, on the hill or by the river.

Noosa International, Edgar Bennet Avenue, Noosa Heads, (071) 47 4822, is a three-storey complex of two bedroom units centred around a swimming pool and overlooking Laguna Bay from the hill. Its staff will arrange activities for guests if they so desire. $140, $260 during school holidays.

Netanya Resort Hotel, 75 Hastings Street, Noosa Heads, (071) 47 4722; a long low beachfront complex of 29 luxury holiday units. One bedroom $120 no beach view, $170 beach view; two bedroom $170 no beach view, $240 beach view.

Seahaven Resort, Hastings Street, Noosa Heads, (071) 47 3422; one- and two-bedroom holiday units with balconies overlooking the beach. One bedroom $80, $120 during school holidays; two bedroom $110, $150 during school holidays.

Ocean Breeze, Corner Hastings Street and Noosa Drive, Noosa Heads, (071) 47 4977; one of the larger unit complexes in Noosa, located on the short stretch of Hastings Street which is not on the beachfront but a very short walk away. Has one-, two- and three-bedroom holiday units with balconies or courtyards. One bedroom $75, $95 during school holidays; two bedroom $90, $120 during school holidays; three bedroom $110, $145 during school holidays.

EATING OUT

Restaurants are so close together on Hastings Street that you can walk from one to another without straining at all.

Annabelle's Beach House, (071) 47 3204, has the pick of the beachfront settings in an old holiday house shaded by coconut palms. Seafood, piles of local crab, lobsters, prawns etc is the speciality, accompanied by a good wine list. Licensed. Upper price range.

Gingers's at Seahaven Resort, (071) 47 5111, adds a touch of the Orient to its seafood such as spanner crabs in soy sauce and ginger or squid stuffed with lobster and scallops. Licensed. Upper price range.

La Plage, (071) 47 3308, deviates from the seafood norm by serving classic French food of which desserts are undoubtedly the highlight. Licensed. Upper price range.

Grenny's, (071) 47 4611, serves local seafood from a blackboard menu so dishes change from day to day, prawns (shrimps) and smoked salmon wrapped with fresh brie in filo pastry is an example of what you might find. BYO. Mid price range.

Michelle's, (071) 47 4722; for satays, reef fish and steak. Licensed. Low to mid price range.

Cafe Le Monde in Ocean Breeze Apartments, (071) 47 4091; for coffee and inexpensive eating early morning or late night on a terra-cotta terrace. Low price range.

TOURS

Sunseeker Tours and **Wintons Suncoast Tours** run full day bus tours from Caloundra to all parts of the Sunshine Coast and as far south as Brisbane. Some tours pick up at Maroochydore and Mooloolaba. Tours to Fraser Island depart from Noosa and surrounding towns, especially Rainbow Beach, many also take in the Coloured Sands. **Noosa 4WD Tours** go into the rainforest of Cooloola National Park.

Cooloola Cruises and 4WD Tours, (071) 49 7884, carries tourists via launch and four-wheel drive vehicle along rivers, across lakes and to forests and beaches otherwise inaccessible to them. There are three itineraries for which prices vary from $27 to $35.

Seven Flags Information Centre, on the Noosa Tewantin Road sells at least 20 other tours to the sights around Noosa as well as being a centre for private 4WD hire.

Mary Valley

The Mary River runs between the towns of Maryborough and Gympie north of the Sunshine Coast. It has a rousing history of timber getting and gold rushes but these days is a quiet backwater and one of the few areas unaffected by the Queensland tourism boom.

GETTING THERE

By Air
Sunstate Airlines flies from Brisbane to Maryborough and Hervey Bay ($74).

By Rail
The *Capricornian* train from Roma Street Transit Centre in Brisbane stops at Gympie ($16.70) and Maryborough ($24).

By Road
Greyhound, Ansett Pioneer and Deluxe coaches departing daily from Brisbane stop at both towns on their services to Townsville and Cairns but only Deluxe continues to Hervey Bay on two of its services. The fare is around $20 to Gympie and $25 to Maryborough.

The Bruce Highway runs through Gympie and Maryborough. Hervey Bay can only be reached by road from Maryborough. The existing railway line does not carry passengers.

It is possible to take a scenic route to Gympie via a westerly diversion from Landsborough, driving into the **Blackall Range** and to the town of Maleny where the **Mary Valley Scenic Way** begins. It passes through **Mary Cairncross Park** where there are excellent views of the coast as far south as Brisbane, as well as walking trails and picnic spots, and runs along the course of the Mary River to **Gympie**.

Gympie

Gympie is a small country town these days but it was once the saviour of Queensland. The town is built on numerous steep hills and when rain falls heavily, the main street fills with water. This occurs so often that the people break out their boats as a matter of course. In September 1867 an English immigrant prospector from Wiltshire named James Nash found gold on the banks of the Mary River in the middle of a forest of gympie-gympie trees, stinging trees that could blister human skin at a touch. Despite their defences, the trees had gone by 1868 and the hills around the Mary River were covered with prospectors tents. The first of Queensland's many gold rushes had begun with a vengeance and continued into the first decade of the twentieth century. Nash himself managed to keep some of his pile and remained living comfortably in the town until he died in 1913. There is a simple monument to him in **Memorial Park** and he is buried in the town cemetery. The locals say there is still gold under the streets and gold fever has not died. In the 1970s a new mine called **El Dorado** was sunk beside the Bruce Highway to look for a reef of gold supposedly under Albert Park, the town's main sporting arena.

Maryborough and Hervey Bay

Maryborough stands at the mouth of the Mary River and was the region's major port in gold rush days. Hervey Bay is the beach town north-east of Maryborough and provides access to Fraser Island, one of the great natural sights along the Queensland Coast.

The gold rush which made Gympie eventually helped to make Maryborough as well, although its early stages stripped the town of much of its population. Maryborough sits at the end of a long protected passage of navigable water where the Mary River blends with the sea. As Gympie grew, drawing thousands from the southern cities to its gold fields, Maryborough added gold business to the timber trade which had previously been its only staple. When timber and gold declined, sugar and its attendant quasi slave trade, called 'blackbirding', came into their own. 'Blackbirders' were ships' captains who ostensibly brought indentured labourers from the Pacific Islands to work in Queensland's cane fields. They were often accused of luring natives on board their vessels only to knock them over the head and throw them in the hold. Those who didn't die from this treatment were sold from the wharves at Maryborough and other port towns, and went to work as semi-slaves in the cane fields. This practice continued into the late nineteenth century and threatened to make Queensland a plantation economy not unlike the southern United States. Fear of this, combined with racial prejudice against black workers, saw blackbirding banned in the late nineteenth century. Whatever its human cost, it helped generate great wealth which in turn funded a building boom in the late nineteenth and early twentieth centuries.

Maryborough is little known to tourists moving up and down the Queensland coast. It has neither beaches nor mountains but it has much to offer for anyone interested in the fascinating history of this area. That the town's people have paid some attention to preserving their historical buildings is an added bonus.

The old **riverfront** where steamers used to move passengers and cargo is graced by pubs with lacy verandas that look old, quiet and innocent to the passer-by but still bear a reputation as 'bloodhouses' where more than one drug haul has come in up the river from the east. A fine old **customs house** and **courthouse** stand above the bend in the river. The courthouse has a barristers' walk down one side overlooking a pretty riverfront park. The town's band, a frequent competition winner, plays regularly in the park's exuberant rotunda. Maryborough is also full of beautiful Queensland high-set houses built before World War II. Modelled on cane farmers' residences, they stand on wooden stilts, high enough to walk under, have wide verandas closed in by louvres, steep steps up to their front doors and are decorated with turned and fret-sawed wood.

Hervey Bay, is a beachside settlement about twenty km (12 miles) from Maryborough. It is a popular holiday spot for families from Brisbane who pack up at school holiday time and repair to the camping grounds, caravan parks and motels along the beachfront. Maryborough workers who crave proximity to the sea tend to live there. The settlement is rather ragged and not very classy but it has much more accommodation for travellers than does Maryborough.

WHERE TO STAY AND EATING OUT

Maryborough has about a dozen motels which one would be hard put to separate for quality. The two most central are **Maryborough City Motel**, 138–140 Ferry Street, (071) 21 2568, and **Maryborough Motor Inn**, Corner Ferry and Queen Streets, (071) 22 2777; both charge around $40 for a double room.

The **Royal Hotel**, Corner Kent and Bazaar Streets, Maryborough, (071) 21 2241; is allegedly modelled on one of Cairo's extravagant examples of hotel architecture. Its foyer would certainly lead one to believe so. The hotel has motel units attached with private facilities as well as rooms in the old building with shared bathrooms. Units single $20, double $30; rooms single $12, double $20.

Melanesia Village Resort, Elizabeth Beach, Urangan, Hervey Bay, (071) 28 9702; is the best accommodation at Hervey Bay. It is a combination of motel units and 'cabanas'—accommodation with separate bedrooms, set in charming tropical gardens around an artificial lake. Hervey Bay social life seems to gravitate to its bars and restaurants. Its only drawback is a three block walk to the beach. Single $38, double $46.

Fraser Island

Fraser Island lies east of Hervey Bay and Maryborough. The second largest island off Australia, beaten only by Tasmania, it is made entirely of sand and always dubbed 'the world's largest sand island'—perfectly true but likely to mis-inform the visitor for the island looks nothing like the Sahara. It accommodates a wide range of habitats from high sandhills and wide beaches to fresh-water lakes and thick forests. Fraser became a *cause célèbre* throughout Australia in the 1970s when the damage being done to its fragile environment by sand mining was brought to national attention. The island became such a focus of public concern that despite the resistance of governments and miners, mining was banned. Notoriety also brought a flood of daytrippers which continues, especially during summer school holidays but there is no doubt that Fraser Island is worth seeing if you have the time. Perhaps its oddest feature in the four-lane highway on 75 Mile Beach. There is no 'road' as such but the beach sand is so tightly packed that cars and buses traverse it four abreast without damage.

GETTING THERE

Travel is by four-wheel drive vehicle over most of Fraser Island and the best way to see it is to book a tour. Independent minded travellers can hire 4WDs in Noosa.

TOURS

Tours depart from Rainbow Beach north of Noosa or from Noosa itself. **Sun Safari Tours**, **Fraser Island Nature Tours** and **Fraser Island Excursions** operate daily. The tours are full day and start early, around 6 am. The cost around $60 to $70 and can be booked at **Seven Flags Information Centre** in Noosa.

The Great Barrier Reef

Variously acclaimed as the world's largest living thing, the eighth wonder of the world and the marine equivalent of Ayers Rock, the Barrier Reef lives up to all that. Its dimensions cannot fail to impress. The 2000 km (1240 miles) of ever-changing coral blanket the Queensland coast from Gladstone to Cape York and extend into the Torres Strait beyond, practically to New Guinea; they stretch to the edge of the continental shelf where the reef ends in an undersea cliff hundreds of feet high. There is a vast number of islands within the reef boundaries. Some are coral cays (formed by the accumulation of coral skeletons), others are continental islands (the peaks of submerged mountains). Innumerable outcrops of coral also surface and disappear with the changing tides. The reef is so full of life and colour that it seems almost profligate to the casual visitor; to the scientists who study it, it appears a world worth more attention than one mere lifetime can provide. Australians themselves only recently came to appreciate the Barrier Reef en masse but once aware of its significance declared it a marine park in 1983, dedicated to preserving a unique expression of natural life.

How the Reef is Formed

The Great Barrier Reef is actually a necklace of many reefs which constantly shift and change. The present reef began to grow about 10,000 years ago at the end of the

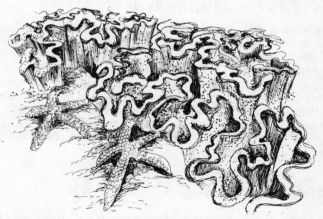

Coral and Starfish on the Barrier Reef

last ice age when the sea rose to cover a range of coastal mountains. It was not the first time such geological events had occurred and the new coral took up where old coral had lived in previous warm periods. The remains of the old reefs are now invisible under existing coral.

Coral is made by animals called coral polyps. They are carnivorous plankton-eaters which produce a hard limestone skeleton to support a soft body equipped with stinging tentacles. In most cases, swimmers don't see these tentacles because coral polyps are night feeders, remaining firmly lodged in their tiny, house-like, skeletons during daylight. Coral outcrops are colonies of coral polyps. They build by budding one from another in a reproductive process akin to cell division but once a year, usually on the fourth or fifth night after the full moon in early spring, they spawn, squirting into the warm tropical waters a pink cloud of microscopic larvae which, in a delicious irony, join the plankton until they can find a suitable base on which to begin another coral colony. The annual coral spawning is usually witnessed by hundreds of enthusiastic locals and tourists. Seeing it is a once in a lifetime experience.

Coral's colour is drawn in most cases not from the coral polyps themselves but from zooxanthellae, single-celled plants that live in coral tissues and aid the production of polyp skeletons.

Fish populate the coral reefs in millions, grazing, preying, pecking at the polyps, moving in startlingly coloured schools or sweeping by alone. They come small, medium and large. Small fishes swim close to the coral outcrops and are the brightest coloured. Striped, ringed, spotted and daubed with yellow, blue, red, black, green and orange, they use their colours and markings to attract mates, deceive predators and warn of their defences. Middle-sized fishes have less colour, they rather shine and glisten, bouncing the light from their reflective scales as they flash by in large schools. Cod are the reef giants, huge lumbering fishes with few predators. Their staring eyes and gaping mouths belie their placid nature.

Discovery of the Great Barrier Reef

Captain James Cook, RN discovered the Barrier Reef and was less than glad that he did since it kept him prisoner for many months and finally wrecked his ship, the *Endeavour*. The barque ran aground on Endeavour Reef off the far north coast of Queensland in June 1770. It was floated off and well enough patched with its own sails to limp to the present site of Cooktown where repairs were made. It seemed, however, that despite having a seaworthy ship, Cook and his companions, including Sir Joseph Banks, might never reach the open sea again because they had yet to find a way through the reef. It was only when they stopped at Lizard Island, 90 km (56 km) to the north, and climbed the high hill now known as Cook's Look that the great seafarer saw his passage to the open sea.

The Great Barrier Reef Marine Park

The ruling contemporary question is how to allow people to see the reef, scientists to research and fishermen to fish, and preserve it all at the same time. This is being

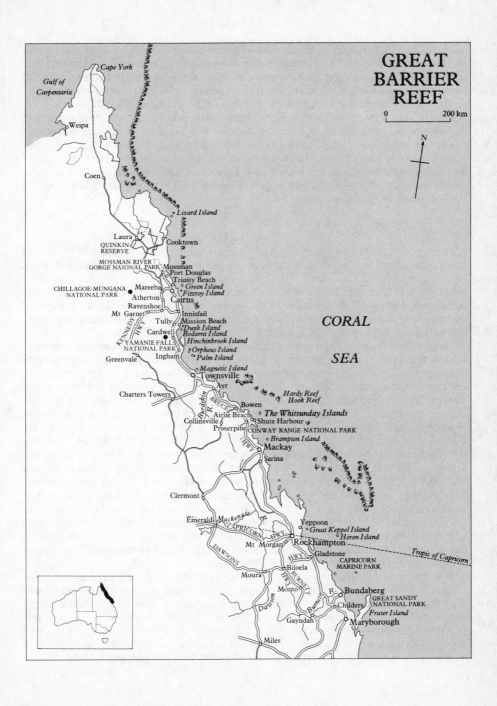

GREAT BARRIER REEF

0   200 km

N

Gulf of Carpentaria

Cape York

Weipa

Coen

Lizard Island

Laura
QUINKIN
RESERVE
Cooktown

MOSSMAN RIVER
GORGE NAIONAL PARK   Mossman
Port Douglas
Trinity Beach
CHILLAGOE-MUNGANA   Mareeba   *Green Island*
NATIONAL PARK   Atherton   *Fitzroy Island*
Ravenshoe   Cairns

Mt Garner   Innisfail
Tully   Mission Beach
Cardwell   *Dunk Island*
Bedarra Island
YAMANIE FALLS   *Hinchinbrook Island*
NATIONAL PARK   *Orpheus Island*
Greenvale   Ingham   *Palm Island*

Magnetic Island
Townsville
Ayr

CORAL

SEA

Charters Towers   *Hardy Reef*
Bowen   *Hook Reef*
Airlie Beach
Collinsville   *The Whitsunday Islands*
Proserpine   Shute Harbour
CONWAY RANGE NATIONAL PARK
Brampton Island
Mackay
Sarina

Clermont

Emerald   *Mackenzie*
CAPRICORN   HWY
Yeppoon   *Great Keppel Island*
Mt Morgan   *Heron Island*
Rockhampton   *Tropic of Capricorn*
Gladstone
CAPRICORN
Biloela   MARINE PARK
Moura
Monto   Bundaberg
GREAT SANDY
Childers   NATIONAL PARK
Gayndah   *Fraser Island*
Maryborough

Miles

undertaken by a management programme under which the reef has been declared a marine park with some areas completely closed, some open only to researchers, some to tour operators and some to anyone. Most of the islands, in keeping with the conservationist mood, have been declared national parks. The resorts on most take up only a very small and restricted proportion of the available area; the rest is open but strict rules apply to its use and no building is allowed. In fact, strict rules apply to the whole reef area. Basically they say that nothing must be disturbed. No matter where you are, you can't take away any coral, living or dead, or any shells, and neither must you remove anything from the islands. After all, you wouldn't break off a bit of a Greek temple to take home, would you? Live coral has some defences of its own, too. It can very often sting prying fingers. Fishing is allowed in many places but it's best to check before setting out.

Seeing the Reef

It's very hard to appreciate the beauty of the marine life and coral of the Barrier Reef unless you get under the water. Coral dies in the open air and the best of it is in deep water, generally 50 to 70 km (31 to 43 miles) off the coast on the outer reef. The water on the outer reef is also very clear, much more so than the water close to the coast and islands. This means that to see the biggest and best looking parts of the reef you have to journey from the coast or an island but wherever you come from, the pattern of your excursion is likely to be pretty much the same.

Here's how it goes. A fast boat, usually a huge twin-hulled aluminium launch, runs to the outer reef and ties up at a big pontoon where the passengers disembark. Some of these pontoons have underwater viewing chambers for anyone anxious to see coral immediately. Once on the pontoon, passengers can choose to go coral viewing in various kinds of glass-bottomed boats or dive either with a snorkel or scuba equipment. This is by no means as difficult as it may sound, so long as you can swim, you can probably snorkel; scuba diving is another matter but lessons are available in many places. The old glass-bottomed boat is still around but any self-respecting reef operator has a semi-submersible these days. They look a bit like a surfaced submarine and allow those in them to get completely underwater without swimming. They work well but you don't come as close to the coral as a swimmer.

Such trips generally last a day and include lunch and refreshments as well as videos and talks about the reef. People who choose to stay on a coral cay have other options as well. A good strong pair of sandshoes (sneakers) allows you to go reef walking at low tide and gain a close acquaintance with smaller reef life. This appeals to keen photographers without underwater equipment and to children. Island coral also means you can go snorkelling at any time.

It is also possible to join aircraft which fly over the reefs and land at pontoons where their passengers indulge in the same pursuits as those brought there by boat. The flights allow passengers to see the reef from above. It breaks from the bright blue water in green and yellow rings and lines like a rash on the surface of the sea.

Many islands have 'fringing reefs', coral close to their shorelines. In a few cases these are interesting and good to dive on but often they are not nearly as impressive as the outer reefs. Heron Island probably has the best fringing coral.

Island Resorts

About 20 islands have been turned over to tourist development. The resorts vary in standard, size and tone from all-muck-in holiday camps to some of the world's most exclusive and pampered places to stay. Their most common feature is full board because there's nowhere else to go when you're there. All have swimming pools, restaurants and bars and a plethora of water and land sports equipment—usually available free unless motorised. Each island resort also runs boats to the nearest reef and further for snorkelling and coral viewing. The islands are detailed later in this section but it is worth keeping in mind that not all islands are in the tropics and those on the southern reef can become quite chilly on winter evenings.

Until recently it was not possible to stay on the reef itself. The introduction of the **Four Seasons** floating hotel on John Brewer Reef off Townsville has changed this to an extent but not for the majority of travellers. For costs and details see Townsville section, page 231.

The Coastal Cities

For those travellers who don't stay at island resorts, a holiday along the gigantic stretch of coastline covered by the reef means staying in one or more large towns between **Gladstone** and **Cairns** and boating to the reef and the islands. The coastal towns are useful centres from which tourists can radiate not only to the reef but to nearby islands for day trips, to the water for cruises through protected coastal passages and inland to mountains and wild country.

Though called cities, the urban areas are more like very large towns and so retain their country charm whilst having city characteristics such as an occasional tall building, department stores and self-awareness. Their country feel is appealing to travellers, their city conveniences make travelling easier. Staying in a coastal city can also reduce the cost of your holiday while opening up a larger range of possibilities than resorting to an island. As well as day trips, 'stand-by' overnight or two day stays on nearby islands are often available for as much as 40 percent less than the published resort rates, provided there are rooms available. May and June are good months to take advantage of these 'stand-by' rates.

The Southern Reef

This section of the reef extends from **Gladstone** to the Tropic of Capricorn which runs through the city of **Rockhampton**. It has neither as many islands as the Whitsunday Passage nor as many inland attractions as Cairns and so is rather jumped over by tourists. Its advantages are that it is not as hot and sticky as the north, not so commercialised and doesn't have stinging jellyfish and crocodiles to make you jittery every time you go swimming.

Gladstone

Perhaps this city is not the best at which to begin one's acquaintance with the Great Barrier Reef but, as geographical accident would have it, it is where the coral begins.

Gladstone was established in 1853 and named after the then British Prime Minister, William Gladstone. It was a small and unimportant river-mouth town until the 1960s when a decision was made to develop its port for the coal and bauxite trade. The result could cruelly be described as something of an industrial wasteland, especially around its port, a place of frightening coal loaders, giant grain and alumina terminals and oil storage tanks. It happens to be vastly important to the Australian economy but it's certainly not pretty. It does, however, have some advantages such as closeness to Brisbane (it's only one and a half hours flying time, 550 km (341 miles), a comfortable day's drive) and mud crabs—this is where they begin to populate the mangroves. Gladstone also gives access to the Capricorn and Bunker island groups.

GETTING TO AND AROUND
Sunstate Airlines flies from Brisbane to Gladstone. The fare is $119. Air travellers from other states land at Brisbane and take on-flights from there.
The *Sunlander*, the *Queenslander* and the *Capricornian* trains from Brisbane's Roma Street Transit Centre stop at Gladstone. The fare is $64.40 first class, $40.50 economy.

TOURIST INFORMATION
Information on the Gladstone region is available from the Gladstone Area Promotion and Development Bureau, Shop 6, City Centre Plaza, Goondoon Street, Gladstone, (079) 72 4000.

WHAT TO SEE
Port Curtis, as the harbour is called is protected by two islands standing in its mouth, **Curtis Island** and the much smaller **Facing Island**. There are other, smaller islands in the harbour. The port is able to take the enormous coal ships which trade between Australia and Japan and moves many tens of millions of tons of cargo each year, employing a goodly proportion of the town's nearly 30,000 people but its development has been undertaken without any regard for aesthetics. Two rivers, the **Boyne** and **Calliope**, empty into the harbour and, with the islands, provide plenty of waterways for enthusiastic local boat-owners.

Tannum Sands is the best beach within striking distance of the city. It is a relatively safe surf beach south of Boyne Island, an island set at the mouth of the Boyne River and home to the Boyne Smelter, the world's largest alumina refinery.

Harbour Islands
Curtis Island runs close to the mainland for nearly all its length and is reached by crossing Port Curtis or a via narrow passage called **The Narrows** a short distance to the north. Most of the island is given over to cattle raising. Ferries operate from **Auckland Inlet** in Gladstone harbour to the permanent settlement at **South End** where there is accommodation and facilities for day visitors including a licensed kiosk. Other areas of the island are best approached by hired vessels. A six-km (four-mile) surf beach runs from South End to a number of rocky headlands of which the most prominent is Connor Bluff. Four and a Half Mile Beach, south of

the settlement, is a turtle rookery between September and March. A lighthouse on **Cape Capricorn** at the northern end of the island overlooks huge sand hills and nearby is **Yellow Patch,** a pumpkin-coloured sand dune set on a small inlet. The area is a popular crabbing and fishing spot in winter. Camping is allowed but water must be taken in. On the seaward side of the Curtis Island is a 30-km (21-mile) stretch of beaches and bluffs, accessible by boat in all but the worst northerly weather. It is also possible to circumnavigate the island, weather and tides permitting.

Facing Island, the smaller of the harbour islands, lies off the mouth of the Boyne River and Tannum Sands Beach. It has neither the beaches nor the facilities of Curtis Island although there are some interesting geological features such as the old exposed reef remnants at 'The Gnome Homes' on the track to the eastern beach and Castle Rocks near the same beach. There are holiday shacks, toilets and barbecues at Gatcombe Head on the southern end of the island.

Hinterland

The **Dawson Valley** and the **Callide Valley** lie about 100 km (62 miles) to the west of Gladstone, centred on the town of **Biloela**. The area has one or two features worth visiting if you have a spare day. **Mt Scoria** south from Biloela on the Burnett Highway via **Thangool**, is an odd volcanic formation consisting of scoracious basalt columns which echo and vibrate when struck with a metal object, heavier blows set up a bell-like echo. The columns have symmetrical shapes and look like a broken stairway with some pieces laid down horizontally and others standing upright. **Cania Gorge National Park** is a short distance further south on the Burnett Highway. Palms, tree ferns and other exotic plants grow in the gorge and there are easy walks leading to quiet fresh-water rock pools and caves.

WHERE TO STAY

Highpoint Motor Lodge, 22–24 Roseberry Street, Gladstone, (079) 72 4711; the most central of Gladstone's motels, a seven-storey building with 54 two-room units. Kitchens and laundry in each unit, air conditioning. Some rooms have city views. Swimming pool. Single $68, double $75.

Mid City Motor Inn, 26 Goondoon Street, Gladstone, (079) 72 3000; another well-located motel with air-conditioned units quite comfortably if plainly furnished. Swimming pool. Single $32 double $38.

Siesta Villa Motor Inn, 104 Glenlyon Street, Gladstone, (079) 72 4922; Air-conditioned units. Swimming pool. Single $39, double $43.

EATING OUT

Swaggy's Australian Restaurant, 56 Goondoon Street, Gladstone, (079) 72 1653; specialises in steaks, mud crabs, kangaroo tail soup and damper. Licensed. Mid price range.

TOURS

Lady Elliot, (079) 75 7162; a luxury cruiser which runs fully catered tours to your choice of destinations off Gladstone for diving, snorkelling and fishing. The vessel has nine berths, including up to two doubles. $1800 for a two day cruise.

MV *Pentana*, (079) 79 2217; another cruise boat operated along the same lines as the one above. Cruises arranged to suit your desires.

Tours of the **Boyne Smelter**, a very large alumina smelter which is very important to the people of Gladstone, can be booked on (079) 73 0211.

ACTIVITIES
Boats are available for hire from **Gladstone Marine Centre**, 34–36 Lord Street, Gladstone, (079) 72 2226, and from **Boyne Kiosk**, 1 Orana Avenue, Boyne Island, (079) 73 7472. Canoes can be hired from **Tannum Sands Canoe Hire**, on the beach at Wild Cattle Creek, phone (079) 73 7201.

Heron Island

Heron Island is the main resort island off Gladstone. It is one of the few Barrier Reef resorts on a coral cay and one of the few actually on the reef. The island is particularly prized by divers since the reefs which surround it are some of the best around any island on the reef and the water is very clear. Heron is what most people picture when thinking of tropical islands, although, strictly speaking, it is not in the tropics. The island is small, low in the water, green at the centre and fringed by white sand. Heron's natural attractions are not only its appearance and position. The island is called Heron because it is a favoured nesting place of herons but gannets and mutton birds also migrate there to breed, some from as far away as Siberia (seems understandable). Green turtles nest there from October to February and during September, migrating whales can be seen from the island shores.

GETTING THERE
Heron Island is 70 km (43 miles) from Gladstone. It can be reached quickly by helicopter or slowly by ferry. Lloyds Helicopter Service charges $217 for its return flights from Gladstone. A launch called the MV *Heron II* leaves Gladstone for Heron Island at 8 am each day except Thursday. The trip takes up to three hours. The return boat leaves at 12.30 pm and the trip takes two and a half hours. Return fare $100.

THE RESORT
Heron Island accommodates 280 people at various standards from luxury beachfront and mid-range units with private facilities to lodges with communal showers and toilets. None of the rooms have televisions or phones. The resort overlooks the island's boat harbour. Full board tariffs are $80 per person per day in the lodges, and $124 to $145 in the units. Private use surcharge is $27 per day. There is also a beach house which costs $163 per day. Diving and, at low tide, walking on the reef are the main activities. Diving costs extra and lessons are available. Fishing is also popular.

Rockhampton

Sometimes called the Beef Capital of Australia which betrays the rural industry truly supporting the local economy, **Rockhampton** sits just above the **Tropic of Capri-**

corn and begins that section of Queensland whose climate can truthfully be called tropical. It is built on the **Fitzroy River**, a short distance inland, and was first settled in 1850s by farming members of the Archer family but it was the almost simultaneous discovery of gold and copper at **Mount Morgan**, about 120 km (74 miles) to the west, that fostered rapid growth through the middle years of the nineteenth century.

GETTING TO AND AROUND
Air travel from Brisbane is by Ansett and Australian Airlines ($142). The latter also flies direct from Sydney ($235).

The *Capricornian* train leaves Brisbane six days a week in the early evening, arriving in Rockhampton next morning at breakfast time. The fare is $73.50 first class, $46.20 economy. The *Sunlander* and *Queenslander* from Brisbane to Cairns also carries passengers to Rockhampton.

Ansett Pioneer, Greyhound, Deluxe and McCafferty's serve Rockhampton from Brisbane and the northern cities of Cairns and Townsville. Fare from Brisbane is around $45.

TOURIST INFORMATION
Tourist information is available from Capricorn Tourism and Development Organisation, Gladstone Road, Rockhampton (079) 27 2055.

WHAT TO SEE
Rockhampton is lucky to have retained much of its historically charming waterfront although its days as a port for anything but a few casual coastal sailors are long since gone. Twenty of the buildings gathered along **Quay Street** on the southern bank of the river are preserved by order of the Queensland National Trust as are another 30 scattered throughout the city. The best of them is the **Customs House** in the middle of Quay Street over-looking the Fitzroy River. It is a sandstone rotunda with two short wings and a high domed roof and expresses the power, optimism and possibly the folly of the gold economy which built it. Quay Street's other nineteenth-century buildings spread on either side of the Customs House and include pubs, bond stores and shops, all kept in something like their original condition. The **Rockhampton Post Office** on the corner of Denham and East Streets in the town mall has also been restored with great attention to detail.

Rockhampton also has some of the best of Queensland's unique domestic architecture in its exclusive suburb called **The Range**. The suburb stands west of the town, set on a series of high hills. The area around the **Mater Hospital**, not itself a distinguished building, is occupied by beautifully tended and very large high-set bungalows with elegant wide verandas, decorated with lattice and turned wood and shaded by mango and banyan fig trees. A house built by the original manager of Mount Morgan mine stands in the hospital grounds. It is a Victorian stone and brick building which goes against the tropical style of its nearby companions and shows that the builder's heart was not at home in his chosen country.

Other places to visit could include the **Rockhampton Botanic Gardens** at the end of Spencer Street on the town's southern outskirts. Set along the banks of

Murray Lagoon, the gardens cover 10 peaceful acres and include a couple of magnificent banyan trees, a small, rather tired zoo and a rather exposed Japanese Garden. The **Rex Pilbeam Theatre and Art Gallery** in Victoria Parade is the town's most prominent modern building. It houses touring stage productions of which there are quite a few in this part of Queensland, and a fair collection of contemporary paintings.

WHERE TO STAY

Riverside International, 86 Victoria Parade, Rockhampton, (079) 27 9933; set by the Fitzroy River, a short walk from Rockhampton's charming waterfront. Restaurant and pool, comfortable rooms on eight storeys, including six luxury top-floor rooms. Single $65, double $80.

Caravilla Motor Inn, corner Bolsover and Archer Streets, Rockhampton, (079) 27 7488; modern air-conditioned accommodation near the new bridge over the Fitzroy River. Swimming pool. Single $34, double $42.

Duthies Leichhardt Hotel, Bolsover Street, Rockhampton, (079) 27 6733; central city location with 120 units of three standards from ordinary motel to tower block, all air-conditioned. Restaurant. Single $30 to $60, double $36 to $66.

EATING OUT

Vijay's Curry House, 41 Denham Street, Rockhampton, (079) 22 2345, will heat your curry how you like from mild to very hot. BYO. Low price range.

La Vieille Terrasse, 120 William Street, Rockhampton, (079) 22 3012; the city's most adventurous French restaurant. Licensed. Upper price range.

Pickles Restaurant, 75 High Street, Rockhampton, (079) 28 6490; buffet style with entertainment and 'one price, eat all you can' approach. Licensed. Mid price range.

ACTIVITIES

Rockhampton's Aquatic Adventureland, Bruce Highway, North Rockhampton, (079) 28 3869; a water fun-park with all kinds of rides where people are propelled by water, also barbecues, a kiosk, picnic areas, trampolines and volley ball courts. From 10 am daily.

Waterskiing is available at Ski Gardens, Fitzroy River, Rockhampton.

Around Rockhampton

Mount Morgan is an old mining town, 38 km (24 miles) south west of Rockhampton, was responsible for much of the city's early wealth. It was established in 1882 as a centre of gold and copper mining and did not cease to be so until 1981 when its giant open-cut mine, a huge and ugly hole, was closed in the face of collapsing copper prices. Although filling with water, the mine remains a tribute to human determination and corporate endeavour. The town is sited on the Dee River and originally had six **suspension bridges** running across the river from town to mine. Only two remain, the others having been destroyed by floods, but they allow visitors to picture the daily procession of miners which proceeded for the best part of

80 years. The bridges are in Tipperary Street. The **Mount Morgan Museum** records the mining days mostly in a collection of photographs showing the growth of the town. It also houses relics of the more primitive mining methods by which the lode was opened up. It is open from 10 am to 1.30 pm Monday to Saturday and 10 am to 4 pm on Sunday. Tours of the mine itself depart from its car park at 9.30 am and 1.30 pm each day.

Caves

Two cave systems, **Cammoo Caves** and **Olsen's Capricorn Caverns**, are located around 20 km (12 miles) north of Rockhampton near a village called **The Caves Township**. Both are dry limestone caves, that is to say, they do not house rivers but rather have been hollowed out in limestone mountains by the action of acidic rainwater seeping through the earth. Like other limestone caves, they are very large and furnished with laceworks and cascades of stone as well as the occasional giant tree root. The caves are inhabited by Ghost Bats, the largest carnivorous bats in Australia which flock there in considerable numbers. Guided tours of both systems take place each day.

Capricorn Coast

This name is given to the coast north-east of Rockhampton which centres on the town of **Yeppoon**. A town of 9000 people, it is 50 km (31 miles) from and is best known for being the site of the **Capricorn Iwasaki Resort**, a 20,000 acre development especially built for Japanese tourists. The resort includes a wildlife sanctuary populated by beautiful grey brolgas, tall water birds famous for their mating dance. **Yeppoon Beach**, extending 20 km (over 12 miles) to the north of the town is characterised by clear water and safe swimming but is not a white sand beach so can disappoint your tropical fantasies. It is also a popular spot for sailing races. **Rosslyn Bay**, four km (two and a half miles) south of Yeppoon is the departure point for cruises to Great Keppel Island and for charter boats serving any of the 32 islands, mostly uninhabited, within reach of this area. A scenic drive runs from Yeppoon to the small town of **Emu Park**, 19 km (12 miles) south, along a succession of attractive beaches ending at the **Singing Ship** on the headland at Emu Park. The 'ship' is a sculpture constructed of singing pipes that imitate the sighing of rigging on old sailing vessels.

WHERE TO STAY
Bayview Tower, corner Adelaide and Normanby Streets, Yeppoon, (079) 39 4500; a new motel with views of Keppel Bay and comfortable rooms. Also has two restaurants and a swimming pool. Single $45 to $50, double $50 to $55. $10 surcharge during school holiday periods.

EATING OUT
Seafood and Eat It, Anzac Parade, Yeppoon, (079) 39 2233; on the beachfront, eat in or take away including oysters from the owners' own leases. Big servings. BYO. Low to mid price range.

TOURS

Rothery's Bus Service, (079) 22 4320, runs day and night coach tours of Rockhampton as well as day tours to the caves, around the Capricorn Coast and to the Koorana Crocodile Farm. The tours depart Monday to Friday and pick up from local accommodation. Not all tours depart every day.

Young's Coaches, (079) 22 3813, runs a tour of the Capricorn Coast which departs from Duthie's Leichhardt Hotel, corner of Denham and Bolsover Streets, Rockhampton each morning. The bus picks up at accommodation around Rockhampton and the tour takes all day.

Romantique, (079) 39 2226, a catamaran sailing vessel leaves Rosslyn Bay Terminal, south of Yeppoon, each day at 9.15 am. It cruises the Capricorn Coast and islands, anchoring at beaches and pausing for snorkelling and scuba diving.

Great Keppel Island

Great Keppel Island lies 48 km (30 miles) east of Rockhampton. It is the largest of the 27 islands in the Keppel group and the only one with resort accommodation. The island is continental, has 17 beaches and covers 1400 hectares (3460 acres). Cook discovered it in May 1770 and named it and its group after Rear Admiral Augustus Keppel, First Lord of the Admiralty. It was used for sheep grazing during the 1930s and developed as a tourist island in the 1960s.

GETTING THERE

Sunstate Airlines flies from Rockhampton to Great Keppel island daily. Boats to Great Keppel depart from Rosslyn Tourist Terminal, south of Yeppoon at 9 am each day. Great Keppel Island Tourist Services operates a commuter boat called *Aquajet* and a larger double hulled launch called *Victory*. A water taxi also operates from Rosslyn.

THE RESORT

The Great Keppel Island Resort is largish, accommodating nearly 400 people when full. It occupies a site overlooking Fisherman's Beach on the southern end of the island. It has double, twin and family units with private facilities, facing the beach or gardens in two and single storey blocks. Tariff is full board and varies between $119 per day for a single person in a beachfront unit during the high season (20 December to 16 January) to $83 per person for two people in a garden room during the low season. Intending visitors to Great Keppel should keep in mind that it directs itself to the unceasing amusement of 18-year-olds or thereabouts with the sales accent on libido and alcohol. There is an activity every minute of the day and a disco every minute of the night.

DAY TRIPS

The *Victory*, described above, as well as operating as a ferry for Great Keppel, carries day-trippers through the Keppel Islands, providing lunch and a stop at Middle Island Underwater Observatory on the way. A bus carries passengers from Rockhampton, Yeppoon and Emu Park to join the Victory.

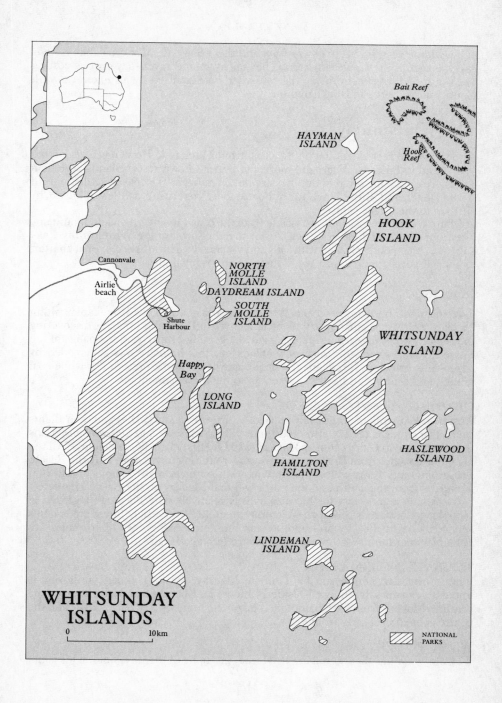

Bait Reef

HAYMAN
ISLAND

Hook
Reef

HOOK
ISLAND

Cannonvale

Airlie
beach

NORTH
MOLLE
ISLAND
DAYDREAM ISLAND

Shute
Harbour

SOUTH
MOLLE
ISLAND

WHITSUNDAY
ISLAND

Happy
Bay

LONG
ISLAND

HASLEWOOD
ISLAND

HAMILTON
ISLAND

WHITSUNDAY
ISLANDS

LINDEMAN
ISLAND

0   10km

NATIONAL
PARKS

Two large vessels, MV *New Horizons* and the TSMV *Coralita* cruise the islands and the reef in the Capricorn area. They take five-and seven-day cruises costing $625 and $858 respectively. Aerial tours can be organised by arrangement with Countryair Services in Rockhampton.

The Whitsundays

The section of reef extending up the coast from **Mackay** to **Bowen** centres on the **Whitsunday Islands**. There are more and better-known resort islands here than anywhere else along the reef but they are linked rather to the coastal settlements of **Airlie Beach** and **Shute Harbour** by boat and to **Proserpine**, a little way inland, by air than to the larger centres.

Many Whitsunday islands are visible from the coast. Rising green and mountain-like from the silver-blue sea, they cluster together around the **Whitsunday Passage**, a calm stream splashed with sails and touched by gentle breezes. Boat charter, either bare or skippered, is a big industry in the Whitsundays.

Mackay

The most southern town on the Whitsunday coast was named by Captain John Mackay, a British seaman who took up land there in 1862 after officially discovering the region two years earlier. He established a grazing property on the banks of the Pioneer River where the town now stands but that industry was superseded by sugar-cane growing. It remains the major activity up to the present day while coal mining and tourism add extra sweetening to the local economy.

GETTING TO AND AROUND
Ansett and Australian Airlines fly to Mackay from Brisbane ($184) and their flights south from Cairns ($212) also land there. The *Sunlander* and *Queenslander* trains from Brisbane to Cairns stop at Mackay ($103.60 first class, $69 economy). All the big name coaches from Brisbane and from surrounding towns such as Airlie Beach, Proserpine and Townsville stop there as well. Fare from Brisbane is about $65. Motorists from the south and the north will find Mackay on the Bruce Highway.

Mackay is a good city for bicycles as it is relatively flat. They can be hired at Hodgkinson's Barty's Bikes, 164 Victoria Street, (079) 57 4484. There are two bus services, one in the city and another for the northern beaches. Timetables are available from the tourist information centre in Nebo Road.

TOURIST INFORMATION
The information centre run by Tourism Mackay, the local tourist authority, is impossible to miss. It is housed beside a Chinese junk beached on Nebo Road on the way into Mackay from Rockhampton. The phone number is (079) 52 2677 and the centre is open every day from 9 am.

WHAT TO SEE
The old buildings that do remain in Mackay are none of them very old. This is not

due to human destructiveness but to a simultaneous cyclone and flood which demolished the town in 1918. Thus the Customs House, Police Station, Court House and banks—those usual representatives of high architecture in Queensland country centres—were all built during or after 1920, nothing remains of town buildings before that date. There is a local museum at **Greenmount Homestead**, 16 km (10 miles) away just off the Peak Downs Highway past Walkerston. The homestead sits on a piece of the estate marked out by Captain John Mackay in 1862, a mere 12-hectare (30-acre) patch of a claim which once stretched to the mouth of the Pioneer River. It contains memorabilia, including the diaries of Albert Cook covering the period 1891 to 1927, and a great clutter of period furniture and bric-à-brac. All its contents are owned by the Cook family whose members lived in the homestead from the time of its construction. The museum is open on Sundays only between 10 am and 4 pm.

Mackay has a couple of beaches close to town on the southern side of the river, **Town Beach** and **Illawong Beach**. The tide which sometimes comes in and out as much as six metres (20 feet) along this coast tends to make them a bit like mud flats when it is low—they look more attractive at high tide. There is a small 'fun park' with trampolines and a waterslide at Illawong Beach. **Blacks Beach** and the beaches of **Eimeo**, **Bucasia** and **Shoal Point** lie about 15 minutes drive or bus ride to the north of the town.

WHERE TO STAY

A lot of motels are strung along Nebo Road, which is also the Bruce Highway as it enters Mackay.

Tourist Village Motel, 34–38 Nebo Road, Mackay, (079) 51 1811; older than some but closer to town. Has some two-room suites with kitchenettes. Double $44.

Miners Lodge Motor Inn, 60 Nebo Road, Mackay, (079) 51 1944; not quite so close. Double $44.

White Lace Motor Inn, 73 Nebo Road, Mackay, (079) 51 4466; offers 24-hour room service and has rooms on two levels of a modern building in the style of a nineteenth-century pub. Single $44, double $45.

Ocean Resort Village, 5 Bridge Road, Mackay, (079) 51 3200; self-contained one-, two- and three-bedroom apartments on Illawong Beach. Single $40 to $80, double $46 to $80.

EATING OUT

Most of the eating places are in hotels. Try **The Brasserie**, Oriental Hotel, Wood Street, Mackay (079) 57 7286 and **The Balcony**, Wilkinson's Hotel, corner Victoria and Gregory Streets, Mackay, (079) 57 2241, but don't expect too much. The Balcony offers dining in the open air on a balcony but the tables and chairs are plastic. Prices are low.

TOURS

Roylen Cruises, Harbour Road, Mackay, (079) 55 3066, operates a twin-hulled cruise launch from Mackay to the Great Barrier Reef on Monday, Wednesday and Friday. Roylen also has a charter launch called the *Endeavour* used for five-day cruises.

You can take in the city sights on **Cowan's Horse Drawn City Tours**, (079) 56 4334, which travel by horse drawn tram. Tours leave the Information Centre hourly from 9.30 am to 3.30 pm Monday to Friday.

Scenic flights over the reef and islands are operated by **Air Pioneer** (079) 57 6661, ($110), and **Lindeman Aerial Services** ($142) from Mackay.

ACTIVITIES
Scuba diving courses, equipment and dive trips are available from Barnes Reef-diving, 153 Victoria Street, Mackay, (079) 51 1472.

Pioneer Valley

The valley formed by the **Pioneer River** is a quiet retreat in the ranges west of Mackay, approachable only by car. Topped by the town of **Eungella**, it is a sugar-growing and dairy-farming area where one of Queensland's largest national parks has been established. Most of the park is over 800 metres (2600 feet) high and rainforest covered. Walking tracks lead among skyscraping trees, strung together with jungle vines and teetering over rocky creeks. It is sometimes possible, with a great deal of patience, to spot a platypus or two feeding in the water. The best time is very early morning before the sun strikes the water.

The **Pinnacle Power Plant** near the village of **Mirani**, lower down the valley, is a museum which, beside the usual bric-à-brac, houses a number of nineteenth-century engines in working order which are switched on each morning for the interest of visitors.

WHERE TO STAY
The Chalet, P.O. Box 6, Dalrymple Heights, (079) 58 4509; a superbly sited, older style guesthouse overlooking the valley, with rolling lawns and gardens as well as a ramp for launching your hang-glider. Horse riding available. Double and family rooms. Three only with private facilities. Licensed. $20 to $55. The guesthouse is at the top of Eungella Road.
Broken River Holiday Cabins, Eungella National Park, (079) 58 4528; budget priced but good quality cabins designed for families and set in the forest across the river from Broken River Picnic Area. The proprietors also run tours of their dairy farm and guide their guests to walking trails in the park. Canadian canoes for river rowing available.

EATING OUT
Pinnacle Cottage, Eungella Road, Pinnacle, (079) 58 5148; devonshire teas and light meals. Low price range.

Meals are also available at **The Chalet**.

Brampton Island

Brampton Island lies 32 km (20 miles) from Mackay and is part of the Cumberland Group at the southern end of the Whitsundays. It is a small mountainous island with mostly open forest and some rainforest pockets as well as fine stands of hoop pines. The island has a coral fringe.

GETTING THERE
Brampton Island can be reached by air on daily Air Queensland flights from Mackay and by launch from Mackay harbour. Launch fare is $12 per person.

THE RESORT
Brampton Island accommodates 200 people in units, each with a patio, housing up to three people. The units have private facilities and some are air-conditioned. They are served by a central dining room and entertainment complex. There is a bank agency on the island. Costs range from $63 to $127 per person per day, full board in high season (20 December to 16 January) and $59 to $120 the rest of the year. The standby rate is $65 per day, sharing.

Proserpine

All many people see of Proserpine is the airport since they are really on their way to Airlie Beach, Shute Harbour and the islands. The town devotes itself to the production of sugar and its main attraction is a very big sugar mill which is open to the public for guided tours during the harvesting season from July to November each year.

The road south from Airlie to Proserpine and Conway Beach runs by Myrtle Creek, a watercourse lined with palm trees and reputed to hold a family of crocodiles. Cedar Creek Falls, 21 km (13 miles) along the road, has deep fresh-water swimming holes, round, greeny-brown and calm, below a picturesque waterfall set in dense rainforest. Conway Beach, at the mouth of the Proserpine River, is a long, narrow strip of white sand with barbecues and toilets.

GETTING TO AND AROUND
Ansett and Australian Airlines fly to Proserpine from Brisbane ($201). The *Sunlander* train on its merry way to Cairns stops at Proserpine ($109.10 first class, $72.70 economy). The Ansett Pioneer and Greyhound Brisbane to Cairns services stops in Proserpine (fare about $75) and there are daily bus services from Mackay which take one and a half hours to reach Proserpine ($15). Drivers will find that Proserpine, like the other Queensland coastal cities is on the Bruce Highway.

WHERE TO STAY
Proserpine Motor Lodge, Bruce Highway, Proserpine, (079) 45 1588; single $38, double $45.

Airlie Beach and Shute Harbour

Airlie Beach and Shute Harbour, although about seven km (four miles) apart, tend to be mentioned in one breath as they constitute the major jumping off point for the Whitsunday Islands. People generally stay in Airlie and jump off from Shute

221

Harbour hence Airlie Beach is a fairly lively spot in its own right and has quite a few passable and even good restaurants for a place its size. It even has some nightlife.

GETTING TO AND AROUND
A bus service operated by Sampsons Tours, (079) 45 2377, runs up to seven times a day in each direction from Proserpine to Airlie Beach and on to Shute Harbour. The buses depart from Mill Street, Proserpine, and also pick up at Proserpine Airport. The trip to Airlie Beach takes about 45 minutes and costs $8.

Cars and small motor cycles are for hire from Soft Top Car Rentals, 58 Shute Harbour Road, Airlie Beach, (079) 46 7444.

WHAT TO SEE
Airlie Beach fronts onto Pioneer Bay which during the winter months (June to August and called cruising season by the locals who have a tropical sense of the seasons) fills with a splendid assortment of pleasure craft from timber schooners to radar-equipped game-fishing boats. The town consists of little more than a single strip of shops, restaurants and accommodation houses bunched up on either side of Shute Harbour Road running part-way along the edge of Pioneer Bay with the Whitsunday Islands looming in the distance and a high hill with a spectacular view behind. The town behaves rather like a stranded island, insisting on calling its hotels 'resorts' and presenting luaus and fancy-dress nights at the local pubs. It does, however, have a veneer of sophistication which some island resorts lack and presents lots of opportunities to book island visits and days out in the Whitsunday Passage. Airlie Beach does have a **town beach** within walking distance of the main street. It is small and calm but hardly bears comparison with what places further afield have to offer.

Shute Harbour is the sheltered bay from which day trips to the islands depart and where a large flotilla of bare boats lies moored waiting for charter. It also has an airport used by Air Whitsunday, a small airline taking passengers to islands and operating joy flights.

Shute Harbour sits on the edge of **Conway Range National Park**, surrounded by its rainforested hills. The national park covers 19,000 hectares (47,000 acres) and is Queensland's biggest coastal park. Walkers can find their way to secluded beaches along some of the tracks through the eucalypt and rainforest.

WHERE TO STAY
Whitsunday Terraces, Golden Orchid Drive, Airlie Beach, (079) 46 6788; set high on the hill overlooking Airlie, this collection of terrace style units with balconies has excellent views of Pioneer Bay. The rooms, either studios or one-bedroom suites, are generous and have stoves and sinks. Two swimming pools, restaurant and lots of organised activities. Studio $95, one bedroom $105, includes breakfast.

Whitsunday Village, Shute Harbour Road, Airlie Beach, (079) 46 6266; the lower cost sister of Whitsunday Terraces, managed by the same group but without the views. It has motel style units and units with cooking facilities. There is entertainment every night in the streetside restaurant and bar which seem designed to hold a large number of people in a minimum of comfort. Toad races take place every Monday night. $65 to $80.

Coral Sea Resort, 25 Ocean View Avenue, Airlie Beach, (079) 46 6458; a smaller and more elegant place to stay a little away from the crowds and good value for the price. Swimming pool and views. Single $90, double $98.

Coral Point Lodge, Harbour Avenue, Shute Harbour, (079) 46 9232; a small place with simple accommodation somewhat in need of refurbishing but has fabulous views over Shute Harbour and the islands. Also houses the offices of Whitsunday Rent-a-Yacht. From $50 a double.

Reef Oceana Village, Shute Harbour Road, Airlie Beach; it has cheap accommodation in holiday units and four-bed rooms, a swimming pool, licensed bar restaurant and laundry. They run a courtesy bus into Airlie Beach twice a day.

EATING OUT

Romeo's Italian Restaurant, Beach Shops, Shute Harbour Road, Airlie Beach, (079) 46 6337; run by a former Melbourne restaurateur who did very well in the south but got sick of the pace, the menu emphasises pastas and classic Italian fare. Licensed. Upper price range.

Angelo's Restaurant, Coral Sea Resort, (079) 46 6278; despite the plain Jane name, a restaurant of international reputation concentrating on seafood. Licensed. Upper price range.

Turtles Restaurant, Whitsunday Terraces, (079) 46 6788; a Japanese chef here can sometimes actually be persuaded to cook Japanese food but mostly does a first class job on the wide ranging European menu. Licensed. Upper price range.

Spice Island Bistro, 66 Shute Harbour Road, Airlie Beach, (079) 46 6585; it tries to do a little too much in covering Asian and Indian food as well as plain steaks and seafood. BYO. Low to mid price range.

KC's Char Grill, 50 Shute Harbour Road, Airlie Beach, (079) 46 6320; char-grilled steaks and seafood. Cooks, in every sense of the word, until late at night. Licensed. Low to mid price range.

TOURS

Air Whitsunday, Whitsunday Airport, Air Whitsunday Road, Shute Harbour, (079) 46 9133; full day flying boat trips over the Whitsunday Islands to the outer Barrier Reef, landing in Hardy Lagoon for reef walking, snorkelling and coral viewing. Scenic flights and joy flights in a Tiger Moth also available as well as helicopter flights.

Capricorn and Reef Cats, South Molle Travel Centre, Airlie Beach, (079) 46 6900; daily cruises to the outer reef and the islands.

Coral Explorer Cruises, Shute Harbour Jetty, Shute Harbour, (079) 46 6224; half-day coral viewing trips and night coral viewing.

ACTIVITIES

Scuba diving is practised all over the Whitsundays on the fringing reefs of most islands and on the outer Barrier Reef. Non-divers who want to try it for the first time, diving novices and qualified divers are all catered for.

Down Under Dive and Sports, Hacienda Building, The Esplanade, Airlie Beach, (079) 46 6869; courses and dive trips to the reef.

Flying Dutchman Sail/Dive Adventures, 17 Iluka Street, Cannonvale, (079) 46 6508; fully crewed and catered yacht trips to the reef and islands with on-board diving courses.

Whitsunday Rent-a-Yacht, Bay Terrace, Shute Harbour, (079) 46 9232; five-, seven- and 11-night diving trips for student and qualified divers.

Game-fishing trips can be organised aboard the *Lady Ruby*, a 42-foot game-fishing boat, phone (079) 46 6239.

Whitsunday Sailboard Centre, Esplanade, Airlie Beach, (079) 46 6869, will rent you a sailboard and teach you to use it as well.

Mandalay Water Sports, Mandalay Road, Mandalay, (079) 46 6211.

Dinghies, boats and paddle skis are available from **Whitsunday Aquatic Centre**, Abell Point, Airlie Beach, (079) 46 6053.

Sailing in the Whitsunday Passage

The Whitsunday Passage, a peaceful tract of turquoise water running between the inner and outer Whitsunday Islands, is one of nature's gifts to sailors. In good weather, which is most of the year, even rank amateurs under sail can make a reasonable fist of island hopping without too much muscular effort. Once under way, there is plenty of time to appreciate the scenery and lots of uninhabited islands with tempting little beaches to drop anchor at as well as just enough other sailors around to make the experience social without being crowded. Sailors are always welcome at island resorts where they can stop for dinner or a night on terra firma but the main attraction is the hundreds of uninhabited islands and unoccupied beaches scattered around the passage.

People attracted by the activity of sailing usually bare-boat charter, ie, rent a boat without crew and provision it themselves or pay extra for provisions provided by the charterer. Anyone bare boating is required to undergo a practical sailing test which usually means sailing around the bay under the eye of someone who knows about such things. Those who like the idea of being under sail but refuse to raise a finger to achieve it can take fully crewed and catered cruises and the minority which actually prefers the throb of an engine will find motor launches for hire as well. The major charter companies are listed below with summaries of what they offer from day trips to long cruises.

Whitsunday Rent-a-Yacht, Shute Harbour (the office is on a pontoon floating in the harbour), (079) 46 9232; the largest boat chartering operation in the southern hemisphere, this operator offers all types of charters including motor launches although it specialises in bare boats. It has a fleet of around 70 craft including some very famous vessels, for example, the America's Cup 12-metre *Gretel*—used for day cruises from Shute Harbour to Langford Reef ($35), the round-the-world single-handed boat, *Solo*, and the Sydney to Hobart race winning maxi, *Apollo*. The boats range from six to eight berth and cost between about $1500 and $2000 per week bare. Provisioning is extra. The crewed and catered cruises are usually for divers and people who wish to learn to sail. This operation also conducts a sailing school.

Australian Bareboat Charters, Shute Harbour Jetty, Shute Harbour, (079) 46 9381; a bare-boat specialist running five- to eight-berth craft including a couple of motor cruisers from about $1000 to $2500 per week. Provisioning and sail guides (part-time skippers) available at extra cost.

Mandalay Budget Boat Charters, Mandalay Point, Airlie Beach, (079) 46 6298; crewed and bare-boat charters including motor cruises. Five- to eight-berth bare boats from about $1400 to $2500 per week. Crewed and catered charters are on 50- to 75-foot ketches taking four to 10 passengers. Day charters also available.

Whitsunday Boating Holidays with Queensland Yacht Charters, book from Sydney (02) 331 1211; very much the same as the others but charges by the day from about $300 to $450, fully crewed yachts cost up to nearly $2000 per day for an eight-berth Formosa 70.

A number of **day cruise** yachts depart daily from Airlie Beach and Shute Harbour. Their cruises usually include lunch, stops at uninhabited islands and opportunities for snorkelling. Each boat takes between six and a dozen people and the cruises are relatively inexpensive. If you want to play Robinson Crusoe on one of the uninhabited islands and have a camping permit from the National Park Office, these boats will do a drop-off/pick-up service for a small fee.

Trinity (079) 46 6224, a trimaran, sails from Airlie Beach to North Molle Island, $20.

Nari (079) 46 6224, a wooden twin-masted vessel which has been sailing the Whitsundays for 16 years, departs Shute Harbour taking various routes through the islands. $28.

Bacchus D (079) 46 6848, departs Shute Harbour taking various routes through the islands. $28.

Jade (079) 46 6848, catamaran, departs from Airlie Beach and allows 'boom netting' along the way. In boom netting a large piece of rope netting attached to a boom is cast into the water while the boat is moving and passengers who feel like a thrill climb onto it. $20 not including lunch.

The Whitsunday Islands

The Whitsunday islands are all continental. There are 74 of them of which the biggest by far is uninhabited Whitsunday Island. The islands were discovered by Captain James Cook who sailed through them in 1770 whilst threading his way up the Queensland coast inside the Great Barrier Reef. They were named for the Christian feast day on which he came upon them. Only seven of the islands are settled. The others, including Whitsunday Island are uninhabited national parks, accommodating the occasional camper or sheltering wandering sailors. Some, for example South Molle, have been used in the past for farming and so cleared of much of their forest; others are covered in the same rainforests which have protected their soils for thousands of years. They are nearly all high, sticking their hills and even mountains up out of the Coral Sea with almost volcanic aggression. Their beaches are not always as pretty or as useful as travel brochures would have you believe, especially as the tides drop very low, exposing wide expanses of wet sand, rocks and coral outcrops.

Hamilton Island

This island is the most developed of all the islands and claims to be the biggest resort in the southern hemisphere. It is one of the few islands without national park status and has more buildings than any other, including such things as a supermarket and butcher as well as a number of multi-storey buildings. The beach in front of the resort is better than many elsewhere in the islands and gets a great deal of use for water sports. The rest of the island is hilly, rising to around 200 metres (680 feet) at Passage Peak and covering about 500 hectares (1200 acres) in area. It lies 12 km (seven miles) from Shute Harbour. Opinions about Hamilton are, in my experience, divided. Some find it appalling, others love it. It tries to appeal to a wide range of pockets within a very narrow range of taste and will certainly satisfy those whose only experience of a beach is pebbles at Pevensey. Its great advantage is accessibility and proximity to other islands such as South Molle and Hayman.

GETTING THERE
Hamilton Island serves as a transport centre for all the Whitsunday Islands. Other than Proserpine, it has the only airport capable of taking jets in the region. Ansett and Australian Airlines fly to Hamilton from Brisbane ($204), Sydney ($286) and Melbourne ($334) as well as from Proserpine ($68 Ansett only), Mackay ($77 Ansett only), Townsville ($106) and Cairns ($151). Ansett N.T. has a direct service from Ayers Rock about twice a week ($372). Air Whitsunday flies into Hamilton from Shute Harbour. Other islands are served by ferries which meet planes at Hamilton. Ferries to and from Shute Harbour, operated by Hamilton Island, as well as a water taxi connect with the island.

THE RESORT
Hamilton Island resort can easily take over 1000 guests. It's accommodation is a hotch-potch of styles varying from mock Polynesian to a couple of structures which would not look out of place in a military camp. It has six swimming pools, one of which is the biggest and most elaborate in the Whitsundays, six tennis courts, six restaurants, a bakery, a sports complex, a medical centre and a number of shops. There is a taxi service on the island which costs $1 no matter how short or long your journey and a 400-berth marina in the water. Some accommodation is on the beachfront but most of it is set back from the beach in neat rows behind the main entertainment complex with multi-storey units built furthest away at the back of the resort area closest to the airport. There are motel style and self-contained units with up to three bedrooms. Tariffs (no meals) are charged per suite rather than per person and vary from $160 to $350 per night. Almost every kind of water-going craft from tiny catamarans and dinghies is for hire; beachfront activities include parasailing and waterskiing; cruises to the reef and other islands, fishing trips and joy flights leave the island daily. Hamilton works on the principle that once you are there, nothing in the way of activities and amusements is lacking but keep in mind that almost all of them, as well as your meals, are an added cost on top of your accommodation which can make a stay there expensive.

DAY TRIPS

Quick Cat II and other fast vessels leave Shute Harbour daily for Hamilton Island. Bookings can be made at the Hamilton Island Mainland Administration Office in Shute Harbour, (079) 46 9444.

Long Island

A mountainous, bushy island only a few km from the mainland, it is only one and a half km (one mile) wide but 11 km (seven miles) long. It has 13 km (eight miles) of walking trails and one tropical style beach at Happy Bay.

GETTING THERE

Launch from Hamilton Island ($24) or Shute Harbour.

THE RESORTS

There are two resorts on Long Island, Whitsunday 100 and Palm Bay, about two km (one mile) apart. **Whitsunday 100** is aimed squarely at the 18- to 35-year old market and is a lounge-around or sport-all-day, rage-till-dawn type of place which holds 120 guests in double and twin units, each accommodating up to four people. The resort is built on a beach which shelves down into the ocean, making for safe swimming and well suited to water skiing. Full board tariffs are $90 per head for two and $75 for three or four in high season (27 December to 17 January) and $85 and $70 respectively during the remainder of the year. No standby.

The other resort on Long Island, **Palm Bay**, a 15-minute bushy walk from Whitsunday 100, has nine one-storey basic cabins housing four to six adults each, with toilets and showers in separate blocks. You provide your own food, buy provisions from the island shop or go to Whitsunday 100 to eat. Daily, room only, rates are $54 and $66.

DAY TRIPS

Jacqueline, a power vessel taking 22 passengers leaves Shute Harbour at 8.45 am each morning for a day at Whitsunday 100. Bookings on (079) 46 9400. There are 20 moorings available for day and night hire at Whitsunday 100.

South Molle

Situated in the centre of the Whitsundays, eight km (five miles) out from Shute Harbour, this island has been used for grazing and so is cleared in many places which relieves walkers of a struggle through the bush. There are some good views of the islands from South Molle's peaks, especially Spion Kop in the interior where you overlook the whole Whitsunday Passage. The island is four km (two miles) long and about two and a half km (over a mile) wide and fringed with not very good quality coral. The main beach at South Molle is neither wide nor especially sandy and tides move the water up and down a good distance, exposing rough brown coral outcrops when they are low.

GETTING THERE

There is no airport on South Molle. Transfers are by launch from Shute Harbour which takes up to 40 minutes and operates three times daily. $20 return. There is also a helicopter service between Proserpine airport and South Molle and a launch from Hamilton Island ($24).

THE RESORT

South Molle Island resort seems to appeal especially to families. It has bungalow style units which are air-conditioned and have private facilities. Some are on the beachfront, some are set high over looking the water and others are surrounded by the resort buildings. Many have recently been re-decorated and are much more comfortable than they were. There is a rather small swimming pool in the middle of the central eating and entertainment complex. The resort has two restaurants, one set menu and the other, which has a good reputation throughout the Whitsundays, à la carte. There is a small golf course at the back of the resort, tennis courts and a squash court. When full, the resort holds close to 500 guests. There are daily boat trips from South Molle to other Whitsunday Islands such as Hamilton and Day-dream and to the underwater observatory at Hook Island. Tariffs vary from $94.50 to $117 in the high season (December 19 to February 3) and $82.50 to $105 in the low season. Standby rates are available.

DAY TRIPS

Two boats, *Capricorn* and *Reef*, carry day-trippers to South Molle from Airlie Beach at 9 am each day. Bookings from South Molle Travel Centre, Airlie Beach, (079) 46 6900.

Daydream Island

This is the smallest of the resort islands and the closest to Shute Harbour. The resort buildings take up the southern end of the island, the middle is covered with a small forest which has lots of jungle vines and the northern end has a small beach. Daydream is long, very narrow and only about 10 minutes' boat ride from Shute Harbour. It has a very small beach called Sunlovers Beach where snorkellers can view fringing coral. Water sports such as windsurfing, paddleboards etc are free but parasailing from the east side of the island costs $25 and waterskiing, $10.

GETTING THERE

Launches run from Hamilton Island ($24) and Shute Harbour several times a day.

THE RESORT

At the time of writing, Daydream Island had just been sold to a new operator and changes may be on the way. Here is the existing establishment. Daydream Island resort centres on an enormous swimming pool which was once the pride of the Whitsundays but has been surpassed by Hamilton and Hayman Islands. Most of the accommodation is built around the pool as are the resort's eating and entertainment complex. Up to 160 guests are accommodated in two standards of units, all with private facilities. Full Board tariffs are $99 and $109 all year. Standby rate $59 for bookings made less than 24 hours in advance.

DAY TRIPS
MV *Daydream* departs Shute Harbour at 9 am each day for day trips to Daydream. Bookings on (079) 46 9200.

Hayman Island

This most northerly of the Whitsundays carries much tropical vegetation in its forested ravines where butterflies breed in profusion. The headlands are spectacular and walking trails, some only for the very fit, abound. The island is 33 km (20 miles) from the coast and 400 hectares (1000 acres) in area with a circumference of eight km (five miles). It has some tall hills, the highest being 250 metres (850 feet) and, unusually for the islands, is forested with eucalypts.

GETTING THERE
Hayman has an airport which takes direct Ansett flights from Cairns ($186) and Mackay ($112), and Air Whitsunday from Airlie Beach ($41) and Townsville ($129).

The other option is launch transfer from Hamilton Island airport to the resort on Hayman ($25). Helicopters also fly from Hamilton Island and Proserpine to Hayman.

THE RESORT
Hayman Island has gone from having some of the oldest accommodation in the Whitsundays to having the newest and most prestigious. A resort for the wealthy and tired who wish to escape the messy business of making money for the desirable pastime of spending it, its design has won universal praise. Suites whose balconies rake back up the sloping face of pristine white buildings, overlook a vast swimming pool perched on the seafront and broken into geometric shapes by walkways. The grounds have been landscaped within an inch of their lives and the style is style. Guests dress for dinner—and don't imagine they're not competing. The service is as impeccable as the served. Of course, you pay for these privileges; room only price varies from $85 to $150 per day from Monday to Thursday and $112 to $200 from Friday to Sunday. No standby.

Lindeman Island

At the southern entrance to the Whitsunday Passage, Lindeman Island is a great island for walkers and those who appreciate the bush in general, having 800 hectares (2000 acres) of undisturbed national park with 20 km (12 miles) of trails. The island is fringed by coral reefs, has seven beaches, an inland lake, high hills and is largely uninhabited.

GETTING THERE
Ansett Airlines flies direct to Lindeman from Cairns ($166) and Mackay ($92). Launch from Hamilton Island costs $15.

THE RESORT

Lindeman Island resort closed in 1987 and is scheduled to re-open in 1988 by which time it will have been largely rebuilt. The new resort is expected to have 150 rooms in three grades and a new central facility. Adventure Valley, a supervised camping site set aside for children is a special feature of Lindeman.

Other Islands

There is bunkhouse accommodation, $15 per night, and a frequently visited under-water observatory on **Hook Island**. The uninhabited **North Molle** and **Whitsunday Island** tend to be frequently visited by sailors and day-trippers. Camping is permitted on some of the uninhabited islands but permits must be obtained from the National Parks and Wildlife Service.

Bowen

Bowen is the town at the top of the Whitsunday group. It is one of those places that get neglected because they are so ugly to drive into. The road into Bowen lies through salt pans and factories which is a shame because it has some lovely beaches to make up for them.

GETTING THERE

Take the *Sunlander* or *Queenslander* train from Brisbane ($113.40 first class, $75.60 economy). The major coach operators stop in Bowen but some services arrive at ungodly hours of the night or morning. The fare is around $80. Drivers continue on the Bruce Highway.

WHAT TO SEE

Bowen is only worth visiting for a day or so. Its attractions are the small, crescent-shaped beaches and inlets around Horseshoe Bay where the waters of the Coral Sea reach a startling intensity of blueness. The beaches are backed by rough rocky hills where wild kapok trees grow in profusion, producing quantities of pillow stuffing that nobody has any use for. In fact, Queensland's gung-ho tourist developers have not found very much use for Bowen itself which is another of its charms. The town is also famous for its mangoes and in season, November to January, they fall off the trees around town or you can buy them from street stalls.

TOURS

Blues Barge, Bowen Travel Service, corner Williams and Hubert Streets, Bowen, (077) 86 1611; takes half day cruises around Bowen harbour for a look at the scenery and some coral viewing.

Townsville

Townsville is the biggest city in north Queensland. It has a population of about 110,000 people and is situated at the mouth of the Ross River on Cleveland Bay.

The city attracts many less tourists than Cairns which means it is quieter, less touristic and tries harder for the tourists it has than does its northerly rival. The climate is truly tropical with seasonal variation being in humidity more than temperature. Summer is very sticky with temperatures in the low 30s °C, winter not so sticky with temperatures in the mid- to high 20s. In summer particularly you will find little variation between day and night heat. There is supposed to be a wet and dry season but the wet has failed to arrive for more than 10 years so the locals are beginning to wonder. In any case, Townsville does not suffer nearly as much rain as its northern rival Cairns. The small town of Tully, which stands between them, is reputed to be the most rained-on burg in Australia.

GETTING TO AND AROUND
Townsville has an international airport but only Qantas flights via Singapore and Darwin land there. It is well served by Ansett and Australian Airlines which fly from Brisbane ($227) and Cairns ($106) as well as operating direct services from Sydney ($297). Fares shown are one way economy. Australian Airlines serves Townsville from western Queensland. A bus connects the airport with major city hotels and motels between 6 am and 9.30 pm. Enquiries on (077) 79 7290.

The *Sunlander* and *Queenslander* trains from Brisbane stop in Townsville ($122.70 first, $81.80 economy). The railway station is at the end of Flinders Street, a short distance from the city centre.

Ansett Pioneer, Greyhound, Deluxe and McCafferty's use Townsville as a major arrival and departure point for their services to and from Brisbane ($77), Cairns ($25), Darwin ($145) and Alice Springs ($120).

Motorists enter via that old faithful, the Bruce Highway.

Townsville city area is easily covered on foot but there are taxis as well. **Hermit Park Bus Service, Campbell's Coaches** and **Melville's Coaches** serve the suburbs.

Mini mokes and cheap cars can be hired from Sun City Rent-a-Moke, (077) 72 2702, Brolga Mini Vehicle Hire Company, (077) 71 4261, Rent-a-Relic, (077) 75 4488, and Rent-a-Rocket, (077) 72 6880. When renting remember to ask about mileage limits, delivery charges, collision damage waiver, personal insurance and other hidden costs. The cars cost about $25 a day. Hourly hire rates are also available in some cases.

Bicycles are available from Downtown Travel, 121 Flinders Street, (077) 72 5022.

TOURIST INFORMATION
Information about Townsville and its surroundings is available from the **Coppertop Information Centre** in the middle of Flinders Mall. **Reef Travel Centre**, 181 Flinders Street, Townsville, (077) 72 4688, is a travel agency specialising in north Queensland and often has good bargains in tours and cruises.

WHAT TO SEE
Townsville is very easy to find your way around in. The city area ranges over a small grid of streets on the western bank of **Ross Creek** with its heart in **Flinders Street**

231

Mall, one of the most pleasant civic centres throughout the cities of Queensland. The town's most prominent natural feature is **Castle Hill**, a brown lump visible from just about everywhere which misses out on being the required height for a mountain by a metre or so. The top of Castle Hill is occupied by a look-out, a monument to Robert Towns, the beef cattle baron after whom the city is named, and a seafood restaurant. The look-out is worth visiting by day and night since it is by far the highest point in the area and gives an excellent view of the wide flat curve of Cleveland Bay, Magnetic Island and the city limits in daylight and an arresting display of lights at night.

The city centre has grown along the edge of Ross Creek, a somewhat detached arm of Ross River. A complex of marinas, wharves, breakwaters, jetties and a bulk sugar terminal is gathered on one side of the creek at the eastern end of Cleveland Bay. The margin of the bay which has a long beach, is marked by **The Strand** a pretty street with houses and hotels on one side and gardens of multi-coloured tropical blooms, especially bougainvillaea decorating its water's edge park. **Customs House** and the old **Queen's Hotel**, now the studios of North Queensland Television, stand at the eastern end of The Strand opposite **Anzac Park**. **Flinders Street**, the main street, runs along the edge of Ross Creek from south to east. The street contains a city centre mall lent more than average grace by the tropical plots planted within its bounds. Most points of interest in Townsville are either on or within easy distance of Flinders Street.

Flinders Street East is the city's showpiece. This short section runs from the Denham Street end of Flinders Mall to the end of the street and was Townsville's heart in the late nineteenth century. Enough of the original buildings remain to convey some ambience of that time to the casual observer but it is hard to gain the full effect from Flinders Street itself. A better option is to cross Ross Creek by George Roberts Bridge and walk along Tomlins Street for a wide view across the wharves to the old buildings. Many have been restored and put to uses in keeping with the modern amusements to which Flinders Street East has been lately dedicated. Thus the old bank in the middle is now a nightclub, the gentlemen's residential at the left-hand end is a backpackers' hostel and other buildings contain art galleries, bookshops, restaurants and travel agencies. Flinders Street East is also the departure point for the big twin-hulled motor catamaran that takes tourists to the Barrier Reef and the smaller craft tending Magnetic Island.

The new **Great Barrier Reef Wonderland** rises at the eastern end of Flinders Street as a modern concrete counterpoint to its wrought-iron lace and awnings. It is recognisable by the fanciful concrete spiral wave rising from its roof. The Wonderland re-creates the Barrier Reef in huge aquariums and its display is the most impressive of its kind in Australia, though no substitute for the real thing. It contains two tanks, one filled with living coral and small fishes, the other with sea predators including sharks. They are divided by a transparent acrylic tunnel through which visitors walk in the illusion of being underwater. An omnimax screen cinema and a museum complete the facilities. The museum is a branch of the Queensland Museum and houses technological and biological exhibits relevant to North Queensland as well as visiting shows from the Brisbane headquarters of the museum. Open 9 am to 5 pm every day. Entry $18.

The **Percy Tucker Art Gallery** at the corner of Flinders Mall and Denham Street is the city's major public art gallery. It houses monthly exhibitions including the the works of local and visiting artists such as Michael Mulcahy, Martin Moore and Richard Lane as well as travelling displays from the big cities. Townsville also has a small **historical museum** at the corner of Sturt and Stokes Streets which records in some detail through the use of photographs, furniture, tools and scale models of horse-drawn vehicles the social history of the region from the 1860s to 1900.

Townsville Town Common, five km (three miles) from the centre of town, entered via a turn-off from Cape Pallarenda Road which runs along the edge of Cleveland Bay from the suburb of Belgian Gardens. The common is not at all what one would expect from its title. It is a landscape of beach ridges, lowlands and ranges exhibiting a variety of habitats from closed forest to mangroves and salt marsh and is frequented by flocks of water birds such as sacred ibis, herons, spoonbills and egrets as well as brolgas. In addition to the wetland and forest birdlife there are wallabies, goannas and other reptiles in the park. Information about walks and other park matters is available from the **National Parks and Wildlife Service** office at the end of Cape Pallarenda Road.

WHERE TO STAY

Sheraton Breakwater Hotel, Sir Leslie Thiess Drive, Townsville, (077) 72 4066; definitely the flashiest hotel in Townsville but with more than one or two things to learn about service. Contains a casino which seems to draw more attention than the running of the hotel. The rooms are as comfortable and well supplied with mod-cons as one would expect in a brand new hotel but it has been built right on the end of the new Townsville breakwater which means a 10-minute walk to town and there are no courtesy buses at night. See what I mean! $106 to $130.

Townsville International, Flinders Mall, Townsville, (077) 72 2477; the most convenient hotel in town, right in the middle of the city in an outstandingly ugly cylindrical building known locally as the 'Sugar Shaker' or the 'Muffler'. Comfortable rooms and courteous service. Some rooms with good views. $95 to $99.

Townsville Reef International, 63–64 The Strand, Townsville, (077) 21 1777; recently finished accommodation house of stylish design on the waterfront at Cleveland Bay about 10 minutes walk from town. Swimming pool and restaurant. $63 to $75 depending on the view and room size.

The Townsville Travelodge, 75 The Strand, Townsville, (077) 72 4255; also faces Cleveland Bay but some distance further down the Strand. A multi-storey hotel which is a little run down. Popular with businessmen. $107.

Central City Gardens, 270–286 Walker Street, Townsville, (077) 72 2655; self-contained, spacious one-, two- and three-bedroom apartments some with two bathrooms and all with separate living area, balconies front and back. Swimming pool. One bedroom $60, two bedroom $90, three bedroom $120.

Townsville caters well for backpackers and has lots of budget accommodation. Prices range from as little as $7 per person per night at **Barrier Reef Hostel,** 537 Flinders Street, (077) 21 1691, to $20 at **Pacific Coast Budget Accommodation,** 287 Sturt Street, (077) 71 6874, and standards vary accordingly. **Backpackers**

International, 205 Flinders Street East, (077) 72 4340, is the most conveniently sited.

Four Seasons Barrier Reef, John Brewer Reef, Townsville, (02) 251 3433; a floating hotel moored on John Brewer Reef, 70 km (43 miles) from Townsville. Lots of luxury but not many places to go. Has a floating tennis court and is a pick-up point for fishing and reef exploring trips. $165 to $790 room only.

EATING OUT
Flinders Street East is flanked by restaurants. Here are some suggestions along that strip.

Higgins Fine Food Restaurant has large windows looking out on the street and a cosy atmosphere, ie the tables are close together. The wide menu ranges from buffalo steaks to mud crab and daily specials are listed on a blackboard. Licensed. Mid price range.

Fanny's Restaurant is a very relaxed place popular with locals, housed in a cavernous ground-floor room with booths against one wall. Serves good reef fish. Licensed. Low to mid price range.

Toppos Spaghetti House, hearty basic Italian fare here in generous servings. Licensed. Low to mid price range.

Luvit has a bright and breezy atmosphere with a black and white theme. Specialises in pancakes and coffee, good place for breakfast but not to be neglected at other times. BYO. Low price range.

TOURS AND CRUISES
Reef Link, Flinders Street East, (077) 72 5733; this group runs day tours to John Brewer Reef and the Palm Islands on a very large and impersonal catamaran taking 400 passengers when it is full. The trip to the reef takes about two and a half hours and includes a pick-up stop at Magnetic Island on the way. The boat moors at an old wooden pontoon on the reef from which a semi-submersible viewing boat departs and where snorkellers can enter the water. Reef Link is by no means the best value in such trips but it is the only one leaving Townsville. The reef trip costs $75. The Palm Island trips allow snorkelling on fringing reefs.

Coral Princess Cruises, 78 Primrose Street, Belgian Gardens, Townsville, (077) 72 4675; the *Coral Princess* is a large motor launch which cruises through the islands from Townsville to Cairns and vice versa. The cruise takes four days and costs $560. The boat also takes a five day cruise from Townsville to Dunk Island and return.

The Travel Company of Townsville, Northtown, Flinders Mall, Townsville, (077) 71 5024; they sell a very large number of tours from half-day city sights to day tours to Magnetic Island and the inland; three-day tours extend to more islands and to the real outback and some packages are up to eight days long.

Farm and bush camping holidays can be booked at Reef Travel Centre (see below). The holidays take place on a property called Belemahar, 45 km (28 miles) south of Townsville near Giru in the foothills of Mount Elliot and include participation in whatever phase of farm life is passing during your visit. This can mean planting beans, mustering cattle or witnessing cane firing.

ACTIVITIES

Aussie Game Fishing Agencies, (077) 73 1912; fishing trips to the reef and other noted angling spots. Boats leave from the public landing pontoons at the southern end of The Strand. Reef trips $85 per head.

Scuba Diving is available from **Mike Ball Watersports**, 252–256 Walker Street, Townsville, (077) 72 3022, which runs very elaborate cruises to the reef and a ship wreck for qualified divers. It also teaches diving.

Home Hospitality offers the opportunity to visitors to join an Australian family for lunch, dinner or drinks. The meetings are organised by the **Magnetic North Tourism Authority**, 303 Flinders Mall, Townsville, (077) 72 4947. The families participating in the scheme are volunteers and there is no charge.

Magnetic Island

This island, a large and highly visible mass rising out of Cleveland Bay, is actually a suburb of Townsville occupied by a couple of thousand commuters who travel each day to and from the city by ferry. The island has four settlements of which the largest is **Picnic Bay** where the ferry from Townsville arrives. The others are **Nelly Bay**, **Arcadia** and **Horseshoe Bay**. They are fairly scratchy little beachfront settlements usually with a few shops and a milk bar or two but Picnic Bay has a paved esplanade near the jetty which is a fairly pleasant place to wander.

The island's climate is rather dry and very hot in summer, hence the bush, a proportion of which has been set aside as national park, is not so lush as on other islands but there are many walking trails leading to some of the small sandy bays around the island shores. Swimming from October to May can be dangerous as the island waters are frequented by box jellyfish.

GETTING THERE

Hayles Magnetic Island Cruises runs a ferry service between a terminal at Flinders Street East in Townsville and the settlements of Picnic Bay and Arcadia every day of the week. The return fare is $7.50. Tickets which include lunch and on-island transport are also available.

A bus service hops from settlement to settlement across the island, its longest journey, to Horseshoe Bay, taking about 15 minutes. Mini Mokes can be hired from Magnetic Movie House, Picnic Bay and Pandora's Hut, Arcadia Holiday Resort, Arcadia, for around $20 a day.

THE RESORTS

Staying on Magnetic more resembles a mainland than an island holiday as there is a wide range of accommodation to select from rather than just one resort. A great deal of it is budget level, some of it is positively crude and there's a good deal of camping and bunkhouse accommodation as well as lots of holiday flats. Here are some recommendations:

Latitude 19 Resort, Mandaly Avenue, Nelly Bay, Magnetic Island, (077) 78 5200; comfortable and fairly close to the beach at the base of Mount Cook, the island's highest point. It has rooms of three standards, a restaurant, swimming pool and tennis courts. $75 to $100.

Arcadia Holiday Resort, Arcadia, Magnetic Island, (077) 78 5177; run by the ferry operators, Hayles, and consists of motel style units on two floors with small verandas. Offers a higher standard than most other places on the island. $65 per night twin share.

Orpheus Island

A long narrow island with low, forested hills, set about 15 minutes flying time north of Townsville, 10 km (six miles) from the coast. Guests are able to walk across it and back before lunch but would be hard put to walk it end to end in less than a couple of days. The island has some fringing coral and seven white beaches.

GETTING THERE
Air Whitsunday flies to Orpheus from Townsville airport, meeting Ansett flights from Melbourne, Sydney and Brisbane each Wednesday, Saturday and Sunday.

THE RESORT
Orpheus Island prides itself on the exclusivity of its resort. It takes only 50 guests staying in studio rooms and small beachside bungalows. The studios have terracotta flooring, rattan furniture, one double bed and a sofa. They have showers but no baths. The bungalows have baths and courtyard gardens. The resort also has a swimming pool and a dining area open to the sea breezes. The usual variety of watersports equipment is available including catamarans and windsurfers, a yacht and powered craft for trips to the reef. There is also a tennis court. Full board tariff $170 to $200.

Hinchinbrook Island

Hinchinbrook looks like a piece of New Guinea that broke off and floated south. It is precipitously mountainous. Impenetrable jungles, thick with looping vines blanket its sides rising darkly from wide green mangroves round the island's shores. Clouds often trip and stick on the peaks. So close is the island to the coast that the passage between seems almost swimmable. The island is 160 km (100 miles) north of Townsville and its highest peak, Mount Bowen, rises around 3000 metres (10,000 feet); a couple of other high points along its length come close to the same height. It has more grandeur than any other Barrier Reef island but those contemplating a stay should consider that it is also the furthest island from the reef and offers no reef visits.

GETTING THERE
Ferry from the small coastal town of Cardwell.

THE RESORT
Located at the northern end of the island, **Hinchinbrook Island Resort** takes only 30 guests. The accommodation is not luxurious but is roomy, consisting of individual cabins with a bedroom, bathroom, living room and small balcony, some are

duplex. They are said to be sufficient for four adults or two adults and four children. The resort management encourages children and has staff to take care of them. Single $130 to $160, double $120 to $150.

DAY TRIPS
MV *Reef Venture* departs daily, except Monday from Cardwell at 9 am for the resort. It will also ferry campers to the island. The fare is $24 return and bookings can be made at **Hinchinbrook Island Booking Office**, 91 Bruce Highway, Cardwell, (070) 66 8539.

Hinchinbrook Passage
The silvery snake of silent water between Hinchinbrook Island and the mainland looks more like a jungle river than a sea passage. Its edges are overgrown with silky green mangroves, the towering peaks of Hinchinbrook dominate its eastern side, the grey heights of the Great Dividing Range stand within sight to the west. The voyager in this passage is enclosed in one of Nature's secret places and can't help but feel its ancient mystery. Cook who came upon so much during his northward voyage of discovery failed to find it and few modern tourists know of its existence.

There is a quick and a slow way of seeing it. The quick way is aboard *Tekin II*, a motor launch which passes through the passage on daily sightseeing tours from Cardwell at the northern end and Lucinda at the southern end. The tour takes about two hours. The other possibility is to rent a cruising houseboat in Cardwell from the Hinchinbrook Island Booking Office (see above) and spend a couple of days in the passage and around Hinchinbrook Island. **Cardwell** can be reached by bus or train from Townsville or Cairns.

Charters Towers and Ravenswood

West of Townsville the perpetual dry affecting that city bakes the cattle country of the **Burdekin**, a region named for its wide but frequently waterless river, the biggest in Queensland. The country is worn out brown and dusty grey, a few cattle pick at the hard remaining grasses and the trees don't grow very high. Bohinia, the Queensland floral emblem, blooms wild along watercourses that are more trails of muddy pools than rivers. Once through the few low dun-coloured hills that represent the Great Dividing Range outside Townsville, flatness prevails and it is hard to believe that such country could produce the wealth of beef it does.

The towns of **Charters Towers**, 135 km (84 miles) south west of Townsville, and **Ravenswood**, its companion in a rich history of gold mining, are places to gain a feel for the struggles and triumphs of living in a hard land.

GETTING THERE
The *Inlander* train runs to Charters Towers from Townsville station on Tuesday and Friday afternoons. The trip takes about two and a half hours and costs $20.10 first class and $13. Coaches from the Greyhound Terminal take just under two hours and cost $15. There are also services on Deluxe ($20). Drivers take the Flinders Highway from Townsville.

WHAT TO SEE

Charters Towers was originally Charters Tors, named after the mining warden of nearby Ravenswood, William Skelton Eurbank Melbourne Charters, who was supposedly reminded of his English home by hills surrounding the town's site. It came into being on Christmas Day 1871 when an Aboriginal called Jupiter discovered gold in a creek where he was slaking his thirst. As an Aboriginal it probably meant nothing to him but he knew what his master, grazier Hugh Mosman, was looking for and ran to him with the news of the discovery. Mosman reported the discovery to Charters and the rush was on. By the time it went into decline, Charters Towers had earned the nickname 'The World' for the sheer number and variety of diggers and hangers-on who had passed through it. It was at one time the greatest city in north Queensland and its huge crushing batteries produced seven million ounces of gold before they fell silent in the 1920s.

The days of glory have long gone from Charters Towers and most of the mining relics have gone with them but a lately developed sense of history has seen some of the town's major buildings preserved and refurbished. The **Stock Exchange** in Mosman Street at the end of Gill Street, now a shopping arcade, built in 1887 houses the local office of the Queensland National Trust and is a good place to go for information and to see the heights of commercial sophistication to which gold mining raised the town. The trading was done from the floor and the prices recorded by chalkies standing on a bridge under the main arch in the centre of the building. A **mining museum** at the back of the exchange houses gold mining and refining equipment and records of how much gold was gained in various years of the boom. Other architectural sights include the **Queensland National Bank Building** of 1891, now the city hall, a few doors down from the exchange; the 1892 Post Office in Gill Street and also in Gill Street, **Pollard's Store**, a country department store where business is conducted in the old manner, even to the extent of vacuum tubes for money transfers—no electronic banking here but plenty of Akubra hats. Gill Street is the town's main thoroughfare and most of its buildings date from the late nineteenth century. The **Excelsior Hotel** is one of the few original pubs remaining in a town which once boasted scores of them. Charters Towers has a superbly preserved piece of Queensland domestic building in **Pieffer House** in Paull Street. The house has been restored by the Mormon Church which uses it as a chapel but members of the public are welcome to look it over. **Lissner Park** at the eastern end of the town is graced by the **Boer War Memorial Kiosk**, so elaborately decorated with iron lace, pillars and finials that it almost qualifies as a folly.

Anyone with a special interest in gold mining and how the miners worked should also visit the **Venus Battery**, two km (one mile) from the railway station. It is the only piece of such equipment remaining in Charters Towers. **Ravenswood**, 80 km (50 miles) south-west and now almost a ghost town has more such equipment and a number of similar period buildings in various stages of decay. Its abandonment has a lonely charm lacking in bustling Charters Towers.

WHERE TO STAY

Cattlemans Rest Motor Inn, Corner Bridge and Plant Streets, Charters Towers, (077) 87 3555; the newest motel in town, has air conditioning, a swimming pool and a restaurant. Single from $39, double from $46.

There is a **backpackers hostel** at 58 York Street, (077) 87 1028 but this author cannot vouch for its quality.

TOURS

Any number of bus companies in Townsville run tours to Charters Towers as it is the only non-coastal place of interest within striking distance of town, many include Ravenswood on their itineraries. Day and half-day bus tours within and around Charters Towers itself are available from **Gold Nugget Scenic Tours**, (077) 87 1568. The tours depart from the Caltex Service Station in Gill Street and visit Ravenswood. They range in price from $8 to $25.

Cairns

Cairns is a true tropical town set on a flat plain between the muddy, mangrove-edged, often grey waters of Trinity Inlet and the deep green, bush-clad inclines of the Great Diving Range rising sharply to the Atherton Tableland. The town is dead flat, laid out in a grid of streets that seem an acre wide; its waterfront is lined with swaying palms and tall hotels. Game-fishing boats cluster by the score at grey wooden wharves; 300 seat tourist boats, private yachts, the occasional cruise ship and small naval vessels slip up and down Trinity Inlet in a leisurely but continual traffic.

Many small palm-fringed beaches step north where cane fields once ran down to the sand. Suburbs of undistinguished concrete houses front these beaches waiting sullenly for the next cyclone to do its worst against their boring frontages. They house a fast growing population, close to 90,000 which lets Cairns vie with Townsville as North Queensland's major city. It is already the greatest tourist town in north Australia, attracting over one hundred thousand a year but the reef and mountain beauty around the town seems able to cope with them. So far, anyway.

Cairns best weather comes during the Australian winter, May to September. In summer it is very humid and heavy (soaked to the skin in 30 seconds) rain falls frequently. Whatever time of year you arrive there, it is unlikely that you will need more than shorts and t-shirt. A trip to the Atherton Tableland on the high ground west of the city may call for something a little warmer.

GETTING TO AND AROUND

Travellers on Qantas from Europe and North America and Japan Air Lines can choose Cairns as their port of first entry into Australia. Travellers from Sydney ($330), Melbourne ($363), Brisbane ($265) and Townsville ($106) can fly straight into Cairns on Ansett and Australian Airlines.

The *Sunlander* and *Queenslander* trains which run up the Queensland coast from Brisbane, stopping at all major towns, terminate in Cairns. Fares are $134.80 first class and $89.90 economy.

CAIRNS

Trinity Bay

Marin Jetty
Platypus Jetty
Hayles Jetty
Ferries to Green Island

Anzac Park

WHARF STREET

DUTTON STREET

STREET

ESPLANADE

Civic Centre

CITY PLACE

SPENCE STREET

Cairns Railway Station

ABBOTT STREET
LAKE STREET
GRAFTON STREET
SHERIDAN STREET
MCLEOD STREET

SHIELDS STREET

APLIN STREET

Visitors Information

FLORENCE STREET

WINNIE STREET

ESPLANADE
ABBOTT STREET
LAKE STREET
GRAFTON STREET
SHERIDAN STREET
MCLEOD STREET
WATER STREET

UPWARD STREET

Greyhound and Ansett Pioneer, Deluxe and McCafferty's coaches travel to Cairns from Brisbane ($90) and Townsville ($25) as well as other coastal cities.

Sea journeys from Townsville to Cairns and vice versa can be undertaken on the *Coral Princess*. The boat cruises gently from one to the other, taking four days to complete the distance and visiting a number of islands along the way. The fare is $560. Phone (077) 72 4675 in Townsville and (070) 51 4055 in Cairns.

Drivers merely continue along the Bruce Highway which also finishes at Cairns.

Cairns is thick with car rental agencies which rent everything from mopeds and mokes to big sedans and four-wheel drives. Try Cairns Rent a Car, 147c Lake Street, (070) 51 6077 and Cairns Leisure Wheels, 230 Sheridan Street, (070) 51 8988; or take a walk down Lake Street or Sheridan Street.

TOURIST INFORMATION
General tourist information can be obtained from FNQ Promotions Bureau, corner of Sheridan and Aplin Streets (070) 51 3588 in Cairns.

WHAT TO SEE
Trinity Inlet runs in from a wide natural harbour, providing a shelter once used by the region's miners but now chock-a-block with leisure craft. The town's waterfront has two distinct areas, a complex of wharves just inside the inlet mouth and a wide sweep of harbour untouched by shipping because of excessive tides that daily expose wide, unattractive, dark grey mud flats. **The Esplanade** runs along this bayfront with tourist accommodation and restaurants on one side and some seaside lawns and palm trees on the other making a pleasant park at high tide. A phalanx of high-rise hotels (nothing over 14 storeys we are assured) beetling over the boats as they pass to and from the open water has begun to give the street that Gold Coast look. There is no beach and when the tide is out, the hotels overlook the mud flats. The wharves around **Marlin Jetty** at the south-eastern end of the Esplanade and along **Wharf Street** accommodate scores of game-fishing boats available for charter and with their prices chalked on boards. The twin-hulled launches that travel to the Great Barrier Reef and the islands also pick up there and there is a much larger wharf for cruise ships from the South Pacific. Like all truly busy and thriving ports, this area has great atmosphere.

Cairns has a central square called City Place where you can sit and watch the city's life go in and out of the few authentic pubs that remain. The **Cairns Historical Society Museum** is on the first storey of the **Cairns Civic Centre** facing onto City Place. It houses a more than representative collection of period artefacts and photographs including some fine models of coastal steamers from the late nineteenth century to the 1940s, a room devoted to the feats of early railway builders in the Cairns district and a fascinating section on Aboriginal life in the rainforests before and after white penetration. This museum also holds winners of the town's annual art prize whose judges have shown more daring and keener critical capacity than those in some supposedly enlightened cities. They have developed a taste for startling hyper-realist works hung with delightful incongruity among the old butter churns and washing boards.

Its unashamed dedication to the tourist dollar has denuded Cairns of interesting civic and domestic architecture although it does, like all north Queensland ports have a **Customs House**—it faces Wharf Street. The city is, in truth, a tourist dormitory from which the sleepers, once awake, escape to a wealth of surrounding beauties varying from mountains and forests to beaches and islands.

Beaches

Any residents who can't or don't want to fit into the town itself have moved to the newly established beach suburbs stretching north to Buchan's Point. Waterfront cane fields at **Machan's Beach, Holloway's Beach, Yorkey's Knob, Trinity Beach, Kewarra Beach, Clifton Beach** and **Palm Cove** have been sub-divided and sold off in quarter acre suburban blocks, some facing the beach. The cane still lurks along the roadsides in less desirable suburbs. Each beach has a couple of motels and every so often there's a big resort hotel for those who can afford it.

Only where the coastal plain finally narrows to almost nothing and the hillsides touch the sea has development stopped. These beaches north of Cairns have their pros and cons. They generally fulfil the expectations placed on tropical beaches, such as palm trees and casuarinas behind a narrow slope of whitish sand, but some, especially the southern ones have been ravaged to almost nothing by a combination of thoughtless development and cyclones. The further north one goes the better the beach. Palm Cove is the best. The presence of box jellyfish from October to May makes it impossible to swim during that period except in very restricted netted areas. You won't see the 'stingers' as they are called but you'll sure know if you meet one.

WHERE TO STAY

Cairns Hilton, Wharf Street, Cairns, (070) 52 1599; is the newest hotel in Cairns and the most luxurious. It sits on the waterfront overlooking the charter-boat wharves, a short walk from the city centre. Single $165, double $185.

Pacific International, 43 The Esplanade, Cairns, (070) 51 7888; Cairns previous number one accommodation house, comfortable, settled and relatively sophisticated with lots of bars and restaurants. Single $125, double $132.

Trade Winds Esplanade, 137 The Esplanade, Cairns, (070) 52 1111; another of the 'just finished' hotels, eight storeys, 238 rooms in a horseshoe-shaped complex at the north-western end of the Esplanade, overlooking Cairns Harbour. Single $95, double $114.

Trade Winds Outrigger, Corner Florence and Abbott Streets, Cairns, (070) 51 6188; Cairns' most stylishly designed hotel run by the same management as the Trade Winds Esplanade. Not on the waterfront but suffers little for that. Single $77 to $88, double $94 to $105.

Quality Inn Harbourside, 209–217 The Esplanade, Cairns, (070) 51 8999; a step down in quality from the hotels listed above but not by a very great distance. Occupies a central position on the Esplanade and has some self-contained suites. $72 to $97.

City Gardens Apartments, Corner Lake and Minnie Streets, (070) 51 8000; a friendly smaller establishment whose self-contained accommodation is good for couples and families. Studios $75 to $83, one bedroom $85 to $93.

Tuna Towers, 145 The Esplanade, Cairns, (070) 51 4688; a little further down The Esplanade than the big hotels and some years older but a less expensive alternative. Air-conditioned rooms and swimming pool. Single $79, double $85.

Four Seasons Cairns, corner The Esplanade and Aplin Street, Cairns, (070) 51 2311; not a pretty building but has views of Trinity Inlet from its higher floors. Rooms are decidedly unpretentious. Single $42 (budget) to $67 (high-rise), double $52 to $78.

Cairns Colonial Club, 18-26 Cannon Street, Manunda, (070) 53 5111, sells itself as being 'just like staying on an island' which it isn't because it's in a suburb of the city but it does offer pleasantly green surroundings and a range of accommodation from deluxe to economy twin as well as some units with limited cooking facilities. The deluxe rooms are very comfortable and pleasingly decorated and the gardens and pool are exceptional but service should be better to make up for a $6 taxi ride from town. For example, the old trick of having no courtesy bus into the city at night was in evidence during my last visit. The food is also expensive. Single $49 to $84, double $56 to $89.

Kewarra Beach Resort, Kewarra Beach, (070) 57 6666; has adopted the Torres Strait Island and houses its guests in accommodation ranging from motel-style blocks to individual huts. It is right on the water at Kewarra Beach, about 10 km (six miles) from the city, and may be the pick of the 'resort' style places near Cairns, having lovely gardens to wander through a classy dining area and barbecues on the beach (but watch out for mosquitos). Single $121 to $170, double $154 to $170.

The Reef House, The Esplanade, Palm Cove, (070) 55 3633; at the northern end of the beach. It's a low white, latticed and louvered building, a piece of typical Queensland tropical architecture, which tends to alleviate the lack of air con-ditioning in some rooms. Guests stay in small semi-detached houses on stilts, there is a swimming pool, gardens and a good restaurant. It is unusual and has great atmosphere. $150 to $380.

Ramada Reef Resort, corner Veivers Road and The Esplanade, Palm Cove, (070) 55 3999; this hotel is across the road from the beach at Palm Cove, about 25 km (15½ miles) out of Cairns. It is very nice and has a remarkable freeform swimming pool but the service among the slowest I have encountered anywhere in the world. $135 to $170.

EATING OUT

Cairns has lots of restaurants, many have taken prime positions along the Esplanade but there are also some good ones a little away from town. They tend to show an alarming lack of price competition and you can expect to pay between $25 and $30 per head for a full meal at most of them. Cairns does have quite a few BYOs and, naturally, they are cheaper than licensed premises.

Verdi's, 123 Abbot Street, Cairns, (070) 52 1010; Italian cooking specialising in pastas with some unusual sauces such as chilli, garlic and parmesan or tuna and green pepper. Other interesting dishes as well. Less expensive than the Cairns average. BYO. Low to mid price range.

Pier 67, 67 The Esplanade, Cairns, (070) 51 8913; in a very pleasant spot by the bay and specialising in seafood. BYO. Mid to upper price range.

Cookaburra's Corner, 57 Kamerunga Road, Stratford, (070) 55 2480; off the Captain Cook Highway past Cairns airport, this restaurant is housed in an refurbished old Queensland house and serves local produce, especially fish from the reef, cooked in simple and effective style. BYO. Mid price range.

Toko Baru, 42 Spence Street, Cairns, (070) 51 2067; Indonesian food of even quality and passable authenticity. Inexpensive. BYO.

The Reef House, Palm Cove, (070) 55 3305; good food in a delightful ambience from a menu including crocodile kebabs which are not as intimidating as you might think. Licensed. Mid to upper price range.

TOURS AND CRUISES

At first sight, a vast number of tours seems to depart from Cairns to the reef, the highlands and the forests. Although this is true to some extent, the situation is confused by the number of agencies selling such tours. A quick check shows that the same tours are being sold from any number of different agencies and it's worth shopping around, if you have the time, to see who is offering specials.

Cruises

Terri-Too, Cairns Tour Services, 87 Lake Street, Cairns (070) 51 8311; a gentle two-hour cruise leaving three times a day from Marlin Marina and travelling into Trinity Inlet. Morning and afternoon cruises $9.50, lunch cruise $11.

SS *Louisa*, Marlin Jetty, Cairns, (070) 51 3893; a paddlewheeler which operates a similar cruise to *Terri-Too*. $8.50.

Hayles Cruises, Wharf Street, Cairns, (070) 51 5644; cruises to Green Island by high speed catamaran ($23) or slow launch ($12); to Michaelmas Cay via Green Island ($54 which includes lunch) and to Hastings Reef (part of the Outer Barrier Reef) via Green Island ($65 including lunch, morning and afternoon tea and coral viewing). Cruises to Fitzroy Island are also available.

Big Cat, 111 Lake Street, Cairns, (070) 51 0444; half-day ($19) on a fast boat and full day ($12) trips on a slower boat to Green Island. The fast boat also takes half day trips to Fitzroy Island and full days taking in both islands ($29).

MV *Quick Cat*, Down Under Tours and Travel, 10e Shields Street, Cairns, (070) 51 5899; departs from Clump Point Jetty at Mission Beach about 140 km (87 miles) south of Cairns to Dunk Island and to the reef. Coach from Cairns. $35 to Dunk Island and $75 to the reef.

Banyandah Marine Tours, 125 Bruce Highway, Edmonton, (070) 55 4966; a catamaran motor launch takes day trips from Deeral Landing, about 40 km (25 miles) south of Cairns, down the Mulgrave river to the sea and the small uninhabited Frankland Islands, returning via Fitzroy Island. Bus pickup from Cairns. $85.

MV *Coral Reeftel*, North Cairns Tourist Information and Booking Centre, 371 Sheridan Street, Cairns, (070) 51 0989; a two-deck launch with accommodation in two-berth cabins for up to 20 people. Departs from Marlin Jetty for cruises of varying length, also picks up from island resorts.

Tropic Sailer, (070) 51 8868; day sailing to Michaelmas Cay. $40.

Ocean Free, 275 Sheridan Street, Cairns, (070) 51 7133; a 21.5 metre (71 foot) ketch which takes day sailing trips to Michaelmas Cay and the reef. $66.

Jungle Queen, Cairns Hinterland Tours, 82 Sheridan Street, Cairns, (070) 51 8199; half-day cruises the Mulgrave and Russell Rivers south of Cairns. $15.

Road Tours
The Red Bus; this vehicle leaves from the Queensland Government Travel Centre, 12 Shields Street, and covers nine stops in the city area. It leaves every hour from 9 am to 5 pm and passengers can alight from the bus, take a walk and join a later bus at will. $6.

Cairns by Night, Cocos Travel, (070) 57 6799; includes a cruise on Trinity Inlet, dinner and a look at the night lights of Cairns. $45.

Tropic Wings, Reef and Rainforest Travel, 54 Lake Street, Cairns, (070) 51 8433; Cairns largest operator, carrying day, half day and longer tours into the Cairns hinterland. It runs 16 tours in all, many of which include boat trips to islands, river cruises and visits to tourist attractions. Among the most popular day tours are those to the Atherton Tableland including the Kuranda Rail ($26), to Cape Tribulation ($38) and Chillagoe Caves ($65). Also does Cairns city sights.

Ansett Trailways, 58 Shields Street, Cairns, (070) 51 8966; the other large coach tour operator which also sells excursions to islands and river rafting trips. Day tours include the Atherton Tableland ($27.50 to $42), Port Douglas and Mossman ($35), and Cape Tribulation ($48).

Other operators covering the same territory are **Deanes Day Tours** (070) 55 6404; **Cairns Day Tours** (070) 51 7366; **Cairns Hinterland Tours** (070) 51 8199; **Nautilus Tours** (070) 51 7366 which has an $89-four-tours package offer and **Cape Tribulation Coach Tours** (070) 51 8124.

Australian Pacific Tours, 103 The Esplanade, Cairns, (070) 51 9299; day tours to Cape Tribulation ($49) in heavy four-wheel drive coaches.

The Crocodile Express, Cairns Tour Service, 87 Lake Street, Cairns, (070) 51 8311; coach to Port Douglas and through the Mossman Gorge plus a cruise in a small boat on the Daintree River.

Air Tours
Air Queensland, 62 Abbott Street, Cairns, (070) 50 4333; day tours to Lizard Island ($220) and Cooktown ($135) as well as tours of longer duration to Cape York.

Lloyd Helicopters, Number Six Wharf, Cairns, (070) 52 1244; flies to the reef and islands ($150) and the Mossman Gorge ($285) and connects with the Quicksilver reef cruiser at Port Douglas from Cairns ($95 one way).

Falcon Air Services, General Aviation Area, Cairns Airport, Cook Highway, Aeroglen, (070) 53 7910; three tours around the Cairns area, each going further afield and spending longer in the air. $35 to $70.

North Queensland Aero Club, Cairns Airport, (070) 53 1438; reef and coastal scenic flights from $35.

The Casino Express, Ansett Airlines, 84 Lake Street, Cairns (070) 50 2230; this flight leaves Cairns at 6.15 pm on Friday. Its passengers are delivered to the Sheraton Breakwater Casino at Townsville. The flight returns at 1.20 am on Saturday. $125 return.

ACTIVITIES

Scuba Diving
In most cases, if you don't have your own gear, hiring cost is added to the price of the trip.
Pro-Diving Services, Marlin Jetty, Cairns, (070)51 9915; diving courses including pool training and reef dives as well as diving for certified divers and night diving at the reef. $135 to $200.
Deep Sea Divers Den, 319 Draper Street, Cairns, (070) 51 2223; overnight on the reef for certified divers. $150
Down Under Aquatics, (070) 51 6360; one-, three- and six-day diving trips from $76 to $443.
Peter Tibbs Dive Centre, Tobruk Baths, 370 Sheridan Street, Cairns, (070) 51 2604; day dives from $30 to $72 and overnight $150.

Game Fishing
The Coast between Cairns and Port Douglas is called the Marlin Coast by local tourism promoters and not without historical reason. Cairns' first claim to international fame was as the place where Lee Marvin loved to catch marlin. This may have been of more moment to Australians in their crippling remoteness than to anybody else in the world but it has led, in part, to the establishment of a game fishing base in the city. The marlin run between September and December each year but fishing boats can be chartered at any time by showing up at Marlin Jetty where scores of them tout for trade with signs and blackboards showing their rates. They vary, depending on the boat, the season, the tackle and provisions from around $40 to $100 per person per day but you can spend much more if you're determined.

Bushwalking
Wait Awhile Walks, Going Places Travel, 26 Abbott Street, Cairns, (070) 51 4055; day walks in the rainforest $35, nocturnal wildlife trips $45. Both include a meal.
Goanna Tour, book at the same office as the previous listing, full day bird-watching tours to the south, north and west of Cairns. $45 includes lunch and tea.

Rafting and Canoeing
Raging Thunder, 67 Grafton Street, Cairns, (070) 51 4148; rubber rafting on the Tully, Barron and North Johnstone Rivers for anything from half a day ($35) to five days ($550). Very rough but tremendously exciting.
R 'n' R White Water, book at Going Places Travel; very much the same as the previous listing.
In the Wild Canoe Tours, 19 Terka Street, Innisfail, (070) 51 4911; full day canoe tours, six boats, two people per boat on the North Johnstone River. Anyone who has $55 and is not likely to suffer a heart attack can do it.
Butler's Canoe Nature Tours, book at Going Places Travel; canoes on the Mulgrave River, a more gentle trip than the others. $50.

Kuranda

The narrow flat coastal plain on which Cairns sits is backed by a range of rugged mountains that are among the highest in eastern Queensland, some touching 3000 metres (10,000 feet). They protect the 140 km (90 mile) wide and agriculturally rich Atherton Tableland, an area of grassy hills and frequent rain. Its rainforest long ago cut down, the land is grazed by dairy cattle and supplies milk to all of north and much of western Queensland.

The mountains presented a formidable barrier and the tableland was almost impossible to develop until the **Cairns to Kuranda Railway** was completed in 1891. The railway, which terminates at the picturesque mountain town of **Kuranda**, is now almost exclusively a tourist attraction but its construction was a much more serious affair. The original commitment to build it was made in 1882 when the wet season was so bad that tin miners working on the Wild River in the Atherton Tableland could obtain no supplies and nearly starved. They were lucky that 1882 was an election year and won the promise of a railway from the government of the day. The route was not chosen until 1884 when it was decided to take the railway up the Barron River Gorge from Cairns. It was to be built in three sections of which the ascent to the tableland through steep grades, dense jungle and hostile natives was by far the most difficult and dangerous. The work on that section, beginning in 1887, was carried out with hand tools, dynamite, buckets and bare hands. A work force of 1500 men, mainly Irish and Italian, was employed at the height of the project. They coped with extraordinary difficulties. On occasions sections of their work were ruined by landslides and mud-slides. The men themselves were always in danger of death from falling trees and explosive accidents. They lived in small townships of tents pitched at tunnel entrances, on cuttings and convenient ledges. Their working conditions were so poor that they went on strike in April 1888 and had their pay raised from eight shillings to eight shillings and sixpence a day. The Stoney Creek Bridge, straddling Stoney Creek within wetting distance of its gossamer falls, is the line's greatest engineering feat. When it was completed in 1890, the Governor of Queensland came to visit and was treated to a banquet in the middle of the bridge, hundreds of feet over the gorge. No speeches were made that day due to the roaring of the falls! The line was completed in June 1891 when the first train rolled into Kuranda. The quaint station, presently so heavily decorated with tropical pot plants that its sometimes hard to find your way around it, was built in 1915.

Kuranda, which attracted urban malcontents and hippies in the seventies, has been carefully gentrified in an effort to please residents and tourists alike—the effort has been surprisingly successful. The town has an extensive **open-air market** that functions on Wednesday and Sunday mornings, lots of small shops and galleries and quite a few places to take tea. There's a **Nocturnal House** where Australian native animals and birds not normally seen in daylight move about for the edification of tourists and a **Butterfly House** where living butterflies display their beauties. A natural amphitheatre has been carved out of the bush a short distance from town. It is used for concerts and plays. When such things occur they can be a highlight of any Cairns visit so keep your eye out for them.

The Atherton Tableland

The Atherton Tableland, centring on the tobacco-growing town of Mareeba, lies beyond Kuranda. It owes its height to long past volcanic activity and its countryside is dotted with lakes, caves, gorges, waterfalls and hot springs recalling those far off upheavals. **Granite Gorge** on Granite Creek 12 km (seven miles) from Mareeba has marked walking paths leading through gigantic boulders and rock formations to green swimming holes and white creek-side beaches. There are limestone caves at **Chillagoe**, 140 km (87 km) west of Mareeba. The **crater lakes** of Eacham and Barrine on the top of the tableland, and Lake Tinaroo, their man-made companion, dark surfaced, still and reflective make an extraordinary contrast to the heat and energy of the reef islands, barely 200 km (124 miles) to the east.

Port Douglas and Mossman

These small towns, the first about 70 km (43 miles) north of Cairns and the second another 20 or so km (12 miles) further north, will be the next victims of tourist invasion. Port Douglas is busily preparing for it, Mossman hasn't quite woken up yet. Both are still very attractive and unspoiled townships. Port Douglas is an access point for the ocean and the reef and Mossman for the Daintree forest, Cape Tribulation and its own nearby river gorge. The towns grew up in the late 1870s when gold brought prospectors in their thousands to north Queensland. Not long after its foundation, Port Douglas held 12,000 residents and 26 hotels but when the railway went to Cairns it was reduced to a fishing village. Mossman is still largely supported by sugar-cane growing.

GETTING THERE
As there is no rail service to Port Douglas, the James Cook Highway is the only way to get there. Ansett Trailways buses leave daily from Cairns.

Port Douglas

The 50-km (31-mile) run along the Captain Cook Highway from the outskirts of Cairns to Port Douglas abandons the beach suburbs for one of the most beautiful coastal drives in the world. Beach after white beach swings up the coast, nearly all deserted. A sluggish, steamy sea laps against them, the forest grows green almost to the water's edge and the road winds from vantage to vantage for its entire length. **Port Douglas** itself retains a little of its fishing village atmosphere. You can still buy fresh fish from the wharf shop at the north-west end of the town but the industry is just a way of keeping a few people employed these days. 'The Port' as locals refer to it has **Four Mile Beach** on its eastern side, a river estuary on the west. The main street joins one to the other. The beach is a true tropical crescent complete with perfectly spaced palms and whitish sand which make it one of the most photo-graphed in North Queensland. The motels and holiday units along its edge are well set back and not especially intrusive. The estuary shelters fishing and pleasure craft and the giant *Quicksilver*, the best tourist reef boat on the whole Queensland coast. Along the quaint street joining them Port Douglas maintains a charming rustic feel aided by arching shady trees, an old pub, countrified shops and an air of gentle largo, something lost completely to Cairns.

WHERE TO STAY

Sheraton Mirage Port Douglas Hotel, Four Mile Beach (PO Box 172) Port Douglas, (070) 98 5888; mercifully, only three storeys high, it has 300 rooms in a rambling structure which includes a golf course and innumerable other facilities designed to make you not want to leave. The hotel is brand, spanking new and far enough out of Port Douglas township to make walking in a chore unless you do it along the beach. $160 to $200.

Port Douglas Terraces, Four Mile Beach, Port Douglas, (070) 98 5397; self-contained accommodation across the road from Four Mile Beach, very comfortable two-storey, two- and three-bedroom units with breezy balconies where they face the sea. Other end of the beach from the Sheraton. Two bedroom sea view $105, three bedroom sea view $110.

Bali-Hatka, 18 Owen Street, Port Douglas, (070) 98 5598; a small guesthouse in a half-acre garden with a swimming pool, close to beaches, bedrooms in the Balinese style—no walls, just mosquito nets. Three rooms only, all upstairs. $50.

EATING OUT

Nautilus Restaurant, 17 Murphy Street, Port Douglas, (070) 98 5230; run by Sydney chef and Thai food expert Mogens Bay Esbensen and probably the best restaurant in far north Queensland. Serves European as well as Thai dishes. Licensed. Upper price range.

Reef Room Restaurant, 87 Davidson Street, Port Douglas; specialises in seafood and has a smorgasbord lunch every Sunday. BYO. Mid price range.

TOURS

Quicksilver Low Isles Cruises, The Pier, Port Douglas, (070) 98 5373; tours to Argincourt Reef on the outer Barrier Reef and to the Low Isles, actually to a single coral cay occupied by a lighthouse and surrounded by clear water and good coral. The Quicksilver is the best of the outer Barrier Reef cruises. My advice for anyone with only the briefest time to see the reef is put aside a day and book your place on it. The journey out is quick and smooth, the coral viewing takes your breath away, the staff are courteous and knowledgeable and the food is good. The Quicksilver also has a resident marine biologist whose pet subject is the reef. Ask her anything you like about it. A ticket for the Quicksilver costs $70 and coach pick up from Cairns another $8.

Sundancer Cooktown Cruises, book through Big Cat Tour Services, Cairns; a fast single-hulled launch which travels from Port Douglas to Cape Tribulation, Cooktown and return, picking up and dropping off in all places. Port Douglas to Cooktown return $69. A coach pick-up from Cairns adds $10 to the fare.

Thomas Charters, (070) 98 5140 or book through Cairns Convention and Visitors Bureau, 41 Shields Street, Cairns, (070) 51 7366; a day sailing to the Low Isles with lunch and tea thrown in. $42 from Port Douglas, $52 from Cairns.

ACTIVITIES
Tropical Walkabouts, 1st Floor, Reef Anchor House, 40 Macrossan Street, Port Douglas, (070) 98 5239; easy and difficult day and half-day walks into Daintree and Cape Tribulation National Parks; $20 to $40.

Mossman

Away from the coast and quieter than any other north Queensland town, Mossman gives the impression that life moves very slowly on its one almost deserted street. If it were not for the cane trains that clatter along it during harvest time, one might wonder what people do there. Tourists go to Mossman River Gorge, a quiet, cool dell in the nearby rainforest. Easy walks lead to the Mossman River where deep calm swimming holes are protected by grey-green boulders over which cool river waters run. They are excellent places to swim in summer when the box jellyfish make swimming on the coast impossible.

WHERE TO STAY
Silky Oaks Colonial Lodge, Finlay Valley Road, Mossman River Gorge, (070) 98 1666; timber cabins set at the base of the Gorge Mountains overlooking the Mossman River and surrounded by national park. A very beautiful setting and good accommodation. Cabin only, $170.

Daintree

It could safely be said that almost everybody in Australia has heard of the **Daintree River rainforest** although relatively few people have actually been there. The forest is deep, cool and high-canopied like other rainforests but has many plant species not found elsewhere. A savage conservationists versus developers battle took place when it was 'threatened' with the construction of a road through its unsullied wilderness in the early 1980s. The conservationists lost and now an unsealed road cuts it. Arguments continue over whether irreparable damage has been done to the forest and what effect the muddy runoff from the road is having on the Great Barrier Reef. To counter future destruction, the Daintree forest is soon to be proposed for World Heritage listing. To see it for yourself drive from Port Douglas to Daintree via Mossman in a four-wheel drive or take a cruise on the Daintree River, bookable in Cairns. There is no accommodation in Daintree.

Cape Tribulation

The way to Cape Tribulation lies across the Daintree River along a difficult and boggy dirt road which has been chewed up by four-wheel drive tourist buses, some with wheels as tall as a man. The road runs through areas which are neither settled nor wild. However, the coastal rainforest is beautiful and runs to the edge of the cape beach. It is the only place where rainforest and reef meet. There are some points of interest along the way, including a remarkable grove of hessian hair palms and a strangler fig over 100 feet high, bedecked with native orchids. Cape Tribulation is a long day trip from Cairns.

WHERE TO STAY
Bloomfield Wilderness Lodge, Cape Tribulation, book through Going Places Travel, 26 Abbott Street, Cairns, (070) 51 4055; a 'package' lodge where the price you pay includes accommodation, airfares, organised tours, boat trips, meals and fishing tackle. The lodge stands on a point off the mouth of the Bloomfield River at the northern end of Cape Tribulation National Park, takes 30 guests and is recommended for fishermen and people with a special interest in the wilderness. Rooms do not have private facilities. There is a swimming pool but no bar. Package prices vary from around $250 to nearly $1000 depending on your package's duration and inclusions.

For very basic and cheap accommodation, try the **Jungle Lodge**, Cape Tribulation which provides bunks in wooden, jungle lodges set right in the rainforest. There is a pool and bar. $9 per night.

Fitzroy Island

This is a continental island with high, green peaks and narrow, sloping beaches of broken coral. It is particularly known for its fringing reefs and good diving opportunities.

GETTING THERE
The trip takes 45 minutes on the Fitzroy Flyer cat from Hayles Wharf at Cairns. The fare is $24.

THE RESORT
Fitzroy has 'villas', actually small cabins with their own shower and toilet but no air conditioning, and spartan but attractively constructed Budget Rooms near the water with share facilities and a communal kitchen. Villas $79 dinner bed and breakfast, budget $15 room only. There is also a camping ground. There is a dive centre on the island which offers everything from gear hire to seven day diving courses.

DAY TRIPS
Lots of day-trippers come to Fitzroy Island either as a single destination or as part of a cruise to the Barrier Reef or Green Island. The Fitzroy Flyer catamaran costs $24 return without extras but lunch and coral viewing can be bought as extras. Hayles boats and the Big Cat also run day trips to Fitzroy, see the section on Cairns for details.

Green Island

Green Island is a coral cay formed by wave and wind with some intervention from man. Coconut trees were planted there in past centuries for the sustenance of shipwrecked sailors. Now they shelter a resort and beaches. The island is surrounded by coral but has suffered from the sheer amount of human traffic it sustains, especially day-trippers. I have heard it said, 'You can't get off the concrete.' Its popularity with day-trippers is due in part to an underwater observatory, a primitive art collection and pools filled with sharks and crocodiles.

GETTING THERE
Hayles is the main operator serving Green Island. The journey takes about 45 minutes. For details see the Cairns section.

THE RESORT
Green Island has twin, double and family units at two prices—$79 and $64 high season and $69 and $54 during the rest of the year. This is a dinner, bed and breakfast cost only.

DAY TRIPS
These are undertaken by Hayles and Big Cat. See Cairns section for details.

Lizard Island

Lizard Island is the most northerly of the Barrier Reef resort islands by a very considerable distance, being about 90 km (56 miles) north of Cooktown off the coast of Cape York, 50 minutes flying time from Cairns. It is deliberately far from the madding crowd and is distinguished by understated luxury, great natural beauty and very high prices. Lizard is a continental island and one of the few to have been settled before the days of resorts so some of its slopes have been cleared and there are many easy walking trails as well as one or two very demanding ones. There are waterfalls, streams and patches of forests in the island as well. It also has very beautiful beaches with calm crystal waters and a lovely lagoon, all part of 1000 hectares (acres) of national park. It can be truly said that, concerning Lizard, the camera does not lie—believe what you see in the brochures. Those who go in search of silence really can find it.

The island is very popular with game fishermen who follow the black marlin from September to December each year and with scuba divers who migrate to a famous spot on the outer reef called the Cod Hole where a giant cod lives in a coral cave and thousands of fish regularly gather.

GETTING THERE
Air Queensland flies from Cairns to Lizard in small propeller craft. The fare is $107.

THE RESORT
The resort on Lizard Island is called Lizard Island Lodge and strives for a relaxed lodge-ish atmosphere with the accent on game fishing. There are black marlin heads on the walls and prominently displayed catch records. This can be intimidating to the those who don't fish but it's rather a front and one should not take it too seriously. In fact, Lizard is the best resort on the reef for a relaxed holiday. Bedarra

252

runs it a close second and Hayman has more gloss. It takes 64 guests accommodated in very comfortable semi-detached cabins built in gardens behind a fine beach. All have water views. Its open-plan central building houses the reception area, small bar and restaurant. The food is very good. The service is equal to it and the atmosphere is gently, casually friendly without intrusion or excessive arrangement of your days. There are reef trips organised, scuba diving, involving some extra costs, and fishing for those who want them. Lizard's full board tariff is between $230 and $280 per person per day. Children under six are not admitted to the resort.

DAY TRIPS
Air Queensland offers two-day tours to Lizard. One includes Cooktown, lunch at the island and coral viewing in its lagoon ($215) and the other goes straight to the island and boats out to the reef ($220).

Dunk Island

A fairly large continental island lying off Mission Beach about 150 km (93 miles) south of Cairns. The island has one large peak, Mount Koo-tal-oo whose forested slopes rise over the resort.

GETTING THERE
Air Queensland flies to Dunk Island from Cairns ($71) and Townsville ($77). The MV *Quick Cat* runs to the Island from Clump Point near Mission Beach. See the Cairns section for details.

THE RESORT
Dunk Island caters, like the Whitsunday Resorts, for around 200 people and aims at the middle mass or somewhat above. The resort is a complex of wooden buildings designed to blend as much as possible with their site on enchanting Brammo Bay. Guests stay in twin, double and family units and eat etc, at a central complex beside the swimming pool. Single-storey Beachfront 'Cabanas' are very comfortable and attractively decorated. Other cabanas face the gardens as do 'Banfield' units in two-storey buildings. There are lots of organised activities and water sports equipment. The full board tariff varies depending on standard of accommodation and whether it overlooks the beach. Charges are $116, $128, $152 in the high season (20 December to 16 January) and $108, $120 and $144 the rest of the time.

DAY TRIPS
Aboard the MV *Quick Cat*. See Cairns section for details.

Bedarra Island

Bedarra is a small continental island about six and a half km (four miles) from the coast whose two resorts have been constructed so as to have a minimal effect on the surrounding environment.

GETTING THERE
Transfer by Bedarra's own launch from Dunk Island.

THE RESORTS
Bedarra Bay takes only 48 guests and accommodates them in bungalows along the shores of a gloriously colourful bay, surrounded by tropical exotica such as orchids, ferns and coconut palms. There is very little organised fun, no doubt predicated on the presumption that guests want to be quietly elegant and truly away from it all. Full-board tariff $230 per person per day share, $270 sole use. **Bedarra Hideaway**, on the western side of the island takes 32 guests.

Michaelmas Cay
The coral cay called Michaelmas sits on the outer reef, 55 km (34 miles) from Cairns and is a nesting site for thousands of birds. It has no resort but is a very popular spot for day trips, both sailing and motorised, as it has a pretty ring of white sand and fringing coral easily seen by snorkellers.

Cooktown

Cooktown is an isolated settlement close to 250 km (155 miles) north of Cairns, only approachable by difficult and unsealed roads through the mountains behind Cape Tribulation or along the coast. It has an interesting history which began in 1770 when Captain James Cook chose the town's site as a place to repair his fractured barque, *Endeavour*, thus giving the town its name. The site had to wait a century to actually become a town as a port for the Palmer River gold rush which began in 1873. Then it grew fast, attracting tens of thousands of diggers along with its companion towns, Mossman and Port Douglas, and assumed very much its present appearance. Like all such preserved places, its remaining is due more to neglect than deliberation.

WHERE TO STAY
Sovereign Hotel, Charlotte Street (PO Box 100), Cooktown, (070)53 1333; on a site occupied by hotels since 1876. The original building was partially destroyed by a cyclone in the 1920s and re-named the Half Sovereign by witty locals. Its site now accommodates a modern hotel/motel with brightly decorated, air-conditioned rooms, some with cooking facilities. Single $76 to $98, double $87 to $109.

TOURS
Air Queensland flies in on Wednesdays from April to November (dry season). Passengers take a coach tour of the town, lunch at the Endeavour Inn and see the James Cook and Cooktown Sea museums. The fare is $135.

Coaches cannot reach Cooktown and return in a day so the Cairns coach operators **Tropic Wings** and **Ansett Trailways** offer overnight and three day packages to the town. The overnights coach up and fly back or vice versa depending on whether they take the coastal or the mountain road. The three day all-coach tours take both routes. On the Ansett two day option you can choose to take the *Sundancer* boat to Cooktown instead of an aeroplane. Fares are between $220 and $250 for all these tours.

Cape York Peninsula

The cape sticks up like a finger attached to the north-eastern corner of Australia pointing straight at New Guinea. It accords with the true meaning of that favourite tourism cliché, unspoilt, that is, unoccupied, wild, difficult of access in the dry season, impossible in the wet and possessing all qualities likely to reduce human beings to nature's playthings, not the reverse. These include jungles, crocodiles and large areas set aside for the sole use of Aboriginals. Its great peninsula has the northern end of the Barrier Reef to the east and the shallow waters of the Gulf of Carpentaria to the west. Its scenery continues the North Queensland themes of green forests to the water's edge, beaches, some white, others grey, mud flats and mangroves. It is hot and silent but for buzzing insects. The Great Dividing Range peters out about halfway up the peninsula and the flat lands above support a few cattle and lots of emptiness. Small bauxite mining towns cling to the west coast. The denizens of the cape are late twentieth-century pioneers and their lives can be lonely and hard. Nonetheless, holidayers from the world's more civilised climes are warmly welcomed and sometimes leave thinking they have just discovered what real life is about.

GETTING THERE
You can hire a four-wheel drive vehicle in Cairns, equip and provision it and drive right up Cape York if you want to. It's an option best undertaken by experienced bushmen as the roads are unsealed and infrequently used. Anyone undertaking such a journey would be well advised to inform the Cairns police of when and where they are going in case they don't make it. The journey will take one to two weeks, depending on the weather. Troubles you can strike vary from floods to sandy bogs but the most common is vehicle damage from the rough conditions.

Cassowara

255

WHERE TO STAY

Cape York Wilderness Lodge, Cape York, (070) 50 4222; is 400 metres (from the northernmost tip of Australia and caters to fishermen and walkers or those who crave silence in the wilderness. Accommodation is in self-contained cabins with private facilities and fans but no air conditioning.

The Inland

Most of this guide's information on Queensland pertains to the south-east coast, the Barrier Reef and the islands where over 90 per cent of the state's visitors spend 100 per cent of their holiday but west of the narrow coastal strip and the ranges is a vast inland populated by cattle farmers and miners. The colours of this country are a complete contrast to the coast. Stunted olive-green trees and patches of grey spinifex grass scatter a canvas of rusty reds and clay browns, spread under azure skies occasionally flecked with small white clouds. Wide, dusty plains are separated by flat-topped ridges and sudden outcrops of tough rock. Surface water is minimal, insufficient for life. Artesian bores whose derricks and silver wind wheels rise regularly from the plains, tap an underground reservoir of more than one million square kilometres supporting the region's hardy stock and people. Sunsets are unforgettable—the sun becomes a red and orange orb, descending to the low horizon in a purpling sky and leaving behind a velvet black night sparkling with millions of stars.

Quite frankly, unless you intend to spend years in Australia you may not see much of it—as Irish/Australian comedienne Geraldine Doyle says 'You can look further and see less than anywhere else in the world.' Nonetheless this is what many people call the real Australia and, especially for Americans, the kind of frontier territory informing their imagined Australia. Be prepared for temperatures of 40°C as a daily affair in the summer, in the winter days are cooler and nights cold. Be prepared also for distance. Towns and sites of tourist interest are hundreds of miles apart in many cases but little traffic will get in your way. Overcoming the space is as much a state of mind as anything else; locals think nothing of driving a hundred miles or more to a party.

Mount Isa and the Far West

Mount Isa marks about as far west as you can go in Queensland without ending up in the Northern Territory. It is over 900 km (558 miles) west of Townsville and could fairly be described as a very hot place in the middle of a desert. All its wealth is underground, extracted from a mine surrounded by slag heaps and next to a lead smelter pumping smoke night and day from a 270 metre (850 foot) stack. It produces more lead and silver than any other mine in the capitalist world. The city, an isolated patch of 26,000 persons, is spilled like a handful of pebbles on the spinifex plain below a range of lumpy brown hills. From a distance it looks like a good sand storm might bury it but close inspection reveals a modern, brick and tile town which can afford to be spacious and which tries despite the heat and dust to green its bit of desert. The people of Mt Isa are tough and various. Though sixty nationalities are represented in its population, many have come to make their money and get out. The mining life makes them intolerant of ease and softness. They like space and freedom and don't care about having no bidet in the bathroom.

GETTING THERE
Australian Airlines flights to Mt Isa depart Cairns on Monday and Tuesday ($185), Townsville on Monday ($182) and Brisbane ($284) on Tuesday, Wednesday, Friday and Sunday. Flights from northern centres take about 1 hour and 15 minutes and from Brisbane, 2 hours 15 minutes. Fares are one way economy.

The *Inlander* train departs from Townsville station on Tuesday and Friday afternoons. The fare is $103.60 first class and $69 economy and the overnight journey takes about 21 hours.

Ansett Pioneer and Greyhound, Deluxe (both $75) and Bus Australia ($62) coaches travel there regularly on their way to the Northern Territory from Townsville on a journey taking about 10 and a half hours. Greyhound also has a Brisbane to Mt Isa service ($129) which travels through central Queensland and takes 29 hours. Drivers take the Flinders Highway from Townsville.

TOURIST INFORMATION
The Mt Isa tourist information office is in Camooweal Street and is open from 9 am to 5 pm Monday to Friday.

WHAT TO SEE
The Mount Isa City Council oversees an area of 40,977 square km (25,406 square miles) which leads it to claim the title of largest city in the world but points of interest in Mt Isa itself are not legion. A **look-out** off Hilary Street which gives a prospect of the town and its silver, lead, copper and zinc mine. Run by Mount Isa Mines, it directly or indirectly keeps most of the townspeople in work and is the main drawcard. Its ores were discovered in 1923 by John Campbell Miles, a prospector from Victoria. A minor rush followed his discovery but the days of individual prospectors were brief and mining soon became dominated by one large company. Surface tours of its mine, called the **Mt Isa Mine**, depart from the Visitors' Centre at the mine at 8.30 am and 1.30 pm Monday to Friday. Underground tours also take place from Monday to Friday but must be booked by ringing (077) 44 2011.

A **museum of mining life** is housed on the site of the town's first water reservoir in Shakleton Street and in the old mine shaft which runs beneath it. There is a **Flying Doctor base**, open 9 am to 11.30 am Monday to Friday in Camooweal Road (Barkly Highway). A **School of the Air**, responsible for the education of isolated children by radio broadcast, operates from the same complex and can be inspected between 10.30 am and 12.30 pm on school days. The last remaining **tent houses**, built between 1932 and 1952 to house miners remain in Fourth Avenue and have been preserved by the National Trust. The houses had canvas walls and roof with a second corrugated-iron roof erected above the canvas. The air between the roofs kept the house cool.

WHERE TO STAY

Burke and Wills Isa Resort Motel, corner Grace and Camooweal Streets, Mt Isa, (077) 43 8000; across from the railway station and over the river from town, near the School of the Air, air-conditioned self-contained rooms. Single $48 to $51, twin $55 to $58.

Copper Gate Motel, 97 Marian Street, Mt Isa, (077) 43 3081; on the other side of town from the place above, slightly older style rooms, air-conditioned. Single $25, twin $30.

EATING OUT

Don't expect very much in this line. There are hamburger joints and pizza bars in Mt Isa but nothing to write home about.

Bonanza Family Restaurant, corner West and Grace Streets; one of a chain of American-style 'family' cafeterias scattered throughout Queensland.

City Café, West Street; over a dozen different hamburgers available here.

TOURS

Copper City Tours run bush ($30) and mine surface ($5) tours from Mt Isa. The bush tour runs only from May to September. The **Inland Tourist Association** runs a Mt Isa Mines underground tour ($10) from Monday to Friday.

Around Mt Isa

Cloncurry, 130 km east of Mt Isa, has more history but less life. It is a dusty cattle selling centre and produces a little straw gold but was once the most productive copper town in the British Commonwealth. The Great Australian Mine, established there in 1867, rose to that exalted status on the back of World War I only to be knocked on the head post-war when copper prices crashed. Cloncurry was the site of the first flying doctor base in Australia. The doctor, called to isolated injured and sick by pedal operated radio, changed life in the outback making proper medical care available to thousands who would have died without it. The base's establishment is marked with plaques commemorating the history of the service in Uhr Street. The Council Chambers in Scarr Street contain an **museum** which records the known history of the **Kalkadoon Tribe**.

The tribe was warlike and greatly feared by other Aboriginal tribes in the district. Its members tried to drive out white settlers when they took up residence. They killed five policemen and after being defeated at Battle Mountain in the ranges north of the town in 1884 were hunted down and wiped out.

The museum also contains relics of **Burke and Wills**, the white explorers who first came to the west of Queensland in 1861. Both men succeeded in crossing the continent from Melbourne to the Gulf of Carpentaria but died on the return journey. Two **cemeteries** betray the ethnic history of the town. Afghans who ran camel trains carrying ore from the Selwyn and Argylla ranges to Cloncurry's smelters are buried east–west in a section of the town's main cemetery. They were brought to the outback in the early 1900s when camels were the only reliable long distance cargo transport. Horses died in the heat and there were no trains. Herds of camels, released when they were superseded by railways, now run wild in the western deserts and some are still used, mostly for tourist amusement, in the Northern Territory. Chinese gold miners had a cemetery of their own which is on the Flinders Highway beside the Cloncurry River.

A monument 41 km (25 miles) west of Cloncurry on the Barkly Highway commemorates Burke and Wills crossing of the Corella River on January 22, 1861. **Lake Corella**, a little further on, is a sanctuary for many species of birds and formerly supplied water to the uranium mine at Mary Kathleen for which purpose it was created in the 1950s. Mary Kathleen closed in 1982 and no trace of it remains. **Battle Mountain** where the Kalkadoon Tribe met its end lies north of the dam wall at Lake Julius, 81 km (50 miles) north of the highway. Mount Isa is 18 km (11 miles) west of the Lake Julius turn-off.

Birdsville

Birdsville in the far south-western corner of Queensland is possibly Australia's most infamous outback town. The **Birdsville Track** runs from here to Maree in South Australia through Sturt's Stoney Desert which does a good job of living up to its name. The track is a byword for every danger associated with travel in the outback. Travellers over its 520-km (322-mile) length have frequently died of thirst and exposure to the desert sun, in the past some have disappeared altogether but, though the track is still dangerous, it is better than it was. Despite improvements, however, anyone who wants to try it must register their travel plans with the Birdsville Police before setting off so that a search can be instituted if they don't appear at the other end within a suitable period. Birdsville itself was originally a customs post, which proves the tenacity of bureaucracy, but when Australian Federation brought free trade in 1901 it lost that function and fell into decline. The population is now 30 but explodes at the **racing carnival** held each September when thousands of punters flock in from surrounding districts. The carnival is now so fashionable that people from the big cities come for a sticky-beak at outback life. The locals are sometimes not amused.

The notorious **Simpson Desert** lies 65 km (40 miles) to the west of the town where the 505,000 hectare Simpson Desert National Park begins. Orange and yellow sand dunes, spinifex grass and desert wildlife are to be found there, entirely without flowing water. Almost no one visits the desert except to make scientific studies or gain publicity.

Central Queensland

The towns of Winton, Longreach and Barcaldine with their wide brown streets, corrugated-iron roofed hotels, deep, shady verandas and few trees define the cattle raising territory of Central Queensland. In this country nugetty horsemen in broadbrimmed hats appear out of the dust with a mob of beasts at their side and road trains full of cattle hurtle by on the few narrow highways. The region has given birth to two vitally important features of modern Australia, labour politics and Qantas Airways.

GETTING TO AND AROUND

Trains run from Rockhampton through Barcaldine ($66.50 first class, $41.80 economy) and Longreach ($78.40 first class, $49.30 economy) to Winton ($97 first class, $64.70 economy). They depart on Tuesday and Friday evenings at 6 pm and arrive at Winton around 2 pm the following day.

Greyhound coaches on the Brisbane to Darwin run set down at Longreach ($80.10) and Winton ($94). The trip takes between 15 and 20 hours and coaches arrive around midnight in Longreach, 5.30 am in Winton. The Capricorn Highway from Rockhampton travels through Barcaldine to Longreach where it joins the Lansborough Highway to Winton.

Winton

Originally known as Pelican Watering Hole, Winton was established in 1875 and rapidly became the centre of a wide cattle and sheep grazing area but when Australia fell into depression in 1890, the area was badly affected. Attempts to load the economic difficulties onto the back of rural workers backfired when shearers struck in 1891, a strike which became a milestone in Australian labour relations. Five hundred strikers gathered from all over the region and camped on the local common. Riots were feared and the police brought in but the strike ended in failure.

Local legend has it that Waltzing Matilda was written somewhere near Winton in 1895 and had its first public performance there. Needless to say there is a statue of a swaggie (itinerant bushman who carried his belongings in a cloth swag attached to the end of a stick held over his shoulder) in the main street, bearing witness to this lore. The billabong at which the events of the song's narrative took place is said to be Combo Waterhole, 145 km (90 miles) to the north. A bush verse competition is held in Winton annually to promote this aspect of its heritage. A fossilised record of a dinosaur stampede consisting of hundreds of small dinosaur footprints can be seen at Lark Quarry Environmental Park, 111 km (69 miles) south of the town. The prints were left in an old creek bed by about 200 small dinosaurs thought to have been panicked by the approach of a predator.

Queensland and Northern Territory Air Services, the precursor of today's QANTAS, was founded at Winton in 1920 by Hudson Fysh but soon moved to Longreach where some of its history is preserved.

WHERE TO STAY

Matilda Motel, 20 Oondooro Street, (P.O. Box 17), Winton, (074) 57 1433; has 13 air-conditioned rooms. Single $30, double $38.

TOURS

Day tours of **Carrisbrook Station**, 80 km (50 miles) south-west of Winton where Lyndon B. Johnson force landed a Flying Fortress in 1942, can be arranged at the Winton Pharmacy or by ringing (074) 57 1684. There is lots of wildlife, an old opal mine and some Aboriginal paintings on the property. It also has some cabin accommodation to which you must bring your own groceries and blankets.

Longreach

Longreach is 178 km (110 miles) south-east of Winton on the Landsborough Highway. The town was settled in the 1870s and is now the largest in central western Queensland.

After its first couple of years at Winton, QANTAS moved to Longreach where it was centred for 12 years until 1934 when the airline made its first overseas flight. Its original hangar, Australia's first **aircraft factory** from 1926 to 1930, is still in use. Longreach makes much of its history as a centre where drovers and cattlemen came during the pioneering days and where they still wet their whistles in the pubs after a hard few days driving the road train. The **Australian Stockman's Hall of Fame** recalls some of the great characters who rode, explored, built and told stories during those times. It is opposite the airport and open every day from 8.30 am to 5 pm.

WHERE TO STAY
Starlight Motel, corner Wonga and Cassorwary Streets, Longreach, (074) 58 1288; has a swimming pool. Single $32, double $40.

TOURS
A tour of Longreach by horse-drawn carriage is available from the Stockman's Hall of Fame, (074) 58 1748.

Barcaldine

Barcaldine, 106 km (66 miles) east of Longreach, was the centre of the 1891 shearers' strike and a meeting in the town during the stoppage led to the formation of the Australian Labor Party, Australia's oldest political party. The meeting took place under the somewhat ironically named **Tree of Knowledge** which stands outside the railway station in Oak Street. The strike itself was brought to failure by the arrest of its committee whose members were charged with conspiracy but it remains a watershed in modern Australian history. **Red Mountain**, 55 km (34 miles) east of the town, is split by high-walled ironstone gorges and escarpments. Bushwalks and picnics are allowed but as the mountain is on private property, arrangements must be made with the Barcaldine Tourist Association.

WHERE TO STAY
Barcaldine Motel, Corner Box Street and Landsborough Highway, Barcaldine, (074) 51 1244; single $25, double $35.
Landsborough Lodge, Landsborough Highway, Barcaldine, (074) 51 1100; single $39, twin $49.

Station and Farm Holidays
Station and farm holidays in this part of the country give an authentic taste of outback life. Guests are generally encouraged to join in the day to day business of being a pastoralist (cattle or sheep farmer), especially where it involves animals. **Dalkeith Station** via Longreach, 4730, about 230 km (143 miles) from the town runs cattle and sheep. Guests can take part in shearing, gem fossicking and riding.

Full-board tariff is $60 per day. **Lorraine Station Outback Resort,** Winton 4735, is 54 km (33 miles) south of Winton and takes guests from April to October. Full board $40 per person twin share. Any arrangement should be made well in advance by writing to the addresses given as these isolated places need to make preparation for their guests and do not function like hotels. Winter (June to August) is the best time to travel to this hot part of the country. Bookings are heaviest during school holidays, especially around September/October and Easter.

FESTIVALS

Outback people live so far apart that they like nothing better than an excuse to get together. Attending any such occasion is a great way to absorb some of the outback ethos and witness displays of horsemanship and other agricultural skills. Here is a short list:

May—Cloncurry Festival, Winton Campdraft

June—Mount Isa Agricultural Show, Longreach Heritage Ball

August—Mount Isa Rodeo, Cloncurry Rodeo and Merry Muster

September—Birdsville Races, Mount Isa Festival of Arts

Part VI

THE NORTHERN TERRITORY

'Ghost Gums'

A 650-million-year-old monolith and a 15-year-old city encapsulate the tremendous contrasts and wonders of the Northern Territory. The monolith is Ayers Rock, symbol of the hot dry 'Red Centre', a temple to its Aboriginal owners and site of mythical ceremonies for 40,000 years. In the huge, red deserts round its base the smallest action—a germinating seed, a drop of rain, the movement of a passing animal—is significant to life's continuance and has a world of repercussions, each vital in ensuring human and animal survival. Its owners are an ancient people struggling with the demons of twentieth-century life.

The city is Darwin, centre of the Top End, reconstructed after Cyclone Tracy with hardly a building older than an average adolescent. In its tropical surroundings profligate nature grows whole gardens in a year, supports a fantasy of birdlife and works one dramatic annual change of season by means of rain alone. The city's people are air-conditioned pioneers, struggling to govern an ancient land which likes to disregard them.

The 'Red Centre' grows only low shrubs, spinifex grass and spindly, narrow-leaved trees except around its watercourses where magnificent, river red gums cluster. The usually bone dry rivers flash flood when rain falls and the desert becomes a carpet of tiny wild flowers. The 'Top End' is thick with tropical greenery, wetlands and rivers where ancient canyons and escarpments have long resisted the endless onslaughts of nature.

Over 1500 km (930 miles) of the straight two-lane Stuart Highway, fully surfaced only in the last five years, make a lifeline between the Top End and the Red Centre, linking small towns across vast stretches of flat, dusty country. The Territory's tiny

263

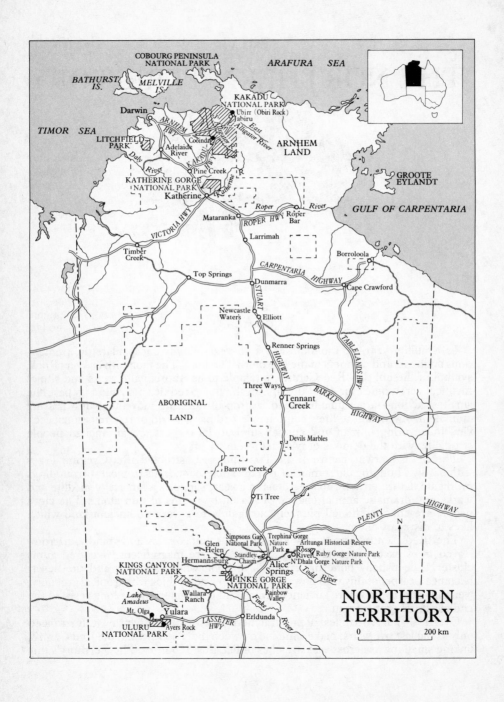

NORTHERN TERRITORY

0   200 km

population (138,800 with well over half living in Darwin and Alice Springs) is spread thinly. About one third of the people are Aboriginal and many live outside the towns, retaining strong tribal traditions, speaking little or no English and caring nothing for the white man's way of life. Town dwellers live roughly in creek beds and parks and often suffer from the ravages of alcohol.

Climate

The climate of the Top End is most like north Queensland. It has a wet season from October to April and a dry season from May to September. In Darwin the height of the 'wet' is known as suicide season, so oppressive does the heat and humidity become. During the 'dry' it doesn't rain for months on end, the temperature hovers around 30°C and days are clear, humidity low.

The Red Centre is dry all year round and can have 14 year droughts. In summer, temperatures climb as high as 50°C, in winter they can drop to less than 0°C overnight although days are around 20°C.

History

History is blissfully little in the Northern Territory. The Dutch who mapped the northern and western coasts of the continent in the seventeenth century were the first to bring the place to European attention but such attention was minimal and contemptuous. In colonial times, settlements were attempted from about the late 1830s but all failed until Darwin in 1869. Further spurts of interest occurred in 1874 when gold was discovered at Pine Creek, and following other mineral discoveries in the 1880s and early 1900s. In 1911, the Commonwealth Government took over Territory administration from the state government of South Australia. Cattle farming was by then the main occupation of the few thousand white residents. The new government attempted to upgrade stock routes and build a railway but the Great Depression put a stop to that.

The Japanese bombing of Darwin during World War II changed the Territory's perceived importance overnight. Money was poured in for the improvement of facilities and communications. Darwin became an Allied base. At the end of the war Territorians returned to raising cattle and mining, cutting the land up into huge pastoral leases, thousands of square miles in extent. They remain a crucial economic base, though tourism seems determined to outstrip them. The greatest changes in the last ten years have been the granting of full self-government in 1978 and the awakening of Aboriginal consciousness which has seen the granting of limited land rights to these long dispossessed people.

GETTING TO AND AROUND

By Air
Darwin and Alice Springs are the major domestic airports in the Northern Territory. International carriers fly into Darwin and national carriers fly into both. Many flights to Darwin from the south go via Alice Springs. There is also a domestic airport at Ayers Rock. **Ansett NT** is the Northern Territory's internal airline.

265

By Rail
Only Alice Springs is linked to the rest of Australia by rail. Bookings should be made well in advance as services are few and Alice Springs is a popular tourist destination, especially in winter. The famous *Ghan* runs between Adelaide and Alice Springs and takes 24 hours.

By Road
Ansett Pioneer, Deluxe, Greyhound and **Bus Australia** coaches enter the Northern Territory via the Stuart Highway from Adelaide, the Barkly Highway from Townsville (joining the Stuart at Three Ways) or around the coast of Western Australia from Perth (to Darwin only). Ansett Pioneer has an extra route through the middle of Western Australia to Ayers Rock and Alice Springs. All are very long trips of anywhere from around 1500 to well over 4000 km (930 to 2,480 miles). Within the Territory, coach travel is the only real alternative to air travel. The same companies' vehicles regularly zoom up and down the Stuart Highway between Alice Springs and Darwin, taking about 20 hours. The main stops are Tennant Creek and Katherine. Services run at least twice daily between Alice Springs and Ayers Rock, a distance of 450 km (279 miles).

Travelling by car is much more practical in the Northern Territory now than it was a few years ago as many more km of road have been surfaced lately. The Stuart Highway is asphalt (tar) for its entire length as are the Barkly, Lasseter and Victoria Highways and the Arnhem Highway into Kakadu National Park. Unsealed roads, however, are many and treacherous and anyone travelling off the beaten track should invest in a well-equipped four-wheel drive vehicle and notify the police of their intended route.

TOURIST INFORMATION
The splendidly well-organised Northern Territory Government Tourist Bureau is responsible for spreading the word about what to see and do in the NT. It issues a helpful publication called *Tours and Services Guide of Australia's Northern Territory* which lists a vast range of tours, who operates them and what they offer. Travellers who scorn tours should try to keep in mind the distance and the inaccessibility of some sights in this still very wild region. The booklet named and other information about the Territory is available from offices at the following addresses:

31 Smith Street Mall, **Darwin**, (089) 81 6611
9 Hindley Street, **Adelaide**, (08) 212 1133
415 Bourke Street, **Melbourne**, (03) 67 6948
48 Queen Street, **Brisbane**, (07) 229 5799
89 King Street, **Sydney**, (02) 235 2822
62 St George's Terrace, **Perth**, (09) 322 4255
35 Ainslie Avenue, **Canberra**, (062) 57 1177
93 Liverpool Street, **Hobart**, (002) 34 4199

Time
The Northern Territory follows Central Time, as does South Australia. It is half an hour behind the eastern states.

266

MAJOR SIGHTS

Nature's great deeds take pride of place in the Northern Territory. **Ayers Rock** has become such a cliché that its Aboriginal owners have lately stopped it being used for every advertisement and rock video but no matter how white folks try to trivialise it, the Rock remains an extraordinary formation with more than a touch of the supernatural about it. Probably equal to it but less known are the nearby **Olgas**. The gorges and gaps on the **Finke River** in the Alice Springs region and the **Katherine Gorge** near Katherine are spectacular, the waters of **Kakadu National Park** are broad and beautiful and the ancient Aboriginal rock paintings in the same park are among the most fascinating cultural relics in Australia.

ACCOMMODATION

The Northern Territory is short of accommodation, especially in remote but increasingly popular locations such as Ayers Rock and Kakadu National Park. What's more the number of beds is likely to stay limited because of natural problems such as lack of water and nobody comes in the wet. Any person coming during the dry and cooler winter months would be well advised to book—being turned away when the next bed is over 400 km (248 miles) distant can be a levelling experience to say the least. Darwin has more accommodation but it too fills up as does Alice Springs. The quality and range of what there is, especially in new development, is judiciously spread from Sheratons to camping grounds.

Bed Tax

The Northern Territory government is the only one in Australia to levy a tax directly on tourism. Charged at the rate of 2.5% of the price of your room, it is collected by the accommodation at which you stay. It is likely that anyone buying a package holiday will pay the tax as part of the holiday cost but a check with your agent would be wise. The accommodation prices shown in this part of the guide do not include the tax.

FOOD AND DRINK

Territorians, especially Darwinians, are reputed to be serious drinkers in the sense that they consume vigorously and vastly anything cold and remotely resembling beer. Buffalo (often called buff) and a fish called *barramundi* are Northern Territory food specialities. Barramundi is firm fleshed, sweet and excellent eating when simply cooked but remember it is caught in the Top End and is naturally freshest there. Buffalo varies from flat and tough as old boots to thick and tender. It is frequently marinated and barbecued. Crocodile, a white meat which tastes like a cross between chicken and fish, is also available in some Darwin restaurants.

ACTIVITIES AND SPORTS

Bushwalking is popular and whether hiking in the gorges or following the nature trails in Kakadu, watch out for snakes and wear long trousers because spinifex is very prickly. Hunting with guns and fishing with lines, spears and pots are common in the Northern Territory. Hunters go after ducks, geese and buffalo but native animals are protected and licence and private property conditions relate to all hunting.

267

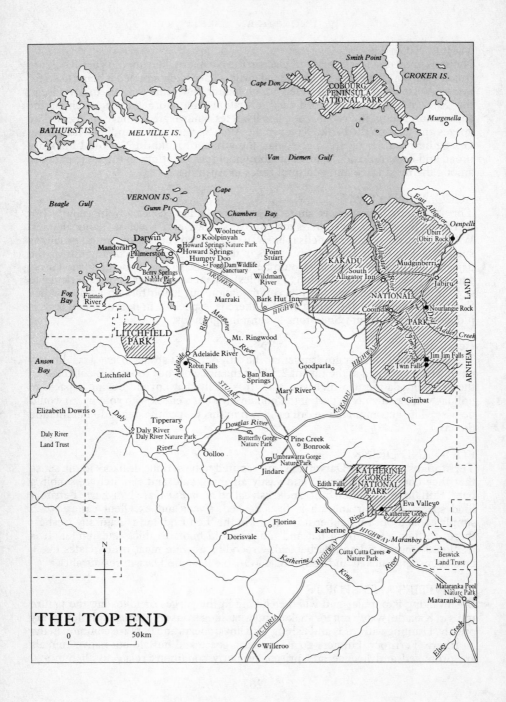

THE TOP END

0   50km

Information regarding the use of firearms is available from the police. Fishing with hand lines, rods and spears is generally permitted in rivers and billabongs through-out the year but there are strict limits on the number of barramundi any one fisherman may take. Mud crabs are also common in the Top End and may be caught in pots provided only one pot is used. Fishing information is available from the Department of Ports and Fisheries, Corner Harry Chan Avenue and Cavenagh Street, Darwin.

There is canoeing in the Katherine Gorges and from Alice Springs it is possible to go ballooning over the Macdonnell Ranges or gliding. Darwin and Alice Springs have tennis courts, squash courts and golf courses.

The Top End

DARWIN

Darwin is the capital of the Northern Territory and the centre of the 'Top End', the name given to that part of the Territory in the torrid zone. It is a truly tropical city, as close to Jakarta as it is to Adelaide and closer to Manila than to Sydney. Its population is 70,000, about as much as a good sized provincial city in any other part of the country but by far the largest settlement in its own region and growing fast. The seasons are akin to those in northern Queensland, wet and dry, with the wet extending from October to May and the dry from June to September. The 'dry' is by far the most pleasant time of year since humidity, the great difference between seasons, is low and days are clear and sunny. People in other parts of the world would call the 'wet' the monsoon season.

Darwin could take the title as Australia's most wrecked city. It was bombed flat by the Japanese during World War II and reduced almost to rubble by Cyclone Tracy on Christmas Day 1974. The cyclone also killed 50 people, not quite so many as the Japanese who managed over 200. The result is that almost any historical building is either reconstructed or exceptionally lucky. 'Historical' in Darwin also tends to mean before 1930.

History

An Aboriginal group called the *Larrakeyah* were the first occupants of the shore where Darwin stands. They had camps at Government House and Stokes Hill and had been there for tens of thousands of years when white men arrived to 'settle' the Top End. Their succession of failed attempts must have made those ancient people laugh. An outpost was established at Melville Island, 80 km (50 miles) north, to ward off the Dutch and French in 1824 and abandoned in 1829. Two further attempts were made on the Cobourg Peninsula north east of Darwin between 1827 and 1849.

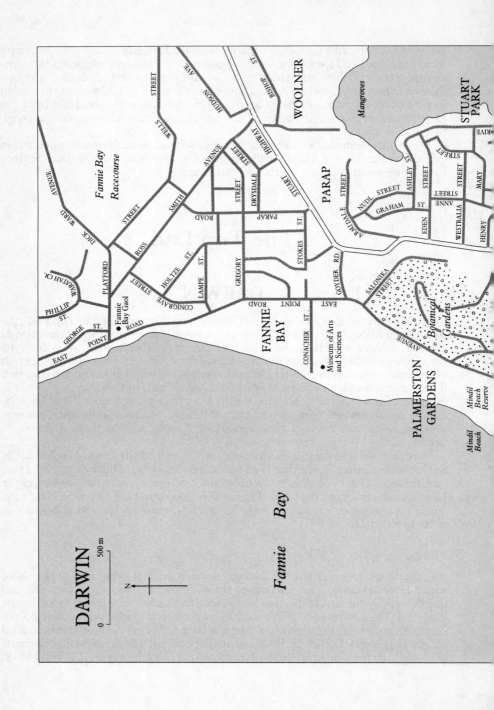

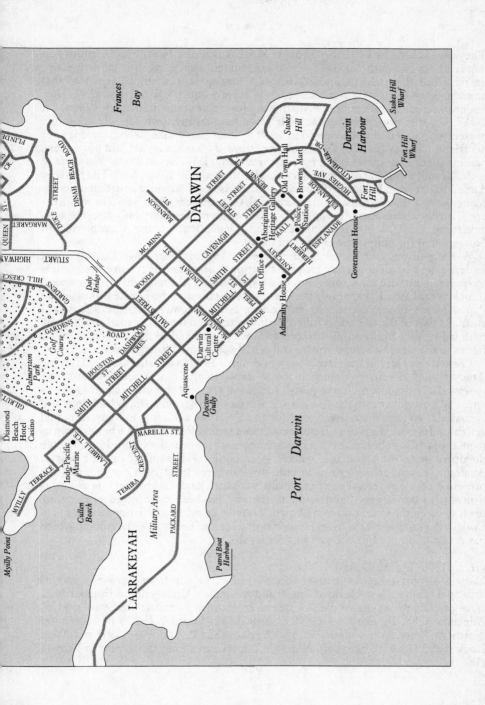

They also failed. In 1863 the whole of what is now the Northern Territory was handed over to South Australia whose government sold parts of it to prospective graziers and then had to undertake some development to fulfil its part of that bargain. A town was started at Escape Cliffs in 1864 but only lasted until 1867. Now under some pressure, the South Australian Government sent its Surveyor General, G. W. Goyder, north to find a suitable place for a lasting township. He chose the present site of Darwin, discovered in 1839 by John Lort Stokes who named it after his friend Charles Darwin, author of *The Origin of Species*. Goyder laid out streets, naming them after members of his surveying party, J. W. Bennett who was speared to death while working on the project, A. H. Smith and A. J. Mitchell. The town he named Palmerston but it rapidly became known as Port Darwin, a situation officially recognised by the Australian Commonwealth Government when it took over Northern Territory administration in 1911. The Northern Territory only became self-governing in 1978 but remains financially dependent on the Commonwealth Government for almost the entirety of its budget.

When gold was discovered at Pine Creek in 1871, it looked like Darwin might undergo the kind of boom that ensured the growth of other Australian cities but this too petered out without earning the city a lasting place in the national consciousness. It took World War II, especially the War in the Pacific and the Japanese invasion of Papua New Guinea, to make its importance as the gateway to northern Australia clear. As part of the war effort Allied troops were based there, the road south to the railhead at Alice Springs was surfaced and the city attacked 64 times by Japanese air forces in the nearest scrape Australia has had with armed foreign invasion.

Present day Darwin has largely been built since 1975 in the aftermath of Cyclone Tracy which effectively demolished the town. In the city's consciousness, the temporal divisions pre-Tracy, post-Tracy have some of the same significance as ante and post diluvian to the rest of us. It has its share of multi-storey buildings and is basically an administrative centre for the Territory's mining and governmental activities. It is not, despite a carefully cultivated reputation, as wild a frontier town as it once was though buffalo hunters haunt the pubs between stints in the bush. People do drink quite a lot and the 'stubby' beer bottle, 375 millilitres in the rest of Australia, has somehow grown to hold two full litres in Darwin but that and the presence of a rich racial mix, especially of Asians and backpackers, is about as frontier as Darwin gets. Palmerston, by the way, has been resurrected as a satellite town to catch the overflow from Darwin's rapidly growing population who come to work in the mining and tourism industries and for the Territory Government which has a vast number of public servants for its size.

GETTING TO AND AROUND

Darwin airport takes some international traffic, mostly from Indonesia but its principal business is made up of Ansett and Australian Airlines flights from all other state capitals which arrive daily. Fares from mainland capitals are Sydney $453, Adelaide $388, Brisbane $410, Melbourne $453. Ansett NT flies in from other Northern Territory towns such as Alice Springs ($252), Katherine ($91) and Ayers Rock ($293 via Alice Springs). A shuttle bus operates from the airport to Darwin city.

272

Ansett Pioneer, Greyhound, Deluxe and Bus Australia coaches operate to Darwin from Alice Springs, Perth via Broome and from Townsville via Mt Isa. Fares are around $100, $200 and $150 respectively.

Darwin has a town bus service called **Darwin Bus Service** whose city terminal is in Harry Chan Avenue. Its routes, especially numbers four and six, pass many points of tourist interest in and around the city and operate with acceptable frequency from Monday to Friday, but hardly at all on Saturdays and not at all on Sundays. Fares are very cheap.

There are some cheap car rental companies in Darwin as well as the big four. They are **Cheapa Rent-a-Car**, 149 Stuart Highway, (089) 81 8400; **Rent a Rocket**, 9 Daly Street, (089) 81 6977; **Rent-a-Dent**, Corner Smith and Maclachlan Streets, (089) 81 1411.

Bicycles are for hire from **City Cycle Rental**, 69 Mitchell Street, (089) 81 9733.

TOURIST INFORMATION
The **Northern Territory Government Tourist Bureau** is at 31 Smith Street Mall in the centre of Darwin, phone (089) 81 6611. It is open from 9 am to 5 pm Monday to Friday and 9 am to noon on Saturday and closed on Sunday. The **Northern Territory National Trust** has an office at the corner of Knuckey Street and The Esplanade where a brochure setting out a walking tour of the city is available. The main **Post Office** is on Knuckey Street between Mitchell and Smith Streets.

City Centre

Darwin's city centre stands on a small peninsula pointing into Darwin Harbour. It is not big and finding your way around is easy as most places of interest lie between Knuckey Street, The Esplanade, Cavenagh Street and Harry Chan Avenue.

Cyclone Tracy demolished so many of Darwin's prominent buildings that the tourist who goes looking for them finds only bits and pieces incorporated in structures that are part of the glossy new city. In fact, following Tracy, the town planners had almost a *tabula rasa* on which to build their dreams. The general opinion is that they greatly improved a rather dowdy town especially in the construction of **Smith Street Mall**, the city's pleasant, even languid main shopping area between Bennett and Knuckey Streets. The **Victoria Hotel** overlooks the centre of the Mall. Built in 1894, it has been partly demolished by cyclones on three occasions and each time, including Tracy, survived and was restored to its place as Darwin's premier watering hole. **The Star Village**, a shopping arcade opposite the hotel, began life in 1930 as an open air cinema called The Star. The original Star's projection booth has been incorporated in the façade of its contemporary replacement. The 1884 **Commercial Bank** façade on the corner of the Mall and Bennett Street is one of the few structures remaining from the days when Darwin was known as Palmerston.

The **Old Town Hall** in the section of Smith Street between Bennett Street and The Esplanade is a reminder of Tracy's savagery, only its walls survived the onslaught. The stone building opposite is **Browns Mart** another cyclone victim

273

which has been restored. Originally built as a mining exchange in 1885, it later became a fruit and vegetable market and is rumoured to have housed Darwin's first police station as well as a brothel. The building was wrecked by a cyclone and reconstructed previously in 1897. **Christ Church Cathedral** and the **Police Station**, both almost completely wrecked by Tracy are located on opposite corners of Smith Street and The Esplanade. They have been reconstructed incorporating what was left of their originals.

More cyclone savaged and resurrected buildings face The Esplanade. **Government House**, built in 1870 has made it through three cyclonic demolitions, each time restored to its oddly gabled tropicality and its gardens re-created with the bountiful assistance of kinder Darwin weather. It was known as the Residency until 1911. The **Darwin Hotel**, one of the city's oases is on the corner of The Esplanade and Herbert Street. **Admiralty House** on the corner of The Esplanade and Knuckey Street is one of the few tropical houses from the 1920s remaining in Darwin. Until recently it housed the Naval Officer Commanding Northern Australia but is now an art gallery and tea house where you can eat in the open air. Across Knuckey Street is **Lyons Cottage** built in 1925 as a residence for employees of the British Australian Telegraph Company. It came to Darwin in the early 1870s when the telegraph line was extended from Java and the overland telegraph to Adelaide established.

One of Darwin's more unusual attractions, **Aquascene**, is located at Doctors Gully on the sea end of the esplanade. At high tide on most days thousands of fish school at Doctors Gully waiting to be fed. The ritual began 20 years ago when a local resident started throwing food scraps to mullet riding in on the tide. The fish grew to like the idea and after some years their daily feeding frenzy became a Darwin sight. Now tourists can wade knee deep among a crush of milkfish, catfish, mullet, bream, batfish and other species, distributing bread like St Peter at the Loaves and Fishes. They are charged $2 for the privilege. Since feeding takes place only at high tide times can vary from around 8 am to 6 pm. The show lasts anything from one to two hours. Phone 81 7837 to find out when the fish appear on any given day.

Fannie Bay Area

Outside the immediate city centre in the direction of Fannie Bay are the **Darwin Botanical Gardens**. They were almost totally destroyed by Cyclone Tracy in 1974 when 78 percent of the trees, the fern house, the nursery and the original gardener's cottage were blown away, but that was only the last in series of disasters including cyclones in 1897 and 1937 and a fire in 1902. The gardens are returning to beauty but things that take a long time to grow, such as avenues of palm trees, are still fairly short. Post Tracy the garden boundaries have been extended down to Mindil Beach on the bay and new features such as a rainforest gully and coastal wetlands section are being developed. The cottage once occupied by Dr Maurice Holtze, a German settler who established the gardens in 1879, has been restored and converted into a restaurant. It is open every day from early morning to sunset.

The **Northern Territory Museum of Arts and Sciences** is a new building in East Point Road on Bullocky Point, Fannie Bay, which houses an especially good collection of South East Asian art and artefacts, Aboriginal art and some quality paintings by white Australian artists but two of its most arresting exhibits are on the lawns outside the museum. They are a pearling lugger and a vessel in which a group of Vietnamese refugee 'boat people' arrived at Darwin in the late 1970s. The museum is open 9 am to 6 pm from Monday to Friday and 10 am to 6 pm on the weekend. Entrance is free. Darwin Bus Service routes four and six pass by it. **Fannie Bay Gaol** at the intersection of East Point Road and Ross Smith Avenue is a museum of different preoccupations. Built in 1883, the gaol has seen many a hanging, the last, a two victim affair, taking place in 1952. In 1920 the gaol housed a group of Darwin's leading citizens who had refused to pay taxes on grounds similar to those which brought about the Boston Tea Party—they were not represented in the government of their own country. The situation was relieved two years later when the Territory was allowed one member in the Commonwealth Parliament. This remains the position to the present day. In 1942, all prisoners were released following Japanese bombing raids on Darwin and the gaol was turned over to the Royal Australian Airforce as an operational point. Most of its buildings have been restored and it is open 2 pm to 3.30 pm from Monday to Friday.

Fannie Bay also has two beaches, **Mindil Beach** and **Vestey's Beach**. They have fine, fawn coloured sand, are gently sloping and their water is tepid and relatively calm. Swimming is not allowed between October and May because of the presence of deadly box jellyfish, often called simply 'stingers'. And, while on the subject of marine matters, **Indo Pacific Marine** in Smith Street West is one of the few places in the world where you can see coral and the entire reef ecosystem existing away from its natural habitat. The re-constructed reef and its colourful fishes are held in glass-fronted tanks which allow an easy close-up view. An informative talk about the reef is included. Indo Pacific Marine is open seven days a week from May to October; 10 am to 4.30 pm and 6 pm to 8.30 pm on Wednesday evenings. Information about hours at other times of the year is available on (089) 81 1294.

SHOPPING

Darwin is not a shoppers' mecca. There are some 'art galleries' selling work by black and white artists—that they double as coffee shops and small restaurants is a measure of their dedication to art. The **Raintree Gallery**, 29 Knuckey Street, specialises in Aboriginal arts and crafts and **Opal House**, Smith Street Mall, sells Australian gemstones.

ENTERTAINMENT

Diamond Beach Casino, the heartland of good times in Darwin is at the southern end of Mindil Beach. As casinos go it is neither so crass as those of Queensland nor so elegant as that of Adelaide but it is a good a place as any to lose your money. Gambling runs from noon to 4 am every day. The casino also has a 24-hour coffee shop and a 350-seat cabaret room.

Next door to the Casino you can browse in the **food market**. In the dry season on Thursday and Saturday evenings, Mindil Beach plays host to a giant communal 'picnic'. Just before sunset, the car park begins to fill up with food stalls offering all types of South East Asian delicacies, from satay sticks and curries to wonderfully

275

refreshing tropical fruit drinks. These are supplemented by Greek and Italian stalls and the ubiquitous True Blue Barbies, so there is something to suit all tastes. Locals bring picnic chairs, tables and 'eskies' which they set up on the dunes and beach to enjoy the food and the sunset. Craft stalls are also represented.

Of all the places in the world to have a **dress code**, Darwin and the Territory in general, tends to be rather strict about such things. The minimum for anywhere with pretensions, including some bars is the 'Territory Rig', shorts, open necked shirt, long socks and shoes. Thongs, singlets, bare feet, sneakers and jeans are unacceptable.

WHERE TO STAY

The Beaufort Hotel, The Esplanade, Darwin, (089) 82 9911, is Darwin's smartest hotel in the architectural sense and one of the city's most interesting modern buildings. It is also a high quality hotel and includes a Japanese and a French restaurant among its features as well as a six lane swimming pool. There are 233 rooms. Darwin centre is a few minutes walk away. Single $115, double $135.

Sheraton Darwin Hotel, 32 Mitchell Street, Darwin, (089) 82 0000, is new but totally uninspired in its design, simply ten storeys of Sheraton hotel placed very conveniently in the centre of Darwin. $120 to $160.

Diamond Beach Hotel Casino, Gilruth Avenue, The Gardens, Darwin, (089) 81 7755; is on the beach and offers accommodation in a hotel with all the extras but, be aware, the concentration is definitely on the casino. There's also a cabaret room and a swish restaurant and a swimming pool. Single $110, double $130.

Four Seasons, Dashwood Crescent, Darwin, (089) 81 5333; nine storeys tall and square, this hotel has cane furniture in its rooms to give a tropical atmosphere and plastic furniture in other places. Single $75, double $88.

Darwin Travelodge, 122 The Esplanade, Darwin, (089) 81 5388, is primarily a base for businessmen because of its convenient position near the centre of Darwin but has the features of a big hotel including bars, restaurants, a fairly big swimming pool and height. $114.

Marrakai Luxury Apartments, 93 Smith Street, Darwin, (089) 82 3711, a two storey complex of serviced two bedroom apartments with full kitchens, lounge and dining areas in central Darwin. Daily serviced $105 January through March, $140 April through September, $120 October through December. Weekly serviced $95, $125, $110.

Poinciana Inn, corner Mitchell and McLachlan Streets, Darwin, (089) 81 8111, is a centrally placed motel of medium standard whose four stories of rooms overlook its car park and the street. Single $55, double $62.

Paravista, 5 Mackillop Street, Parap, (089) 81 9200, is a tall motel, closer to Fannie Bay and the museum than to the city centre. Rooms are rather small and cluttered. Some have balconies. Single $60.50 November through March, $76 April through October, double $67 and $84.

Larrakeyah Lodge, 50 Mitchell Street, Darwin, (089) 81 7550; air-conditioned rooms with fridges, tea and coffee making facilities. Share bathrooms. The building used to be used by Qantas staff and was renovated as budget accommodation about five years ago. It has singles, twins and family rooms. $25 to $55.

276

EATING OUT

The Beagle, N.T. Museum of Arts and Sciences, Conacher Street, Fannie Bay, (089) 81 6474; is the only restaurant in Darwin on the seafront and a great place to watch the city's beautiful sunsets. Smorgasbord lunch on weekdays and à la carte in the evening. Licensed. Mid price range.

Asian Gateway, 58 Aralia Street, Shopping Centre, Nightcliff, (089) 85 1131; is Darwin's top Thai restaurant. The house speciality is a delicious boneless duck. Licensed. Mid price range.

Rock Oyster, Cavenagh Street, Darwin, (089) 81 3472, offers outdoor dining when the weather suits or air-conditioned when it doesn't. Naturally, there is seafood on the menu, especially barramundi. BYO. Mid price range.

Lee Dynasty, Workers Club Building, Cavenagh Street, Darwin, (089) 81 7808; has won some prestigious awards for its Chinese dishes which are cooked by chefs imported from Hong Kong. Licensed. Mid to upper price range.

TOURS

A great variety of tours departs from Darwin by land, sea and air and in many cases allow you to see places that would otherwise be beyond reach. One of the best ways to appreciate their variety and make an informed choice is to obtain a copy of *Tours and Services Guide of Australia's Northern Territory* published by the Northern Territory Government Tourist Bureau. It lists day and extended tours from Darwin as well as Territory-wide tours and tours in the Red Centre. Here are day tour possibilities, they can all be booked at the Bureau office, 31 Smith Street Mall, Darwin, (089) 81 6611.

City Tours

Arura Safari Tours operates historical tours of the city ($25) and to the wildlife parks around the city ($30).

Buck's Safaris runs personal tours of the city on demand ($45 per hour).

Coop & Co Horse Drawn Tours short horse drawn tours of the Botanical Gardens ($10), historical sights ($5) and city lights ($20).

Go Tours city and sunset tours 4 pm daily ($20).

Keetley's Tours three hour coach tour of Darwin sights ($20).

Harbour Cruises

Billy 'J' morning ($15), lunch ($25) and afternoon ($17), catamaran cruises as well as an evening cruise which includes a barbecue and corroboree ($38).

Schooner Algerias is a 75 foot sailing boat on which you can enjoy a seafood lunch whilst cruising Darwin Harbour. Evening cruises as well. $67.

Adelaide River

Adelaide River Queen cruises the tidal Adelaide River east of Darwin where there are thousands of birds and crocodiles. Cruise only, $18, cruise and bus from Darwin, $38.

Go Tours conducts morning, afternoon and full day cruises on the tidal reaches of the Adelaide River. $45 to $75, some with coach transport.

Around Darwin

It's easy to see Top End wildlife in Kakadu National Park but if that opportunity isn't available you can find buffaloes, crocodiles, emus, brolgas and the like penned at **Yarrawonga Zoo**, 20 km (12 miles) south of Darwin on the Stuart Highway. The **Darwin Crocodile Farm**, a similar distance further south, houses over 5000 crocodiles whose meat ends up on restaurant tables and whose skins will one day be shoes and handbags, some giants among them are preserved to attract tourists. The farm is open every day from 9 am to 5 pm. The crocs are fed at 3 pm on Wednesday and Sunday and 11 am on Friday.

Coastal swimming is out from May to October in Darwin but there is freshwater swimming at **Howard Springs** and **Berry Springs** south of the city. The turn-off to Howard Springs lies just beyond Yarrawonga. Its reedy swimming hole is frequently very crowded. Berry Springs attracts lesser numbers because it is further away and harder to get to. Take the turn-off 46 km (29 miles) south and continue for another 10 km (six miles) to the reserve. There is a walking track as well as swimming.

Mandorah, across Darwin Harbour from the city, is a popular coastal resort where you can swim between November and April. It is reached by ferry from Stokes Hill Wharf. **Fogg Dam Conservation Reserve**, is 68 km out of Darwin on the Arnhem Highway. The Lillie covered dam is an important refuge for thousands of birds, geese, ducks and fish during the dry season and is a worthwhile hour or two's stop-over on the way to Kakadu National Park.

Bathurst and Melville Islands

These islands lie close together about 80 km (50 miles) north of Darwin. They are the home of the *Tiwi* people, a group of Aboriginals who developed a distinct culture through being cut off from their mainland brothers for many centuries. They are generally of a more outgoing and less formal character than mainland Aboriginals and welcome tourists, although the welcome is strictly on the Tiwi's own terms. Individual tourists are generally not admitted to the islands and the only way to experience Tiwi life and culture is to join a tour, usually of a day's duration, to Melville Island. See Tours below for a list of options.

Half and full day tours are operated by **Tiwi Tours** which flies you out, shows villages and workshops and introduces the island Aborigines. $125 and $185.

Katherine Gorge National Park

Katherine is a small town 330 km (205 miles) south of Darwin on the Stuart Highway. It is the access point for **Katherine Gorge National Park** which centres on a spectacular sheer walled sandstone canyon cut by the Katherine River. It is another of the fantastic natural wonders with which this part of Australia abounds. Although there are 100 km (62 miles) of walking tracks over 10 different walks in the park most visitors see Katherine Gorge on boat tours so as to be fully impressed with the size of its walls. They generally come during the dry season when the river is quiet and slow moving, in the wet it flows much faster and there are more waterfalls and greenery. Day tours to Katherine Gorge operate from Darwin or are available from Katherine township, see Tours listed below. Canoes in which to take your own tour are available from the BP Roadhouse, Katherine, for $20 per day. A commuter bus service operates around the Katherine area, linking accommodation with the gorge.

The fare from Springvale Homestead to Katherine Gorge is $4.50.

GETTING THERE
Greyhound buses run daily from Darwin. The journey takes three and a half hours and the fare is $28.

WHERE TO STAY
Springvale Homestead, Shadforth Road, Katherine, (089) 72 1044, has a range of accommodation from motel units, single $32, twin $39.50, to air-conditioned budget rooms, single $18, twin share $12.50, to tents with mattresses for $6 per person. The homestead is right beside the Katherine River and canoes can be hired for $20 per day or $5 per hour. Free walking tours of this historic homestead are available daily 9 am to 3.30 pm from April to October.

TOURS
Dial-a-Safari operates one- ($99), two- ($249) and three- ($349) day tours from Darwin including gorge cruises and visits to other landmarks around Katherine. They operate with much reduced frequency during the wet season.
Breakwater Canoe Tours: seven-day canoe trips on the Katherine and Daly Rivers. $675.
KGTA operates a very wide range of tours from the town of Katherine from 2 hour cruises in open flat bottomed aluminium boats ($8.50) to package tours of several day's duration. Almost all operate only in the dry season.
A five day **Wilderness Walk** to Edith Falls can be arranged at the Ranger Visitor Centre.
Tillair on Katherine Terrace operate scenic flights over Katherine Gorge and Edith Falls and 'Outback Mailman' flights on Wednesday, Thursday and Friday.

Other attractions around Katherine

These include the **Cuttacutta Caves**, 26 km (16 miles) south of Katherine—a series of limestone caverns 500 million years old with stalacmite and stalagtite deposits in the 700 m cave in karst landscape—Ranger Tours from $1.50, open 10.30 am to 1.30 pm, April to October; **Mataranka**, 120 km (75 miles) south of Katherine—crystal clear thermal pools in a fan palm setting but they do get very crowded. Mataranka is based on the Elsey station, made famous in the book *We of the Never Never* by Mrs Aeneas Gunn. Tours of the Roper river can be taken from here.

Crocodile

Kakadu National Park

Kakadu is where *Crocodile Dundee* was filmed. It is a natural wonderland unlike any other you are ever likely to see. To do it justice, come twice—in the 'dry' and in the 'wet'. Receding rains in March herald the dry. Clouds disappear and the sun begins to burn. Initially, the park is green, water lies on the plains and the rivers are full but the sun, beating down unabated for months, sucks up the moisture and dries out the land. Thousands of birds, long-legged wide-winged waders to tiny insect eating species, flock in the remaining creeks, lagoons and tidal river reaches as the water levels fall, engaging in a ferocious struggle to gather the last sustenance left by the cruel sun. Fish, plentiful at the close of the wet, die off, stranded and penned by the lessening water and birds feed in frenzied multitudes, rising and clamouring in the hard blue sky around their remaining water holes. Fat, water-living plants shrivel and in places the earth cracks.

When the wet arrives in late October or early November, the air grows palpable, you wear it. The sky blackens, rain falls in sheets and pours down from the **Arnhem Land** escarpment over **Jim Jim** and **Twin Falls** in spectacular white torrents. Streams overflow into lagoons and onto flood plains. Deep tropical green is all around, on heights and flats, floating on the water and in it. Flowers bloom in purple, red and white. The birds, assured of plenty, breed. The fish return and vigorous life is everywhere. Many species of both fauna and flora are unique to Kakadu.

Kakadu also has a dark side, not all of which is provided by crocodiles despite their great abundance. History and compromise have left it with some legacies one would not expect to find in such a place. They include a uranium mine called 'Ranger', located close to **Jabiru** township, and a meatworks at **Mudginberri** north of the same town.

The park begins 150 km (93 miles) east of Darwin and stretches a further 100 km (62 miles) or so at its widest point, to the western border of Arnhem Land, a huge area controlled by the Aborigines of the Northern Territory. Its northern boundary is the coast from which it extends anywhere from 80 to about 200 km (50 to 124 miles) south.

The Park and the Aborigines

Northern Territory Aboriginals are designated 'traditional owners' of Kakadu National Park, indeed it is named after one of the first tribes, the *Gagadju*. A third of the park staff is Aboriginal and many are park rangers. They have added a new dimension to land management, employing ancient means of husbanding such as mosaic burning as standard practices. It has emerged that far from being a 'primitive race' these people worked the land with such subtlety that their conquerors failed until recently to recognise their activities as part of a coherent system. The lesson is vitally important for without the understanding gained from traditional owners, white management no matter how well intentioned may have destroyed the park.

The natural environment plays a fundamental role in Aboriginal spirituality. Their cathedrals lie among the rocks in Kakadu's great galleries of painting and engraving whose works include human, animal and spirit beings in detailed renderings of considerable expressive power. They are among the best and most accessible of such 'exhibitions' in the country and have the added advantage of being part of a living culture. Though the practice of rock painting may be gone, a degree of its meaning is current and explicable to white visitors even if their understanding of it will be at the most primitive level.

Arnhem Land

Arnhem Land, the large tract of country bordering Kakadu to the east, is set aside exclusively for Aboriginals and white people may only enter by special permit. Such permits must be obtained from the Aboriginal council in charge of the area. They are not issued to tourists.

GETTING THERE

The Arnhem Highway gives access to the park. It is a sealed road running from Humty Doo, 35 km (22 miles) south of Darwin to **Jabiru** close to the eastern edge of the Park. It crosses the South Alligator River and meets the Kakadu Highway, a partly sealed road leading to Cooinda and Jim Jim Creek both also in the park. Ansett Pioneer coaches travel from Darwin to Kakadu stopping at South Alligator ($25) and Cooinda ($35). They leave Darwin at 7 am each day. The Greyhound Darwin to Katherine service travels through Kakadu and includes Jabiru ($27) as well as the other stops (South Alligator $21.40 and Cooinda $34). It leaves Darwin at 7 am on Monday, Wednesday, Saturday and Sunday during the dry but on Wednesday and Friday only during the wet and arrives in Cooinda an hour later than its opposing service because of the diversion.

TOURIST INFORMATION

Park headquarters is a couple of km south of Jabiru on the Kakadu Highway. Information is also available at the South Alligator Motor Inn and at the Tasbureau office in Darwin.

281

WHAT TO SEE

The park has a number of must-see sights. The section of the **South Alligator River** between the Arnhem Highway and the coast is a wide tidal reach tremendously rich in birdlife and a favourite haunt of salt-water crocodiles (the man-eating kind) and buffalo. The other wetland of greatest note is **Yellow Waters Lagoon**, where, as the dry lengthens and water becomes scarce in other sections of the park, thousands of birds including whistling ducks, jabiru, egrets, spoonbills, pelicans and the ubiquitous magpie geese take refuge. The streams which rise in the **Arnhem Land Escarpment** in the east of the park spill over in waterfalls of which the most impressive are **Jim Jim Falls** and **Twin Falls**, a 40 km (25 miles) drive from the Kakadu Highway near Cooinda on a track sometimes closed in the wet season, although they are then at their best. There are two 'galleries' of Aboriginal rock art open to the public although there are over 6000 examples of rock art in the park. **Nourlangie Rock**, a short drive off the Kakadu Highway about halfway between Jabiru and Cooinda, is a massive outcrop painted with mythological figures, some dating back 20,000 years, and containing the only known blue paintings. **Obiri** (renamed **Ubirr**) in the north of the park close to the Arnhem Land boundary, is a 'skeleton' painting site where animals important both as food sources and totemic spirits are depicted. They include kangaroos and barramundi. Ubirr hill top also has magnificent views over Kakadu and Arnhem Land.

In the dry season there are several walking trails around the tropical wetlands such as **Mamukala**, where a viewing area and bird hide overlook the thousands of water birds at the end of the day when other wetlands in the Top End dry up.

WHERE TO STAY AND EAT

South Alligator Motor Inn, Arnhem Highway, Kakadu National Park, (089) 79 0166, is the best accommodation in Kakadu for both convenience and comfort. Rooms in the 'resort complex' are above average motel style with high ceilings and air-conditioning. There is a pool and licensed restaurant. Single $66, double $98 May to October, $50 and $80 the rest of the year.

Four Seasons Cooinda Motel, Cooinda, Kakadu National Park, (089) 79 2545, is newly constructed in a rustic outback style, inside the park close to its eastern boundary. Rooms, in separate blocks of four each, have absolutely no frills but are self-contained and air-conditioned. There is a restaurant and swimming pool. Single $72, double $92.

TOURS

Tours to and in Kakadu are many but they travel over predictable ground, covering assorted combinations of the sights mentioned above.

Tours from Darwin

These vary from hard driving one day jaunts, some of which fly part of the way, to eight day packages and cost between about $100 and $800. You can join a small group in a four-wheel drive or take a bus tour. Generally speaking, tours link up with in-park cruise operators on the South Alligator River and Yellow Waters Lagoon, take passengers to one of the rock art sites and, on longer durations, to Jim Jim and

Twin Falls and the Arnhem Land Escarpment. Some tours include the Ranger Uranium Mine and both rock art sites. The major operators are **Australian Kakadu Tours**, **Dial-a-Safari** and **Terra Safari Tours**. **Air North** is the major air tour operator into Kakadu. Bookings for all tours can be made through the Northern Territory Tourist Bureau, 31 Smith Street Mall, Darwin, (089) 81 6111.

Tours from Kakadu
Once in Kakadu you can independently take cruises and tours to the major sights. **Yellow Waters Lagoon** cruises cost $18 (for dawn and dusk and $15 during the day), depart six times a day and last one and three quarter hours.
Kakadu Princess operates various cruises on the South Alligator River in slow and fast boats with special runs in the wet season over the Kakadu floodplain. They depart from the South Alligator River Bridge and cost from $16 to $40.
Kakadu Air Services takes half hour ($35) and one hour ($60) scenic flights from Jabiru Airport.

Canoeing
This is an unusual but effective way to see Kakadu at a slow pace without too many other sightseers close by except at major sites. The major operators of such tours are **Pandanus Canoe Safaris** and **Dial-a-Safari** in combination with **Breakwater Canoe Safaris**. The average duration is seven days and the cost around $700 to $800. Some travel into remote parts of the park. Dry season (May to October) only. Book through the Northern Territory Tourist Bureau, 31 Smith Street Mall, Darwin, (089) 81 6111.

The Gove Peninsula

This isolated area of rainforest and white beaches is on the far north eastern tip of Arnhem Land. The Peninsula was first chartered by Matthew Flinders in 1803 but the main town of Nhulunbuy only developed as a mining centre for bauxite and aluminium processing in 1969.
   Gove is cut off from the rest of the Northern Territory because no made up roads penetrate this far into the region. There is a rough four-wheel drive track which connects to Katherine, but as this passes through Arnhem Land, a permit is required from the NT Police and the track is impassable in the wet. Air and sea transport are the mainstay of Gove and its remoteness and inaccessibility are a part of its attraction.
   Reef fishing and big game fishing are the major pulls of the region and you can take in a crocodile or buffalo safari. Camping is allowed on some of the offshore islands. There are beautiful beaches but crocs and stingers make swimming dangerous.

WHERE TO STAY
Arnhems Hideaway Motel, PO Box 769, Nhulunbuy, (089) 87 1833; single $45, twin $30, restaurant, pool and tennis court.

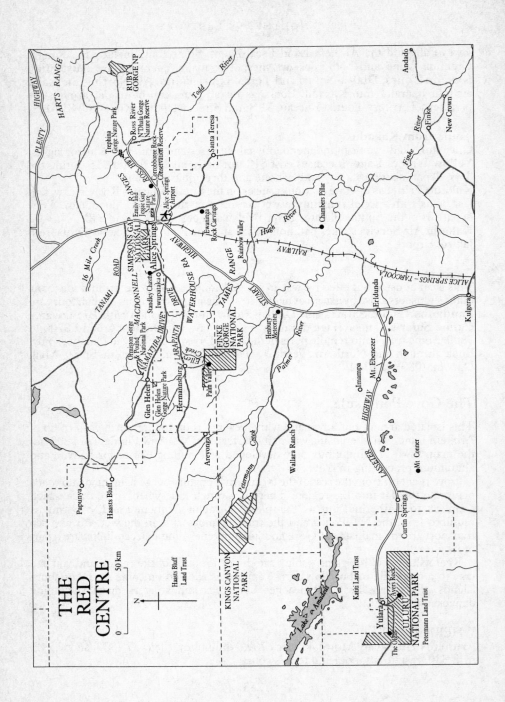

THE RED CENTRE

N

0   50 km

HARTS RANGE

PLENTY HIGHWAY

RUBY GORGE NP

To Ross River
N'Dhala Gorge Nature Reserve

Trephina Gorge Nature Park

Todd River

Corroboree Rock Conservation Reserve

Santa Teresa

Emily and Jessie Gap Nature Park

Alice Springs Airport

Chambers Pillar

Ewaninga Rock Carvings

Rainbow Valley

Hugh River

RAILWAY

ALICE SPRINGS – TARCOOLA

Finke River

Andado

New Crown

Kulgera

SIMPSONS GAP NATIONAL PARK

Alice Springs

MACDONNELL RANGES

16 Mile Creek

TANAMI ROAD

Standley Chasm

Iwupataka

STUART HIGHWAY

WATERHOUSE RA

JAMES RANGE

Eridunda

Ormiston Gorge & Pound National Park

NAMATJIRA DRIVE

Glen Helen

Glen Helen Gorge Nature Park

Hermannsburg

LARAPINTA DRIVE

Ellery Creek

FINKE GORGE NATIONAL PARK

Palm Valley

Henbury Meteorites

Palmer River

Wallara Ranch

Imanpa

Mt. Ebenezer

STUART HIGHWAY

Mt Conner

Papunya

Haasts Bluff

Haasts Bluff Land Trust

Areyonga

Petermann Creek

KINGS CANYON NATIONAL PARK

Lake Amadeus

Kaitii Land Trust

LASSETER HIGHWAY

Curtin Springs

Yulara

The Olgas

Ayers Rock

ULURU NATIONAL PARK

Petermann Land Trust

TOURS
Arnhem Land Adventure Safaris (089) 87 1833, run tours of the mines, reef fishing, crocodile safaris in Dalwoi Bay and Island exploring.
Sweet Surrender (089) 87 1549, charter boats for fishing and diving and also run cruises.

The Red Centre

ALICE SPRINGS

The Red Centre takes its name from the burnt umber colour of the soil which together with the piercing blue sky create some memorable scenery. Set in an enclosed area between the Macdonnell ranges, the Alice (never simply 'Alice' as some have been heard to say) holds a legendary place in Australian thinking as the town in the red heart of the continent but it pricks as many balloons as it pumps up. Its isolation and the severity of its climate—although the Alice averages over 9 hours sunshine per day, temperatures range from lows under 0°C in winter nights to summer highs over 50°C—combine in the national mind with a 'she'll be right, avago (have a go) mate' life-style and a tendency to drink oceans of beer, to encapsulate all that Australians fear and love about the outback. In reality, fast transport, fast food and fast tourists are making the Alice less and less outback all the time. The real outback where you can die of thirst in a day has been left lurking just a little outside the shiny, expanding town, proud of its first set of traffic lights, brand new pedestrian mall and incessant tourist accommodation building. Alice is a great base for exploring the outback but it isn't the outback anymore.

GETTING TO AND AROUND

By Air
Ansett and Australian Airlines fly direct to Alice Springs from Perth ($328), Adelaie ($253), Sydney ($332), Melbourne ($315) and Darwin ($252), Ansett alone from Brisbane ($326). Flights depart every day from all these capitals with the greatest number of direct flights leaving Sydney and Adelaide.

By Rail
The *Ghan*, one of Australia's great rail journeys, runs between Adelaide and Alice Springs, although it's not the adventure it once was. The line, formerly an ill-laid track through Maree and Oodnadatta which suffered frequent washing away and changed grade halfway along, was re-laid in 1980 through Tarcoola and Maria further west, reducing the time taken to reach the Alice to a mere 24 hours. The journey lies through the central Australian desert and is a comfortable way to see it.

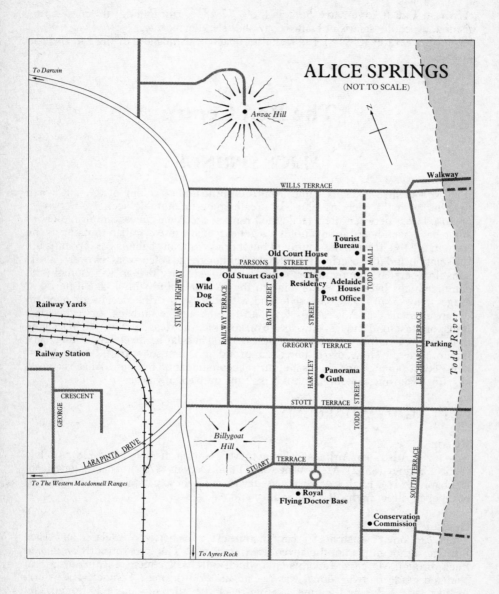

The fare is $282.50 first class and $200 economy which include meals. Trains depart Adelaide at 11 am on Thursdays, arriving in Alice Springs at 8.50 am on Friday. The *Alice* connects Sydney with Alice Springs via western New South Wales and South Australia. The fare for the all first class train is $506 and you need to book ahead. Trains depart at 1.40 am on Monday, arriving in Alice Springs at 12.30 pm on Wednesday.

By Road

Coach travellers will find that Bus Australia runs express services from Adelaide ($99), Darwin ($99) and Townsville ($110); Deluxe from Darwin ($105), Adelaide ($105) and Townsville ($119); Greyhound from Adelaide ($106), Darwin ($106), Townsville ($121) and Brisbane ($172); Ansett Pioneer from Adelaide ($106), Darwin ($106), Brisbane via Townsville ($172) and Cairns via Townsville ($131). The journey from Adelaide takes 23 hours, from Townsville 26 hours and from Darwin 20 hours.

You have to be a very dedicated driver to travel the 1525 km (946 miles) from Darwin to Alice Springs but the road is sealed all the way. There is only one and it's called the Stuart Highway. It takes even more courage to take on the 1,938 km (1202 miles) from Adelaide.

There is no public transport in Alice Springs other than taxis but the central city area is small and easily covered on foot. A shuttle bus operates between the airport, railway station and accommodation houses. The fare is $4 from the airport, $2 from the railway station.

The national car rental companies have Alice Springs offices and airport desks. Mokes can be rented from Centre Car Rentals, Ford Plaza, Todd Mall, (089) 52 1405 from $18 a day. Four-wheel drive vehicles are for hire from most car rental shops.

TOURIST INFORMATION

The Northern Territory Tourist Bureau has an office at 51 Todd Street, Alice Springs. Phone (089) 52 1299.

Town Centre

The centre of town occupies a grid of short streets bounded by Stott Terrace to the south and Wills Terrace to the north with Railway and Leichhardt Terraces forming the western and eastern boundaries. Most places of historical interest are found in or near this area.

Almost none of Alice Springs is much over a century old. Almost all of it is less than half that. The town's main historical attraction is the **Old Telegraph Station**, established in 1872 as a repeater station along the route of the overland telegraph which linked Adelaide and Darwin. The line was a milestone in opening the centre of Australia to such development as it would bear (not very much) but, more importantly, it established relatively speedy contact between South Australia, at that time a British colony, and London. Messages which formerly took three months to make the distance were transmissible in seven hours thanks to the overland line. The Alice Springs Telegraph Station was the largest of several repeater stations established through the Northern Territory. It accommodated a Station Master who, aside from his telegraphic duties, was the local magistrate, had charge of Central Australian Aborigines and even acted as an emergency doctor when the occasion called for it. His family lived at the station along with a small contingent of linesmen-telegraph operators, a cook, a governess and a blacksmith. In the earliest days, they constituted almost the entire settled white population of the area. The station, which stands on the banks of the Todd River (at a permanent water hole originally thought to be a spring—hence the name) in Telegraph Station Road a short distance north of Alice Springs Centre, is a small group of stone buildings including the Station Master's house, the Telegraph Office, Post Office, Blacksmith's Shop, Power House, Barracks, Cemetery and Weather Station. The Northern Territory Conservation Commission has restored it to the way it appeared between 1895 and 1905 and established exhibits of telegraphic equipment, domestic utensils, tools and photographs of the initial occupants in some of the buildings. Open 8 am to 9 pm. Entry is free.

As with many an Australian town, the next building of historical note which remains intact is the gaol. Called the **Old Stuart Gaol**, it was built in 1907 by which time the township, then known as Stuart, had seen enough life to merit it. The gaol is in Parsons Street and is open on Saturdays only from 9.30 am to 11.30 am. Other buildings considered worthy of preservation date from the 1920s and reflect two aspects of Alice life, a desultory administrative interest on the part of governments and a lively commitment on the part of religions, especially the Lutheran Church. **The Residency**, a single storey stone structure with surrounding verandas was constructed in 1927 as a home for the town's first Government Resident, John Charles Cawood. It now serves as an eclectic museum, housing meteorite fragments and paintings by Aboriginal watercolourist Albert Namatjira as well as displays about local wildlife. The building is on the corner of Parsons and Hartley Streets and is open 9 am to 4.30 pm weekdays and 10 am to 4 pm on weekends. The Lutheran interest is represented by **Adelaide House** in Todd Street. It was built as the first Alice Springs hospital between 1920 and 1926 by the Australian Inland Mission, an organisation established by Lutheran minister John Flynn who was known as Flynn of the Inland for his dedication to the isolated souls of central Australia. When a government hospital was opened in the town in 1939, Adelaide House became an accommodation and convalescent centre for outback women and children. Now a museum, it is open from 10 am to 4 pm weekdays and from 10 am to noon on Saturdays. Entry costs $1.20. The ugly church next door is a memorial to Flynn whose work did not end with the establishment of Adelaide House—he also founded the Royal Flying Doctor Service, an airborne emergency medical service which continues to serve outback families today. The Service's Alice Springs headquarters in Stuart Terrace, a block south of the town centre, contains a radio room which keeps 130 outback stations in touch with medical advice as well as providing regular telegram and radio telephone communications. A small museum contains obsolete equipment including the pedal driven radio developed in the early 1920s which enabled distant stations without electricity to contact the RFDS base. Tours of the base occur half hourly between 9.30 am and 1.30 am and 2 pm and 3.30 pm on weekdays and 9 am to 11 am on weekdays.

Alice Springs has developed the 'mall complex'—a current mania of Australian urban planners and banned cars from its central section around the junction of Todd and Parsons Streets. The resulting mall has been paved with bricks, planted with boxes of native flora and given over to pedestrian shoppers. It includes the town's first glass fronted shop, Marron's Newsagency, built in the early 1930s, and its latest example of commercial architecture, a concrete shopping centre with obligatory splashing fountain underneath the escalators.

Where tourists become the lifeblood of a town, private museums, displays and exhibitions automatically spring up for their amusement and the Alice is no exception to this rule. **Stuart Auto Museum, Pitchi Ritchi Sanctuary** and **Mecca Date Gardens** are gathered together just off the Ross Highway at Heavitree Gap. The museum houses vintage and veteran cars and motor-cycles, old phonographs, telephones and steam engines and is open every day from 9 am to 5 pm. The sanctuary features clay sculptures of Aborigines by William Ricketts, a collection of Central Australian artefacts and lots of birds; open 9 am to sunset daily. The gardens are Australia's only commercial date farm and are open to the public from 9.30 am to 4.30 pm every day. A **Camel Farm** is located a small distance further along the Ross Highway. It offers short, inexpensive and uncomfortable camel rides and has a museum giving some history of the Afghan cameleers who brought the first camels to the Red Centre as cargo transport. An **Aviation Museum** and a **Pioneer Cemetery** where legendary gold prospector Harold Lasseter is buried, along with Aboriginal painter Albert Namatjira and other Alice Springs identities, can be found in Memorial Avenue on the western side of town. Lasseter died in 1931 whilst searching the desert for a fabled reef of gold. Although later expeditions have also failed to find Lasseter's Reef, many still believe it exists.

The Alice also has two staggering examples of tourist bad taste, **Panorama Guth**, an exhibition of hideous, cliché-ridden 'bush paintings' arranged like a circular stage set and **Diorama Village**, Aboriginal dreamtime legends rendered in luridly lit and painted shop-dummy groups.

SHOPPING

The burgeoning trade in Aboriginal artefacts is well represented in Alice Springs, although it is just about impossible to find a shop or gallery actually staffed by Aborigines. There is no end of spears, woomeras (spear throwers), boomerangs, digeridoos (a long wooden pipe used as a musical instrument), dilly bags (women's painted carry-all bags) and paintings to be had and it's hard to pick the difference between one and another as the dreary sameness of repeated folk art infects them all. 'Sand' paintings (actually executed on canvas) offer the largest variation. They are a development of story pictures originally sketched in sand to accompany the narration of a personal story (many old tribal Aboriginals still do this almost unconsciously when telling stories). Each is individual and although similar in style they are various in content. A genuine work should be accompanied by a text telling the story of which it is the expression, otherwise it is meaningless, though it may be visually interesting.

ENTERTAINMENT

The **Araluan Cultural Centre**, at the western end of Alice Springs in Larapinta Drive is the town's main entertainment venue, presenting everything from movies to ballet and theatre performances. It is used by touring professional companies and by local amateur groups. Although the building exterior resembles a tin shearing shed, its interior is more attractive.

Lasseter's Casino, in Barrett Drive is a privately run casino which offers all that is expected of such places in the way of gambling as well as a disco open until 4 am. The other late opening discos in town are **Bojangles Nightclub** in Todd Street, the **Todd Tavern** on the corner of Todd Street and **Wills Terrace** which also has a piano bar.

Chateau Hornsby, the only winery in Central Australia, is located 11 km (seven miles) south of the Alice. I include it under Entertainment because **Ted Egan**, the outback's most famous singer, performs there. Egan's humorous songs about outback life deal with subjects from drinking to black–white relations and are sung to the sole accompaniment of a cardboard beer carton on which the singer beats a regular rhythm. The chateau also holds wine tastings, lunches and dinners. For further information ring (089) 52 5771.

WHERE TO STAY

There is plenty of good accommodation in Alice Springs but the demand for it still well outstrips the supply, especially when the weather is cool in July and August. Booking well ahead is a wise move.

Sheraton Alice Springs Hotel, Barret Drive, Alice Springs, (089) 52 8000; 252 rooms in a swimming pool centred complex where one hopes a garden will grow soon. The hotel is almost brand new and has two restaurants and bars but is a long walk from town. $135 to $145.

Four Seasons, Stephens Road, Alice Springs, (089) 52 6100; even more recent than the Sheraton, even less garden and a longer walk but all the most modern and comfortable appointments including movies on two channels. Single $93, double $109.

Oasis Motel, 10 Gap Road, Alice Springs, (089) 52 1444; partly new and partly from the previous era of Alice accommodation which was a couple of steps below what now prevails. New rooms are very comfortable and spacious and the new swimming pool is stylish. Also has an acceptable restaurant and is about five minutes walk from the town centre. Single $62, double $68.

Alice Springs Pacific, Stott Terrace, Alice Springs, (089) 52 6699; low roofed buildings centred on a swimming pool, close to town centre, across the Todd River bridge. Single $63 and $69, double $69 to $75.

Larapinta Lodge, 3 Larapinta Drive, Alice Springs, (089) 52 7255; a new hotel offering motel-style rooms in the mid-range of comfort and price at two levels, standard and deluxe. Single $42 and $55, double $55 and $65.

Elkira Motel, 134 Bath Street, Alice Springs, (089) 52 1222, has new deluxe rooms and older, smaller rooms described as moderate. Some have cooking facilities. Single $49 and $59, double $74 and $80.

Youth Hostel, Corner Todd Street and Stott Terrace, Alice Springs, (089) 52 5016; $6 per night.

EATING OUT

The eating out scene in Alice Springs tends to be dominated by steak houses which barbecue their servings in the traditional Aussie style (well done) and dish them up with chips (French fries) and salad. In other words, the food is crude but inoffensive. These places also usually offer water buffalo and barramundi as well. The former is marinated to tenderise it and the latter comes to this very isolated town as one would expect, frozen.

Hindquarter Steakhouse, Melanka Lodge, 94 Todd Street, Alice Springs, (089) 52 2233; a barn of a place with a bar in one corner, a barbecue along one wall and laminex tables. Licensed. Low price range.

Aussie Tucker, Pioneer Theatre, Corner Leichhardt Terrace and Parsons Street, Alice Springs, (089) 52 7829, is part of a complex which was once one of Alice Springs' first outdoor cinemas. Includes kangaroo soup and *damper* (like sour dough bread) on its menu. Licensed. Low price range.

Other eating houses where you will occasionally find more interesting items include:

Lilli's Restaurant, Heavitree Gap Motel, Ross Highway, Alice Springs, (089) 52 4260; offers some Indonesian dishes. Licensed. Mid price range.

Mr Pickwicks, 20 Undoolya Street, Alice Springs, (089) 52 9400; includes Atlantic salmon on its menu. Licensed. Upper price range.

Liana's Restaurant, Verdi Club, Undoolya Road, Alice Springs, (089) 52 3922; traditional Italian fare. Licensed. Mid price range.

TOURS

Alice Springs serves as a departure point for a great variety of outback tours from day trips by coach to the Western Macdonnell Ranges to lengthy four-wheel drive safaris into the desert. Here are some of the options.

Coach trips

Ansett Trailways, (089) 52 2422; day tours to Palm Valley ($55), the Western Macdonnell Ranges ($50); two-day tour to Palm Valley and Glen Helen ($180); three days to Ayers Rock and Kings Canyon ($285).

CATA Tours, (089) 52 1700; day tours to Western Macdonnells ($53), Eastern Macdonnells ($54), Palm Valley ($55), Alice and the Chasms ($45); half-day tours to Standley Chasm and Simpson's Gap ($29); two days to Western Macdonnells and Palm Valley ($187).

AAT Kings, (089) 52 5266; one day Palm Valley ($55), one day Western Macdonnells ($53), one day Ross River Country ($54); half-day Standley Chasm and Simpson's Gap ($29); two day Western Macdonnells and Palm Valley ($187); three day Kings Canyon and Ayers Rock ($439).

All the above operators also run afternoon tours of the Alice itself for around $25.

Four-Wheel Drive

Although most of these travel to the same places as the coach tours, the groups are smaller and the operators are able to move off the beaten track.

Outback Experience, (089) 52 3389; day tours to Palm Valley, Eastern and Western Macdonnells and Rainbow Valley (all $45) and a long day to Kings Canyon (6.30 am to 9.30 pm, $125).

Spinifex Tours, (089) 52 2203; day tours to Macdonnells and Palm Valley (both $45); two days to Kings Canyon ($80).

Worana Tours, (089) 52 5710; day tours to Kings Canyon ($65) and Western Macdonnells ($45), four day tour to Mt Conner, Ayers Rock, the Olgas and Kings Canyon ($460).

Rod Steinert

This gentleman receives special mention because of his relationship with the Aborigines living in the countryside around Alice Springs. He operates a number of short tours which illuminate the living habits and culture of the centre's earliest people. His tours include corroborees, witchetty grub eating, Aboriginal mythology and suchlike as well as a visit to a working cattle station. The tours can be booked through Ansett Trailways except for the Dreamtime Tour (on which one samples bush tucker) which is the province of CATA. They cost between $50 and $60 and are worth it.

Air Tours

Tillair, (089) 52 6666; Macdonnell Ranges ($35); Yulara, Palm Valley, Kings Canyon, Ayers Rock and the Olgas ($175); Outback Mailrun which visits scattered cattle stations ($157).

Canyonair, (089) 52 9440; overflies the Western Macdonnells and Palm Valley and joins a four-wheel drive tour of Kings Canyon ($180).

Capricorn Helicopter Tours, (089) 52 4202; short flights varying from 10 to 30 minutes east and west of Alice Springs over the Macdonnells ($30 to $75).

Oddities

Camel trips, usually lasting about half a day are available from Ansett Trailways.
Balloon flights over the sight with a 20 km radius of the Alice are operated by **Aussie Balloons**, (089) 52 4369, and **Toddy's Tours and Safaris**, (089) 52 1322. They cost $98 for half an hour and $150 for an hour.

Around the Alice

Alice Springs sits neatly between the western and eastern spurs of the Macdonnell Ranges, a wide scattering of relic mountains of about the same age as Ayers Rock, 650 million years or so.

The Macdonnell Ranges

The mountains are low, rusty looking and rocky, weathered down to the hardest rock and in parts resembling ruined walls, so little is left of their original material. Occasional rain brightens up the mulga bushes and spinifex grass on their slopes and adds a tinge of olive and darker green to the predominating ferrous red. If enough falls, small brightly coloured flowers appear. Occasionally the ramparts break apart where intermittent but violent rivers have cut their softer parts, forcing a passage through narrow gorges with high, red walls topped by a bright blue sky and scattered with the rubble of a million years. Deep green water sometimes lies at the bottom of the gorges and stretching away at either end, a dry river bed with river red gums growing right down the middle of its course. Which gorge the individual traveller prefers is entirely a question of taste.

In their youth, the Macdonnell Ranges were about 3000 metres (10,000 feet) high and thus high mountains by anyone's standards but in the ensuing millennia they have been worn down to a shadow of their former selves, about one tenth to be precise. Those outcrops that remain are generally hard quartzite and sandstone which has refused to give way under constant weathering.

West Macdonnell Ranges

Namatjira Drive runs west into the Macdonnells from Alice Springs to Glen Helen. It passes some of the most scenic gorges. **Simpson's Gap**, is the closest, 22 km (14 miles) out of town. Here the dry watercourse with its stands of river red gums is wide and noble and the break sudden, filled with deep green water and with a tantalising prospect of ghost gums and grass in the daylight beyond. Rock wallabies are often seen around the rocks near Simpson's Gap.

Standley Chasm, further west, is perhaps the most spectacular. It is short but extremely narrow, the break which forms it being only four or five metres wide between walls 70 metres (230 feet) high. A natural spring fills a small, rocky waterhole in the centre of the chasm and beyond its end is another giant red cliff where ghost gums perch in seemingly impossible places. Standley Chasm is especially impressive around the middle of the day when the sun reaches a height sufficient for it to shine straight down between the walls, lighting up the normally shaded rocks and the water. **Ormiston Gorge**, a short distance north east of Glen Helen, is much wider and has enough sand and water to resemble a beach in some places. Its walls are less overpowering and more varied in their formations and the gorge is long, leading to a 'pound' or enclosed area past its waterhole.

Glen Helen Gorge, is found at the end of the Namatjira Drive on the ancient Finke River, reputed to be the oldest river in the world still occupying its original bed. It opens into a narrow valley following the river southwards. The way into the valley is blocked by a small lake stretching across the opening between high cliffs. The lake supports water birds, fish and some aquatic plants. The river bed turns sharply at the gorge and its search for a place to flow through is clear where it has had to skirt the huge hard cliffs before making that decisive turn. Access to the valley is possible by climbing over the walls bordering the dry river bed which, despite being practically vertical have walking tracks winding up their sides.

The Finke River

The Finke River or, more accurately, its dry course continues south into Finke Gorge National Park where it has cut two further remarkable gorges, both of which have permanent waterholes. The **Palm Valley**, is an extraordinary relic of days when the ancient inland sea of Australia supported a much more temperate climate.

The valley accommodates 400 plant-types including a variety of cabbage-palm found nowhere else on earth. The park also abounds in quaintly named rock formations such as Initiation Rock and the Amphitheatre. Finke Gorge itself is another sandstone-walled watercourse a short distance south. The park is 323 km (200 miles) from Alice Springs and can be reached from Larapinta Drive but the final track requires four-wheel drive. Tours depart regularly from Alice Springs for Palm Valley. See 'Tours' section above.

East Macdonnell Ranges

More gorges and gaps occur east of Alice Springs along the Ross River Road, a mostly unsealed but reliable track. **Emily and Jessie Gaps**, 16 and 24 km (10 to 15 miles) away, are popular picnic spots for the townspeople. Emily Gap is one of the few gaps to have flowing water with any frequency. **Corroboree Rock**, 43 km (27 miles) beyond the point where the bitumen runs out, is said to have been a favourite ceremonial place of the Aboriginals in past times. Its weird formations lend credence to the legend. **Trephina Gorge**, the widest and longest of the eastern gorges is about 75 km (46 miles) east. A track from it leads to **John Hayes Rockholes**, deep in a cool sheltered cleft which retain water long after more exposed locations have dried up. **N'Dhala Gorge** around 20 km (12 miles) south of Trephina beyond the Ross River Homestead has some Aboriginal rock carvings and rock wallabies appear there.

Kings Canyon

Kings Canyon is the largest but also the furthest gorge from Alice Springs, being 323 km (200 miles) south west. It has huge sheer walls up to 200 metres high of which the southern is the most impressive thanks to its smoothness and somewhat threatening angle. Other features of the canyon are the Garden of Eden, a shady oasis of cycads, and the Lost City, a closely gathered collection of oddly weathered outcrops resembling round-topped houses.

WHERE TO STAY

Glen Helen Homestead Lodge, Namatjira Drive, Glen Helen, radio telephone 137; the lodge is about 100 metres from Glen Helen Gorge on the banks of the Finke River, looking out at majestic red cliffs. It has a few small motel rooms, not luxurious but with bathrooms; units without private facilities; a bunkhouse and a caravan (trailer) park. The motel units are $44 single, $55 double. Book by writing to PO Box 3020, Alice Springs, NT 5750 or phone the Northern Territory Government Tourist Bureau (089) 52 1299.

Ross River Homestead, office at 64 Hartley Street, Alice Springs, (089) 52 7611; is at the eastern end of the Macdonnell Ranges and has quaint cabins taking up to 6 people, and a bunkhouse as well as camping and caravan (trailer) sites. A number of tours, including horse and camel rides depart from the homestead. Cabins $53 single and double.

Ayers Rock and The Olgas

The Rock, as it tends to be called in Australia, is a universal symbol of the red heart of the country. Indeed, it stands almost at the centre of that vast desert region making up most of the Northern Territory and a fair slice of Queensland, South Australia and Western Australia. Its fashionable Aboriginal name is *Uluru*, meaning shady place. Uluru is also the name given to the National Park which surrounds it and includes the Olgas, a nearby formation of similar geology.

Sensible visitors come in the Australian winter when, although nights and early mornings can be as cold as 0°C, daytime temperatures are in the low twenties. In the summer, daytime temperatures of over 40°C are not uncommon and when the wind is strong, dust storms regularly occur.

Ayers Rock and the Aborigines

Ayers Rock is owned by the Northern Territory Aboriginal tribes of *Pitjantjatjara* and *Yakuntjatjara*, who together call themselves *Anangu*. They do not actually live there but in the past have used the Rock for sacred ceremonies including male and female initiation and regard many parts of it as taboo. The Rock is also an important source of permanent water of which there is little in the surrounding desert. From a European perspective, a visit to Ayers Rock may be most easily compared to visiting a great cathedral although this does not present a perfectly true picture of its place in *Anangu* culture.

Aboriginal beliefs concerning the formation and significance of Uluru centre on an existential concept called *Tjukurpa* which is expressed in the natural features of the land and in the daily life, spiritual and physical, of its people. There are many stories associated with the *Tjukurpa* of Uluru which tell how it was formed. In the time when the earth was created (the dreamtime), beings of great power moved about the land in the shape of humans, animals and plants performing extraordinary feats of creation and destruction. The initial makers of Uluru were two young boys at play in the desert but its present form is the result of re-making by other *tjukurpa* creatures. These included the *Kuniya* (carpet snake creatures) and *Liru* (poisonous snake creatures) who fought a war from which battle scars and casualties remain at Uluru. There was also a conflict between *Mala* (hare wallaby) people and *Kurpanngu* (the devil dingo) resulting in the formation of other features. As part of *tjukurpa* these events were and are celebrated in the Anangu religion. *Tjukurpa*, however, is not religious in the discrete sense common to modern western thinking. It gives meaning to and explanation for all creatures, plants, natural formations and actions in the whole of *Anangu* life and is a closed system of law and cultural perception as much as an expression of spirituality.

Ayers Rock and the Whites

The exploratory expedition of Ernest Giles surveyed and named the main features of the area south west of Alice Springs during the 1870s. Ayers Rock was named after the then South Australian Premier, Henry Ayers, and the Olgas after Queen

Olga of Wurttemberg but the country surrounding it proved useless for European pastoralists and white people hardly ever appeared there. In 1920 the Commonwealth Government declared the 'corner country' where the borders of Western Australia, South Australia and the Northern Territory meet, including the Rock, a reserve for Aborigines. During the following decades, especially after World War II, a series of misguided attempts to 'deal with' the *Anangu* whose culture was perceived to be in decline as they drifted into Alice Springs and other outback settlements, followed. In general, the Aborigines were herded into mission stations where attempts were made to 'civilise' them. Their own culture proved more resilient than expected and, to the frustration of WASP officialdom, they continued to wander the countryside in keeping with its dictates while taking from European materialism what seemed good to them, especially faster transport.

Tourism began to have a material effect on the Ayers Rock area in the late 1950s and early 1960s when motels were built close to its edge. Feeling the presence of a new threat to their sacred sites, the *Anangu* began a long fight for recognition of their right to govern the future of the area. After over twenty years of struggle, the Rock and the Olgas were handed over provided the *Anangu* agreed to lease them back to the government for tourism and research purposes.

Geology of Ayers Rock

Ayers Rock is a sandstone monolith, a single rock. Some argument exists as to whether it is the largest such formation in Australia. Western Australians say that their Mount Augustus is bigger although, strictly speaking, it is a monocline and thus of slightly different geological origin. Whatever the case, Ayers Rock draws more crowds than any similar feature anywhere else. It is three and a half km long, 348 metres high and nine km (six miles) around the base but, like an iceberg, most of it is unseen. It is speculated that another 600 metres (2000 feet) of sandstone penetrates into the earth in a curved formation beneath what can be seen above the desert plain. The Rock arose around 650 million years ago in an upheaval which also saw the formation of the Olgas, Mount Conner and the MacDonnell Ranges around Alice Springs as well as other, now completely destroyed, mountains. What remains is the hardest rock which has refused to give way under many millions of years of weathering by water and wind. The red colour characteristic of all these formations comes from a small quantity of iron in their make-up which, as it is exposed to air, begins to oxidise. In other words, Ayers Rock is rusty and only its surface is red. If you could crack it like an egg it would be grey except for a thin crust of oxidised stone.

GETTING TO AND AROUND

By Air
Flights straight to Ayers Rock operate from Sydney and Perth on East West Airlines and Ansett WA ($330). Air NSW flies direct from Sydney ($330). Ansett NT flies non-stop from Cairns ($335) and Alice Springs ($106).

Yulara Airport is about ten minutes drive from the Yulara tourist village where

Ayers Rock visitors are accommodated. The bus fare from airport to village is an extortionate $5 but there's no other way.

By Bus
Coaches run the 450 km (280 miles) from Alice Springs to Ayers Rock in about five hours. They are operated by **Ansett Trailways**, (089) 56 2066, **CATA**, (089) 56 2075; and **Deluxe Coachlines**, (089) 56 2171. The fare is around $45.

Early each morning, buses depart from Yulara for the main viewing area and there are evening buses for sunset viewing.

TOURIST INFORMATION
The **Yulara Visitors' Centre** is probably the best place to open your acquaintance with the Rock. It has generous space given over to an informative display on the geological history, present environment and desert surroundings of the monolith as well as its significance in Aboriginal life. The display contains many spectacular photographs that you won't have seen before, especially of the Rock during occasional rain storms when clouds obscure its top, lightning flashes against its sides and water cascades down its many gullies. The plants and animals of the desert, poisonous and benign, are described and the ingenious uses to which Aborigines have put them are shown. Regular slide and video shows take place at the centre by day and night and its staff can help with questions about the Rock from the complexities of its geology to when the next tour leaves.

There is also an **information centre** staffed by park rangers close to Ayers Rock itself. It has a traditional Aboriginal camp beside it where visitors can buy artefacts and talk to the people living there. The rangers, who speak much better English than the Aboriginals, will explain why the camp looks the way it does for, although its appearance seems random, it is not. Admission is free. Taking photos of the Aboriginals is not allowed.

Ayers Rock

Ayers Rock is so famous that, on first sight, it looks rather too much like the photographs in every magazine article about central Australia—dropped on the plain like a huge spoonful of Milo and so neatly etched by the clear blue sky that it might be a cardboard cut-out. On closer acquaintance, the photographic cliché—always taken from a distance of about eight km (five miles)—is swept away and the mysterious and imposing personality of the Rock emerges in its place.

Climbing Ayers Rock
Would-be rock climbers can try ascending the western side of the Rock from the main viewing area. This is best done as early in the day as possible before any wind arises. The ascent is very steep and very dangerous and a slight breeze at ground level means a roaring gale on top. At the time of writing this book, 15 people had died while climbing, most from heart attacks but a fair number because they pursued hats, cameras and other paraphernalia blown away by the gale which is an almost permanent feature of the Rock's higher slopes and summit. Such innocent fools and

their foolhardy companions, who wander from the marked path to prove their independence, pay a very high price because the Rock's smooth sides offer no way to break a fall other than by arriving at the bottom. Whether the climb pays a sufficient dividend for the effort required to accomplish it is at the least an open question. After hauling himself up with the aid of a chain attached to poles set in the side of the Rock and weaving across its top in a cheek-ripping gale, the climber learns that the smooth appearance gained at a distance is illusory and that, in fact, many small hollows and gullies deep enough to hide a man pit and cross its surface in a pattern of deep wrinkles which covers the top as well as the sides. The view from the summit is of a flat desert, featureless at this height, except for the Olgas and Mt Conner which rise to the west and east respectively. People generally reach the top, take some photographs and commence their descent by retracing their steps along the wind-blown top before heading back down the steep and slippery side.

Around the Base
Those who remain below can if they wish walk the entire nine km (six miles) around the Rock, stopping at caves and waterholes to absorb some of their rugged beauty and speculate on the meaning of a cave painting or two. Alternatively you can drive or take a bus trip. The margin of the Rock is surrounded by desert vegetation including ghost gums, desert oaks and spinifex grass, and pitted with caves, each of which has meaning for the Anangu. In the morning it is cool and quiet and the spirits of the Rock sites seem perceptible even to a thoroughly materialistic westerner. Some sacred areas are fenced off and no one may enter them except suitably qualified Aboriginals. The most prominent of these are *Pulari* the birth cave and the male and female initiation caves of *Tjukajapi* and *Warayuki* but they are large and open enough to be seen from the roadside. There are two caves near the climbing trail. The largest, a kind of natural theatre, was used for corroborees and the other, smaller cave contains graffiti-like paintings depicting animals, snakes and journeys. More paintings can be seen at **Maggie Springs**, *Mutitjulu*, a permanent waterhole on the southern side of the Rock where Ernest Giles made the first climb. All the paintings are decayed as they have not been renewed for many decades.

Sunset Viewing
Sunset viewing is without doubt the great whitefellas' ritual of a visit to Ayers Rock. It is the third and usually the last perspective that tourists gain before wrapping up their acquaintance and turning to other matters. The five thousand guests that Yulara Resort accommodates pour out to a bump in the desert about eight km (five miles) west of the Rock with their cameras and binoculars. There they stand about in the red, sandy bush while the sun sets behind the Olgas, turning the Rock deeper and deeper shades of terra cotta. The plain in front of it glows gold and green and the sky darkens from electric blue to mauve. When the show is over everybody goes back to the twenty buses and one hundred other vehicles in the parking area and returns to Yulara in an insulated, air-conditioned convoy whilst the desert fades into dark silhouettes, the Rock turns purple and the whole vision is at last consumed by the black desert night. Although the viewers are outstandingly uniform in their behaviour, no two sunsets are the same.

The Olgas

This collection of monoliths 32 km (20 miles) west of Ayers Rock is called *Kata Tjuta*, 'Many Heads' by the *Anangu* and there is much in their observation. The Rocks, once a huge individual monolith much larger than Ayers Rock, have been weathered down to resemble a convocation of featureless heads, some high and narrow, others low and broad, all with the same red tone as their more famous counterpart. They are divided up by gorges and valleys and, like the Rock, present very different faces at varying times of the day, from various angles and distances of viewing. They are, if anything, more various than the Rock itself and arguments rage amongst those who have seen both as to which is the more impressive. Certainly Mt Olga is a good deal higher at 546 metres and there is the **Olga Gorge** running between that mountain and Mount Wulpa which is only a little shorter. The gorge is narrow, deep, walled in by sheer cliffs, strewn with boulders and stoppered at the eastern end with a huge stone block 12 metres high. **The Valley of the Winds**, on the northern side of the Olgas is another vast and mysterious location. A 2.5 km (one and a half mile) walking track leads into the valley from the road around the Olgas.

Yulara

Accommodation for the Ayers Rock and Olgas region is at **Yulara**, a purpose-built tourist village 20 km (12 miles) from the Rock. The village offers various standards of accommodation from a camping ground to the Sheraton Ayers Rock Hotel but at peak times, July and August, it can be almost impossible to get a room. Its capacity is about 5000 people on any given day, the majority in the camping ground and caravan (trailer) park.

Yulara is one and a half km (one mile) from end to end and has staff quarters, shops, a pub, an amphitheatre and a community centre mixed with its tourist accommodation. Their design is consciously uniform, making them strikingly similar if not inseparable.

The Olgas

WHERE TO STAY

Sheraton Ayers Rock Hotel, Ayers Rock (089) 56 2200, is a luxury hotel with 234 large rooms built around a central grassy courtyard with a swimming pool in one corner. Parts of the courtyard are shaded with canvas sun sails. The hotel is at the southern end of the village. $155 to $175.

Four Seasons Ayers Rock, Ayers Rock, (089) 56 2100; four-star standard hotel with 100 air-conditioned rooms, restaurant, swimming pool and half-sized tennis court. It has less glass and more corrugated iron than the Sheraton and the rooms are not as big or smartly furnished. $120.

Ayers Rock Lodge, PO Box 10, Yulara, (089) 56 2170; budget dormitories, air-conditioned cabins and family units, two swimming pools, barbecues, shop. Self catering. Linen not provided but can be hired. Units and cabins $48, dormitory $12.

EATING OUT

This is almost universally done in the hotels which offer various levels of dining.

The **Sheraton** has a brasserie with buffets and à la carte, a 'fine dining' restaurant called the Kunia Room and a snack bar beside the pool. The **Four Seasons** has an upmarket restaurant called the Stuart Room and a snack bar in the Oasis Lounge. **Ayers Rock Lodge Food Bar** offers extremely simple cooking and takeaway food.

Ernest Giles Tavern is the Yulara's pub and serves counter and bistro meals at about $10 for a main course. There is a takeaway bar selling hamburgers and chicken in the shopping area.

TOURS

Several coach operators run Ayers Rock and Olgas tours. They generally offer an early morning transfer to the Rock, a drive around its base with some stops, afternoon trips to the Olgas with a stop at the Sunset Viewing hill and evening tours of the monoliths. There is little to choose between them for content or comfort, the main difference being how amusing or dull your bus driver is. **Ayers Rock Touring Company**, **Deluxe Coachlines**, **CATA**, and **Ansett Trailways** are the major operators and their tours can be booked at the Yulara Visitors' Centre or through your hotel reception. Prices range from around $15 to $20 for these tours except the evening one which costs about $40 and includes dinner. The same operators offer two and three day packages departing from Alice Springs.

Rangers of the Conservation Commission of the Northern Territory conduct tours daily, showing and explaining subjects as varied as the southern hemisphere night sky and foods of the desert. They can be booked at the Yulara Visitors' Centre. Australian National Parks and Wildlife Service rangers conduct one hour tours around the Rock from the base of the climb every day. These do not need to be booked and can simply be joined at their departure point. Teams of white and Aboriginal rangers also conduct a two hour guided walk three times a week. Details and bookings, which are essential, can be obtained from the ranger station near the Rock. Phone (089) 56 2988. The tours are free.

Scenic flights are operated by **Ayers Rock Air Services**, (089) 56 2389; **Chartair**, (089) 56 2280; and **Central Australian Helicopters**, (089) 56 2114. Fixed wing flights cost around $25 and helicopters $35. The former depart from Yulara airport and the latter from a helipad in Yulara village.

Part VII

VICTORIA

Wilson's promontory

By Australian standards, the state of Victoria is small but clever. It settles comfortably into the south-east corner of the continent, making no big noises about its place as the nation's number two economy but having at its heart the richest farm lands and in its capital the wealthiest corporations. Delineated by the meanders of the Murray, Australia's largest river, in the north and the dead straight South Australian border in the west, it holds a population of 4.1 million, more than half of whom live in Melbourne. Except in fits and starts the state lacks Nature's dramatic gestures so common elsewhere in Australia. Rather it is settled and neat; busily, productively farmed and much more closely populated than its counterparts in statehood. Except in the remoter parts, no driver toils long on the road without encountering an outpost of civilisation.

The state's coast faces south into Bass Strait, the passage separating mainland Australia from Tasmania. Melbourne has a position roughly in the middle where the deep, circular inlet of Port Phillip Bay makes a safe haven for ships. The Australian Alps, source of the Murray River, reach into the north-east from New South Wales. The river itself flows west and north, irrigating the land right to the South Australian border and beyond. Only the scrubby mallee, as the middle-west is known, is relatively unproductive.

Climate

Victoria is one of the few places in Australia to have four recognisable seasons. In autumn (March to May) trees change colour and temperatures fall; in winter (June to August) you can rely on fairly cold weather, under 10°C is not uncommon but

302

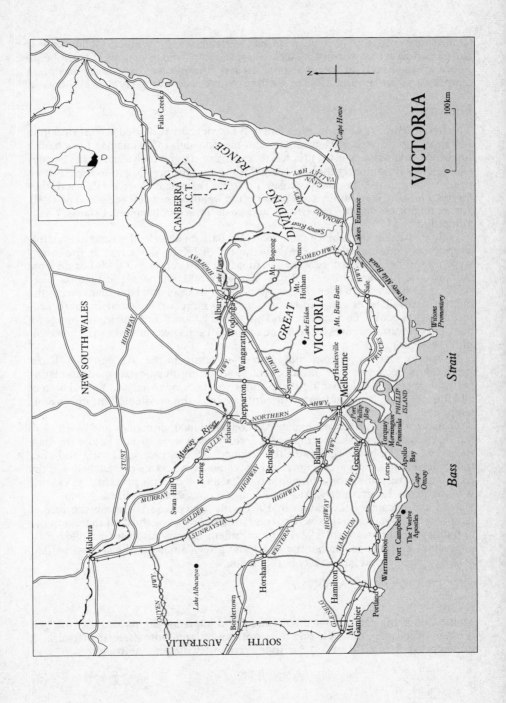

VICTORIA

100km

NEW SOUTH WALES

CANBERRA
A.C.T.

GREAT

DIVIDING

RANGE

Falls Creek

Cape Howe

Snowy River

CANN VALLEY HWY

ORBOST

OMEO HWY

Omeo

Mt. Bogong

Mt. Hotham

Lakes Entrance

Ninety Mile Beach

Sale

Wilsons
Promontory

Lake Eildon

Mt. Baw Baw

VICTORIA

Healesville

Melbourne

Lake Hume

Albury

Wodonga

Wangaratta

Seymour

Shepparton

NORTHERN

HUME HWY.

HIGHWAY

STURT

HIGHWAY

Echuca

Kerang

Swan Hill

Murray River

MURRAY

VALLEY

CALDER

SUNRAYSIA

OUYEN HWY

Mildura

Lake Albacutya

Bordertown

Horsham

WESTERN

HIGHWAY

Bendigo

Ballarat

HAMILTON HWY.

HIGHWAY

PRINCES

Geelong

Torquay

Lorne

Apollo
Bay

Cape
Otway

Port Campbell

The Twelve
Apostles

Warrnambool

Hamilton

Portland

Mt.
Gambier

GLENEG HWY

SOUTH

AUSTRALIA

Port
Phillip
Bay

Mornington
Peninsula

PHILLIP
ISLAND

Bass

Strait

AUSTRALIA

snow is rare except in the alps; in spring (September to November) blooms appear and trees turn green, weather is excellent for travelling and in summer (December to February) the heat is on but not so much as in northern Australia, average maximum temperatures are around 25°C in southern Victoria but can go higher in the west.

History

The first attempt to settle Victoria failed. A convict party dumped at Port Phillip in 1803 gave up the struggle a year later and moved south to Tasmania. They hadn't found Victoria's rich heart, a task left to a string of rugged individuals from Sydney who opened it up during the 1820s and '30s. Eager farmers began to trickle down from New South Wales and percolate up from Tasmania. Once established, they forged a grazing community strong enough to weather the rural recession of 1840, attract migration direct from Britain and push for separate colonial status, finally granted in 1851.

Gold was discovered almost immediately at Ballarat and Bendigo and irreversibly altered the Victorian colonial scene. By the end of 1851 half the men in the colony were on the fields and more were pouring in from overseas; 200,000 came from Britain, 25,000 from China. By 1860 there were 600,000 people in Victoria.

The boom was short-lived. Depression struck in 1854 and later that year, in the nearest Australia ever came to revolution, gold miners rebelled at Ballarat, protesting outrageous licence charges and official corruption. Their fight was put down but their grievances redressed with the coming of self-government in 1855. Revolution was not to be.

Prosperity made a welcome but short-lived return in the '70s and '80s. Rural landholders became almost an aristocracy, acquiring huge estates, accumulating political power and establishing sheep and wheat farming dynasties. Speculation of all kinds, especially in land, grew rife until in 1891 the inevitable but unthinkable happened.

Wheat and wool prices crashed, banks collapsed in all directions and by 1893 all but three had shut up shop completely. Twenty years were to pass before the state recovered and only the really wealthy retained any confidence. During and after those hard times rich arch-conservatives came to rule and entrenched a Tory tradition that remains strong, though somewhat blighted, in the present day. Victoria is home to the Liberal Party, Australia's largest conservative political group.

Australia became a federation in 1901 with Melbourne taking on the role of temporary national capital. The Federal Parliament was established there and did not shift to Canberra until 1927. The twentieth century also saw a largely rural population gravitate to Melbourne which has grown almost to the size of Sydney, making it the second largest city in the nation.

GETTING TO AND AROUND

By Air

Melbourne is the gateway for international and interstate flights into Victoria but, because of its small size, Victoria does not have a large intra-state air network. A small operator called **Kendell Airlines** serves a few larger country towns.

By Rail
Trains travel direct to Melbourne from Sydney and Adelaide only. **V/Line**, as the Victorian train network is called, runs trains to major country centres throughout the state and links some major railheads to nearby towns by coach.

By Road
Depending on where you're coming from and where you're going to, there are four main coach routes into Victoria: via the Hume Highway from Sydney (busiest), via the New South Wales south coast also from Sydney (most scenic) via central New South Wales from Brisbane and via Ballarat from Adelaide. These are all covered by **Ansett Pioneer, Greyhound, Deluxe** and **Bus Australia**. Once in Victoria, the same companies can drop passengers at major towns on their routes. All serve Geelong, Ballarat and Albury but Greyhound has the most extensive network including also Bendigo, Echuca and Mildura.

Roads in Victoria are good by Australian standards and there's hardly any dirt except in remote places. A couple of freeways run in and out of Melbourne but otherwise it's two lanes even when the sign says highway.

TOURIST INFORMATION
Victour is the state run tourist authority. It produces brochures, gives tourism advice and makes bookings but don't have high expectations. The brochures are poor and the organisation's attitude can vary from off-hand to downright unhelpful. Regional tourism associations within the state are better motivated and more useful. The **Melbourne Tourism Authority** and **Gold Centre Tourism** (Ballarat and Bendigo) are among the best. See the relevant sections for their addresses.
Victour addresses are:

230 Collins Street, **Melbourne**, (03) 602 9444
192 Pitt Street, **Sydney**, (02) 233 5499
221 Queen Street, **Brisbane**, (07) 221 4300
16 Grenfell Street, **Adelaide**, (08) 51 4129
Jolimont Centre, Corner Northbourne Avenue and Rudd Street, **Canberra**, (062) 47 6355
SBT Building, Corner Murray and Collins Streets, **Hobart**, (002) 31 0499
St Georges Court, 16 St Georges Terrace, **Perth**, (09) 325 1243

MAJOR SIGHTS
Although **Melbourne** is not a city of great natural beauty, it has style and plenty of cultural interest, especially in its National Gallery and Performing Arts Centre. It is also a city of fine parks and gardens and has the attractive **Dandenong Ranges** on its doorstep. The most spectacular natural sight in Victoria is the **Twelve Apostles**, a line of detached cliffs near Port Campbell on the south coast. The central Victorian gold towns of **Ballarat** and **Bendigo** played a vital part providing the state's early wealth and they retain much of that history, re-created at its best in **Sovereign Hill** a convincing replica of a gold-mining town in the 1860s. Cruising on the **Murray River** is among the most delightful activities of a Victorian holiday.

305

ACCOMMODATION

Aside from an occasional gem such as Burnham Beeches Country House in the Dandenong Ranges, Victoria is a decidedly undistinguished middle-weight in the accommodation stakes. Melbourne has a couple of truly fabulous new hotels (Hyatt and Regent) and enough mid-level ones to cope with the traffic but in the rest of the state it's motels, motels and motels.

FOOD AND DRINK

BYO restaurants are encouraged by Victorian licensing laws so they tend to appear more in Victoria than in any other state. In Melbourne, which has a weighty stock of culinary expertise thanks in part to its high immigrant population, eating out is something of a religion. This sophistication extends to the centre and, less so, the north of the state where there are respectable restaurants in most sizeable towns but it runs out beyond these areas. Despite the quality of dining, Victoria has no special regional foods but it does have a wine industry which produces some quality reds. Brown Brothers is a name to look for.

ACTIVITIES AND SPORTS

Victoria is the home of **Australian Rules Football**, the only truly Australian ball game. It is enthusiastically played and followed in Melbourne and more about it can be found on page 320. Gentle **watersports** such as windsurfing and sailing are pursued on Port Phillip Bay and some of Australia's best board-riding conditions are to be found at Bells Beach, near Torquay on the south coast (see p. 338). **Fishing**, especially for Murray Cod, a huge native fish occurring not only in the Murray but in other inland waters, is popular. There are tennis courts in practically all towns, squash courts and golf courses in those of reasonable size. A special running track for joggers exists skirting the Botanical Gardens in Melbourne.

MELBOURNE

Three million Australians call it home; it has the biggest Greek population of any town in the world outside Athens and Thessaloniki; it is Australia's most southern mainland city and considers itself the country's capital of serious thought though its first wealth was based on gold lust. Melbournites cling to their 'Kulchur', slighting Sydneysiders as shallow, glittering, ephemeral, geeing-up an argument begun in colonial times and now a national sport. Melbourne is grey, conventional, hidebound, boring says the opposing view. Neither is true but both hold grains. Melbourne isn't loud like Sydney, rather it's self-assured, sophisticated, a little formal, more like a European city than any other Australian capital; a place of wide avenues, trees and gardens meant for walking in. Though its winters may be cold and windy, summers are glorious, sometimes hot, springs full of lovely flowers and autumns richly coloured. The joke goes that all too often these seasons occur in the one day, a discomfort for which the city is famed and which can throw your suitcase into chaos. This aside, early or late summer is a good time to be there.

History

The city site on the banks of the Yarra was originally occupied by the Wuywurrung tribe who were driven out during the 1830s by waves of migratory pastoralists heading south from New South Wales and north from Tasmania, at that time still known as Van Diemen's Land. Edward Henty and his sons, who arrived at Portland Bay in 1834, were prominent in this process. They were followed in May 1835 by John Batman who explored the country north and west of Port Phillip Bay. In August of the same year, another group arrived from Launceston in Tasmania. None of this movement was strictly legal according to the government of New South Wales, which had officially restricted the taking up of land outside Sydney, but the occupation had gathered such momentum that within a year recognition of the new settlement was forced on the Colonial Office in London. T. E. Mitchell, the Surveyor General of New South Wales, took a party south in 1836 and more immigrants followed in his wagon tracks, opening up further pastoral lands to the east. In August 1842, the village on the Yarra was declared a municipality and separation of the whole colony of Victoria from NSW occurred in 1850.

Melbourne's status as the leading city of the new colony went for nothing in 1851 when gold was discovered at Ballarat and Bendigo. The population dwindled as everyone from vagrants to shop assistants to the sons of wealthy merchants made for the diggings. The loss, however, was distinctly short-lived and a year later the city had become a huge staging camp for the gold fields accommodating 76,000 residents. The wealth pouring from Victoria's golden heart helped to construct civic monuments in the capital where a Parliament House, a Treasury, Public Library and grand Post Office were built in the next 20 years. Yarra River traffic grew to such proportions that a bend was cut from its meanders in 1879 and a great complex of new docks constructed between the river bank and Spencer Street Station. Melbourne had begun to rival Sydney as chief among the colonial cities. In 1901 it was appointed temporary capital of the new Australian nation and remained so until 1927 when Federal Parliament moved to its new home in Canberra, after a quarter of a century in the Royal Exhibition Buildings, Carlton.

Twentieth-century, especially post-war migration from Europe has affected Melbourne more than any other Australian city. Census figures show that nearly 50 per cent of the city's population has at least one parent born overseas and 21 per cent regularly use a language other than English.

GETTING TO AND AROUND

By Air

Melbourne's International Airport is at Tullamarine, up to an hour's drive north-west of the city, depending on traffic. It is Australia's second busiest airport, planes land there from all over the world and chances are that travellers who don't land in Sydney from overseas will do so in Melbourne.

Ansett and Australian Airlines fly to Melbourne from Sydney almost hourly during morning and evening peak times. The flight takes about an hour. East West Airlines and Air NSW also operate very regular services between those cities. There are also frequent services direct from all other state capitals and Canberra on Ansett

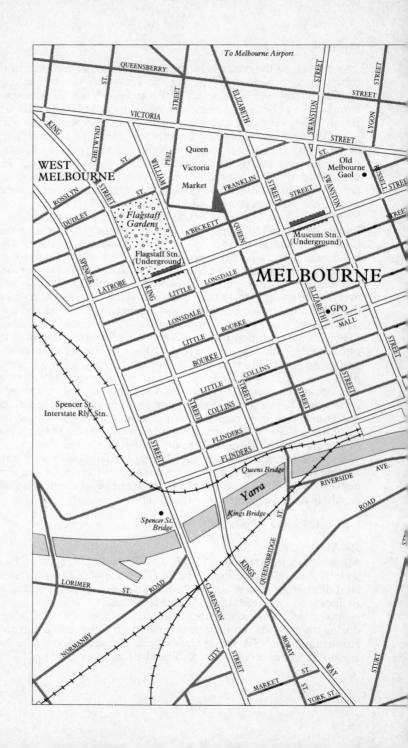

and Australian. Darwin flights travel via Alice Springs. Fares from mainland capitals are Sydney $171, Brisbane $261, Adelaide $161, Perth $396, Darwin $453 and Canberra $134. The smaller airlines are a little less expensive. Kendell Airlines is the major intra-state airline in Victoria.

Skybus operates buses from the airport to its Franklin Street terminal from 6.30 am until 11.30 pm. They depart approximately every half-hour during daylight hours, less frequently after dark. A shuttle bus runs from the terminal to city hotels. The fare of $6 includes both services. **Taxis** do frequent the airport in quantity but the fare is expensive, around $20.

By Rail
Trains called the *Melbourne Express* (overnight) and the *Inter-Capital Daylight Express* ($94 first class, $67 economy, sleeping $129) link Sydney with Melbourne. *The Overland* (overnight) performs the same service for Adelaide ($101 first class only) as well as a train/coach service called Daylink ($66 first class, $47 economy). Canberra and Melbourne are connected by a similar service called Canberra Link ($48.40 and $39).

By Road
Ansett Pioneer, Greyhound, Deluxe and Bus Australia coaches hurtle up and down the 890-km Hume Highway between Sydney and Melbourne with punishing frequency. The fare varies between about $35 and $40. The route is also serviced by cut-price operators who generally offer nothing but the bus. The big boys also run from Adelaide to Melbourne for the same price and have services from Brisbane via the Gold Coast and Toowoomba for around $75 to $85. Services from elsewhere go via one of the aforementioned capitals.

The Hume Highway is the main route from Sydney. It is sometimes a dangerous and unpleasant road, parts of which are in ill repair and all of which is crowded with barrelling trucks. A longer but more peaceful route runs down the coast and through eastern Victoria via the Princes Highway. The Western Highway is the main route from Adelaide.

Getting Around the City
Melbourne has a well organised public transport system in which its famous trams (street cars) play a prominent part. They run throughout the city and into the near suburbs as well as out to the beachside at St Kilda. The old green 'boneshakers' have the most charm and the least comfort and their modern yellow/brown counterparts the reverse. They are really all anyone needs to get around the inner city. If speed is of the essence, take a taxi. There are also buses which run to the suburbs not served by trams.

Spencer Street is Melbourne's central railway station. It lies to the east of the city centre, within walking distance provided you're not carrying anything heavy there are tram and bus stops outside. It is where inter- and intra-state trains arrive and depart. Four underground stations plus Spencer Street ring the inner city. They are Flinders Street on the banks of the Yarra River, Parliament on Spring Street to the west and Museum and Flagstaff on Latrobe Street to the north. Compared to trams, they are not the best available city transport although they are modern and quiet. Flinders Street station, as well as being a Melbourne landmark is the main commuter station and where you will catch a train to the Dandenong Ranges or the Mornington Peninsula on the city outskirts.

The whole system of buses, trains and trams which serves metropolitan Melbourne is called *The Met*. Tickets covering the inner Melbourne area cost $1.20 for two hours of travel, $2.30 for all day and $11.20 for a week and are transferable from tram to bus to train.

TOURIST INFORMATION
The excellent, informative **Melbourne Tourism Authority** has an office on the 20th Level, Nauru House, 80 Collins Street, Melbourne, (03) 654 2288. **Victour** is at 230 Collins Street, (03) 619 9444. **Transport information** for the Melbourne metropolitan area is available from Met Customer Services (03) 617 0900; for country areas ring (03) 619 1500.

Orientation
Melbourne is built on the banks of the Yarra River with its main streets to the north and gardens and the state arts centre to the south. The Princes Bridge links the two parts. The city has some attractive nineteenth-century buildings and although the centre fell prey to a mild form of high-rise mania during the 1960s, the last ten years have moderated if not halted the destruction of architectural heritage. This may be due to a consciousness that Melbourne's city is its main attraction rather than the landscape in which it is set. The city is laid out on a square grid of streets which, when you look at a map, seems to make it blissfully easy to find your way around. However, these streets are linked by a network of narrow lanes which can become a maze to the innocent tourist. None the less, the basic idea is straightforward. Swanston Street runs north to south through the centre, becoming St Kilda Road on the southern side of the Princes Bridge and carrying traffic to Carlton and the northern suburbs in the opposite direction. The rest of the city centre rises to the east and west of Swanston Street along Bourke and Collins Streets.

City Streets

Melbourne is a city of boulevards inhabited by a bustling traffic of pedestrians, cars and trams. The city's standing glories are man-made and there is no great natural prospect to be seen anywhere. Hence the most commanding sight is the length of St Kilda Road striding south from the city centre, flanked on the west by the Victorian Arts Centre and on the east by Kings Domain, a long and wide park which also takes up the eastern foreshores of the Yarra River. The Yarra itself is no wide and noble stream but rather muddy, narrow and skirted by traffic.

Spring Street
The city's distinguished buildings fall distinctly into two classes, old and ultra-modern. The best of the old reflect the fact that Melbourne is one of the few cities in the world to have grown into a fully-fledged metropolis during the Victorian era.

The buildings which remain from that period include the large public edifices in Spring Street at the eastern extremity. **Parliament House** is the biggest and most impressive. Building commenced in 1854 and, according to the original plans, has not yet been finished, nor is it ever likely to be. The completed sections include a Legislative Council Chamber described by Sir John Betjeman (of all people) as the 'best Corinthian Room in the World', a library, Queen's Hall and vestibule and, finally added in 1892, the wedding cake facade and grand steps. The building stands at the top of Bourke Street above the bustle of the city's commercial centre. The **Old Treasury** also in Spring Street at the top of Collins Street was built between 1857 and 1862 of sandstone from Bacchus Marsh, north-west of Melbourne. Originally called the New Treasury, the building was designed by the then 19-year-old government architect, J. J. Clark, and his compatriots in the Public Works Department. Its basement vaults housed gold from Ballarat and Bendigo.

The very green and English **Treasury Gardens** slope away from the Old Treasury along Spring Street, their wide lawns shaded by well-established trees and in their midst an incongruous monkey compound occupied by a large extended family of mandrills. The open space continues across Landsdowne Street into **Fitzroy Gardens** which contains **Captain Cook's Cottage**. The cottage, where the infant Cook grew up, was removed from its original site at Ayton in Yorkshire to the gardens in 1934. It is open every day from 9 am to 5 pm. Admission costs 80c. The gardens also contain a memorial to John F. Kennedy. They serve as a place of escape for the city's people at lunchtime or on a summer evening.

The other great Victorian edifice on Spring Street is the **Windsor Hotel**. It lies across the road from the public buildings and was the project of George Nipper, a ship-owner who, in 1883, commissioned architect Charles Webb to design and build it. The hotel later fell into the hands of a temperance campaigner, James Munro, who turned it into a coffee palace. Re-licensed in 1920, it became a watering hole for the wealthy but declined over a long period, reaching its nadir and a considerable state of scruffiness in the 1970s. The hotel was saved by an agreement between the State Government which now owns it and the Oberoi Hotel company which runs it and has done a glorious and faithful job of restoration. Taking high tea in the Windsor lounge on any afternoon is a pleasure of a restrained but delightful kind and the dining room, although not recommended for eating in, is a stirring, high Victorian sight.

George Nipper also commissioned Charles Webb to design and erect **Tasma Terrace** in nearby Parliament Place. The **Princes Theatre** at 163 Spring Street completes this precinct of Victorian extravaganzas. The Second Empire-style palace of entertainment was built in 1886 on the site previously occupied by a theatre of the same name built in 1857. It had been preceded by Astley's Amphitheatre, one of the city's first palaces of popular entertainment. **Carlton Gardens** lie at the end of Spring Street where it meets Victoria Street. They are bounded by Rathdowne and Nicholson Streets and extend to Moor Street. The gardens house the **Royal Exhibition Building**, constructed in 1880 as an echo of London's Crystal Palace. It is a cavernous wedding cake of a place with a tremendous octagonal dome in its centre and a high arched entrance flanked by two three-storey towers. It remains a major venue for trade shows and public exhibitions.

Collins Street

This street, which runs downhill, west from Spring Street to Swanston Street and then up again to Spencer Street, is often cited for its Parisian charm, especially at the parliamentary end where many small exclusive shops once preened themselves and their customers behind decorative facades. The exclusive shops remain but skyscrapers now vie to top each other where the little doorways once invited. Biggest are the **Regent** and **Hyatt**, Melbourne's most ritzy hotels which compete head to head within a block of each other but lesser lights from office blocks to shopping centres have also lately sprouted on the Bourke Hill end off Collins Street. They have, however, the merit of being among the more striking of Melbourne's late twentieth-century architectural boom babies. These creatures of 'facade-ism', a style which, whatever it may say about lack of direction in design, does relieve the oppressive blight of internationalism, include **Number One Collins Street** and the **Rialto** between King and William Streets; both have used the faces of former city landmarks to front steel and glass towers.

   City Square occupies the junction of Swanston and Collins Streets. It must be confessed that the square is rather bleak and anything but a thriving centre of civic activity, although occasional demonstrations and speeches take place there. It is the victim of a grey, stoney flatness which is off-putting despite a network of fountains, waterfalls and small aqueducts designed perhaps to relieve it. **St Paul's Cathedral** stands on the south side of the square on a site which accommodated the Victorian colony's first place of worship, a tent where all-comers were welcome. From 1842 to 1847 a corn and hay market occupied the land but when that moved elsewhere the church re-acquired it. The first St Paul's was built in 1851 but superseded in 1880 when the foundation stone of the existing church was laid. It was consecrated in 1891 but the spires were not added until 1933. The lugubrious building on the opposite corner to City Square is **Melbourne Town Hall**.

Bourke Street

Bourke Street is the next major east–west thoroughfare north of Collins Street. It is the city's main shopping street, making room between retailers for many of Melbourne's cinemas. Its main feature is a semi-pedestrian mall; the mall, though closed to cars is open to thundering trams and it seems to suffer from the same pedestrian inspiration as City Square though not quite so badly. **Bourke Street Mall** runs from Swanston Street to Elizabeth Street with the city's major department stores, Myer and David Jones, on one side and smaller shops and arcades on the other. The **Melbourne General Post Office** is at the Elizabeth Street end and a booth called 'Half Tix' which sells discounted theatre tickets stands close to the centre. Trams retain right of way through the mall and insist upon it without fear or favour. Those unaccustomed to them should be aware that in Melbourne they do not indicate their approach by sounding a horn but ring a pitiful and easily neglected bell. The tourist who is not used to being 'belled' off the road can find several tons of green metal bearing down at high speed about two feet from his or her right ear. This is disconcerting and embarrassing, more so if you're not a passable sprinter. Be warned! Despite the danger, shoppers congregate there in thousands and on sunny days city workers pour in at lunchtime. In winter the wind, whipping around the shop fronts, drives people into the heated department stores and the mall is deserted.

Little Bourke Street

Melbourne's **Chinatown**, more authentically crowded and narrow than Sydney's and Brisbane's dressed-up versions, occupies Little Bourke Street, running parallel to Bourke Street. There are many good restaurants of all Asian persuasions. Live crabs and lobsters swim in buckets and tanks awaiting their culinary fate in a steamer or on a plate of black bean sauce. The restaurant and shop frontages are highly coloured and there is much bustle. Do, however, remember to bring your money with you if you come to eat on this street—it is aware of its privileged position. Cheaper Asian eateries spill round the corner in **Lonsdale Street** which also has quite a few Greek and Lebanese establishments.

North–South Streets

The streets described above are crossed north–south by Swanston, Russell and Exhibition Streets. **Swanston Street** is arguably Melbourne's main street and leads across Princes Bridge into St Kilda Road. The edifice at the junction of Swanston and Flinders Streets is **Flinders Street Station**, where commuter trains from Melbourne's 6000 square km (3720 square miles) of suburban sprawl pull in. Opposite is **Young and Jackson's Hotel** the city's most famous pub. Chloe, whose naked portrait graces the main bar, looks tame in contemporary terms but when she first went up in Victorian times there was an uproar of monumental proportions.

The **Old Melbourne Gaol** and the **National Museum** (not really national) are close together at the northern end of Russell Street. The gaol was the site of over 100 hangings during its period of service from 1841 to 1929. It is now a penal museum whose cells, ranged along two storeys with a wide central well and iron walkway hugging the walls, contain death masks of its victims, the most famous being bushranger Ned Kelly. Kelly led a gang of thieves whose contempt for the colonial police force in particular, and civil authority in general, won them many friends in their own time and has made them Australian folk heroes ever since. Kelly was Irish and believed himself and his family oppressed by an ignorant and savage English colonial administration, an oppression which forced them into crime. On these grounds he justified shooting policemen and stealing horses. He was captured at Glenrowan in north-eastern Victoria during a siege in which he wore crude armour to protect himself against the police guns. He was hanged at Melbourne Gaol on gallows which can be seen on the building's second storey. His armour is also on display. The penal museum is open from 10 am to 5 pm each day. Admission $3.50.

The National Museum which includes the Victorian Science Museum, is a pot-pourri of scientific and cultural exhibits of distinctly variable quality. Ingenious pieces of agricultural machinery including harvesters and bailers manufactured in surprisingly primitive engineering shops and foundries during the late nineteenth and early twentieth centuries are among the most interesting. Easily the most bizarre is the stuffed corpse of Phar Lap, Australia's best known racehorse which died in mysterious circumstances in the United States and threw a considerable cloud over

Australian-American relations. There is also a fine collection of weapons, which should impress gun enthusiasts, and a planetarium. The museum is open from 10 am to 5 pm daily and admission is free except for the planetarium which costs $2.20.

South of the City

The Victorian Arts Centre
The spire of the Victorian Arts Centre rises over the southern part of the city beyond Princes Bridge. The centre is the state's cultural pride and joy. Where the Sydney Opera House is a triumph of form over function, it could be jokingly described as the opposite. The centre consists of three grey, rather undistinguished-looking buildings: the circular structure by the river contains the **Melbourne Concert Hall**, a **Performing Arts Museum**, a kiosk and an elaborate coffee shop; the next door theatre complex which bears the scaffolding spire contains the **State Theatre**, **Playhouse**, and **Studio** theatre and the **Vic Restaurant**; the **Victorian National Gallery** occupies the last of the buildings.

The Concert Hall is a multi-purpose venue used for everything from symphony and rock concerts to graduation ceremonies and the occasional musical. It is built into an enormous hole in the ground so that its outward appearance belies its depth of several storeys which has room for 2677 concert-goers. The theatres are laid out clover-leaf pattern in a building which also descends into the earth. The State Theatre is a good-sized lyric house, seating 2000 patrons on three levels as well as having a big stage which is often used by the Victorian State Opera; the Playhouse is smaller, accommodating 880 on two levels, and the Studio is a flexible space for less conventional productions and seats 250 to 400 depending on its layout.

Such attention has been paid to the technical design and decoration of the hall and theatres that internally, all make up for their outward dreariness. They share the theme 'Australia's Mineral Wealth' and their foyers are decked out in colours drawn from copper, silver and gold, including ceilings leaved with those precious metals. The foyers also contain a collection of contemporary Australian painting equalled in no art gallery in the country. Each is devoted to the works of a single giant of the last quarter century. The Concert Hall and and State Theatre foyers share *Paradise Garden* a huge work by Sir Sidney Nolan, made up of 1320 individual paintings in 220 panels; it depicts the germination, flowering and death of a desert bloom and took two years to complete. The Circle Foyer of the State Theatre contains Arthur Boyd's electrifying paintings of the Shoalhaven River in southern New South Wales; in other foyers you will find work by Jeffrey Smart and John Olsen. Hugh Oliveiro painted the lustrous mural decorating the St Kilda Road entrance to the theatres and the Playhouse foyers feature works by Aboriginals of the western desert. Tours which include both buildings leave regularly from the tour desk on the left of the St Kilda Road entrance to the theatre complex. They cost $3.50 and last an hour.

The **Victorian National Gallery** occupies a grey, rectangular block of a building which, I'm afraid, reminds me of nothing so much as a prison but again, do not judge the book by its cover. The four-level gallery is built around three square courtyards, two glassed-in to admit natural light, containing sculpture from monumental to environmental, and a third court, at the northern end, used for exhibitions of contemporary work. Most of the gallery's collection is shown on the ground and second floors and it has some considerable highlights. Chief among them is the best survey collection of Australian painting between 1840 and 1940 (and a little beyond), chronologically arranged so the viewer can easily perceive the constant theme which dominates that century and remains a continuing focus of Australian art— landscape and its meaning. Other preoccupations, from domestic life to nationalism, intrude but all are dominated by varying perceptions of the land. The Anglicised romanticism and aggrandisement of John Glover gives way to the fiercely nationalistic painters of the 1890s such as Tom Roberts and later Frederick McCubbin. The migratory Edwardians, Rupert Bunny and E. Phillips Fox, who went to Europe to learn fashionable ways of painting, turn away for a time to mannered and decorative domesticity in a country seemingly tamed. Their successors, the angry young men of the forties and fifties like Albert Tucker and Arthur Boyd, reject comfortable urbanity for harsh desert-inspired images. These last-mentioned uncomfortable painters are balanced by the less jarring efforts of William Dobell and Russell Drysdale. The survey contains some images seminal in the Australian national consciousness, especially Tom Robert's *Shearing the Rams* and Fred McCubbin's *The Pioneers*.

The clue to what happens next in this artistic battle to perceive the land, and be perceived by it, is probably to be found in a small display of Aboriginal art on the first floor. It is a gathering of tremendously exciting works whose pictorial power reflects an entirely distinct, mythologically inspired expression of the Australian outback, drawn from a completely enculturated understanding of it and man's place within it. The mostly non-representational paintings are accompanied by short explanations serving to partially clarify them for the white observer.

Although these collections are the best the National Gallery has to offer, they by no means exhaust it. It has other surprising strengths such as Pre-Columbian and Asian art. Its Great Hall on the ground floor is also worth seeing. The space is roofed with stained glass and it is not unheard of for gallery visitors to lie on the floor, looking up for extended periods of time, working out the roof's patterns. The gallery is open from Tuesday to Sunday, 10 am to 5 pm. Admission costs $1.20. There is a restaurant and cafeteria in the building.

The Kings Domain

The Kings Domain is the large park on the opposite side of St Kilda Road to the Victorian Arts Centre. More than a simple park, it includes Alexandra and Queen Victoria Gardens and the Myer Music Bowl where Melbourne's major outdoor musical and theatrical performances take place. The city's war memorial, called the Shrine of Remembrance stands in the southern section of the domain. The eastern edge accommodates Government House and entrances to the Royal Botanic Gardens which slope down to, but don't actually meet, the bank of the Yarra River. **La Trobe's Cottage** also stands on this side of the park. La Trobe was Victoria's first governor and the simple white weatherboard house he occupied makes a telling contrast with the opulence of the present governor's official residence. The **Royal**

Botanic Gardens are reckoned to be one of the sights of Melbourne. They stretch over 41 hectares (100 acres) and contain around 12,000 species of native and exotic plants which is impressive in itself but their fine landscaping, hilly location, ornamental lakes and great variety of birdlife make them especially soothing to the tired soul. We have largely to thank William Guilfoyle for the setting. He reigned over the gardens for 33 years from 1873 and drew his inspiration from the great English gardens of the eighteenth and nineteenth century. Free guided tours take place on Tuesdays and Thursdays at 10 am and 11 am from the Plant Cottage. The gardens are open from early morning to around sunset each day.

Southern Suburbs

Further south of the city, the exclusive and expensive suburbs of **Toorak** and **South Yarra** cosset the most entrenched of Australia's establishment families. This is the heartland of the country's conservative politics and the money is old and copious, just like the houses. Toorak Road, South Yarra, is where the rich folk shop—Italian designer labels crowd out the windows and no-one bothers to check their prices. Non-shoppers should head for **Como House**, a mansion built in stages during the 1850s and occupying two hectares (five acres) of splendid gardens overlooking the Yarra River. The two-storey house is the height of airy, early Victorian elegance, entirely white with wide verandas and a minimum of Italianate decoration. It was built for George Armytage, a pastoralist and leading citizen of Melbourne in the mid- to late nineteenth century and is now owned by the National Trust which has furnished it in period. Como is open each day from 10 am to 5 pm. You'll find it in Como Avenue, South Yarra; entry costs $3.50.

Also south of the city, in the much less salubrious South Melbourne, is the *Barque Polly Woodside*, a deepwater, square-rigged, commercial sailing ship built in 1885 and said to be the last such vessel still afloat in Australia. The ship is the main attraction at the Melbourne Maritime Museum on the corner of Normanby Road and Phayer Street. Open weekdays 10 am to 4 pm and weekends noon to 5 pm. Admission $4.

North of the City

No true feeling for Melbourne can really be gained without walking along **Lygon Street**, Carlton, north of the city. The street pulsates with the life brought by Melbourne's migrants. Its footpaths are shaded by sloping awnings. Italian coffee shops and restaurants of all descriptions abound and the clothing stores are more adventurous and trendy than their South Yarra counterparts. Any deviation left or right moves you past rows of Victorian terraced houses for which the area is justly famous. **Brunswick Street**, Fitzroy, to the east, on the other side of Carlton Gardens and the Royal Exhibition Buildings, has some of the same character—restaurants galore but not so many trendy shops.

Other Sights

Rippon Lea, perhaps the most famous of Melbourne's grand old houses, as much known for its gardens as for the house, hides behind a high wall at 192 Hotham

Street, Elsternwick. The house was built in 1868 in a rather heavy-handed Romanesque style by Sir Fredrick Sargood and has fifteen rooms including a ballroom. The gardens, with their lovely use of ponds and bridges provide a restful counterpart to the house. Open daily 10 am to 5 pm most of the year except for mid-June when it's Wednesday, Thursday and Friday 11 am to 3.30 pm only, and mid-August, weekends only 10 am to 5 pm.

The **Royal Melbourne Zoological Gardens** in Elliot Street, Parkville, is the world's third oldest zoo. It occupies 22 hectares (60 acres) and is home to 400 species of Australian and other animals, a large variety of them displayed in open range enclosures. The zoo's most unusual feature is a Butterfly House where 20 species of butterflies float freely among tropical plants. Open daily 9 am to 5 pm. Admission $4.40.

The **Meat Market Craft Centre** is a large craft gallery and workshop complex established by the Victorian Ministry for the Arts in the old Metropolitan Meat Market, 42 Courtney Street, North Melbourne. The original space has been converted to a long exhibition hall flanked with workshops, some of which are open to the public. Exhibitions change regularly and there is also a permanent collection on show. Open 10 am to 5 pm daily. Admission free.

When dealing with Melbourne one cannot pass over that temple of Australian sport the **Melbourne Cricket Ground**. The ground has no architectural or cultural merit but attracts more people than any other sporting venue in Australia. It was built as the central stadium for the 1956 Olympic Games and has room for over 100,000 spectators. More than this number turns up each year in September for the Grand Final of the annual Australian Rules Football competition which dominates Melbourne's sporting consciousness more than the Melbourne Cup, if such a thing is possible. Cricket is played there in the summer and also attracts big crowds so long as the competition is international. The **Melbourne Cricket Club Museum** which contains sporting trophies for Australia's past, is housed there. Open Wednesdays from 10 am, 40 cents admission. The MCG, as it is universally known, is in Yarra Park, Wellington Parade, Jolimont.

Melbourne's closest seaside suburb is **St Kilda** on Port Phillip Bay. It is an odd mixture of seaside jollity and sleaze. The jollity comes out on fine weekends when the city people spill onto Fitzroy and Acland Streets for coffee and mountains of cake or browse the amateur art market along the esplanade each Sunday. It's also reflected in Luna Park where roller coasters tumble and kids scream with delight, and in the old Palais Theatre, a looming relic of the 1920s. The sleaze, nothing so abandoned as Sydney's Kings Cross, comes out at night when prostitutes cruise Fitzroy Street and drug deals are done in back alleys. 'Adult' entertainment is the order of the night but the coffee shops are still good and St Kilda remains the only place in Melbourne with much late night action.

SHOPPING

Clothes shopping is good in Melbourne, good enough for Sydneysiders to make seasonal expeditions in search of just the right addition to their wardrobes. The fashion centre is South Yarra where the dedicated shopper can easily dispense with an afternoon or even a whole day, breaking for lunch at one of the glitzy restaurants in which that suburb delights. Do not, under any circumstances, expect bargains. The boutiques are stocked with Italian originals to which import duties, sales taxes and hefty profit margins have been added. Bring your credit cards with you.

ENTERTAINMENT AND NIGHTLIFE

Buy the *Melbourne Age* newspaper on Friday for a useful, comprehensive guide to what's on around the city and suburbs. It caters as well to the needs of the classical concert-goer and the theatrically minded as the pub rock devotee.

Theatre is a very busy and serious business in Melbourne but the city has no designated theatre district. The major city theatres are **Her Majesty's** and the **Comedy Theatre** on Exhibition Street and the **Princess Theatre** on Spring Street. They usually run musicals and commercial plays. The **Russell Street Theatre**, near the Flinders Street end of Russell Street, is a smaller venue which houses productions by the prestigious Melbourne Theatre Company, usually of full length Australian and overseas plays. The **Atheneum**, an old theatre, somewhat tatty but historical, near the corner of Collins and Swanston Streets, has two spaces catering for fringe and straight productions and there are, of course, the Arts Centre theatres in St Kilda Road, described above, of which the State Theatre houses ballet and opera as well as plays. The most prominent suburban theatres are **La Mama**, 205 Faraday Street, Carlton, an independently minded group which maintains strong contacts with the 1970s, and **Anthill Theatre**, 199 Napier Street, South Melbourne, which specialises in new work by Australian playwrights. The Australian Opera and Ballet companies spend part of each year in Melbourne and appear at the Victorian Arts Centre State Theatre. Opera late March to May and ballet June, October and November.

Melbourne has its own symphony orchestra which performs regularly along with visiting artists and Australian soloists at the **Melbourne Concert Hall** in the Victorian Arts Centre; concerts also take place at **Robert Blackwood Hall**, Monash University, Clayton. The **Melbourne Town Hall** often hosts free concerts on weekend afternoons and weekday lunchtimes in which the music can range from jazz to organ classics. Rock concerts mostly occur at **Festival Hall**, Dudley Street, West Melbourne, and at the **Melbourne Sports and Entertainment Complex**, Batman Avenue, Melbourne.

Bookings for any of these major events can be made at **BASS** (Best Available Seating Service) ticket agencies. There is one in the Smorgon Family Plaza, Victorian Arts Centre and others scattered through the city. (Phone (03) 654 1914). The previously mentioned Half Tix booth in Bourke Street Mall sells half-price tickets to many theatre shows on the day of performance but be there at 9 am when it opens as people queue and tickets to the best shows go early. A board lists what is available.

Melbourne theatre of the last two decades has had a rich fringe and nowhere is it so visible as in the **theatre restaurants** which rose to prominence in the late 1970s. Their leading light is the **Last Laugh Theatre Restaurant**, 64 Smith Street, Collingwood, where around 200 diners are entertained nightly by anything from stand-up feminist comics to fully produced musical madcappery, usually with a pungent sauce of local politics, sometimes more than a little blue. The show is frequently better than the food but you pay for both, about $25 a ticket.

Melbourne considers itself the **rock music** capital of Australia which means, in practice, that hundreds of hopeful bands play the pubs searching for their big break. This would make Melbourne no different to Sydney were it not for a tendency to play up to rock's working class origins in sweaty public bars whilst abhorring the corporatisation of the music industry. Mind you, Melbourne was the birth place of Men at Work, The Little River Band and many an Australian 'muso' who finds himself more at home in Los Angeles these days. Their possible successors can be seen at **Billboard**, 170 Russell Street, Melbourne, and **The Palace**, Lower Esplanade, St Kilda.

The city also has **dance clubs** where crowds of physical and mental teenagers grind, twitch and thrust to extended disco-mix tracks and the manic flickering of video screens. The top names in this game are all in King Street, City. They are **Inflation**, 60 King Street, **The Hippodrome**, 14–20 King Street and **Melbourne Underground**, 22–24 King Street. Late night places for older people (over 25) are **Lazar International**, 240 King Street, and **Melbourne Ritz**, corner Princes and Fitzroy Streets, St Kilda. Don't appear at these latter joints in jeans or collarless shirts.

SPORT
Some people go so far as to say sport has taken the place of religion for your average Melbournite. It is certainly popular, especially so in the case of Australian Rules football, a local code derived from Gaelic Football. Australian Rules Competition has recently come to involve teams from all states of Australia but its home is Melbourne. Sunday games at the Melbourne Cricket Ground draw enormous crowds bedecked with sweaters and scarves in team colours. Indeed, the Sunday football crowd on a Melbourne tram is a sight to be seen nowhere else on earth. On grand final day, the last Sunday in September, over 100,000 of the citizens join the Australian Prime Minister to find out who will be the Victorian Football League Champions for the season. The occasion is one of the most prominent in the national sporting calendar.

WHERE TO STAY
Melbourne is less well endowed with international hotels than Sydney but it also attracts fewer tourists so accommodation is generally easier to come by except at very specific times of year, namely Melbourne Cup week (first week of November) and Football Grand Final time (last weekend in September). A large number of good serviced apartments is one of Melbourne's great attractions. Both in and near the city, they offer a useful alternative to hotels, especially for the longer term visitor. The hotels and apartments listed below are in a rough order of comfort and cost; their distance from the city is also taken into account.

Hyatt on Collins, 123 Collins Street, Melbourne, (03) 657 1234, is the most recently built of Melbourne's few really swish hotels and goes to the full extreme: acres of pink marble, bronze statues and a foyer big enough for the cast of Ben Hur.

The hotel is entered via a sparkling shopping arcade from Collins Street, the limousines pull up around the corner in Russell Street, the hotel rooms rise in a glossy stack many storeys tall above both entrances. Single $185, double $210.

Regent Melbourne, 25 Collins Street, Melbourne, (03) 653 0000, has lately been somewhat eclipsed by the bright Hyatt only a block away but was the new boy in town only a couple of years ago and has lots of style as well as a dizzying atrium decorated with huge bolts of glimmering fabric. $225.

Menzies at Rialto, 495 Collins Street, Melbourne, (03) 62 0111, is Melbourne's leading example of 'facade-ist' architecture, a high-rise hotel erected behind the facade of an old building in order that the old building's appearance may be preserved without the inconvenience of its contents. It's at the unfashionable end of Collins Street close to Spencer Street Station but this is about its only drawback. Single $210, double $230.

The Windsor, 103 Spring Street, Melbourne, (03) 653 0653, is a hotel in the grand old manner now run efficiently by the Oberoi management company. Rooms tend to vary in size; ask for an external room to avoid the small ones. Single $155, double $180.

Rockman's Regency Hotel, corner Lonsdale and Exhibition Streets, Melbourne, (03) 662 3900, promotes itself as Melbourne's small hotel but actually has over 180 rooms and is a medium-sized high-standard property close to the city centre. $195.

Southern Cross Hotel, 131 Exhibition Street, Melbourne, (03) 63 0221; built 25 years ago, this hotel would be getting out of date were it not for recent refurbishment and a very high standard of service. It still has a certain social cachet in Melbourne. Single $140 to $160, double $160 to $170.

Hilton International Melbourne, 192 Wellington Parade, Melbourne, (03) 419 3311; a mid-quality Hilton which is closer to the Melbourne Cricket Ground than to the city proper but at least the walk to town is through Fitzroy and Treasury Gardens. Single $200, double $220.

Noahs Hotel Melbourne, 182 Exhibition Street, Melbourne, (03) 662 0511, has one of best locations in Melbourne but the rooms are rather small and have begun to need renovation. $126.

Park Royal On St Kilda Road, 562 St Kilda Road, Melbourne, (03) 529 8888; is far enough south of the city to necessitate a tram (street car) ride but makes up for the distance with well-appointed rooms in various configurations and a view of Kings Domain. A good hotel. $163.

Gordon Place, 24–38 Little Bourke Street, Melbourne, (03) 663 5355; a classy collection of serviced apartments in a National Trust classified building next door to Chinatown. Sometimes hard to get into but the pick of this type of accommodation in Melbourne, it has studio, one-and two-bedroom apartments. Single $120, double $150.

Chateau Melbourne, 131 Lonsdale Street, Melbourne, (03) 663 3161; is done up in the now unfashionable pseudo-antique look but is none the worse for that. The hotel is actually a tall, thin building close to the city centre near Melbourne's Greek and Lebanese restaurants almost across the road from Rockman's Regency. It caters to many business men as well as tourists. $150.

Sheraton Hotel Melbourne, 13 Spring Street, Melbourne, (03) 63 9961; don't be fooled, this is not a member of the Sheraton chain but a budget option which has the advantage of a convenient location. Single $105, double $119.

Interwest Settlers Old Melbourne Hotel, 5–17 Flemington Road, North Melbourne, (03) 329 9344, is built in a studied mock-colonial style in which turned wood plays a strong part. Like the Park Royal, it is far enough from town to enforce the pleasure of a short tram ride but the hotel is not of equal standard. Seems popular with Americans. Single $110, double $120.

St Kilda Road Travelodge, corner St Kilda Road and Park Street, South Melbourne, (03) 699 4833; a largish hotel (228 rooms) which stands in about the middle of Melbourne hotel standards. The city is a short tram ride or 15 to 20 minute walk away along St Kilda Road. $135.

City Gardens, 335 Abbotsford Street, Melbourne, (03) 320 6600; is a complex of serviced apartments in one- and two-bedroom configurations furnished to about the standard of a medium motel but with much more space. Also has more luxurious town houses available. Northern side of the city. One bedroom $80, two bedroom $90.

Victoria Hotel, 215 Little Collins Street, Melbourne, (03) 63 0441; a large hotel right in the centre of the city which will suit the budget-conscious traveller. Most rooms are small, very simply furnished and do not have private facilities but some have been brought up to a higher standard and include ensuites and other conveniences. $63 to $85.

The President Melbourne, 63 Queens Road, Melbourne, (03) 529 4300; recent additions to this hotel have raised its standard somewhat; it now has a tower where rooms have views of Albert Park Lake. The hotel is south of the city area. Single $102 to $175, double $110 to 180.

City Limits Motel Apartments, 20–22 Little Bourke Street, Melbourne, (03) 662 2544, is an inexpensive inner city motel next door to Gordon Place. Small rooms, laminated furniture but you can eat next door or in Chinatown. $71 to $83.

Townhouse Hotel, 701 Swanston Street, Carlton, (03) 347 7811, is well worth considering if you'd rather stay in one of Melbourne's more exciting suburbs than in town. It a short tram ride to the city and a quick walk to Lygon Street and has bright comfortable rooms if a little squeezy. Two bedroom $135, three bedroom $145.

Station Pier Condominiums, 15 Beach Street, Port Melbourne, (03) 647 9666; one- and two-bedroom serviced apartments in duplex style with plenty of space, light and comfortable furniture. They stand near the waterfront at Port Melbourne and some have views of Port Phillip Bay. They are about four km (two and a half miles) from the city. One bedroom $125, two bedroom $150.

Magnolia Court, 101 Powlett Street, East Melbourne, (03) 419 4222; centres on an 1862 building, once a girls' school and now renovated complete with iron lace balcony and other Victorian features. Guests can stay in this part but will need to ask for it specifically as most of the accommodation is housed in a motel wing added in more recent times. Rooms in this wing are of slightly above ordinary motel standard. The nearest tram stop is two blocks away in Wellington Parade from where the city is a short ride away. Single $70, double $75.

South Yarra Hill Suites, 14 Murphy Street, South Yarra, (03) 268 8222; serviced apartments of from one to three bedrooms in ritzy South Yarra, one block from the shopping mecca of Toorak Road. The suites are comfortable and spacious with lounges, kitchens and baths. $75 to $155.

Oakford Executive Apartments, Oakford House, 180 Toorak Road, South Yarra, (03) 267 4401; has 170 serviced apartments in nine locations south of the city, mostly in South Yarra and Toorak. They vary from bed-sits to apartments and town houses of one, two and three bedrooms. A 25-square-metre penthouse is also available. Some have gardens or courtyards and others are two-storey. All have separate dining/living areas and are furnished to luxury standard. A grocery delivery service is offered if you can't be bothered shopping for the necessaries yourself. $60 to $140.

EATING OUT

A marvellous and, no doubt, entirely fortuitous combination of Commonwealth immigration policies and State licensing laws has served to make Melbourne one of the best and least expensive cities in which to eat anywhere in the world. Successive Australian governments' encouragement of European and lately Asian immigration has made Melbourne's racial and cultural mix extremely diverse thus providing unparalleled culinary variety. Victoria's licensing laws make full restaurant licences expensive and difficult to obtain but BYO licences the opposite, thus fostering low-priced eating. The spectrum of cuisines probably surpasses Sydney with special strength in Italian, Greek and lately Turkish and Vietnamese cooking. Melbourne also has a very long suit in up-market restaurants and has cornered that market in Australia for years.

Its long history as a foodie's dream does not protect the city from fads and fashions. Food halls are the most recent vogue. They inhabit warehouses and the like divided into numerous booths serving a variety of food styles, although their inspiration is South-East Asian. They are down-market and often astonishingly inexpensive. In the opposite direction lies the 'deli'. This again is more a design concept than a cuisine, although deli menus do tend to have certain common features such as pasta, light main courses, rich cakes and coffee. Whatever the menu, pastel is their code in decor, lack of formality in service and neon somewhere in the place is *de rigueur*. Their inspiration seems to come from New York.

A subsidiary, but immensely convenient, delight of dining out in Melbourne is the habit restaurateurs have of congregating along particular streets in particular districts. So uniform is this tendency that I have divided the following guide to restaurants into areas rather than cuisines, trying to choose a representative variety in each location. Just to confuse everybody, the division begins with a non-geographic grab bag of the best dining Melbourne has to offer, in other words, the best dining Australia has to offer.

The Best

Stephanie's, 405 Tooranga Road, Hawthorn East, (03) 20 8944, named after chef Stephanie Alexander who is a national treasure of Australian cuisine. She not only cooks and, with her husband, runs Melbourne's best restaurant but also writes on food for a national magazine. Ms Alexander draws her influences from places as far apart as France, Italy and China. Menus are seasonal and dishes are never repeated.

The restaurant is in the grand manner with three dining rooms, all imposingly furnished. Licensed. Upper price range. Stephanie's actually has set-price menus for lunch and dinner. Lunch is by far the less expensive, about half the cost of dinner. Expect to spend well over $100 for two at dinner time.

Fleurie, 40 Ross Street, Toorak, (03) 241 5792; Iain Hewitson has a hand in three successful restaurants in Melbourne but he does his cooking here. The restaurant is small and deliberately limits its menu to four starters, four main courses and four desserts. Although basically French the food strikes out to the Pacific Rim for variations in flavour. BYO. Upper price range. Set price is the rule here as well, expect over $100 but not quite so much as the previous listing.

Mietta's, 7 Alfred Street, City, (03) 654 2366; superb fish and game dishes here, in a restaurant which is famous throughout Australia. The dining is in two areas: downstairs—lounge which serves drinks and light meals until 3 am; and upstairs—formal restaurant whose inspiration is French, extending from the regional to the modern. Licensed. Upper price range.

Glo Glo's, 3 Carters Avenue, Toorak, (03) 241 2615, is flowers, comfort, quietness and service but above all food that tastes as good as it looks. Simple and complicated dishes on a modern French menu of seven starters and eight main courses as well as a selection of fantastic desserts. Licensed. Upper price range.

Maria and Walter's, 166 Rathdowne Street, Carlton, (03) 347 3328; a small restaurant which pays more attention to its food than its decor but the food is so decorative that it well and truly makes up for any surrounding drabness. Desserts are particularly good. The style is French. BYO. Upper price range but not as expensive as the previous listings.

Marchetti's Latin, 55 Lonsdale Street, Melbourne, (03) 662 1985; is an Italian institution in Melbourne, having been around with one name or another for 30 years. The dishes range from what one would expect to what one wouldn't, such as spaghetti with a sauce of squid ink. Licensed. Upper price range.

City

The city area defies the trend to restaurant streets and scatters its eating houses around, except for Chinatown in and near Little Bourke Street. Lunch is sometimes a better option than dinner as many places shut once the workers have gone home.

Gordon Place Bistro and Terrace, 24–32 Little Bourke Street, Melbourne, (03) 663 5355, has one of the city area's most charming settings in the courtyard of Gordon Place Apartments where potted palms and wrought-iron, marble-topped tables abound. You'll find the food has Italian ancestry but moves in other directions in saucing its pastas. Meat, fish, chicken and salads also available. Breakfast and lunch. Licensed. Mid price range.

McKillop Food Hall, 21 McKillop Street, Melbourne, (03) 600 0195, is one of the '57 varieties' places described above. The multitudinous stalls include French cakes and croissants, sandwiches, Turkish meat dishes, Italian and very basic Asian. Expect nothing fancy, you eat with plastic off plastic at laminex tables. Closes 6 pm. BYO. Low price range.

Asian Food Plaza, 196 Russell Street, Melbourne, (03) 663 3536; a great place to introduce yourself to Asian food since the varieties available here range from

Malaysian to Mongolian, touching on Vietnamese and Cantonese on the way. It's a big bustling place which allows mix and match eating from its wide range. BYO. Low price range.

Little Malaysia Restaurant, 26 Liverpool Street, Melbourne, (03) 662 1678, has lots of good noodle dishes and splendid curries on the mild side. Also mild is the soft pink decor and general open airiness of the place. BYO. Low price range.

Tsindos Bistrot, 100 Bourke Street, Melbourne, (03) 663 3076, is something of a fashionable institution in Melbourne which advertises itself as cooking French and Italian but is, of course, owned by a Greek and therefore has Greek specialities as well. Licensed. Upper price range.

Tsindos the Greek's Restaurant, 197 Lonsdale Street, Melbourne, (03) 663 3194, is owned by the nephew of Tsindos (see above) but is a much simpler proposition which limits itself to Greek food. Moussaka, souvlaki, octopus as well as combinations and salads are served along with seafood and daily specials. BYO. Low to mid price range.

Florin Deli, 490 Flinders Street, Melbourne, (03) 614 3466, has a blackboard menu which lists some unusual pastas such as *macaroni Genovese* and *fusilli arrabbiata* as well as more substantial offering like schnitzels and T-bone steak. There are pizzas and good seafood as well. BYO. Low to mid price range.

Sinatra's, 177 Exhibition Street, Melbourne, (03) 663 2718; don't let the Frank Sinatra movie posters lead you astray, this is a basic but good quality Italian, very convenient to the theatres with an unpretentious approach to decor and service. BYO. Low price range.

Rick's Brasserie, 412 Collins Street, Melbourne, (03) 67 2280; a slick and extra chic establishment which specialises in big salad lunches, pasta or steak if you prefer. Diners feel very elegant in the blue pastel with yellow and pink trim surroundings—nothing harsh, of course. Licensed. Low to mid price range.

The Bourke Street Deli, 75 Bourke Street, Melbourne, (03) 663 4654, is one of the best delis in the city and has the advantage of early and late hours, opening for breakfast at 7.30 am and not retiring until 1 am. The menu is wide to say the least including savoury pancakes, pastas, fish and roasts of the day, soups, steaks and ribs to name a few selections. A pre-theatre set price dinner is available from 5.30 to 7.30 pm. BYO. Low price range.

Rosati's, 95 Flinders Lane, Melbourne, (03) 654 7772; worth seeing for what has been described as 'Italian railway station' decor, ie, mosaic floor tiles, huge central bar with stools, booths and an enormously high ceiling. It's noisy and very full at peak eating times; the food is traditional Italian; pastas, chicken, veal, and the wines are expensive. Licensed. Mid price range.

Carlton

Lygon Street is the main drawcard in Carlton, Melbourne's Italian quarter and one of the city's best places to eat, but there are good restaurants in nearby streets as well. Neither is the selection limited to Italian food as the area attracts restaurateurs and diners of all persuasions.

Chenny's Chinese Bistro, 320 Lygon Street, Carlton, (03) 347 0241, is a Chinese which looks like its been done by a designer from Vogue and not to displeasing effect, either. The soft pink walls and carpet and the black lacquer furniture only add to the pleasure of excellent Chinese with an occasional touch of Malaysian. BYO. Mid price range.

Kiss At Ten, 63–73 Pelham Street, Carlton, (03) 663 3365, is near the corner of Pelham and Lygon Streets and is one of my Melbourne favourites though some will find the menu a little odd. Starters listed are likely to include sashimi, terrine or tagliatelle, main courses to range from yakitori to rabbit salad or fillet of beef. The idea is to take a little of the best from everything and it works. Light meals and good coffee also available. BYO. Mid to upper price range.

Carlton Curry House, 204 Rathdowne Street, Carlton, (03) 347 9632, is a good value and very popular place with menu highlights being vegetable dhal, beef vindaloo and a range of Indian desserts. BYO. Low price range.

Nyonya, 191 Lygon Street, Carlton, (03) 347 8511; Nyonya is, as the menu here explains, a cuisine combining Chinese and Malay elements and it's well represented here in examples like aubergine (eggplant) curry, fish cutlets in tamarind curry, marinated chicken and pork ribs. BYO. Low to mid price range.

Le Bouchon, 401 Rathdowne Street, Carlton, (03) 347 8792, is a classic French restaurant whose atmosphere is a little time-worn but whose quality of food is always reliable and thoughtful. Starters may be snails cooked in white wine and served with pastry caps and light velouté sauce or crudités with Julienne of cold pork tongue; main courses move into fish meat and casserole territory, including couscous and there are blackboard specials as well. BYO. Mid price range.

Tiamo Restaurant and Bistro, 303 Lygon Street, Carlton, (03) 347 5759, is possibly the social centre of Carlton and certainly a great place to see and feel the life that goes on there. The walls are poster-covered and the clientele is entertaining, often by profession. The food—minestrone, pastas, veals, osso bucco, etc.—is straight Italian. Breakfast is served from early morning to 11 am. BYO. Low price range.

Il Pronto, 298 Lygon Street, Carlton, (03) 347 7080; smart decor with lots of green and an air of the café about this Italian which does the standard fare plus some unexpected things like salads and quiches for light eaters. BYO. Low price range.

Café Sport, 262 Lygon Street, Carlton, (03) 347 7461; pastas are especially good at this upstairs restaurant which is an old favourite in Carlton. BYO. Mid price range.

Fitzroy

As Lygon Street is to Carlton so Brunswick Street is to Fitzroy only more, in fact, it is probably the city's most patronised strip of restaurants and offers well over 20 places to eat between Gertrude Street and Alexandra Parade.

Thai Tani, 293 Brunswick Street, Fitzroy, (03) 419 6463, captures all the delicacy and flavour of great Thai food in pleasant surroundings. The menu is wider than average for Thai and includes such items as calamari with mint salad, vegetable green curry and omelettes. Can be very busy which slows down the service. BYO. Mid price range.

Seagoing Vegetable, 304 Brunswick Street, Fitzroy, (03) 419 9206; has such an odd name because it used to specialise in vegetarian and seafood dishes but has lately expanded to include pasta and meat. The food is fresh and deliciously simple. BYO. Mid price range.

Annicks, 153 Brunswick Street, Fitzroy, (03) 419 3007; has a strong reputation among those in the 'know' as making the very best of straightforward ingredients with delicious sauces. This French leaning results in duckling with port sauce and rabbit with grain mustard appearing on the menu beside similar concoctions. The restaurant's green and white decor, linen napkins and decorative cutlery add to its attractions. BYO. Mid price range.

Middle Kingdom, 197 Smith Street, Fitzroy, (03) 417 2438, has a terrific specials menu including Cantonese style calamari—fried in batter with spices and sauces, stuffed scallop shell or stuffed quail with oyster sauce and sizzling chicken, also prepared with an oyster sauce. BYO. Mid price range.

Colmao Flamenco, 60 Johnson Street, Fitzroy, (03) 417 4131, is one of the better places in 'Little Spain' along Johnson Street. It specialises in seafood including, of course, paella and garlic prawns (shrimp) as well as sardines in vinegar. Flamenco dancing is a feature on Friday and Saturday nights. It's done in the restaurant window. BYO. Mid price range.

Café Melbourne, 135 Greeves Street, Fitzroy, (03) 417 5399; is rather more up-market than many other Fitzroy eateries and features carefully prepared home grown ingredients in romantic surroundings. BYO. Mid to upper price range.

Brunswick Street Deli, 384 Brunswick Street, Fitzroy, (03) 417 7863; offers a fairly wide selection of light food in light, airy surroundings decorated with soft colours. Salads of smoked salmon, ham or tuna, hamburgers cooked on charcoal, omelettes and interesting open sandwiches are on the menu. BYO. Low price range.

South Yarra

The eating places along Toorak Road and Chapel Street are the southern equal of those in Carlton and Fitzroy but their setting, especially that of Toorak Road, means higher prices and a more refined, sometime more pretentious, approach to food and setting. The streets cross one another so access to restaurants in both is easy.

Players, 176 Toorak Road, South Yarra, (03) 241 8377, is the kind of place that has become the symbol of eating in South Yarra—glass, chrome, metal and gloss everywhere and an eye to the young market. What's surprising is the quality and originality of the food. Breakfast on avocado and bacon omelettes or tomatoes on toast with pork sausages; lunch on an open trout sandwich or satay platter; dine on spatchcock or avocado with mustard marinated scallops. There is an original range of pasta sauces available too including *penne alla vodka*! The menus are peppered with odd 'cool' slogans which sensible eaters ignore. Licensed. Low price range.

Yarra's, 97 Toorak Road, South Yarra, (03) 266 5002, has a pretty courtyard and an uncomplicated home-cooked simplicity to the food. Seasonal menu changes assure variety and freshness but you'll find light fare in summer and filling hot lunches in the cold season. BYO. Low price range.

Tre-Galli, 34 Toorak Road, South Yarra, (03) 266 5708, offers alfresco dining in the street café manner and the food is good too, particularly pastas but the comment extends to seafood, chicken, scallopine and steaks. Summer lunch should be the preferred option here. BYO. Mid price range.

Kanpai, 569 Chapel Street, South Yarra, (03) 241 4379, is a small Japanese restaurant which offers good value in the straightforward manner of the best such places. Tofu (bean curd) dishes, deep-fried sardines, tempuras and sashimi are among the selections here. BYO. Low price range.

The Deli, 26 Toorak Road, South Yarra, (03) 266 8545, is the place for a Saturday morning breakfast of toasted bagels (the fillings are too numerous to list here) while surrounded by the chic folk of the district. Greek, pasta, bean shoot and potato salads are among the 20 or so options at lunch time. Seafood and steak from the chargrill at night. BYO. Low to mid price range.

The Greek Deli, 583 Chapel Street, South Yarra, (03) 241 3734; well, everything's a deli around here, but you'll actually find Greek food cooked on a charcoal grill in this establishment. The fare includes fish of the day, calamari, lamb on a spit, souvlaki and quails. BYO. Low to mid price range.

Fungies, 445 Toorak Road, Toorak, (03) 266 2575; a Pritikin restaurant—no fat, no sugar, no oil in the teriyaki chicken, the cabbage rolls, the seafood avocado or much else on the menu. Deli-style decor. BYO. Low price range.

There are rumoured to be around 1600 restaurants in the Melbourne metropolitan area, so this list does not even dent the world of possibilities open to the serious diner. Other suburbs to try include **Richmond** which is to Greeks what Carlton is to Italians but has also lately taken in some Vietnamese and **Prahran** into which Chapel Street extends. Pubs are not to be neglected either. Among the best are **Zanies Hotel Bistro** on the corner of Lonsdale and Russell Streets in the city, **Lord Jim's** and the **Loaded Dog**, which brews its own beer, in North Fitzroy and **The Flying Duck** in Prahran.

TOURS AND CRUISES

Australian Pacific Tours, (03) 63 1511, operates a pick up and drop bus called the City Explorer every day except Monday. It leaves from the Swanston Street side of Flinders Street Station at 10 am and you can alight at any designated stop along the route, picking up the bus again an hour later. There are seven stops including the major museums, Lygon Street and Melbourne Zoo. A ticket costs $8.

Ansett Pioneer (03) 668 2422, **Australian Pacific**, (03) 63 1511 and **AAT Kings**, (03) 666 3363 operate half-day city sightseeing tours which include many of the sights listed above. These tours take place in the afternoon and cost around $20. There are also half-day tours which include Mt Dandenong Lookout and Sherbrooke Forest but they only amount to a very cursory look indeed. They are morning tours and cost the same. Australian Pacific and AAT Kings depart from 181 Flinders Street and Ansett Pioneer from the corner of Franklin and Swanston Streets. All pick up from major hotels.

The same operators run full day tours which include a longer look at the the city and the Dandenongs, cost around $35 and depart every day. You buy your own lunch. Other options for a full day are city and Victoria Farm Shed (a tourist farm where sheep are sheared); Dandenongs and Phillip Island; Victoria Farm Shed and Phillip Island.

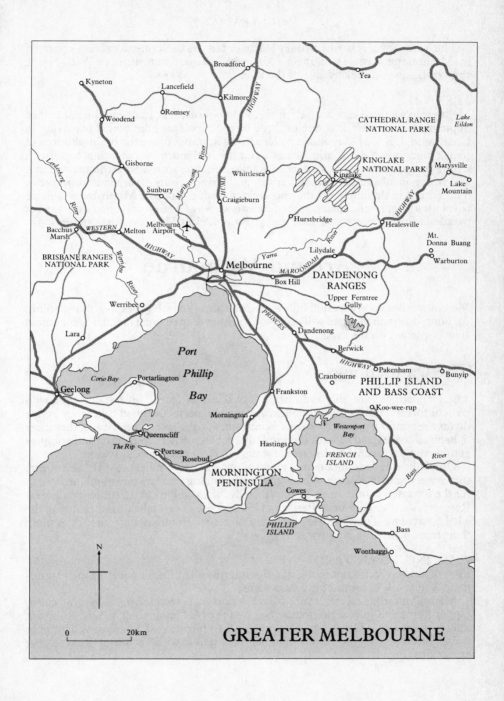

GREATER MELBOURNE

The Yarra River is hardly Sydney Harbour but you can cruise it in boats operated by **Melbourne Cruises**, (03) 63 2054, which depart from Princes Walk beside Princes Bridge on the city side of the river.

FESTIVALS
Melbourne's annual arts festival, Spoleto Melbourne, takes place in the last half of September each year. It is one of three linked 'Spoletos', the others occurring in Charleston, USA, in May and in Spoleto itself in June. All are the brain-children of Italian composer Gian Carlo Menotti and the Melbourne version puts together a strong programme of music, dance, drama, film, literature and art in mainstream and fringe involving performers, critics and writers from Australia and overseas. The accent is definitely on the the serious business of·art. **Moomba** is a more frivolous affair. It takes place in the first two weeks of March and ends with a street parade of floats, bands and marching girls on the last Monday of its celebrations.

Around Melbourne

Melbourne has cool, forested hills to the east and yellow bay beaches to the south. An hour or two on the road will carry you to either of them for a lunch by a mountain view or picnics on the sand.

The Dandenongs

The Dandenongs are hilly and lush, full of shade and steep hillsides covered with ancient forest. Discrete communities appear with perfectly timed frequency as one drives the winding mountain roads. Accustomed to the local tourist trade, they cater to its need for tea and scones; their quietly spoken retailers spill crafts and antiques gently onto pavements and roadside stalls sell roast chestnuts in season.

Officially called mountains and rising about 40 km (25 miles) east of Melbourne, they are more truly a patch of high ground, providing fine city views and bush parks for the harassed suburbanite. Ferntree Gully National Park, Mt Dandenong Forest Reserve, Sherbrooke Forest Park and Olinda State Forest take up either side of the Mt Dandenong Tourist Road, the main north–south mountain route. In autumn their trees blaze with colour.

GETTING TO AND AROUND
First of all, be careful not to mistake the suburb called Dandenong for the Dandenong Ranges. It is south of the mountains.

Metrail suburban electric trains from Flinders Street Station in Melbourne run to Upper Ferntree Gully at the southern end of the Mt Dandenong Tourist Road but not to Olinda or Mt Dandenong. Belgrave, a little further east, is also served by these trains. It is where *Puffing Billy*, a mountain steam train which is one of the area's big attractions, departs.

Drivers can get to the Mt Dandenong Tourist Road (Metropolitan Route 22) from the south via Upper Ferntree Gully on the Burwood Highway or from the north via Ringwood on the Maroondah Highway. The trip takes about 40 minutes either way.

Bicycles can be hired at **Healesville Bike Hire**, 297 Maroondah Highway, Healesville, (059) 62 5198.

TOURIST INFORMATION
Since the area is really part of Melbourne, it tends to be dealt with by the information outlets in the city.

Mt Dandenong Tourist Road
Driving this road is the best way to enjoy the greenery and coolness of the Dandenongs if your time is short. It winds serpent-like between Upper Ferntree Gully and Montrose through forests of tall eucalypts. It gives access to similarly pretty sights on Sherbrooke Road and Basin–Olinda Road as well as running through the mountain centres of Sassafras, Olinda and Mt Dandenong to the Mt Dandenong Lookout.

Puffing Billy
Puffing Billy is a steam train service which runs on a narrow gauge line from Belgrave to Lakeside via Menzies Creek. A relic of the early 1900s when four such railways were constructed as an experiment in rural development, Puffing Billy, actually three trains working to a schedule, winds 13 km (eight miles) through thick bush and over an old wooden trestle bridge to finish beside Emerald Lake. There are intermediate stations at Menzies Creek and in the small town of Emerald. During most weekdays there is only one run per day, leaving Belgrave at 10.30 am. At weekends and throughout school holidays there are usually four trips a day between 10.30 am and 2.50 pm. The complete round trip takes about two hours. Things to see along the way include a steam museum at Menzies Creek (open Sunday 11 am to 5 pm) and a model railway with over 2000 metres of track at Lakeside Station. Emerald Lake Park where the journey ends is blighted with the presence of two huge waterslides and a rapacious approach to tourism. Paddle boats are available on the lake. The return fare from Belgrave to Lakeside is $8.20 and current timetable information is available on (03) 870 8411.

Sassafras and Olinda

These towns are in the middle of the range. They typify the craft shop and tea rooms mentality but their well-watered, temperate climate has lent itself willingly to the establishment of English-style gardens such as the **Australian Rhododendron Gardens** in The Georgian Road, Olinda and the **R. J. Hamer Arboretum** off Woolrich Road, Olinda. Both gardens are part of Olinda State Forest which covers 716 hectares (1719 acres) in all and is crossed with walking trails through mountain vistas.

William Ricketts Sanctuary
William Ricketts has reached legendary status in Australia. He and his sanctuary,

which is filled with sculptures inspired by Aboriginal myths, have been the subject of documentary films here and overseas. Although he is an old man, he continues to live and work in the sanctuary set beside the Mt Dandenong Tourist Road, on the slopes of Mt Dandenong. His sculptures stand in ferny grottoes set beside winding tracks on the forested mountainside. They are idealised representations of Aboriginal women, children and elders joined with the rocks and trees of the surrounding bush and endeavouring to depict *Pmara Kutata*, the everlasting home and universal soul of Aboriginal belief, as understood by Ricketts. The sculptor appears in his work, protected by spiritualised Aboriginal friends. Although the overall effect is rather contrived, repetitive and static, much of it looking like sentimentalised Aboriginals as William Blake might have drawn them (lots of swirling beards), the execution is skilful and the setting superb. Open 10 am to 4.30 pm every day. Admission free.

Mt Dandenong Lookout
The lookout is placed underneath the television towers on Mt Dandenong, the highest point in the vicinity of Melbourne. It is a fairly generous area as lookouts go and on a clear day Melbourne spreads out like a toyland, its skyscrapers and suburbs down to Port Phillip Bay.

Healesville

Healesville is a little over 30 km (19 miles) from Mt Dandenong on the Maroondah Highway in the foothills of the Great Dividing Range. The distance is worth travelling to see the **Healesville Sanctuary** where Australian native animals are kept in a bushland setting. Open range marsupials such as kangaroos and wallabies live in wide natural enclosures and birds including the rarely seen lyrebird, are numerous. A number of special enclosures and houses allow visitors to see nocturnal animals such as Tasmanian Devils (open 10.30 am to 4 pm) and reptiles (open to 4.30 pm) and there is a glass-sided tank where a platypus appears from 1.30 pm to 3.30 pm each day. The sanctuary opens at 9 am and closes at 5 pm each day. Entry cost $5.30.

WHERE TO STAY
The short distance between the Dandenongs and Melbourne means that accommodation is relatively scarce but one gem makes up for the lack of a string of motels. **Burnham Beeches**, Sherbrooke Road, Sherbrooke, (03) 755 1903, is one of the best country house hotels in Australia. It occupies a mansion once home to the Nicholas family who made their fortune from analgesic pills called Aspro. The house, constructed in the 1930s, is a prime example of Art Deco domestic architecture and the addition of extra guest accommodation has been achieved with extraordinary sympathy for the original design. It stands in 56 acres of landscaped grounds and rooms vary from standard doubles to doubles with lounges and larger suites. The Burnham Beeches restaurant enjoys a reputation throughout Australia for the excellence and style of its French cuisine. Children under 12 years old are not permitted as guests. $155 to $425 room only.

Sanctuary House Motel, Badger Creek Road, Healesville, (059) 62 5148, is off the highway at Healesville and has medium standard motel rooms and a BYO dining room. Single $73, double $46 bed and breakfast.

Strathvea, Myers Creek Road, Healesville, (059) 62 4109; at one time there were over 50 guesthouses in the Healesville area. This is one of the few still operating. It is surrounded by beautiful gardens and mountain views and the accommodation is comfortable, some rooms having ensuite bathrooms. The dining room serves fresh country food and is open to casual diners. Single from $70, double from $110 dinner, bed and breakfast. Restaurant is BYO and mid price range.

EATING OUT

Lunch and afternoon tea in the Dandenongs are something of a Melbourne tradition. The number of restaurants is not huge but the standard is excellent in the best places. Tea rooms abound in the mountain towns.

Burnham Beeches, Sherbrooke Road, Sherbrooke, (03) 755 1903; the restaurant in this hotel, the best in the Dandenongs, is open to the public as well as house guests. The cooking is French influenced, including some startling delicacies such as sage leaf fritters with tomato sauce. Afternoon teas also available. Reservations are essential. Licensed. Upper price range.

Kenloch Restaurant, Mt Dandenong Tourist Road, Olinda, (03) 751 1008; is another old mansion, though somewhat more eccentric than Burnham Beeches. It is surrounded by nine acres of gardens with fountains and hedges so you lunch with a very pleasing prospect on uncomplicated food from an international menu. Licensed. Mid to upper price range.

Olinda Chalet Restaurant, 543 Mt Dandenong Tourist Road, Olinda, (03) 751 1844; is a small restaurant whose menu changes every two months but is always good eating. Past menu items have included terrine of scallops, roulade of lamb with rosemary; home made ice cream is usually among the desserts. BYO. Mid to upper price range.

TOURS

Many of the day and half day coach tours listed for Melbourne include the Dandenongs because they are so close to the city. One of the best itineraries includes a ride on Puffing Billy and a visit to Healesville Sanctuary. It is available from AAT Kings and Australian Pacific for around $50.

Mornington Peninsula

The Mornington Peninsula occupies the eastern shore of Port Phillip Bay and the western shore of Westernport Bay. It swings in an almost semi-circular arc from **Frankston**, 40 km (25 miles) south of Melbourne to **Portsea** near the narrow entrance to Port Phillip called The Rip. Narrow, yellow, calm-watered beaches called 'front' beaches face north into the bay all along this coastal strip and draw big crowds in summer. Less crowded are the 'back' beaches on the southern side of the narrow peninsula tip where Cape Schanck Coastal Park protects some wilder surfing spots.

GETTING TO AND AROUND

Trains run from Flinders Street Station in Melbourne to Frankston from where buses depart regularly to Portsea. There is also a hovercraft service which connects Port Melbourne and Frankston. Phone (03) 781 2766 for bookings. The hovercraft fare is $8. The Nepean Highway (Metropolitan Route 3) joins Melbourne to the peninsula along Port Phillip Bay. The distance from Melbourne to Portsea is close to 100 km (62 miles).

TOURIST INFORMATION

Tourist information is obtainable at Australian Colonial Travel, 54 Playne Street, Frankston, and also at Dromana, halfway between Frankston and Portsea. Walkers contemplating the trails in the coastal park should contact the National Parks and Wildlife Service in Melbourne and ask for its brochure on the peninsula. Phone (03) 651 4011.

Beaches

The beaches of Mornington Peninsula offer safe swimming, some surfing and have their share of rugged beauty, especially along the shore of Cape Schanck Coastal Park. The 'front' beaches are narrow fringes of creamy sand occasionally broken by low scrubby heads and short stretches of steep sand hills. Their gentle waves are popular with families and boardsailors (windsurfers) who make a colourful and busy scene on hot weekends. A wide highway, stacked with sun-bleached houses and take-away food shops runs close to many of them. The 'back' beaches, particularly those along the margin of the park, can be extremely rocky with broad platforms exposed beneath low cliffs when the tide is out. They are often dangerous, indeed, it was at Cheviot Beach on the end of the peninsula that Harold Holt, Australian Prime Minister, was drowned in 1967. His body has never been found. Around Frankston sunbathers will find themselves lying within sight and earshot of the passing traffic, but around Mornington and Mt Martha the highway dips inland and leaves the beaches a little more secluded, although this hardly prevents the summer hordes reaching them. The back beaches are easiest to reach at Sorrento and Portsea at the narrow end of the peninsula. A connected series of walking tracks called the Peninsula Coastal Walk has been developed from Portsea to Cape Schanck. It covers 30 km through the shoreline park and is sometimes cut by high tides. To traverse the full distance takes about 12 hours but the track can be easily reached at various points. Maps are available from the National Parks and Wildlife Service.

Colonial Houses

Ballam Park, in Cranbourne Road, is the headquarters of the Frankston Historical Society. It was one of the area's first brick homes, built in 1850 by Wilburham Liardet, a local farmer who was living well for his time. The two-storey, green and white country house has a pretty garden and 64 acres of gardens where picnics and barbecues are encouraged. A museum in the grounds contains photographs and records of Mornington Peninsula's past. There is also a vehicle museum and blacksmith's shop on the premises. Open Sunday 2 pm to 5 pm. Admission $1. **Sage's Cottage**, Sages Road, Baxter, about six km (four miles) from Frankston, was the home of John Edward Sage who managed Carrup-Carrup, a 15,000-acre property on the peninsula during the 1840s and '50s. He came from Sydney in 1840 and married his employer's daughter, Maria Baxter, in 1853, also building the cottage in that year. It is a classic Australian weatherboard farm cottage with a low pitched roof and a veranda at the front. Its wide grounds include an orchard and herb garden. Open 10 am to 4 pm daily in summer, Friday, Saturday and Sunday in winter. Two other colonial houses worth seeing are **McRae Homestead** on the slopes of Arthur's Seat near Dromana and **Cooltart** on Sandy Point Road, Balnarring.

Dromana

Arthur's Seat is a quaintly named peak above Dromana from whose apex you can see the whole peninsula. A chairlift runs up the face of the mountain but only operates during summer holidays and on weekends.

Sorrento

Sorrento has the distinction of being the first place settled in Victoria. A party arrived from England in 1803 believing that their presence would forestall the French who were nosing around Australia's southern foreshores at the time. Due to lack of water, the settlement lasted less than a year and all that remains of the attempt is a pioneer memorial and cemetery at Sullivan Bay. The settlers moved on to Hobart but one among them, John Pascoe Fawkner, only 11 years old at the time, returned 25 years later as one of the first settlers of Melbourne. Later history, including the great paddle steamers which used to carry thousands of passengers from Melbourne to the peninsula during the late nineteenth and early twentieth century, is displayed in the **Mechanics Institute Building** in Old Melbourne Road.

WHERE TO STAY
Since the peninsula is a prominent holiday location places to stay are not hard to come by, except of course in peak holiday time around Christmas and Easter each year when long advance booking is necessary.
Ambassador Motor Inn, 325–331 Nepean Highway, Frankston, (03) 781 4488; may be the only motel in Australia which features stained glass windows in its reception area but does offer a good range of accommodation from standard motel rooms to two-bedroom apartments and 'penthouse' suites. Standard $65, apartments $90, penthouse $155 to $225.
Frankston Colonial Motor Inn, 406 Nepean Highway, Frankston, (03) 781 5544; lots of dark furniture and turned wood here in keeping with the 'colonial' idea and the rooms have plenty of natural light which is unusual in motels. Also a good range of facilities including guest laundry and a place to wash your car. Single $44, double $50.

EATING OUT
Pettifoggers, 40 Playne Street, Frankston, (03) 783 1541; is a restaurant with no pretensions about appearance—plastic tablecloths and rough chairs but the food, especially salads and fish, is excellent. BYO. Mid price range.

Checkers, 42 Lochiel Avenue, Mt Martha, (059) 74 2733; is a stylish place with an international menu tending to sauced seafood and pasta. Licensed. Mid to upper price range. There is a deli next door serving lunches.

Knockers, 182 Ocean Beach Road, Sorrento, (059) 84 1246; is a bustling restaurant serving straightforward char-grilled steaks and fish from a blackboard menu which changes each day. BYO. Mid price range.

Phillip Island

This island stands at the mouth of Westernport Bay, 128 km (79 miles) south-east of Melbourne. A **penguin parade,** the best attended tourist attraction in Victoria, occurs there nightly but the island is also a summer resort favoured by Melbourne's millions. Beaches are the best within easy distance of the city and the atmosphere is 'away-from-it-all'. Cowes, on the north side of the island where the ferries land, is the main town. The penguin parade takes place at Summerland Beach near the south-west corner. There are protected beaches on the north shore and surf beaches on the south shore.

GETTING TO AND AROUND
The public transport journey from Melbourne to Phillip Island is a three stage affair. Train from Melbourne (Flinders Street Station) to Frankston, bus from Frankston to Stony Point on Westernport Bay and ferry to Cowes on the northern side of the island. Ferry times vary considerably between winter and summer. For information phone (059) 52 1014. The one way fare is about $5 and the entire trip from Melbourne takes around two and a half hours. Anyone going merely for the penguin parade can take the 5 pm bus from Dandenong railway station which travels down the east side of Westernport Bay to Newhaven via the bridge which links Phillip Island to the mainland at San Remo. Drivers should take the same route, that is, the South Gippsland and Bass Highways.

TOURIST INFORMATION
The island has information centres at its main entry points, 71 Thompson Avenue, Cowes, and in Phillip Island Road, Newhaven. Phone (059) 56 7447.

Penguin Parade
A large colony of fairy penguins lives in burrows on Summerland Beach in the island's south-west. Its adult members fish each day and come home just after sunset to feed the chicks and rest. Their homecoming is a spectacle witnessed by thousands of humans, to a man overcome with its cuteness. The tiny dinner-suited creatures struggle heroically through the surf and waddle comically up the beach, oblivious to the storm of spotlights and appreciative sighs which greets them. The parade is best seen in summer with the breeding season in full swing and penguins

present in hordes. The winter is so bleak that Melbourne hotels, on hearing their guests are taking a tour to the parade, have been known to issue blankets. Certain rules do contain the tourist horde, among them, no getting in the penguin's way and no flash photography.

Other animals
Kingston Gardens Zoo, Tourist Road, Cowes, is a 5-hectare (12-acre) collection of Australian native fauna along with the kind of farm animals that children love. Open 8.30 am to 6 pm daily, admission $3. Thousands of fur seals inhabit **The Nobbies**, a group of rocks off Grand Point, the extreme south-west tip of the island. You can't get out to them but they can be observed with binoculars. Also at Grand Point is a blowhole which really shoots when the seas are high. Mutton birds make an annual migration to the island in spring from Japan and Alaska, taking up residence in established rookeries around Cape Woolamai on the south-east tip of Phillip Island until April. The same cape has a walking track through rugged territory right out to its end.

EATING OUT
Restaurants in Cowes tend to gear themselves to the Penguin Parade, opening both before and after to catch late and early diners. Seafood is the rule which is hardly unexpected.
The Jetty Restaurant, The Esplanade, Cowes, (059) 52 2100; a seafood specialist residing in a brick, stone and timber building with high ceilings, lots of exposed surfaces and potted palms. Has an open fireplace and bay views from some tables. Licensed. Upper price range.
Hollydene Restaurant, 114 Thompson Avenue, Cowes, (059) 52 2311; seafood too but offers a children's menu if you're travelling with the rug rats. Licensed. Mid price range.
Shearwater Restaurant, Lot 5, Phillip Island Road, Cowes, (059) 56 7371, is an attractive bluestone building set close to a mutton bird rookery on the south side of the island. Straightforward menu includes steak, fish and lobster but the real drawcard is the setting. BYO. Mid price range.

TOURS
AAT Kings and Australian Pacific coach tours to Phillip Island go for the Penguin Parade and so don't arrive back in Melbourne until late at night, usually around 10.30 pm or 11.30 pm during daylight saving. Most leave in the afternoon around 2 pm but some are full day tours which include the Dandenongs. They cost around $50 for the parade only option, dinner not included.

West of Melbourne

Melbourne's west is basically a run of unattractive suburbs but a couple of features outside the suburban sprawl are worth seeing if you are a long term visitor to the city.

Hanging Rock
This mysterious pile of stone columns, extruded from the earth in a long past age

and now jutting from surrounding flats like a ruined Tower of Babel, was the setting for *Picnic at Hanging Rock*, Joan Lindsay's novel which became the first notable success of Australia's new film industry. In the story, a group of schoolgirls picnicking at the rock disappears under unexplained and perhaps unnatural circumstances. One re-appears just as mysteriously three days later unable or unwilling to explain the episode. Any visitor will attest to the surreal and disturbing atmosphere of the place, especially at dusk when the grey, riven columns cast long shadows on the plain but the views from its top are worth clambering for and daytime picnics around it are very popular. Fine views are also to be had from nearby **Mt Macedon**, a 1013-metre (3323-foot) extinct volcano.

Kyneton and Malmsbury

These little towns lie in granite country on the Calder Highway beyond Mt Macedon. The grazing land surrounding them is broken by outcrops and boulders of blue-grey stone and many old homesteads, barns, mills and town buildings have been built of it. Known as bluestone, it is unique to the area and the massive buildings constructed of it are unlike those anywhere elsewhere in Victoria. Some in Kyneton have been restored but the most dramatic, often still occupied, are to be seen in the open countryside.

The Great Ocean Road

The Great Ocean Road passes through some of the most extraordinary, beautiful and startling landscapes in Australia. Its western section is unsurpassed for dramatic coastal scenery but there is hardly a boring moment on the whole 300-km (186-mile) journey from Torquay to Warrnambool. Summer resort towns where you can go surfing and walking scatter its length, dominated by a wild and undeveloped coastline to which the road defiantly clings, winding around seemingly innumerable headlands or climbing the hills of Cape Otway.

GETTING THERE
Driving is the only option. The road is reached via Geelong, a large town 75 km (46 miles) from Melbourne on the western side of Port Phillip Bay which can be safely ignored by the tourist. Torquay lies 40 km (25 miles) south of it.

Torquay to Apollo Bay

Torquay, Anglesea, Lorne and Apollo Bay are the main resort towns between the beginning of the Great Ocean Road and the point where it turns inland to cross Cape Otway. Each has an east-facing beach which catches the Bass Strait surf, the most famous being Bells Beach near Torquay where the Australian Surfing Championships take place each Easter holidays. The road in this section clings to hills that plunge steeply down to the ocean; it twists in and out of small bays, over the mouths

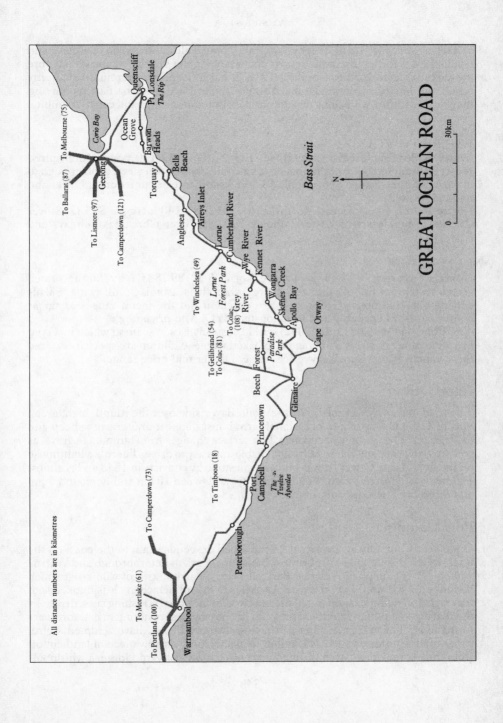

GREAT OCEAN ROAD

All distance numbers are in kilometres

To Portland (100)
To Camperdown (73)
To Mortlake (61)
Warrnambool
Peterborough
To Timboon (18)
Port Campbell
The Twelve Apostles
Princetown
Beech Forest
Glenaire
Paradise Park
To Colac (81)
To Gellibrand (54)
To Colac (108)
Grey River
Lorne Forest Park
To Winchelsea (49)
Cape Otway
Apollo Bay
Skénes Creek
Wongarra
Kennet River
Wye River
Cumberland River
Lorne
Aireys Inlet
Anglesea
Bells Beach
Torquay
To Camperdown (121)
To Lismore (97)
To Ballarat (87)
Geelong
To Melbourne (75)
Corio Bay
Ocean Grove
Barwon Heads
Queenscliff
Pt. Lonsdale
The Rip

Bass Strait

N

0   30km

of creeks and past small beaches. **Lorne,** about halfway between Torquay and Apollo Bay, is the largest of the resorts and was a popular seaside escape even before the Great Ocean Road was built in 1932. It has a deep, semi-circular bay, pretty beach and lots of accommodation. Around Apollo Bay, the coast flattens out and there are beautiful, wide, long beaches backed by feminine hills and caressed by blue green surf.

WHERE TO STAY
Motel Kalimna, Great Ocean Road, Lorne, (052) 89 1407; is an uninspired red-brick building but front rooms have balconies with ocean views good enough to make you forget. Single $46, double $55. $15 surcharge per unit during Easter and on long weekends.
Lorne Hotel, Great Ocean Road, Lorne, (052) 89 1409; Single $35 ($48 over Christmas holidays and Easter), double $40 ($55 over Christmas holidays and Easter).

EATING OUT
Kosta's Taverna, 48 Mountjoy Parade, Lorne, (052) 89 1883; is a wildly decorated Greek restaurant full of noise and energy when the season is in full swing. Salads and dips in traditional Greek style are excellent but the menu ranges as far as Moroccan lamb casserole and local lobster. BYO. Mid price range.
The Pier, on the Pier, Lorne, (052) 89 1119; specialises in seafood which is served in a wide range of styles from ragout to baked whole. Children are specially catered for at lunch. BYO. Lunch low price range. Dinner mid price range.

Cape Otway

The road makes its way inland from Apollo Bay, rising over the round, high, green hills of Cape Otway where occasional farm houses appear and grazing sheep and cattle seem to be the only occupants. The surface changes from bitumen to gravel as you cross the cape but the road is still reliable and easy to drive. There is a lighthouse on the tip of Cape Otway. It was built of limestone by convicts in 1848 and is almost 100 metres (333 feet) high. You'll find it open between 10 am and noon and 2 pm and 4 pm on Tuesdays and Thursdays.

Port Campbell

Once over Cape Otway the Great Ocean Road descends again to the coast on the final stretch through the Port Campbell National Park to Peterborough and Warrnambool. Port Campbell National Park takes up a narrow strip of wild coast which includes the extraordinary **Twelve Apostles,** a line of detached cliffs hundreds of feet high and rising straight out of the sea close to the coast. Crashing seas, driven by the roaring forties have cut them off from the nearby land resulting in extraordinary formations. The waves, boiling a dizzying distance below, have sculpted weird, gargantuan landforms such as London Bridge, a long, narrow piece of land cut off from the shore with an arch through its centre, and Loch Ard Gorge, a whirlpool-like hole cut deep into the cliffs and named for a migrant ship wrecked there in 1878. Only two people survived the disaster. Some of the 48 dead, including entire families, are buried in a small cemetery nearby. Port Campbell is the only town in the national park which bears its name. It is located on yet another teetering sea gorge. There are walking trails on the wild coast and the hills around the town.

Warrnambool

The Great Ocean Road ceases to be a scenic route at Peterborough and heads off to join the Princes Highway just outside Warrnambool. This medium-sized town has a beach too, protected by a big stone breakwater near which it is long and narrow but becoming wider as it stretches away. Late last century, the town accommodated a primitive naval base designed to ward off, of all things, a Russian invasion. The invasion never came and the base is now a maritime museum, located near the lighthouse on Flagstaff Hill. Its old weatherboard buildings and the ships tied up by them are open from 9.30 am to 4.30 pm daily.

WHERE TO STAY
Warrnambool is probably as far as you will get in a day. It has lots of motels due to its cachet as a summer resort. The journey can be broken at Lorne as well.
Tudor Motor Inn, 519 Raglan Parade, Warrnambool, (055) 62 8877; newish, average standard motel decked out in mock tudor fashion. Has a restaurant which specialises in seafood. Single $43, double $50. Surcharges up to $10 per unit during Christmas holidays, at Easter and on long weekends.
Timbertop Motel, 349 Raglan Parade, Warrnambool, (055) 62 2755; slightly lower standard than the above but still OK. Also has a seafood restaurant which is BYO. Single $36, double $42.

EATING OUT
Coterie Restaurant, 72 Liebig Street, Warrnambool, (055) 62 3714; a French-style restaurant serving steaks, pork, duck and quail with the expected sauces plus fresh seafood. BYO. Mid price range.
Samessa Bistro, 62 Liebig Street, Warrnambool, (055) 62 4208; excellent steaks here on a straight menu which also includes turkey breast marsala, roast duckling and beef curry. Fresh fish and lobster are served when available. The restaurant is housed in a generous double-fronted shop. BYO. Mid price range.

The Victorian Gold Fields

Gold, the lust for it and the adventure of its acquiring brought fantastic wealth, violent conflict and huge population to central Victoria in the 1850s. The towns of Ballarat and Bendigo were made by it. Beginning as filthy, rowdy, lawless camps full of refugees from the failed Californian fields, they became elegant cities designed by men of vision with gardens in their streets, parks full of statuary, admirable public buildings and permanent populations of skilled Cornishmen, housed in neat white cottages.

Both fields produced vast quantities of gold, financing Melbourne's growth and never following the swift decline so many other gold towns suffered.

Ballarat

Before gold was discovered in 1851, Ballarat was a sleepy pastoral spot, sparsely settled and dull. The wave destined to engulf it began haltingly. In mid 1851, small finds were made north and south of the real wealth. In August, sheltering from a mid-winter storm, prospecting mates John Dunlop and James Regan hid under a stand of trees at Ballarat itself. As rain poured down, pecking the ground at their feet they saw the first gold of that legendary field. News spread fast but the diggers were fickle. By September 1000 hopefuls worked the field; by December, fired by rumours from elsewhere, most were gone. Only the hardy stayers won a just reward and soon Melbourne heard of Ballarat.

Shops emptied of their staff, businesses lost their clerks, farms hands and owners left the harvest. 'Gold in the Streets' the papers said and soon the world rushed in. On the tented field, no one could count their numbers but 60,000 during the fever's height is a good estimate. The luckiest made fortunes—one party fossicking 3000 ounces in three days—but most were disappointed, many turned away from the hideous squalor without raising a shovel.

Alluvial gold, easily dug and sluiced, was rapidly consumed. Miners worked longer and deeper for less but staggering finds went on among the buried river beds and golden reefs under the earth. As mines spread west and south beneath the town, the newly rich—miners, storekeepers and publicans—formed companies to tunnel in ways impossible for individual men. Diggers in need of a crust became their workers. Foundries and engineering workshops opened up to feed the big mines' appetite for huge steam-driven machinery and ten years after the rush began the railway came to Ballarat making it western Victoria's railhead. A base for the future was established but the romance was gone.

Ballarat's last gold mine closed in 1918. It is impossible to calculate the value of the field with accuracy as much of the early gold went unrecorded but if only that offically accounted for were loaded onto ten-ton trucks, it would take 63 of them to carry it.

The Eureka Stockade

The events at Eureka on the Ballarat gold fields in late 1854 are the closest Australia has ever come to a revolution. A gaggle of miners' grievances led to a small revolt which came to a bloody and unsuccessful end on 3 December of that year. Mining licences were the main upset. Diggers were required to buy a licence, fee three pounds a month, a sum beyond the means of many and beyond the willingness of all. The police and magistrates enforcing licences were corrupt, lazy, vindictive, discriminatory and often drunk. That many were retired English army men with a special dislike for Irish miners did not help the situation and it was further compli-cated by blind officialdom in Melbourne which kept raising the cost of licences and refusing to hear protests.

In October 1854, a miner named Scobie was murdered near the Eureka Hotel. The publican of that establishment was tried and acquitted of the killing but the magistrate, the publican's bosom friend, was accused of acting corruptly. The diggers burned down the pub. Arrests followed and tempers all round were about to blow. On 25 November, those arrested for the arson were convicted and a local newspaper, *The Ballarat Times*, openly espoused a miners' revolt. The ugly situation caused the government to surround the police compound with troops.

Events got thoroughly out of hand when on 28 November, the police conducted a licence 'hunt' and made more arrests. Miners met at Bakery Hill and elected a fiery Irishman called Peter Lalor as their leader. They hoisted a flag representing the Southern Cross which had been designed by one of their number, actually an American, and erected a primitive stockade at Eureka where they armed themselves for a showdown with the police and the military. They were attacked on the morning of 3 December and suffered a quick and ignominious defeat despite acts of personal bravery. Some soldiers acted brutally but some were heroic. The licensing law was eventually revoked and the whole system abandoned, and Peter Lalor went on to become a prominent conservative citizen of Ballarat, entering State Parliament a quarter of a century later. The Southern Cross flag lives on as a lasting reminder of one of the few armed conflicts between officialdom and the people in Australian history. It has been adopted by those who would see Australia a republic and not a nation titularly headed by the Queen of England.

GETTING TO AND AROUND

Ballarat is 112 km (69 miles) almost due west of Melbourne.

Trains run from Spencer Street Station in Melbourne to Ballarat on a trip taking about two hours. There are six services a day during the week, less at weekends. Economy fare $8.40.

Greyhound and Ansett Pioneer coaches on their way from Melbourne to Adel-aide stop in Ballarat. The fare is around $12 and the trip takes about two and a half hours.

Drivers can reach Ballarat in close to an hour and a half along the Western Freeway from Melbourne.

TOURIST INFORMATION

The gold fields region is well organised for tourism. Its Ballarat office is at 202 Lydiard Street, North Ballarat, just across the railway line overlooking Ballarat Railway Station. It has a vast number of publications on the area and very helpful staff. Hours are 9 am to 5 pm Monday to Friday and 10 am to 3 pm on weekends.

For information about transport to Ballarat, phone (03) 619 1500.

The Town

Ballarat's town centre is not very large. It has an imposing main street, **Sturt Street**, divided by a median strip wide enough to accommodate substantial shady trees and a decorative bandstand called the Titanic Memorial Rotunda. The street is flanked with buildings from the late nineteenth century as well as more recent structures reflecting the contemporary life of the town. There are many lace verandas and the whole makes a standing catalogue of the popular public building styles Australia has inherited from Europe. The equally interesting Lydiard Street crosses Sturt near the **Bridge Street Mall**.

Ballarat Fine Art Gallery, 40 Lydiard Street, is the oldest regional art gallery in Australia and one of the best. It was established in 1884 although its present building was constructed in 1887 and extended in 1987. From the first, the gallery collected Australian paintings and now has one of the best collections of work from the late colonial and early Federation periods anywhere in the country. They combine to show how European romantic and impressionist painting, in the hands of migrant and Australian born artists, gradually adjusted itself to depicting the harsh and challenging Australian landscape and followed the progress of exploration from temperate south-eastern coastal regions to the hot deserts. Domestic scenes and genre paintings also move from European domination to the nationalism of the 1890s. Artists to look for in this collection include the Viennese Von Geurard, the Swiss Bouvelot and Chevalier, and the Englishmen Clark, Eustace, Prout and Gritten who were the first generation to come to grips with the landscape. They were followed by names now better known in Australia such as Long, McCubbin, Roberts and Streeton whose work is also represented. These later painters show a new capacity to deal with the intensity of Australian light, aided in part by their trips to the salons of Paris. Indeed, the first and last of the quartet eventually chose to stay there. Other items of interest in the Ballarat Gallery include a large print collection dating from Cook's voyage to the present day and the original Eureka flag, now somewhat tatty, but the centre-piece of an historical exhibit on the gold fields in which the lively watercolour cartoons of S. T. Gill are well represented. The gallery is open 10 am to 4 pm. Admission around $2.

Ballarat is was also endowed by its thoughtful early citizens with a **Botanic Gardens** and an ornamental lake called **Lake Wendouree**. They lie on either side of Hamilton Avenue off the western end of Sturt Street. The lake, once a swamp, is small with gently sloping grassy banks and shady trees at its margin, a haven for water birds, picnickers, cyclists and rowers and was the venue for rowing events at the 1956 Olympic Games. The gardens were commenced in 1858 as the result of a town competition over what to do with a horse paddock. Aside from providing a swathe of delightful greenery, they are something of a Victorian sculpture gallery thanks to two immensely wealthy miners, James Thompson and Thomas Stoddard. Thompson was a Glasgow Post Office clerk who came to the diggings unskilled in manual work but went on to earn himself a reputation and a fortune as an expert in the most dangerous kinds of mining in loose ground and wet sand drifts. His collection is housed in a statuary and includes an extravagant piece called 'Flight from Pompeii'. Stoddard donated 12 statues to the city on the occasion of Queen Victoria's birthday in 1884. They stand outdoors among the trees and flowers.

Other town attractions include **Montrose Cottage**, an old miner's dwelling furnished in period, and the cottage once lived in by poet Adam Lindsay Gordon which stands on the shores of Lake Wendouree.

Sovereign Hill

Many people come to Ballarat with the sole purpose of seeing Sovereign Hill. The hill, overlooking Ballarat's once golden mile, is a re-creation of the town as it was during the 1860s. It was constructed in the 1970s by a group of Ballarat businessmen with help from people who retained skills and knowledge from gold mining days. They used period drawings and plans for the layout and buildings of the town. The success of the project can hardly be overstated and has exceeded all expectations. Sovereign Hill works—that is to say every store, workshop, foundry, steam powerhouse, stable and battery is fully operational. Nearly all items sold from the bakery and the sweet shop to the metal shop are made on site. Coaches and drays work the main street and even the school, set up in 1860s fashion, is in use. Students from around the state visit once a year for a week of nineteenth-century education complete with uniforms of the period.

About half the fascination of Sovereign Hill resides in the original steam engines, many made in Ballarat between 1880 and 1914, providing power for the complex. These gleaming emerald green and brass machines power belt-driven lathes in the metal foundry and woodworking shop, drive the huge pump which drags water from the hill's mine shaft and operate the crushing battery at regular intervals throughout the day. On the lower side of the hill, below the street of retailers and workshops, are examples of the tents and rough houses in which miners lived on the diggings, and a small Chinese quarter complete with temple and apothecary's shop. The government camp, a part reconstruction of the 1857 original in the Ballarat gold fields, stands on top of the hill overlooking the entire scene. Sovereign Hill also extends underground. Conducted mine tours, somewhat sanitised compared to the reality, but interesting none the less, are part of the price of your ticket. The complex is open every day from 9 am to 5 pm. Admission $8.

Gold Museum

This stands opposite Sovereign Hill in a low modern concrete building. It has two sections, one devoted to the story of gold and the other recording the social history of Ballarat. The first will be of interest to people who find gold fascinating in itself. It contains examples of the various natural manifestations of the mineral on the gold fields and delves into the history of its use for ornament and coinage. Its layout is confusing, jumping from one subject to another in seemingly random fashion. The social museum provides an interesting record of how ordinary people lived during Ballarat's heyday. It also has displays about the Aboriginals who inhabited the area before white settlement. Open 10 am to 5 pm. Admission $1.50.

WHERE TO STAY

Ballarat is within easy driving distance of Melbourne so that many travellers treat it as a day trip but it also has plenty of accommodation for overnight or longer stays.
Bakery Hill Motel, 1 Humffray Street, Ballarat, (053) 33 1363, is a new motel located close to the end of Bridge Street Mall. Single $41, double $47.
Lake Terrace Motel Apartments, 20 Wendouree Parade, Ballarat, (053) 32 1812, is an undistinguished three-storey brick building containing one- and two-bedroom apartments, quite pleasingly decorated, with kitchens. Some apartments overlook Lake Wendouree. Single $45, double $50.

Mid-City Motor Inn, 19 Doveton Street North, Ballarat, (053) 31 1222, also has a good location just off Sturt Street but is now one of the older motels in Ballarat. Single $41, double $49.

Craig's Royal Hotel, 10 Lydiard Street, Ballarat, (053) 31 1377; one of the older hotels in Ballarat, most rooms with hot and cold water but share bathrooms. Single $26, double $37 includes breakfast.

Mt Buninyong Homestead Lodge, Midland Highway, Ballarat, (053) 41 3001, is outside the town on 10 acres and has country views. All rooms with private facilities. Single $32, double $38.

EATING OUT

Taste of Life Café, 24 Doveton Street South, Ballarat, (053) 33 2788, is quite an unexpected restaurant for Ballarat. It is housed in an attractive two-storey residence with iron lace around its veranda, set in an English country-style garden but the food is the main interest. Food writer Julie Stafford, who specialises in low-cholesterol, low-fat, sugar-free, salt-free food and whose cookery book *A Taste of Life* is one of the most successful ever published in Australia, is involved in the restaurant which specialises in preparing her recipes. Don't be fooled into thinking the dishes are boring: they include rare peppered beef, turkey buffee, terrines and patés as well as delicious cakes and slices. BYO. Mid price range.

The Crossing, 206 Burbank Street, Ballarat, (053) 39 1439; a small restaurant set in a 100-year-old brick butcher's shop although the decor has long left the butchering days behind. There's quite a lot of pink and the walls have been stripped back to reveal the original brick. Dishes include chicken romano, surf and turf, beef and burgundy shashlicks. BYO. Mid price range.

Lillian's, 312 Main Road, Ballarat, (053) 31 7533; has seasonal menus which can often feature unusual meats such as buffalo and venison. Housed in the Main Lead Motor Inn close to Sovereign Hill. Licensed. Mid to upper price range. Set lunch less expensive.

Dyers Steak Stable, Little Bridge Street, Ballarat, (053) 31 2850, is in an 1860s hotel, pleasantly furnished and decorated with a hotch-potch of artworks. As far as food is concerned, the name says it all. A 'pound-and-a-half monster' is the house speciality but many other cuts of steak are available. Licensed. Mid price range.

The Winery, 118 Lydiard Street, Ballarat, (053) 33 1166; pink seats, low hanging lights and small tables in this bistro. The menu changes monthly but has run chicken with spring onion and ginger sauce and freshly smoked eel in the past. Licensed. Mid price range.

TOURS

The Talking Bus, (053) 31 2655, takes a 35 km-hike around the sights of Ballarat. It picks up from the Railway Station at 9.30 am Monday to Friday, 10 am on Saturday and 11.30 am on Sunday. There are afternoon pick-ups from Sovereign Hill as well.

Wineries

Although not widely known for wine growing, the Ballarat area has two vineyards

346

well worth visiting if you have the time. Both are established makers of *methode champenoise* sparkling wines. **Taltarni** is about 70 km (43 miles) north-west of Ballarat in the Avoca area. Run by Dominique Portet whose family has a long and distinguished history in French wine making, this winery has produced a number of award-winning vintages including a 1979 Cabernet Sauvignon judged top of its class in 1983 by the *Los Angeles Times*. Its sparkling wines include a Blanc de Blancs and a Brut Taché, slightly blushed by the addition of some red wine. The winery is open Monday to Saturday 9.30 am to 4 pm and Sunday noon to 4.30 pm. **Yellowglen**, fifteen minutes drive south of Ballarat near Smythesdale on the Glenelg Highway, has specialised in *methode champenoise* with outstanding success on the domestic market. It produces three chardonnay-based styles—Brut Non Vintage, Brut Rosé and Brut Crémant.

Bendigo

Bendigo's gold history began in 1851 when Margaret Kennedy, wife of the manager at a sheep run called Ravenswood, discovered some alluvial gold. Landowners tried to keep the find a secret but by 1852 a rush of similar proportions to that at Ballarat was in full swing. The field was, if anything, richer than its southern counterpart. It continued to produce until the 1950s and, in the face of a rocketing world gold price, is beginning to feel the old itch again. The Central Deborah Mine close to the centre of town is being pumped out in anticipation of assays proving it worth re-opening. Tourist dollars support the work.

GETTING TO AND AROUND
Bendigo is 152 km (94 miles) from Melbourne.

Trains depart from Spencer Street Station four times a day on weekdays and less on weekends. They take about two hours to reach Bendigo and the economy fare is $13.20.

Greyhound Coaches on the Melbourne to Broken Hill route stop in Bendigo. Fare is $13.20 and the trip takes around two and a half hours.

Drivers take the Calder Highway from Melbourne which passes through the pretty and historical towns of **Kyneton** and **Malmsbury**. It is possible to deviate from the highway at Woodend and drive to **Hanging Rock** where the mystery film *Picnic at Hanging Rock* was made.

Bendigo has a good public bus service for which there is a route map at the end of Hargreaves Mall.

TOURIST INFORMATION
The tourist information office for Bendigo is on the Calder Highway, four km (two miles) south of the town. There is a second office in Charing Cross, Bendigo's central city roundabout. Hours are 9 am to 5 pm Monday to Friday and 10 am to 3 pm at weekends.

The Town

Bendigo is flatter and more spread out than Ballarat. It centres on Charing Cross, a circle with a sculptural fountain in the middle, from which four major thoroughfares radiate. They are Pall Mall to the north, High Street to the south, Mitchell Street to the east and View Street to the west. The fountain is named **Alexandra Fountain** after the Princess of Wales whose two sons, Albert and George, declared it open in July 1881. It stands over Bendigo Creek which used to carry the sludge of the diggings and now runs under the roadway between View and Mitchell Streets.

Pall Mall, the name reflects the city fathers' desire to recreate the glories of London on their gold fields, is Bendigo's main street. Its civic buildings, many in French Renaissance style, date from the late 1880s and the 1890s when the town was ruled by men of fabulous wealth. George Lansell whose statue surveys the street was one of the most prominent. The rigid bronze burgher holds a lump of quartz in his hand as a tribute to the rock that brought him so much. Some of the old magnificence still surrounds him in the 1887 **Post Office,** the largest outside Melbourne, the 1890 **Law Courts,** the **Soldiers Memorial Hall** and **Roslyn Gardens.** The other side of life is represented by the gargantuan **Shamrock Hotel,** built in 1897, whose immense double veranda, iron laced through 18 bays, shades the footpath. The hotel is the third on that site and began life as a restaurant, at one time also serving as the town theatre.

Bendigo Art Gallery in View Street, which slopes up from Charing Cross, holds some paintings by Louis Bouvelot, the Swiss artist who had a profound effect on the nationalist painters of the 1890s as well as an eclectic group of works by minor European painters of the Victorian period and some contemporary paintings by feted Australians including Melbourne *enfant terrible* and animal rights campaigner Ivan Durrant. Further up the hill is **Dudley House** one of Bendigo's first government offices, dating from the 1850s. A simple but charming two storey Georgian building, it originally served as house and office for Richard Larritt, the area's first surveyor, and is now the Bendigo Historical Society headquarters.

The gothic cathedral south of Charing Cross in High Street is **Sacred Heart Cathedral**. It occupies a dominant position overlooking the town centre and has the odd distinction of being the only gothic cathedral completed during the last half of the twentieth century. The building was begun in 1887 but abandoned at the turn of the century with the church incomplete. It was not resumed until after World War II by which time stonemasons had to be imported from England and Italy to finish it. There were not enough skilled individuals in Australia.

Talking Trams

Bendigo gave up its trams (street cars) in 1972 after they had served the city for 69 years but their absence proved extremely short lived. They were in service again by early the next year. The cars are a tourist attraction, travelling from the Central Deborah Gold Mine to the Chinese Joss House via High Street, the Alexandra Fountain and Pall Mall on a route which passes most of the historic sights. During the journey, passengers are regaled with a taped commentary on Bendigo's history and architecture. The **Bendigo Tram Museum** is a highlight of the tour. It contains restored trams which once travelled the city streets. The Talking Trams run hourly from 9.30 am on weekends and during school holidays and twice a day, at 9.30 am and 2 pm on ordinary weekdays. The fare is $3.50.

Central Deborah Gold Mine

Central Deborah was the last of the mines to operate at Bendigo, closing down in 1956. It has been resurrected partly as a tourist venture and in the hope of mining more gold. Muddy crosscuts and drives, gold seams visible in the walls and a mess of mining machinery under the lift derrick show how authentic the mine is. Tourists who join the fascinating underground tour are fitted out with miner's hard hat, light and battery and taken down the mine shaft in a cage to the second level about 60 metres (200 feet) below ground. An informative guide leads a circular walk of several hundred metres through the mine, explaining the kinds of geological formations which excite gold miners and eventually coming to gold seams in the tunnel wall. Novice members of the party are asked to decide which of the seams is fools' gold and which the real McCoy. The tour also deals with old and new mining methods and the unique interconnections of mines in Bendigo. Central Deborah Mine is open from 9 am to 5 pm daily. Tours last about an hour and cost $6.

Other attractions

Chinese, who came to the gold fields in great numbers, are represented in the **Dai Gum San Wax Museum**, View Street, where highly decorated regal and military figures of Imperial China are arranged, and in the **Joss House**, a small Chinese temple complete with guarding lions and carved inscriptions, now preserved by the National Trust. Also in View Street is the **Bendigo Militaria Museum** where medals, war posters, uniforms and weaponry are displayed.

The **Bendigo Pottery**, at Epsom north of Bendigo proper, is Australia's oldest existing pottery. It was established in 1858 by George Guthrie, a Scottish potter who came to prospect but recognised the quality of Bendigo clay and returned to his old trade with astonishing success. Some of the kilns he built remain in use. The pottery is open 10 am to 3 pm on weekdays and 10 am to 4 pm on weekends. Tours take place six times a day, $2.50.

WHERE TO STAY
Most of the motels in Bendigo are on the outskirts of town.
Lakeview Motor Inn, 286 to 288 Napier Street (Midland Highway), Bendigo, (054) 42 3099, is a comfortable newish motel a short drive north of town. Single $42, double $50.
Golden Square Motor Inn, 508 High Street, Bendigo, (054) 47 7455; about the same distance away on the southern side of Bendigo. Single $40, double $48.
Ravenswood Homestead, Ravenswood, via Harcourt, (054) 35 3284, is a Georgian-style homestead built in 1857 and one of the loveliest houses remaining near Bendigo from that period. It has seven units, all with bathrooms and furnished with antiques and is 15 minutes' drive south of the town. Double $58 Sunday to Friday, $75 Saturday bed and breakfast.
Marlborough Lodge Guest House, 49 Rowan Street, Bendigo, (054) 41 4142, is

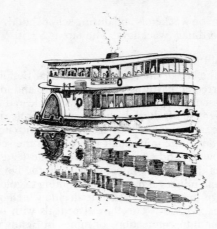

Paddle Steamer

a small guest house (four suites) in a residence dating from 1869. Rooms are comfortably furnished in Victorian style. Share facilities. Dining room BYO. Double $50 bed and breakfast.

EATING OUT

The Metropolitan, corner Bull Street and Hargreaves Street, Bendigo, (054) 43 4916, is a charming old pub with two restaurants, one a casual brasserie where pastas, salads and light meals are served and the other a formal restaurant with a high reputation for French cooking. Licensed. Low, mid and upper prices depending where you choose to eat.

Maxine's, 15 Bath Lane, Bendigo, (054) 42 2466; the subtle pinks of this restaurant's interior are equalled by the subtlety and imagination of the food, especially magnificent desserts. BYO. Upper price range.

Pears Café Restaurant, 61 High Street, Bendigo, (054) 42 2362, is situated in a long narrow shop with a warm atmosphere aided by cut back brick walls, wooden furniture and lots of old fashioned Pears prints. Good for a simple lunch or afternoon tea. BYO. Low price range.

TOURS

Bendigo Goldseeker Tours, show how to prospect for gold in the modern fashion—with a metal detector. Bookings by phone only on (054) 47 9559. Tours are full day and cost around $100.

Wineries

There are eight wineries within a fairly wide radius of Bendigo. The most prominent is **Balgownie**, 10 km (six miles) west of the town on Hermitage Road, Maiden Gully. Others the leisurely visitor might try are **Chateau Doré** at Mandurang Valley, eight km (five miles) south and **Chateau Le Amon**, 10 km (six miles) south on the Calder Highway.

350

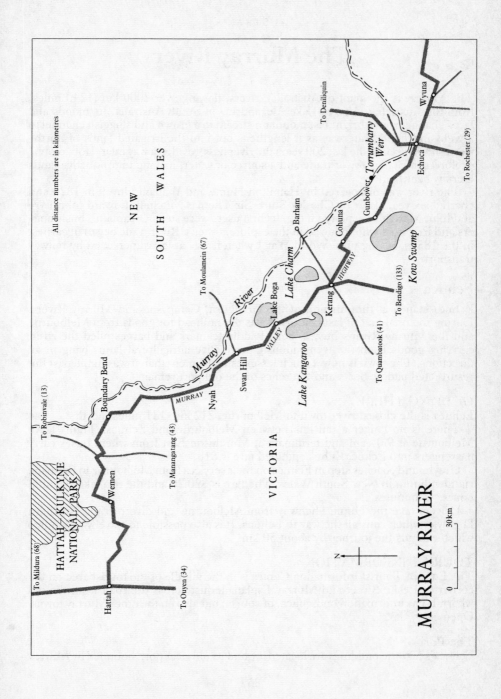

MURRAY RIVER

The Murray River

The Murray is the giant of Australian rivers, flowing over 2000 km (1240 miles) from the Australian Alps to Lake Alexandrina in South Australia. Its moods and faces change from a bright fast mountain stream to a brown and sluggish channel to a wide and noble waterway as it lengthens out into the irrigated lands of north-western Victoria. In the last 200 years the river has provided a way inland for colonial explorers, a vital artery of trade and a source of water, making unproductive lands literally bear fruit.

The river was discovered by Hamilton Hume and William Hovell in 1824 and charted six years later by Charles Sturt. Sir Thomas Mitchell, Edward John Eyre and John McKinlay explored it too. Its first users were steamer captains, bushrangers and irrigators who followed in the explorers' steps. River trade began in earnest in the 1850s, lasting until World War I when it was at last superseded by railway transport.

Echuca

Echuca stands at the junction of the Goulburn, Campaspe and Murray Rivers. During the final half of last century it was the railhead for goods from Melbourne and the Murray River's busiest port. Paddlesteamers and barges plied the river, carrying goods from the tremendously productive agricultural lands lying in all directions. The town is now a much lesser establishment than it was in the past but resurrected paddle boats and the relics of the old port remain.

GETTING THERE
Echuca is the closest river town to Melbourne, 212 km (131 miles) north.

There is no longer a rail link between Melbourne and Echuca. Trains leave Melbourne at 9.07 am and terminate at Murchison East from where buses carry passengers into Echuca. The combined fare is $18.

Greyhound coaches stop in Echuca on their services from Melbourne to Brisbane via Deniliquin in New South Wales. The fare is $20.20 and the trip takes about 3 hours, 45 minutes.

Drivers take the Hume Highway from Melbourne and divert to the Northern Highway which runs all the way to Echuca. It is also possible to travel via Bendigo which extends the journey by about 50 km.

TOURIST INFORMATION
The Echuca Tourist Information Centre is in the middle of the tourist area on the corner of Leslie Street and Murray Esplanade just across the road from the old wharf. It has information on Echuca, of course, but also on the other Murray towns. Open every day.

The Port
Echuca's historic buildings are located around its old river port, bounded by Murray

Esplanade and High Street. The area small, easy to walk around and shamefully commercialised—absolutely nothing is free, even down to inspecting the old Bridge Hotel, still a licensed premises and restaurant. The **old wharf** is a rough redwood structure that stands high out of the water and is fenced with corrugated iron so that passers-by must pay to see what is in there. Inside is an old steam train, some cranes and two restored paddle boats, the *Pevensey* and the *Adelaide* which are open for inspection but do not cruise the river. There is also an audio visual display and diorama.

The opposite side of the street is crowded with small buildings among which is a tea house and a wax museum. The lovely old **Bridge Hotel** is at the end of this block. 'Passports' allowing entrance to the old wharf, Star and Bridge Hotels are available from the Star Hotel in the middle of the block and cost $2.75.

The local **historical society museum** occupies the 1867 Police Station and Lock-up across from the port in High Street. It is open on weekends and during school holidays from 1 pm to 4 pm and includes old river charts and photographs in its collection. Admission 80 cents. There is also a museum of horse-drawn vehicles on Murray Esplanade, $2.

River Cruises

Two paddle steamers, the *Canberra* and the *Pride of the Murray*, run one hour river trips from a pier near the old wharf. They are not 'river boat gambler' style craft but more like small ferries with a wheel on either side rather than a large one at the back. The craft operate four times a day during school holidays, once a day on other days in summer and on weekends only during winter. The fare is around $5. Tickets for Canberra from the Bond Store and for Pride of the Murray from the Coach House, both opposite the old wharf.

Longer cruises are available on board the *Emmylou*, a vessel with cabins, some quite small. The cruises are two nights and two days over a weekend or midweek and the boat takes 20 passengers when full. Two berth cabins range from $265 to $295 per person and there is a double cabin for $315. Phone (054) 82 3801.

WHERE TO STAY

Steam Packet Motel, 610 High Street, Echuca, (054) 82 3411, is a two-storey sandstock brick corner building with a bullnose awning over the street, located in the Port and contemporaneous other buildings there. Rooms are furnished in something approximating 1880s style but have modern comforts as well. Single $34, double $44.

Port of Echuca Motor Inn, 465-477 High Street, Echuca, (054) 82 5666, is a bit of a hike down High Street from the port area but has queen-sized beds and air conditioning you can adjust in your room. Single $46 to $64, double $52 to $68.

EATING OUT

Savarin, 463 High Street, Echuca, (054) 82 4845; fresh produce from the Murray River and northern Victoria area is used to great effect here in high quality, classical French cooking. One of Victoria's best country restaurants housed in an 1857 building. Licensed. Upper price range.

MV *Echuca Princess*, 57 Murray Esplanade, Port of Echuca, (054) 82 5244, is a floating restaurant which has the courtesy to travel in the opposite direction to the cruise boats so diners can see different scenery. Lunch and floodlit dinner cruises. Licensed. Mid price range.

Steam Packet Steak Tavern, 610 High Street, Echuca, (054) 82 3411, is a char-grill steak and seafood restaurant housed in a National Trust classified building which stands on a corner and has been carefully restored down to its shady awning and colonial windows. BYO. Mid price range.

Humble Bull, 601 High Street, Echuca, (054) 82 5782; dinner menu features spit-roasted beef, pork and lamb. BYO. Low price range.

BOAT HIRE

You can take your own river cruise or go fishing by hiring a boat from **Echuca Boat Hire** at the Victoria Park Boat Ramp. It has canoes and kayaks as well as six-person motor boats and also hires out camping equipment for overnight trips. Motor boat rates vary from $20 for one hour to $85 for eight (this includes petrol), canoes and kayaks $8 to $30 for the same periods.

Swan Hill

Swan Hill owes its name to Major Thomas Mitchell, Surveyor General of New South Wales. While exploring the Murray in 1836, he camped at the present town site and was kept sleepless all night by honking swans. The noisy birds failed to deter permanent settlers who followed the major's trail in ruts made by his giant bullock drays. They didn't need to hurry; it is said the ruts remained for up to ten years. The first properties were taken up in the 1840s but it was the punt crossing of 1847, the first on the river, and the riverboat trade of the 1870s and '80s which built the town.

GETTING THERE

Swan Hill is 345 km (214 miles) or about half a day's drive from Melbourne, roughly halfway between Echuca and Mildura.

Trains run to Swan Hill from Spencer Street Station in Melbourne Monday to Friday at 5.40 pm, Saturday at 6 pm and Sunday at 6.35 pm. The fare is $26.

V/Line Coaches northern district service from Spencer Street Station runs to Swan Hill, leaving at 10 am. The fare is the same.

Drivers should take the Calder Highway to Bendigo and the Loddon Valley Highway from there to Swan Hill.

TOURIST INFORMATION

There is a tourist information centre 306 Campbell Street, Swan Hill.

Pioneer Settlement

The settlement is a re-creation of a river port as it was in the heyday of trade on the Murray. It centres on a big paddle steamer called the *Gem*, in its day the largest such vessel to work the Murray and Darling rivers and now moored permanently at the Pioneer Settlement wharf. Around the wharf are shops, houses and workshops constructed and operating in the manner of the 1880s. A newspaper office, saddlery store and blacksmith's forge are among the more interesting reconstructions. Residences include a log cabin, drop log homestead and a pre-fabricated steel kit home shipped from England and claimed to be Australia's first such structure. There is also a farm and shearing shed. Transport through the township is by horse-drawn carriages and a stage coach. Open 8.30 am to 5 pm each day. Admission $7.50. A sound and light show takes place each night at Pioneer Settlement and there are river tours aboard the paddle steamer *Pyap*. These also cost $7.50 each. Bookings on (050) 32 1093.

Murray Downs and Tyntyndyer

The banks of the Murray were 'squatter' country, first settled illegally by squatters who defied bans on taking up new land. Their defiance occurred so often and with such success that squatters gradually acquired vast tracts of valuable land for little or no payment. Some became a kind of landed aristocracy, known colloquially as the 'squattocracy' and built mansions to house their wealthy dynasties. Swan Hill has two great relics from their era.

Murray Downs, opposite Swan Hill on the New South Wales bank of the river, was developed in the 1840s and had at that time a 50 km river frontage. What remains is a rather ostentatious and undisciplined country house set on the river bank in four acres of gardens. It has a single- and a double-storey wing, ground level verandas shaded by fan-shaped awnings and many bay windows overlooking level lawns and gardens. The whole is a hotch potch of architectural styles ranging from Australian homestead to Venetian townhouse. Some of the opulent furniture and paintings which once filled the house are on display inside. The grounds of Murray Downs contain an animal park, nursery, tea room, souvenir shop and children's playground. Open 9 am to 4.30 pm each day except Monday. Admission $4.50.

Tyntyndyer, 17 km (11 miles) north of Swan Hill is an older homestead than Murray Downs. Built in 1846, it is a low, more severe and undecorated house but has greater colonial charm. Shady verandas surround it and parts of the house are vine covered. Tyntyndyer has been owned by the Holoway family from 1876 and takes a low key approach to visitors, no souvenir stores, no children's playground. Open 9 am to 4.30 pm every day. Admission $4.

WHERE TO STAY
Travellers Rest Motor Inn, 110 Curlewis Street, Swan Hill, (050) 32 9644, is the newest motel in Swan Hill and has particularly spacious rooms which makes up for the exposed brick walls in them. The motel is quite close to the river.
Swan Hill Motor Inn, 405 Campbell Street, Swan Hill, (050) 32 2726, has decor which, in parts, makes one long for exposed brick walls but that aside it is an excellently run establishment.

EATING OUT
Captain Beattie's Riverboat Restaurant, P.S. Gem, Pioneer Village, Swan Hill, (050) 32 2463, is on board the riverboat tied up at Pioneer Settlement wharf and

serves dishes with uniquely Australian ingredients such as yabbies (small freshwater crustaceans), Mallee turkey, Mallee pig and fish from the Murray river, not to mention witchetty grub soup. The restaurant is decorated in the chintzy style expected of river boats. Licensed. Mid price range.

Silver Slipper Restaurant, Swan Hill Motor Inn, 405 Campbell Street, Swan Hill, (050) 32 2726; menu includes starters such as smoked trout and lambs' brains, main courses like spatchcock and rack of lamb and desserts such as cream caramel and profiteroles. The less said about the hideous blue decor the better. Licensed. Mid to upper price range.

Houseboats

Sun Centre Houseboats, (050) 32 2320, hires out three-bedroom houseboats in which you can cruise the river from Swan Hill to Barham, about 50 km (31 miles) upstream towards Echuca. They have bathroom and kitchen and a flat roof for sunbathing. Write to PO Box 10, Murrabit, Victoria 3579.

Mildura

Mildura is an island of greenery in a dry and desert-like region, closer to Broken Hill and Adelaide than Melbourne. The town was founded by William and George Chaffey who arrived in 1887 under the patronage of Alfred Deakin, later Prime Minister of Australia, and established an irrigation scheme using the waters of the Murray. The grape- and orange-growing industries that now support the town are a measure of the Chaffeys' success but the desert sun continues to shine unabated, making Mildura one of the sunniest places in Victoria. Its average summer temperature is 33°C.

Mildura supports a number of commercial tourist attractions including a small zoo called **Golden River Fauna Gardens** where there are deer, camels, lions and birds as well as native animals, but the town is essentially a departure point for the largest paddle steamers cruising the Murray. The *Coonawarra*, which accommodates 36 passengers and has recently been re-fitted takes five-day cruises, leaving Mildura each Monday. It travels downstream and into the Darling River, the large inland waterway the flows into the Murray some distance beyond Mildura. The *Melbourne* is a day boat carrying passengers on two-hour cruises which pass through Lock 11, a large lock close to Mildura Wharf.

Other attractions can be found in Cureton Avenue, Mildura. They include Fosketts' Fuchsia Farm, the Miniature Railway Complex, the Humpty Dumpty Tourist Farm and Woodsies Gem Shop.

GETTING THERE

Mildura is 550 km north-west of Melbourne. Sunstate Airlines, (03) 665 3333, flies to Mildura from Melbourne ($224) and Adelaide ($170).

Trains run from Melbourne to Mildura on Monday, Tuesday and Wednesday at 8.30 am and Tuesday, Friday and Sunday at 9.35 pm on a trip taking about 10 and a half hours. The economy fare is $34.50.

Greyhound coaches run from Melbourne to Broken Hill via Mildura. Fare is $30.80 and the trip takes around 17 hours, leaving Melbourne at 10.30 pm on Friday and Sunday.

Drivers who take it easy will need a day or two to reach Mildura from Melbourne via the Western Freeway to Ballarat and the Sunraysia Highway the rest of the way. Drivers from Adelaide travel via Renmark on the Sturt Highway. The River City Highway runs between Mildura and Broken Hill.

TOURIST INFORMATION
The Mildura City Tourist Office is at 41b Langtree Avenue.

WHERE TO STAY
Mildura has at least 20 motels of various ages, states of repair and levels of interest. Many are strung along the Sturt Highway, known as Deakin Avenue when it reaches Mildura.

Grand Hotel, Seventh Street, Mildura, (050) 23 0511, has self contained rooms with the usual motel appointments ranging in comfort from deluxe to budget in a building with a certain amount of style since it wasn't a motel to begin with. Almost opposite the railway station. Single $30.50 to $73.50, double $49 to $92.

Commodore Motel, corner Deakin Avenue and Seventh Street, Mildura, (050) 23 0241; an ordinary motel close to the city centre. Single $40, double $46.

Four Seasons Inlander, 373 Deakin Avenue, Mildura, (050) 23 3823, is a 'resort'-style place with a big heated swimming pool, two tennis courts, putting and bowling greens and a children's playground but is four good-sized blocks from the town centre and eight from the river. Single $44, double $54.

EATING OUT
Restaurant Rendezvous, 34 Langtree Avenue, Mildura, (050) 23 1571, has two sections, one for formal dining which goes the full distance into French classic and one for informal pastas, charcoal grills and blackboard specials. Licensed. Mid to upper price range.

TOURS
Ron's Tourist Centre, 41 Deakin Avenue, Mildura, (050) 23 6160, is the departure point for day tours throughout the district. As well as doing the town sights they include a sultana farm, wineries and Wentworth. Some go as far as Broken Hill.

Wentworth

The small town of **Wentworth** over the New South Wales border at the Murray Darling junction, 33 km (20 miles) from Mildura, has a number of buildings left over from the days of its prosperity during the 1880s. They include an eye-catching gaol and a 100 year old courthouse. The gaol is open every day. Tourist information is available at the Old Gaol.

Wineries

The grape-growing industry around Mildura, though largely devoted to sultana grapes, supports some wineries. **Mildara Wines** at Merebein is a large producer of brandy and fortified wines as well as table wines. The **Stanley Wine Company** over the border at Buronga, next door to **Orange World,** an orange farm which welcomes tourists, produces varietal table wines and is stronger in fruity whites than other styles. **Lindemans Wines** at Karadoc uses its fields for grape growing but you can taste its wines from other areas at the vineyard. **Fitzpatrick Estate** at Irymple, is a small self-contained winery producing mostly whites. Its featured wine is a 1986 Chardonnay.

The Victorian Alps

The Great Dividing Range begins to rise in a spur called the Dandenong Ranges just east of Melbourne but doesn't reach snow catching height until close to 200 km (124 miles) north-east of the city. The mountains here climb close to 2000 metres. Like the nearby alps of New South Wales they are covered with scrubby eucalypt forest and when the snow falls, present a patchwork of bright white and grey green. The spring and summer bring mountain wild flowers and autumn clothes the foothills in a cloak of golden leaves.

Winter is a busy time. Skiers come from Melbourne by the thousand, many for cross-country as well as downhill skiing. In other seasons bushwalkers take over but in far lesser numbers.

GETTING TO AND AROUND
The mountain resorts are rather scattered and there is no airport very close to them. Bright, 308 km (191 miles) from Melbourne, is the most central town to the northern mountains of Falls Creek, Mt Hothham and Mt Buffalo, each between about 30 and 60 km (19 and 37 miles) away.

Kendell and East West Airlines fly daily from Melbourne to Albury at the northernmost point of the region. The one way economy fare is $87 and the journey takes 50 minutes. There are extra services during the ski season. Buses operate from Albury to the ski fields.

Hoy's Coaches run from Melbourne ($37) to Mt Hotham and from the central mountain town of Bright to ski fields at Mt Buffalo, Mt Hotham and Falls Creek.

V/Line buses run from Melbourne to Mt Buller in the south of the region. The fare is $29. Mansfield–Mt Buller Bus Lines also run from Melbourne during the ski season and operate a fleet of four-wheel drive vehicles on Mt Buller itself.

The main road route from Melbourne is the Hume Highway. Turn onto the Midland Highway for Mt Buller and the Ovens Highway for the other resorts.

Bright

Settled deeply into the Ovens Valley surrounded by the Great Dividing Range foothills, Bright is the only town central to the northern ski fields of Mt Hotham, Falls Creek and Mt Buffalo. Crowded in winter and a centre of bushwalking in summer, the town is at its best in autumn when the leaves turn gold and red. That season is a lovely time to try the many walking trails around it. A small museum in the Bright Railway Station, long unvisited by trains, recalls the riots of 1857 when Chinese gold miners were forced off their claims in and around Bright. It also contains relics of the first skiing days. Gold mining by dredge continued at nearby Harrietville until 1956.

WHERE TO STAY

Bright has more tourist accommodation than any other town in the alpine region but most of it is holiday flats and lodges designed for long term ski holidays. There are also seven motels.

Colonial Inn, 54 Gavan Street, Bright, (057) 55 1633, stands in an attractive garden setting underneath a forested hill. Rooms are furnished in ersatz colonial style. Single $36, double $44, surcharges during ski season, public and school holidays.

High Country Inn, 13–17 Gavan Street (Ovens Highway), Bright, (057) 55 1244; the Canyon Walk, one of Bright's best trails, runs directly behind this modern motel set on the bank of the Ovens River. Single $38, double $47. Ski season and holidays $50 and $51.

Bogong High Plains

Mt Bogong, Victoria's highest mountain at 1986 metres lies east of Bright at the top of Bogong National Park. The park contains the Bogong High Plains, a granite plateau with sheer cliffs, rounded tors and fabulous mountain views. Old wooden stockmen's huts built in the 1880s and still used today are scattered across the plains. Each year from November to March, wild flowers bloom in thousands of colours and rare shrubs flower. Huge Bogong moths are found there; in past ages, local Aborigines held yearly gatherings to feast on them. The best way to see the plains is on horseback and trail rides can be organised at Falls Creek Alpine Village.

Ski Fields

Large parking areas, equipment hire, ski schools and lodges are common to the Victoria ski fields. They operate much the same as those in New South Wales except that they are more widely scattered and their snow is, generally speaking, less reliable.

Mt Buffalo is the oldest Victorian ski resort. Thirty-two km (20 miles) from Bright and in the midst of a national park, it has no private lodges but there is one chalet, bookable through Victour on (057) 55 1500. Its two ski areas, Cresta and Dingo Dell, are quite separate and neither is any use if you're a good skier. They suit beginners or cross country. There are two chair lifts at Cresta, pomas and a bambi lift only at Dingo Dell. The snow cover here is not reliable and the skiable area is small. Entry price $3.50 per day. Lifts $14.50 per day.

Mt Hotham is 55 km (34 miles) from Bright and has the most reliable snow of Victoria's resorts but its lifts are long distances apart and getting from one to another can be very tiring. Cross-country skiing is a big deal here, perhaps because the resort village is so strung out you need to ski from end to end of it. Entry price $10.50 per day. Lifts $30 per day.

Falls Creek has the best downhill skiing in Victoria when the snow cover is good. The resort nestles in a natural bowl in the heart of the Bogong High Plains and has 22 lifts—three are chairlifts and the rest mostly pomas. The resort has a carefully laid out lift and return system which allows skiers to ski from lodges to lifts and back again. Most of the trails are of intermediate standard with some for beginners and advanced. There is also cross-country skiing to the top of Mt Bogong. Accommodation is in the Falls Creek Alpine Village and at Mt Beauty, a small town on the road from Bright. The alpine village also has restaurants and a couple of entertainment venues which operate during the ski season. Entry price $11 per day. Lifts $30 per day.

Mt Buller is much closer to Melbourne (241 km, 149 miles) than the other north-eastern resorts and so attracts greater weekend crowds. It is the largest of Victoria's ski fields and a huge plan has just been put forward to re-develop it, a job not expected to be complete before 1992. The slopes are served by 23 lifts (eight chairs) operated by two companies so that you need two tickets for your day's skiing. The nearest town with accommodation is Mansfield and there are lodges in Mt Buller Alpine Village. Entry price $8.50 per day. Lifts $30 per day.

Mt Baw Baw is the most southerly of the resorts, 185 km (115 miles) from Melbourne, but has the least reliable snow cover and does not attract crowds equal to Mt Buller. It is kind to inexperienced skiers. There is one chairlift and some long platter and t-bar lifts. Entry price $5 per day. Lifts $23 per day.

WHERE TO STAY

Lodges and flats dominate accommodation in the alpine villages. The **Falls Creek Motel**, Falls Creek Road, Falls Creek, charges $50 per person dinner bed and breakfast in the off-season but rates go up during winter.

The only accommodation at Mt Buffalo is in **Mt Buffalo Chalet**, $55 per person full board, and **Tatra Inn**, Cresta, $46 dinner, bed and breakfast. Both prices are off-season.

Generally speaking, prices rise sharply and rooms go quickly during the ski season, especially if the snow is good. Out of season, many lodges close. Falls Creek has the most accommodation of the alpine villages but it is also the most crowded. People who want to avoid the crush and a little of the expense stay in Mt Beauty, close to Falls Creek, where there are motels, holiday flats and a chalet. Bright is the option for Mt Hotham and Mt Buffalo.

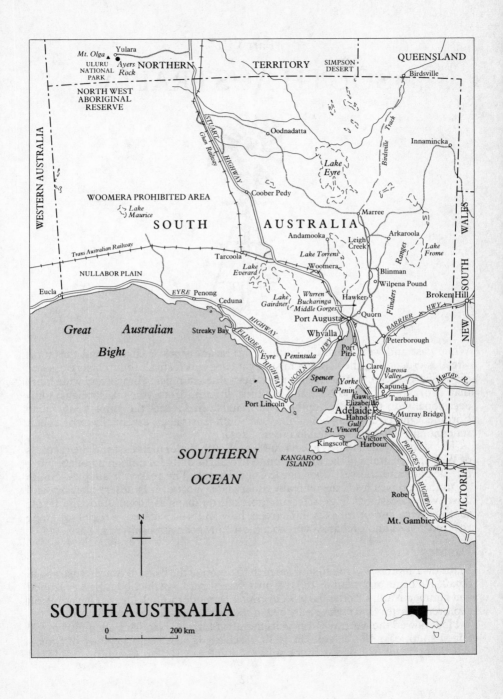

SOUTH AUSTRALIA

0   200 km

Part VIII

SOUTH AUSTRALIA

While east and west Australia battle it out on the stock exchange and the north wrestles crocodiles, the south is busy organising arts festivals, church services and dinner parties. South Australians insist they value art, music, theatre and wine more than sport, sun, TV and beer and are thus different from other Australians. Only occasionally do they suffer outbreaks of loutish hedonism, the annual Australian Formula One Grand Prix being one, but South Australia is essentially more sober, reticent and self-contained than other states.

The state is walled in by Victoria and New South Wales to its east and the vastness of Western Australia to the west. Around two thirds of its 1.4 million population live in Adelaide and the rest does not live far from it. The reason is simple—South Australia receives less rain than any other state, most of it is desert, flat, dry and dusty with occasional huge salt pans (marked on maps as lakes). Only the fertile south eastern corner relieves. It is green, hilly and well watered, a region of grape covered slopes and orchards with an almost European atmosphere in parts.

History

Matthew Flinders was the first white man to examine the coast of South Australia in detail. He came and went in 1801. Thirty years later Captain Collet Barker landed and climbed Mount Lofty, the peak overlooking modern Adelaide, but it was inland explorer Charles Sturt who really began the push to settle Australia's south.

He followed the Murray River to its mouth at Lake Alexandrina about 80 km (50 miles) south east of Adelaide, in 1830, discovering rich country. News of Sturt's expedition reached London in the wake of articles by Robert Gouger and Edward

Gibbon Wakefield, the 'Systematic Colonisers', proposing that unemployment in Great Britain be relieved by colonising South Australia. The new colony would raise revenue by selling land. Land ownership would motivate free settlers to work hard and no convicts would be required. The new colonial society would be diligent, religious and clean.

In 1832 the South Australian Land Company was formed to further the project and Colonial Office recognition came two years later. In late 1836 the colony was established under the governorship of Captain John Hindmarsh, RN. The Colonial Office took charge of government and a Colonisation Commission was made responsible for land sales, emigration and financing.

As soon as the colony was established, ferocious squabbles blew up between government and colonisation representatives. Land speculation was soon rife, little food was produced before 1840, administrators proved inept and self-aggrandising and the colony became expensive to the government. In 1842 the commission was scrapped and the whole operation handed back to the Colonial Office.

Ironically, by 1844 the small landholders were beginning to fulfil the promises Wakefield had made for them. The colony became self-supporting and before long was exporting wheat and wool. In 1845 rich copper deposits prompted a mining boom. Migration was heavy and the population reached 67,000 in 1850, just prior to the Victorian gold rush. When the rush came, population flowed out but money flowed in as the South Australian wheat fields fed the Victorian diggers.

The garden continued to bloom until a succession of droughts and the 1890s depression stripped it bare. Its people discovered they had no other resource. The land was all and the land had let them down. Their economy was so badly shattered that real recovery did not come until nearly World War II, delayed by a continuing, almost bloody-minded, dependence on agricultural production.

During and after the war industrialisation was at last seriously adopted and is now a considerable force in the South Australian economy, so much so that in 1987 the state succeeded in winning a huge defence contract over the much more industrially powerful state of New South Wales.

GETTING TO AND AROUND

By Air
Adelaide has the only airport in South Australia taking international traffic. **Kendell Airlines** and **Lloyd Aviation** are the main interstate operators in South Australia.

By Rail
Adelaide is again the gateway. Trains run from Sydney, Melbourne, Perth and Alice Springs and there are also train/coach services from Sydney and Melbourne. A small rail network also exists around the city but there is little rail in other parts of the state.

By Road
Ansett Pioneer, Greyhound, Deluxe and **Bus Australia** coaches serve South Australia from the east, west and north. Greyhound coaches on their way through

the state set down in Renmark, Murray Bridge and Mt Gambier to the east and Port Pirie, Port Augusta, Ceduna and Coober Pedy to the west and north.

TOURIST INFORMATION
The **South Australian Government Tourist Bureau** has offices at:
    18 King William Street, **Adelaide**, (08) 212 1644
    25 Elizabeth Street, **Melbourne**, (03) 614 6522
    143 King Street, **Sydney**, (02) 232 8388

Time
South Australia runs to Central Time, half an hour behind the eastern states and $1^1/_2$ hours ahead of Western Australia.

MAJOR SIGHTS
Adelaide is the only true city in South Australia. It has a very attractive centre built to a rigid plan and surrounded by parkland. The Mount Lofty Ranges, really a spine of pretty hills and small valleys, surround the greater Adelaide area. Australia's best wine is produced in the **Barossa Valley** north of the city, a region of neatly arranged vineyards attached to gentle slopes surrounding some charming small towns. Where the fertility around Adelaide runs out it gives way to the dry but spectacular **Flinders Ranges** which are the highlight of South Australia's desert regions.

ACCOMMODATION
South Australia has not undergone the rapid hotel development that has lately characterised other parts of Australia. It's probably five to ten years behind the pace set by the eastern states in terms of modernity but, except at very specific times of year, e.g., Easter and the Australian Grand Prix, rooms are not difficult to secure— the state doesn't do a great tourist trade. It does, however, pride itself on an elegant life-style so service is often of a more professional standard than in some more touted destinations.

FOOD AND DRINK
South Australian wines are the best in the country. The best, from the Barossa Valley, are covered on page 383. Extensive winelists feature in many restaurants but there are fewer BYOs than in other parts of the country. Adelaide has plenty of quality restaurants but they are a rarer sight elsewhere, even the Barossa Valley is rather short of them. Restaurant menus and the approach to dining and service are frequently traditional and male diners would be wise to carry a tie and leave their shorts at home.

ADELAIDE

Adelaide is Australia's prettiest city. Its old mansions and villas are superbly cared-for, its many parks and gardens are delightfully inviting, its stone churches are placed to the most picturesque effect and even its cricket oval is regarded as a masterpiece of sporting gentility.

Adelaide residents call their home 'The Athens of the South', affirm the paramountcy of cultured life over commercialism and point to their theatres, museums, art galleries, carefully conserved old buildings and biennial arts festival as practical evidence of that affirmation. The city, circumscribed by boundaries set over a century and a half ago and restricting industrial unsightliness to its margins, wears refinement like a rose. Its people are exceptionally polite and friendly and often a touch more 'cultured' than the residents of other Australian cities. They can also be stiff, straight laced and parochial.

History
Adelaide city was planned by Colonel William Light, an army man who loved straight lines. Light chose a flat plain between the Mount Lofty Ranges and Gulf St Vincent as his site and stuck to it despite continuous sniping from the chief naval and government representative, Governor Hindmarsh. By 1837 Light had succeeded in confirming the simple but elegant shape that Adelaide city bears today and there is no doubt that history has proved him the wiser man. His vision is celebrated in a statue which stands overlooking the Torrens River and the city on Montefiore Hill.

GETTING TO AND AROUND

By Air
Qantas is the only international airline that flies into Adelaide and that only from New Zealand. Ansett and Australian Airlines flights operate several times a day from Sydney and Melbourne to Adelaide, up to twice a day from Perth, three times a week from Canberra and four times a week from Brisbane. Non-stop flights from Perth take four hours, from Brisbane one hour, from Sydney one and a half hours, from Canberra one hour and from Melbourne 40 minutes. In practice, your flight from Sydney can take three and a half hours if it goes via Melbourne, the same is true of flights from Brisbane. Fares from major cities are Sydney $234, Melbourne $161, Perth $342, Alice Springs $253, Canberra $208. Adelaide airport is located about ten minutes' drive east of the city.

A private bus service run by the Transit Company operates between the airport and the city, setting down at prominent hotels and the Adelaide Rail Passenger Terminal at Keswick on the Western outskirts of the city. It also picks up city and airport passengers at Keswick which is the rail terminal for passengers from interstate. The fare is $2.60 airport to city. Trains run from Keswick to Adelaide city as well.

By Rail
The *Indian Pacific* train from Sydney to Perth passes through Adelaide and is the only rail connection between Sydney and that city. The journey takes about 30 hours and costs $249 first class, $186 economy. Perth to Adelaide rail travellers take the *Trans Australian*, a journey of 37 hours, costing $454.50 first class $333.50 economy. The *Overland* operates from Melbourne to Adelaide, taking 12 hours and

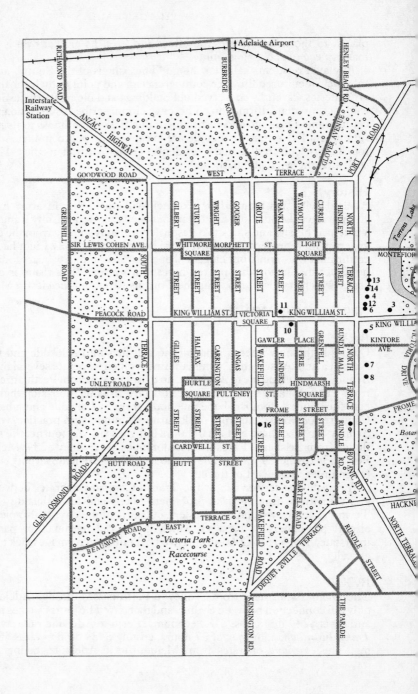

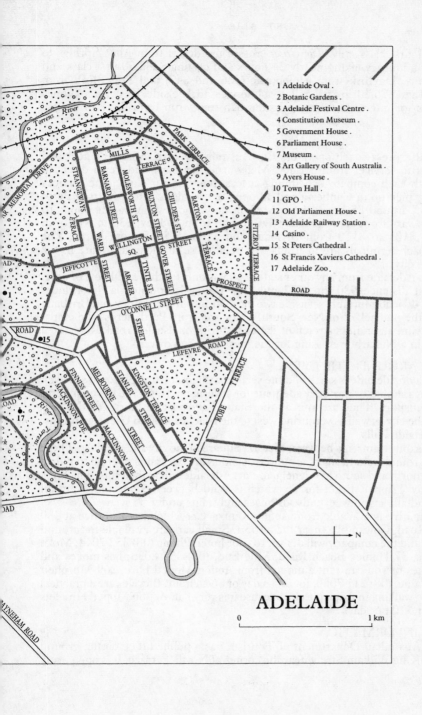

1 Adelaide Oval .
2 Botanic Gardens .
3 Adelaide Festival Centre .
4 Constitution Museum .
5 Government House .
6 Parliament House .
7 Museum .
8 Art Gallery of South Australia .
9 Ayers House .
10 Town Hall .
11 GPO .
12 Old Parliament House .
13 Adelaide Railway Station .
14 Casino .
15 St Peters Cathedral .
16 St Francis Xaviers Cathedral .
17 Adelaide Zoo .

ADELAIDE

0   1 km

costing $101 first class only. *The Ghan* crosses the desert from Alice Springs to Adelaide on a journey taking nearly 24 hours and costing $282.50 first class and $200 economy. **Daylink** from Melbourne ($66 and $47) and **Speedlink** from Sydney ($79 and $76.20) are two rail-coach services to Adelaide. Keswick Station is the terminus for interstate trains and suburban trains run from there to central Adelaide.

By Road
The national express coach operators Bus Australia, Deluxe, Ansett Pioneer and Greyhound run services from Sydney, Melbourne, Brisbane and Perth direct to Adelaide with each company scheduling at least one bus per day. Some services from Sydney pick up in Canberra and all operate overnight. The trip from Perth takes longest, around 35 hours, from Melbourne is shortest, averaging about 10 hours. Fares vary from approximately $70 to $80 from Sydney, $35 to $45 from Melbourne, $105 to $110 from Brisbane and $100 to $115 from Perth. The interstate coach terminals are in Franklin Street, close to Victoria Square in the centre of the city.

Driving to Adelaide from any other state capital is only for those with lots of time. The shortest distance 930 km (577 miles) is from Melbourne via the Princes Highway, to do it comfortably set aside two days. Routes from Sydney and Brisbane lie through the outback of of New South Wales and from Perth across the empty Nullarbor Plain, an endless stretch of flat desert with one sealed road. Roos are a real danger in a Nullarbor crossing for the inexperienced driver.

GETTING AROUND THE CITY
The city area of Adelaide is small and the section with interesting places to see even smaller so legs should be perfectly adequate for covering it. Buses are the main form of public transport. They are run by the State Transport Authority (STA) and criss-cross the city as well as venturing west to the beaches around Glenelg and east into the Adelaide Hills.

Adelaide's only tram runs between Victoria Square in the city and Glenelg. There is no underground train network around Adelaide City but trains operate to points on the coast north and south of Glenelg, to Port Adelaide and to the Hills. The STA issues a 'Day Tripper' ticket for $5 which is valid between 9 am and 3 pm on weekdays and all day on weekends for buses and trains under its sway.

Cheap **car hire** is available from Action Rent-a-Car which has its office at 280 Burbridge Road, Cowandilla, near the airport. Small cars are available for around $35 per day and the company will deliver to your hotel. Phone (08) 352 7044. Moke Rent-a-Cars, 37 Henley Beach Road, Mile End, (08) 352 8033; has mokes and other cheapies or you can rent a moped from Action Moped Hire, 269 Morphett Street, Adelaide, (08) 211 7060, for $25 a day or $6 an hour. Bicycles are a practical alternative to walking in Adelaide city because it is very flat. Action Moped Hire lets them out for $10 per day.

TOURIST INFORMATION
The South Australian Department of Tourism has a public office on the ground floor at 118 King William Street near the corner of North Terrace. It is open every

day and carries information about the rest of South Australia as well as Adelaide. Phone (08) 212 1644. For information about public transport in Adelaide phone (08) 210 1000 or visit the State Transport Authority information centres in Adelaide Railway Station, North Terrace, or the corner of William and Currie Streets in the city.

Orientation

Adelaide is easy to navigate. The city area is practically square, bounded by **North, South, East** and **West Terraces** (streets) which mark the outer edges of a grid centred on **Victoria Square**. This square you will recognise by the tram parked in its middle, Adelaide's only such conveyance, which runs from the city to the beachside at Glenelg. There is also a fountain in the square. King William Street, Adelaide's main north–south thoroughfare runs through the square. Most of the city's 'action' happens to the north around Rundle and Hindley Streets and North Terrace.

North Terrace

Adelaide's major public edifices stand along North Terrace. The Adelaide Casino, the Constitutional Museum, the South Australian Parliament, Government House, the State Library, the South Australian Museum, the Art Gallery of South Australia, the University of Adelaide, the South Australian Institute of Technology and Royal Adelaide Hospital stand cheek by jowl along the northern side; shopping centres, pubs, cafés, airline offices, churches and the historical Ayers House are along the southern side. You can spend a morning on North Terrace and not slow down.

The much promoted **Adelaide Casino** is the classiest in the country—if you like casinos. It is small and has no poker machines or video games, just tables for roulette, blackjack and the like, and a ring for the Australian coin-tossing game Two-up. It is housed in a grand old railway station whose original function continues downstairs. Commuters march through the casino's marble-floored foyer twice daily. The gambling is so popular that, on weekend nights, patrons queue into the street. The casino is open every day from 10 am to 4 am, dress is expected to be 'smart' but how smart is left to the security guards to determine. Clean jeans do not seem to be out of place but don't wear shorts or thongs.

Old Parliament House stands next door to the casino as you head towards King William Street. The 1855 building housed South Australia's first Legislative Council. It was threatened with demolition in 1978 but underwent resurrection instead and serves as a constitutional museum covering the political history of South Australia in audio-visual displays. The displays aim to tell the state's story from discovery to the present day and take place in the restored chambers of the House of Assembly. Changing exhibitions on political themes are held in other parts of the building and there is also a coffee shop and a book shop. Open Monday to Friday 10 am to 5 pm, weekends noon to 5 pm. Admission $3.50.

The existing **Parliament House** stands next to its older counterpart on the corner of North Terrace and King William Street. Their contrast is marked to say

369

the least. Whereas the older building looks rather like a simple church, its replacement is a neo-classical extravaganza built of grey Kapunda marble with ten tall Corinthian columns along its façade and an odd little Victorian Juliette balcony tacked on the back. It took 56 years to build, beginning in 1883 and not being completed until 1939. It is not as large as one might expect given the time taken to construct it but quite imposing in an appropriately stolid way.

Government House, the official residence of South Australia's governor occupies the opposite corner. Its east frontage was built between 1838 and 1840, very soon after the first colonists arrived and is Adelaide's oldest surviving example of the Regency building style.

The South Australian Museum has whale skeletons in its front window but its true value lies in a very large collection of Australian Aboriginal and New Guinea native artefacts. Though the collection is large, the museum space is small and anyone with a yen for studying these items would be well advised to bone up on their significance beforehand as they are not very completely explained, especially the quite startling array of Pacific Island masks, spears, shields and other bits and pieces on the third level. The Aboriginal display is on level five. The museum is open from 10 am to 5 pm Monday to Saturday, except Wednesday when it does not admit the public until 1 pm. Sunday hours are 2 pm to 5 pm. Admission is free.

The Art Gallery of South Australia, not to be confused with the **Gallery of South Australian Art** which stands behind it, is next door to the museum. It houses the state art collection displayed chronologically in two wings, one devoted to Australian painting and the other to works from elsewhere, especially Europe. The colonial art collection which begins the Australian wing is interesting for its comparison of stylistic developments, especially in the depiction of landscape, in the various states. The interest is mainly historical as the artistic standard of some paintings is low. The following rooms lead visitors through the development of an Australian impressionist style from Tom Roberts to Rupert Bunny, to painters of the mid-twentieth century and finally to recent Australian painting of which the most fascinating is undoubtedly by Aboriginal painters of the western desert. It is worth comparing their understanding of landscape with that shown by their European counterparts. The back sections of the gallery are devoted to changing retrospective shows of individual artist's work and touring exhibitions. The gallery is open daily 10 am to 5 pm and admission is free.

Ayers House, on the south side of North Terrace is a carefully preserved specimen of how a local member of the Adelaide establishment lived in Victorian times. The residence was designed by Sir George Kingston for Sir Henry Ayers, once Premier of South Australia. It was constructed in stages, beginning with the central, one storey section in 1846 and, over the next 30 years, having the bow windowed dining and drawing rooms added. It is now the headquarters of the South Australian branch of the National Trust and also houses two restaurants. Ayers House is open from Tuesday to Friday 10 am to 4 pm and on weekends 2 pm to 4 pm. Admission $2.

The Festival Centre
This theatrical complex is Adelaide's best modern architecture. It occupies the city's

loveliest site, a short distance north of the intersection of King William Street and North Terrace, overlooking Elder Park with its 1882 band rotunda, Torrens Lake and wide lawns towards North Adelaide. It holds pride of place in panoramic photographs of Adelaide.

The centre looks like three huge white tents pitched on the river bank, although it is rather more substantial than such a description implies. The effect comes from its very low roofs which narrow down to triangular corners at ground level, making them resemble stretched sheets. It contains four theatres, a concert hall which doubles as a lyric theatre, a playhouse, an experimental space and an open air amphitheatre. All are excellent auditoriums, especially the concert hall and playhouse which are among the best in Australia. Guided tours take place hourly from 10 am to 4 pm Monday to Friday and at 10.30 am, 11.30 am, 2 pm and 3 pm on Saturday but are sometimes cancelled without warning. They cost $2.

Rundle Mall

The mall is Adelaide's main shopping centre and is linked to the south side of North Terrace by arcades of small shops and a big department store called John Martin's. It is a pleasing, tree-lined thoroughfare flanked by fashion stores, specialty shops, cinemas, restaurants and small commercial art galleries. Cars are excluded. Pieces of modernist sculpture, fruit carts and an outdoor restaurant complete its promenade atmosphere. At weekends, buskers inhabit favoured shop entrances in the evenings.

The section of Rundle Street stretching from the Mall to East Terrace past the East Market is more ragged but also more interesting. It's a good place to go in search of breakfast, lunch, dinner or an Italian coffee.

Hindley Street

Every city has its low life quarter and this is about as low as Adelaide goes—not really very low. When last there I saw a laughable street fight between two gangs of fourteen year olds; probably not typical. Whatever the case, Hindley Street is the only part of Adelaide (excluding the casino) that doesn't shut down at 10 pm. Along its crowded couple of blocks are movie houses, discos, pubs, bars and restaurants which open to the wee small hours. A couple of breakfast places, opening around 7.30 am strive to give the street a 24 hour look. Hindley Street runs west from King William Street to West Terrace.

Botanic Gardens

The **Botanic Gardens** and **Botanic Park** lie between North Terrace and the Adelaide Zoo. The gardens cover 16 hectares and include the usual range of Australian and exotic plants as well as hot houses where some unexpected tropical species can be found. Open 9 am to 6 pm during summer and 9 am to sunset in winter. Admission free. Guided tours depart at 10 am on Fridays from the kiosk.

Adelaide Zoo

The century old Adelaide Zoo is one of Australia's longest established. Standing on the banks of the Torrens River, it is entered from Frome Road on the north east outskirts of the city area. Although the zoo is old, it has adopted modern trends in animal display including moated enclosures for apes, hoofed animals and marsupials, a nocturnal house and a reptile house as well as three large walk-through aviaries where many of the 1200 birds in the zoo's collection are displayed. The aviaries contain rainforest species, waterbirds and parrots.

A collection of rare and beautiful yellow-footed rock wallabies is exhibited near the entrance. Aside from its displays, the zoo is known for its rare and endangered species breeding programmes. Some of the species on such programmes include the golden lion tamarin, ctontop tamarin, Pygmy hippopotamus, red panda, Persian leopard and Przewalski's horse. The zoo is open daily from 9.30 am to 5 pm. Admission is $5.

Churches

Adelaide's original inhabitants were great church builders, consequently the city has a number of old stone houses of worship which, though not masterpieces of architecture and art, deserve mention because they reflect the plain middle class Protestantism which played a major part in the history of South Australia.

St Peter's Cathedral on the corner of Pennington Terrace and King William Street, north of the city across Adelaide Bridge is the most visible and is notable as one of the few churches in Australia with twin spires. The church building was constructed between 1869 and 1876 but the towers and spires did not go up until 1902. They contain the heaviest peal of bells in the Southern Hemisphere. **Holy Trinity Church** in North Terrace is the oldest of Adelaide's major churches. Its foundation stone was laid by Governor Hindmarsh in 1838 but only the clock from the original building remains in the present structure, built fifty years later. **St Francis Xavier's Cathedral** in Wakefield Street was constructed in two widely separated stages. Its southern section took from 1856 to 1858 but the rest had to wait until 1922 before it was begun. It was finally completed in 1926.

Old Pubs

Adelaide has more charming late nineteenth century pubs than any other Australian capital. The two great examples of the heights of exuberance that pub building reached in the heady 1880s are **The Botanic Hotel** on the corner of East and North Terraces and the **Newmarket Hotel** on the corner of West and North Terraces. Their lacework verandas and decorative interiors make the average drinker feel like a king. **The Earl of Aberdeen** on the corner of Carrington and Pulteney Streets is another grand old dame and serves an excellent lunch.

North Adelaide

When Colonel Light planned the Athens of the South he added just one suburb, North Adelaide, which has become the city's most exclusive living area. Like the city which it overlooks, it is a small, self-contained grid, centred on a town square. North Adelaide is linked to Adelaide proper by King William Street and the Adelaide Bridge and begins at St Peter's Cathedral but most of it stands on a hill above the river and the city. It is undoubtedly one of Australia's most fascinating and eccentric parades of domestic architecture.

Almost every admirably kept house has another unexpected tower, roofline, iron filigree or stone façade. Stone—ranging from honey coloured sandstone to granite, and the tasteful grandeur of its houses distinguish it from inner city suburbs in other parts of Australia. Elsewhere, when the rich built, they generally outdid themselves in tastelessness but not in North Adelaide, even its eccentricities are more whimsical than crass. Examples of what Adelaide people call 'Villas', single storey, bay windowed stone houses with red brick architraves, tuckpointing between the stone blocks and verandas decorated with iron lace, are frequent.

North Adelaide's contemporary face appears on **Melbourne Street,** the area's exclusive shopping strip, somewhat overburdened with hairdressers and frock shops but with a number of restaurants as well. Many working men's cottages of the Victorian era have been converted into commercial premises.

WHERE TO STAY
Adelaide has one big new glossy hotel, the rest (bar the Hilton) were built about 20 years ago and ought to be up to their third or fourth re-furbishment but some don't seem able to raise the wherewithal.

Hilton International, 233 Victoria Street, Adelaide, (08) 217 0711, faces Victoria Square in the middle of Adelaide's City area, a little removed from the 'fun' end of town. Eighteen floors with 387 rooms. Single $150 to $190, double $170 to $210.

Adelaide Parkroyal, 226 South Terrace, Adelaide, (08) 223 4355; located at the southern end of town about 15 minutes walk from the city and main tourist attractions. Recently refurbished foyer but the rooms although large, are older style with 'hear-through' walls. Pleasant restaurant and bar area off the foyer where there is restrained entertainment on some nights. $130.

The Gateway, 147 North Terrace, Adelaide, (08) 217 7552; opposite Parliament House. Has some narrow rooms whose decoration will make you wish you hadn't woken up with a hangover but offers the other facilities common to large hotels such as restaurants, bars and 24 hour room service. $120.

Hotel Adelaide, 62 Brougham Place, North Adelaide, (08) 267 3444, stands high on the hill over Adelaide, not far from where Colonel Light had his vision and enjoys lovely views over the city. The hotel itself is well and truly due for an up-date. Single $105, double $115.

Travelodge, 208 South Terrace, Adelaide, (08) 223 2744; next door to the Parkroyal with some rooms overlooking the park across the street. The hotel shows some signs of age and is frequented by coach groups. $106.

Grosvenor, 125 North Terrace, Adelaide, (08) 51 2961, is an elegant old hotel at the low end of North Terrace which used to be Adelaide's premier accommodation house but is now somewhat below the ruling standard. Rooms range from deluxe to budget but are not luxurious even at the top. Single $50 to $90, double $60 to $100.

Meriden Lodge, Melbourne Street, North Adelaide, (08) 267 3033, is in North Adelaide's smart street of shops and restaurants. Standard rooms $65, executive $75.

Adelaide Paringa Motel, 15 Hindley Street, Adelaide, (08) 231 1000; central motel in an old commercial building on Adelaide's street of night-time action. All rooms air-conditioned and 24 hour room service. Single $55, double $60.

Ambassador, 107 King William Street, Adelaide, (08) 51 4331; an older hotel whose public rooms have undergone renovation but whose rooms remain somewhat vintage. Near Victoria Square. Single $47, double $59.

Austral Hotel, 205 Rundle Street, Adelaide, (08) 223 4660; ordinary pub accommodation, narrow rooms, share facilities but cheap and clean. Single $20, double $36.

Hyatt Regency, North Terrace, Adelaide, (08) 231 1234; opens mid 1988 and will outstrip any other Adelaide offering, leaving the rest of the city's hotels with plenty of catching up to do. Overlooks the Torrens, is next door to the casino and a few steps from the Festival Centre. Bound to be expensive.

EATING OUT

Adelaide restaurants gather together in identifiable locations and have almost universal licensing, which puts up the price of your meal if you drink alcohol with it but, by way of compensation, food prices are reasonable. Generally speaking, try the eastern end of Rundle Street from Rundle Mall to East Terrace for Italian restaurants and one or two places which dare to bend the norm; the Central Markets area has Asian and fish restaurants, especially Gouger Street for the latter, and Hindley Street has a variety. Other good eating places are scattered throughout the city.

Da Clemente, 227 Rundle Street, Adelaide, (08) 223 2211, is one of the city's best Italian establishments where you can see the cooking done in a central exposed kitchen and eat either in a formal dining room or facing the kitchen. Try the kid stew (goat kid, of course). Licensed. Low to mid price range.

Ruby's Cafe, 255 Rundle Street, Adelaide, (08) 224 0365; an old established eating place in the East Market area which has taken a turn to modernity in the last couple of years. The menu is short and changes weekly but everything is so attractive that it's hard to decide what to have. Avocado and fennel bulb salad with mustard cress; cauliflower, camembert and basil charlotte in silverbeet with hollandaise sauce are just two examples. BYO. Low to mid price range. Good breakfasts are available here early when the market traders come in to eat.

La Mensa, 527 Rundle Street, Adelaide, (08) 223 2764, is another Rundle Street Italian but a little plainer and less ambitious than Da Clemente. Licensed. Low price range. Lunch is very cheap here.

Mezes, 287 Rundle Street, Adelaide, (08) 223 7384, is a Greek restaurant, prefers to be called Mediterranean and looks like a post-modernist stage set for *Iphigenia in Aulis*—back-lit false columns and other souped-up, cut-down classical paraphernalia bathed in blue light. The effect is not as alarming as it sounds and the food is surprisingly unaffected and hearty: souvlaki, moussaka and other Greek domestic delights. BYO. Low to mid price range.

Bangkok, corner Rundle and Frome Streets, Adelaide, (08) 223 5406; the best Thai restaurant in Adelaide for which you must book. Everything is good from green and red curries to vermicelli with minced pork. Licensed. Mid price range.

Hawker's Corner, 141 West Terrace, Adelaide, (08) 211 8182; is actually a collection of food stalls selling various Asian cuisines including Thai, Indian, Malaysian and Chinese. The decor is best described as minimal, tables take up most of the room with the stalls ranged along one wall. Very popular with the student fraternity. No alcohol permitted. Low price range.

Jolleys Boathouse Bistro, Jolleys Lane, Adelaide, (08) 223 2891, is housed in a boathouse on the Torrens river and has a wide veranda for delightful summertime dining. Food is in a French vein but saunters at liberty through the best of local ingredients. Licensed. Low to mid price range.

Glo-bo's, 125 Gilles Street, Adelaide, (08) 223 6271; a continuous bistro offering service from noon to midnight every day except Tuesday. BYO and licensed. Low price range.

Chloe's, 36 College Road, Kent Town, (08) 363 1001; close to the city and set in a villa with several opulently furnished dining rooms. Consider this one for your splurge night out in Adelaide. The food is classic French with a little help from a modern perspective and includes duck liver mousse with madeira sauce and wood fungus, boned duck and kumquats. Chloe's is also known for the excellence of its wine list. Licensed. Upper price range.

Duthy's, 19 Duthy Street, Malvern, (08) 272 0465; in the southern suburbs and therefore somewhat out of the way but well worth the travelling for Wayne Hargreave's fine cuisine based on nouvelle but not enthralled by it. Past selections from an ever-changing menu are prawn quenelle poached in red wine with tiny onions; rare fillet of aged ox with fresh roasted chestnuts, chestnut butter and beef glaze; halva bavarois with caramel sauce and chocolate shards. BYO. Mid price range.

Mawson House, 51 King William Road, Unley, (08) 271 3098, is a converted Adelaide villa complete with honey coloured stone walls and red brick exterior architraves. A restaurant very much in the grand manner with a number of dining rooms and a reputation for table-side cooking. Steak tartare is a speciality. Licensed. Upper price range.

Magic Flute, 109 Melbourne Street, North Adelaide, (08) 267 3172; nestles among the exclusive frock shops and offers indoor dining in cool elegance or a courtyard for summer. The food on the regularly changing menu is in keeping with the surroundings, showing delicate French influence and a way with the occasional oddity such as water buffalo. Licensed. Upper price range.

TOURS

The **Adelaide Explorer**, a bus dressed-up as a tram, departs from the South Australian Government Travel Centre at 18 King William Street at 9.30 am, 11 am, 12.30 pm and 3.30 pm every day except Saturday. It travels through the centre of the city, a short distance into North Adelaide and west to Glenelg on a journey taking about an hour and a half. Passengers can climb on and off buses to take walks and so extend their exploration throughout a whole day. Tickets cost $10. **City Sights Tours** are operated day and night by Briscoes Coach Holidays (08) 212 7344, Premier's (08) 217 0777 and Transit (08) 381 5311. They cost between $7 and $14.

Glenelg and the Beaches

Glenelg lies about fifteen minutes' drive south west of Adelaide on the edge of Cape St Vincent and is where the locals go for a summer swim. A tram from the centre of the city will take you there but do not expect too much, the beaches are not the equal of those on the east coast of Australia by a long chalk. In fact, at times of high tide they seem to have no sand at all and the water can be as grey as it is sometimes blue. Glenelg is netted against sharks. South Australia is home to the *white pointer*, one of the more deadly members of the shark family. The settlement surrounding Glenelg Beach has that rather tatty and temporary-seeming appearance common to resorts populated for only half the year. It has an **amusement park** on the beachfront and a sailing ship called the *Buffalo* moored at a wharf in the small harbour behind the main beach.

The ship is a replica of that which brought the first South Australian colonists to Glenelg where settlement began. It was built to plans drawn up in 1813 for the original *Buffalo* and houses a restaurant, bar and small museum containing items related to the *Buffalo*'s voyage from Portsmouth to Glenelg in 1836.

The **Grange** north of Glenelg past Henley Beach is the site of a museum dedicated to Captain Charles Sturt whose exploratory feats inspired the settlement of South Australia. The house was built in 1840 and Sturt made it his home between further expeditions and trips to England until 1853 when he left Australia permanently. It is furnished in the style of his time and contains memorabilia of the Sturt family. Sturt's Murray riverside camp is reconstructed in the grounds of the Grange. Open 1 pm to 5 pm Wednesday to Sunday. Admission $1.50.

WHERE TO STAY

If staying in Adelaide does not attract, you can stay by the water at Glenelg and take the tram into the city.

Pier Hotel, 2 Jetty Road, Glenelg, (08) 295 4116; is an old style seaside hotel where some rooms have a few mod cons such as air conditioning, private bathrooms and TV. Single $42, double $47.

Colley Motel Apartments, 22 Colley Terrace, Glenelg, (08) 295 7535; is opposite grassy and attractive Colley Reserve and has cooking facilities in all rooms. Single $30, double $35.

Port Adelaide

Adelaide's port facilities are concentrated in Port Adelaide north west of the city. A busy port until World War II, activity came almost to a standstill following the end of coastal steamer trade and increased competition from Sydney and Melbourne. A laudable result of this setback was the unintended preservation of Port Adelaide's nineteenth-century wharf precinct, now a **maritime museum**.

The museum ranges through the **Bond and Free Stores** built in 1854 and 1857 and now housing the main display galleries, **Weman's Building**, a sailmaker's shop and ships chandlery built in 1864 and the **Old Port Adelaide Lighthouse** of 1869 which was re-sited in 1986 from its former position on South Neptune Island. The buildings are surrounded by restored façades of merchant houses, banks, pubs and official buildings including the **Customs House**, **Police Station** and **Court House**.

Two vessels are moored at **No. 1 Wharf**, the *Nelcebee* built in Port Adelaide in

1883 and the *Yelta*, a 1949 tug boat, the last steam tug to operate in the port. The museum buildings are open from 10 am to 5 pm Saturday to Wednesday. Combined admission to Bond Store and No. 1 Wharf $3.50, Lighthouse $1.

Cruise

The *Captain Matthew Flinders* cruises from Port Adelaide into Gulf St Vincent. The boat leaves from North Parade Wharf usually around midday and takes three hours to complete its journey. Cruise cost is about $20. Phone (08) 47 1966 for bookings.

EVENTS

Each year Adelaide hosts the **Australian Grand Prix**. Formula One Racing cars roar and grunt their way around the closed-off city streets in a deafening procession of unabashed egotism. Racing fans cause such congestion in accommodation that camp sites are established in parks and private homes let out their bedrooms and balconies. The race is relatively new but fiercely contested because it is the last race of the year and can decide the world champion but unless you're a car racing fan, Adelaide is to be avoided like the plague when the thing is on. If you are a fan and want to be comfortable, book about a year ahead. The event happens around the middle of November and lasts three days with the big race on the last day.

The **Adelaide Festival of Arts** occurs biennially on even numbered years. Although almost all Australian state capitals convene similar festivals annually, Adelaide's is the oldest and by far the most prestigious. It behaves like other arts festivals in having mainstream and fringe events and attracts a wide range of overseas artists. Writers' Week is its most controversial and amusing forum. Novelists, poets and journalists gather from around Australia and overseas, argue, drink, make prophecies and display their wounds to the bewilderment and outrage of the general public. The festival occupies three weeks in March and enquiries can be made by writing to Adelaide Festival, GPO Box 1269, Adelaide, South Australia 5001 or phoning (08) 216 8600. Bookings should be made well ahead of the event.

The Adelaide Hills

Adelaide lies neatly set out on a flat plain between the Mount Lofty Ranges and Gulf St Vincent. The ranges are not really mountains but attractive hills dotted with picturesque townships within easy reach of the city. The towns are conscious of their attractiveness and play upon it gently so as to draw residents and visitors from the city.

GETTING TO AND AROUND

Trains run from the city to the hills via a rather circuitous route through Adelaide's southern suburbs. Buses from Adelaide also travel into and around the hill towns. Drivers should take the Glen Osmond Road from South Terrace to the Mount Barker Road.

Mount Lofty

In Adelaide's early days, Mount Lofty was climbed by anyone who wanted to see the surrounding countryside and it still gives the best view of the city's clean and dirty faces. The mountain is about 20 km (12 miles) from town and its summit is reached by a road ending in a large look-out where a column stands as a monument to Matthew Flinders. From the look-out you can see Colonel Light's perfect city core isolated by a ring of greenery and modern Adelaide's suburbs, as full of concrete and wire as those of any other twentieth century city, sprawling north and south. A look in the opposite direction encounters the greenery of the Adelaide Hills where a couple of small farmhouses rest quietly under timbered slopes. There could not be a greater contrast.

Mount Lofty Botanic Gardens has been established near the summit and can be entered from Mawson Drive off Summit Road. The gardens range over 42 hectares of hilly ground and are planted out with exotic plants of cool and sub-alpine regions which means they are at their most beautiful during autumn. The gardens are closed during winter months.

Bridgewater

Bridgewater Mill, a stone water-mill built in 1860, has been restored and converted to a winery by one of Australia's most prestigious new producers, **Petaluma Wines**. Visitors can taste Petaluma's Bridgewater Mill wines at the mill as well as have lunch in the Granary room, a high ceilinged hall with tables on three levels. The giant water wheel attached to the side of the building and turned by a reticulated flow of water from a nearby creek can be closely inspected from a viewing deck built beside it. There is also a restaurant and cellar for bottle fermented sparkling wine on other floors of the mill. Grapes for this wine, named 'Croser' after its maker Brian Croser, come from the Piccadilly Valley under Mount Lofty as do those for Petluma's Chardonnays.

Hahndorf

Hahndorf, the main town in the Hills, is the oldest surviving site of German settlement in Australia. East Prussian victims of religious persecution repaired here under the sponsorship of George Fife Angas, one of the original Systematic Colonisers. Angas believed they would be well behaved and hard working. He was right. The town is named after Captain Hahn, captain of the ship *Zebra* on which the settlers undertook a difficult journey from Europe, arriving at Port Adelaide in January 1839.

Modern day Hahndorf, preserved and pickled, is aimed right between your touristic eyes. A dumplings and lederhosen atmosphere prevails in cafes and coffee shops touting goulash and other mid-European culinary delights or quaint white-windowed stores selling dreadful folksy crafts.

The **Hahndorf Academy** has a more serious purpose. Opened as a private institute of higher learning in 1857, it has survived various official attempts at demolition to become the town museum. Paintings by Sir Hans Heysen, who came to Hahndorf as a boy and lived there most of his life, are the pride of the museum's collection. Heysen lived from 1877 to 1968 and gained considerable fame for his landscapes of the Adelaide Hills and the Flinders Ranges, earning a prominent place among the representational depicters of Australian regional scenes. His European training and the gentle appearance of the Hills he painted are especially well expressed in his watercolours. The museum is open from 10.30 am to 5.30 pm Monday to Thursday and Saturday, Sunday hours are 11.30 am to 5.30 pm. Admission is $4.

WHERE TO STAY AND EATING OUT

Mt Lofty House, 74 Summit Road, Crafers, (08) 39 6777; is perhaps the pick of country accommodation houses in South Australia. It seems to have everything, delightfully furnished bedrooms, sitting rooms with open fires and a superb food. The house itself was built between 1852 and 1858 and overlooks the glorious Piccadilly Valley. $180 to $275 room and breakfast. There are two restaurants, Hardy's and Piccadilly. The first is a formal room decorated in High Victorian style where you eat with silver and drink from crystal, the second is more relaxed, having a glass roof to let the sun in, a lovely view over Piccadilly Valley and a minimum of decoration. The menu in both is modern Australian with the expected French influences plus a touch of Mediterranean. Lunch is served daily in the Piccadilly room and dinner in Hardy's. Licensed. Mid price range for lunch, upper price range for dinner.

    Petaluma Restaurant, Bridgewater Mill, Mount Barker Road, Bridgewater, (08) 339 4227; is the exclusive restaurant in the Petaluma Winery and has one of the most original menus around Adelaide. I remember a pigeon pie done Moroccan style appearing on one occasion. The wines are also excellent. Licensed. Upper price range.

TOURS

Premier's, (08) 217 0777, runs coach tours to Hahndorf and the Adelaide Hills on Mondays, Wednesdays and Sundays. It takes three and a half hours and costs $15. **Transit**, (08) 381 5311, runs a full day coach tour to Hahndorf and surroundings on Saturdays ($26) and a half day to Mount Lofty and Cleland Wildlife Reserve on Sundays and Wednesdays ($16).

The Fleurieu Peninsula

The Fleurieu Peninsula south of Adelaide is near enough to the city to encourage day-trips. The peninsula has fine beaches along its Gulf St Vincent side, just south of the urban sprawl from Christie's Beach to Maslins Beach and further south at Aldinga and Sellick's Beaches. Hang gliders leap from the high cliffs at Cape Jervis on the peninsula tip and Kangaroo Island lies within view across Backstairs Passage.

    Victor Harbour, the main peninsula town stands on the southern side looking out onto Encounter Bay, its waters protected by Granite Island whose tall peak offers fine views of bay and town, eased by a chairlift to the top. The island is connected to the shore by a causeway. Views are also available from a high headland called The Bluff. Below is Rosetta Bay and Whale Haven where reminders of the town's early whaling days (1837 to 1869) are preserved.

The **Southern Vales** wine growing area is also on the peninsula. McLaren Vale, which supplies grapes to many of the best Barossa Valley vignerons, has a number of wineries and more can be found at Reynella, Willunga and Langhorne Creek.

Kangaroo Island

The large island, 150 km (95 miles) long by 30 km (18½ miles) wide, is a summer resort for Adelaide. It has protected beaches on its northern shore and a wild, cliff edged southern coast. With an environment undisturbed by exotic animals, the island is an excellent place to see wildlife such as koalas, kangaroos, wallabies and seals. It has a large national park, Flinders Chase, at its western end and three small towns, Kingscote, American River and Penneshaw at the eastern end.

GETTING THERE
The ferry *Philanderer III*, (085) 59 2276, runs three return trips daily to Penneshaw from Cape Jervis 10 km away on the tip of Fleurieu Peninsula. The *Troubridge*, (08) 47 5577, runs from Port Adelaide to Kingscote, a journey of six and a half hours. Both ferries take cars.

Four airlines, Albatross (0848) 22 296; Airtransit (08) 352 3128; State Air (08) 267 2400; Lloyd (08) 352 6944, serve the island from Adelaide.

The Barossa Valley

The Barossa Valley has low round hills, fast flowing streams and fields striped with rows of grape vines, pruned to picking height, but its rural tranquillity belies the commercial punch packed by the huge wine companies which dominate the valley and the Australian wine market. These old companies, Seppelts, Orlando and Penfolds are three, some established for over a century, make very public faces of their history but behind their castellated façades are huge steel holding tanks containing millions of litres of wine, often made from grapes grown far away, and destined for cardboard casks in corner liquor stores around the country. The valley also has its small fry. Rusticity is no marketing ploy for them—it's the truth but some make very fine wines indeed. Hard to come by in the discount stores of Sydney and Melbourne, they are the special delight of a Barossa Valley visit.

History

Colonel William Light named the Barossa Valley in 1837 in memory of Barrosa in Spain where he had fought a decisive battle in 1811 under the command of Lord Lynedoch. The lord had defeated the French and turned the tide of the Peninsular War. Light, reminded of Barrosa by the hills around the valley, named them the Barrosa Range. A subsequent mis-spelling of the name caused it to be rendered Barossa.

The Barossa's cultural heritage is German but it might not have been without Englishman George Fife Angas. Angas funded a group of East Prussian Lutherans in their escape from religious oppression by King William the Third. The Prussian king wished to impose his Calvinistic state religion on them. They wished not to have it. Angas, always on the look-out for a good colonial prospect, financed their migration to South Australia. Some found their way to Hahndorf in the Adelaide Hills but the majority followed their leader, Pastor August Kavel, to the Barossa.

The region had been explored in the late 1830s by an eccentric Silesian mineralogist called Johannes Menge who had noted the country's potential for viticulture and its resemblance to parts of what is now Poland. The new arrivals established the towns of Bethany, Angaston, Langmeil (now Tanunda) and Lyndoch Valley which they called Hoffnungsthal meaning Valley of Hope. Arriving in 1842, by the late 1840s they had planted vines. Although they lived at first in tents and wattle and daub huts, their building skills were soon displayed in the rising spires of Lutheran churches and the stone cottages and shops they constructed for permanent living. Once the towns were established, there was little reason to alter them and their centres retain a sometimes disorienting German look.

GETTING TO AND AROUND

The Barossa Valley is small and close to Adelaide, about 60 km (37 miles) or an hour's drive from the city, and the wineries cluster conveniently between the towns of Lyndoch and Nuriootpa which are about 20 km (12 miles) apart. Tanunda, the Barossa's other settlement, stands between the two. Although the main business for the traveller is wine tasting, travelling's associated pleasures, dining, taking in the scenery and learning about local history are not lacking.

The Barossa Valley has no large towns or airports. It must be approached from Adelaide by road. The Barossa Adelaide Passenger Service operates buses from the city to Lyndoch, Tanunda, Nuriootpa and Angaston. They leave the Franklin Street Bus Terminal, 101 Franklin Street, at 9.30 am, 1.30 pm and 5 pm from Monday to

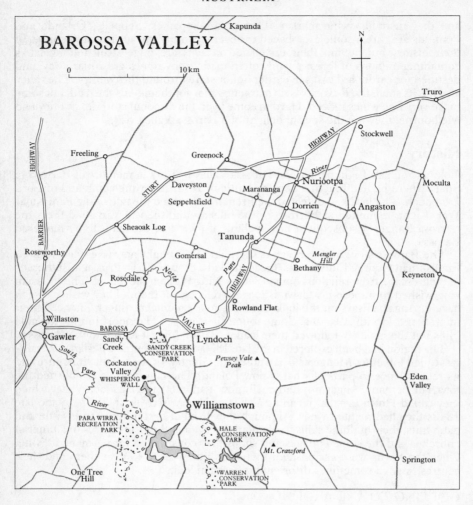

BAROSSA VALLEY

0   10 km

Friday, 12.15 pm and 5.45 pm on Saturday and 5.45 pm only on Sunday. The journey to Tanunda takes one and a quarter hours and costs $4.60. For more information phone Barossa Adelaide Passenger Service, Ebenezer Road, Ebenezer, (085) 65 6258.

Drivers can select from two routes; through Elizabeth and Gawler to Lyndoch at the southern end of the valley, is a direct but rather boring passage, or via the Hills, entering the valley at its northern end through Angaston and Nuriootpa. This is a more scenic but longer path.

Although the Barossa Valley is surrounded by hills, it is not itself especially hilly so that fairly comfortable cycling is possible. Bicycles can be hired at **Kell's Gift Centre**, 63 to 67 Murray Street, Tanunda, (085) 63 2177 which is open seven days a week or from Elderton Wines, 3 Tanunda Road, Nuriootpa, (085) 62 1058.

TOURIST INFORMATION
Information is available from Coulthard House, 66 Murray Street, Tanunda, (085) 62 1866. The house is open from 8.30 am to 5.30 pm Monday to Friday and from 9.30 am to 4.30 pm on weekends and is the major tourist information centre for the Barossa Valley.

Wineries

There is a great range and number of wineries in the short stretch of valley between Lyndoch and Nuriootpa, about 50 in all, but to visit each one is neither necessary nor wise. The selection offered here can easily be covered in a day and represents the historical wineries with interesting buildings, tours, restaurants and the like as well as smaller places that concentrate wholly on producing excellent regional wines.

Chateau Yaldara is at the bottom of the Valley just outside Lyndoch, a short distance off the Barossa Valley Highway. It was established in 1947 and is a large though not enormous enterprise. The stone 'chateau' that fronts the winery was built on the ruins of a nineteenth century flour mill and houses a collection of antique furniture and porcelain which can be viewed by visitors on hourly tours from 10.15 am to 3.15 pm Monday to Friday. Yaldara wines are not expensive and, though not of premium quality, are frequently good value for money so don't disregard the tasting room here. The winery produces fortified as well as table wines. It is open for tasting and sales from 9 am to 5 pm seven days a week.

The **Orlando Winery Complex** at Rowland Flat, five km (three miles) north of Lyndoch, is one of the biggest in the valley. The first vines in the area were planted by Johann Gramp in 1847 at Jacobs Creek, a name now carried by Orlando's best known claret. The history of Orlando since the 1950s parallels the growth of big Australian winemaking. Once the producer of truly terrible sweet carbonated muck, it has followed a path of technological innovation through flagons to table casks while maintaining a foothold in the bottled quality wine market. The result has been a fabulous business success and a complex resembling more a factory than an old winery. Although the approach to Orlando's is unspectacular, it caters well to the interested public with hourly winery tours from the Public Relations Area every day of the week. The tours cost $1 and will show you how winemaking can be turned into agribusiness. Those who wish to see grape crushing should visit from February to April. The winery is open from 9 am to 5 pm on weekdays with slightly shorter hours on weekends.

Rockford, a tiny winery on Krondorf Road, a right turn off the Barossa Valley Highway about three km (two miles) from Rowland Flat, could not be more of a contrast to Orlando. The tasting room is in a narrow stone shed, once a stable, behind winemaker Robert O'Callaghan's house and your initial greeting will probably be from the family dog—he's very friendly, but inside there are wonders for the palate. O'Callaghan's reds, especially his basket pressed 1986 McLaren Vale Shiraz (a wine so big it almost talks), have other Barossa winemakers wondering what they have to do to catch up. He specialises in premium regional wines, using grapes from McLaren Vale south of Adelaide and from the Clare Valley as well as from the Barossa and can tell you precisely from which vineyard the vintage you are drinking came. The winery is open seven days a week, 11 am to 5.30 pm.

Krondorf Wines, a short distance along Krondorf Road from Rockford was, until recently, the preserve of Burge and Wilson two young winemakers who have earned an international reputation in the past ten years for the quality of their output. Like O'Callaghan, they did not limit their choice of grapes to the Barossa but also bought from outside, taking the best they could find from growers' annual offerings with special concentration on individual grape lots. The results in both reds and whites were outstanding and Krondorf produced some of the Barossa's best high quality table wines, especially in its Burge and Wilson range. The winery has now been taken over by Mildara, a giant of Australian wine production, and the original winemakers have gone their separate ways. It is yet to be seen what the effect will be. Tastings occur seven days a week from 10 am to 5 pm.

Seppeltsfield, the home of Seppelts Wines is visually the most exciting and unusual of the Barossa's wineries. It is also one of the biggest. The winery is approached via the small town of Marananga where an avenue of date palms begins, not stopping until it reaches the old winery several miles away. The effect of date palms among the Barossa hills is exotic and a little bizarre. The winery has a long history, having been established by an energetic Silesian migrant, Joseph Seppelt in 1851. Seppelt brought his wife and family, thirteen other families and nine single men with him, all of whom had worked in his snuff factory in Wusterwaltersdorf. They started a tobacco farm on the present winery site but, although the tobacco grew well, it was too rank for sale. Not easily defeated, Seppelt took up viticulture and winemaking which proved much more successful.

His eldest son, Benno, took over management of the winery at the age of 21 and developed it so successfully that his wines won awards in Australia and Europe. The company also produced brandy, rum, gin and pharmaceutical spirits.

A huge building programme began in 1875 and included port maturation cellars, a distillery, a vinegar factory, a brandy bond store and vintage cellars described by the *London Gazette* in 1892 as 'the most modern in the world'. These and other period structures constitute the carefully preserved public face of Seppelts. They are solid, practical works of the late nineteenth century but Seppeltsfield also has a folly. Travellers down the avenue of date palms come upon a small, classical Greek style, sandstone temple perched on a roadside hill and approached by a huge flight of stairs flanked, naturally, by date palms. Isolated from but overlooking the winery, it is the Seppelt family mausoleum. Hourly tours of the winery, costing $1, take place seven days a week. Tasting hours are Monday to Friday 8.30 am to 5 pm, Saturday 10.30 am to 4.30 pm and Sunday 11 am to 4 pm.

Wolf Blass Wines, Sturt Highway, Nuriootpa, is the domain of Wolf Blass who made his mark in South Australia much more recently than Joseph Seppelt but who would seem to emulate that patriarch. Blass earned his reputation as a maker of fine wines in the mid 1970s when he won the Jimmy Watson Trophy, Australia's most prestigious red wine prize, three years running—a feat yet to be equalled, but his aggression and some would say guile as a marketer have earned him intermittent industry brickbats since those heady days. His marketing strategy was simple, win awards and crow about it, then make every label look the same whether its on an award winner or not. This play has been very successful but whatever one thinks of it, there's no denying the wines are uniformly good and some are excellent. The winery is open seven days a week, from 9.15 am Monday to Friday and from noon on weekends.

Henschke near Keyneton, a small town west of the Barossa Valley, is that rarest of creatures, an old family winery which is still small and run by family members. It is one of Australia's most respected wine producers, a giant in reputation if not in production which celebrates its 120th anniversary in 1988. Henschke's shiraz vines are among the oldest in the Barossa area, dating from the 1890s and the Hill of Grace red that they produce is the kind of wine auctioneers long to get their hands on. Stephen Carl Henschke who presently runs the winery is the fifth generation of the family to do so since Johann Christian Henschke first planted at Keyneton in the 1850s. The cellar lies in a small valley five km (three miles) north of Keyneton township and is open from 9 am on weekdays and Saturdays.

Other wineries which could be profitably included on a tour of the Barossa Valley are **Penfolds**, the giant of Nuriootpa which covers 3 hectares and has storage for over 22 million litres of wine, **Heritage** at Marananga on the way to Seppeltsfield and **Elderton** in the Nuriootpa township, both small, interesting, friendly places and **Saltram** and **Yalumba**, two more old Barossa stalwarts situated on either side of Angaston, east of Nuriootpa.

Other Sights

When not making wine, the jolly Lutherans of the Barossa Valley loved to go to church and they ensured their **churches** reminded them of the old country. **Tanunda** has four good examples. The Langmeil Church, surrounded by lawns and cypress pines, whose adjacent cemetery contains the grave of Pastor August Kavel and other prominent figures in Barossa history, is in Murray Street, the town's main thoroughfare. The Tabor Lutheran Church at the street's northern end has an orb-topped spire. St John's in Jane Street contains some fine wooden statuary and St Paul's on the corner of Basedow Road and Murray Street has a beautiful organ and some lovely stained glass. The Gnadenfrei church at **Marananga**, though it lacks a spire, is one of the prettiest in the valley.

Collingrove Homestead in Eden Valley Road, Angaston, was the home of George Fife Angas' descendants until 1976 when it was presented to the National Trust. The Trust now runs it as a combined museum, restaurant and accommodation house. The single storey building is more a big rambling home than a grand country mansion, though it has great elegance. Its two almost identical wings spread from a central living area, giving the impression of two semi-detached houses with a tiny third in their midst. Verandas run along the wings, each ending in a room with long bay windows. The house contains antique furniture, memorabilia and documents relating to the Angas family. From October to May, it is open 10 am to 4.30

pm Wednesday to Sunday and from June to September 2 pm to 4.30 pm on Sunday only. Cost $2.

Undoubtedly the greatest eccentricity in the Barossa Valley is the **Kev Rohrlach Collection**. Mr Rohrlach was a builder whose work took him to many parts of South Australia and gave him the opportunity to collect a vast, eclectic assortment of mechanical bric-à-brac which would otherwise have been lost. His museum is housed in a former winery on the main road between Tanunda and Nuriootpa. Its highlight is a transport collection ranging from a Maharaja's barouche to a mobile steam engine and the car that won the 1955 Australian Grand Prix. Clearly it's a case of anything that goes, goes. Open 9 am to 5 pm Monday to Saturday, 10 am to 5 pm Sunday. Admission $3.

WHERE TO STAY

Yaldara Barossa Motel, Barossa Valley Highway, Lyndoch, (085) 24 4268, is a highly recognisable building centred on a very ugly two-storey dining room and standing on a hill close to the Yaldara winery just outside Lyndoch. The motel suites are arranged in a curve around a garden and swimming pool. Single $37, Double $45 includes breakfast.

Barossa Junction, Barossa Valley Highway, Tanunda, (085) 63 3400; a motel made out of gutted railway carriages which also features one of the Barossa's better known restaurants. Single $45 to $160, Double $53 to $160.

Blickinstal, Rifle Range Road, Tanunda, (085) 63 2716; motel-style accommodation with kitchenettes, has lovely views over the valley. Single $41, Double $49 includes breakfast.

Collingrove Homestead, Eden Valley Road, Angaston, (085) 64 2061; National Trust property and ancestral home of the Angas family. Accommodation is in the old servants' quarters. Double $48 bed and breakfast.

The Hermitage of Marananga, Corner Seppeltsfield and Stonewell Roads, Marananga, (085) 62 2722; large, comfortable suites with French doors opening onto the establishment's own vineyards, and a good restaurant. Single $64, Double $70 includes breakfast.

Broadoak, 6 Murray Street, Tanunda, (085) 63 3054, is a guesthouse set in an old bluestone cottage just outside the centre of Tanunda. Share facilities. Single $30, Double $50 includes breakfast.

Lawley Farm, Krondorf Road, Tanunda, (085) 63 2141, is a country property where the old farm cottage and its nearby barn have been restored and converted into bed-sitting rooms with en suite bathrooms. Owners Mike and Janica Nichols also conduct two day wine tours. Single $59, Double $69 includes breakfast.

EATING OUT

Producers of good drink can usually be expected to attract producers of good food and this is no less true in the Barossa than in other such places.

Pheasant Farm, Off Seppeltsfield Road, Nuriootpa, (085) 62 1286; enjoys an Australia-wide reputation for excellent country cooking. Pheasant is on the menu of course as well as trout and yabbies (small, freshwater crustaceans) from the artificial lake which does double service as a diners' view. You may also discover champagne and stilton soup, rabbit sausage and kangaroo with quince glaze on the menu. Licensed. Mid to upper price range. To find the restaurant follow the signs from Seppeltsfield Road. Closed during February.

Marananga Restaurant, Seppeltsfield Road, Marananga, (085) 62 2888, occupies a one roomed stone cottage with a fireplace at one end, thick wooden posts and roof beams, and rustic furniture. The food is plain but hearty and the wine list features some local quality. Licensed. Low to mid range prices.

Die Gallerie, 66 Murray Street, Tanunda, (085) 63 2788, prides itself on German food such as wursts and dumplings. Diners share pleasant surroundings in any season with a cosy, fire-warmed room in winter and a courtyard for summer eating. Licensed. Mid price range.

Vintners, Nuriootpa Road, Angaston, (085) 64 2488, is run by a restaurateur couple from Melbourne who cook in the French style with some interpolations from other cuisines. Prime beef is a feature. Their wine list is excellent and the premises a study in space and local stone. Licensed. Mid price range.

Zinfandel Tearooms, 58 Murray Street, Tanunda, (085) 63 2822; is a great place to eat so much afternoon tea that you can forget about dinner. The tearooms specialise in strudels and crumbles as well as chocolate Bavarian cream pie. Lunches with a German flavour are also available. No alcohol. Low price range.

TOURS

Tours of the Barossa Valley depart daily from Adelaide. The **Premier Roadlines**, (08) 217 0777, tour approaches the valley from the south through Gawler and returns through Angaston; the **Briscoes**, (08) 212 7344, travels through the Torrens Gorge, approaching the Barossa from the north and returns through Gawler. Both tours cost $26 which includes lunch.

Those who want to learn something about grape growing can take a walk in a vineyard with **Ray Hahn**, a fifth generation grape grower. He conducts tours of his own vineyard at 2 pm from Monday to Saturday from October to June. Phone (085) 62 1045. The tour costs $3.

Vintage Festival

The Barossa celebrates a Vintage Festival over Easter each year. The festival includes grape picking and treading contests, concerts, dinners, a fair, art shows, a wine auction and town days when individual settlements celebrate their histories. Anyone who wants to stay in the valley for this sometimes riotous event needs to secure accommodation well beforehand. Information about the festival can be obtained from Coulthard House, 66 Murray Street, Tanunda, (085) 62 1866.

Outback South Australia

South Australia is one of Australia's least settled states. Outside the south-east the land is barren and inhospitable and anywhere north of Spencer Gulf is thinly populated, surfaced roads are few and good quality gravel roads are not many.

Towns are small and scattered. The further a traveller goes, the closer he comes to the red heart of Australia—the temperature rises and the water runs out but in parts of the outback, especially the Flinders Ranges, the landscape is spectacular.

Desert Banded Snake

The Flinders Ranges

The Flinders Ranges begin to rise between Peterborough and Crystal Brook, about 240 km (149 miles) north of Adelaide and spread over a wide section of country as far as Marree, 430 km (267 miles) to the north. They are not high mountains but a range of very ancient weathered sedimentary rock formations pushed up from the sea about 1600 million years ago. Folded and buckled into multi-coloured cliffs and peaks, they have been worn down over an immense time, exposing their hard cores in convoluted shapes and arresting formations such as St Mary's Peak and Wilpena Pound. Minerals laid down in their age-old sediments colour the hills with purples, mauves, reds and yellows.

The Flinders Ranges also exhibit a startling climatic change as the traveller moves north from their temperate and relatively well-watered southern slopes to the arid, hot desert which overtakes their northern peaks.

Quorn

A railway town which came to life in 1879 when connected to Port Augusta by narrow gauge line, Quorn rose to become an important junction on both the east–west and north–south trans-continental routes during the 1920s and 1930s. By-passed by the standard gauge railway in 1956, it fell into decline, only to be revived a little by Flinders Ranges tourists during the past couple of decades.

GETTING THERE
There are no trains or regular commercial flights to Quorn, the only public transport is by Stateliner coach from Adelaide. The trip takes 6 hours and costs $23.20.

Services run three times a week leaving Adelaide on Monday and Wednesday at 9 am and Friday at 4 pm. Phone (08) 217 0777.

The shortest driving route to Quorn from Adelaide is via Clare, Gladstone and Wilmington, a distance of 376 km (233 miles) which can be covered in about half a day. It is all sealed except for a section of 20 km (12 miles) on the Wilmington to Quorn road.

TOURIST INFORMATION
There is an information bay in Railway Terrace, tourist information is also available from the District Council Office in Seventh Street.

WHAT TO SEE
The town has resurrected its railway history by reconstructing part of the old track through the **Pichi Richi Pass** which leads to Port Augusta. Tourists can take a two and three quarter hour steam train ride into the pass from the old Quorn Railway Station (1916). The train crosses century-old stone bridges and embankments through a narrow pass which also accommodates road traffic and the Pichi Richi River. The journey includes Pichi Richi township, abandoned in the 1880s when the railway passed it by. The restored train runs during school holidays and on long weekends; information about its timetable is available from the Quorn Motel (086) 48 6016.

The style of late nineteenth-century Quorn remains in three **historical buildings**, the public school (1880), Bruses Hall (1885) and the Town Hall (1891). The town's oldest building is Quorn Mill, built in 1878 as a flour mill and later used for grain storage. It's now a tourist site with accommodation, a restaurant and arts and crafts shop.

The Yarrah Vale, Warren, Buckaringa and Middle **Gorges** cut into the ranges north of Quorn. They are approached by unsealed roads but the trip is worth it as they are the most naturally beautiful places in the district. In the same direction but easier of access are the ruins of **Kanyaka,** a once great homestead which in its heyday, from the 1850s to the 1870s, supported 70 families and was almost a township of its own. Only the ruins of the stone homestead buildings and the graveyard remain, south of the signs that point to Kanyaka settlement. There is a second group of ruins a short distance further along the road behind a rise. The road ends at Death Rock Waterhole, a pretty site despite its name, about a kilometre and a half further on. Walking trails run south of Quorn to Devil's Peak and Dutchman's Stern where there are views over the town and its picturesque valley.

WHERE TO STAY
Criterion Hotel Motel, Railway Terrace, Quorn, (086) 48 6018, has both motel rooms with private facilities and hotel rooms with share facilities. Single $28, double $35 motel; single $20, double $25 hotel. Includes light breakfast.

EATING OUT
It's a case of counter meals at the **Austral Hotel** or the **Criterion Hotel**, both in Railway Terrace. Hamburgers and take-away chicken are available from **Big Al's Fun Parlour** in Sixth Street.

TOURS
Intrepid Tours, 29 First Street, Quorn, (086) 48 6277, operates day and half-day trips north and south of the town to the gorges, the Kanyaka ruins and to Wilpena.

Hawker and Wilpena

The small outback town of Hawker is the main access point for the northern Flinders Ranges, especially Wilpena Pound, an extraordinary geological formation and the highlight of the ranges.

GETTING THERE
There are no trains or regular commercial flights to Hawker, the only public transport is by Stateliner coach from Adelaide. The trip takes 7 hours on the same services as travel to Quorn. The fare is $30.50. The Friday afternoon bus continues to Wilpena which extra distance brings the fare to $32.80. Phone (08) 217 0777 for bookings.

The shortest driving route is via Clare and Orroroo, a distance of 374 km (232 miles) of which the last 100 or so km (62 miles) are unsealed. Anyone not wanting to attempt the unsealed section can reach Hawker via National Route 47 from Quorn which is sealed. The run from Hawker to Wilpena is also sealed.

TOURIST INFORMATION
Hawker Motors, in Cradock Road is the local tourist information centre.

WHAT TO SEE
Hawker is another of the railway heads that fell away when by-passed in the 1950s and came to a new life thanks to the tourists. Places of historical interest in the town include the recently restored **Railway Station** (1880) and its associated complex of yards and workshops as well as other late nineteenth-century buildings such as the Hawker Hotel, Flinders View Cafe, Post Office and Institute Building.

The sad stories of failed dreams in which this country abounds can be found in the **ruined wheat stations and settlements** near the town. They include Hookina, Willow Waters, Wilson and Wonoka. A more ancient and much longer history is present in the Aboriginal rock paintings at **Yourambulla Cave** 10 km (six miles) south of the town.

Wilpena Pound, 55 km (34 miles) north of Hawker on the edge of Flinders Ranges National Park, is the great natural sight of the Flinders Ranges. The pound is a basin of about 80 square km (50 square miles), encircled by a ring of mountains, some rising to well over 1000 metres. On the outer edge of the circle, multi-coloured cliffs rise in an almost impenetrable barrier but on the inside, the basin slopes relatively gently from its high edge to a central plain. It is a natural refuge for wildlife, especially kangaroos and birds from multi-coloured parrots and budgerigars to wedge-tailed eagles. The only access to Wipena Pound is on foot through a narrow gorge above Sliding Rock near the Wilpena Pound Motel. Walking trails in the pound include a climb up St Mary's Peak, at 1190 metres the highest on the circle, for a magnificent panorama of the whole basin, and walks across the basin floor to Malloga Falls and Tanderra Saddle. The pound is not Flinders Ranges National Park's only attraction, Bunyeroo and Brachina Gorges provide scenic variety and at Aroona more ruins show what drought and hostile Aborigines could do to even the most persevering settlers.

WHERE TO STAY

Bookings for accommodation can be made in Adelaide at Flinders Ranges Tourist Services, 32 Whitmore Square, (08) 212 6386.

The Hawker Hotel Motel, Elder Terrace, Hawker, (086) 4891, when connected ask for 95; is an old style bush pub which has modern, air-conditioned motel units behind. Single $38, Double $47.

Flinders Ranges Outback Motel, Hawker, (086) 4891, when connected ask for 111; air-conditioned units and a dining room. Single $46, double $51.

Wilpena Pound Holiday Resort, Wilpena, (086) 48 0004; is the only settlement on the edge of Wilpena Pound and has motel units, a swimming pool and camping area. Single $60, double $65, includes light breakfast.

Yappala Station, off Leigh Creek Road, via Hawker, (086) 4891, when connected ask for 24; is a working sheep station nine km (five and a half miles) from Hawker where there are air-conditioned holiday units of various sizes from single rooms to a three bedroom family unit. Write to PO Box 35, Hawker, SA 5434 for bookings.

EATING OUT

As the town has a permanent population of 350, restaurateurs have a hard time making a living but travellers can dine at the **Hawker Hotel Motel** and the **Flinders View Cafe** in Elder Terrace.

TOURS

Flinders Ranges Safaris, (086) 4891, when connected ask for 49; operates four-wheel drive tours of the area.

Scenic flights and the hire of four-wheel drives can be arranged at the **Flinders Ranges Outback Motel**.

Wilpena Pound Motel is the centre for scenic flights over and tours into Flinders Ranges National Park.

Rawnsley Park Homestead, 20 km (12 miles) south of Wilpena on the Hawker to Wilpena Road, offers saddle and pack horse treks into the pound. The station also holds sheep shearing demonstrations every Sunday at 10 am in September and October and has some accommodation available.

Coober Pedy

Coober Pedy is South Australia's centre of opal mining. It stands on the Stuart Highway, the road between South Australia and the Northern Territory, 850-odd km (530 miles) north of Adelaide and its name is thought to mean 'white man's hole in the ground' from the words 'kupa' meaning white man and 'piti' meaning hole or burrow. The name is apt—the people of Coober Pedy live underground to escape daytime temperatures of around 50°C and night-times of equally uncomfortable cold. The climate is so dry that water has to be imported.

The town's drifting population, most of whom come in the hope of striking it rich and don't, is drawn from any number of nationalities. They dig for opals in thirty different fields in and around the town, the furthest being Shell Patch, 35 km (22 miles) north.

GETTING THERE

Kendell Airlines flies from Adelaide to Coober Pedy on Monday, Wednesday, Friday and Saturday. The fare is $192. Phone (08) 212 1111 for bookings.

Coach services from Adelaide to Alice Springs on Greyhound, Ansett Pioneer and Deluxe stop at Coober Pedy. The trip takes about ten hours and the fare is around $60.

Drivers take National Route 1 from Adelaide to Port Augusta and continue on Route 87 (Stuart Highway) to Coober Pedy. The distance is 855 km (530 miles).

WHAT TO SEE

Visitors to Coober Pedy who expect beauty are likely to be sadly disappointed. The universally used descriptive word for town and its surroundings is 'lunar' and I cannot offer a more appropriate adjective. Anyone who has seen Mad Max III will know what is meant from the searing red desert scenes which characterised that film—they were shot close to Coober Pedy. What there is to see is man-made and underground and will give you an education in opal mining.

Opals are mined in quantity at various places in Australia which would otherwise be deserted, Coober Pedy is the largest of them and produces more opal than anywhere else in the country. Opals are a precious stone of relatively low value compared to diamonds, emeralds and the like but valuable enough to be worth mining. They are not uniquely Australian but Australia produces more opal than anywhere else in the world by a long stretch. The multi-coloured stones come in three cuts, **cabochons** which are domed-topped stones of pure opal, **triplets** which consist of a layer of opal with opaque backing and a transparent cap and **doublets** with the same backing but no cap. Black and crystal opals are the most valuable, semi-black and semi-crystal come next and milk opal is least sought after. High-domed opals are better than flat ones and big ones, provided they are clear and have no flaws are also worth more.

Coober Pedy has been an opal mining centre since about 1915, the stone was first discovered there in 1911. Mining, originally done with picks and shovels, is now carried out with more sophisticated machinery but the manual labour required remains hard and dangerous. The trick of living underground to escape the heat and cold was learned in the mines and miners turned their skills to making 'dugouts' for their families when they were not chipping away for opal. A couple of display mines which include underground homes and, of course, opal shops are open to visitors. The **Opal Cave** and **Umoona Opal Mine Museum** are two such places of which the latter, run by the local Aboriginal community, covers Aboriginal history as well. The town also has two **underground churches**, St Peters and St Pauls.

WHERE TO STAY
Opal Inn Hotel Motel, Main Street, Coober Pedy, (086) 72 5054; one of the few things above ground, air-conditioned. Has counter meals and à la carte dining room. Single $42, double $48.
Umoona Opal Mine, Museum and Motel, Main Street, Coober Pedy, (086) 72 5288; yes, travellers can stay here as well as tour the mine. $12 per person.

EATING OUT
Traces Restaurant, Hutchinson Street, Coober Pedy, (086) 72 5147; charcoal grills and some Greek specialities. Licensed. Mid price range.

TOURS
Town and mine tours are operated by Coober Pedy Tours (086) 72 5333, Prospector's Opal Tours (086) 72 5338 and Kmets Tours (086) 72 5163.

Camel Trecks
If the idea of riding a camel into Australia's outback stirs your adrenalin, try a company called **Transcontinental Safaris** which operates such adventures into the Flinders Ranges and even wilder places. The Flinders camel train has its base at Merna Mora Station on the Hawker to Leigh Creek Road west of Wilpena and operates regular one day, overnight, five day and seven day treks in the Flinders region which usually include Wilpena Pound. They cost between $45 and $625. Much longer journeys, up to 24 days, venture into the wastes of the Simpson Desert and Sturts Stony Desert. Four-wheel drive safaris are also available from the same company. For more information contact Rex Ellis, Transcontinental Safaris Pty Ltd, PMB 251, Kingscote, Kangaroo Island, South Australia 5223. Phone (0848) 93 256. Details are also available from South Australian Government Travel Centres in Sydney, Melbourne and Adelaide.

Part IX

WESTERN AUSTRALIA

Western Australia is a giant among Australian states in terms of territory, a dwarf in population. In over 2.5 million square kilometres, nearly one third of the continent, it fits 1.4 million people, less than one tenth of the population. The state sprawls from the western borders of South Australia and the Northern Territory to the Indian Ocean. Its coastline is over 5000 km (3100 miles) long and vast areas of it and the huge inland expanse it borders are unpopulated. The Great Sandy Desert, the Gibson Desert and the Great Victoria Desert form the greater part of the state's arid centre from the Kimberley Ranges in the north to the Nullarbor Plain in the south.

The population is concentrated in the south-west corner, in and around Perth, protected by the fertile Swan and Avon Valleys and tall karri and jarra forests of the Margaret River region. These areas are famous for magnificent wild flowers which cover the fields and forests with all the hues of the painter's pallet each September. Away from the south-west, population thins east through a wide wheatbelt to the outback gold mining communities of Kalgoorlie and Coolgardie or north to the huge iron ore mines of the Pilbara. The Kimberley in the far north, much closer to Darwin than Perth, is cattle country, red, rugged and riven with ironstone gorges. Its coast around Broome has the starkest, most brilliant colours on the continent and the sea there gives up pearls to Japanese and Filipino divers.

Their isolation—Perth is 4000 km (2480 miles) from Sydney—gives Western Australians a strong regional consciousness that pays no heed to the niceties of life on the east coast. This is particularly so in business where Perth millionaires—there are more millionaires per head of population in Perth than anywhere else in the country—have a tendency to walk in and take over old eastern states business

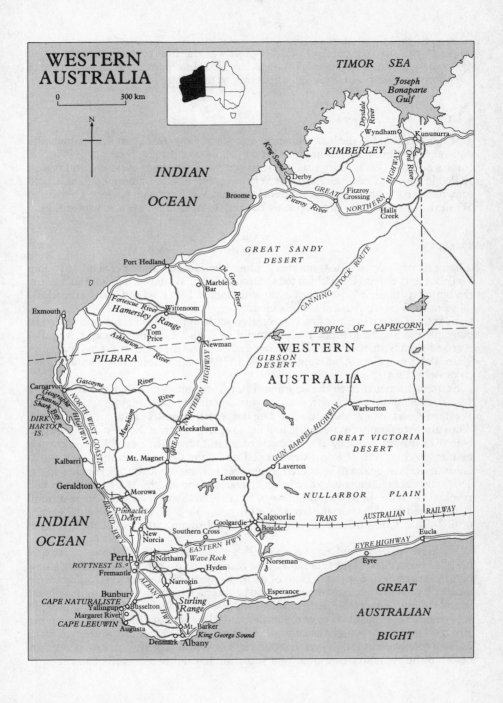

WESTERN AUSTRALIA

0   300 km

N

TIMOR SEA

Joseph Bonaparte Gulf

Drysdale River

Wyndham

Kununurra

KIMBERLEY

Derby

King Sound

Broome

GREAT

Fitzroy Crossing

NORTHERN HIGHWAY

Fitzroy River

Halls Creek

Ord River

INDIAN

OCEAN

GREAT SANDY DESERT

Port Hedland

Marble Bar

De Grey River

Exmouth

Fortescue River

Hamersley Range

Wittenoom

Tom Price

CANNING STOCK ROUTE

TROPIC OF CAPRICORN

Newman

Ashburton River

WESTERN

GIBSON DESERT

PILBARA

River

AUSTRALIA

Carnarvon

Gascoyne River

Geographe Channel

Shark Bay

DIRK HARTOG IS.

NORTH WEST COASTAL

Murchison River

GREAT NORTHERN HIGHWAY

Meekatharra

Warburton

GREAT VICTORIA DESERT

GUN BARREL HIGHWAY

Kalbarri

Mt. Magnet

Leonora

Laverton

Geraldton

Morowa

NULLARBOR PLAIN

INDIAN

OCEAN

Pinnacles Desert

BRAND HWY

New Norcia

Southern Cross

Coolgardie

Kalgoorlie

Boulder

TRANS AUSTRALIAN RAILWAY

Eucla

Perth

ROTTNEST IS.

Fremantle

Northam

EASTERN HWY

Wave Rock

Hyden

Norseman

EYRE HIGHWAY

Eyre

Narrogin

Bunbury

CAPE NATURALISTE

Yallingup

Busselton

Margaret River

CAPE LEEUWIN

Augusta

ALBANY HWY

Stirling Range

Mt. Barker

Denmark

Albany

King George Sound

Esperance

GREAT

AUSTRALIAN

BIGHT

empires with no 'beg pardons.' Although it was the first part of Australia to be discovered, the state is distinctly younger than its counterparts in the development of a modern economy and it retains something of the frontier about it.

Climate

The Perth region has the best climate of any Australian city, a great deal of sunshine and very little humidity, although winters can be wet if mild. The north is in the tropics and has wet and dry seasons, with occasional summer cyclones, and is best visited in winter. The desert parts are very hot (over 40°C) in summer and have cold (down to zero) nights but pleasant days in winter. Wherever you go, take a hat as the Western Australian sun is ferociously burning to pale skins, even in winter time.

History

The coast of Western Australia was explored by Dutch sailors between 1616 and 1699 but not settled. The British too showed little initial interest in it, only extending the boundary of their 1788 colony as far as longitude 129° East and leaving the whole of modern Western Australia unclaimed.

Fear of a French landing finally motivated settlement 38 years later and a party of convicts and soldiers under the command of Major Edmund Lockyer was dispatched from Sydney to claim King George Sound on the south coast in December 1826. Perth and Fremantle were settled in 1829 but the farming was poor and most colonists returned east.

Settlement schemes to the south and north struggled or failed and by the late 1840s it seemed that isolation and a severe labour shortage might drive the whole Western Australian venture to ruin. The desperate colonists cried out for convicts. Thus almost as transportation finished in the east, it began in the west, enabling that colony to survive and grow if not exactly prosper. During the next 20 years, grazing country to the north of Perth was opened up by the Gregory Brothers and wheat lands to the east began to be settled. A number of trans-continental crossings in the 1870s also helped increase knowledge of grazing land and by 1880, cattlemen had reached as far north as the Kimberleys. Small gold discoveries were made around Perth and in the Pilbara in the late 1880s but really big gold rushes did not take place until 1892 at Coolgardie and Kalgoorlie, finally bringing substantial population to the colony.

Western Australia did not receive self-government until 1890 and so was an understandably reluctant federator. The resentment over being swept into a new nation almost before it had a taste of its own independence was re-kindled in the Great Depression when the state suffered badly and felt poorly treated by its fellows. A movement for secession arose and in 1933 a referendum recommending the split was passed by almost two to one. Despite this clear wish on the people's part, the British Parliament, which was empowered to rule on such matters, refused to do so and the secession question lapsed in the glare of World War II. Post-war prosperity resolved the economic questions and secession has not been heard of since.

GETTING TO AND AROUND

Getting to Western Australia from anywhere else is a time-consuming, expensive and intermittent business. The nearest city to Perth is Adelaide and it is over 2000 km (1240 miles) away.

By Air

Perth is the only air gateway to Western Australia. It takes both international and interstate flights. **Ansett WA** operates between Perth and major towns along the north coast and in the Hamersley and Kimberley regions. **Skywest** links Perth with 17 Western Australian towns including Kalgoorlie and Albany.

By Rail

The *Indian Pacific* train links Sydney and Perth via Adelaide and the *Trans Australian* travels from Adelaide to Perth. Rail travellers from other states must join these trains at either Sydney or Adelaide. Western Australia has a small rail network radiating from Perth into the south of the state.

By Road

Coach transport into and around Western Australia is on the big four operators **Ansett Pioneer, Greyhound, Deluxe** and **Bus Australia**. There are two routes into the state, one across the Nullarbor Plain from Adelaide and the other through the Kimberley and down the coast from Darwin. Greyhound travels through the inland via Newman and Meekathara on the way from Darwin and Ansett Pioneer uses an inland route to Perth from Ayers Rock. The distance from Adelaide to Perth is 2815 km (1745 miles, 35 hours), from Darwin via the coast 4444 km (2755 miles, 57 hours) and inland 4364 km (2706 miles, 33 hours). Adelaide to Perth coaches pass through Norseman and Kalgoorlie and all important coastal towns are served by the northern route. Only Deluxe runs south to Albany.

The road across the Nullarbor Plain from South Australia is sealed as are major highways north and south of Perth. Minor roads in the south-west are also generally surfaced but once off the main routes elsewhere, it's strictly dirt.

TOURIST INFORMATION

The **Western Australian Tourism Commission** publishes a wide-ranging series of brochures on towns and districts in Western Australia. They are not fantastically informative but they give a general run-down on what's to be seen in particular places and what sort of accommodation is available. The commission's offices are called Holiday WA and can be found at:

772 Hay Street, **Perth**, (09) 322 2999
92 Pitt Street, **Sydney**, (02) 233 4400
2 Royal Arcade, **Melbourne**, (03) 63 3692
307 Queen Street, **Brisbane**, (07) 229 5794
108 King William Street, **Adelaide**, (08) 212 1344

The local tourist information centres listed under individual towns are generally open from 9 am to 5 pm Monday to Friday and 9 am to noon on Saturday. In larger centres and during holiday periods they often open on seven days a week.

Time

Western Australia sets its time two hours behind the eastern states and one and a half hours behind Central Time. When there is daylight saving on the east coast the margin extends to three hours as the Western Australians don't follow this convention.

MAJOR SIGHTS

There's no doubt that **Perth** has one of the most beautiful settings among Australian cities and probably has the best climate. It also doesn't suffer the smog and snarl of the big eastern cities though it is quite big enough to have plenty of life. **Fremantle**, since it was painted-up for the 1987 America's Cup has charm and the old gold rush town of **Kalgoorlie** is romantic in a decidedly rough way. The **Margaret River** where vineyards and surf beaches lie within a few kilometres of each other is unique in Australia as is the north-west coast around **Broome** with its red sand and tropical greenery. The desert country of the **Pilbara** and the ancient mountains of the **Kimberley** offer dramatic desert scenery—gorges and escarpments, similar to that of the Northern Territory.

ACCOMMODATION

When the Americas Cup came to Western Australia two presumptions were made, that it would stay and that it would be the progenitor of a tourist boom in the west. Neither happened. The cup went back Stateside and the tourists, who hadn't lived up to expectations even when the battle was in full sail, reverted to their former trickle. The result is that there's no lack of good quality rooms in Perth or Fremantle and that accommodation prices are lower than in the rest of Australia. Unusual places to stay exist in the Avon Valley east of Perth where some colonial houses have been turned over to the tourist trade. South of Perth is where the locals take their summer holidays and it can get crowded at that time of year. Motels and caravan (trailer) parks are the norm here as well as occasional 'resorts' a little distant from towns and offering extra inducements such as tennis courts and their own beachfronts.

FOOD AND DRINK

The great Western Australian delicacy is Rock Lobster but we won't mention the prices asked for it as they are enough to frighten anyone away. Most of them are consumed in places other than the west. A local speciality is an ugly-looking, black-shelled freshwater crustacean called the marron. It is farmed and served in the Margaret River area south of Perth and is quite good eating—difficult of access but sweet. The Margaret River and Swan Valley are Western Australia's wine districts and their vintages are well worth trying. You'll find these wines strongly represented on most wine lists and in bottle shops. They are discussed at length in this guide's sections on where they are grown.

Eating out can be a very pleasant experience in and around Perth. The city has many interesting BYOs and licensed restaurants with strong representation from Italians and Vietnamese. There is also good eating in the Avon and Margaret River Valleys.

ACTIVITIES AND SPORTS

Australian Rules Football and cricket are the main spectator and participatory sports in Western Australia. Big matches take place in Perth at the WACA (pronounced wacker), the Western Australian Cricket Association ground. International competition is limited to cricket which supplies a few one day encounters and one test per year.

Sailing and windsurfing are popular in the Swan River and off the coast at Fremantle and Yanchep, north of Perth, the best surfing is to be had on the south-west and south coasts and fishing is common to all coastal locations. As with the rest of Australia, tennis courts exist in all but the smallest communities, the town council office will tell you where they are.

PERTH

The city on the Swan River is credited with being Australia's 'young' state capital. In reality it is about the same age as Adelaide but has earned a brash, youthful reputation in the last twenty years during which time the city and its state have undergone extraordinary growth, developing from a backwater to a centre of aggressive commerce.

Thankfully, the city's people often have more time to talk than the residents of other Australian cities. They drive more slowly and seem rather bemused by the ever climbing storeys. They perceive the advantages of their isolation from the rest of Australia as much as its drawbacks and enjoy the presence of tourists who, despite energetic promotion, remain relatively few.

Perth also likes to see itself as a city of millionaires. Moguls such as Lang Hancock, Alan Bond and Robert Holmes a Court have become legendary names in Australian business, wheeling and dealing establishment east coast money out of its own territory and moving into international markets like hungry predators. The houses of Dalkeith and Peppermint Grove, on the Swan's northern shore, are evidence of no shame in late twentieth-century wealth and almost every time one arrives in town, the buildings are higher. Bond, the man who funded Australia's much fêted Americas Cup win, is the latest contributor with a glass tower overlooking everything in the city centre by storeys.

History

The site of Perth was discovered in 1697 by a Dutch navigator named de Vlamingh who named its river the Swan after the black swans he found there. In 1829 Captain James Stirling arrived with the first settlers and founded a colony that struggled—almost failing on more than one occasion—until the 1860s when it finally could be said to have found its feet. Perth was proclaimed a city in 1856 at the height of a 20-year convict era which provided many public buildings and gave the community breathing space in which to establish a firm economic base. Few of those buildings remain but the gaol and courthouse, so necessary to a penal colony, have been preserved as part of the Western Australian Museum.

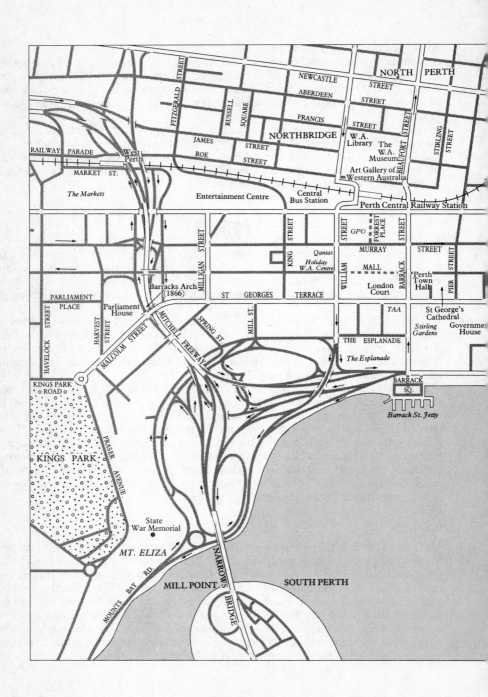

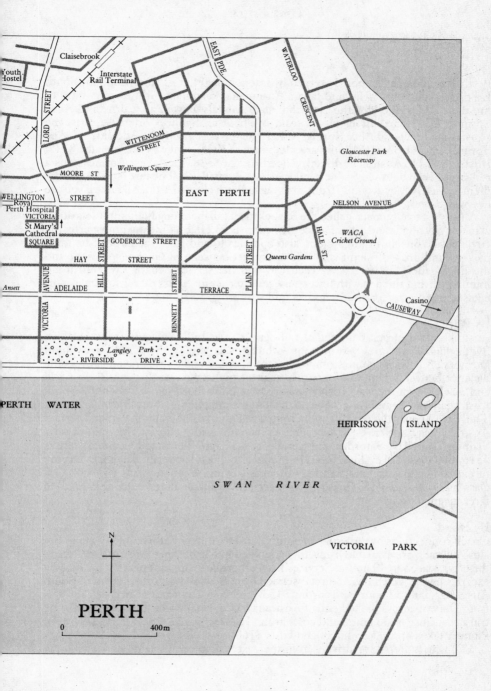

Claisebrook

Youth Hostel

Interstate Rail Terminal

EAST PDE

WATERLOO

LORD STREET

CRESCENT

WITTENOOM STREET

Wellington Square

MOORE ST

WELLINGTON STREET

Royal Perth Hospital

VICTORIA

St Mary's Cathedral

SQUARE

HAY

GODERICH STREET

STREET

HILL STREET

VICTORIA AVENUE

ADELAIDE

Ansett

STREET

BENNETT STREET

TERRACE

PLAIN STREET

EAST PERTH

Gloucester Park Raceway

NELSON AVENUE

HALE ST.

WACA Cricket Ground

Queens Gardens

Casino

CAUSEWAY

Langley Park

RIVERSIDE DRIVE

PERTH WATER

HEIRISSON ISLAND

SWAN RIVER

VICTORIA PARK

N

PERTH

0   400m

GETTING TO PERTH

By Air

Perth International Airport is served by international flights from London, South East Asia, southern Africa and Japan. Ansett and Australian Airlines carry most of the domestic traffic into the city from state capitals as well as Cairns and Alice Springs. There are direct flights from Melbourne, Sydney, Adelaide, Brisbane (Australian only) and Alice Springs, otherwise travel is mostly via Adelaide or Alice Springs. Fares from major cities are Melbourne $396, Sydney $444, Adelaide $342, Brisbane $611 (Australian direct), Alice Springs $328. East West Airlines runs a red-eye special between Sydney and Perth via Ayers Rock. The fare is $444 and the flight leaves Sydney around 10 pm, arriving in Perth close to 4 am. All fares given are one way economy.

An airport to city coach called the Skybus meets all incoming flights and sets down at major city hotels and airline offices. The fare is $3.50. Bus 338 on Transperth, the city's public bus and train system, also operates to and from the airport. Its main pick-up and drop-off point is in William Street between St George's Terrace and the Esplanade. The fare is $1 each way and the service departs every 40 to 50 minutes during the day with fewer services after 6 pm. A taxi ride from the airport takes about 20 to 25 minutes and should cost around $10 to $15.

By Rail

Australia's only trans-continental rail service, the Indian-Pacific, runs between Sydney and Perth. Beloved of train enthusiasts as 'one of the world's great train journeys', it takes its name from the oceans at either end of the line and covers the distance between them in 65 hours over three nights passing through Broken Hill and Adelaide on the way. It shoots across the Nullarbor Plain between the South Australian border and Kalgoorlie on the longest straight of railway line in the world. Those who cover the entirety of its route see almost all the kinds of inland terrain Australia has to offer, especially some of its more arid sections. The train departs Sydney Thursday, Saturday and Sunday at 3.15 pm. The single economy fare is $516, first class $696. The *Trans Australian* also links Perth with Adelaide. Departures are Wednesday and Saturday 6 pm and 9 pm. Economy fare $333.50, first class $454.50. Adelaide to Perth seats are also available on the *Indian Pacific*. All fares given are one way.

By Road

Coach connections by the usual operators, Ansett Pioneer, Greyhound, Deluxe and Bus Australia are available from Adelaide. The fare is between $100 and $120 and the trip takes 35 to 40 hours. Services from other state capitals operate via Adelaide except Deluxe which has a 'direct' service from Sydney via Port Augusta in South Australia taking 52 hours and costing $153. The same companies run coach services from Darwin across the top end of Australia and down the west coast to Perth. The trip takes close to 60 hours and costs around $200. Ayers Rock to Perth on Ansett Pioneer takes around 33 hours and costs $160.

The way to Perth for drivers from the east is also via Adelaide and across the

Nullarbor Plain, a distance of over 2700 km (1674 miles). The road is sealed all the way but the difficulties of the trip may be gathered from the fact that those Australians who haven't done it treat those who have with added respect. It is also possible to follow the coast from Darwin via Broome, a distance of over 4400 km (2728 miles).

GETTING AROUND
Perth is an easy city to walk but it has a tempting an inner city bus service which might have been designed for tourists. Free buses called **City Clippers** take routes which cover almost all the tourist spots except the Cultural Centre which is so close to their departure point that it doesn't matter. The routes are colour coded yellow, red, green and blue. Information about them and about all local transport is obtainable from their departure point, the **Central Bus Station** in Wellington Street. Perth's **Central Railway Station**, from where trains depart to all points outside the city, is next door. Information about public transport in and around Perth can also be obtained at the Transperth office, 125 St George's Terrace, (09) 325 8511. The MTT as it is known also operates river ferries from Barrack Street Jetty. The jetty is on the blue City Clipper route.

TOURIST INFORMATION
Information about Perth is available from a tourist booth in Hay Street Mall and from the Holiday WA Centre, 772 Hay Street, Perth, (09) 322 2999, which is just outside the mall across William Street. It is open from 9 am to 5 pm from Monday to Friday and on Saturday mornings. The Post Office is in Forbes Place Mall between Murray and Wellington Streets.

Orientation
Perth's streets are arranged in a long narrow grid. The city centre is bounded to the south by St George's Terrace, the main business district, which stands high over parks and gardens, flanked by hotels and history; to the east by Barrack Street which runs down to the edge of Perth Water; to the north by Wellington Street which runs past the bus and railway stations and to the west by King Street, connecting Wellington Street and St George's Terrace.

Hay Street Mall
Hay Street, which runs through the centre of Perth city, has been converted into a pedestrian mall between Barrack and William Streets. The mall is Perth's main shopping centre and makes a feature of arcades that lead off on both sides to Murray Street and St George's Terrace. They are full of bright shops and coffee lounges as well as housing the city's cinemas. The mall is excellent for general shopping and a good place to start your walking tour of Perth. **London Court** is the most eccentric of its arcades. The court is an open laneway of little shops built in 1937 in an hilarious mock-Tudor style complete with medieval clocks around which mechanical knights joust in tune with the passage of time. It was built by Claude de Bernales who made his fortune on the Kalgoorlie gold-fields.

St George's Terrace

Although stacked with high rise buildings, St George's Terrace is the city's most historical street. A Hollywood touch has been added to it by the insertion of bronze plaques in the pavement recalling the names of contributors to the Western Australia's history, a few true relics also remain. **Barracks Archway**, all that is left of the 1860 Pensioners Barracks, stands at the western end of the terrace behind **Parliament House**. The somewhat incongruous arch, a castellated, three-storey, 'toy-soldierish' gateway made of Flemish-bond brickwork was left standing as a memorial to the state's pioneers only after a bitter civic fight some years ago. **Government House**, built between 1859 and 1864 and still the residence of the Western Australian Governor, stands at the eastern end of the terrace. The building is an exuberant Gothic revival structure which caused no end of protest at the time of its construction. On completion, its cost was $30,000, twice the original estimate. The elaborate gardens which surround it are opened to the public on celebratory occasions. Government House is flanked by two modern buildings, the **Council House**, Perth's centre of civic administration, and the **Perth Concert Hall**, the city's venue for musical performances including opera.

The **Supreme Court** stands below Government House. Its complex of buildings includes **The Old Court House**, built in 1836 and now one of Perth's oldest surviving structures. In its early days it saw double duty as a boys' school and court. The boys had to move out when legal proceedings were in session. It is now a museum of legal history, open 9.30 am to 12.30 pm on Tuesday. The **Supreme Court Gardens** whose wide lawns and tall Norfolk Island Pines front the court buildings, provide breathing space for city workers during summer lunchtimes and provide a lovely walkway down to **Barrack Street Wharf** where ferries and river cruise boats depart.

Schools and Churches

As always in Australian cities, the churches staked out some of the best property early and have hung onto it. **The Deanery** on the corner of Pier Street and St George's Terrace was occupied by the first Anglican Dean of Perth in 1859 and remains a church administration centre today. **The Cloisters** between King and Milligan Streets was the city's first secondary school for boys, established by Bishop Hale in 1858. **The Old Perth Boy's School** on the southern side of the terrace between William and Mill Streets was built in 1854 and despite being a government school, one need look no further than its medieval church architecture to feel the influence of religion. It later became the Perth Technical College and is now the headquarters of the National Trust of Western Australia. Open on weekdays from 10 am to 3 pm.

Two other prominent nineteenth-century buildings stand just off St George's Terrace. First is **St George's Cathedral** next door to the Deanery but approached from Cathedral Avenue. The site has seen three churches, an original wood and rush building—the colony's first place of worship—hurriedly constructed in 1829, a later stone church which served until 1841, and the present structure. The other is **Perth Town Hall** on the corner of Hay and Barrack Streets. The town hall is convict built in the style of an English market—there were once stalls beneath its arches, and some windows in its tower resemble reversed broad arrowheads, the British Government's mark for convicts.

Cultural Centre

The Perth Cultural Centre lies over the railway tracks in the close city suburb of Northbridge. It is within easy walking distance of the city centre and can be reached by crossing Horseshoe Bridge over the railway. The centre consists of several buildings gathered around an open space which would be called a piazza or square in Europe but is designated a mall in Australia. Seats, sculpture and brightly decorated shade sails lift what is otherwise a rather bleak and wind-blown space. Its main attractions are the Art Gallery of Western Australia and the Western Australian Museum.

The Art Gallery of Western Australia is closest to Horseshoe Bridge and just to the right as one enters the Cultural Centre Mall. It is not a large or overwhelming gallery and much of its collection consists of works by contemporary Australian artists few overseas or even interstate visitors will have seen before. Consequently, there is a lot of painting that is hard to contextualise but also the occasional startling piece, especially amongst the gallery's small but impressive sculpture showing. Some esoteric interest can be drawn from the works by middle ranked Australians of the early and mid twentieth century including the stagey works of Roy de Maistre, Grace Cossington Smith's electrifying post-impressionism and Margaret Preston's unique paintings of native flora. Hans Heysen's *Droving into the Light* and Frederick McCubbin's *Down On His Luck* are perhaps the gallery's most recognisable Australian works. There is also a comprehensive gathering of paintings by Clifton Pugh.

The gallery has also made an assiduous collection of work by Aboriginal artists ranging from the Papunya area in central Australia to Arnhem Land and Bathurst and Melville Islands in the Northern Territory. More than the usual level of explanation accompanies these works in a pamphlet detailing the artists' use of modern and traditional media and the commercialisation of their traditional arts as well as some of their mythological significance.

The Western Australian Museum, located on the corner of the mall and Beaufort Street, is centred on the **Old Gaol**, completed in 1856 and used as a courthouse and gaol until 1889. It was built by convicts who made the walls of limestone rubble, filled with mortar and plastered. The building has been restored to something close to its original appearance and serves as an historical and cultural museum of Western Australian life. Its exhibits range from household items of the nineteenth and early twentieth centuries to political documents (including the secession petition of 1933), records of how Western Australia was explored and surveyed and memorabilia of such influential political figures as John Forrest, the state's first Premier, later a Federal politician and lastly Lord Forrest of Bunbury.

The museum's **Aboriginal gallery** is its best feature. The first habitation, art, religion and way of life of Western Australian Aborigines are carefully set out in photographs, text, artefacts and re-creations. Their remarkable adaptation to changes in environment from coasts to inland deserts is elucidated and the coming of the white man—for which invasion is taken as the historical model—is detailed with no shirking from its nastier side.

Other buildings house a negligible show of stuffed animals, a transport display featuring vintage and veteran cars and a few horse-drawn vehicles but the highlight among these eccentricities is the the Mundrabilla meteorite, a boulder-like lump of almost pure iron which landed at Mundrabilla in the western desert many thousands of years ago. It is rusty and pock marked and would probably fit neatly into the back of a pick-up truck except that it weighs enough to squash one. Other examples of planetary debris which have fallen to earth in the same region are also displayed and explained at length.

Northbridge
The Cultural Centre Mall is actually part of James Street which continues west into the Italian suburb of Northbridge. Although it is rather run down and neglected in comparison to the glittering city across the tracks, this is where many of Perth's good, small restaurants are found and it's a great place to get a cup of coffee, have an easy lunch or just soak up some atmosphere. Perth's tiny Chinatown, Chung Wah Lane, is also here. It runs between James and Roe Streets.

Kings Park
Perth residents were left a great city park by their prescient forebears. Kings Park covers 400 hectares of ground to the west of the city, most of which is completely untouched bush. Its most prominent feature is Mount Eliza, the knoll overlooking the Swan River from which one gains the best city view by day or night. The mount and its surroundings are places of manicured lawns, wishing wells, plots of annuals, lookouts and the like. The freeway system which carries traffic into, out of and past the city, itself set amongst lawns skirting the river's edge, rushes beneath. The city view you see reproduced on postcards is taken from the **State War Memorial** in the the park. There is another lookout on top of Dumas House in Kings Park Road. The park is decorated in spring by displays of the wildflowers for which Western Australia is famous.

The Beaches
Perth's western suburbs stretch along the coastline of the Indian Ocean. A string of beaches run north from Cottesloe, on the banks of the Swan River, and can be followed right out of the metropolitan environs. They have fine white sand, vivid blue water and gentle surf. Most of the beaches are backed by sand-dune vegetation with the exception of Scarborough, where Alan Bond's 'Observation City' dominates the skyline. Coastal roads skirt nearly all of the beaches and you can get to them by bus from the Central Bus Station in Wellington Street. **Cottesloe**, **City Beach**, **Trigg** and **Scarborough** are the best known and there is a nude beach at Swanbourne. Perth also has riverside beaches between the yacht-clubs at Matilda Bay, Crawley, Peppermint Grove and Como.

NIGHTLIFE
Perth is not over-endowed with opportunities to let your cultural juices flow—unless you are there during its annual cultural festival in January/February—but it does have a couple of major theatres and concert venues. High-brow music is

usually confined to the **Perth Concert Hall** on St Georges Terrace but that hall also accommodates touring rock bands that don't expect huge audiences. Huge audiences go to the **Perth Entertainment Centre** in Wellington Street which seats 8,000 but can also accommodate smaller audiences, especially for musicals. The West Australian Ballet, the West Australian Opera Company and the West Australian Arts Orchestra are all headquartered in **His Majesty's Theatre**, corner King and Hay Street. The Western Australian Theatre Company makes its home at the **Playhouse Theatre**, corner Hay and Pier Streets where it presents contemporary plays and classics.

Perth has a **casino** on Burswood Island in the middle of the Swan River, east of the city. It has a show room, restaurants and bars as well as gambling. For specific information about who and what is appearing at these venues, consult the Friday edition of **The West Australian**, Perth's morning newspaper which carries of comprehensive listing of what's on in town called *Where to Go*.

WHERE TO STAY

Merlin Perth, 99 Adelaide Terrace, Perth, (09) 323 0121; an Asian style luxury hotel with a huge atrium, is one of the latest additions to Perth's crop of up-market places. Has over 400 rooms some of which overlook the Swan River. Single $120, double $140.

The Orchard Perth, 707 Wellington Street, Perth, (09) 327 7000; a luxury place with marble foyer and marble bathrooms and every mod con in the rooms. Opposite the Perth Entertainment Centre and surrounded by a complex of shops and restaurants. Single $110 to $130, double $130 to $150.

Parkroyal, 54 Terrace Road, Perth, (09) 325 3811; has one of the best views in town, overlooking the Swan River. A good hotel but showing its age a little against some of the newer places. Restaurant, two bars. Longer walk to the city centre than other city hotels but still not far. $118.

Parmelia Hilton, Mill Street, Perth, (09) 322 3622; another with views over the parks to the river. Again, amongst the older places in high rise establishments. Has the usual Hilton manner. Single $110 to $160, double $125 to $175.

Sheraton Perth Hotel, 207 Adelaide Terrace, Perth, (09) 325 0501; is one of Australia's older Sheratons but then so many Sheratons in Australia are practically brand new. Standard room $125, deluxe $125.

Ansett International Hotel, 10 Irwin Street, Perth, (09) 325 0481; very glossy place with every comfort including bars, restaurants, gym and sauna. 243 rooms mostly in a tower block. $110.

Perth Ambassador Hotel, 196 Adelaide Street, Perth, (09) 325 1455; a good, middle-of-the-road hotel. $110, $130 deluxe rooms.

The Mount Plaza Hotel, 24 Mount Street, Perth, (09) 481 0866; is one remove from the city centre but close to Kings Park. Rooms are a good size and some include cooking facilities. A good value option. Single $80, double $90.

Greetings Hometel, 875 Wellington Street, West Perth, (09) 322 6061; one and two bedroom apartment style accommodation aimed at families. Decoration and furnishings are basic motel level. One bedroom $55, two $72.

Paradise Hill Hotel, 15 Constitution Street, East Perth, (09) 325 1866; a step

down in standard from the previous listings, this hotel has a variety of accommodation from single rooms to four bedroom apartments. You will need to take a bus or
taxi into town. Hotel single $44 to $50, studio room $70, family room $91. One
bedroom apartment $80, two $100, three $137, four $160.

Miss Maud European Hotel, 97 Murray Street, Perth, (09) 325 3900; a small
hotel whose rooms are decorated and furnished with complete disregard for aesthetics but whose location is very convenient. Rooms have the usual colour TV, tea
and coffee making facilities etc. Single $52.50, double $65 includes breakfast.

Jewell House Private Hotel, 180 Goderich Street, Perth, (09) 325 8488; a big
unlicensed hotel which is best for budget conscious travellers who want to be close
to the city centre. Expect to get what you pay for. Single $22, double $32, twin $34,
family (sleeps five) $55.

Observation City Resort Hotel, Scarborough Beach, (09) 245 1000; is a high rise
resort hotel on the beachfront at Scarborough and looks like something moved from
the Queensland Gold Coast by mistake. Standard room $95, superior $120 to $170.

EATING OUT

For a small city, Perth has a goodly number and variety of restaurants although few
will challenge you with an adventurous menu. Lots of small, inexpensive Asian and
Italian places can be found in the Northbridge and Mt Lawley area close to the city
but in no case will you have to wander far from town for a meal.

The Plum, 47 Lake Street, Northbridge, (09) 328 5920; is a silver service restaurant where lightly sauced fresh ingredients make the food a delight. The atmosphere, low lights and romance, is equal to the menu. BYO. Upper price range.

Vino Vino, 27 Lake Street, Northbridge, (09) 328 5403; has won many awards for
the best in traditional Italian fare. BYO. Mid to upper price range.

Casa Latina, 254 William Street, Northbridge, (09) 328 1769; offers a wide choice
of cheap or expensive items ranging from pastas to baramundi in entrées and veal to
lobster in main courses. Chicken Queen Victoria, a white wine casserole with
mushrooms and onions is especially good. BYO. Low to mid price range.

Quoc Nam, 318 William Street, Northbridge, (09) 227 9017; unlike many of the
so-called Vietnamese restaurants in Perth, which are actually Chinese, this has an
extensive menu of authentic Viet dishes such as South and North Vietnamese
varieties of noodle soup, prawn and pork cole slaw and a number of vegetarian
dishes. The food comes hot and fast and a uniformly dark brown decor is just about
the only drawback. BYO. Low price range.

Hawkers Paradise, 234 William Street, Northbridge, (09) 227 9704; simple decor
and very obliging service lead the way to some excellent Malaysian eating. BYO.
Low price range.

India, 10 Lake Street, Northbridge, (09) 328 4171; offers a small but high quality
range of Indian staples. Try chilli crab or charcoaled prawns. BYO. Low price
range.

Satay Inn, 253 William Street (Brittania Private Hotel), (09) 328 2398; takes its
inspiration from the subtle flavours of Singapore, offering such delicacies as fried
white bait with roasted peanuts in chilli and delicious home-made spring rolls for

starters. Main courses take up the satay theme—marinated meats served grilled on skewers. BYO. Low price range.

Copacabana, 37 Lake Street, Northbridge, (09) 328 2730; offers a fixed price menu with various selections for each course. Charcoaled chicken, pork rib and prawn (shrimp) dishes are specialities and there is a pleasant if small alfresco dining area. BYO. Low price range.

Nonnatina's, 147 Beaufort Street, Northbridge, (09) 328 1229; excessively plain decor but extremely good Italian food in uncomplicated style. BYO. Low price range.

Jessica's, Shop 1, Merlin Centre, Merlin Hotel, Adelaide Terrace, Perth, (09) 325 2511; may be the best seafood restaurant in Perth and adds a view over the Swan to its attractions. Selections are from a blackboard menu and the staff helps diners unaccustomed to local fish varieties. Licensed. Upper price range.

Hana of Perth, Mill Street (opposite the Hilton Hotel), Perth, (09) 322 7098; is one of Perth's best Japanese, has tatami rooms and a sushi bar, à la carte dining or set menu. Licensed. Mid to upper price range.

Me and You, Shop 1, Doric Street, Scarborough, (09) 341 6929; a touch of French modernity near the beach. BYO. Mid price range.

Clementina's, 279 Rokeby Road, Subiaco, (09) 381 8398; housed in a restored cottage with an intimate atmosphere and log fires in the winter. An interesting menu with French influence. Subiaco is a suburb a little west of Perth city. BYO. Mid price range.

Farqies, Clyde Street, Mosman Park, (09) 384 2539; a favourite of Perth's yuppies who seem to like venison and roast duckling amongst other things. On Sunday nights it lowers its prices and allows the less well-heeled in. Licensed. Upper price range.

Pubs and Cafés

A recent cosmopolitan legacy, Perth's coffee shops and cafés—many with gardens or terraces—provide delightful lunch-time, or late-night, venues where you can either linger over a coffee or eat a full meal. Here are a few favourites: **Sonny's Le Café**, Rokeby Road, Subiaco. **Bar Bazaar**, Hay Street, Subiaco and **The Desert Café**, Beaufort Street, Northbridge.

Live music, be it from a chamber orchestra or rock band, can be heard in many of the pubs in Perth, particularly at the Sunday lunchtime 'session'. **Steves**, The Broadway, Nedlands, **Queens**, Beaufort St, Northbridge and **The Brewery**, Stirling Highway are just three on the pub circuit.

TOURS AND CRUISES

Ansett Pioneer, (09) 325 8855, and **Parlorcars**, (09) 325 5488, are the major day tour operators in Perth. They run run half and full day coach tours of Perth city sights, some including Fremantle. **Feature Tours**, (09) 271 1131, specialises in evening tours of the city which include dinner and drinks but has a range of day tours as well. The **Perth Tram**, actually a bus mocked up to resemble a tram, takes one and a half hour trips around the city sights from 9.30 am to 6.30 pm every day. It picks up from 124 Murray Street (near Barrack Street).

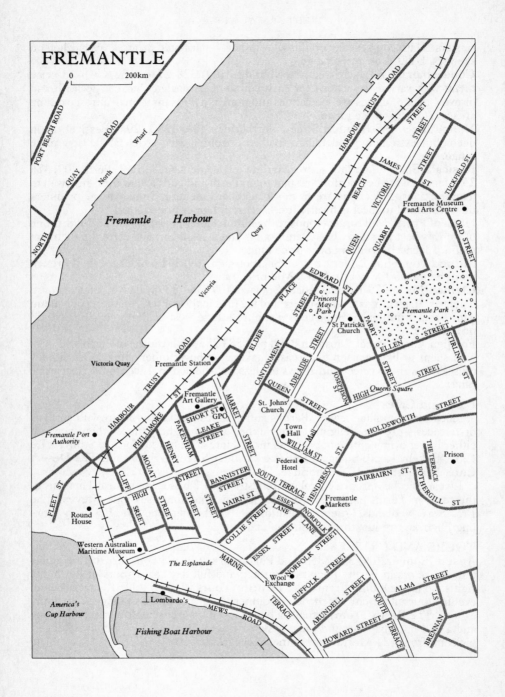

FREMANTLE

0   200km

Fremantle Harbour

PORT BEACH ROAD
QUAY ROAD
North Wharf
NORTH
Victoria Road
HARBOUR TRUST ROAD
Quay
BEACH
QUEEN
Victoria Quay
Fremantle Station

HARBOUR TRUST RD

PHILLIMORE ST

Fremantle Port
Authority

FLEET ST

CLIFF

MOUAT STREET

HIGH SREET

Round
House

Western Australian
Maritime Museum

America's
Cup Harbour

The Esplanade

Fishing Boat Harbour

HENRY STREET

PAKENHAM STREET

Fremantle
Art Gallery
SHORT ST
GPO
LEAKE STREET

MARKET STREET

BANNISTER STREET

NAIRN ST

COLLIE STREET

MARINE
TERRACE

Lombardo's
MEWS ROAD

ELDER STREET
PLACE

CANTONMENT

EDWARD ST

Princess
May
Park

QUEEN

ADELAIDE STREET

St. Johns
Church

Town
Hall

Federal
Hotel

SOUTH TERRACE

WILLIAM ST

HENDERSON ST

Fremantle
Markets

ESSEX LANE

ESSEX STREET

Wool
Exchange

SUFFOLK STREET

ARUNDELL STREET

HOWARD STREET

NORFOLK LANE

NORFOLK STREET

JAMES STREET

VICTORIA STREET

ST

TUCKFIELD ST

Fremantle Museum
and Arts Centre

ORD STREET

St Patricks
Church

Fremantle Park

PARRY STREET

ELLEN STREET

STIRLING ST

STREET

HIGH
Queens Square

JOSEPHSON ST

Queens Square

HOLDSWORTH STREET

THE TERRACE

Prison

FOTHERGILL ST

FAIRBAIRN ST

SOUTH TERRACE

ALMA STREET

BRENNAN ST

River cruises depart from Barrack Street Jetty. They run either up river to the vineyards of the Swan Valley, down river to Fremantle or just around Perth. Prices vary from $8 to over $30, depending on the length of the cruise and whether food and drink are provided. The major cruise boats are *The Captain Cook*, (09) 325 3341MV Countess, (09) 425 2651, the *Lady Houghton*, (09) 325 6033, and *Miss Sandalford*, (09) 325 6033. The last two are vineyard cruise boats.

Fremantle

Fremantle is Perth's port district. As well as being the place where Kevin Parry lost the Americas Cup in 1987, it is a suburb of history and charm. The auld mug, supposed to 'put Fremantle on the map', didn't stay long enough to do so and now the old port has returned to the quiet of former days. Race fever did rouse the locals to paint up their nineteenth-century shop fronts and pubs, open enticing sidewalk cafés and spruce up some historical buildings: an easy-going day's sightseeing is the result.

GETTING THERE

Fremantle stands at the mouth of the Swan River and, although this impression seems to be encouraged, is not a separate settlement from the rest of the metropolis. It is reached by driving about 20 km (12 miles) through the suburbs, a half-hour journey from the city centre.

Buses depart regularly from St Georges Terrace. Trains leave Perth Central Railway Station in Wellington Street with equal regularity. The Stirling Highway is the main traffic route from central Perth to Fremantle. If you have a map, you could follow the river along roads through Nedlands, Dalkeith, Claremont and Peppermint Grove for some of the best views of the city.

TOURIST INFORMATION

Information is obtainable from a small cottage two doors down from the Round-house in Cliff Street. It has brochures of walking tours, places of historical interest and activities and is open the same hours as the Roundhouse.

WHAT TO SEE

Fremantle is first and foremost a port and parts of it have all the grime, grit, run-down sheds and buildings, cranes and storage silos one associates with such places. However, these unsightly items are not a reflection of the old town which has been carefully preserved for the amusement of tourists and Perth residents alike. Provided one keeps to the streets and wharves of that district, the modern port does not intrude.

Historical sites

Fremantle is named after Captain Charles Howe Fremantle who claimed the west coast of Australia for the British crown in May 1829. Very shortly afterwards,

Captain James Stirling arrived in the '*Parmelia*' with Western Australia's first white settlers. By 1831 they had built a gaol. **The Roundhouse**, as it is called, stands today as an empty, roofless tribute to the necessity of locking people up even in the earliest days of colonisation. It is Western Australia's oldest remaining public building and stands overlooking the Indian Ocean at the end of High Street. It is actually a dodecahedron made of limestone with cells around the walls and a well in the central courtyard. After its construction, the prisoners were required to dig a tunnel beneath it, not for escape, but to allow products brought ashore from the whaling fleet easy access to High Street. The look-out in front of the Roundhouse neatly divides Fremantle in half with the working port to the right and the pleasure port to the left. The Roundhouse is open from 11 am to 1 pm and 2 pm to 4 pm Wednesday and Thursday, 10.30 am to 1 pm and 2 pm to 4.30 pm Friday, and 10.30 am to 12.30 pm and 1.30 pm to 4.30 pm on Sunday.

The Western Australian Maritime Museum at the junction of Cliff Street and Marine Terrace, also of convict construction, was built in 1850 as a commissariat store. It now houses fascinating exhibits salvaged from seventeenth-century Dutch merchantmen wrecked off the Western Australian coast. Most prominent among them is the *Batavia* which came to grief off the Abrolhos Islands in 1629 carrying a cargo of gold and silver coins. A section of the *Batavia*'s hull is being reconstructed in a side gallery. Viewing platforms allow visitors to see conservators undertaking this painstaking but fascinating process.

The museum also houses cannons and coins, including pieces of eight, from the *Batavia* and other wrecks. One of its most riveting pieces is Dirk Hartog's Plate. Hartog is the first European to have left documentary evidence of his landing on Australian soil. He was captain of the United East India Company's ship *Eendracht* which came, by mistake, upon the coast of Western Australia on 25 October 1616, whilst sailing from the Cape of Good Hope to Bantam in Java. Hartog anchored off an island close to the coast where the ship remained for two days while he examined the mainland. He found nothing profitable and moved on, leaving behind on the island a pewter plate tacked to a post and bearing a short inscription recording his landing. He continued up the coast, making a chart between 26° South and 22° South where he finally left the still-barren land behind. The museum is open from 10.30 am to 5 pm Monday to Thursday and 1 pm to 5 pm Friday to Sunday. Admission $1.

Fremantle Museum and Arts Centre in Finnerty Street was built as the Swan River Colony's lunatic asylum between 1861 and 1865 and has since served as an old ladies' home and the World War II headquarters of the US forces stationed at Fremantle. Slated for demolition in 1957 but saved at the last moment, the large sandstone rather gothic building took 13 years to restore, re-opening in 1970. The museum section is devoted to records and relics of Fremantle's growth and also contains more debris from the wreck of the *Batavia* as well as the arms and armour collection of the Western Australian Museum. It is open the same hours as the Maritime Museum. The arts centre houses studios, workshops and exhibitions by Western Australian artists and crafts people. It is open 10.30 am to 5 pm Monday to Saturday and 1 pm to 5 pm on Sunday. The extra hours of 7 pm to 9 pm are added on Tuesday and Thursday.

Other places of historical interest include **Fremantle Prison** in The Terrace (off Fairbairn Street), built between 1851 and 1859 by convicts to house convicts and still doing so, the properties in Cliff and Ord Streets associated with the **Samson Family**, who came to prominence in Fremantle during the late nineteenth century and remain so today, and the **churches**, St John's (corner Adelaide and Queen Streets), St Patrick's (corner Adelaide and Parry Streets), the Wesley Church (corner Market and Cantonment Streets) and Scots Presbyterian (corner South Terrace and Norfolk Street), all built during the late nineteenth century.

Pubs and the Market

Fremantle had some rollicking pubs in its young days. The rollicking has faded but a couple of excellent pubs recall its heyday. The **Sail and Anchor** in South Terrace is a fully restored 1903 building but the site, formerly the Freemasons' Hotel, has been occupied by pubs since the 1850s. Other than atmosphere—of which it has plenty—its main claim to fame is in-house brewing.

The new Australian trend to individual hotels brewing their own beer in the face of boring mass-produced product started here and has ballooned into a national obsession. Known as 'boutique brewing' it has produced such unforgettable drops as the **Dog Bolter**, a beer of such alcoholic thump that it takes only one to lay you on your back. Fremantle's other grand old pub is the **Federal Hotel** opposite the Town Hall in William Street. It dates from 1887 and was extended in 1904.

The Fremantle Markets are a weekly institution whose local prominence has grown metro-wide over the past few years. The markets take place in a building constructed for that purpose and dating in part from 1897. As well as the fruit, vegetables and other produce, gifts and work by many Perth and Fremantle crafts people are available from market stalls. The markets are on the corner of South Terrace and Henderson Street opposite the Sail and Anchor and operate from 9 am to 9 pm on Friday, 9 am to 5 pm Saturday and 11 am to 5 pm on Sunday.

The Waterfront

The coming of the Americas Cup to Fremantle saw extensive commercial development of the waterfront. The wharves opposite the Western Australian Maritime Museum, which used to support a fish shop or two, have been edged with elaborate boardwalks over which restaurants, from up-market glass and steel extravaganzas to refurbished fish and chip joints, beetle threateningly. They look across Fishing Boat Harbour to the berths once occupied by those great 12 metres which fought for the 1987 cup. The whole effect is a little sad now and there must be one or two worried restauranteurs in town but a walk around the boards in the sun loses nothing for the absence of yachting glories.

WHERE TO STAY

Esplanade Plaza Hotel, Marine Terrace, Fremantle, (09) 430 4000; the only substantial hotel close to the centre of Fremantle. $120. Large reductions on weekends.

Norfolk Hotel, 47 South Terrace, Fremantle, (09) 335 5405; one of Fremantle grand old pubs which has the advantage of some rooms with private facilities. Single $30 share facilities, $45 private, twin $55 private.

Tradewinds Hotel, 59 Canning Highway, Fremantle, (09) 339 8188; Fremantle's new hotel built to accommodate Americas Cup visitors. It overlooks the Swan River near Stirling Bridge and so is a mite too far from the town centre to make walking there a realistic option. Single $60, double $65.

EATING OUT
Some people come to Fremantle for the express purpose of eating out. The food is not great but is of reasonable quality and the atmosphere is delightful. There are waterfront restaurants, sidewalk cafés along South Terrace and one or two elegant eating houses in old buildings. The emphasis is on Italian and seafood since both have played a long, honourable and inseparable part in Fremantle's history. It was Italian immigrants who established the port's fishing fleet after World War II.

Lombardo's Fishing Boat Harbour, Mews Road, Fremantle; is the major water-font complex and offers indoor and outdoor dining of various classes from full à la carte to takeaway fish and chips. **Harbour Lights**, (09) 430 4343, is the major high cost venue. Licensed. Mid to upper price range. **Sea Shells Bistro**, (09) 430 4346; serves excellent seafood at reasonable prices. Licensed. Low to mid price range.

Papa Luigi's, 33 South Terrace, Fremantle, (09) 336 1599; is a Fremantle institution which has grown from a corner café to a sunny terrace overlooking the street. It serves everything from coffee and cakes to pasta meals and family dinners. BYO. Low to mid price range.

Domenic's, Hampton Road, Fremantle, (09) 335 7251; a busy, noisy family-run restaurant with seafood and pasta on the menu as well as steaks and roast chicken. BYO. Low price range.

Wray Bar, Corner Wray Avenue and South Terrace, Fremantle, (09) 335 9892; white linen and fresh flowers characterise this intimate place which pushes the menu a little further than most Fremantle eateries. Try New Zealand mussels or *pasta e fagioli*. BYO. Low price range.

Koto, 39 High Street, Fremantle, (09) 336 2455; consistently successful Japanese which some say is the best such restaurant in the whole of Perth. Small, café-style place with some sidewalk seating and delectable food. BYO. Low to mid price range.

Bengal, 48 High Street, Fremantle, (09) 335 2400; here you would be well advised to ask the waiter how hot the curry is as the restaurant is known for its authenticity. The lamb korma is especially good and not too hot. BYO. Low price range.

TOURS
Fremantle is so close to Perth that it is included in many coach tour itineraries covering the city. For tours contact the operators mentioned in the Perth section.

The Fremantle Tram, a local version of the Perth tram, departs hourly from the car park in front of the Maritime Museum for tours around Fremantle streets. The cost is $3.

Rottnest Island

This island lies 18 km (11 miles) off Fremantle and is an extremely popular day trip and short holiday destination for the people of Perth and is a good place for relaxing and lying around on the beach.

Dutch seaman Willem de Vlamingh named the island, when he landed there in 1696, after the *quokkas*—small marsupials related to wallabies—which he mistook for giant rats, hence Rottnest. Quokkas are now a protected species, unique to the island, and can be found in many bushy places.

Originally used as a prison for Aborigines, Rottnest has been an official tourist resort since 1917. Cypress pines around Thompson Bay, the main resort area, afford some of the only shade on an island with sparse vegetation and intermittent wind-bent tea trees. It is universally sandy, has few hills but does boast many small, rocky bays and white sand beaches where it is possible to escape the the summer crowds. There are some small, shallow, salt lakes in the centre of the island but the most attractive thing about Rottnest is the colour of the water that encircles it—true turquoise blue.

The reef surrounding the island provides protected lagoons and some interesting **shipwrecks** for snorkelling. These are pointed out, although not all actually to be seen, on a marked trail around the island. There are 12 shipwrecks in total. **The Basin** is the island's most popular swimming spot. It lies a short distance north of the main settlement and is protected from wind by rocky headlands at either end.

GETTING TO AND AROUND

Rottnest Airlines flies daily from Perth Airport. Boats depart from Barrack Street Jetty in Perth and from Fremantle. If you leave from Perth, there is a commentary for the Swan River section of the trip; $22.50 or $25 day return depending on whether you take the slow or the fast boat. Once on the island, people usually hire bikes to get them from beach to beach. Rottnest Bike Hire, behind the Rottnest Hotel, has the bike hiring concession ($6 per day with a $10 deposit).

TOURIST INFORMATION

There is a Tourist Information Centre at the end of the main jetty.

WHERE TO STAY AND EAT

Accommodation on Rottnest is mostly in the Thompson Bay area and consists of small cabins, some hotel and motel rooms, a guest house and a camping ground. Units can also be rented at Geordie Bay and Longreach Bay. All accommodation is controlled by the Rottnest Island Board and at peak times it can be very difficult to acquire as Perth holidaymakers head for the island in droves. For information on tariffs and bookings, phone the board on (09) 292 5044.

Note: Rottnest suffers from severe water shortages so all the showers in accommodation are salt water. You can buy salt water soap and shampoo on the island but it is cheaper on the mainland.

Hotel Rottnest, which overlooks the main beach and a small jetty, used to be the summer residence of Western Australian Governors. It was built in a a style suitable to such eminent persons between 1858 and 1864 but was converted to flats in 1919.

The Pinnacles Desert

It became a hotel in 1953 and has recently been renovated. It is the main rendezvous, nicknamed the 'Quokka Arms'.

You can buy wonderful doughnuts from the Rottnest Bakery but for the main part food is DIY and shops on the island are very expensive.

TOURS
A **Round the Island** bus tour operates from the Tourist Information Centre at the main jetty. The trip takes two hours and returns in time to meet ferries for Perth. An **Underwater Explorer** boat also departs regularly from the main jetty and cruises over shipwrecks and some of the primitive corals which grow off the island.

North from Perth: The Pinnacles Desert

Just inland from the crayfish port of Cervantes, about 250 km north of Perth lies the extraordinary Daliesque **Pinnacles Desert**. The area is one of fine yellow sand covered in limestone pillars of varying heights, mostly between one and three metres (three and ten feet). Rainwater seeping down through the sand dunes gathered minerals from the sand. The calcium carbonate leached into seepage channels and, in this way, cemented into pinnacles, later to be uncovered by wind erosion of the surrounding sand. The best time to see them is just before sunset, when they cast long shadows—a photographer's delight. The desert is in the Nambung National Park. **Pinnacle Tours** run a day trip from Perth for $38. By car, follow the Brand Highway north from Perth to the turnoff to Jurien and the Pinnacle Desert.

Monkey Mia

Monkey Mia is 26 km (16 miles) from Denham, the most westerly town in Australia, between Geraldton and Carnarvon. There is a marine reserve there where you can literally swim with the dolphins. The dolphins come right into the

416

beach and are tame enough to be petted. They come in during the dry months from April to November. In nearby **Shark Bay** is a unique landscape created by stromatolites. These cauliflower- and mushroom-shaped fossils are remnants of one of the earliest known life forms, and are formed by very slow-growing algae.

Swan Valley

Perth is the only city in Australia to have a wine-making district on its doorstep. The Swan River, on which the city stands, runs north-east into the Swan Valley, a wide, flat valley edged with low hills where mixed farms alternate with wineries. As the city's fertile hinterland, the district has been occupied since early days. Ever-expanding Perth has swallowed up the valley edges so that once separate rural communities are now suburbs and country wineries are almost in the urban area.

GETTING TO AND AROUND
Trains depart regularly from Perth Central Station for Midland, the gateway to the Swan Valley, stopping at the historical town of Guildford.

The Swan Valley is served by Transperth buses from Perth city. They travel through the valley to Upper Swan along Middle Swan Road and there are frequent services.

The Swan Valley is about 30 km (19 miles) from Perth, around half an hour to forty minutes driving time. The route from town runs along Guildford Road or the Great Eastern Highway as far as Midland and then onto the Great Northern Highway which runs through the centre of the valley.

TOURIST INFORMATION
The Swan Valley Tourism Association is headquartered under the clocktower of Midland Town Hall, Great Eastern Highway, Midland.

Guildford

This town was once a separate settlement east of Perth but has been consumed by the quiet suburban push of Perth's nearly one million people. It has clung to its historical character and trades on it to some extent. Places to see in the town include **Woodbridge House**, built in 1885 on the banks of the Swan River as a summer retreat for the Perth personality Charles Harper. Harper led a rich life, and was an explorer, pastoralist, pearler, inventor, educationalist, newspaper proprietor and politician. His house has been restored by the National Trust in the style of its period and is open 1 pm to 4 pm on Monday, Tuesday and Thursday to Saturday, and 11 am to 1 pm and 2 pm to 5 pm on Sunday. Closed on Wednesday. **St Matthew's Church** in Stirling Square and the **Courthouse Gaol** on the corner of Swan and Meadows Streets are other nineteenth-century buildings.

Like many places close to rural fields but not far from the city, Guildford has attracted more than its share of craftspeople. Their works can be seen at the **Guildford Potters**, 105 Swan Street, Guildford. Open 10 am to 3 pm daily.

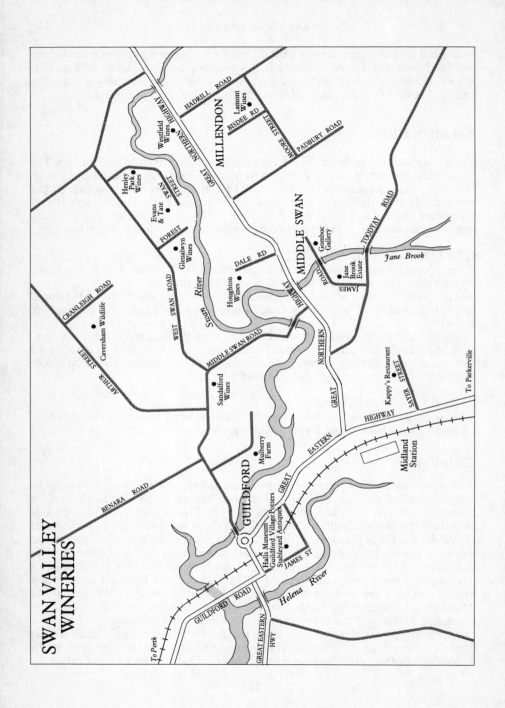

SWAN VALLEY
WINERIES

Vineyards

The Swan's first vines were planted in the 1830s around Guildford but the current high production is based on much more recent plantings in the Middle Swan area. Except for a couple of heavyweights, the wineries are run by committed individuals or couples who produce generally good but not remarkable regional wines. Grapes come from the Swan Valley or the Margaret River area in south-west Western Australia with some from the cooler Frankland River region further south. Varieties such as Verdelho and Zinfandel, rarely grown in other parts of the country, tend to pop up here quite regularly.

Houghtons

This is the best known and largest of the Swan Valley wineries. It produces a White Burgundy, among Australia's top selling wines but only one of a wide range, concentrated in the whites. Houghtons produced its first commercial wines in 1859. It is one of the most prettily sited wineries in the valley, set among tall trees and carefully overgrown with vines, in a dale reached by driving through close packed, hilly vineyards along the river's edge. The complex of low timber and sandstock brick buildings is set-up to receive large groups of visitors who are welcome to picnic on the surrounding lawns. The winery can also be reached by boat from Perth (see River Cruises). Your reception here is tuned to the mass-market inclination of the winery and, in my experience, the staff at the tasting counter are not expert. The winery is in Dale Road, Middle Swan, off the Great Northern Highway. Open 10 am to 5 pm Monday to Saturday, noon to 5 pm Sunday.

Sandalford

Next down the ladder in size and, once again, a producer of mass market vintages made largely from Margaret River grapes. Sandalford is refreshingly simple and accurate in its labelling and produces a very good Rhine Riesling, generally drier than wines of the same name from South Australia and the east. The Sandalford complex is not so luckily sited or so rustic as Houghtons but the tasting staff are polite, knowledgeable and chatty. The winery also does a considerable trade in wine cruise patrons who ride up the river from Perth (see River Cruises). It is in West Swan Road, Caversham, near the corner of Middle Swan Road. Open 10 am to 5 pm Monday to Saturday, noon to 3 pm Sunday.

Evans and Tate

Evans and Tate is one of the few Swan Valley wineries to specialise in reds. Their wines are hard to find in states other than Western Australia as they are not produced in large quantities and tend to be snapped up by the wise people of their own state. The vineyard is new, established in 1975, but its Gnangara Shiraz has already won a number of awards and is backed up by other reds produced from Margaret River grapes. It also produces a Chardonnay. The winery and tasting room is in a small brick building with a sunny courtyard and your welcome there will be friendly and informative. The winery is in Swan Street, Henley Brook, and is open 10 am to 5 pm Monday to Saturday and noon to 3 pm on Sunday. It operates a gift service to the United Kingdom.

Westfield Wines
A small winery, established in 1922 and best known in recent times for its chardonnay. Tastings take place in an informal atmosphere among the barrels in the
cellar. The winery is just off the Great Northern Highway at Baskerville at the
northern end of the valley. Open 8.30 am to 5.30 pm Monday to Saturday.

WHERE TO STAY
The Swan Valley's proximity to Perth has discouraged tourist accommodation but
the **Rose and Crown Hotel/Motel**, 105 Swan Street, Guildford, (09) 279 8444,
has private facilities and air-conditioning in all rooms. Single $32, double $40.

EATING OUT
Swan Valley Restaurant, 15 Benara Road, Caversham, (09) 279 2815; a lovely
place to dine in winter by the open fire, or in summer, alfresco under the vines. Chef
Peter Hill cooks French with a modern touch. Good wine list. Licensed. Mid price
range.

RIVER CRUISES
Miss Sandalford, (09) 325 6033, plies the Swan River from Barrack Street Jetty to
the Sandalford Winery. The cruise includes lunch and Sandalford wines. *Lady
Houghton*, on the same number, does the same cruise to Houghtons' Winery.
Evening cruises with a dinner and cabaret are also available.

Avon Valley

The Avon River is a branch of the Swan which turns east from its mother stream in
the Swan Valley and takes a winding arc, eventually swinging south about 100 km
(62 miles) east of Perth and running through the towns of Toodyay, Northam and
York. This pleasingly hilly area was settled early in Western Australia's history and is
the closest thing to a rural idyll anywhere in the state but, for reasons known only to
themselves, the people of Perth neglect it, preferring to head south.

Nostalgic first settlers named the valley after England's own Avon. In winter good
rainfall makes the countryside richly green. In summer the Western Australian sun
takes its toll and the grass can turn a crusty brown never seen on the banks of this
Avon's gentle Shakespearian namesake. The best time is spring when the greenness
remains but is decorated with pastel coloured everlastings, bright red kangaroo paws
and other beautiful wild flowers.

GETTING TO AND AROUND
Westrail, the rail service which connects Western Australian country centres with
Perth, runs a daily train (except Saturday) called the *Prospector* to Kalgoorlie which
stops at Toodyay and Northam. The train leaves Perth at 3 pm on Sunday, Monday
and Wednesday, 9 am on Tuesday and Thursday and 4.15 pm on Friday.

Westrail also runs a coach service to Northam and York which leaves Perth every
morning. The fare is $7.40. Greyhound bus services from Perth to Port Headland
stop in Toodyay ($9.10).

Drivers go to Midland from where two routes branch, the Toodyay Road to Toodyay and the Great Eastern Highway to Northam and York. It takes a little over an hour to reach any of the three towns, the distance between them is roughly 30 km (19 miles) from town to town.

TOURIST INFORMATION
There are tourist information centres at Connors Mill, Stirling Terrace, on the banks of the Avon River in Toodyay, at Brabazon House, 3 Beavis Place, Northam, and at 105 Avon Terrace, York.

Toodyay

Western Australians call this town 'Two Jay' and pronouncing it any other way is frowned on or not recognised. Though all the Avon Valley towns are intimate, Toodyay is most so—it is the smallest and its hills are rounder and a little steeper than those along the rest of the river's course. It inhabits the crook where the river turns from east to south and its name is appropriately derived from *Duidgee*, an Aboriginal word meaning 'place of plenty'. The present town is not the first to bear the name. The first Toodyay was established eight km (five miles) downstream in the 1830s but proved to be flood prone. The present site was chosen in 1860 for a town called Newcastle. The old Toodyay declined as Newcastle prospered and, in a final act of pillage, the new town took it predecessor's name in 1910.

Thirteen buildings in Toodyay have been classified, i.e. declared worthy of preservation, by the National Trust of Western Australia but few of them are open to the public. **Connors Mill**, in Stirling Terrace which functions as the tourist centre contains a small museum recounting the exploits of Joseph Bolitho Jones. Jones was a bushranger who, after he escaped from the old Toodyay lockup in 1861, committed robberies in the Swan and Avon Valleys. He became known as 'Moondyne Joe' and such is his lasting local fame that a festival is held in his honour on the first Sunday in September each year. The mill is open 9 am to 5 pm Monday to Friday and 10 am to 5 pm on weekends. Closed Saturdays from December to March.

The **Old Newcastle Gaol Museum** in Clinton Street, houses colonial relics and a reconstructed courtroom. Open 1 pm to 4 pm Saturday, 11 am to 4 pm Sunday. A prospect of the town can be gained from **Pelham Reserve Lookout** in Duke Street where there are picnic sites and toilets. **Wild flowers** grow around Toodyay during the spring. The White Gum Company in Sandplain Road, Toodyay, grows some of these blooms commercially but also has access to 700 acres of bushland where they grow wild and where anyone can take a walk..

WHERE TO STAY
Appleton House, Harper Road, Toodyay, (096) 26 2622; a house in the wide-verandaed colonial style set in the hills close to Toodyay. Double $60 Monday to Friday, $70 weekend bed and breakfast.

Northam

Northam, largest of the Avon Valley towns, is the second largest inland settlement in Western Australia but it isn't really very big at all. In keeping with its place on the

Avon River, white swans have been induced to populate the area around the town's road bridge. The **Avon Valley Arts Society** is housed in two well preserved buildings, the Old Girls School of 1877 and the Old Post Office of 1892. The centre's shop sells ceramics and craft work made by local artists and is open 9 am to 4 pm from Tuesday to Friday. The **Old Railway Station Museum** in Fitzgerald Street was the headquarters of the Eastern District railway for 30 years from 1886 when it was built as part of the Eastern Goldfields Railway. Its PMR 721 locomotive, carriages and light railway vehicles are strictly for the railway enthusiast.

Two properties close to Northam represent the highs and lows of colonial life and show how the Avon Valley, once permanently settled, made a good living for its landholders. **Morby Cottage**, east of the town along Avon Drive, was built in 1836 by John Morrell whose family was amongst the first in the valley. It has mud brick walls and floors of stone flagging and was the first home in the valley to have glass in its windows. As well as being the Morrell home, it functioned as Northam's first church and school as well as a flour, milk and cheese factory. The house is open from 10.30 am to 4 pm, on Sundays only. Admission $1. **Buckland**, a 'stately home' 12 km (seven miles) north-west of Northam, marks the opposite end of the scale. Although parts of it date from the same year as Morby Cottage, the valley had undergone nearly 40 years of development by the time it took on the elegant proportions it has today.

Buckland was settled by Charles Pratt who was granted 8,000 acres on the site in 1836. He built a cottage which now forms the east wing of the house. A second cottage, built for his daughter Ann and her husband James Dempster a few years later, forms the west wing. Family difficulties caused the daughter and son-in-law to leave in 1848 and take up a farming lease on Rottnest Island but Pratt died in 1853 and the two returned to found what became an Avon Valley dynasty. The two storey Georgian style stone mansion with wide verandas and spacious rooms which is now Buckland was built onto the northern ends of the two cottages in 1874. Until a few years ago it had been left derelict but has now been restored as a family home by Tony and Penny Motion and furnished with their collection of antiques and paintings. They open the house and grounds every day from 10 am to 5 pm. Admission $3.50. There is also bed and breakfast accommodation at Buckland (see 'Where to Stay' for details).

WHERE TO STAY
Buckland, Buckland Road, Irishtown, Northam, (096) 22 1130; is an elegant old country mansion described in the section on Northam. It offers accommodation in two lovely rooms upstairs in the main part of the house. Breakfast is part of the deal and is usually served English stately home style in the dining room downstairs. Single $45, double $80.

WHERE TO EAT
O'Hara's Restaurant, Shamrock Hotel, Northam, (096) 22 1092; is in a part of the old Shamrock Hotel which has been studiously returned to its former glories by very fastidious owners. It has an international menu. Licensed. Mid to upper price range.

York

York enjoyed great prosperity during early gold-rush days when it was the staging point for gold-fields development. The good times were expressed in energetic building and commercial life but in 1894, by-passed by the railway, York declined, leaving a legacy of architecture appreciated by no-one until the 1970s when the town woke up to its hidden treasure.

Avon Terrace, York's main street, is flanked by pubs, shops and a police station which represent architectural styles from the 1860s to around 1900. The **Old Police Station**, which dominates the street, has been restored with painstaking attention by the National Trust of Western Australia. Its oldest section, the cell-block, now in the centre of the building, dates from 1852. The cold, narrow cells reflect the mania for imprisonment so prevalent in the early settlement of Australia and their date records the time when convicts first began to appear in Western Australian society. Around them is built a complex of law enforcement in all its stages—the original police quarters, now a courtyard, stood in front; a courtroom dating from 1874 is to the south; another more elaborate wing of similar function, built in 1895, fronts the street and beside it stands another police station, built in 1900. They are linked by a confusing network of doorways and passages, which seem designed to keep the offenders at bay and enhance their captors' and judges' authority. The Old Police Station is open from 11 am to 3 pm on weekdays and from 10 am to 4pm on weekends. Admission $2.

The **York Motor Museum** occupies an old shopfront next door. Car enthusiasts will find in it one of the best veteran and vintage car collections in Australia. The vehicles include street cars, racing cars, motor-cycles and even fire engines. The museum is open every day. Admission $3.50. The elaborate and ugly **Town Hall** at the corner of Avon Terrace and Jonquina Street, was built in 1911. It was once the largest such hall in Western Australia.

Historic interest extends beyond Avon Terrace. The **Residency** in Brook Street is the oldest house in the town. It was built between 1842 and 1859 for Resident Magistrate William Goldsmith Meares and is a good example of comfortable colonial living. The single storey house has wide verandas with French doors opening onto them from spacious, airy rooms. It houses a museum of colonial life in York to which many heirlooms from local families have been donated. They include photographs of commercial buildings and private homes still standing in the town, antique furniture and decorative pieces. The Residency is open from 1 pm to 3 pm, Tuesday to Thursday and 1 pm to 5 pm on weekends. Closed Friday and Monday. Admission $1.

Balladong Farm, just outside the York, on the road to Beverley, presents colonial life from a different angle. It is a working farm which operates according to the principles of the mid 1800s when it was first established. The farm buildings date from the 1850s and include a milking shed, shearing shed, granary and stables, hay shed, butcher's shop and blacksmith's shop, all of which have been restored to working order along with much farm machinery. Visitors are likely to see different aspects of farm life depending on when they arrive. Spinning, blade shearing (of sheep), crutching, drenching, milking, chaff cutting with horse powered machinery, ploughing, harrowing and seeding are among the skills displayed at various seasons. The blacksmith works year round. Balladong Farm is open from 9 am to 4 pm, Tuesday to Sunday. Admission $3.

The places mentioned above by no means exhaust the colonial sights of York although they do mark the limit of those regularly open to the public. The town also has two fine churches, **St Patrick's** on Howick Street and **Holy Trinity Church** on Newcastle Street of which the latter contains historical scenes in stained glass depicting the travels of John Ramsden Wollaston, Archdeacon of Albany in the 1850s. Wollaston wrote a journal which includes an account of the church's construction. Western Australian wild flowers and landmarks of the York area can also be seen in the windows. The **Old Hospital** of 1896, now a community centre, is next door to the Residency and there are two old pubs, **The Castle** and **The Imperial** on Avon Terrace in the centre of town. **Mount Brown**, a steep hill with a look-out on top, provides a view of the whole settlement and its surrounding countryside.

WHERE TO STAY
Settlers House, 125 Avon Terrace, York, (096) 41 1096; is probably the best in the valley. It has 21 rooms all double except for one twin and three family units. They are attached to the old Settlers' Precinct in the heart of York (see 'Eating Out') and each is furnished individually with period furniture. One room has a four-poster bed. $65 per person Sunday to Friday, $80 Saturday.

Hillside, Forrest Road, York, (096) 41 1065; is an Edwardian house owned by artist James Cumberland Brown who produces hand-turned woodwork and scrimshaw. Accommodation is available in twin rooms with ensuite and private sitting rooms and includes breakfast. Hillside has a swimming pool, tennis court and bicycles the use of which is included in its tariff. $35 per person bed and breakfast.

EATING OUT
Ensign Dale Restaurant, Settlers' House, 125 Avon Terrace, York, (096) 41 1096; is part of the Settlers' Precinct, a square of shops and accommodation built of local stone in the 1840s, surrounding a leafy courtyard. Good food in an authentic atmosphere. Licensed. Mid price range. There is also a cafe attached where lunch, and morning and afternoon teas are served.

The Avon Descent
On the first weekend in August each year when the Avon River is full and flowing fast around 800 canoeists assemble at Northam to participate in the Avon Descent. The descent is a fast, furious and exciting race which dumps many a paddler in the water before it finishes in Perth, 133 km (82 miles) away. Good natured crowds gather along the river bank to cheer the racers on, carouse and rescue any non-finishers.

Darling Ranges
This range of hills east of Perth and parallel to the coast draws city crowds for weekend and holiday picnics. From September to November over 4000 species of

wild flowers bloom there. They are best seen in **John Forrest National Park** about 40 minutes drive from Perth. Other attractions of the district include look-outs over the city and suburbs to the coast from Kalamunda and some pretty, dell-like spots along the Brookton Highway around Araleun. The **Cohunu Wildlife Park** in Mill Road, Gosnells, allows its patrons to hand-feed native animals.

Hyden and Wave Rock

The small town of Hyden is in the wheatlands between the Avon Valley and the Goldfields. Three km (two miles) from the town is **Wave Rock**; a huge, granite outcrop, shaped into a perfect ocean wave form by wind and rain. It is 15 metres (50 feet) high and mineral washes have streaked the rock with colour.

A nearby formation is **Hippos Yawn** and there are Aboriginal rock paintings at **Bates Cave**, where ancient *gnamma* holes show where Aboriginals exploited cracks in the bedrock to bore for water.

Pinnacle Tours run one day excursions to this area from Perth.

The South-West

Travelling south from Perth, you must first pass through the unsightly agglomeration of nickel smelters and engineering works between Kwinana and Bunbury before reaching the greener and gentler landscape of the Great Southern and south-west region. Once beyond the heavy industry, there are forests of towering jarrah, tuart and karri trees, windswept capes of romantic dreaminess, patchwork fields of wild flowers in spring and small bays of almost story-book arrangement for summer swimming. The rivers give good trout and marron fishing in season. The Stirling Ranges and Porongorups provide good bushwalking and some lovely views.

Busselton

Busselton stands on Geographe Bay, a wide, flat arc, 32 km (20 miles) long, protected at its western end by Cape Naturaliste and running away east and north towards Bunbury. The town is built close to the Vasse River estuary and is a good access point for sights in the northern part of this region.

Busselton's atmosphere is more akin to an English seaside resort than Australian beachsides. There isn't any surf, the beach is flat and narrow, there is a long wooden jetty jutting out into Geographe Bay where people fish and go crabbing—an unassuming amusement park and oceanarium provide beachfront diversion. It is a very safe beach for both swimming and water skiing.

John Garret Bussell, who gave his name to Busselton, migrated to Western Australia from England in 1829 with several of his brothers and took up residence at Augusta near Cape Leeuwin. When the settlement there failed, they moved north to take up land on the shores of Geographe Bay. The track which they cut from the bayside beach to the Vasse River is the main street of present day Busselton. The great stands of timber which grew in its district fed an export industry that, by 1850, saw Busselton as the area's main port but in the twentieth century it lost this role to Bunbury and became a summer resort town.

GETTING TO AND AROUND
Trains from Perth travel only as far as Bunbury but Westrail provides coaches from that city to points south. Coaches run to Busselton daily except Tuesdays and Sundays. The cost for train and coach is $13. The trip takes about 4 hours.

A once daily service on South West Coachlines (09) 322 5173, departs Perth at 1.30 pm Monday to Saturday and 8 pm on Sunday. The fare is around $15.

Drivers take the South West Highway or the Coast Road from Perth to Bunbury and then the Bussell Highway to Busselton.

TOURIST INFORMATION
The Busselton Tourist Bureau is on Southern Drive at the southern outskirts of town. It has brochures and maps covering the town and its surroundings and local tours can be booked there.

WHAT TO SEE
St Mary's Church, the first stone church to be built in Western Australia, is a modest village house of worship constructed in Peel Terrace in 1834 by the Bussells and their fellow settlers with financial help from their supporters in England. The **Old Courthouse** at 4 Queen Street, dates from the early 1900s. It houses a gallery and studios where you can see pottery, weaving, painting and glasswork by local artists. There is also a coffee shop in the building. Busselton has a **museum** in Peel Terrace, run by the local historical society. Period furniture, clothing, marine items, whaling equipment and photographs of life in the old town can be seen there. It is open 2 pm to 5 pm on weekends and during school holidays.

WHERE TO STAY
On the Vasse Motel Resort, 70 Causeway Road, Busselton, (097) 52 3000; is not a resort by any stretch of the imagination but rather a relatively new and quite well appointed motel on the outskirts of Busselton within a short walk of the town centre. Single $43, double $50.

The Geographe, Bussell Highway, West Busselton, (097) 55 4166; is on the beachfront about six km (four miles) west of Busselton township. It has more facilities than your average motel including tennis courts and a gym as well as a restaurant and bar. Single $41, double $46 to $52. Holiday surcharges.

The Ship Resort Hotel, 2 Albert Street, Busselton, (097) 52 3611; once again stretches the meaning of resort a little since it is actually a new motel centred on a small stone building established as a wayside inn in 1847. Next door is the big Ship Hotel, a favourite local watering hole with a good plain restaurant. Guests have the use of a tennis court and swimming pool. Single $49, double $59.

EATING OUT
The Naturaliste Restaurant, 34 Queen Street, Busselton, (097) 52 1612; is a good quality restaurant which lists plenty of local seafood, especially crayfish, on its

blackboard menu. Housed in a colonial shopfront with large windows looking out on the street. BYO. Mid price range.

Newtown House, Bussell Highway, Vasse, (097) 55 4485; is an 1851 farmhouse eight km (five miles) west of Busselton which has been restored and specialises in Devonshire teas and lunches. It is the most charming place in the district to eat simply. Low price range.

Cape Naturaliste

Cape Naturaliste, west of the Busselton, is wide and green. Sheep graze nonchalantly on its low rolling hills in fields graced by tall spreading trees and wild lilies, even in winter. In spring, wild flowers bloom in profusion along the road out to **Cape Naturaliste Lighthouse** which stands on the nose, 37 km (23 miles) from Busselton. Small rocky bays such as Bunker Bay and Eagle Bay can be found along the Cape's eastern side. They are more rugged, challenging and infinitely more scenic than their Busselton counterparts, sometimes with an almost Japanese quality in the minuteness and detail of small rococo forms in rocks and vegetation. Salmon are caught and brought ashore at these bays during Easter each year. The lighthouse is open every day except Wednesday from 9.30 am to 3.30 pm.

The pretty township of **Dunsborough** lies on the Cape west of Busselton. It is closer to both cove and surfing beaches and is a popular holiday spot for Perthites.

Wonnerup House

Wonnerup House stands a short drive through a majestic tuart forest, off the Bussell Highway, about ten km (six miles) east of Busselton. The house has been restored by the National Trust of Western Australia. It was built in 1859 by George Layman, son of George Layman, whose family had settled in the area in 1834. Among the surrounding buildings are an older homestead of 1838, built by the first George Layman, and a complex of school buildings dating from 1874. The house is a simple single-storey, rectangular structure with a wide, shaded veranda. The school buildings typify the timber classrooms where bush schooling was usually conducted and sometimes still is.

Yallingup Caves

Yallingup Caves, 32 km (20 miles) west of Busselton on the Yallingup Road are the most northerly of several limestone cave complexes in the south-west. The caves are close to the Indian Ocean coast and there is good surfing at nearby **Yallingup Beach** as well as rugged coastal scenery and rock formations a little further south around Sugar Loaf, Canal Rocks and Torpedo Rocks. The caves are open from 9.30 am to 3.30 pm every day.

TOURS

South West Coachlines, (097) 52 1500, operates a Busselton Highlights tour costing $12 and a Cape Naturaliste and Yallingup tour for $25. **Geographe Bay Tours**, (097) 52 1034, offers a similar selection. Bookings from the tourist bureau. Milesaway Safari Tours, (097) 55 3574, operates one day tours to Cape Naturaliste and the caves with a barbecue lunch and billy tea thrown in. The cost is $44. The same company offers tours of from three to 12 days' duration which cover the whole of the south-west.

Margaret River

The Margaret River flows through the middle of the south-west. It is only a short stream but the country surrounding it has proved ideal for viticulture, so much so that the Margaret River valley has come to match the Swan Valley as a wine-growing district. The township of Margaret River is about ten km (six miles) from the coast, making it uniquely close to the sea for wine growing and adding swimming and surfing to the district's other lures.

In historical terms, Margaret River also felt the developmental hand of the Bussell family. Alfred Bussell settled there in 1851 and farmed the good land he found around the Margaret and Vasse Rivers but few followed his pioneering efforts. Only in the aftermath of World War I was a greater effort made to work the area. Margaret River was chosen in the 1920s as a site for the Group Settlement Scheme, a plan to settle returned soldiers, but the economic storms of the 1930s practically ruined it. Recent successes, attributable to wine and tourism, date from the 1970s.

GETTING TO AND AROUND

Coaches connect with trains at Bunbury on Monday, Wednesday, Friday and Saturday. The fare is $13.

The South West Coachlines service which runs from Perth through Busselton terminates at Margaret River. The fare is $18.

Drivers can continue along the Bussell Highway to Margaret River or deviate a little to the west and drive down Caves Road. The vineyards generally lie between the two roads and are approachable from both.

TOURIST INFORMATION

The Margaret River Tourist Bureau is on the Bussell Highway in Margaret River township. It will supply you with good guides to the wineries as well as information about restaurants and accommodation in and around the town.

Margaret River Town

The town is a one street affair with small, thoughtful modern buildings of timber and corrugated iron. It sits on a rise just above the river and, like similar tourist-geared towns in Australia, has tea rooms, small shops, restaurants and motels along the main street. **The Old Settlement Craft Centre**, stands by the river at the northern entrance to the town. It has been constructed to resemble a group settlement of the 1920s and functions in part as a museum of those days. It also provides a public work place for a blacksmith, potter and wood turner. Their work and that of other local talents is available from a shop in the settlement. Open every day. Admission 50 cents.

Wallcliffe House, built by Alfred Bussell in 1864 is located on the Margaret River banks near the coast. A house in the English country style with gables and attic windows, it was built of stone and timber hewn and cut on the property by Bussell's convict and Aboriginal workers. The house is still occupied by descendants of the Bussell family but is open to the public every day.

Wineries

There are over 20 wineries in the Margaret River area. Most are small operations and although the valley has some larger establishments they are not to be compared to the giants of the Barossa and Hunter Valleys. Here are some worth visiting.

Vasse Felix in Harmans South Road, Cowramup, is the oldest existing winery in the Margaret River area. Its first vintage was released in 1971 and came from four-year-old vines. The winery has more to offer in whites than reds and concentrates on classic varieties such as Riesling, Semillon and Sauvignon Blanc. Available red varieties are Cabernet Sauvignon, Malbec and Hermitage. The winery is set close to the road in well-timbered surroundings with green lawns. Tastings take place from 10 am to 4.30 pm Monday to Saturday in the cellar.

Cape Mentelle is one of the prettiest and most interesting wineries in Margaret River. It is set in a small valley off Wallcliffe Road about halfway between Margaret River and the coast. The winery buildings are constructed of rammed earth (pise), a building method frequently used over the last ten years in this area. They are a rich fawn colour and give a marvellous impression of natural solidity. An inviting garden of shady tress, climbers and annuals with a small stream running through it and swing seats in attractive locations stands between the car park and the buildings. Good quality regional wines are produced at Cape Mentelle in small quantities which means it is hard to predict what will be available at any given time. The winery's Cabernet Sauvignon is particularly well known; it also produces a Zinfandel, something of a rarity in Australia. Cape Mentelle is open from 10 am to 4.30 pm from Monday to Sunday and you will find the staff very knowledgeable and friendly.

Leeuwin Estate, Gnarawary Road, Margaret River, is also set in fine gardens but on a much grander scale. It makes no secret of its appeal to tourists and, aside from a big tasting room, has a restaurant and wide grounds where visitors can picnic. None of this, however, is overstated and the public buildings are in such a delightful setting under a steep, green hill beside Boodjidup Brook, and so decorated with vines that the effect is tremendously pleasing. The winery is a fairly big producer of table wines, managing over 100,000 bottles a year including a Late Harvest Rhine Riesling and a Pinot Noir as well as the classic varietals common to this region. Open every day.

Margaret River's biggest resident is **Sandalford Wines**, Metricup Road, Willyabrup, whose Swan Valley winery is mentioned in the section on that region. The same range of wines is to be found at this complex which has adopted the rammed earth building style seen throughout the area. Sandalford is open from 11 am to 4 pm each day.

Other wineries to visit if you have time to spare are **Wrights Wines** Harmans South Road, Cowramup, near Vasse Felix, **Redgate Wines**, Boodjidup Road,

429

Margaret River, and **Cape Clairault Wines**, Henry Road, off Pusey Road, Willyabrup.

WHERE TO STAY
Captain Freycinet Motel, corner Bussell Highway and Tunbridge Road, Margaret River, (097) 57 2033; is the biggest motel in Margaret River and offers a high standard as motels go but also has rooms for travellers on a budget. It is perhaps a little too surrounded by grey asphalt parking areas but this is forgivable in a motel. The swimming pool is quite inviting. Single $39 to $45, double $50 to $62.
Gilgara Homestead, Caves Road, Margaret River, (097) 57 2705; is a reconstruction of a colonial mansion of the 1830s set on a rise overlooking the bush and a nearby creek. It takes only 14 guests. Double $56 bed and breakfast. Dinner set menu $18. The dining room is open to the public. BYO. Low price range.
Margaret River Guest House, Valley Road, Margaret River, (097) 57 2349; is located in an old convent in the street behind the motel mentioned above but hidden in a secluded, leafy depression. The manner here is casual and simple. Single $30, double $50 bed and breakfast. The establishment has a restaurant where guests can eat dinner on demand for $12. It opens to the public from Thursday to Saturday for set price à la carte at $18. BYO.
Margaret River Lodge, 220 Railway Terrace, Margaret River, (097) 57 2532; a good budget place with a selection of double rooms, twins bunk rooms and dormitories. Share facilities. About ten minutes walk from town. $7.50 per person in the dormitories to $20 per room for doubles.
Merribrook, off Cowramup Bay Road, (PO Cowramup), Cowramup, (097) 55 5490; is a working farm which has six rammed earth cottages in its grounds. The cottages can take up to two adults and four children and have their own bathrooms. Meals and recreation are taken in a central 'lodge' overlooking a small lake. The emphasis here is on adventure which means challenging outdoor activities such as abseiling, rock climbing, canoeing and caving but you can also visit the wineries and go on cycle trips around the area. Guests are not expected to undertake the more dangerous pastimes mentioned unaided, hosts, Richard and Lorraine Firth are expert and make a point of helping novices. Full board.

EATING OUT
Leeuwin Estate, Gnarawary Road, Margaret River, (097) 57 6253; is the site of the area's best restaurant, housed in the main winery building overlooking a wide lawn and creekside garden. Food is French style. Licensed. Mid to upper price range.
1885 Restaurant, Farrelly Street, Margaret River, (097) 57 2302; is a cosy establishment in an old house where winter dining is done beside a log fire. Menu is international and you can choose your wine from the cellar. Licensed. Mid price range.
The Old Stone House Restaurant, Bussell Highway, Margaret River, (097) 57 2425; is also in a charming old house close to the river. A la carte menu includes fish, chicken and steak. BYO. Mid price range.

TOURS
Margaret River Scenic and Vineyard Tours, (097) 57 2775, operates day and half-day tours north and south of the town including the wineries, the coast and the Old Settlement Craft Centre. The tours run only on weekends and cost around $25.

Caves

The **Mammoth, Lake** and **Jewel Caves,** can be reached from Caves Road between Margaret River and Augusta. The Mammoth is 21 km (13 miles) from Margaret River, the Lake 23 km (14 miles) and the Jewel 37 km (23 miles). The Mammoth Cave is big, a storehouse of animal bones including those of extinct creatures such as giant kangaroos and wombats as well as animals now only found in other parts of Australia such as the Tasmanian Devil. The Lake Cave is known for its great beauty and was once called 'The Queen of the Earth.' Its entrance, located at the bottom of a steep crater, formerly a cave itself, is thickly vegetated with karri trees as much as 1000 years old. The cave contains an underground lake and a formation called the Suspended Table. The Jewel Cave is the largest tourist cave in Western Australia and contains one of the longest 'straws' in the world. A straw is a fragile tube, usually around five millimetres in diameter, formed by water droplets containing calcite. This one is 5.9 metres long and has probably taken over 3000 years to grow to its present size.

Unusual Farms

Marrons and kiwi fruit (Chinese gooseberries) are grown in the Margaret River region. Marrons are dark shelled freshwater crustaceans unique to south-west Western Australia. They look and taste like a cross between a giant prawn (shrimp) and a crayfish. The **Margaret River Marron Farm** grows them in ponds and serves them at its restaurant 11 km (seven miles) south of Margaret River township in Wickham Road. The farm is open every day from 10 am to 4 pm with guided tours at 10.30 am, 11.30 am, 1.30 pm, 2.30 pm and 3.30 pm.

Kiwi fruit are grown at The Berry Farm on Bessel Road, 13 km (eight miles) from Margaret River. The enterprising berry farmers have used them in jams, pickles, chutneys and wine. They also produce strawberries, loganberries, raspberries and boysenberries (a cross between the last two) depending on the season. Visitors can pick their own strawberries from mid-October to early April. The farm is open every day from 10 am to 4 pm.

Gypsy Caravans
Vardo Horse-Drawn Holidays, (09) 276 9666, rents out gypsy vans, each with a Clydesdale draught horse. The vans are self-contained and hirers drive them around designated back country roads in the Margaret River area for a minimum of three days, presumably enjoying the slow pace and rustic delights of such trundling. Costs range from $250.

Augusta

Augusta stands on a hill overlooking Hardy Inlet where the Blackwood River flows into the sea. It is the closest town to the south-western tip of Australia and has white beaches and wide blue waters.

The town is named after Princess Augusta, the second daughter of George III. It was first settled in the 1830s by the Bussell, Molloy and Turner families but they subsequently moved north to the Vasse River when starvation threatened. The abandoned settlement rose again in the 1880s when a strong timber industry developed under the hand of Maurice Coleman Davies who became the timber baron of the south-west. From the late nineteenth century to nearly World War I he and his sons built a huge business based on exporting jarrah and karri, the excellent hardwoods native to the south-west. The area is now devoted to beef, sheep and dairy farming and attracts a few tourists in summer. The timber industry also remains a force.

GETTING TO AND AROUND
Augusta is 43 km (27 miles) south of Margaret River and the most southerly of the towns along the Bussell Highway. It is the last stop on the Westrail train and coach service to Busselton and Margaret River. Coaches to Augusta meet the Australind train at Bunbury on Mondays and Fridays.

Drivers continue to the end of the Bussell Highway or Caves Road, both of which finish at Augusta.

TOURIST INFORMATION
The Augusta Margaret River Tourist Bureau has a small office on the Bussell Highway at the northern end of the town. Information is also available at Leeuwin Souvenirs in Blackwood Avenue.

WHAT TO SEE
Augusta has an **Historical Museum** in Blackwood Avenue recording the hardships suffered by its early settlers, the building of the Cape Leeuwin Lighthouse and the timber empire of M. C. Davies. A more recent event which has earned the town some fame is also commemorated there. In 1986 a school of whales beached itself at Flinders Bay near Augusta. The townspeople banded together to rescue them and their efforts became a focus of national attention. Their success and the world's congratulations are recalled in a display which is the museum's pride and joy. Open 10 am to noon each day. Admission $1.

WHERE TO STAY
Augusta Hotel Motel, Blackwood Avenue, Augusta, (097) 58 1944; is the only motel in town. Single $39, double $45.

EATING OUT
Colonial Restaurant, Blackwood Avenue, Augusta, (097) 58 1658; despite its name, serves French food more of the modern than the classical kind. Licensed. Mid price range.

The Steak Cave, corner Allnutt Terrace and Ellis Street, Augusta, (097) 58 1411; again goes against its name since you can dine in the garden when the weather is fine. Seafood and steaks dominate the menu. BYO. Low to mid price range.

TOURS
Augusta Ferry Service, (097) 58 1600, runs two and four hour cruises around Hardy Inlet and up the Blackwood River. Morning and afternoon tea is included.

Around Augusta

Cape Leeuwin Lighthouse on the tip of Cape Leeuwin, eight km (five miles) from Augusta, is the most south-westerly building in Australia. Plans for it were first made in 1881 but it did not come into service until 1896. The tower is constructed of locally quarried limestone and remains one of Australia's most important navigation beacons. It stands on a flat tongue of rock thrusting out into the sea from the end of the cape and, unlike most other lighthouses in Australia, is not very high above the waves. It is open from 9.30 am to 3 pm from Tuesday to Sunday and guided tours leave every hour. Children under six not admitted. Occasional closures for maintenance mean that intending visitors should check at the tourist information centre before driving to to the lighthouse. The cape itself is named after the Dutch ship Leeuwin (Lioness) whose captain, when passing there in 1622, named the area Leeuwin's Land.

The remnants of M. C. Davies' timber empire remain at Hamelin Bay and Old Karridale, both north of Augusta. **Hamelin Bay** is reached via Caves Road and the Hamelin Bay Road. It was the port from which most of the jarrah and karri logs cut in the south-west were exported. At the height of the early timber trade the bay's jetty was 549 metres (1,800 feet long), and Davies' yacht used to be moored there amongst the timber ships. Only a few of the old wharf's jarrah piles remain today. Hamelin Bay was by no means a safe port. In the winter of 1900 five ships were wrecked there. The bay is now a small holiday centre with a good beach and a lake for still water swimming.

Old Karridale on Karridale Road, north of Augusta off the Bussell Highway, is another example of time's cruelty to the memory of Mr Davies and his sons. It was the seat of their empire and a well-chosen one at that, perfectly placed between the forests and the sea. All that remains now is a lone chimney from the old timber mill which closed in 1913 and has since been the victim of many bushfires.

Albany

Albany is Western Australia's oldest settlement and the southern region's commercial centre. It lies on a saddle between Mt Clarence and Mt Melville, high hills surrounding land-locked Princess Royal Harbour. York Street, the main thoroughfare, slopes gently down to a wide harbour front where jetties jut into the bay, silos and wharf sheds rise, and an occasional yacht bobs quietly. King George Sound, discovered and chartered in 1791 by Captain George Vancouver RN, lies on the south-easterly side of the town. It is edged by lawned recreation areas and caters to the other side of Albany, summer holiday fun.

Fears of other colonial powers motivated the initial British settlement at King George Sound. Major Edmund Lockyer and a party of soldiers and convicts aboard the brig *Amity* arrived on Christmas Day 1826 and established a military outpost of New South Wales. The venture teetered on the edge of failure for the next quarter century but matters improved for Albany when it became a coaling station for steamers on the way to Perth. Whaling also helped pay for the necessaries of life until as recently as 1978.

GETTING TO AND AROUND
Albany is 412 km (256 miles) south of Perth. Skywest Airlines flies daily from Perth. Coach services are operated by Westrail and Deluxe. There are no passenger trains to Albany.

The quickest driving route is the Albany Highway from Perth which takes about four and a half hours. Drivers can reach Albany from Augusta via Nannup and the South West Highway, a distance of 407 km (252 miles) and so about equal driving time or perhaps a little more as not all roads on this route are highways.

A local bus company, Loves Bus Service, covers the town and surrounding areas such as Middleton Beach, Spencer Park, Emu Point and destinations along the Albany Highway.

TOURIST INFORMATION
Albany Tourist Bureau is in the town centre on the corner of York Street and Peel Place close to the harbour front.

WHAT TO SEE
York Street runs from the Albany Highway to a harbourside railway line and has the open feeling typical of streets leading down to the sea. Once flanked by nineteenth century façades, it is now simply a modern street of right-angle awnings and aluminium shopfront though the occasional relic remains. The Town Hall, built in 1887, is one. Buildings of older times in nearby streets include the Parish School of 1869, Pyrmont House of 1858 and St Josephs Church (1878) and Community Centre (1881), formerly a convent.

There are more historical buildings on Stirling Terrace and the harbour foreshores. The **Residency Museum**, covers regional history from discovery to settlement and whaling. There are also displays concerning the geography and environment of the southern region. The museum occupies a single storey colonial house built in 1850 and originally part of the convict hiring depot. Between 1873 and 1953 it served as the local magistrate's house and later became a naval training facility. Open 10 am to 5 pm Monday to Saturday and 2 pm to 5 pm Sunday. Admission free. A full scale replica of the brig **Amity**, built in 1975, has been erected on the water's edge nearby. The **Old Gaol** and the town's original **Post Office** can also be found in this area.

Albany's last whaling station, at Cheynes Beach in Frenchman's Bay 21 km (13 miles) from the town, has been converted into a museum of whaling called **Whaleworld**. Its attractions include, ironically, a beached whale chaser complete with loaded harpoon gun and an exhibition of marine mammal paintings by a New York

434

resident specialist in such works, Richard Ellis. Open 9 am to 5 pm daily. Guided tours hourly from 10 am to 4 pm. Admission $3.50.

Strawberry Hill Farm set in attractive gardens on Strawberry Hill is the state's oldest farm. It was built in 1836 and the stone house has been restored to its early Victorian style. Both house and gardens are open to the public and Devonshire teas are served in an adjoining cottage. cottage.

The beaches of King George Sound, especially Middleton and Emu Point are ideal for still water swimming as is Jimmy Newhills Harbour to the south of the town along Frenchman Bay Road. The major natural sights are **The Gap** and **The Natural Bridge** two coastal rock formations in Torndirrup National Park also to the south of the town.

WHERE TO STAY

Albany has eight motels plus some guest houses and a number of hotels in the old Australian style. The following are reliable.

Travel Inn, 191 Albany Highway, Albany, (098) 41 4144; two blocks north of the York Street Albany Highway junction, has standard and deluxe rooms as well as two bedroom units. Single $45 and $52, double $52 and $58. Two bedrooms $69.

Hospitality Inn, 234 Albany Highway, Albany, (098) 41 2200; is aimed at family trade. It stands three blocks north of the junction between the Highway and York Street and has a licensed restaurant which offers a child's menu and live music on weekends. Single $42 to $44, double $49 to $51.

EATING OUT

The Penny Post Restaurant, Stirling Terrace, Albany, (098) 41 1045; occupies a section of the Old Post Office. It includes an à la carte restaurant which specialises in seafood and a grill room where you can cook your own steak and dine overlooking the harbour. Licensed. Low to mid price range.

Nona Maria Restaurant, 135 York Street, Albany, (098) 41 4626; specialises in northern Italian cooking. Licensed. Mid price range.

The Stirling Ranges and the Porongorups

North-east of Albany, the Stirling Ranges and the Porongorups rise majestically out of the flat plain, contrasting sharply with the surrounding wheat and grasslands. They provide good bushwalking tracks for day and half-day walks but you will need a car to get to them. Bluff Knoll is the highest peak in the Stirling Ranges and Toolbrunup has particularly commanding views.

Esperance

Esperance is set in the Bay of Isles, facing the many islands of the Recherche Archipelago. Originally settled in 1863, in the last 30 years the town has developed as an agricultural centre and grain loading port for the rich surrounding land.

A number of excellent beaches stretch to the west of the town. Nine, Ten and Eleven Mile Beaches are named for their distance from town rather than their size.

They do boast, however, some of the most vivid turquoise seas. Closer to town, Twilight bay is a popular swimming and picnic spot.

GETTING THERE
Esperance is 894 km (559 miles) from Perth and 476 km (298 miles) from Albany. Skywest Airlines flys from Perth. De Luxe is the only interstate coach service to stop in Esperance on the Perth–Adelaide route. Westrail run buses from Kalgoorlie and Perth two or three times a week.

WHAT TO SEE
Places of interest in the town itself include the **Museum** on the corner of James and Dempster Street which houses early agricultural machinery and pioneer memorabilia as well as remnants of the American Skylab, which crashed to Earth in 1979, landing close to Esperance. At the **Craft Village** next to the museum, there is a collection of craft and work shops selling Australiana from stained glass parakeets to blackboy wooden bowls and sheepskin rugs. Here too you can find the **Tourist Bureau**.

The 'Scenic Loop', a 26-km (16-mile) road constructed for the Bicentenary, takes in the **Pink Lake** just three km (2 miles) north of Esperance and continues through bush to meet the Ocean Road. The Lake's bright pink colour derives from salt deposits and varies in intensity with the weather. The lake also supports many species of birds. East of Esperance is the rugged coastal scenery of Cape Le Grand National Park.

From the jetty you can take day trips to see the seals and penguins in the wildlife sanctuary of Woody Island or visit other islands in the Archipelago.

The Goldfields

The goldfields country is red, dry, hot and flat, scattered with mulga, spinifex, desert oaks, eucalypts and occasional ruined pubs. The horizon looks a million miles away and the sky is bigger than anything else in the landscape. Towns have streets 'wide enough to turn a camel train around in' and skylines broken by head frames, cranes and conveyers. Tailings dumps rise like shattered pyramids on their outskirts. They exist for the unashamed pursuit of wealth, wealth that comes from far below the earth to be stacked up and locked away where most of us can't afford to get at it.

History

Western Australia was a mere contingent outpost of the eastern colonies when gold was unearthed at Southern Cross, a little less than halfway between Perth and Kalgoorlie, in 1887. Although that discovery soon ran out, prospectors pushed further east in search of more.

At Coolgardie in 1892 Arthur Bayley and William Ford staked a claim at Bayley's Reward, about three km (two miles) east of the present town, opening a mine which continued producing until 1963. Within six months a thousand prospectors had arrived and during a short but vigorous period the population of Coolgardie is estimated to have touched 15,000. The frenzy was over by 1905 and today the town supports less than 1000 citizens.

At Kalgoorlie three Irishmen, Patrick Hannan, Tom Flannigan and Daniel Shea discovered gold in 1893 near a small hill now called Mount Charlotte. Their good luck was followed by that of Brookman and Pearse, first to strike it rich on the 'Golden Mile', a square mile of legendary wealth where, when Kalgoorlie was at its height, over 100 mines worked simultaneously.

It used to be said that miners watched their waterbags more closely than their gold so severe was the lack of water during the early days. Men often died of thirst or poisoning from polluted water. The water problem lasted until 1903 when a 536-km (350-mile) pipeline from Mundaring Weir, close to Perth, to Kalgoorlie was opened. The pipe was the brainchild of engineer C. Y. O'Connor who persevered in the face of continuous vilification for attempting the impossible. So savage was the mockery that, when the water pumps were started and no water appeared a mere three days later, O'Connor broke down and shot himself. His lack of self-confidence was not justified—water took two weeks to travel the 536 km (335 mile) pipeline but when it flowed the problem was solved at a single stroke.

Kalgoorlie's rush went the way of all such phenomena, surface gold ran out quickly and companies with the resources to dig deep for the precious metal took over from individual miners. Diggers who dreamed of vast wealth found themselves slaving underground in deadly conditions for three pounds a week. Storekeepers and publicans made more money than anyone else. None the less Kalgoorlie proved a long-lasting field and continued to produce through the low price years of the 1920s. It picked up again during the Depression, fell away after World War II and now, when gold is again among Australia's top five exports, is enjoying a new boom.

Kalgoorlie

Kalgoorlie was the greatest of the gold-rush towns and the only one still producing. It has an absurdly wide and straight main street where spindly old hotels teeter like turn-of-the-century grand dames, one clock tower gives a thumbs up to the visitor and you can count the parked cars on your fingers. The town was founded on the Golden Mile, a square mile of hugely wealthy mines which stands, largely abandoned, to the south.

GETTING TO AND AROUND
The goldfields region is about 600 km (375 miles) east of Perth. Ansett WA and Skywest Airlines flights depart daily for Kalgoorlie from Perth. The fare is $142.

A train called the *Prospector* leaves Perth for Kalgoorlie each day except Saturday and takes about 6 hours to make the distance. Fare $47.10 and departure times Sunday, Monday and Wednesday 3 pm, Tuesday and Thursday 9 am, Friday 4.15 pm.

Greyhound and Ansett Pioneer coaches stop at Kalgoorlie on their way to Adelaide. The fare is $39.

The entire Golden Mile can be skirted on the *Rattler*, formerly the Kalgoorlie Boulder Loop Line, a train that linked Kalgoorlie with its service town of Boulder. A tourist train runs the length of the line at 11 am from Monday to Saturday and at 1.30 pm and 3 pm on Sunday. Cost $5. There is another museum dealing with the history of the eastern goldfields at Boulder Station along the train's route.

TOURIST INFORMATION
There is an information centre at 250 Hannan Street, Kalgoorlie.

WHAT TO SEE
Hannan Street, the main street in a grid of tree-lined avenues, has the stolid brick public buildings and lacey old pubs typical of gold-rush towns throughout Australia. The **Exchange Hotel** is an absolutely typical early 1900s pub—deep lacey verandas shading the footpath supported by narrow columns, gables roofed in red corrugated iron and Fosters sign outside but the **Cornwall Hotel** is just as impressive. Kalgoorlie **Town Hall** (1903) and **Post Office** (1899) with its domed clocktower represent the official side of the argument. A crudely executed statue of Paddy Hannan holding his water bag which incorporates a drinking fountain stands outside the Town Hall. An identical statue stands inside.

The **Hainault Gold Mine** dominates Kalgoorlie's tourist offerings. Part of the Golden Mile, it was a working mine from 1898 until 1968. Underground tours, led by a former miner, begin with a 60 metre drop in a miners' cage and conduct groups through the drives and crosscuts of the mine, explaining how gold was won from deep underground. The tours take place daily at 10.30 am, 1 pm, 2.30 pm and 3.45 pm and cost $6.50. The surface area of the mine, a hotch potch of corrugated iron and timber buildings and rusting old machinery, is also open and inspection is free. More gold mining machinery and even a few picks and shovels are on show at the **Golden Mile Museum** in the former British Arms Hotel, Outridge Terrace, open 10.30 am to 4.30 pm each day. Admission $2.

Mount Charlotte Reservoir where C. Y. O'Connor's pipeline ends is still Kalgoorlie's major source of fresh water. There is a **look-out** at the reservoir which gives a good view of the town but not the water, covered to minimise evaporation. You will find both near the end of Hannan Street, off Park Street.

WHERE TO STAY
Accommodation can be hard to come by in the cool months of August and September when most tourists come to this region. Anyone who wants to stay in the centre of town is limited to the old hotels as the motels built in recent years are a little further away.

Exchange Hotel, 155 Hannan Street, Kalgoorlie, (090) 21 2833; has some rooms with private facilities. Single $20 and $30 (with facilities), double $30 and $45.

The better motels are the **Hospitality Inn**, corner Hannan and Throssell Streets, Kalgoorlie, (090) 21 2888; single $55, double $65; and **Sandalwood Motel**, Hannan Street, Kalgoorie, (090) 21 4455; single $48, double $60.

EATING OUT

Since meals in this part of the country are designed to fill empty stomachs rather than appeal to gourmet tastes, take the unpretentious route and eat at the pubs, especially the **Exchange Hotel** in Kalgoorlie and the **Denver City Hotel** in Coolgardie. Neither is expensive.

TOURS

Goldrush Tours, Kalgoorlie, runs town tours of Kalgoorlie, excursions to Coolgardie and goldfield ghost towns as well as wild flower tours in August and September.

Boulder

Boulder is the close satellite of Kalgoorlie, so close it is difficult to tell them apart. It grew up as a service town for the mines of the Golden Mile but is not as interesting as its close companion. The **Eastern Goldfields Historical Society Museum** in the Boulder City Railway Station is another place to soak up some mining history, the **Cornwall Hotel** is Boulder's contribution to memorable pubs and the Boulder Town Hall has an elaborate clock tower.

Coolgardie

Coolgardie is a gold-mining ghost 40 km (25 miles) west of Kalgoorlie on the Great Eastern Highway. Re-living the glory days is now the town's principal occupation and takes place in the **Wardens Court Building**, on Bayley Street in the centre of town. When erected in 1898 it was the largest stone building in Western Australia outside Perth, contained the local court and mining registrar's office and was the centre of official business in the wild mining community. The mines department still maintains an office there but the Warden's Court is primarily a museum of mining, concentrating on how life was for the individual digger on the goldfields during the boom and on the rise and fall of Coolgardie itself. It also houses the local tourist bureau and a bank agency. Museum open 9.30 am to 4.30 pm every day.

Coolgardie's history is also recounted in a series of markers, placed at intervals throughout the town. There are 150 in all, each endeavouring to show, by the use of photographs and text, how their location looked at the height of the rush. A guide to the markers' positions is located next door to the Wardens Court.

TOURS

Tom Neacy's Adventure Tours, Coolgardie, (090) 26 6090, runs half and full day tours around Coolgardie including general sightseeing, gold panning expeditions and wild flowers in season.

Fossicking

There is still gold to be found around the goldfields towns, although it's unlikely to pay your fare home. Equipment for finding and unearthing it, from the most modern metal detectors to picks and pans, as well as advice on how to behave like a real prospector, is available from the **Safari Village** 2 Renou Street, Coolgardie.

439

Nullarbor Plain

East of the Goldfields lies the treeless Nullarbor, a flat, waterless plain extending over 700 km (438 miles) to the South Australian border and a further 520 km (325 miles) to the tiny South Australian town of Ceduna where the thin line of bitumen which crosses it, the Eyre Highway, comes to an end. The huge cliffs of the Great Australian Bight, beaten continuously by a raging southern ocean, stand to the south of the plain.

Until 1976 when the last section of the highway was surfaced, people who drove across the Nullarbor threw their cars away afterwards. The surfaced road runs a little south of the true plain but driving it is still no push-over. Petrol supplies are an average of 200 km (125 miles) apart and inexperienced night drivers can easily hit big kangaroos that frequently cross the road. Anyone attempting the journey must carry minimal spare parts, first aid and water—it's a long wait between cars.

The easy alternative is to take the Indian Pacific train which crosses the Nullarbor north of the highway.

The North

Although in the tropics, north Western Australian is not what one would imagine as typically tropical. In Western Australia the Tropic of Capricorn borders the Pilbara, first of the two huge regions taking up the state's north. Here red rules the land: red earth, red sunsets and red skins if you don't apply sun screen. Rain is rare. For over half the year, temperatures are hot enough to fry eggs on a rock. Gigantic open-cut iron ore mines rip raw wealth from the Hamersley Ranges and vast quantities of natural gas are tapped from the Burrup Peninsula.

The Kimberley Plateau, north of the Pilbara, is an ancient reef now raised above the sea to form a rugged dome. Red earth, worn down mountains, green waterways, orange beaches, a wide blue sea and, most of all, boab trees, are its symbols. Cattle raising, diamond mining and irrigated agriculture keep its few people occupied.

Both regions, despite increasing interest, remain hard work for the tourist. Broome in the Kimberley has some awareness as has Wittenoom in the Pilbara but elsewhere tourists are something of an oddity. Distance is tyrannous. Towns and points of interest are hundreds and hundreds of kilometres apart. Roads are unsealed, many suitable only for four-wheel drive vehicles and travel consumes time. Public transport is almost totally lacking.

The Pilbara

Outside a few ports and inland mining towns almost no-one lives in the Pilbara, there are fewer than 50,000 people in 510,335 square km of land. The former asbestos mining town of **Wittenoom** at the northern end of **Hamersley Range National Park** is the area's scenic centre. It features hills whose colours change

Boab tree

with the light, wild flowers in the cool season and more than 20 dramatic gorges on the range escarpment.

The winter season, April to October, when temperatures average between 25°C and 30°C, is the most comfortable time to visit this area. What little rainfall there is comes in summer, making roads impassable, and temperatures hover around 40°C (37°C is 100°F).

GETTING THERE
This is not easy. There are no planes, trains or buses to Wittenoom. Travellers must reach Karratha, over 350 km (217 miles) of largely dirt to the west, Port Headland, 286 km (177 miles), half dirt, to the north, or Newman, 280 km (174 miles) of dirt to the east, and arrange their own transport. There are daily Ansett WA and East West Airlines flights from Perth to each of these towns. One way economy class fares are $264 to Karratha, $273 to Port Headland and $223 to Newman. There are also irregular flights to the iron ore mining town of Tom Price, 130 km (81 miles) from Wittenoom ($228) on Ansett WA. They leave about every two days.

Greyhound coaches operate to Newman on Thursday, Friday and Sunday from Perth. The trip takes 14 and a half hours and costs $69. The same company operates to Tom Price on Monday evenings. The journey takes 21 hours and costs $69. Coaches on their way from Perth to Darwin pass through Port Headland ($92).

TOURIST INFORMATION
Wittenoom Tourist Centre, Second Avenue, Wittenoom has brochures and can make bookings for tours and accommodation. It is open every day from 7.30 am to 6.30 pm. Phone (091) 89 7046.

Wittenoom Gorges

Deep, narrow, red walled gorges—some with water-holes and streams, penetrate the edges of the Hamersley Range from the Fortescue River basin east and west of

Wittenoom. Most are only accessible by climbing down from the top rather than walking in from the mouth. The biggest are Wittenoom, Kalamina, Yampire and Dales, lined up east of the township. Bee, Hamersley and Rio Tinto Gorges lie to the west.

Bolitho Road runs 12 km (seven miles) from Wittenoom township into **Wittenoom Gorge** meeting a walking trail which leads to Red Gorge. The road passes through a dry, wide passage with steep red cliffs on both sides, narrowing as it approaches the walking trail. The trail rambles along a creek bed, over occasional red boulders sheered off from the walls, past trickling waterfalls and by clear freshwater pools. Cycads, palms and ghost gums grow in the watered sections. **Red Gorge**, where the walk ends, is a deep rusty split, exposing bands of strata 100 metres into the earth. It is one of four much shorter but very deep chasms spreading like cracks where Wittenoom Gorge finishes, some with crystal pools and waterfalls in their depths. Test your vertigo index at **Oxers Lookout** where the gorges converge.

Dales Gorge, approached via the broad and sandy **Yampire Gorge**, 25 km from Wittenoom, has long wide stretches of delicious transparent water, so clear that rock platforms and strata are visible beneath the surface. Its loveliest parts are Fortescue Falls, Circular Pool and Dignams Gorge. **Hamersley Gorge** to the west of Wittenoom has a deep green swimming hole almost completely surrounded by rock walls.

WHERE TO STAY AND EATING OUT
Wittenoom has one hotel, the **Hotel Fortescue**, (091) 89 7055. It has motel style rooms with air conditioning as well as a restaurant and swimming pool. It charges $53 single, $64 double. There are camping and caravan facilities in the town.

TOURS
Bus tours to the gorges depart most days from the Wittenoom Tourist Centre. **Scenic Tours** (091) 89 7052 fly over the gorges and the Hamersley Ranges. **Pathfinder Tours**, (09) 332 3332, run six-day tours into the Pilbara from Port Headland and **Nor-West Explorer Tours**, (091) 85 2474, operate tours from Karratha.

Broome

Broome is the gateway to the Kimberley. The town is small, stained and spotted with orangey red dust. The dust lies by green mangroves and round the rough tin sheds at Streeters Jetty where black and white pearling luggers tie up. The jetty, an old wooden finger, points out into opalesque Roebuck Bay. Boab trees stand everywhere like fat old men, grey-trunked with short, startled branches on their heads.

GETTING THERE
Ansett WA flies to Broome from Perth every day except Saturday with two flights on Saturday. The one way economy fare is $342. There are also flights from Darwin ($247).

The major coach companies serving the coastal run from Perth to Darwin stop in Broome. The journey takes about 22 hours and costs around $120 from Perth. From Darwin it is 10 and a half hours and $113.

TOURIST INFORMATION
The Broome Tourist Bureau is on the Great Northern Highway just past the airport about a block before you enter the town. It stands opposite the crashed Garuda Airlines DC-3 which once housed it. The office is open 9 am to 5 pm Monday to Friday and 9 am to noon on Saturday.

WHAT TO SEE
A once thriving pearling industry, established in the 1880s, has left undying marks on Broome. Its population and appearance were 'orientalised' by the Japanese, Malays, Koepangers (Timorese) and Filipinos who crewed the 400 luggers operating during the early 1900s. They produced 80 per cent of the world's mother of pearl but plastic put them out of business. A few luggers remain, their divers combing the sea bed for live shell oysters which they sell to cultured pearl farmers.

Chinatown on Carnarvon Street at the southern end of town, close to Streeters Jetty, is a thoroughfare of ricketty wooden shops and restaurants dating from the early days of the town. One of the few open air cinemas still operating in Australia, Sun Pictures, stands near the corner of Short and Carnarvon Streets. It was built in 1916. The old Roebuck Bay Hotel nearby is something of a bloodhouse on weekend nights. Corrugated iron shops along the waterfront sell **pearls**, etched mother of pearl jewellery and shells. In some shops you can see craftsmen carving oyster shells.

Pearl divers and seamen died in droves during the early 1900s, more as a result of cyclones (1908 killed 150) than nitrogen narcosis, though it scored a fair share. They are buried in a **cemetery**, just off Cable Beach Road outside the town. The Japanese section is carefully maintained. It has inscribed marble headstones, many recently renewed, and a column erected to commemorate the 40 Japanese who died in 1908. The stones reflect the setting sun. The graves of white and Aboriginal dead have been left to the weather but are interesting to wander through.

Pearling industry memorabilia is displayed in the old customs house on Saville Street, now the **Broome Historical Society Museum**. Hours are officially 10 am to 2 pm Thursday and Saturday but not exactly reliable.

The Japanese also have a less touching connection with Broome. The town was used as a clearing station for refugees from the Dutch East Indies (now Indonesia) during World War II. In March 1942 it was bombed by a squadron of Zero fighters which had trailed a refugee plane. Seventy people were killed, 15 flying boats sunk in Roebuck Bay, and several land-based aircraft destroyed. The remains of the flying boats are visible at low tide.

Cable Beach, is a short distance east of Broome township. It wears the orange tinge typical of everything in this part of the country but stretches of it are white as well. It has coarse sand, a low surf and endless blue horizon. At one end stands a long unused jetty. Stingers prevent summer swimming. English property developer Lord McAlpine, something of figure in Western Australia, has opened a a 27 hectare wildlife park at Cable Beach called the **Pearl Coast Zoological Gardens** which holds a vast and varied collection of exotic and Australian native birds.

Broome's saddest sight is some of its unfortunate Aboriginals idly but earnestly drinking themselves to death in and around the Louis Street bar of the Continental Hotel.

WHERE TO STAY AND EATING OUT
Some people think Broome will be the next great tourist centre in Australia but it has a long way to go in developing accommodation and restaurants.
Club Cable Beach, Cable Beach, Broome, (09) 381 6433; has accommodation in beachside bungalows with private facilities. There is a swimming pool, tennis court and fitness centre. Two km from town. One bedroom bungalows $150, two bedroom $195.
Broome Overland Motor Inn, corner Saville and Robinson Streets, Broome, (091) 92 1204; is a good quality motel. Single and double $45.

The Kimberley

Word about the far-flung beauties of the Kimberley keeps filtering insistently down to the civilised southern parts of Australia. It has tremendous gorges, striped beehive-shaped hills and meteorite craters.

Kimberley weather can be positively dangerous, especially in the 'wet' when rivers expand from metres to kilometres wide, cutting roads and isolating settlements on the strength of two days' rain. Temperatures at this time rise above 40°C and tourist attractions are simply inaccessible. April to September, the 'dry', is the best time to visit. Roads, though lately improved, are bad and four-wheel drive is a necessity for off-highway excursions.

GETTING THERE
The tiny coastal town of **Derby**, 216 km (134 miles) north of Broome is the turn-off point for the gorges and national parks of the Kimberley. Few travellers I have met have anything good to say for it, its greatest asset being the **Great Northern Highway** which departs the town for the major sights of the region.

Ansett WA flies from Perth to Derby daily. The one way economy fare is $344. The same airline also serves Kununurra at the other end of the Great Northern Highway ($428). Flying from Darwin to either destination is much cheaper; $221 to Derby and $129 to Kununurra.

Coaches on their way from Perth to Darwin along the coast stop in Derby ($139) and Kununurra ($192) as well as Fitzroy Crossing ($166) and Halls Creek ($176). You arrive at night or very early morning (before dawn) in all the towns. Coaching from Darwin is again much less expensive, $61 to Kununurra and $91 to Derby. The Great Northern Highway is surfaced only as far as Halls Creek.

TOURIST INFORMATION
There are tourist bureaux in Derby (091) 91 1426, Halls Creek (091) 68 6087 and Kununurra (091) 68 1177.

Gorges

Windjana Gorge on the Lennard River is part of the Napier Ranges. Surrounded by a small national park, it is about 150 km (93 miles) west of Derby. The gorge has 90 metre (300 feet) limestone walls, relics of Devonian age coral reefs, between which the river charges in the wet, reducing to a chain of pools during the dry.

    Tunnel Creek a few kilometres south towards Fitzroy Crossing, has cut a half mile tunnel through the Oscar Range. During the dry, the tunnel can be explored with a torch. It has a shaft in the centre, exposing the sky above. Look out for flying foxes and be prepared to wade.

    Geikie Gorge on the Fitzroy River is 20 km (12 miles) from the tiny settlement of Fitzroy Crossing. The gorge is full of wildlife and vegetation including freshwater crocodiles (less dangerous than salt-water), kangaroos and wallabies. Visitors are restricted to walking on the west bank and swimming is permitted. There are boat trips in the gorge during the dry season. National Parks Rangers are based at Windjana and Geikie Gorges during the dry season.

Wolf Creek Meteorite Crater

Halls Creek, 296 km (184 miles) west of Fitzroy Crossing, the site of a short-lived gold rush in 1886, is the turn-off point for the Wolf Creek Meteorite Crater. The oft-photographed crater is 835 metres (2780 feet) wide, 50 metres (170 feet) deep and as red as the face of Mars. Discovered in 1947, it is said to be the second largest such depression in the world. It lies 135 km (84 miles) south of the town.

Bungle Bungle

The Bungle Bungle Range, 160 km (99 miles) north of Halls Creek, is the Kimberley's greatest sight. Its thousands of low, round peaks look like hives pushed together by a bee-keeping giant. Some are pointed towers, some hats, others faces.

Barnett Gorge

445

Their wrinkled, rusty brown surfaces, pitted and broken like the skin of a centenarian, are striped across with narrow bands of lichen. Seen from above, the stripes blur vision, from below they defy belief. The steep slopes, deep indentations and maze of passageways between the peaks are covered with a yellowy green furze of spinifex grass and mulga. Desert oaks and similar spindly trees grow here and there. The Bungle Bungle Range has just been declared a national park but is still very difficult to get into. A rough road leads from the highway and is impassable in the wet. Before visiting, seek information about park conditions from the tourist office in Halls Creek or Kununurra. Scenic flights and tours to Bungle Bungle depart from Kununurra during the dry season.

Kununurra

This town was built in the 1960s as the centre of the Ord River Scheme, an irrigation scheme once expected to turn the north of Western Australia into a rice bowl. The rice growing experiment failed but hope sprang eternal and the farmers turned their attention to sorghum, soybeans, peanuts, mung beans, maize and melons with better if not spectacular success.

An unexpected piece of luck was the discovery of the world's largest deposit of diamonds at Smoke Creek south of the town in 1979. The diamonds are mostly yellow and are being mined for industrial use although jewellery is made with them. The mine, called the Argyle Diamond Mine, has a visitors' centre.

Lake Argyle
Lake Argyle 70 km (43 miles) by road from Kununurra, is an artificial lake created for the Ord River scheme. It holds nine times the water of Sydney Harbour and its shores are surrounded by wide green fields of irrigated crops. A tourist village with accommodation and a restaurant has been created on the lake shore and the old Argyle Homestead, moved when the lake was filled, has been turned into a pioneer museum. Bus and boat tours leave from the village.

WHERE TO STAY
Overland Motor Inn, Duncan Highway, Kununurra, (091) 68 1455; has 60 air-conditioned motel units, a swimming pool and licensed restaurant. Single $74, double $84.

Part X

TASMANIA

Tasmanian Devil

Tasmania, the island state, is made in miniature. Towns, farms, minds and life in general are smaller and closer than in the wide, open spaces of mainland Australia. The settled east, an area of farms, orchards and villages reeking with history, is as close to English countryside as Australia ever comes; the land gently green and welcoming, wet, misty and enclosed; the settlements small, their houses old and made of tawny sandstone or white painted timber. In the untouched west a wild grandeur of landscape utterly unlike the rest of Australia appears. Nature's triumph is dramatic, mountainous and squally; deep, dark and silent rivers flow into impenetrable forests and the coastal cliffs are windswept, grey and uninviting. Mining towns, luckily few, are the only blot on an otherwise intimidating beauty.

The Bass Strait, 500 km (310 miles) wide, is the physical barrier between the continent and Tasmania but the state is limited in other ways. Its population is the smallest, 437,000. Its capital, Hobart, is the smallest (population 175,700). It is the poorest state by far and struggles constantly to develop its minuscule economy.

Climate

There are four distinct seasons in Tasmania and climate generally is much more like temperate parts of Europe than the rest of Australia. Summers never reach mainland heat and winter temperatures are consistently lower than any other state, freezing point being a common occurrence. Winter conditions are milder in the east than the west which has extremes of cold and snow on the mountains throughout winter.

447

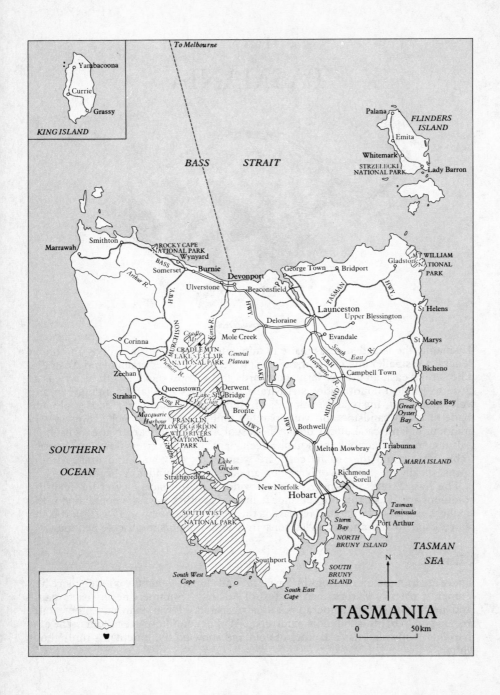

KING ISLAND

Yarrabacoona

Currie

Grassy

To Melbourne

BASS STRAIT

Palana
FLINDERS ISLAND
Emita
Whitemark
STRZELECKI NATIONAL PARK
Lady Barron

Marrawah

Smithton

ROCKY CAPE NATIONAL PARK
Wynyard
Somerset
BASS HWY.
Burnie
Devonport
Ulverstone
Beaconsfield

George Town   Bridport
Gladstone
MT WILLIAM NATIONAL PARK

Arthur R.

MURCHISON HWY.

Corinna

Cradle Mt.
CRADLE MTN.
LAKE ST CLAIR NATIONAL PARK

Mole Creek

Deloraine

TASMAN HWY.

Launceston
Upper Blessington

St Helens

Forth R.

Central Plateau

Evandale
St Marys

Zeehan

Pieman R.

LAKE HWY.

South East R.

Bicheno

Strahan

Queenstown
King R.

Derwent Bridge
Lake St Clair

Campbell Town

MIDLAND HWY.

AMH.

Macquarie R.

Coles Bay
Great Oyster Bay

Macquarie Harbour

Bronte

FRANKLIN LOWER GORDON WILD RIVERS NATIONAL PARK

Bothwell

Triabunna

MARIA ISLAND

Lake Gordon

Melton Mowbray

Strathgordon

New Norfolk

Richmond
Sorell

Hobart

Tasman Peninsula
Port Arthur

SOUTH WEST NATIONAL PARK

Southport

Storm Bay

NORTH BRUNY ISLAND

SOUTHERN OCEAN

South West Cape

South East Cape

SOUTH BRUNY ISLAND

TASMAN SEA

N

TASMANIA

0   50km

History

Tasmania, initially known as Van Diemen's Land, was the second Australian colony to have white occupants. The people, mostly convicts, came from a failed attempt to settle Port Phillip in Victoria and from Norfolk Island off the New South Wales coast. They established Hobart in 1804 and Launceston in 1806. Both were ruled from Sydney until 1825 when the crown declared Van Diemen's Land a separate colony, re-naming it Tasmania.

Early years were characterised by speedy material progress and a hideous war with the Aboriginals who were effectively wiped out, less than one hundred remaining alive at the time of 'reconciliation' in 1829. At the same time wheat production soared and Tasmania began exporting to New South Wales. Prosperity seemed assured by 1847 when the population reached 70,000 but 10 years later the dream collapsed into a 25-year depression. The way to disaster was laid open by too great a dependence on convict labour and precipitated by the end of convict transportation, protectionist moves by the government of Victoria and gold discoveries on the mainland.

Revival came when mines opened in the north-east and the west of the island during the 1880s, timber production also helped resurrect the colonial economy. Tasmania's staples are the same today except for the addition of huge and controversial hydro-electric schemes in the south-west which have encouraged the development of some secondary industry.

GETTING TO AND AROUND

By Air
The only international flights to land in Tasmania are **Qantas** and **Air New Zealand** (which services New Zealand). They land in Hobart. Flights from east coast capitals arrive at Devonport, Launceston and Hobart. **Airlines of Tasmania** connects the population centres of Hobart, Launceston, Devonport, Queenstown, Strahan and Wynyard as well as flying to King and Flinders Islands in Bass Strait.

By Rail
No passengers are carried on trains in Tasmania.

By Sea
A ferry called the *Abel Tasman* crosses Bass Strait from Station Pier in Melbourne, leaving at 6 pm on Mondays, Wednesdays and Fridays. It runs to Devonport on the north coast of Tasmania, arriving at 8.30 am the next day and beginning the return journey at 6 pm. The ferry has cabins on four decks ranging from A Deck double-bedded suites with private facilities to C Deck four-berth with shared facilities. Fares are charged according to three seasons, bargain (May to mid-September), shoulder (September to mid-December and February to April) and holiday (mid-December to end January). The cost varies from a lowest possible fare of $70 to a highest possible of $197 per person. The ferry also takes vehicles to which a complicated formula taking into account length, height and time of year is applied resulting in charges from $82 to $313. Bicycles get on board for from $9 to $12. Meals are extra.

449

Deluxe Coaches offers a combined bus/ferry ticket from places as far away as Cairns, Darwin, Alice Springs and Perth as well as from Sydney, Canberra and Brisbane. It is based on the lowest level of cabin accommodation and costs between $105 (Canberra to Devonport, low season) to $316 (Darwin to Devonport, high season).

By Road
Redline Coaches which run between all the major towns and cities, up the east and west coasts and through the middle of the island. They meet the *Abel Tasman* at Devonport for transfers to Launceston and Hobart. **Ansett Pioneer** also operates in a circle linking Hobart, Launceston, Devonport, Burnie and Queenstown.

Drivers will find sealed roads between major centres in Tasmania but wherever there is little settlement they run out pretty rapidly.

TOURIST INFORMATION
Tasmania calls its tourist information service **Tasbureau**. It acts as a distribution point for various publications including those produced by the Tasmanian Visitor Corporation, an active private organisation involved in tourism promotion, and a monthly newspaper called *Tasmanian Travelways* which carries up-to-date information including prices on transport and accommodation throughout the state. The offices of Tasbureau are at:

80 Elizabeth Street, **Hobart**, (002) 30 0211
129 King Street, **Sydney**, (02) 233 2500
256 Collins Street, **Melbourne**, (03) 653 7999
217–219 Queen Street, **Brisbane**, (07) 221 2744
32 King William Street, **Adelaide**, (08) 211 7411
55 William Street, **Perth**, (09) 321 2633.

MAJOR SIGHTS
Port Arthur on the Tasman Peninsula south of Hobart is the best convict site in Australia. It is the largest and best preserved of the prisons that played such an important part in the early days. **Cradle Mountain-Lake St Clair National Park** in the middle of the island contains Australia's most praised mountain walking track and has remarkable natural beauty as does the **Gordon River** area on the west coast.

ACCOMMODATION
Your accommodation can be a real highlight when visiting Tasmania. A goodly number of colonial residences from farm cottages to mansions have been converted to tourist accommodation in two forms; holiday flats and guesthouses. The former are self-contained self-catering establishments that require you to provide for your own needs in food and groceries, the latter are bed-and-breakfast establishments, some with private facilities, some without. They are called **Colonial Accommodation** and to qualify as such must have been built before 1901 and have been restored, decorated and furnished in colonial style. As well as these there are **Country Accommodation** establishments which provide bed and breakfast and offer accommodation in country homes or on host farms, sometimes within the main house, otherwise in self-contained cottages on the property.

The more common types of accommodation exist as well. In the cities of Hobart and Launceston there several motels and hotels, those of the **Inkeepers Group** are of a reliable standard. A brand-new Sheraton Hotel has just been opened in Hobart.

FOOD AND DRINK

Tasmania was once known as the 'Apple Isle' for the quantity and quality of its apples which thrived in the cool island climate. They are still there but the tag is not heard so much these days. The island is also famous for its crayfish which are sought after as far away as Japan. They are expensive but the fuss over them is justified. Atlantic salmon are farmed in the cold waters off the island's coast. The dairy industry of King Island, one of Bass Strait's two islands, produces fine soft cheeses, especially Brie. A small wine industry produces bottled table wines for an almost exclusively island market. Its products are usually collected under the heading 'Tasmanian Wines' on wine lists. Its leading name is Heemskerk, producer of a respectable Chardonnay.

ACTIVITIES

Tasmania's many lakes and rivers make it ideal for **trout fishing**, and companies regularly organise fishing holidays. Tasbureau can supply details. Tasmania also has some of the best **bushwalking** territory in the country, especially in the Cradle Mountain area and in the south-west. Commercially organised wilderness tours will guide you through some of these areas. Contact the Adventure Tours Association of Tasmania, c/o R. H. Geeves, Arves Road, Geeveston, 7116, (002) 97 1384, for details or see the Wilderness section of this chapter, beginning on page 470. Skiing is available during the winter at Ben Lomond, 61 km (38 miles) from Launceston, and Mt Field, 96 km (60 miles) from Hobart, but neither field has accommodation. Tasmania has 60 golf courses, about 20 of which allow non-members on payment of a green fee.

HOBART

Hobart is Australia's smallest state capital by a very long way, with a population of 175,700 which is smaller than some provincial cities in other states, but what it lacks in citizens, and the energy they bring, it makes up for in history. The city is situated on the south-east coast of Tasmania beside the west bank of the Derwent River. The river is so wide and close to its mouth at this point that it is more akin to a harbour. Mount Wellington, 1270 metres of forested slopes, stands behind the city, often cloud topped and sometimes snowcapped. There are few high-rise buildings and almost no bustle in the city streets.

Hobart's climate is much cooler than that of other Australian cities. For example, the average summer maximum is only around 20°C (70°F) and the minimum 10°C (50°F). In winter the respective levels are 12°C (54°F) and 4°C (40°F). The seasons of the year are more marked in Tasmania than elsewhere as well, their distinction being more European or north American in character than Australian.

History

Almost as soon as Sydney and New South Wales came into being, the colonial authorities had two problems to face: what to do with incorrigible convicts and how to prevent other European powers encroaching on Australia. The meeting of both problems was instrumental in founding Hobart. It was there that the prison colony of New South Wales established its own prison colony which also served as an outpost to discourage French interest.

Risdon Cove, near Hobart, was the site of the first landing on 7 September 1803, by Lieutenant John Bowman. He was followed, on 20 February 1804, by Lieutenant Governor David Collins, sent from Sydney to run the new outpost, who established the official settlement at Sullivan's Cove on which the city now stands. He named it Hobart Town after the British Secretary of State for Colonies. The early history of this new settlement parallels that of Sydney where convicts were used as de facto slave labour to ensure the continuation of an otherwise doubtful establishment. The early industries of whaling and sealing brought the town to prominence as a port and later the near surroundings were opened up to wool growing. Hobart was officially declared a city in 1842 but the extremely rugged and inhospitable terrain of much of Tasmania, its small size and especially the absence of mineral wealth, such an important factor in helping other parts of Australia to grow, saw the city fall behind all others and limited its growth.

GETTING TO AND AROUND

Air New Zealand and Qantas flights from New Zealand land at Hobart and some Qantas flights from London and West Coast USA to Sydney and Melbourne continue to Hobart. Domestic carriers Ansett, Australian, East West and Air NSW fly daily from Sydney and Melbourne and anyone coming from other states must make connections in those cities. The economy fare from Sydney is $218 and from Melbourne $157. A shuttle bus run by Redline coaches connects Hobart airport with the city, a journey of about 35 minutes. The fare is $3.50. Taxis are also available and cost around $14.

The MV *Abel Tasman*, car and passenger ferry from Melbourne to Devonport in northern Tasmania, is connected to Hobart by Redline Coach. The fare is $25.60. Redline coaches also connect Hobart with other large centres in Tasmania.

The central area of Hobart is without useful public transport other than taxis but it is compact and easily covered on foot. The Metropolitan Transport Trust (MTT) buses operate from Hobart's city centre into the suburbs and an unlimited travel ticket called a **Day Rover** is available for these from the MTT enquiry counter at Tasbureau, 80 Elizabeth Street, Hobart. The desk is open from noon to 5 pm, Monday to Friday.

Bicycles can be hired from Graham McVilly Cycles, (002) 23 7284, for $3 an hour or $15 per day.

TOURIST INFORMATION

Tourist information is available from Tasbureau, 80 Elizabeth Street, Hobart. Not only does this office cover Hobart but it is also the main tourist office for all of Tasmania and a good place to take your queries about other parts of the island.

452

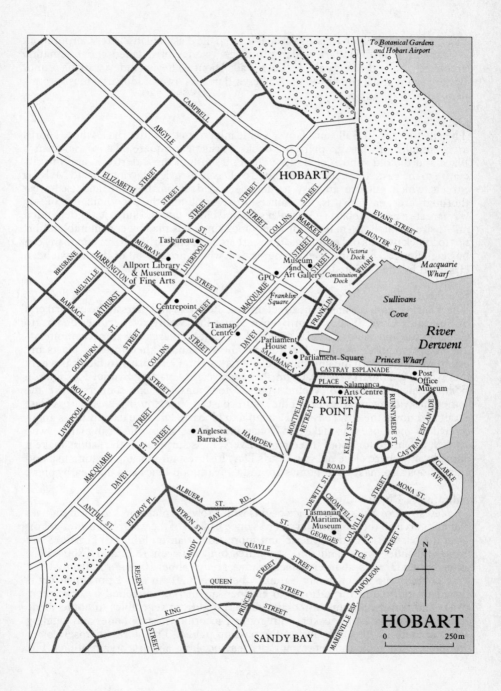

Information about Hobart is also available from the Tasmanian Visitor Corporation, 7 Franklin Wharf, Hobart, which produces a series of detailed and fascinating brochures under the general title 'Let's Talk About'. They include a walking tour of Battery Point and a run-down on Anglesea Barracks, two of Hobart's most prominent attractions.

Orientation

The city focuses on Sullivan's Cove, a wide inlet from the wider river, whose shores are a complex of wharves, piers and docks. Parliament Square, historic Salamanca Place and the old suburb of Battery Point lie south of the waterfront, and the city centre to the east. The centre is bounded by Davey, Argyle, Harrington and Melville Streets which enclose an easy to negotiate grid of north–south and east–west thoroughfares; easy, that is, for walkers; drivers will find the predominance of one way streets a pain. Hobart is Australia's second oldest city and since it has depended on Australian holiday-makers for a very long time, has made a considerable effort not to knock over its old buildings. They are its most endearing charm and many can be seen along Davey and Macquarie Streets where around 60 of them have been classified by the National Trust.

Franklin Wharf

The wharf is really a waterfront street linking the docks and piers at the eastern end of Sullivan's Cove. It runs from Brooke Street Pier where river cruises depart, to Constitution and Victoria docks, enclosed and gated squares of water accommodating private yachts that sail the Derwent on fine weekends. Their forest of masts and bright white hulls are the city's most exuberant sight. **Constitution Dock** is where the Sydney to Hobart ocean race finishes each year. Departing Sydney Harbour on Boxing Day, hundreds of yachts from 70 foot maxis to one tonners brave the sometimes vicious weather down the south coast of New South Wales, across Bass Strait and down the east coast of Tasmania to Hobart. The race usually takes about three days and those who make it to Constitution Dock, always fewer than those who started, celebrate for about three more. Everyone is surprised if the sailors make it home by anywhere close to New Year's Day. Fish restaurants and floating fish and chips shops also make their homes around Constitution Dock and the nearby piers.

Salamanca Place

The old street of Salamanca Place begins with a row of bond stores and warehouses that has survived the whaling days. It was once in sight of the water but is now cut off from it by later, less atmospheric and more utilitarian buildings. The stores are three-and four-storey sandstone structures built between 1835 and 1860 whose undecorated facades, standing cheek by jowl, stretch about 100 metres, fronted by a wide cobblestone street. Every Saturday between 8.30 am and 1 pm the street is closed to traffic and turned over to an open-air market inhabited by craftsmen, artists and trinket, antique and craft sellers. Food from vegetables to home-made cakes is also on sale and buskers with guitars, accordions, saxophones and juggling balls compete for the attention of the passing public. The stores themselves are occupied by a combination of restaurants, fashion shops and arts organisations. The

Peacock Theatre, a swish shopping arcade called the **Galleria** and the **Salamanca Arts Centre**, shared by printmakers, leather workers and other artists, are among the major tenants.

Parliament Square

This square, containing Parliament House and a small, shady park, takes up an intervening triangle between Salamanca Place and Brookes Pier. Parliament House was built between 1836 and 1840 to a design by John Lee Archer, responsible also for the Government Stores and other prominent Hobart buildings. It was originally a Customs House and is one of the oldest buildings in the city. The public is admitted to the parliamentary gallery when State Parliament is sitting.

Battery Point

Salamanca Place leads from the warehouses to Battery Point, Hobart's oldest suburb. The battery which gave the point its name was set up there in 1818 and later became a signalling station, relaying news of incoming ships from a similar station on Mt Nelson to the south. The suburb's appearance has changed little from the 1850s when it was populated by seafaring men from the harbour master to mariners, merchants, shipwrights, coopers, boatbuilders and fishermen who chose it for its unique position between Sullivan's Cove and Sandy Bay Creek. They drank at 'The Whalers Return', 'The Neptune Inn' and 'The Shipwright's Arms' and went to church at St George's in Waterloo Crescent. This church still stands and is one of the most striking in any Australian city.

Built between 1836 and 1847 it is a combination of designs by the two leading architects of the time, John Lee Archer and James Blackburn. Although based on the Gothic cross, the church appears determined to out-Greek the ancient Greeks since it has a columned portico and pediment complete with acroteria. Its three-tiered, octagonal and columned central tower is one of Battery Point's landmarks. Many of the point's residences are in the simple, elegant, double-fronted, single-storey style typical of the Georgian period and in this feature alone the suburb is unlike any other in Australia. It also has a small circular 'village green' in Arthur Circus. Guided walking tours of Battery Point depart from Franklin Square in the city at 9.30 am each Saturday morning and cost $3.

Anglesea Barracks

The old barracks stand at the eastern limit of Battery Point, facing Davey Street. The barracks are the Tasmanian headquarters of the Australian Army and the oldest military establishment in Australia still occupied by the military. The site was selected by Governor Lachlan Macquarie of New South Wales on his first visit to what was then known as Van Diemen's Land in 1811 but despite his constant cajoling, the buildings took until 1818 to complete. They were occupied by British forces until 1870 and then put to various uses including a boys' school, a girls' industrial school, a girls' reformatory, old women's home, a weather bureau and the headquarters of the Royal Hobart Bowling Club.

The barracks contain some of Hobart's best preserved buildings and certainly the greatest concentration of them. They consist of white painted convict brick houses dating from 1814 to 1838 and more imposing sandstone buildings built between 1838 and 1870. Entry is from Davey Street and, although tourists are welcome to wander around the outside of the buildings, entrance to them is generally not permitted except by invitation. Guided tours take place at 11 am on Tuesdays.

Tasmanian Museum and Art Gallery

The museum and gallery complex is on the corner of Davey and Argyle Streets, just behind Constitution Dock. They are entered through a 1960s glass, steel and linoleum foyer but penetrate the **Old Commissariat Store**, Hobart's oldest building, constructed in 1808. The gallery has a large room devoted to pieces from the colonial era whose display includes not only paintings by the artists John Glover (1767–1849) and W. C. Piguenit (1836–1914) whose work is important in the history of Australian painting, but furniture, silverware, crockery, sculpture and even musical instruments. 'The Conciliation', painted by Benjamin Dutterau in 1840 is the focus of this room. A large work taking the central position on one wall, it depicts George Augustus Robinson conciliating with the Aborigines of Tasmania during the 1830s when, after the whites had tried and failed to wipe them out, it was thought better to persuade them to move to Flinders Island in Bass Strait. The persuasion succeeded but was disastrous for the Aborigines, who died out. In the present atmosphere of black–white relations in Australia the work is, to say the least, ironic.

The Tasmanian Aborigines' sad history, including the survivors and their descendants, is recounted in the museum half of the complex. The story is one of an ill-armed group trying to defend their land against very well armed invaders who, although they did not set out to commit genocide, practically did so. The museum and art gallery are open from 10 am to 5 pm daily.

Other Museums

One of Hobart's most gracious old houses, Narryna, built in 1836 at 103 Hampden Road, Battery Point, now houses the Van Diemen's Land Folk Museum. The two-storey house is of brick construction with a sandstone facade, all in the refined, understated style of the Georgian period. It is approached through wide iron gates and has a fountain in the centre of the front garden. The museum concentrates on how the people of Tasmania lived day to day in pioneering times. The **Tasmanian Maritime Museum** at 21 Secheron Road, Battery Point, holds bits and pieces of the state's extensive maritime history from whaling and sealing to trade. The **Allport Library and Museum of Fine Arts**, attached to the Tasmanian State Library at 91 Murray Street, features rare books, paintings, prints, antique furniture, silverware, glass and ceramics. The **Post Office Museum**, 19 to 21 Castray Esplanade, shows how the communications system in Tasmania has developed.

Botanic Gardens

Hobart's Botanic Gardens are under the lee of Government House. They stand in a prime position on the northern side of the city where there are lovely views over the river. The site is decidedly steep with paths down the hillside through a thoroughly

European layout of plants and trees, especially the tall pines and fir trees. The gardens are a great spot to picnic.

Mount Wellington

The mountain that looms behind Hobart is the best place for an overall view of the city and its waters. The Mt Wellington lookout is 20 km (12 miles) by road from central Hobart and at any time of year it is a cold and windy place but the view is tremendously wide. There are also subsidiary lookouts on the way up the mountain that take in views to the north and south. A view of the city is also to be had from **Mount Nelson**, south of the Olinda Grove Nelson Road where you look up and down the Derwent River but don't see so much of the suburbs.

WHERE TO STAY

Sheraton Hobart, corner Davey and Evans Streets, Hobart, (002) 23 4499, is an almost brand-new hotel which is now the largest building on the Hobart waterfront. One former Hobart town planner has described it as a 'pile of bricks' and no one could argue with him but it offers the highest standard of service and accommodation in the city. $98.

Wrest Point Federal Hotel Casino, 410 Sandy Bay Road, Sandy Bay, (002) 25 0112, was the top hotel in Hobart until the Sheraton came along. It is a high-rise tower on the point at Sandy Bay and suffers from being an unwalkable distance from all Hobart's interesting places. It has the city's only casino. Tower rooms $135 and $260. There is also a motel attached to this hotel where rooms are available for $65 and $75 per night. The more expensive ones overlook the Derwent River.

Four Seasons Downtowner, 96 Bathurst Street, Hobart, (002) 34 6333; next step down from the above, ie, no 24-hour room service, not quite the level of decoration but comfortable rooms with most other facilities and a good location on the margin of the city area. The building looks like a multi-storey office block. Single $72, double $82.

Four Seasons Westside, 156 Bathurst Street, Hobart, (002) 34 6255; a more up-market twin of the above hotel situated a block and a half further west. Single $85, double $95.

Innkeepers Lenna of Hobart, 20 Runnymede Street, Battery Point, (002) 23 2911, is one of Hobart's grand old houses which has been converted to tourist accommodation. The restaurant, reception and other public areas are in the old house and the guest rooms have been built onto the back overlooking Sullivan's Cove. The addition could not be described as sympathetic but the rooms are large, some have two bedrooms and the house is very close to Salamanca Place. $115.

Innkeepers St Ives, 67 St George's Terrace, Hobart, (002) 30 1801; located a little south of Battery Point, the accommodation here has been built behind a refurbished old hotel in modern motel style (rooms entered from the outside like apartments) over its own car park but the standard is higher than ordinary motels. Single $65, double $75.

Hadley's Orient Hotel, 34 Murray Street, Hobart, (002) 23 4355, is one of Hobart's grand old pubs which recently underwent a well-deserved face-lift, including a considerable enlargement of its rooms. Centrally located. Single $60, double $20.

457

Tantallon Lodge, 8 Mona Street, Battery Point, (002) 23 3124, is a two-storey house, dating from about 1910 and overlooking Sandy Bay. Rooms have private facilities and some take advantage of the view. Accommodation for seventeen persons. Single $38, double $50 bed and breakfast.

Colville Cottage, 32 Mona Street, Battery Point, (002) 23 6968, is one of Battery Point's most delightful old cottages converted to a guesthouse accommodating twelve guests. Shared facilities. Delightful garden. Single $40, double $50 bed and breakfast.

Imperial Mansions, 138 Collins Street, Hobart, (002) 23 7509, is, despite its grand name, a budget option. Share facilities, no phones or TV in the rooms but a central location and charming old building. Single $25, double $40 bed and continental breakfast.

Argyle Motor Lodge, corner Argyle and Lewis Streets, North Hobart, (002) 34 2488, is, once again, an old house converted to tourist accommodation by the addition of a totally unsympathetic wing. It specialises in accommodation for families and has cooking facilities in its rooms. You will need to take a bus into town. Single $48, double $52.

EATING OUT

Dear Friends, 8 Brooke Street, Hobart, (002) 23 2646, is set in an old waterfront building where you might choose to go for an intimate dinner rather than a rowdy night. The cuisine is delicate in the modern French manner and the extensive wine list includes vintages grown on the island. Licensed. Upper price range.

Mure's Fish House, 5 Knopwood Street, Battery Point, (03) 23 6917, has been awarded the accolade of 'Best Fish Restaurant in Australia' by the big selling local news magazine *The Bulletin* and is an institution in Hobart. Licensed. Upper price range. There is a cheaper branch of Mure's on the waterfront near Brooke Pier.

Alexanders, Innkeepers Lenna of Hobart, 20 Runnymede Street, Battery Point, (002) 23 2911, occupies one of the best rooms in a sumptuous old mansion which also serves as one of Hobart's better hotels. The menu makes much of local seafood, especially crayfish. Licensed. Upper price range.

Dirty Dick's Steak House, 22 Francis Street, Battery Point, (002) 23 3103; despite its dreadful name, you will find this restaurant in a charming small shopfront surrounded by the old houses of Battery Point. The menu is basic with steaks done as you like them and a second line in seafood. No frills but open fires. Licensed. Mid price range.

One Five Nine Davey Street, 159 Davey Street, Hobart, (002) 23 1538, occupies an 1830 cottage where the fireplaces still glow in winter time. The restaurant does original work with fresh ingredients and prides itself on its sauces and desserts. Licensed. Mid price range.

Mondo Piccolo Ristorante, 196 Macquarie Street, Hobart, (002) 23 2362, is the place to go if you're in the mood for Italian. Licensed. Mid price range.

Miss Victoria's Parlour, 4 Victoria Street, Hobart, (002) 34 7480; simple, 'home made' food in pretty surroundings. A good place for morning and afternoon teas but serves breakfast and other meals as well. BYO. Low price range.

TOURS AND CRUISES

A selection of day and half day tours can be booked at the Tasbureau office, 80 Elizabeth Street, Hobart, (002) 30 0211. The half day options include Hobart and environs ($15), Mt Nelson and city sights ($12). As Tasmania is so small, full day tours tend to skip the city sights and go further afield.

Visitors who want to travel on the Derwent River have a choice of ferry-like motorised launches with a capacity for over one hundred passengers or sailing vessels which take only a few people. The major motorised river cruisers are *Commodore I* (002) 34 9294, two hour cruises departing from Brooke Street Pier at 10 am, noon and 2 pm and an 8 pm evening cruise, all $11 except noon which includes lunch and costs $22; MV *Derwent Explorer*, (002) 34 4032, offers some more elaborate cruises including such things as a 'Craybake' and dinner with jazz, prices range from $11 to $38; MV *Emmalisa*, inexpensive cruises from Brooke Street Pier at 12.05 pm, 1.05 pm and 3 pm for $3. The 48-foot ketch *Prudence* (002) 34 9921, has lunch cruises from Monday to Friday, $40, and all day Sunday, $70, plus morning ($30) and lunch cruises on Saturday ($45). The boat departs from Watermen's Dock.

Port Arthur

Port Arthur is the best preserved, most extensive and most interesting convict relic in Australia. It stands on the Tasman Peninsula 102 km (63 miles) south-east of Hobart, a little over an hour's drive from the city. The convict settlement was established there in 1830 as a replacement for Macquarie Harbour on the island's west coast, considered too remote to justify its continuance. Port Arthur was used to house criminals who offended in Tasmania and served until 1877 by which time 12,500 convicts had passed through its complicated system of graduated gaols, workshops, mines and punishments.

Port Arthur

The site was named after Governor Arthur who selected it, noting its natural qualities as a prison. The only land access is by Eaglehawk Neck, a spit of land so narrow that a single line of ferocious dogs successfully guarded it against escaping prisoners. The dogs and fear of swimming the waters on either side of the neck kept prisoners on the peninsula even if they managed to escape the actual prison.

The prison operated under a regime which seems unutterably cruel but was enlightened for its time. Prisoners were graded according to their crimes and behaviour. The worst slaved in the coal mines at Saltwater River on the north side of the peninsula, the best lived in comparative luxury in the dormitories of the main penitentiary at Port Arthur. Lashings were meted out for even the most petty offences such as not saluting an officer, and those who continued to misbehave were sent to the 'model' prison.

In that dreadful place they dwelt in solitary silence except for religious services and during those were isolated in cubicles and masked to prevent them recognising each other. They remained masked when moving around the prison and were required to stay 15 feet apart; they could not pass face to face but had to turn to the wall as one walked by another. Their only utterance was hymn singing. The idea, which came from the Model Prison at Pentonville in England, was that they should reflect on their crimes and reform. The effect was to drive many of them mad. Those who did not succumb to madness or physical punishment frequently died from respiratory infections fostered by the almost continuous damp and cold of Port Arthur. Ironically, in later years a lunatic asylum was attached to the model prison building.

When closed in 1877, Port Arthur was put up for sale at £800. There were no takers and the site was allowed to decay, falling victim to savage fires in 1895 and 1897 which reduced most of the large buildings to shells. By early this century enough time had passed for it to be recognised as a place of tourist interest and guesthouses were established in some of the old residences which were part of the complex. During the 1920s it became a holiday spot with tennis courts in front of the penitentiary and sailing boats on the bay, but despite the interest nothing was done to preserve it. The buildings continued to decay under attacks from weather and the peninsula locals who used them as a source of second-hand building materials.

In 1979 the National Parks and Wildlife Service embarked on a nine million dollar programme of preservation and restoration. That programme is now complete and Port Arthur has become Tasmania's most popular tourist attraction, drawing about 300,000 visitors a year.

GETTING THERE

The choices are distressingly few. Either you take the Peninsula Coach Service which leaves Tasmanian Motors, Centreway Arcade, Collins Street, Hobart at 3.45 pm and effectively means staying two nights as the return coach leaves Port Arthur at 7.45 am each day, or you hire a car. The return coach fare is $14. The alternative is to join a coach tour for the day (see below).

Drivers take Route A3 from Hobart to Sorell and Route A9 to Port Arthur.

TOURIST INFORMATION

There is an information centre in the car park where tours can be booked and guide books purchased.

WHAT TO SEE

Its many surviving buildings, all constructed by convicts, are an important reason for Port Arthur's pre-eminence among convict sites. Because the settlement was distant from other centres of civilisation, it grew to be a township as much as a gaol and the houses in which its clergy, overseers, medical and military personnel lived are better preserved than the various gaols occupied by the convicts. All the buildings are loosely gathered around a small harbour protected by an island called Isle of the Dead, where dead convicts were buried, and by a promontory known as Point Puer on which a boys' prison was established in the 1840s. The sloping grassy site with its wide lawns and spreading trees is more like a peaceful English country village than a prison.

The settlement is divided between official residences and prison buildings, the latter constructed of sandstone and showing a great deal of skill in their design and execution. They include the penitentiary, a cylindrical castellated guard tower, the facade of the prison hospital, the prison administrative offices and the model prison and asylum which houses the site's main museum. This last building is the only one where an admission charge ($3.50) is levied. It holds relics of convict life from leg irons of various weights—heavy ones were used for punishment as were heavy shovels—to pieces of the mast and semaphore signal system that warned the troops at Eaglehawk Neck of an escape.

The only residence in the prison area belonged to the prison commandant. It has been fully restored and is open from around 11 am most days, depending on staffing. Other residences open to the public include the chaplain's house and the medical officer's house on the hill overlooking the prison. Near these is the Port Arthur church, possibly the most photographed convict ruin in Australia. It is a superbly proportioned colonial Gothic church with the austere and mysterious grandeur that seems to typify all ruined religious sites and the bonus of an approach through a long avenue of arching trees. On entering, since there is no roof or decoration left, the bare essentials of its crucifix design are utterly exposed. In a surprising dose of ecumenicism, the church was used for services of all denominations and never consecrated to any one of them. It, too, was burned by the disastrous fires of 1895 and '97.

Nearby Attractions

The area around Port Arthur is one of rugged beauty and has some spots where nature deserves to be marvelled at. To reach them, take the road from the settlement marked **Safety Cove and the Remarkable Cave**. **Palmers Lookout**, a short distance along this road gives a superb view to the north over the ruins of Port Arthur. The drive to Remarkable Cave runs by beachfront farms and some pleasant beaches and finishes at **Maingon Bay Lookout**. From here you can look south-west to Cape Raoul where huge pillars of Jurassic dolomite rear up hundreds of feet from the sea like a cluster of organ pipes. The cape is named after the pilot of Bruny D'Entrecasteaux's 1792 expedition which stirred the New South Wales government into settling Tasmania. Unfortunately, the pillars are not as huge as they once were—the Royal Navy used them for target practice sometime before World War II. The surf which boils below Maingon Bay Lookout comes directly from the Antarctic, an unencumbered 2500 km (1150 miles) due south. The **Remarkable Cave** is reached via a flight of steps near the lookout. It is a natural tunnel into which surging waves rush without warning, clashing the stones at its entrance and filling the rocky sink before it with creamy foam. At low tide the tunnel is empty and safe enough for tourists to walk into.

WHERE TO STAY AND EATING OUT

There is enough interest in the Port Arthur area to warrant an overnight stay and enough passable establishments to make it comfortable but there are few restaurants other than in the accommodation houses themselves.

Four Seasons Port Arthur, Port Arthur, (002) 50 2101; set immediately above and overlooking the historic site, it is undoubtedly the most convenient place to stay and has the best views. Of good motel standard. Single $63, double $71.

Fox and Hounds Holiday Resort, Arthur Highway, Port Arthur, (002) 50 2217, is a complex of mock Tudor family villas and motel rooms with a roadside tavern in the same style. It stands right on the highway about three km (2 miles) from the Port Arthur site and has water views. $65.

New Plymouth Holiday Village, Stewarts Bay, (002) 50 2262, is a group of wooden cabins standing on a hillside with balconies overlooking a lovely small green bay. They have kitchens and come in two, three and four room sizes. For those who don't want to cater for themselves, there is a seafood restaurant in the middle of the layout. The cabins are just off the highway right outside the Port Arthur historic site. $50.

Cascades, Koonya, Tasman Peninsula, (002) 50 3121, was once a convict out-station of Port Arthur, now converted to a tourist outstation. Accommodation is in two buildings, an old hospital converted for groups up to six and officers' quarters consisting of three conjoined cottages, each of which takes two people. All have private facilities and kitchen, log fires and colonial-style furniture. The property consists entirely of original buildings and includes the remains of a prison, workshop and solitary confinement cell. It is 15 km (nine miles) from Port Arthur on the edge of Norfolk Bay. Double $50 bed and breakfast.

TOURS

Many people choose to see Port Arthur on a day coach tour from Hobart. They can be booked at Tasbureau, 80 Elizabeth Street, Hobart, (002) 30 0211. A tour of the historic site alone departs on Mondays at 10 am ($26). A tour including Tasman Peninsula commercial tourist attractions such as the Bush Mill and Tasmanian Devil Park departs on Wednesday, Friday, Saturday and Sunday at 9 am ($48).

Tours are also available at the historic site itself. **National Parks and Wildlife Service** guides conduct free tours from the information booth in the car park at 9.30 am, 11.30 am, 12.30 pm, 1.30 pm, 2.30 pm and 3.30 pm. An 'audio tour' costing $4 is also available from the information office. You are supplied with a cassette tape machine, earphones and recorded commentary and walk around at your leisure. Other tour options include a minibus which continues to the Remarkable Cave and boat trips to the Isle of the Dead.

Richmond

Richmond is a small village 26 km (16 miles) north of Hobart which is also a major historical site. It has a quantity of well-preserved buildings including the usual gaol, a famous bridge, Australia's oldest Catholic church and many other places dating from the 1820s and '30s. The village has the advantage of being set in green, undulating, placid countryside which was among the first farmed in Tasmania and whose grain proved a salvation for the whole colony in the early 1800s.

GETTING THERE
Other than a tour, a car is the only way to get to Richmond. Take Route A3 out of Hobart and Route B31 to Richmond.

WHAT TO SEE
A plethora of tawny, sandstone Georgian buildings lines Richmond's main street. They include Buscombe's General Store (1829), the Bridge Inn (1833), old bakehouse (1840) and other stores from 1836 to 1850 most of which are now tea rooms or private museums. **Richmond Bridge**, on which convicts slaved for two years from 1823 to 1825, is the oldest freestone bridge remaining in Australia and stands in perfect order, its three arches straddling the Coal River less than symmetrically but to the required result. The best way to see it is from the river bank picnic grounds.

Richmond Gaol, built in 1825 and so pre-dating Port Arthur by five years, accommodated convicts who worked on Richmond's public buildings and fine houses. It later served as a stopping point for bushrangers and Aboriginal fighters on their way to Hobart to be hanged. The gaol is a squat sandstone walled building set in a green lawn overlooking sheep-strewn countryside. It has been fully restored as a penal museum and is rich in anecdotal detail concerning those who stayed there. Among them were Isaac Solomon, a London brothel keeper, swindler and fence who is reputed to have been the original model for Fagin; the bushranger Martin Cash and the Aboriginal warrior Yummarra who organised resistance to white settlement. The gaol is open from 9 am to 5 pm each day. Admission $2.50. The town's Catholic church, St Luke's, built in 1836, is Australia's oldest.

WHERE TO STAY AND EATING OUT
Prospect House, Richmond, Tasmania, (002) 62 2207, is one of the area's graceful old homes built during the 1830s. Guest rooms with private facilities and colonial furniture are situated in converted barns and haylofts adjacent to the main house which contains the restaurant. About two km (one and a quarter miles) outside Richmond. Single $50, Double $62.

TOURS

Half-day tours to Richmond depart from Hobart each Wednesday and Sunday at 2 pm. Cost is $15. Book with Tasbureau, 80 Elizabeth Street, Hobart, (002) 30 0211.

Launceston

Launceston is Tasmania's second city and the major centre of population in the north of the island. About 87,000 people live there. It is a hilly city, full of

European-style gardens, flowers in spring (September to November), coloured leaves in autumn (March to May) and cool greenery in summer (December to February). The city stands where the North and South Esk Rivers join to form the Tamar River, a wide but short stream which empties into Bass Strait at Port Dalrymple 64 km (40 miles) north. Although it lacks the historical buildings of Hobart, some of Tasmania's best National Trust properties are within easy driving distance.

Launceston was originally named Patersonia after Colonel Paterson who founded and commanded settlements on the Tamar River from 1804. The river had first been noted by George Bass and Matthew Flinders on their 1798 voyage around Tasmania. They named its wide mouth Port Dalrymple. Further explorations were carried out over intervening years but no settlement undertaken until 1804 when Colonel Paterson took possession of the site on the eastern shore of the bay now occupied by George Town. Paterson moved a few weeks later to the site of present day York Town at the end of a long cove on the opposite shore and finally, three and a half years later, abandoned that settlement for Launceston which had already been settled by farmers. They, it seems, knew what they were doing. Paterson, in a fit of humility or possibly servility, changed the name of the settlement to Launceston after the town in Cornwall where Governor Philip Gidley King of New South Wales, his commanding officer, had been born.

GETTING TO AND AROUND

Australian Airlines and Ansett fly to Launceston from Sydney ($201), Melbourne ($135) and Hobart ($79), the latter city also being connected by Airlines of Tasmania ($54.50).

Redline coaches travel between Hobart and Launceston six times a day from Monday to Friday and twice on Saturdays and Sundays via the Midland Highway. The trip takes around two and a half hours and costs $12.60 one way. Phone (002) 34 4577 for bookings.

Drivers should take Route 1, also known as the Midland Highway.

TOURIST INFORMATION

The Tasbureau office is on the corner of Paterson and St John Streets, (003) 32 2488.

The City

Cameron Street has a grey paved, modern **Civic Square** towards its western end. The new City Library and Police Headquarters beetle over its edges; the old St Andrew's Kirk (1850) is on the corner and the older **Macquarie Museum** (1830) is bang in the middle. The last is a plain two-storey sandstone building of perfect regularity in the Georgian manner that is everywhere in Tasmania. It was originally a warehouse but was used more as a military barracks and later an office building. It now houses a branch of the larger Queen Victoria Museum and Art Gallery. The prospect east and west along Cameron Street where many nineteenth-century buildings remain gives an excellent idea of how Launceston must have looked in that time.

The **Queen Victoria Museum and Art Gallery** in Wellington Street just across from its junction with Cameron Street is Launceston's major museum and art gallery. It houses a particularly good collection of convict artefacts including puzzle carvings and other folk art from Port Arthur which is better preserved than the material at the port itself. There is also an excellent small collection of modern sculpture and some colonial paintings although these are not a match for Hobart. A complete Joss House, donated by the descendants of Chinese settlers who took part in a small gold rush in north-eastern Tasmania at the turn of the century, is among the historical displays. The natural history section concentrates on Tasmania's unique fauna. The museum is open from 10 am to 5 pm Monday to Saturday and 2 pm to 5 pm on Sunday. Admission is free.

Although Launceston has fallen prey to mall mania and has a city shopping mall on Brisbane Street, it also possesses a far more enjoyable city shopping area in **Yorktown Square**, at the north-eastern end of the main shopping centre off George Street. This square of shops, boutiques, restaurants and coffee shops in mock colonial style encloses a sunny space not overwhelmed by featureless facades.

Parks

Launceston has parks and gardens to play with. They are scattered around the city centre, enhanced by the cool temperate climate of north-eastern Tasmania and composed by skilful landscape artists. **City Park** (main gate in Brisbane Street) is the most formal of the gardens. It is a flat space taking up a single block on the north-east margin of the city centre and broken up into carefully arranged open prospects peppered with tall, spreading trees and occasional ornamental beds. A year round display of plants in bloom is held in the John Hart Conservatory in the centre of the park. There is also a monkey pit and a waterbird pond. **Albert Hall**, on the edge of the park facing Brisbane Street, was built in 1891 for the Tasmanian International Exhibition. It is now a convention centre. Just outside the park gates on the corner of Brisbane and Tamar Streets is the **Design Centre of Tasmania**, a gallery and shop containing work by the Tasmania's leading crafts people. The pieces on display range from dining suites to pencil boxes but their common thread is the use of Tasmania's superb timbers, especially huon pine. You will also find ceramics and fabric at the centre. It is an excellent place to hunt for an unusual souvenir and prices are reasonable considering the quality of the goods.

Launceston's other fine parks include **Royal Park** which slopes down to the banks of the Tamar River behind the Queen Victoria Museum and Art Gallery and **Princes Square** where a bronze fountain, purchased at the Paris exhibition of 1858, is the visual focus of an English garden featuring rhododendrons and trees native to that country.

Cataract Gorge

William Collins who explored Port Dalrymple and the Tamar in 1804 aboard the 'Lady Nelson', discovered Cataract Gorge. He wrote, 'Upon approaching the entrance I observed a large fall of water over rocks, nearly a quarter of a mile up a straight gully between perpendicular rocks about 15 feet high. The beauty of the scene is probably not surpassed in the world.'

The gorge lies on the western edge of the city centre where the South Esk flows into the Tamar. It is narrow and precipitous and its fast flowing waters are a result of the area's unusual geology. Where the Tamar and North Esk have cut wide channels through the soft bed of an ancient lake, the South Esk has had to carve its way through hard dolerite, making the most of fissures in the rock and forming a channel which remained higher than its fellow rivers. It is surrounded by very steep hills, especially on the north-western side and has a wide pool called the **First Basin** at the head of the gorge proper. A recreation area called Cliff Grounds Reserve surrounds it.

The best access is from the end of Basin Road where a chairlift straddles the First Basin, a distance of 457 metres. There is a public swimming pool surrounded by a wide lawn, as well as a café and kiosk on the city side and a more elaborate restaurant perched on the opposite, steeper, hill which also has limited picnic spots and is much shadier. A suspension bridge built in 1934 crosses the First Basin at its narrow southern opening. Walking tracks, some paved, lead off from the First Basin to **Kings Bridge** at the northern end of the gorge (15 minutes) and to the **Second Basin** and Ducks Reach Power Station, a disused hydro-electric facility, south of the suspension bridge (40 minutes). There are also short walks on the western side of First Basin including one to **Cataract Lookout** which gives a view of the whole gorge.

Two commercial tourist attractions are placed close to Cataract Gorge. They are Penny Royal World and Ritchies Flourmill Art Centre. **Penny Royal World** is an entertainment and accommodation complex partly built in the old Cataract Quarry at the Kings Bridge end of the gorge. It began with the stone by stone removal of an 1825 corn mill from Barton, 60 km (37 miles) from Launceston, to the quarry. Many of the buildings surrounding the old mill are faced in a similar rough stone and mortar and the whole has a unity usually uncharacteristic of such places. Inside the complex are working examples of nineteenth-century wind- and water-powered mills grinding gun powder as well as flour. The water is gathered in large open tanks where miniaturised sailing vessels take rides and there are blacksmith's, millwright's and wheelwright's workshops in the corn mill. The gunpowder mill resides in the old quarry, along with a cannon foundry, and is reached by an old restored tram. Entry to Penny Royal World costs $9. The **Ritchies Flourmill Art Centre**, across the road from Penny Royal World and ranged down the hillside near the river has four levels of wooden buildings built in 1845, most of which are devoted to displays of work by local artists. There is also a tea house in the miller's cottage.

WHERE TO STAY
Colonial Motor Inn, corner Elizabeth and George Streets, Launceston, (003) 31 6588, is another accommodation development typical of Tasmania. In this case Launceston's Old Grammar School of 1847 has been turned over to tourists. The quality restaurant and public areas are in the white and gabled old main school building and any accommodation which faces the street is built in the same style but the bulk of the rooms, behind the impressive facade, is just like any other motel only bigger. A second, less expensive restaurant and bar are behind the old school. $86.
Penny Royal Watermill Motel, 147 Paterson Street, Launceston, (003) 31 6699,

is part of the Penny Royal World next to Cataract Gorge and has motel rooms of good quality. $79. **Penny Royal Village**, part of the same complex, has one-, two-, three- and four-bedroom self-catering suites starting at $75.

The Old Bakery Inn, corner York and Margaret Streets, Launceston, (003) 31 7900, is a short distance from Penny Royal and housed in a bakery dating from 1870 which has been sympathetically restored and converted to modern accommodation. The owners have kept the inn small, enabling them to maintain its character. There are 14 rooms. Single $48, double $54.

Batman Fawkner Inn, 35–39 Cameron Street, Launceston, (003) 31 7222, is Launceston's oldest pub, established in 1822 and right in the centre of the city. Since the building is very old, some rooms are small but all have private facilities. Single $45, double $50.

Kilmarnock House, 66 Elphin Road, Launceston, (003) 34 1514, is an elegant two-storey Edwardian merchant's town house built in 1905 which has been restored and furnished to period. There are nine guest rooms with private facilities. The house is about 15 minutes' walk north-east of the city centre. Single $40, double $50 bed and continental breakfast.

Hillview House, 193 George Street, Launceston, (003) 31 7388, is a two-storey house of about 1840 with nine guest rooms. It overlooks the city and the estuary of the Tamar River. Single $39.50, double $49.50 bed and breakfast.

Molecombe Cottage, Mt Leslie Road, Prospect, (003) 31 1355, is a three-bedroom country cottage about seven km (four miles) south of Launceston off the Bass Highway. The cottage, built around 1830, has bedrooms up and downstairs, a kitchen, living, sitting and breakfast rooms. Double $50 bed and continental breakfast.

EATING OUT

Shrimps, 72 George Street, Launceston, (003) 34 0584, is housed in a classical Georgian terrace built in 1824. The food is among the best in Launceston, with seafood being the house speciality. The wine list is good. Licensed. Mid price range.

Georgie's, Yorktown Square, Launceston, (003) 34 1666, looks down on the pretty square from wide windows. The menu is international, ranging from prawn (shrimp) cocktails to trout and making contact with the standard meat and fowl along the way. Licensed. Mid to upper price range.

La Cantina, 63 George Street, Launceston, (003) 31 7885; hearty Italian food here which runs from the straightforward pastas to veal and chicken dishes. Licensed. Low to mid price range.

Sotto's, 150 George Street, Launceston, (003) 31 2679, is housed in a charming cream and green cottage built in 1834, in fact charm is everywhere in this place from the linen table cloths to the cosy corners of the dining area. BYO. Mid price range.

Images Restaurant, 95 George Street, Launceston, (003) 34 0560; a French restaurant whose menu extends to venison and quail. BYO. Mid price range.

O'Keefe's Hotel, 124 George Street, Launceston, is a good place to go for a counter meal of steak, fish or sausages if you must. Licensed. Low price range.

TOURS AND CRUISES

A half-day city sights tour departs at 9.15 am each Tuesday, Thursday and Sunday. Tickets ($15) from the Tasbureau office, corner Paterson and St John Street, (003) 32 2488.

The MV *Lady Stelfox* (003) 31 6699, is a paddle steamer which takes 45-minute cruises on the Tamar River leaving on the hour from 10 am to 5 pm daily. The boat departs from Ritchies Mill Landing Stage and cruises up Cataract Gorge and around Launceston harbour. $3.

Colonial Houses

Three very fine colonial houses owned by the National Trust lie close to Launceston. **Franklin House**, six km (four miles) south on the Midland Highway in the former village of Youngtown, now a light industrial suburb, was built in 1838 for a successful brewer named Britton James. Mr James spared nothing in the construction of his elegant residence, importing red cedar from New South Wales for the doors, architraves, skirting and other woodwork. He occupied Franklin House until 1842 when it became the W. K. Hawkes School for Boys. The school grew over some years to be one of Launceston's finest until its progenitor gave it up and went into politics. The house then passed through a succession of owners and fell into disrepair. When the National Trust bought it in the 1960s it was derelict but has now been restored and furnished in the period of its origin. The house is of simple design with a columned portico over the front door, a central hallway with large symmetrically arranged rooms on either side and service wings at the back. Its best feature is undoubtedly the upstairs front room which extends the full width of the house and is a masterpiece of space and light. Franklin House is open daily from 9 am to 5 pm except in the months of June, July and August when it closes at 4 pm. Admission is $2. The original Youngtown Village church, directly across the road from Franklin House has also been restored.

Twenty km (12 miles) further south on the same road, near the small village of Nile, is **Clarendon**, the greatest stately home in Tasmania. It was completed in the same year as Franklin House but far outdistances it as an ostentatious display of wealth. James Cox was its lord and master. The Wiltshire-born son of New South Wales' great road engineer William Cox, James Cox settled in Tasmania in 1814 and in 1817 was granted 700 acres of land. In 1819 he petitioned successfully for another 6000 which was to become Clarendon, an estate eventually increased to 20,000 acres by purchase. Cox became a County Magistrate in 1817 and served in the Tasmanian Legislative Council from 1829 to 1834 and behaved throughout his life like an English country squire, despite his antipodean location. He established the merino sheep industry in Tasmania with sheep from James MacArthur's flock at Camden south of Sydney. He bred Hereford cattle and raised thoroughbred horses. He founded the Clarendon Hunt and established a deer park to raise suitable quarry for it. Lastly he founded the village of Lymington, now called Nile, and endowed its church.

The house that he had built as an expression of his paramountcy has 16 rooms on two floors with its service rooms in a deep basement. Its most imposing feature is a gigantic portico like that of a Roman temple but lacking a pediment. Its four Ionic columns, rising the full two storeys of the house, stand on a podium divided by stairs which break left and right to reach the ground floor level but do not approach the wide front door directly. The central columns frame the door and the outer ones the long windows of reception rooms left and right of the wide hallway. Inside, the hall is unbroken between the front and back doors. Staircases to the upper and lower floors are relegated to secondary hallways behind the front rooms. The back door leads out to a large walled garden laid out in formal beds with a central sun dial. The house is surrounded by another nine acres of landscaped grounds. Clarendon is open the same hours as Franklin House and admission is $2.

The older **Entally House** is at Hadspen, a small town 13 km (eight miles) west of Launceston on the Bass Highway. Entally is an example of the close connection between Sydney and Tasmania in early colonial days. The house was built in 1819 by Thomas Reibey, son of Mary Reibey after whom Reibey Place near Sydney's Rocks is named. Mary Haydock was transported to New South Wales for horse stealing in 1790 at the age of 13. She met a sub-lieutenant who worked for the British East India Company, Thomas Reibey, on the way out and subsequently married him. Not of the usual convict mould, Mrs Reibey worked hard in her enforced new home and built a business empire that eventually sent her son Thomas to Tasmania to look after the family trade and agricultural interests.

He built Entally on a 1050-hectare (2595-acre) property near Launceston and settled down to the life of a colonial worthy, founding a Tasmanian dynasty of Reibeys which saw his son, another Thomas, become one of the state's first premiers. Unlike many of his fellows, he did not copy the houses of the English gentry but built one of the earliest examples of the wide veranda, low roof, single-storey farm houses which have come to typify Australian rural architecture. The house, its lovely gardens, outbuildings and bluestone chapel are cared for by the National Parks and Wildlife Service and are in splendid condition. Open daily 10 am to 12.10 pm and 1 pm to 5 pm. Admission $2.50.

The Tasmanian Wilderness

Tasmania is a Jekyll and Hyde state. The settled east coddles its history and tries to look sophisticated but the west is savage, wild, careless and abandoned, its landscape a mix of undisciplined thick forests, towering mountains and wide, silver lakes. So remote and difficult are some parts that they have never been explored. The accessible regions, especially Cradle Mountain, Lake St Clair and the Gordon River are the jewels in Tasmania's crown, places to walk on a mountain heath with only the wind for company, or paddle on a river so dark and deep you might be dreaming.

However, there are a number of shocks on the way—mutilated forests, drowned lakes and denuded hillsides, legacies of rapacious, thoughtless industries which have not stopped destroying. When you drive along the narrow, broken country roads, be prepared to meet careering timber trucks, storeys high with 'Killer', 'Crusher' and 'Death' stencilled on their grilles. No landscape is so damaged by pollution as that of Queenstown on the west coast and no greater environmental tragedy than the drowning of Lake Pedder in the south-west has occurred in Australia. The smallest state seems determined to ruin its heritage if the rest of Australia doesn't stop it first.

Cradle Mountain–Lake St Clair National Park

Cradle Mountain and Lake St Clair are at the north and south extremities of a huge (131,915 hectares: 325,962 acres) national park containing Mt Ossa (1617 metres: 5305 feet), Tasmania's tallest peak and a number of other rugged, heady mountain tops. The region has sudden changes of weather in all seasons and its high places should be treated with the greatest respect. Its alpine scenery—jagged snow-capped mountains looming over blue glacial lakes—is unlike anywhere else in Australia.

GETTING TO AND AROUND
Stafford's Coaches, (004) 24 3628, runs buses from Launceston Airport to Cradle Valley ($32) and Lake St Clair ($40) and from Devonport, on the north coast, to the same destinations for $20 and $35. **Mountain Stage Line**, (003) 34 0442, has charter buses available on demand from Launceston to Cradle Mountain ($25) and Lake St Clair ($20).

Devonport is the jumping off point for driving to Cradle Mountain. The trip takes about an hour and a half via Sheffield and Gowrie Park and the final 30 km (19 miles) to Waldheim and Dove Lake is unsealed and narrow. Lake St Clair is most easily reached from Hobart. Cynthia Bay on the southern shore is six km (four miles) from Derwent Bridge, a small town on the Lyell Highway 175 km (108 miles) from Hobart and 83 km (51 miles) from Queenstown. Lake St Clair is also approachable from Launceston via Cressy, Poatina and the Marlborough Highway which involves about 40 km (25 miles) of unsealed road in a distance of 190 km (118 miles), much of it through ugly, damaged timber country.

There is no road through the park. The only way to get from Cradle Mountain to Lake St Clair is to walk the 85-km track which runs between them. It takes five to six days.

TOURIST INFORMATION
Information about the park and its walking trails is absolutely essential to anyone undertaking even a short exploration. It can be obtained from the National Parks and Wildlife Service which has ranger stations at Cradle Mountain (003) 63 5187 and at Lake St Clair (002) 89 1115, as well as offices in Hobart and Launceston. The service publishes a walker's pamphlet on the park and the rangers have current information about the weather and the state of the track.

WHAT TO SEE
The park's terrain varies from high mountains and fast flowing streams through glacial lakes and deep valleys to high plains and dense forests. It was opened up by an Austrian, Gustav Weindorfer, who built Waldheim Chalet at the northern end in

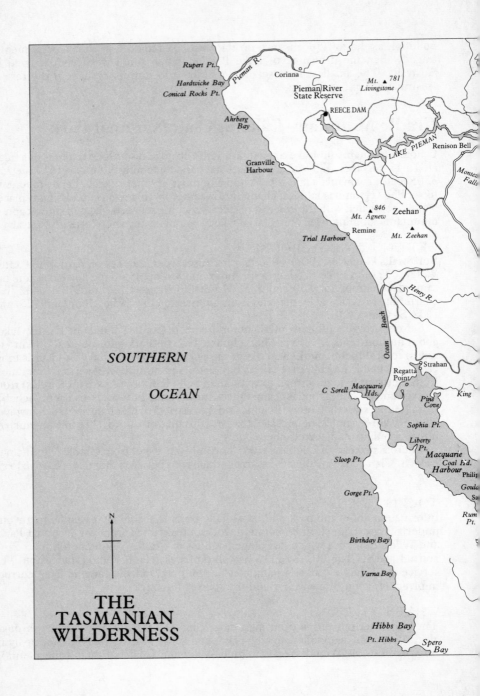

Rupert Pt.

Pieman R.

Corinna

Mt. ▲ 781
Livingstone

Hardwicke Bay
Conical Rocks Pt.

Pieman River
State Reserve

REECE DAM

Ahrberg
Bay

LAKE PIEMAN

Renison Bell

Montez
Falls

Granville
Harbour

▲ 846
Mt. Agnew

Zeehan

Remine

▲
Mt. Zeehan

Trial Harbour

Henry R.

SOUTHERN

OCEAN

Ocean Beach

Strahan

Regatta
Point

C Sorell

Macquarie
Hds.

Pine
Cove

King

Sophia Pt.

Liberty
Pt.

Macquarie

Sloop Pt.

Coal Hd.
Harbour

Philip

Goula

Gorge Pt.

Sa

Rum
Pt.

N

Birthday Bay

Varna Bay

THE
TASMANIAN
WILDERNESS

Hibbs Bay

Pt. Hibbs

Spero
Bay

660
rns
ak

MACKINTOSH
DAM

●WALDHEIM

▲ 1545
CRADLE MTN

Western Bluff

DEVILS
GULLET

L. Mackenzie

*Borrowdaile
Plains*
Arm River
Forest Reserve
Mersey White
Water FR
ROWALLAN

Fisher Bluff

Mersey R.

1300 ▲ ▲ 1408
Deception point

1348
▲
Blue
Peaks

Ironstone
Mt. ▲
1443

Lake
Mackintosh

BASTYAN
DAM
Rosebury

Tullah
712
▲ Mt. Farrell

MURCHISON DAM
949

1275 Victoria
Peak

February
Plains

LAKE
ROWALLAN

Howells
Bluff

▲ 1449

Clumner Bluff

1245 ▲

1353
Forty Lakes

WALLS OF
JERUSALEM
NP ▲ 1458

MT.
MURCHISON

lliamsford

Lake Murchison

Mt. Jerusalem

CRADLE MTN

LAKE ST CLAIR

NATIONAL PARK

▲ 1617
MT. OSSA

DU CANE RANGE

TRAVELLER RANGE

GREAT PINE TIER

CENTRAL PLATEAU
CONSERVATION AREA

NTY
CIAL
AINE

▲ 1439
Eldon Peak

▲ 1147
Mt.
Sedgewick

Gormanston

▲ 1447
MT. OLYMPUS

CHEYNE RANGE

LAKE ST CLAIR

Queenstown
1146 ▲ Mt.
Owen

Lynchford

NELSON VALLEY

RAGLAN RANGE

*COLLINGWOOD
RANGE*

Derwent
Bridge

Bronte Park

WEST COAST RANGE

Proprietary
Peak ▲ 1103
MT.
TUKES
1168
Crotty

Mt. Arrowsmith 981 ▲

LODDON RANGE

LAKE KING
1324 WILLIAM
Mt. King William I

WENTWORTH HILLS

▲ 1031

44 ▲
Mt. Darwin
t. Sorell

FRANKLIN LOWER GORDON

ENGINEER RANGE

▲ 1443
FRENCHMAN'S CAP

WILD   RIVERS

ADAM RANGE

NATIONAL   PARK

CRACROFT HILLS

Mt. McCall

DECEPTION RANGE

*SURVEYOR
RANGE*

NORWAY RANGE

KING   WILLIAM   RANGE

Guelph
Basin

▲ 1359
MT. KING WILLIAM II

TUNGATINAH

Tarraleah

Gordon R.

ELLIOT RANGE

Franklin R.

PRINCESS RANGE

PRINCE OF WALES RANGE

1028
▲
MT. HUMBOLDT

THE PLEIADES

DENISON RANGE

▲ 1337
Wylds Craig

GORDON RANGE

m

D'AGUILAR RANGE

734
▲
Mt. Lee

*KING BILLY
RANGE*

1912 and explored much of the area now occupied by the park. The surroundings are at their most beautiful and safest in the summer (December to February) when the mountain flowers appear and the weather is more predictable, although sudden snow storms sometimes occur. The best way to see it all is to walk the 85 kilometre Overland Track from Cradle Mountain to Lake St Clair or vice versa, a journey of about five or six days.

A fit person should be capable of taking on the track which is well marked and maintained and has diversions to waterfalls, lookouts, places to climb and mountain peaks along its length. There are small cabins to stay in along the way. It skirts the western shore of Lake St Clair, Australia's deepest fresh water lake under Mount Olympus (1447 metres), penetrates through some of the world's last remaining temperate rainforest, reaches its midpoint at Mount Ossa (1617 metres with a track to the summit) and continues over alpine moorland and heath to the glacial lakes around Cradle Mountain (1545 metres). Between Cradle Valley and Cradle Mountain there is a number of short tracks that show off some of the area's most beautiful scenery but don't require the same effort as the Overland. There is a park-use fee of $10 for walkers undertaking the Overland Track.

WHERE TO STAY
Cradle Mountain Lodge, Cradle Mountain Valley, (003) 63 5164, is a guest house and the only serviced accommodation in the park. The lodge, a two storey timber shingle building with the proper mountain atmosphere, has share facilities, takes 30 guests and has a dining room. Single $39, double $49, room only. Individual cabins are also available in association with Cradle Mountain Lodge.

Wooden **huts** are scattered along the overland track. They are extremely basic and, during the summer, can be crowded out. Late arrivals should bring their own tent.

There are also more substantial huts at Cynthia Bay on Lake St Clair which can be booked through the National Parks and Wildlife Service. Once again, they are very popular during the summer and even in winter some are occupied.

GUIDED WALKS
Cradle Huts, (002) 31 0983, conducts six-day walks along the Overland Track which include optional climbs of Mt Ossa and Cradle Mountain. You must be able to carry about eight kilograms between 10 and 18 km (six and eleven miles) a day. The cost is $595 per person and includes transport, meals, equipment and accommodation at Cradle Mountain Lodge and in the company's own more comfortable trackside huts. Guides know the region, its flora, fauna and geology well. Tours depart from Hobart each Saturday between December and March. They return to Launceston.

The South-West Coast

The south-west coast of Tasmania is a wild, inhospitable area of awesome beauty characterised by high mountains, deep still rivers, almost impenetrable forests and huge cliffs along its ocean shore. It has only one safe haven from the roaring forties which bang against its precipices—Macquarie Harbour, a long, wide bay penetrating deeply into the island and hidden behind a narrow, sand-barred entrance so treacherous it is known as Hell's Gates.

The west coast of Tasmania might not be inhabited at all but for mineral rich mountainsides a few miles inland from the Southern Ocean shore. Convicts and their gaolers were its first settlers but they gave it up as too bad even for the worst of men and went to Port Arthur instead. They had spent 13 years at Macquarie Harbour, most hideous of the colony's prison camps, where the worst convicts, continuously bound in leg irons, cut Huon pine from dense riverside forests 12 hours a day and rafted it back to their prison on Sarah Island. There, other convicts slaved in sawpits, hand-sawing planks for British naval vessels. In this cold, wet, windy, implacable hell tiny misdemeanours were punished with hundreds of lashes and men died daily of overwork, injury and starvation.

Those who rebelled ended up on Grummet Island, a windblown rock where forty at a time were kept like animals. Escape or death were the other choices. Of the 112 who got off Sarah Island, 15 were recaptured and died by execution, 68 died in the bush and six were cannibalised by desperate fellow escapees. The remainder returned to prison. The whole shameful episode ended in 1834 when the last remaining officers and their charges came to Port Arthur but it is vividly recalled in one of the first landmarks of Australian fiction, Marcus Clarke's *For the Term of His Natural Life*.

Interest in the west coast ballooned again in 1881 when alluvial gold was discovered at Queen's River on the site of Queenstown. Serious mining, which supported the region almost entirely for the next century and has only recently shown signs of collapse, began in 1883 on gold found at Mount Lyell. A relatively low yield of the yellow metal was pursued for nearly all of the next decade while the tremendously rich copper deposits in which it lay were ignored. In 1891 the Mt Lyell Mining Company woke up to the error of its ways and began smelting copper with great success, a success which continued until the severe slump in copper prices of the last ten years. During its heyday in the late 1890s and early 1900s, Queenstown, with a population of 5051, was the third largest town in Tasmania. Its rail link with the port of Strahan on Macquarie Harbour had 48 bridges and grades so steep that a rack and pinion system was necessary to prevent the trains from sliding back along the track. The smelters' copper fumes had begun to pollute the surrounding forests so severely that not a single tree or blade of grass survives on the once thickly forested hills close to the town. Despite prosperity, it took the Great Depression to link Queenstown to Hobart. The Lyell Highway between the two cities was completed in 1932, ending the mining community's dependence on sea transport through Strahan.

Queenstown has dramatic recent history as well. It was the centre of a powerful struggle between environmentalists and the Tasmanian State Government during the late 1970s and early 1980s over a plan to dam the Gordon River below the point where it joins the Franklin. Protesters picketed the dam site and the town. There were fist fights in front of news cameras, some very vigorous arrests and people were almost bull-dozed. The nation was split but at election time it became a case of

Tasmanians versus the rest and the rest put a stop to the nonsense. A national park and World Heritage Area was declared. The Gordon below Franklin remained free of exploitation for hydro-electricity though it had previously been dammed further up-stream. Tourism has since become a strong contributor to the local economy.

GETTING TO AND AROUND
Airlines of Tasmania flies to Queenstown from Hobart ($67.50) and Launceston ($54.50) as well as from Essendon Airport in Melbourne ($122).

Redline Coaches from Hobart to Burnie on the north-west coast operate via Queenstown. The trip takes four hours and costs $22.

Drivers take the Lyell Highway from Hobart, a distance of 258 km (160 miles), which takes a little less than four hours to cover.

TOURIST INFORMATION
Tasbureau has an information office at 39–41 Orr Street, Queenstown.

Queenstown

The landscape on the last few kilometres of the Lyell Highway into Queenstown can only be described as bizarre. The road winds down through naked yellow hills, their faces riven and pitted with erosion gullies from where the last vestiges of soil have long been washed and whose only colour comes from exposed rocks veined with minerals. Before mining began, the hills were covered with thick temperate rainforest. Two decades of rapacious timber cutting combined with uncontrolled sulphur pollution from Queenstown's copper smelters reduced and poisoned the vegetation, making it especially susceptible to fierce bushfires. Each summer the fires raged until no regrowth was possible. Each winter the rain washed more and more soil into the Queen's River. In the end, the hills were dead. The mining, however, continued and Queenstown remained, clinging defiantly to its own fouled nest. It is a sight not easily forgotten and, some would say, shows how the world will look one day if the human race isn't more careful.

Ironies abound in Queenstown. Not the least of them is that the **Mount Lyell Mine**, on its last legs as a copper producer, is being converted to a tourist attraction—a 'living museum' of mining history is its promotional angle, surely a contradiction in terms. Guided tours of the mine and its museum take place at 9.15 am and 4 pm every day and cost $2.50. History of the mining days which makes no claim to be living can be seen at the **Galley Museum** on the corner of Sticht and Driffield Streets. The museum occupies the old Imperial Hotel and features more than 1000 photographs ranging from Queenstown's beginnings as a mining centre to around 1940 and including the development of other towns on the west coast. Personal and household items used by the average miner in early days complete the collection. Open daily 9 am to noon, 2 pm to 5 pm and 7 pm to 9 pm. Admission $2. The history of the Queenstown to Strahan railway is recounted in a display mounted at a public park called **The Miners' Siding** in Driffield Street.

Strahan

The growth of tourism on the west coast is focused on the Gordon River, and Strahan, the small port town at the northern end of Macquarie Harbour, 41 km (25 miles) from Queenstown, is where Gordon River cruise boats depart. The town prospered on the back of Queenstown and its development paralleled that community. Only the Union Steamship Company building and the Post Office remain from Strahan's glory days but they are edifices equal to anything else on the west coast. **Ocean Beach**, a 40-km (25-mile) stretch of high sand dunes and violent surf lies six km (four miles) west of the town. There is a camping and picnic ground there. Strahan has an odd connection to the United States of America. Thomas Gratton Riggs, an American actor who founded the Elks fraternity in his homeland, is buried in the local cemetery.

The Gordon River

The river, such a divisive issue during its national prominence, is an extraordinarily tranquil stream of dark, deep, mirror-like waters, famed for its misty calm and the thick forest that grows along its shores—so thick that walking parties struggle to make two km (one mile) a day through parts of it. The river rises in Lake Richmond, a twisted 193 km (120 miles) from Macquarie Harbour, and has been dammed at The Knob to form a huge lake larger than Sydney Harbour. High speed tourist boats cut their way up the river each day on sight seeing trips, penetrating about 50 km (31 miles) and creating large, damaging washes. The scenic air cruise operator at Strahan also lands his amphibious plane on its peaceful waters.

WHERE TO STAY AND EATING OUT

For what you get, accommodation in this part of Tasmania can be considered comparatively expensive but remember there's not much of it and it is a long way from anywhere else.

Westcoaster Motor Inn, 1 Batchelor Street, Queenstown, (004) 71 1033, is on the north side of the town and has some ordinary family units as well as the usual motel rooms and a licensed restaurant. Single $66, double $72.

Penny Royal Queenstown, Batchelor Street, Queenstown, (004) 71 1005; a motel with one- and two-room units and a licensed restaurant. Close to the preceding listing. Single $70, double $83.

Four Seasons Strahan, Jolly Street, Strahan, (004) 71 7160; well-kept motel about 10 years old. Has a licensed restaurant. Single $63, double $71.

CRUISES

Half-day cruises, taken at a fairly hectic pace, depart from Strahan every day of the week. They run the length of Macquarie Harbour and continue into the Gordon River. On the way you'll see Hells Gates, Sarah Island and Sir John Falls as well as the river. All three boats operating these cruises are large, modern, water-jet propelled, shallow-draft vessels with enclosed and open decks. The boats and their fares are the *Gordon Explorer*, $25, the *James Kelly II*, $25, and the *Wilderness Seeker*, $28. The latter has the shallowest draft and is able to go as far as the Gordon/Franklin River junction, a little further than the other two can manage.

TOURS AND ADVENTURES
Scenic flights aboard float equipped light aircraft run by **Wilderness Air** depart each day from Strahan Jetty. Fares from $25 per person. Phone (004) 71 7280.
Bushventures 4WD Tours, (002) 29 4291, operate a 4-day Franklin River/World Heritage Area tours between September and May. They include the mining towns, the Gordon River cruise and a look at the Franklin River as well as a visit to Lake St Clair and other wild places. $410 twin share basis, all inclusive.
Tasmanian River Rafters, (002) 95 1573, sells a range of white water rafting trips on the Franklin River lasting from four to 16 days and costing from $580 to $1633 all inclusive. All tours depart from and return to Hobart.

INDEX